THIRD EDITION

ADVANCES in MOTIVATION in SPORT and EXERCISE

THIRD EDITION

ADVANCES in MOTIVATION in SPORT and EXERCISE

EDITORS

Glyn C. Roberts, PhD

Norwegian School of Sport Sciences

Darren C. Treasure, PhD

Human Kinetics

Library of Congress Cataloging-in-Publication Data

Advances in motivation in sport and exercise / Glyn C. Roberts, Darren C. Treasure, editors. -- 3rd ed.

p. ; cm.

Includes bibliographical references and index.

ISBN-13: 978-0-7360-9081-0 (hard cover)

ISBN-10: 0-7360-9081-9 (hard cover)

I. Roberts, Glyn C. II. Treasure, Darren C., 1965-

[DNLM: 1. Physical Fitness--psychology. 2. Exercise--psychology. 3. Motivation. 4. Sports--psychology. QT 255]

613.7--dc23

2011035695

ISBN-10: 0-7360-9081-9 (print)

ISBN-13: 978-0-7360-9081-0 (print)

The web addresses cited in this text were current as of October 2011, unless otherwise noted.

Acquisitions Editor: Myles Schrag; **Developmental Editor:** Melissa J. Zavala; **Assistant Editors:** Anne Rumery, Elizabeth Evans, and Kali Cox; **Copyeditor:** Bob Replinger; **Proofreader:** Erin Cler; **Indexer:** Andrea J. Hepner; **Permissions Manager:** Dalene Reeder; **Graphic Designer:** Bob Reuther; **Graphic Artist:** Tara Welsch; **Cover Designer:** Bob Reuther; **Photo Production Manager:** Jason Allen; **Art Manager:** Kelly Hendren; **Associate Art Manager:** Alan L. Wilborn; **Illustrations:** © Human Kinetics; **Printer:** Edwards Brothers Malloy

Printed in the United States of America   10 9 8 7 6 5 4 3 2

The paper in this book is certified under a sustainable forestry program.

Human Kinetics
Website: www.HumanKinetics.com

United States: Human Kinetics
P.O. Box 5076
Champaign, IL 61825-5076
800-747-4457
e-mail: humank@hkusa.com

Canada: Human Kinetics
475 Devonshire Road Unit 100
Windsor, ON N8Y 2L5
800-465-7301 (in Canada only)
e-mail: info@hkcanada.com

Europe: Human Kinetics
107 Bradford Road
Stanningley
Leeds LS28 6AT, United Kingdom
+44 (0) 113 255 5665
e-mail: hk@hkeurope.com

Australia: Human Kinetics
57A Price Avenue
Lower Mitcham, South Australia 5062
08 8372 0999
e-mail: info@hkaustralia.com

New Zealand: Human Kinetics
P.O. Box 80
Torrens Park, South Australia 5062
0800 222 062
e-mail: info@hknewzealand.com

E5081

CONTENTS

PART II   Understanding the Psychological Determinants and Mediators of Physical Activity Behavior   **229**

CHAPTER 7   Self-Determination Theory and Exercise Motivation: Facilitating Self-Regulatory Processes to Support and Maintain Health and Well-Being 233
Martyn Standage, PhD, and Richard M. Ryan, PhD

CHAPTER 8   Self-Efficacy and Motivation in Physical Activity and Sport: Mediating Processes and Outcomes 271
Todd A. Gilson, PhD, and Deborah L. Feltz, PhD

CHAPTER 9   Social-Cognitive Approaches to Understanding Exercise Motivation and Behavior in Cancer Survivors 299
Jeff K. Vallance, PhD, and Kerry S. Courneya, PhD

PREFACE

Motivation research in sport and physical activity has come of age!
When Glyn Roberts began in this field in the late 1960s and early
1970s, only 30 to 40 people attended meetings of the North American Society
for the Psychology of Sport and Physical Activity (NASPSPA), and only 10
people or so attended motivation research presentations. Following the watershed Allerton Conference in 1973, where we had 100 attendees, NASPSPA
grew rapidly, and, at the same time during the 1970s, a revolution occurred
in motivation research and practice. Motivation theories may be viewed as
being on a continuum ranging from deterministic to mechanistic to organismic
to cognitive (for a more extensive treatment of motivation theories, see Ford,
1992). Deterministic and mechanistic theories view humans as being passive
and driven by psychological needs or drives. Organismic theories include innate
needs but also recognize that a dialectic occurs between the organism and the
social context. Until about 1971 the mechanistic and organismic theories had
replaced the more deterministic theories. In Glyn's case, at the time, he was
doing research with the achievement need motivation concepts of Atkinson
and McClelland in which he used approach success and avoid failure tendencies as his independent variables. But Weiner (1972) signaled the beginning of
the new era by arguing that individuals who were high or low in motivation
were likely to think differently about why success and failure occurred. The
notion that thoughts, rather than needs, were the critical variables transformed
the study of motivation and has led to a lively interest in how these thoughts
determine motivation.

As individual differences and the influence of personality and needs waned
in importance in motivation research, the situation and its meaning to the
participants became a more important focus. Motivation is now understood in
terms of mediating cognitions, but not only in terms of control, autonomy, and
competence, but also in terms of purpose and meaning. Cognitive theories view
humans as being active and initiating action through subjective interpretation
of the achievement context. The most popular contemporary theories of motivation in sport and exercise psychology tend to be based on organismic (e.g.,
self-determination theory, Deci & Ryan, 1985; hierarchical goal model, Elliot,
1999) or social-cognitive theories (e.g., achievement goal theory,
Nicholls, 1989; self-efficacy, Bandura, 1986) and are based
on more dynamic and sophisticated conceptions that assume
that the human is an active participant in decision making and
in planning achievement. Some of us in motivation research

eBook
available at
HumanKinetics.com

continue to argue for needs, or the surrogates of needs, as the energizers of motivation but recognize the dialectic that does occur. For those of us who subscribe to the social-cognitive approach to understanding motivation, we eschew needs and accept that beliefs, thoughts, and perceptions are the basis of understanding the process of motivation (Roberts, Treasure & Conroy, 2007). Although organismic approaches are experiencing a resurgence in the literature and are used to good effect in sport and exercise psychology (see Ntoumanis et al., this volume; Standage & Ryan, this volume), most motivation research in sport and physical activity contexts over the past 40 years has adopted a social-cognitive approach, and the specific approach that emerged as the most popular is achievement goal theory (see Roberts, this volume).

As Harwood and colleagues (2008) state, "The past 20 years have been a watershed for our understanding of sport achievement behavior" (p. 158). Harwood and colleagues continue to state that achievement goal theory has "triggered a penetrating wave of research into the interpersonal and environmental influences on athlete behavior in achievement settings" (p. 158). We agree, and we argue that the social-cognitive approach to motivation has given motivation research an impetus and, over the past 40 years, some valuable insights into the motivational equation. In 1987 Csikszentmihali and Nakamura made the comment that the cognitive revolution in psychology in the 1970s and 1980s had given a new life to the study of motivation. The notion that thoughts were the critical variables transformed the study of motivation and has led to a lively interest in how these thoughts determine motivation and achievement behavior. The research effort in education, the workplace, sport, and the exercise setting has increased remarkably as research teams investigate the dynamics of the motivation equation. From a modest beginning, the research effort into motivation processes in sport and physical activity has grown to become a huge literature focusing on the cognitive schema and organismic dynamics that determine achievement striving.

For those of us who were there at the beginning of this cognitive revolution, it is rewarding to see that now our research meetings are packed in conferences worldwide and the number of researchers has increased exponentially. But more important, the quality and conceptual underpinning of the research endeavor has also increased remarkably. And, as this book illustrates, the practical implications of this work are now made more explicit for the people in the trenches—the teachers, coaches, exercise leaders, parents, and so on! In our minds, one of the most important benefits is that we now have evidence on which to base our practice. In 2001 Roberts lamented that there was always a time lag between research and practice. He argued that several years have to pass before research findings enter textbooks and become general knowledge and eventually part of the lore of coaching, teaching, and parenting. Roberts further complained that many practical suggestions remained the exclusive knowledge of the professionals in universities. But that is changing rapidly. Our research knowledge is being integrated more quickly into coaching, teaching, and parenting practice, although the pace may still be too slow for many of us.

Indeed, motivation research in sport and exercise psychology has come of age!

This book reviews and integrates important contemporary contributions to the study of motivation. The authors are distinguished contributors to the conceptual understanding of motivation and to the application of these thought processes to enhance motivation in applied contexts. Each chapter represents an important avenue of research endeavor in the sport or physical activity area. In this volume we have invited distinguished scholars within the motivation research community in exercise, physical activity, and sport psychology. We are pleased that everyone, except one colleague for very good reasons, was able to respond to our request to contribute. Thank you each!

The themes of this volume center on the understanding and enhancement of achievement behavior in sport or physical activity. Each contributor sheds light on the dynamics of the process of motivation and on the variables and constructs that help our understanding of why we are or are not motivated. Each contributor also examines how motivation may be enhanced within the framework that she or he professes. Each contributor has a perspective that differs a little, or a lot, from those of the other contributors. These differences include the determinants of the motivated state (personal goals, personal agency beliefs, basic needs, or values), the way in which the context contributes to the motivated state, and the way in which we can change the motivated state and contribute to the practical side of our work: the enhancement of motivation. But all agree that thoughts and perceptions, or a constellation of cognitions, are major determinants of the energization, direction, and regulation of achievement striving.

If there is one way that we can illustrate the advancement that has occurred in the 20 years between the 1992 book and the current treatise or in the 10 years between the 2001 book and today, it is in the insights that we now have about applying our knowledge in exercise, sport, and physical activity contexts. As befits a field that is applied in character, we have progressed a great deal in our understanding of how to enhance motivation in physical activities. The contributors all address this aspect in their chapters. And it is true that our findings are now being implemented where they can make a difference: in the gym, on the sport field, and in the exercise group.

We thank our fellow contributors and acknowledge their efforts. Thank you for agreeing to our demands. We especially thank the contributors who were timely in their submissions and were patient as we waited and harassed those who took longer than we would have liked! But it was worth the wait. Thank you all. And we thank Human Kinetics staff (in particular Melissa Zavala and Myles Schrag) for their patience and understanding.

ACKNOWLEDGMENTS

In any endeavor, we always stand on the shoulders of others: I have been no different. I would like to acknowledge the significant contributions of former colleagues and friends, especially those who attended that seminar series in 1977 where the first kernels of what became achievement goal theory were presented and debated: John Nicholls, Carole Ames, Carol Dweck, and Marty Maehr. I also acknowledge the contributions of my other colleagues at the Children's Research Center, the Department of Kinesiology at the University of Illinois, and my last port of call, my colleagues in the Department of Coaching and Psychology at the Norwegian School of Sport Sciences in Oslo, Norway.

One of the privileges of being a professor is that you meet so many bright young people. I would like to acknowledge all of my former (and present) PhD students. I learned from each of you, and working and discussing issues with you helped me grow and think better, both personally and professionally. Having such gifted and motivated students (yes, Kevin, there were favorites, but you were always among them!) has been the professional highlight of my career. John Nicholls used to say that having someone take your ideas seriously enough to argue with you is a significant form of respect. I have been fortunate enough to have had many doctoral students who have argued hard and long with me. In the twilight of my career, I deeply appreciate those debates; they forged my ideas and contributed to my modest achievements in sport psychology. But more important to me, and something of which I am proud, is that not only are you valued and respected colleagues, but you are also my friends. I value those friendships more than you know.

I would also like to acknowledge colleagues and friends who were important to me at various stages of my life and career: Ema Geron, who persuaded me to become a member of the Board of Directors of IAAP, which fostered my continued international involvement; John Nicholls, mentor, colleague, and very good friend; Dick Magill and Steven Silverman, good friends, for being there when it was important; the ICHP group, good for my sanity, if not my golf; Darren Treasure, for many things, but most of all for making me part of his family; Nicolas Lemyre, a colleague and friend, for making sure my last two years in Oslo were served with dignity, demonstrating that loyalty is earned not demanded; Marit Sørensen, who eased my professional and personal immersion into Norway, and who reintroduced me to the joy of having dogs and horses in my life; and finally, to Nicolas and Stephanie for the privilege of being a grandfather to Tobias, Kaisa and Ebba.

Last, but not least, I want to thank Marit and my Welsh and Norwegian families for their love and support. I sometimes tax each!

Glyn Roberts

I would like to acknowledge the role of Glyn Roberts in my professional and personal life. His decision to take me on as a doctoral student at the University of Illinois in 1990 was a life-altering event. I have always appreciated his intellect and passion, not simply in regard to the motivation question but also politics, wine, golf, Welsh rugby, premier league, and just about any other topic that grabs his attention. Since the day he accepted me as a student, our relationship has evolved into one of the more significant in my life, and I am proud to call Glyn one of my dearest friends.

A special thanks to my friends, PhD students and colleagues, many of whom contributed to this volume, who have influenced my thinking and played a significant role, perhaps unknowingly, in my professional development: John Kane, John Loy, David Andrews, Jim Denison, Martyn Standage, Kendy Vierling, Nicolas Lemyre, Edward McAuley, and Stuart Biddle.

I also want to thank the many coaches, sport scientists, medical professionals, and administrators I have had the opportunity to collaborate with in my applied work. All share an insatiable desire to learn, get better, and enhance the development, well-being, and performance of the athletes in their respective programs. I would particularly like to acknowledge the athletes I have had the opportunity to work with. It has been an honor to be a part of your personal journey. I learned something from each of you and cannot express how much I appreciate the trust you placed in me.

Lastly, but certainly most important, I want to take this opportunity to thank Chrissy, Emma, Jack, my parents Colin and Rita, and brother Spencer for their ongoing unconditional love and support.

Darren Treasure

PART I

Contemporary Theories of Motivation: New Directions and Interpretations

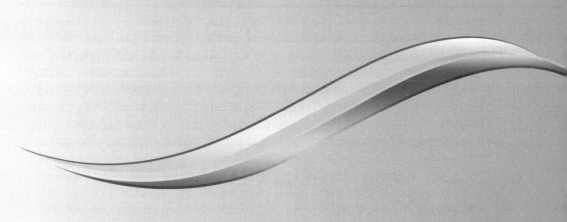

It is quite astonishing to realize that the new and revolutionary approaches to understanding motivation that some of us were engaged in in the 1970s and 1980s have now become the traditional and established theories of motivation. In this first section of the book, we look at the most popular of the motivation theories that have stood the test of time and have been thoroughly examined by multiple researchers in many countries. These new approaches were based on the cognitive revolution that swept through psychology in the late 1970s and early 1980s. Now, these are mainstream theories. But they all have a deep cognitive base to their conceptualization. Some are based purely on social cognitive criteria and believe that thoughts, perceptions, and beliefs govern action, and some believe we need needs to explain the initiation of motivated behavior, even though there is a deep cognitive overlay on these theories.

One of the hallmarks of the contemporary study of motivation in sport and exercise is that we now have so many deeply thoughtful scientists in the field. This book reflects that! This opening segment looks at some of the old theories, with some new insights and interpretations, and some new perspectives on motivation that are becoming popular. But the contributors are all thoughtful and innovative scientists, and they all have something to say.

The first chapter deals with achievement goal theory, and Roberts documents the basic infrastructure of the theory and the wealth of empirical evidence that supports the basic tenets. Roberts makes the point that while the dispositional and contextual determinants have been investigated independently, they should be considered as interactive constructs. In addition, Roberts discusses the counterarguments to the theory, with counterpoints to the counterarguments. But the important message of the first chapter is a call for sport scientists to remember the famous saying of William of Occam (1285-1347): "Entities are not to be multiplied beyond necessity." Known as *Occam's Razor*, it is a call for parsimony. Roberts argues for recognition of parsimony, elegance, and conceptual coherence in sport psychological research, motivation in particular, and concludes with a look at the practical import of achievement goal theory and the new research directions achievement goal theory can follow.

The second chapter is by Papaioannou and colleagues, and they present and discuss the extensions to achievement goal theory of the Hierarchical model of Elliot and colleagues. Papaioannou and colleagues critically look at the original theory and the arguments for the extension by Elliot. They criticize the theory and offer alternative directions that researchers may follow should they wish to investigate valence-based criteria of motivated behavior in sport and physical activity. Of particular interest is the argument that a focus on approach performance goals that may be adaptive for the person, at least in the short term, may be maladaptive for society. Papaioannou and colleagues conclude that parents, coaches, and teachers should not emphasize interindividual competition and performance approach goals because this might have negative consequences for the group and the larger society.

The third chapter is by Ntoumanis, and he focuses on self-determination theory, a theory that is growing in popularity. The fact that we have two chapters on self-determination theory lends credence to its growing popularity in sport and physical activity. Ntoumanis's focus is on sport and physical education with a thorough discussion of the role of self-regulation in the motivational equation. But Ntoumanis also attempts a very difficult, but necessary, task: He attempts to discuss how we may integrate the components of the various theories of human striving. There is no question that the theories overlap to a greater or lesser extent: Just how do mastery, autonomy, and empowerment differ in the various theories? But it is not easy because there are some fundamental conceptual differences in the energization of achievement striving (e.g., needs versus cognitive schema). But we do need to be more thoughtful about the common attributes and attempt to develop a more unifying theory of motivation. The research evidence reviewed in this chapter offers support for the usefulness of the SDT approach for understanding and promoting adaptive motivation in sport and PE.

The fourth chapter is by Hall and colleagues on the relatively new area of perfectionism. In order to evaluate the degree to which the features of perfectionism may be responsible for performance excellence, the chapter examines how perfectionism has been defined. Hall and colleagues argue that in some instances, perfectionism has been defined by its measures rather than by its core features, and as a consequence, empirical evidence has been accrued to support the notion that certain forms of perfectionism may be universally positive or healthy. The chapter reviews empirical literature that has examined perfectionism in sport to illustrate that when perfectionism is measured in a manner that captures its core features simultaneously, it has few positive psychological and performance consequences. This literature challenges notions that perfectionism can be positive and demonstrates that the outcomes are more detrimental when the construct is viewed in its broadest sense. Finally, the authors argue that the empirical evidence points clearly to the fact that although adaptive achievement striving provides a sustainable route to fulfilling a person's sporting potential, perfectionism is not a foundation for excellence.

The fifth chapter is by Vallerand on the concept of passion in sport. This is a new area of research into achievement striving, and Vallerand provides strong support for the model he proposes. He has developed interesting concepts of harmonious and obsessive passion with scales to measure each. A number of social and personal determinants are hypothesized to determine the initial and ongoing development of passion for a given activity. Research has shown that harmonious passion promotes adaptive outcomes to a greater extent than obsessive passion. It was found, however, that under certain specific situations, obsessive passion can lead to some positive outcomes and harmonious passion can lead to less adaptive ones. In its relative infancy, the research to date using prospective and longitudinal designs on passion showed that passion leads to changes in outcomes over time. Finally, directions for future research and applications are proposed.

The last chapter in this segment is by Roberts and Kristiansen on that "oldie but goodie," goal setting. Goal setting is the most utilized motivational enhancement technique in sport psychology. Recent reviews have clearly shown that goal setting consistently works in enhancing performance in sport and that it is effective across a wide array of athletic events and athletic experience. There is still confusion in the literature about what goals people should set, what psychological processes are involved in goal setting, and how people go about setting goals for either themselves or others. Using achievement goal theory, Roberts and Kristiansen argue that achievement goal theory may give a conceptual backdrop to goal setting to explain why the athlete becomes motivated. They conclude that while goal setting is empirically viable, why goal setting works is less clear, and researchers should be more thoughtful about the processes underlying goal setting.

CHAPTER 1

Motivation in Sport and Exercise From an Achievement Goal Theory Perspective: After 30 Years, Where Are We?

Glyn C. Roberts, PhD
Department of Psychology and Coaching
Norwegian School of Sport Sciences

Motivation and motivation issues remain one of the central concerns of modern life. In everyday life we continue to hear of the importance of motivation and ways in which to foster it for desired outcomes. Whether it is banks that provide outrageous bonuses to "motivate" their investors and brokers, politicians who wish to change society, business leaders who are concerned with motivation in the workplace, the health industry that worries about the rise in childhood obesity and sedentary lifestyles, parents and teachers who bemoan the study habits of children and adolescents, or coaches and administrators within the sport and exercise communities who wonder how to get better results—all are concerned with motivation issues. But what is motivation? If we take our cues from everyday life, then it may be arousal, such as the "motivational" tirades of coaches in the locker room. Former players of Manchester United Football Club have often remarked about the halftime locker room "hairdryer treatment" talks of the legendary coach Sir Alex Ferguson. Some believe that motivation is a measure of confidence, a winning attitude that motivates people to better performance. Some believe that motivation is a simple matter of positive thinking: Believe and you will achieve! Some believe that it is a personal entity or is genetically endowed, that either you have it or you don't! All these beliefs and practices have some merit, but these simplistic assumptions do not begin to capture the complexity and richness of motivational matters (Roberts, 2001).

I and others have argued (e.g., Ford, 1992; Roberts, 2001; Roberts, Treasure, & Conroy, 2007) that the term *motivation* is overused and vague, especially in the "trenches"—the classroom, the gymnasium, the exercise room, the playing fields, the sport arenas, the workplace, and so on. We have former successful sport stars, politicians, and business people who earn big money on the lecture circuit giving what are called motivational talks! We have sport commentators and business correspondents who argue that the successful are more motivated to achieve than the unsuccessful. But their definitions and understanding of motivation differ. Even among motivation researchers, motivation is defined so broadly by some that it incorporates the whole field of psychology and so narrowly by others that it is almost useless as an organizing construct. Ford (1992) has argued that there are at least 32 theories of motivation that have their own definitions of the construct. Pinder (1984) claimed that there are almost as many definitions as there are theorists. This contention is especially true in sport and exercise psychology. Read the chapters on motivation in any two textbooks and you find very different perspectives and understandings of what motivation is, or should be. As an example, the recent textbook by Horn (2008) includes three chapters on motivation. Each is fine as it stands. The amazing aspect is that although each deals with motivational issues in sport and exercise psychology, cross-referencing is almost absent! Each chapter has its own perspective and draws on its own body of evidence. This circumstance is not unusual. Even within perspectives we find researchers who are fonder of citing themselves and their former students than they are of embracing the literature. The "toothbrush syndrome" (Frese, 2006) seems to be alive and well in sport and exercise psychology: That is, some motivation theorists would rather use another theorist's toothbrush than his or her theory and research!

In contemporary motivation research, because the term is so vague, the solution has been to abandon the term and use descriptions of cognitive processes such as self-regulation or other self-systems that affect motivation, motivational processes such as striving for personal goals or goal setting, and emotional processes. But the important assumption agreed to by most contemporary theorists is that motivation is not an entity but a process (e.g., Maehr & Braskamp, 1986). Motivation is typically defined as the process that influences the initiation, direction, magnitude, perseverance, continuation, and quality of goal-directed behavior (Maehr & Zusho, 2009). To understand motivation, we must attempt to understand the process of motivation, the constructs that drive the process, and the way in which the constructs apply in sport and exercise.

Motivation and Achievement Behavior

Motivation theories may be viewed as being on a continuum ranging from deterministic to mechanistic to organismic to cognitive (for a more extensive treatment of motivation theories, see Ford, 1992). Deterministic and mechanistic theories view humans as being passive and driven by psychological needs or drives. Organismic theories include innate needs but also recognize that a dialectic occurs between the organism and the social context. Cognitive theories view humans as being active and initiating action through subjective interpretation of the achievement context. The most popular contemporary theories of motivation in sport and exercise psychology tend to be based on organismic (e.g., self-determination theory, Deci & Ryan, 1985a; hierarchical goal model, Elliot, 1999) or social-cognitive theories (e.g., achievement goal theory, Nicholls, 1989; self-efficacy, Bandura, 1986) and are based on more dynamic and sophisticated conceptions that assume that the human is an active participant in decision making and in planning achievement. Although organismic approaches are experiencing a resurgence in the literature and are used to good effect in sport and exercise psychology (see Hagger & Chatzisarantis, 2007; Ntoumanis, this volume; Standage & Ryan, this volume), most motivation research in physical activity contexts over the past 35 years or so has adopted a social-cognitive approach, and the specific approach that emerged as the most popular is achievement goal theory (e.g., Duda, 1992, 2001; Duda & Whitehead, 1998; Duda & Hall, 2001; Harwood, Spray, & Keegan, 2008; Roberts, 1984, 1992, 2001; Roberts, Treasure, & Kavussanu, 1997; Roberts et al., 2007). In 1998 Duda and Whitehead identified 135 research studies reported in the 1990s, and just two years later Brunel (2000) identified 160 studies. As of today, the number stands at well over 300! As Harwood and colleagues (2008) state, "The past 20 years have been a watershed for our understanding of sport achievement behavior" (p. 158). Harwood and colleagues (2008) continue to state that achievement goal theory has "triggered a penetrating wave of research into the interpersonal and environmental influences on athlete behavior in achievement settings" (p. 158).

The history and development of achievement goal theory in sport have been reviewed in several recent publications (e.g., Duda, 2005; Duda & Hall, 2001; Harwood, Spray, & Keegan, 2008; Roberts, 2001; Roberts et al., 1997, 2007). I will not exhaustively review the literature in the present chapter; rather, I will focus on identifying key constructs, tenets, and constraints to the theory; reviewing empirical support; and presenting recent proposals for expanding or restructuring the approach, while offering as well some rebuttals and counterpoints! First, let us review the basic conceptual infrastructure of achievement goal theory.

As a historical aside, it was in 1977 that several of us who were working at the Institute for Child Behavior and Development at the Children's Research Center of the University of Illinois (John Nicholls, Marty Maehr, Carole Dweck, Carol Ames, Russ Ames, Ken Hill, Carol Farmer, and I) decided to have a seminar series in the fall to talk about things motivational. At the seminar series, where we all presented our future research proposals, John Nicholls introduced us to some of his new ideas and the concepts that we would now recognize as integral to achievement goal theory: ego and task involvement. John presented his ideas about having equality of motivation through task involvement, and the ideas eventually became a publication in the *American Psychologist* (Nicholls, 1979). That seminar series changed the research directions of all of us involved and led directly to the first article that introduced the concepts in the form that we would recognize today (Maehr & Nicholls, 1980). All of us who attended became achievement goal people in one form or another. Each of us who were there has acknowledged the importance of the fall of 1977 in the development of achievement goal theory. We all contributed, and many of us went on to develop our own interpretations of achievement goal theory (e.g., Dweck, 1986), but at the time the intellectual leader was clearly John Nicholls. Let me give you my interpretation of achievement goal theory, which tends to be highly influenced by Nicholls.

To understand motivation, we need to understand the psychological constructs that energize, direct, and regulate achievement behavior (e.g., Roberts et al., 2007). Achievement goal theory is a social-cognitive theory that assumes that the individual is an intentional, rational, goal-directed organism and that achievement goals govern achievement beliefs and guide subsequent decision making and behavior in achievement contexts. It is argued that to understand the motivation of individuals, the function and meaning of the achievement behavior to the individual must be taken into account and the goal of action must be understood. People give meaning to their achievement behavior through the goals that they adopt. These goals reflect the purposes of achievement striving. Once adopted, the achievement goal determines the integrated pattern of beliefs that energize approach and avoid strategies, the differing engagement levels, and the differing responses to achievement outcomes. Goals are essentially what give an activity purpose or meaning (Kaplan & Maehr, 2007; Maehr & Nicholls, 1980). In other words, achievement goal theory specifies the kinds of goals (purposes or reasons) that direct achievement-related behaviors. By thus recognizing the importance of the meaning of behavior, it becomes clear that there may be multiple goals of action, not one (Maehr & Braskamp, 1986). Thus, an individual's investment of personal resources such as effort, talent, and time in an activity depends on her or his achievement goal.

The overall goal of action in achievement goal theory, thereby becoming the conceptual energizing force, is assumed to be the desire to develop and demonstrate competence and to avoid demonstrating incompetence in an achievement context (Nicholls, 1984). The demonstration or development of competence is the energizing construct of the motivational processes of achievement goal theory. But competence has more than one meaning. One of Nicholls' (1984) conceptual contributions was to argue that more than one conception of ability exists and that achievement goals and behavior may differ depending on the conception of ability held by the person. Nicholls argued that two conceptions of ability (at least) manifest themselves in achievement contexts, namely an undifferentiated concept of ability, in which ability and effort are not differentiated by the individual, either because they are not capable of differentiating, as is the case with young children, or because the individual chooses not to differentiate; and a differentiated concept of ability, in which ability and effort are differentiated (Nicholls, 1984, 1989).

Nicholls (1976, 1978, 1980) argued that children originally possess an undifferentiated conception of ability in which they are not able to differentiate the concepts of luck, task difficulty, and effort from ability. From this undifferentiated perspective, children associate ability with learning through effort so that the more effort one puts forth, the more learning (and ability) one achieves. Following a series of experiments, Nicholls (1978; Nicholls & Miller, 1983, 1984a) determined that by the age of 12 children are able to differentiate luck, task difficulty, and effort from ability, enabling a differentiated perspective. When using this differentiated perspective, children begin to see ability as capacity and recognize that the demonstration of competence involves outperforming others. In terms of effort, high ability is inferred when outperforming others and expending equal or less effort or performing equal to others while expending less effort.

People approach a task or activity with certain goals of action that reflect their personal perceptions and beliefs about the particular achievement activity in which they are engaged and the form of ability that they wish to demonstrate (Dennett, 1978; McArthur & Baron, 1983; Nicholls, 1984, 1989). The conception of ability that they employ and the ways in which they interpret their performance can be understood in terms of these perceptions and beliefs.

These perceptions and beliefs form a personal theory of achievement at the activity (Nicholls, 1989; Roberts et al., 1997; Roberts, 2001) that reflects the individual's perception of how things work in achievement situations. The adopted personal theory of achievement affects the person's beliefs about how to achieve success and avoid failure at the activity. Therefore, based on their personal theory of achievement, people use different conceptions of ability and criteria of success and failure. Clearly, achievement goal theory is therefore a phenomenological theory.

The two conceptions of ability thereby become the source of the criteria by which individuals assess success and failure. The goals of action are to meet the criteria by which success and failure are assessed. Nicholls identifies achievement behavior using the undifferentiated conception of ability as task involvement and achievement behavior using the differentiated conception of ability as ego involvement. When a person is task involved, the goal of action is to develop mastery, improvement, or learning, and the demonstration of ability is self-referenced. Success is realized when the person attains mastery or improvement. The goal of action for an ego-involved person, on the other hand, is to demonstrate ability relative to others, or to outperform others, so ability is other-referenced. Success is realized when the person exceeds the performance of others, especially when expending less effort than they do (Nicholls, 1984, 1989).

State of Involvement

As we stated earlier, the overall goal of action in achievement goal theory is assumed to be the desire to develop and demonstrate competence or to avoid demonstrating incompetence (Nicholls, 1984). Thus, individuals have the goal of demonstrating competence as they conceive competence. When the conception of ability is undifferentiated, then perceived ability becomes less relevant because the individual is trying to demonstrate or develop mastery at the task rather than demonstrate normative ability, and the individual is task involved. Because the individual is trying to demonstrate mastery or improvement, the achievement behaviors will be adaptive in that the individual is more likely to persist in the face of failure, exert effort, select challenging tasks, and be interested in the task (e.g., Duda & Hall, 2001; Nicholls, 1989; Roberts et al., 1997, 2007).

On the other hand, when the conception of ability is differentiated, then perceived ability is relevant because the individual is trying to demonstrate normative ability, or avoid demonstrating inability, to determine how her or his ability fares with comparative others, and the individual is ego involved. If the individual is ego involved and perceives herself or himself as high in ability, then that person is likely to approach the task by engaging in adaptive achievement behaviors. These people seek competitive contests and want to demonstrate superiority. When perceived ability is high, the demonstration of high normative ability is likely to occur; therefore, the individual is motivated to persist and demonstrate that competence to pertinent others. If the person can demonstrate ability with little effort, then this is evidence of even higher ability. Thus, the ego-involved person is inclined to use the least amount of effort to realize the goal of action (Nicholls, 1992; Roberts et al., 2007). If the perception of ability is low, then the individual will realize that he or she is not likely to demonstrate ability and instead will likely manifest maladaptive achievement behaviors because he or she wishes to avoid demonstrating incompetence (Nicholls, 1989). Maladaptive behaviors are those in which the individual avoids the task, avoids challenge, reduces persistence in the face of difficulty, exerts little effort, and, in sport, drops out if achievement of desired goals appears difficult. These people avoid competitive contests because their lack of competence is likely to be exposed. Although the participant may view these avoidance behaviors as adaptive because the behaviors disguise a lack of ability, they are considered maladaptive in terms of achievement behavior.

One of the most important tenets of achievement goal theory is that the states of involvement are mutually exclusive (e.g., Duda & Hall, 2001; Roberts, 2001; Roberts et al., 2007; Treasure, Duda, Hall, Roberts, Ames, & Maehr, 2001). One is either ego involved or task involved, although this notion has been questioned in light of parallel processing models of information processing (Harwood & Hardy, 2001). The theory, however, is quite explicit: A person's state of motivational involvement may be seen to range on a continuum from task involvement to ego involvement. The goal state is dynamic and can change from moment to moment as information is processed (Gernigon, d'Arippe-Longueville, Delignières, & Ninot, 2004). An athlete may begin a task with strong task-involved motivation, but contextual events may cause the athlete to wish to demonstrate superiority to others. The athlete thus becomes ego involved in the task. As an example, an athlete might be brought out of a state of task involvement by a coach's public highlighting of a mistake or by a competitor's or fan's derogatory comment about the athlete's competence. Similarly, an athlete may begin a competitive event with a strong ego-involved motivation but may realize as the event unfolds that she or he will win easily (or lose emphatically) and therefore may begin to work on mastery criteria instead and become task involved. Thus goal states are dynamic and ebb and flow depending on the perception of the athlete.

The measurement of goal states is a particularly challenging task. It has been done in one of three ways. One has been to take one of the existing goal orientation measures and reword the stem to obtain state measures (e.g., Hall & Kerr, 1997; Williams, 1998). A second has been to use single-item measures asking participants to indicate whether they focus on achieving a personal standard of performance (self-referenced) or on beating others in an upcoming contest (other-referenced) (e.g., Harwood & Swain, 1998). The third way is to use video replays of the event and to ask the participant to view the replay and retrospectively reflect on his or her goal involvement at any one point in the contest (e.g., Harwood, 2002). Although the first two procedures may be more predictive of the initial state of involvement than the orientation measures per se (Duda, 2001), these procedures may not capture the essence of task and ego involvement because they are fluid and dynamic during a competitive event (Gernigon et al., 2004). Because the states are so dynamic, by definition, that even if you were able to reflect the state of involvement at the outset of the competition, as the state of involvement ebbs and flows as task and competitive information is processed, we have no indication of the changes that may have occurred (Roberts, 2001). It is naive and conceptually inconsistent to assume that the state of involvement will remain stable throughout the contest.

The best way of estimating the state of involvement is by the procedure used by Smith and Harwood (2001). At least we obtain the participant's observation of her or his goal involvement at various times of the contest. This superior procedure of determining goal involvement considers the dynamic nature of goal involvement. But the procedure is labor intensive and has to be done with each participant over the course of the contest. What typically happens in research on achievement goals is that researchers measure the achievement goal orientation or motivational climate and assume that the state of involvement matches the goal orientation or motivational climate. Strong evidence indicates that this strategy is reasonable (e.g., Roberts et al., 2007).

Clearly, the development of an assessment procedure for the state of goal involvement is a major task. As has been the case with measuring state anxiety, obtaining repeated measures while an athlete is engaged in competition is a practical nightmare. And we have to recognize that repetitive assessments of goal involvement during a competitive encounter may have the effect of changing the goal of involvement (Duda, 2001)! Certainly, if we ask an athlete who is task involved to assess his or her goal involvement by forcing the athlete to consider why he or she is doing what he or she is doing, the athlete may become more self-aware and ego involved in the task. To reduce the likelihood that this will happen, the strategy of Smith and Harwood (2001) to use retrospective recall is clearly the better procedure, despite its disadvantages.

In this chapter when we refer to the motivated state of involvement of the individual, we use the terms *ego involvement* and *task involvement* to be consistent with Nicholls' use of the terms. In addition, when we refer to individual differences (e.g., self-schemas, personal theories of achievement, dispositions), we use the terms *task orientation* and *ego orientation*. Other motivation theorists (e.g., Dweck, 1986; Dweck & Legget, 1988; Elliot, 1997; Maehr & Braskamp, 1986) have used different terms to describe the same phenomena.

Goal Orientations

It is assumed that individuals are predisposed (e.g., by their personal theory of achievement) to act in an ego- or task-involved manner; these predispositions are called achievement goal orientations. Individual differences in the disposition to be ego or task involved may be the result of socialization through task- or ego-involving contexts either in the home or in significant achievement contexts (e.g., classrooms, physical activities) (Nicholls, 1989; Roberts et al., 1997). The way that Elliott and Dweck (1988) explain it is that each of the achievement goals runs off a different "program with different commands, decision rules, and inference rules, and hence, with different cognitive, affective, and behavioral consequences. Each goal, in a sense, creates and organizes its own world—each evoking different thoughts and emotions and calling forth different behaviors" (p. 11).

Goal orientations are not to be viewed as "traits" or based on needs. Rather, they are cognitive schemas that are dynamic and subject to change as information pertaining to the person's performance on the task is processed. But the orientations do have some stability over time, too (Duda & Whitehead, 1998; Roberts, Treasure, & Balague, 1998). These self-cognitions are assumed to be relatively enduring. As examples, Dweck (1986) considered that a person's theory of intelligence is relatively stable, and Nicholls (1984) considered the conceptualization of ability that a person has to be stable as well. Thus, being task or ego oriented refers to the inclination of the individual to be task or ego involved, respectively, in an achievement task.

To measure goal orientations, researchers have typically created questionnaires that are assumed to assess ego and task goal orientations (e.g., Nicholls, Patashnick, & Nolen, 1985). Although Dweck and her colleagues (e.g., Dweck & Leggett, 1988) conceptualize, and measure, the achievement goals as dichotomous, researchers usually assume that the two goals are conceptually orthogonal and measure them accordingly (Duda & Whitehead, 1998; Nicholls et al., 1985; Roberts et al., 1998).

Nicholls (1989) has argued that to assess personal achievement goals, individuals should be asked about the criteria that make them feel successful in a given situation rather than note their definition of competence. In line with this suggestion, Roberts and colleagues (Roberts & Balague, 1989; Roberts et al., 1998; Treasure & Roberts, 1994b) and Duda and colleagues (Duda & Nicholls, 1992; Duda & Whitehead, 1998) have developed the POSQ and TEOSQ scales, respectively, to measure task and ego goal orientations in sport. Both scales have demonstrated acceptable reliability and construct validity (Duda & Whitehead, 1998; Marsh, 1994; Roberts et al., 1998). Although other scales exist, the POSQ and the TEOSQ are the scales that best meet the conceptual criteria of measuring orthogonal achievement goals in sport (Duda & Whitehead, 1998). When developing scales in the future, the constructs identified must be conceptually coherent with achievement goal theory. This has not always been the case in the past (e.g., Gill & Deeter, 1988; Vealey & Campbell, 1988), a circumstance that has created some conceptual confusion (Marsh, 1994).

The most important attribute of achievement goal orientations is that they are orthogonal! That is, task and ego goal orientations are independent, which means that a person can be high or low in either or both orientations at the same time. Using developmental research with children, Nicholls (1989) concluded that by the age of 12, it is possible for an individual to be high or low in both task and ego goal orientation, or high in one and low in the other. The sport and exercise literature has supported this orthogonality (e.g., Duda, 1988; Lemyre, Roberts, & Ommundsen, 2000; Pensgaard & Roberts, 2000; Roberts, Treasure, & Kavussanu, 1996; Walling & Duda, 1995). For reviews see Duda and Whitehead (1998) and Roberts et al. (1997, 2007).

The implications of the orthogonality of goal orientations are profound. The research evidence suggests that individuals with high task and high ego orientations, as well as high task and low ego orientations, have the most adaptive motivational profiles (e.g., Fox, Goudas, Biddle, Duda, & Armstrong, 1994; Hodge & Petlichkoff, 2000; Pensgaard & Roberts, 2002; Roberts, Treasure, & Kavussanu, 1996; Smith, Balaguer, & Duda, 2006). As we would expect, when an individual has been high in ego and low in task orientation, or high in task and low in ego orientation, then the findings are consistent with the findings reported earlier for task and ego orientation (task orientation is adaptive; ego orientation, especially when coupled with low perception of competence, is generally maladaptive). But we find that high ego orientation when coupled with high (or moderate) task orientation is not maladaptive (e.g., Cumming, Hall, Harwood, & Gammage, 2002; Harwood, Cumming, & Fletcher, 2004; Pensgaard & Roberts, 2002; Smith et al., 2006; Wang & Biddle, 2001). Therefore, rather than focusing on whether an individual is task or ego oriented, it is important to consider the simultaneous combination of task and ego orientation (Kaplan & Maehr, 2002; Roberts et al., 2007).

Two strategies have been used to determine the goal orientation profiles (high in each, high in one and low in the other, and low in each). One strategy has been to create the four profile groups through a mean or median split of the task and ego scores (e.g., Fox et al., 1994; Roberts et al., 1996). A weakness of this approach is that individuals may be misclassified. Even using a criterion of 0.5 standard deviation above or below the mean as a cutoff (e.g., Roberts et al., 1996) eliminates a significant number of participants. An alternative is to use cluster analysis to obtain the goal profiles (e.g., Hodge & Petlichkoff, 2000). Cluster analysis is a data analytical approach that produces groups that possess the greatest amount of within-group similarity and the greatest amount of between-group dissimilarity of participants using goal orientations as the characteristics of interest (Hair, Anderson, Tatham, & Black, 1998; Smith et al., 2006). Researchers in sport have used cluster analysis to investigate goal orientations and in general have supported the use of the cluster analysis to produce goal orientation profiles (e.g., Cumming et al., 2002; Harwood et al., 2004; Hodge & Petlichkoff, 2000; Smith et al., 2006; Wang & Biddle, 2001). The constitution of the clusters has varied across these studies, but moderate levels of goal orientation consistently emerge. More important, participants with high ego and high task goal orientation and those with high task and moderate or low ego goal orientation have consistently reported responses that are more desirable on the variables under study (e.g., greater imagery use, more physical activity, higher self-determination, better social relationships). Thus, the motivational implications of the orthogonality of goals are an important attribute of achievement goal theory.

Elite athletes are likely to be high task and high ego (e.g., Pensgaard & Roberts, 2000) or high ego and low or moderate in task orientation. The individuals most at risk, however, are the high ego and low task oriented. These people are most likely to exhibit maladaptive motivation, drop out of participation, and even be the athletes most likely to burn out when they believe that they cannot demonstrate competence (see Lemyre, Roberts, & Stray-Gundersen, 2007). The low ego and low task people are the least motivated and may not even commit to achievement tasks. The important issues in the present discussion are that the orthogonality of goal orientations has been demonstrated conclusively and that the orthogonality of the goals is an important determinant of motivated behavior. The avenue of research related to achievement goals in the context of physical activity has demonstrated that individual differences in goal orientation are associated with different motivational processes and different achievement behaviors.

Motivational Climate

One of the most powerful aspects of achievement goal theory is that it incorporates not only the individual difference variables of task and ego orientations but also the situational determinants of task and ego involvement. The situation plays a central role in the motivation process (Ames, 1992a; Nicholls, 1984, 1989). Consistent with other motivation research that has emphasized the situational determinants of behavior (e.g., Ames, 1984a; deCharms, 1976, 1984), research within achievement goal theory has examined how the structure of the environment can make it more or less likely that an individual will become task or ego involved in an achievement environment. The premise of this line of research is that the individual perceives the degree to which task and ego criteria are salient within the context. This is then assumed to affect the achievement behaviors, cognition, and affective responses of individuals through their perception of the behaviors necessary to achieve success or avoid failure (Roberts et al., 1997, 2007). When we refer to the achievement cues within the context, the schemas emerging from achievement situations, we will be consistent with Ames (1984a, 1992b) and refer to the task-involving aspect of the context as mastery criteria and the ego-involving aspect of the context as performance criteria.

The premise of the research from a situational perspective is that the nature of an individual's experiences and his or her interpretation of those experiences influence the degree to which a mastery or performance climate is perceived as salient. A performance climate is created when the criteria of success and failure are other-referenced and ego involving (Ames, 1992b), and the athlete perceives that the demonstration of normative ability is valued. A mastery climate is created when the criteria of success and failure are self-referenced and task involving (Ames, 1992b), and the athlete perceives that the demonstration of mastery and learning are valued. The characteristic of the climate is assumed to affect an individual's interpretation of the criteria of success and failure extant in the context and to affect achievement behavior. The individual will adopt adaptive achievement strategies (namely, to work hard, seek challenging tasks, persist in the face of difficulty) in the climate in which he or she feels comfortable. For most people, especially children, this is in the climate that emphasizes mastery (e.g., Biddle, 2001; Roberts et al., 1997, 2007; Treasure, 2001). But we must not forget that some people function well in a performance climate. Within achievement goal theory, these are assumed to be the people who are high in perceived competence at the activity and who wish to demonstrate their competence and superiority to others.

In mastery-oriented situations, an individual is assumed to adopt adaptive achievement strategies such as working hard, seeking challenging tasks, and persisting in the face of difficulty. Certainly, the extant research supports that assumption (e.g., Treasure, 2001). Sometimes, however, ego-involved individuals also adopt adaptive achievement strategies. As argued earlier, these ego-involved people have high perceptions of their ability and enjoy demonstrating their superiority to others. As long as the perception of high ability lasts, these people seek challenging tasks and revel in demonstrating their ability. But as soon as the perception of ability wavers or the perception of ability becomes low for some reason, these people are likely to adopt maladaptive achievement strategies (namely, to seek easy tasks, reduce effort, or give up in the face of difficulty).

The extant literature in physical education and sport suggests that the creation of a mastery motivational climate is likely to be important in optimizing positive (i.e., well-being, sportsmanship, persistence, task perseverance, adaptive achievement strategies) and attenuating negative (i.e., overtraining, self-handicapping) responses (e.g., Kuczka & Treasure, 2005; Miller, Roberts, & Ommundsen, 2004; Ommundsen & Roberts, 1999; Sarrazin, Roberts, Cury, Biddle, & Famose, 2002; Standage, Treasure, Hooper, & Kuczka, 2007; Standage, Duda, & Ntoumanis, 2003a; Treasure & Roberts, 2001a). This pattern of findings has been confirmed in a meta-analysis consisting of statistically estimated effect sizes from 14 studies ($n = 4,484$) that examined the effect of different motivation climates in sport and physical education on cognitive and affective responses (Ntoumanis & Biddle, 1999a). As an example, Parish and Treasure (2003) investigated the influence of perceptions of the motivational climate and perceived ability on situational motivation and physical activity behavior of a large sample of adolescent male and female physical education students. The findings showed that perceptions of a mastery climate were strongly related to more self-determined forms of situational motivation (intrinsic and identified motivation) and were predictive of physical activity behavior. In contrast, perceptions of a performance climate were found to be strongly related to less self-determined forms of situational motivation (extrinsic and amotivation) and unrelated to physical activity. The extant evidence, therefore, supports the position that perceptions of a mastery motivational climate are more associated with adaptive motivational and affective response patterns than are perceptions of a performance climate in the context of sport and physical education.

For the purposes of the present discussion, it is good to realize that dispositional goal orientations and perceptions of the climate are two independent dimensions of motivation that interact to affect behavior (Nicholls, 1989). And the powerful and parsimonious aspect of achievement goal theory is that both the individual dispositions and the perception of the motivational climate are encompassed by the theory. It is true, however, that research to date deals primarily with dispositional goal orientations and perceptions of the motivational climate as separate constructs in isolation from each other. It has been suggested that an interactionist approach that looks to combine both variables promises to provide a more complete understanding of achievement behaviors in the sport and physical education experience (e.g., Duda, Chi, Newton, Walling, & Catley, 1995; Papaioannou, 1994; Roberts, 1992; Roberts & Treasure, 1992; Roberts et al., 1997, 2007; Treasure, 2001).

Interaction Between Orientations and Climate

Although these two lines of research have been conducted in relative isolation, an interactionist approach that looks to combine both types of variables may provide a far more complete understanding of the motivation process. To this end, Dweck and Leggett (1988) suggested that dispositional goal orientations should be seen as an individual variable that will determine the probability of adopting a certain goal of action, that is, a task or ego state of goal involvement, and a particular behavior pattern in achievement contexts. Situational variables, such as perceptions of the motivational climate, however, were proposed as potential moderators of the influence of the individual variables. As Roberts and colleagues (1997) argued, when the situational criteria are vague or weak an individual dispositional goal orientation should hold sway. In contexts where the situational criteria are particularly salient it is possible that perceptions of the climate may override an individual's dispositional goal orientation and be a stronger predictor of behavioral, cognitive, and affective outcomes. It is also proposed that children and young adolescents, who have yet to firm up their personal theories of achievement, may be more susceptible to the influence of situational variables than older adolescents and adults (Roberts & Treasure, 1992).

The result of the limited research that has examined both individual and situational variables has shown that taking into account both of these variables enhances our understanding of the sport context (e.g., Kavussanu & Roberts, 1996; Seifriz, Duda, & Chi, 1992). The limited evidence to date also provides support for Dweck and Leggett's (1988) contention that situational variables may moderate the influence of goal orientations (e.g., Swain & Harwood, 1996; Treasure & Roberts, 1998). When significant interaction effects emerged they did so in a manner consistent with a moderation model. Although finding statistically significant interaction effects is often difficult (see Duda et al., 1995; Papaioannou, 1994; Roberts & Treasure, 1992; Roberts et al., 1997, 2007; Treasure, 2001), the findings of the limited studies that have been conducted are consistent with the fundamental tenets of achievement goal theory and speak to the veracity of investigating the interaction in addition to the main effect of individual and situational variables. But how the researcher measures interaction effects is not a trivial issue.

Measuring Interaction Effects

A study by Seifriz, Duda, and Chi (1992), with male high school basketball players, examined the degree to which intrinsic motivation and attributional beliefs were a function of perceptions of the motivational climate, dispositional goal orientation, or a combination of both. The findings of this study indicated that attributional beliefs were best predicted by an individual's goal orientation. Although perceptions of the motivational climate and dispositional goal orientation emerged as predictors of enjoyment, dispositional goal orientation was the predominant predictor of reported effort exerted and perceived. Treasure (2001) argued that although Seifriz and colleagues claimed to be testing the possible interactive effects of dispositional goal orientations and perceptions of the motivational climate, the statistical analyses utilized were not consistent with this statement. By assessing the unique variance, these are main effect analyses.

The influence of achievement goal orientations and perceptions of the motivational climate has also been examined in a study conducted by Cury and colleagues (1996). In this study the researchers used structural equation modeling (SEM) to examine the interest of adolescent girls in physical education. Cury and colleagues hypothesized that direct paths would emerge from mastery- and performance-oriented perceptions of the climate to the pupils' interest in physical education. The results showed an excellent fit of the data to the hypothesized model. Perceptions of the motivational climate in the physical education class emerged as more important predictors of pupil interest than achievement goal orientations. The researchers concluded by suggesting that their findings supported the positive effects of a mastery-oriented motivational climate in physical education and offered evidence of a possible shaping effect of the climate on an individual's goal orientation.

Structural equation modeling is a useful tool for the development and testing of complex social theories (Duncan & Stoolmiller, 1993). SEM has an advantage over regression analytic techniques in that parameters of a model can be specified simultaneously. SEM statistical packages also provide modification indices that make suggestions about how the model could be improved. Although modification indices are useful tools to aid in improving the model, as Treasure (2001) argued, it is important to recognize that the modification indices are statistically rather than theoretically derived. Consequently, only those revisions that are theoretically coherent should be used in subsequent runs. This is not an insignificant issue. As I have argued (Roberts, 2008) elsewhere, conceptual coherence should take precedence over statistical or empirical convenience.

Although SEM may be an appropriate technique to examine potential relationships among achievement goals and perceptions of the motivational climate, it is limited in that it does not allow for the testing of interactive effects. As Hardy (1998) has stated, the only way that interactive effects can be assessed is through multiple sample analyses or moderated hierarchical regression analyses (Jaccard, Turrisi, & Wan, 1990). The approach, however, may provide some interesting insights into how goal orientations and the motivational climate may be related.

Research has found interesting relationships between orientations and the climate (e.g., Swain & Harwood, 1996; Treasure & Roberts, 1998), but some research has failed to find the hypothesized effects (e.g., Harwood & Swain, 1998). Although moderated hierarchical analysis does enable researchers to examine the separate as well as the interactive effects of goal orientations and the motivational climate, this type of analysis is not powerful. But the fact that significant main effects emerged for both climate and orientations appears to confirm the veracity of investigating the effects of goal orientations and perceptions of the motivational climate that the majority of achievement goal research has taken to date.

Although some have discussed the implications of both goal orientations and the motivational climate within a model (e.g., Roberts, 1992; Treasure, 2001), I have to agree with Harwood and colleagues (2008) that research in sport has not yet fully examined the interaction of dispositions and the situational criteria of the motivational climate on the manifestation of goal involvement.

Motivational Implications of Task or Ego Involvement

Most research in achievement goal theory has focused on the antecedents and consequences of being ego or task involved and has looked at goal orientations and the motivational climate in isolation. As stated earlier, the most important facet of achievement goal theory is that the individual difference variables (self-schemas, personal theory of achievement, valence, dispositions, goal orientations) and the situational variables (motivational climate, emergent schemas) are part of the same theory and are conceptually compatible. The individual difference variables and the situational variables are both determinants of goal involvement. The kernel of the theory is that it is the state of goal involvement that energizes achievement striving. Thus, looking at goals and climate independently is rather artificial (which is what I and everyone else have done previously). The essential issue is that the state of involvement drives achievement striving; therefore, it is more conceptually coherent to look at the effect of being task and ego involved, however one gets there! I have already alluded to the difficulty of measuring task and ego involvement in situ, so I shall be consistent with the vast majority of the literature and assume that when individuals score high on ego orientation or are subjected to a performance climate, then they are more likely to be ego involved. Similarly, when individuals score high in task orientation or are subjected to a mastery climate, then they are more likely to be task involved. It makes conceptual sense, therefore, to look at the literature in terms of state of involvement rather than to break down the literature into orientation and climate, the means to goal involvement. Remember that achievement goal theory is much less concerned with *what* individuals are trying to achieve than with *why* (Urdan & Maehr, 1995). It may be statistically and empirically accurate to relate goal orientations or climate to the cognitive, affective, and behavioral variables that we typically study, but it is not strictly conceptually accurate. Accordingly, in this section I shall briefly review the research on achievement goal orientations and the motivational climate together rather than separately, as has been done in past reviews. I shall address the association between achievement goals of involvement on cognitive, affective, and important outcome variables. As an aside, from this point of view, we may regard the theory as being an Ames–Nicholls achievement goal theory.

Beliefs About Competence and Success

One of the fundamental differences between task-involved and ego-involved athletes is the way that they define and assess competence and success. Task-involved individuals tend to construe competence based on self-referenced criteria and are primarily concerned with mastery of the task, so they are more likely than ego-involved individuals to develop perceived competence over time (Elliott & Dweck, 1988). In contrast, ego-involved people feel competent when they compare favorably with others, so they are less likely to maintain high perceived relative ability or competence, especially those who already question their ability (see Dweck, 1986). This prediction of achievement goal theory has been supported in numerous studies with a variety of conceptualizations of competence perceptions (e.g., Anderson & Dixon, 2009; Boyce, Gano-Overway, & Love Campbell, 2009; Chi, 1994; Cury, Biddle, Sarrazin, & Famose, 1997; Dunn, 2000; Escarti & Gutierrez, 2001; Kavussanu & Roberts, 1996; Nicholls & Miller, 1983, 1984b; Standage et al., 2003a; Vlachopoulos & Biddle, 1996, 1997; Xiang, McBride, Bruene, & Liu, 2007).

Several lines of research suggest that using the task-involving conception of achievement to judge demonstrated competence enhances resiliency of perceived competence. As I and my colleagues (Roberts et al., 2007) argue, the implications of these findings are particularly important in learning contexts. For example, for individuals who are beginning to learn a new physical skill, being task involved may be instrumental in facilitating perceptions of competence, effort, and persistence, and consequently success in the activity. This idea is supported by the Van Yperen and Duda (1999) study with Dutch male soccer players. They found that athletes high in task orientation were judged by their coaches to possess greater soccer skills from pre- to postseason. A task orientation fosters perceptions of competence and success for people who are either high or low in perceived competence and encourages the exertion of effort. An ego orientation, on the other hand, may lower perceptions of success, perceived competence, and thus effort, especially for those who already are unsure of their ability.

Nicholls (1989, 1992) maintained that a person's beliefs about the causes of success in a situation comprise her or his personal theory of how things work in achievement situations. For people with low perceived ability, a belief that ability causes success will likely result in frustration and a lack of confidence, and even lead to dropping out because these individuals believe that they do not possess the natural ability required to be successful. In the physical activity domain, where practice and hard work are essential for improvement, especially at the early stages of persistence, a belief that effort leads to success is the most adaptive for maintaining motivation.

Research has confirmed these arguments with young athletes, high school students, young disabled athletes participating in wheelchair basketball, and elite adult athletes (e.g., Anderson & Dixon 2009; Boyce et al., 2009; Conroy, Kaye, & Coatsworth, 2006; Cox & Williams, 2008; Duda, Fox, Biddle, & Armstrong, 1992; Duda & Nicholls, 1992; Guivernau & Duda, 1995; Hom, Duda, & Miller, 1993; Kavussanu & Roberts, 1996; Lochbaum & Roberts, 1993; Newton & Duda, 1993; Ommundsen & Roberts, 1999; Ommundsen, Roberts, & Kavussanu, 1998; Roberts & Ommundsen, 1996; Roberts, Treasure, & Kavussanu, 1996; Smoll, Smith, & Cumming, 2007; Treasure & Roberts, 1994a; Walling & Duda, 1995; White & Duda, 1993). Whether the criteria for being task or ego involved were determined with achievement orientations or the motivational climate, the findings are similar. Research has consistently demonstrated that being task involved is associated with the belief that hard work and cooperation lead to success in sport. In general, being ego involved has been associated with the view that success is achieved through having high ability and using strategies such as cheating and trying to impress the coach.

Purposes of Sport

In classroom-based research, being ego involved has been associated with the belief that the purpose of education is to provide one with wealth and social status, which is evidence of superior ability. Being task involved, on the other hand, has been linked to the view that an important purpose of school education is to enhance learning and understanding of the world and to foster commitment to society (Nicholls et al., 1985; Thorkildsen, 1988). Similar findings have been reported in sport and physical activity (e.g., Duda, 1989; Duda & Nicholls, 1992; Ommundsen & Roberts, 1999; Ommundsen et al.,

1998; Roberts & Ommundsen, 1996; Roberts et al., 1995, 1996; Treasure & Roberts, 1994a; White, Duda, & Keller, 1998), indicating that world views cut across educational and sport contexts. Being task involved has been associated with the belief that the purpose of sport is to enhance self-esteem; advance good citizenship; foster mastery and cooperation; encourage a physically active lifestyle; foster prosocial values, such as social responsibility, cooperation, and the willingness to follow rules; and develop lifetime skills. In contrast, being ego involved has been linked to the view that sport should provide a person with social status, enhance popularity and career mobility, enhance status, and teach superiority. In addition, being task involved in physical education has been associated with the view that the purpose of physical education is to provide students with opportunities for improvement, hard work, and collaboration with peers and being ego involved in physical education has been associated with the view that the purpose of physical education is to provide students with an easy class and teach them to be more competitive (Papaioannou & Macdonald, 1993; Walling & Duda, 1995).

Affect and Intrinsic Interest

Another consistent finding in achievement goal research has been the link between task involvement and experienced enjoyment, satisfaction, and interest during participation in sport and physical activity (e.g., Balaguer, Duda, & Crespo, 1999; Barkoukis, Ntoumanis, & Thøgersen-Ntoumani, 2010; Boixados, Cruz, Torregrosa, & Valiente, 2004; Cunningham & Xiang, 2008; Duda et al., 1995; Duda & Nicholls, 1992; Jackson & Roberts, 1992; Kavussanu & Roberts, 1995, 1996; Morris & Kavussanu, 2009; Mouratidis, Vansteenkiste, Lens, & Vanden Auweele, 2009; Papaioannou, Ampatzoglou, Kalogiannis, & Sagovits, 2008; Parish & Treasure, 2003; Sage & Kavassanu, 2007; Treasure & Roberts, 2001a; Walling, Duda, & Crawford, 2002). In these studies, being ego involved was either inversely related or unrelated to intrinsic interest, satisfaction, or enjoyment.

An interesting finding is that when studies have looked at goal orientations, participants with a high task orientation, in combination with either a high or low ego orientation, experience greater enjoyment than those who are high in ego orientation and low in task orientation (e.g., Biddle, Akande, Vlachopoulos, & Fox, 1996; Cury et al., 1996; Goudas, Biddle, & Fox, 1994; Vlachopoulos & Biddle, 1996, 1997). Clearly, when high in ego orientation, having a high task orientation seems to have a buffering effect on the resultant state of involvement. Being task involved seems to be especially important in sport and physical activity because it is associated with enjoyment and satisfaction regardless of one's perceived success (Goudas et al., 1994), perceived ability (Vlachopoulos & Biddle, 1997), or intrinsic interest (Goudas, Biddle, Fox, & Underwood 1995).

Probably the most significant study to illustrate the association of goal states with affect was conducted by Ntoumanis and Biddle (1999a). They conducted a meta-analysis with 41 independent samples and found that task orientation and positive affect were moderately to highly positively correlated. The relationship between ego orientation and both positive and negative affect was small. In brief, being task involved fosters positive affect in physical activities.

Anxiety

In 1986 I was probably the first to suggest that athletes who are ego involved (i.e., are high in ego orientation) may experience anxiety as a function of whether they believe that they can demonstrate sufficient competence in an achievement context. Those with a task orientation should be less likely to experience anxiety because their competence and self-worth are not threatened. Research has generally supported this hypothesis and the basic tenets of achievement goal theory (e.g., Roberts et al., 2007). Being task involved has been negatively associated with precompetitive anxiety (Vealey & Campbell, 1988), cognitive anxiety with young athletes (Ommundsen & Pedersen, 1999), somatic and cognitive anxiety (Hall & Kerr, 1997), task irrelevant worries and the tendency to think about withdrawing from an activity (Newton & Duda, 1999), and concerns about mistakes and parental criticisms (Hall & Kerr, 1997; Hall, Kerr, & Matthews, 1998). Further, a task orientation has been associated with maintaining concentration and feeling good about the game (Newton & Duda, 1993). An ego orientation, on the other hand, has been positively related to state and trait anxiety (Boyd, 1990; Newton & Duda, 1993; Vealey & Campbell, 1988; White & Zellner, 1996), cognitive anxiety in the form of worry (White & Zellner, 1996), getting upset in competition, and concentration disruption during competition (Newton & Duda, 1999; White & Zellner, 1996).

The extant research, whether using individual dispositions or the motivational climate to assume task and ego involvement, consistently shows that when task involved, most participants, from children (e.g., Hall & Kerr, 1997) to elite performers (e.g., Pensgaard & Roberts, 2000), reduce their anxiety and concerns about performing. When ego involved, the opposite is true; a positive association is found with anxiety, worry, and concern with mistakes (e.g., Abrahamsen, Roberts, & Pensgaard, 2008; Boyd, 1990; Escarti & Gutierrez, 2001; Grossbard, Cumming, Standage, Smith, & Smoll, 2007; Hall & Kerr, 1997; Hall, Kerr, & Matthews, 1998; Newton & Duda, 1999; Ntoumanis & Biddle, 1998; Ommundsen & Pedersen, 1999; Papaioannou & Kouli, 1999; Pensgaard & Roberts, 2000; Smith, Smoll, & Cumming, 2007; Vealey & Campbell, 1988; Vosloo, Ostrow, & Watson, 2009; White & Zellner, 1996).

Ommundsen and Pedersen (1999) remind us, however, that simply stating that being task involved is beneficial in terms of anxiety is not necessarily sufficient. Ommundsen and Pederson found that being task involved did decrease cognitive trait anxiety, whereas low perceived competence increased both somatic and cognitive anxiety. This finding suggests that being task involved is beneficial but that perceived competence is also an important predictor of anxiety. Being task oriented and perceiving one's competence to be high are both important antecedents to reducing anxiety in sport.

The work cited above indicates the interest in affective and cognitive variables that has been the focus of much research in achievement goal theory. The most interesting aspect of the recent work with achievement goal theory has been the attention paid to achievement strategies and outcome variables, especially performance, exerted effort, peer relationships, perceived well-being, overtraining and dropping out, and cheating in sport. In particular, the emphasis has been on the effect of the motivational climate on these variables. An upsurge has occurred in research on the way that coaches coach and teachers teach! The criteria of success and failure that teachers and coaches impart to participants have important implications for the resultant demonstrated motivation and outcome of the sport and exercise experience. The big gap in the literature that needs to be closed is the effect of the way that parents parent! We have almost no information on the influence of the criteria of success and failure that parents impose on their children within the sport experience.

Achievement Strategies

Lochbaum and Roberts (1993) were the first to report that the emphasis placed on problem solving and adaptive learning strategies was tied to being task involved in a sport setting. Research that measured orientations or the motivational climate has demonstrated that being task involved is associated with adaptive achievement strategies, such as being committed to practice, learning, and effort, and being less likely to avoid practice (e.g., Boyce et al., 2009; Gano-Overway & Ewing, 2004; Keegan, Harwood, Spray, & Lavallee, 2009; Kouli & Papaioannou, 2009; Lochbaum & Roberts, 1993; Magyar & Feltz, 2003; Morgan & Kingston, 2008; Morgan, Sproule, McNeill, Kingston, & Wang, 2006; Ommundsen, 2006; Ommundsen & Roberts, 1999, 2003; Roberts et al., 1995; Roberts & Ommundsen, 1996; Theeboom, De Knop, & Weiss, 1995; Treasure & Roberts, 2001a; Valentini & Rudisill, 2004). Typically, in these studies, being ego involved corresponded to a tendency to avoid practice and to focus on winning during competition.

In regard to posttask feedback, Cury and colleagues (Cury, Sarrazin, & Famose, 1997; Cury & Sarrazin, 1998) found that high-ego-involved climbers who were low in perceived ability were more likely than task-involved climbers to reject task-related and objective performance feedback but that high-ego-involved climbers who were high in perceived ability selected normative feedback and rejected task relevant information. This finding showed that those who were ego involved and had low perceived ability rejected normative feedback because it was likely to be negative, whereas high-ego-involved participants with high perceived ability sought normative feedback because it was likely to be positive.

These studies demonstrate that the achievement strategies endorsed by sport and physical activity participants are meaningfully related to their being task or ego involved. Across the studies, being task involved was coupled with adaptive learning strategies, the value of practice to learn new skills and improve, and seeking task relevant information. In contrast, ego-involved athletes endorsed avoiding practice as an achievement strategy and avoided task relevant information in favor of obtaining normative feedback (but only when high in perceived ability).

Effort and Performance

Little research to date has investigated exerted effort and performance. Vealey and Campbell (1988) were among the first to provide evidence of a performance boost from being task involved. Van Yperen and Duda (1999) also found that when football players were task involved, an increase in skilled performance resulted (as perceived by the coach). Similarly, Theeboom et al. (1995) investigated the effect of a mastery program on the development of motor skills of children and found that the task-involved group reported higher levels of enjoyment and reliably exhibited better motor skills than those who were ego involved.

Probably the best evidence thus far that task-involved athletes performed better than ego-involved athletes has been presented by Sarrazin et al. (2002). We investigated exerted effort and performance of adolescents involved in a climbing task. The results demonstrated that task-involved boys exerted more effort than ego-involved boys and performed better (a success rate of 60% versus 42%). The degree of exerted effort was determined by an interaction of the person's achievement goal of action, perceived ability, and task difficulty. Ego-involved boys with high perceived ability and task-involved boys with low perceived ability exerted the most effort on the moderate and difficult courses; ego-involved boys with low perceived ability exerted the least effort on the moderate and very difficult courses. Finally, task-involved boys with high perceived ability exerted more effort when the task was perceived as more difficult.

In general, the research has shown that when task involved, participants exhibit (or report) greater effort than others (e.g., Cury et al., 1996; Duda, 1988; Duda & Nicholls, 1992; ; Durand, Cury, Sarrazin, & Famose, 1996; Goudas et al., 1994; Ommundsen et al., 1998; Sarrazin et al., 2002; Solmon, 1996; Tammen, Treasure, & Power, 1992; Treasure & Roberts, 2001a), and when ego involved, participants with low perceived ability exhibit reduced effort compared to participants with high perceived ability (Cury, Biddle, et al., 1997). Clearly, there is developing evidence (e.g., Cumming, Smoll, Smith, & Grossbard, 2007; Cervelló, Santos Rosa, Garcia Calvo, Jiménez, & Iglesias, 2007; Papaioannou et al., 2008; Martin, Rudisill, & Hastie, 2009) that being task involved leads to better performance. We may conclude, with the limited evidence thus far, that task-involved people try harder and perform better!

Peer Relationships and Friendship Patterns

Peers play a central role in the lives of adolescents, and peer influence and opinion are salient forces in adolescent development (Bigelow, Lewko, & Salhani, 1989; Smith, 1999; Hartup, 1996). During this period, peers provide emotional support and friendship (Coleman & Byrd, 2003), and positive social preferences by peers during childhood and adolescence can have strong buffering effects on the development of later antisocial psychopathology (Parker & Asher, 1987). Research has demonstrated that the domain of competitive sport is a particularly important context for psychosocial development in that peer status, peer acceptance, well-being, identity, and self-worth are established and developed in that environment (e.g., Dworkin, Larson, & Hansen, 2003; Evans & Roberts, 1987; Fox, 1988; Heuzé, Sarrazin, Masiero, Raimbault, & Thomas, 2006; Kavussanu, Seal, & Phillips, 2006; Keegan et al., 2009; Kouli & Papaioannou, 2009; Ommundsen, Roberts, Lemyre, & Miller, 2005; Roberts & Treasure, 1992; Smoll & Smith, 2002; Stuntz & Weiss, 2009; World Health Organization, 1989; Vazou, Ntoumanis, & Duda, 1995). These psychosocial attributes are based on many factors, but one way that children can gain acceptance and recognition among their peers is to demonstrate competence in an activity valued by other children (Roberts & Treasure, 1994). One area of competence highly valued by children is athletic or physical ability (e.g., Chase & Drummer, 1992; Duda, 1981; Roberts & Treasure, 1992). Being a good athlete appears to be a strong social asset for a child, especially for boys (Roberts & Treasure, 1994).

Sport, therefore, is an important arena for peer interaction and is assumed to provide a vehicle for learning to cooperate with teammates, negotiate and offer solutions to moral conflicts, develop self-control, display courage, develop positive peer relationships, and learn such virtues as fairness, team loyalty, persistence, and teamwork (e.g., Kleiber & Roberts, 1987; Shields & Bredemeier, 1995). Youth sport represents an important contributor to the development of valuable peer bonds (Dworkin et al., 2003). In sport, peers take on a variety of psychosocial roles because peers are identified as preferred sources of competence estimation and self-esteem enhancement, and they have been found to influence young people's friendship patterns and peer interaction (e.g., Duncan, 1993; Heuzé et al., 2006; Kavussanu et al., 2006; Keegan et al., 2009; Kouli & Papaioannou, 2009; Roberts & Ommundsen, 2003; Roberts, Ommundsen, Lemyre, & Miller, 2004; Stuntz & Weiss, 2009; Vazou et al., 2005). Thus, the sport experience should be available to all, and the context should be psychologically constructed to enhance peer interaction and peer bonding.

As reported earlier, one way to enhance peer relationships is to construct a mastery climate in the sport experience. Being task involved is associated with strong beliefs and perceptions that effort and cooperation with others will lead to success and that participation in sport will enhance self-esteem, advance good citizenship, and foster mastery and prosocial values such as social responsibility, collaboration, and cooperation (Duda, 1989; Lochbaum & Roberts, 1993; Ommundsen et al., 1998; Roberts & Ommundsen, 1996; Roberts et al., 1995). It is argued that paying attention to personal improvement, coordinated team effort, and cooperation facilitates constructive peer relationships. Positive relationships between high task orientation and reported attraction to the team and perceived team integration have been reported (e.g., Chi & Lu, 1995; Duda, 2001). In contrast, being ego involved is associated with strong beliefs and perceptions that demonstrating superior ability to others leads to success and that participants will enhance self-importance and social status (e.g., Duda, 1989; Lochbaum & Roberts, 1993; Ommundsen et al., 1998; Roberts & Ommundsen, 1996; Roberts et al., 1995; Smith et al., 2006). It is argued that an egocentric mode of thinking gives rise to less sensitivity, empathy, and cooperation toward fellow team members when a participant is in pursuit of individual achievement. Such egocentric thinking may facilitate intrateam rivalry, interpersonal conflict, and a view of the other players on the team as competitors to be conquered (Duda & Hall, 2001; Roberts et al., 2007; Shields & Bredemeier, 1995; Smith, 2003; Smith et al., 2006). Consequently, mutual peer acceptance, interpersonal attraction, and the quality of friendship may suffer (Chi & Lu, 1995). As we can appreciate, coaching coaches to construct a mastery climate within the sport experience optimizes the potential of the experience to enhance peer relationships and friendship patterns.

Well-Being and Ill-Being

Related to the development of peer relationships and friendship patterns is perceived psychological well-being. It is argued that participation in sport as a child is important for psychological well-being (e.g., Dworkin et al., 2003; Larson & Verma, 1999; Ommundsen et al., 2005; Smoll & Smith, 2002; Steptoe & Butler, 1996; World Health Organization, 1989). As a stark example, Tomson and colleagues (Tomson, Pangrazi, Friedman, & Hutchinson, 2003) found that American children 8 to 12 years of age who did not play sports outside of school had a relative risk for depressive symptoms that were 1.3 to 2.4 times higher than those who reported playing sports outside of school, and those classified as inactive had a risk 2.8 to 3.4 times higher than those classified as active. Thus, sport may lead to well-being. The counterpoint is that organized sport is also a context laden with negative consequences. Participation may create stress, poor relationships between coach and athlete, poor peer relationships, fear of failure and injury, and unreasonable expectations for young people to succeed. This circumstance may lead to perceived ill-being (e.g., Coakley, 2001; Holt, Hoar, & Fraser, 2005).

The study of well-being has increased recently (e.g., Sheldon & Bettencourt, 2002; Zaff et al., 2003), and the approach includes emotional well-being characterized by psychological functioning and an integrated sense of self within the domain of action, in our case sport (e.g., Reinboth & Duda, 2004), vitality and additional positive everyday affective states (e.g., Diener, Suh, Lucas,

& Smith, 1999; Ryan & Frederick, 1997; Steptoe & Butler, 1996), the fulfillment of what are called basic psychological needs (e.g., Ryan, Deci, & Grolnick, 1995), intrinsically regulated motivation (e.g., Ratelle, Vallerand, Chantal, & Provencher, 2004), and harmonious passion (e.g., Vallerand, Mageau, Ratelle, Leonard, Blanchard, Koestner, & Gagne, 2003). In contrast, psychosocial ill-being includes indices of malfunction and disruption, such as amotivation (e.g., Ratelle et al., 2004); negative everyday affective states (e.g., Crawford & Henry, 2004; Diener et al., 1999), dysfunctional achievement behaviors, such as self-handicapping (e.g., Greaven, Santor, Thompson, & Zuroff, 2000); detrimental personal indices, such as maladaptive perfectionism (e.g., Flett, Hewitt, & De Rosa, 1996); and obsessive activity involvement (e.g., Vallerand et al., 2003).

As we would expect, one approach advocated to enhance subjective well-being is to focus on the psychological environment that surrounds the participation of young people. As Biddle and coworkers argue, "While physical activity may enhance psychological well-being, it is likely that the prevailing psychological climate and social interactions inherent in such settings will be more crucial than the physical activity itself" (Biddle, Gorely, & Stensel, 2004, p. 682). The psychological environment may generate conditions conducive for young people to benefit psychologically, as well as conditions that are detrimental for young people (e.g., Reinboth & Duda, 2004; Roberts et al., 2007).

As I have argued earlier for peer relationships, one way to enhance the probability of enhancing well-being is to construct a mastery climate in the sport experience. Being task involved is associated with the multifaceted variables that make up the perception of well-being. Subjective well-being is enhanced by the positive consequences of participation in a mastery climate and embraces positive affective states (e.g., Steptoe & Butler, 1996), perceptions of autonomy and relatedness (e.g., Deci & Ryan, 2000), harmonious passion (e.g., Vallerand, 2005; Ratelle et al., 2004), intrinsic motivation (e.g., Ommundsen & Kvalø Eikanger, 2007; Standage, Duda, & Ntoumanis, 2003a), and subjective vitality (Reinboth & Duda, 2004; Reinboth, Duda, & Ntoumanis, 2004). In contrast, a performance climate fosters ill-being that embraces indices of malfunction and disruption, such as amotivation (e.g., Ratelle et al., 2004); negative everyday affective states (e.g., Crawford & Henry, 2004; Crook, Beaver, & Bell, 1998; Diener et al., 1999); dysfunctional achievement behaviors, such as self-handicapping (e.g., Eronen, Nurmi, & Salmela-Aro, 1998; Greaven et al., 2000); detrimental personal indices, such as maladaptive perfectionism (e.g., Flett et al., 1996); and obsessive activity involvement (e.g., Vallerand et al., 2003). These variables are argued to be important precursors of psychosocial health and well-being in young people (e.g., de Bruin, Bakker, & Oudejans, 2009; Coudevylle, Martin Ginis, Famose, & Gernigon, 2009; Ommundsen, 2006; Ratelle et al., 2004; Reinboth & Duda, 2004, 2006; Steptoe & Butler, 1996). Clearly, when in pursuit of enhancing the well-being of young sport participants, creating a mastery climate is one avenue to investigate.

Moral Functioning and Cheating

Being task or ego involved has also been linked to moral cognitions and moral behavior in sport. A number of studies have identified consistent relationships between task and ego involvement and sportspersonship, moral functioning, and moral atmosphere, as well as endorsement of aggressive tactics. In general, studies have shown that being high in ego involvement leads to lower sportspersonship values of respect and concern for social conventions, rules, officials, and opponents; more self-reported cheating; lower moral functioning (i.e., lower order of moral judgment and greater intention to retaliate; more self-reported cheating, and more self-reported cheating behavior); and greater endorsement of aggression when compared to high-task-involved athletes (e.g., Boixados, Cruz, Torregrossa, & Valiente, 2004; Fry & Newton, 2003; Kavussanu, 2006; Kavussanu & Boardley, 2009; Kavussanu & Ntoumanis, 2003; Kavussanu & Roberts, 2001; Kavussanu, Roberts, & Ntoumanis, 2002; Kavussanu & Spray, 2006; Lee, Whitehead, Ntoumanis, & Hatzigeorgiadis, 2008; Lemyre, Roberts, Ommundsen, & Miller, 2001; Lemyre et al., 2002; Miller & Roberts, 2003; Miller, Roberts, & Ommundsen, 2004, 2005; Morgan, Sproule, McNeill, Kingston, & Wang, 2006; Ommundsen, Roberts, Lemyre, & Treasure, 2003; Ryska, 2003; Sage & Kavussanu, 2007). Males typically cheated more than females, but within gender, ego-involved males and females cheated more than task-involved males and females. For males in particular, being ego involved meant that they were more likely to engage in cheating behavior, to engage in injurious acts, to be low in moral reasoning, and to perceive the moral atmosphere within the team to be supportive of cheating.

Competitive sport often places individuals in conflicting situations that emphasize winning over sportspersonship and fair play. It would be wrong, however, to attribute this issue to the competitive nature of sport. The results discussed earlier suggest that the competitive context itself is not the issue. Rather, it may be the salience of ego involvement in the athletic environment that induces differential concern for moral behavior and cheating, rules, respect for officials, and fair play conventions among players. If sportsmen and sportswomen are to develop sportspersonship behaviors and sound moral reasoning, and eschew cheating, coaches should attempt to reinforce the importance of task-involving achievement criteria in the competitive environment.

Burnout

Another interesting outcome variable that is becoming popular in sport is burnout. Why is it that some athletes burn out, and what are the precursors of burning out? Individuals who experience burnout tend to show a strong commitment to the pursuit of goals and set high standards for themselves. Despite personal investment and great persistence, they often experience depression, depersonalization, disillusionment, and dissatisfaction as their goals are continually unmet. Some recent research from a motivational perspective has given us some interesting findings. For example, Hall et al. (1998) reported a strong relationship between elite athletes' perfectionism, achievement goals, and aptitudes to perform. When athletes continually perceived that their ability and effort were inadequate to meet their achievement goals, the maladaptive nature of their motivational orientation became apparent. Athletes may drop out to maintain any real sense of self-worth. Investigating young elite tennis players, Gould and colleagues (Gould, 1996; Gould, Tuffey, et al., 1996; Gould, Udry, et al., 1996) found that burned-out athletes believed that they had less input into their own training, were higher in amotivation, and were more withdrawn. The burned-out players did not differ from their non-burned-out counterparts in terms of the number of hours that they trained. Consequently, Gould et al. posited that the crucial factors leading to burnout were psychological (motivational) rather than physical in nature.

In a series of studies investigating the psychological determinants of burnout, Lemyre and colleagues (e.g., Lemyre et al., 2008; Lemyre, Stray-Gundersen, Treasure, Matt, & Roberts, 2004; Lemyre, Treasure, & Roberts, 2006) examined the relationship between ego and task involvement at the start of a season for elite athletes in endurance sports and signs of burnout at season's end. As an example, Lemyre, Hall, and Roberts (2008) used elite winter sport athletes and found that when the athlete was ego involved, was low in perceived ability, and had a coach and parents who emphasized performance outcomes, then that athlete was more at risk of developing symptoms of burnout than the more task-involved athlete. The findings suggest that the source of motivation for sport involvement in elite athletes at the beginning of the season and symptoms of overtraining are both independently linked to signs of burnout in elite athletes. These and other findings (e.g., Cresswell & Eklund, 2005a) support a motivational approach to study burnout propensity in elite athletes.

Evidence Summary

The literature reviewed here has addressed achievement goal theory from an integrated perspective by arguing that dispositions and the perceived motivational climate are part of the same theoretical platform and that the energizing force for motivated behavior is the resultant state of involvement. The research supports meaningful relationships between personal goals of achievement and the perceived criteria of success and failure in the motivational climate with cognitive and affective beliefs about involvement in physical activity, as well as achievement striving. In addition, I have shown that outcomes, such as exerted effort, performance, moral behavior, cheating, peer relationships, and burnout are affected by whether one is task or ego involved.

With colleagues (Roberts et al., 2007), I proffered that we may draw two important conclusions from the evidence of the research effort over the past 30 years. The first one is that ego-involving goals, however they have been defined or conceptualized, are more likely to lead to maladaptive achievement behavior, especially when participants perceive competence to be low, are concerned with failure, or are invested in protecting self-worth. In such circumstances the evidence is clear: Motivation ebbs, task investment is low, persistence is low, performance suffers, satisfaction and enjoyment are lower, peer relationships suffer, cheating is more likely, burnout is more likely, and participants feel more negative about themselves and the achievement context. But this does not mean that ego-involving goals are always negative; in some situations, for some people, they are positive. When a person has an ego-involving goal and a high perception of competence, then that goal facilitates achievement and functions as a motivating construct (e.g., Pensgaard & Roberts, 2002). But even then, ego-involving goals are more fragile and can lead to maladaptive achievement striving as context information is processed (Dweck & Leggett, 1988).

Second, the research is unequivocal that task-involving goals (mastery) goals are adaptive. When task involved, whether through personal dispositions or when participants perceive mastery criteria in the context, motivation is optimized, participants are invested in the task and persist longer, performance is higher, satisfaction and enjoyment are higher, peer relationships are fostered, burn out and cheating are less likely, and participants feel more positive about themselves and the task. Being task involved has been consistently associated with desirable cognitive, affective, and achievement-striving responses. The research is now clear that if we wish to optimize motivation in sport and physical activity, we ought to promote task involvement. We can do it either by enhancing socialization experiences so that the individual has a task goal orientation and is naturally task involved (Nicholls, 1989) or by structuring the physical activity context to be more task involving (Ames, 1992b; Roberts & Treasure, 1995; Treasure & Roberts, 2001a). The crucial issue is that the participant has task-involving goals of achievement. This point is particularly true for young athletes who are learning skills, but it is also true for both young and old if we wish to promote active lifestyles for the populace in general. The evidence has led many sport psychologists to conclude that being task involved better enables participants to manage motivation in the sport experience and in other physical activity contexts (e.g., Brunel, 2000; Duda, 1993; Duda & Hall, 2001; Hall & Kerr, 1997; Pensgaard & Roberts, 2002; Roberts, 2001; Roberts et al., 1997, 2007; Theeboom et al., 1995; Treasure & Roberts, 1995). Many sport psychologists believe this, but not all!

Counterarguments

Several counterarguments question the assertions that we, in achievement goal theory work, have made over the years. One of the most provocative has emerged from work on the hierarchical model of achievement motivation (e.g., Elliot, 1999; Elliot & Conroy, 2005). The hierarchical model claims to revise and extend achievement goal theory, in other words, to offer a new and improved version! The theory is based on the premise that approach and avoidance motivation are also important in considering achievement striving. We refer you to Papaioannou and colleagues (this volume) for a more complete explanation, but briefly the hierarchical model of achievement motivation asserts that the dynamic states of involvement are influenced by both the definition of competence and the valence of the goals.

The arguments are similar to arguments made back in the 1960s. Contemporary researchers suggest that an approach and an avoid motivation exist (e.g., Elliot, 1997; Elliot & Harackiewicz, 1996; Middleton & Midgley, 1997; Skaalvik, 1997). They argue that people strive to be competent (an appetitive, or approach, valence) or strive to avoid appearing incompetent (an aversive, or avoid, valence). Thus, it is possible to differentiate goals based on their valence, or the degree to which the focal outcome is pleasant or unpleasant.

In reviewing the achievement goal literature, Elliot (e.g., 1994) observed that performance goals (as Elliot and colleagues term ego goals) that focused on the pleasant possibility of demonstrating competence (approach goals) led to different outcomes than performance goals focused on the unpleasant possibility of demonstrating incompetence (avoidance goals). Performance avoidance goals reduced both free-choice behavior and self-reported interest in a task, whereas performance approach goals did not have any consistent effect on either intrinsic motivation index (Rawsthorne & Elliot, 1999). This finding led to the introduction of a tripartite model of achievement goals comprising mastery (as Elliot and colleagues term task goals), performance approach goals, and performance avoidance goals (Elliot & Harackiewicz, 1996). Following a series of studies (e.g., Cury, Da Fonséca, Rufo, & Sarrazin, 2002a; Cury, Da Fonséca, Rufo, Peres, & Sarrazin, 2003), the model was expanded to include a fourth possible achievement goal: mastery avoidance goal (e.g., Elliot & Conroy, 2005). Thus, the argument was proffered that achievement goals should consider both the definition of competence and the valence of the striving, so the model became two by two, with two definitions of competence (mastery versus performance) and two valences of striving (approaching competence versus avoiding incompetence), yielding mastery approach, mastery avoidance, performance approach, and performance avoidance goals (see Papaioannou and colleagues, this volume; Roberts et al., 2007).

The introduction of the hierarchical model has challenged many of the tenets and underlying assumptions of what may be referred to as traditional achievement goal theory. In particular, it expanded the mastery and performance dichotomy to form a two-by-two model of achievement goals. Thus, the hierarchical model expanded the "old" theory from two goals to four goals. A body of evidence has accumulated to support these assertions (see Papaioannou and colleagues, this volume; Roberts et al., 2007), and some argue that the new model is a better theory to explain motivated behavior (e.g., Elliot & Conroy, 2005). I will debate that later! But it is not the only source of criticism of the traditional model or the only expansion of the number of goals. We have had strong criticism from Harwood and colleagues (e.g., Harwood, Hardy, & Swain, 2000; Harwood & Hardy, 2001; Harwood et al., 2008), who have raised what they consider conceptual and methodological issues. In particular, they have claimed that achievement goal theory does not stand up as well in competitive sport as it does in the education sphere.

Similar to others who have argued for multiple goals, such as process, performance, and outcome goals (e.g., Burton & Weiss, 2008; Gould, 2010; Hardy, Jones, & Gould, 1996; Kingston & Wilson, 2009; see Roberts & Kristiansen, this volume), Harwood and colleagues also argued for multiple states of task involvement and multiple goals (e.g., Harwood et al., 2008). Initially, Harwood and colleagues argued that achievement goal theory was not as useful in sport as in education, and they professed that task involvement, as a state, did not exist in sport because of the ego-involving nature of the sport experience. They argued that the goal pertinent to sport was "self-referenced ego involvement" (Harwood et al., 2000, p. 244). Therefore, they proposed three states of involvement that were termed *task involvement*, *self-referenced ego involvement*, and *norm-referenced ego involvement*. We countered their criticisms in 2001 (Treasure et al., 2001) and demonstrated, quite convincingly I thought, that their logic was flawed and that they had misrepresented achievement goal theory. But it is for the reader to read the articles and decide for himself or herself.

In a later treatise, Harwood and colleagues (2008) are just as critical of achievement goal theory when applied to sport and now suggest that the three goal states and goal orientations are called task involvement–process, task involvement–product, and ego (p. 165). Their model incorporates three goal orientations and states of involvement and has the climate acting as a moderator or a mediator. Their argument revolves around how task involvement may be "corrected" and made to characterize what really happens in sport. Harwood and colleagues state that the failure of researchers to integrate Nicholls' core concepts into research themes "that drive at the heart of sport subcultures and specific contexts . . . will bring to a halt this line of inquiry" (p. 167)! They clearly state that achievement goal theory as originally proposed is not relevant for sport. They conclude by saying that research that "peddles" the original concepts of Nicholls within sport runs the risk of stagnating the research and boring its readers (p. 167)! Further, in their overview of motivation, Harwood and colleagues state that the research that most of us have done with achievement goals is now "old hat or flawed" (p. 175) and shortsighted! Oh, to be young and arrogant again! Well, young anyway!

Counterpoints to the Counterarguments

We have addressed the merit of these challenges elsewhere in some detail (e.g., Roberts et al., 2007; Treasure et al., 2001). Therefore, I refer to them here only briefly and suggest that the interested reader consult the sources. I shall, however, briefly address each criticism in turn, beginning with the hierarchical model.

Valence of the Hierarchical Model

One of the most important differences between achievement goal theory and the hierarchical model pertains to the energization of the motivational process. The proponents of the hierarchical model argue that achievement goals should consider both the definition of competence and the valence of striving. It is assumed that the goals are the manifestation of "needs," or at least the "motivational surrogates," as Elliot and Church (1997) state of the needs of achievement motivation (approach) and the fear of failure (avoid) (Kaplan & Maehr, 2002, 2007). This suggests that achievement goals represent approaches to self-regulation based on satisfying approach and avoid needs that are evoked by situational cues. In traditional achievement goal theory, the goals themselves are the critical determinants of achievement cognition, affect, and behavior. Achievement goal theory is a cognitive theory in that it states that these goals are the product of learning and the individual's interpretation of what it takes to achieve success. The goals give meaning to the investment of personal resources because they reflect the purposes underlying achievement actions in achievement contexts. Once endorsed, the goal defines an integrated pattern of beliefs, attributions, and affect that underlies approach and avoid strategies, various levels of engagement, and the various responses to achievement outcomes (Duda & Hall, 2001; Kaplan & Maehr, 2002). As stated earlier, Elliott and Dweck (1988) explain that each of the achievement goals runs off a different "program" that has different commands, decision rules, and inference rules and therefore has different cognitive, affective, and behavioral consequences. An individual interprets his or her performance in terms of what he or she believes it takes to be successful in a given situation. Achievement goals refer to achievement-oriented or achievement-directed behavior in which "success" is the goal. We argue that these beliefs and perceptions form a personal theory of achievement in the activity that drives the motivation process and that a conceptually coherent pattern of relationships should therefore exist between an individual's achievement goals (the subjective meaning of success) and his or her achievement striving (Roberts et al., 2007). In the achievement goal approach, the issue is not how one defines competence with its attendant valence; it is how one defines success and what it takes to achieve success within that achievement setting. The meaning behind developing or demonstrating competence is the crucial issue. Simply put, the hierarchical approach presents energizing constructs that are different. Indeed, it may be more accurate to state that the merit of the hierarchical model is that it modernizes the traditional achievement motivation arguments of Atkinson and McClelland by introducing the competence arguments of Nicholls, not the other way around!

One other conceptual difference has emerged from the development of measures for the hierarchical model of goals, especially of the two-by-two model, in sport. Duda (2005) has argued that because the interrelationship among the performance approach, mastery avoidance, and performance avoidance goals is low to moderate (e.g., Conroy, Elliot, & Hofer, 2003), and only the mastery approach and performance avoidance goals have demonstrated independence. Then this creates conceptual problems for the hierarchical approach. The proponents of the two-by-two model argue that limited positive correlations should be expected between goals that share either a definition of competence or a valence. But that raises an interesting question: What are the expected relationships between the goals? Should they demonstrate greater independence to be recognized as extending the range of goals? And how does this relate to the evidence that task and ego goals have been demonstrated to be orthogonal (e.g., Maehr & Braskamp, 1986; Nicholls, 1989)?

In addition, do different conceptual assumptions underlie performance approach and avoidance goals? Performance approach tendencies may be based on demonstrating normative ability, but performance avoidance may be based on one of three facets: impression management, that is, a way of "saving face" (Skaalvik, 1997); a fear of failure (Elliot & Church, 1997); or a focus to avoid demonstrating low ability (Middleton & Midgeley, 1997). Smith, Duda, Allen, and Hall (2002) found that impression management explained the most variance (40%), and fear of failure and avoiding demonstrating low ability explained only 9.4% and 8% of the variance, respectively. Given the findings of Smith et al., perhaps it is more important to people who have performance avoidance goals to protect self-esteem than to avoid failing.

Similar arguments may be made for mastery avoidance goals. These goals involve focusing on not making mistakes or not doing worse than a previous performance. Cumming and colleagues (Smith, Cumming, & Smoll, 2008) argued that the measurement technology assumes that the concept is more a worry factor than a mastery avoidance factor! With the traditional achievement goal approach, it is conceptually inconsistent to have a mastery- or task-involved goal with a focus on avoiding appearing incompetent. Traditional achievement goal theory, however, argues that because orientations are assumed to be orthogonal, then the individual may also have an ego-involving orientation, and this is what may affect whether the individual is also concerned with the demonstration of incompetence. It may be that a person who demonstrates mastery avoidance has both ego and task goals and perceives the context to evoke ego-involving criteria. In addition, the person may not perceive herself or himself to have the necessary competence to complete the task. An avoidance strategy then becomes acceptable because the person does not wish to experience failure.

I must admit that the research on mastery approach and performance avoidance goals has been fairly consistent with the traditional approach to achievement goals. Pursuing mastery approach goals has been demonstrated to be largely positive, whereas the adoption of performance avoidance goals has been shown to be mostly detrimental to many important outcomes. But I would argue that the findings concerning performance approach and mastery avoidance goals are remarkably inconsistent. Some agree; some do not (see Maehr & Zusho, 2009). These findings are puzzling, but Elliot (1999) argued that it is good to keep in mind that these goals represent a hybrid of both positive and negative motivation. Therefore, these goals may predict both positive and negative outcomes! Needless to state, this issue needs to be investigated empirically, and only when we have theory informing research and data informing theory will we be able to understand the energizing mechanisms behind mastery approach and performance avoidance achievement striving.

Finally, this brings us to a further point of conceptual departure between the two approaches. In achievement goal theory the orientations are considered orthogonal: That is, a person can have both orientations to one degree or another. This circumstance has been demonstrated many times (e.g., Duda, 1988; Lemyre, Ommundsen, & Roberts, 2000; Pensgaard & Roberts, 2000; Roberts et al., 1996; Walling & Duda, 1995). Being both task and ego oriented is conceptually coherent with achievement goal theory. It may well be that being high in both task and ego orientation is valuable in the learning process because multiple sources of competence information are available to the athlete. Duda (1988) has asserted that achievement and persistence may be increased with both orientations because a person has two sources of determining success. For an athlete, being both task and ego oriented in an athletic context is both intuitively plausible and conceptually consistent with achievement goal theory (e.g., Pensgaard & Roberts, 2000). An athlete may be highly ego involved when competing but become very task involved when training in the same sport. We must not forget that task and ego involvement are dynamic constructs that are subject to ebb and flow as the athlete plays the game or continues with the activity. The issue is not whether an individual should be task involved or ego involved but rather when is it appropriate to be task involved or ego involved. This concept is very different from the hierarchical model, which assumes that a person is either mastery or performance oriented and it is the valence that may ebb and flow.

I should state here that I have nothing against the hierarchical model as a conceptual model to attempt to understand motivation. It is an interesting model that has produced some intriguing findings. My reaction is to the argument that the model "extends" traditional achievement goal theory. In my mind it is a different theory, one that brings "needs" back into the motivation equation when the basis of the original theory is social cognitive and eschews needs. And this brings us back to the second criticism.

The second source of criticism for achievement goal theory comes from Harwood and associates (e.g., Harwood & Hardy, 2001; Harwood et al., 2000, 2008). Some of the many points of contention have been debated in detail in the published literature (e.g., Treasure et al., 2001). I shall briefly address some of the more important issues.

Self-Referenced Ego to Task Product

In their overview of what they refer to as the "original achievement goal theory," Harwood and colleagues (2000) argued that an "individual adopts the achievement goal that most closely reflects his or her cognitive belief about what is required to maximize achievement in that social context" (p. 236). The impression given is that achievement goals serve as some distal construct that will satisfy an individual's personal theory of achievement. They continued with this perception in their chapter in 2008. I believe that they continue to confuse achievement goals (i.e., the subjective meaning of success, as argued earlier) with discrete goals and strategies aimed at fulfilling some particular objective, as one does within the goal-setting paradigm (Roberts & Kristiansen, this volume; Treasure et al., 2001). They are concerned with the *what* of achievement striving, whereas achievement goal theory is concerned with the *why* of achievement striving. It is more accurate to state that a person's theory of achievement reflects how success is defined in a particular achievement context and what he or she believes it takes to be successful in that situation. Nicholls (1989) argued that it is these beliefs and perceptions that form a personal theory of achievement in the activity. He was fond of saying that one's personal theory makes the person ask the question, What does it take to be successful here? It is not a performance or achievement criterion as argued by Harwood and colleagues.

Probably the most controversial argument of Harwood and colleagues is their insistence that a new construct and a new goal need to be introduced into achievement goal theory to reflect the nature of the sport experience. Originally termed *self-referenced ego involvement*, both as a state of involvement and a goal orientation, it is described by Harwood and colleagues as a state of ego involvement relative to oneself. The reason for this new construct is the argument that an individual cannot evaluate her or his own ability against that of another and still be in a state of task involvement. They propose the existence of "pure" task involvement in which "achievement" (sic) is conceived of as effort and hard work, self-referenced ego involvement in which performers focus on the adequacy of personal ability when compared with others, and norm-based ego involvement in which individuals try to achieve superiority to others (Harwood et al., 2000, p. 244). They continue with their arguments and state that task involvement is not present in competitive sport because, by definition, competitive sport is ego involving. They surmise that what we in the achievement goal world have called task involvement is probably self-referenced ego involvement.

In 2001 and subsequently, Harwood and colleagues (e.g., Harwood & Hardy, 2001; Harwood et al., 2008) have modified their arguments somewhat, probably in response to the Treasure et al. (2001) counterarguments, but continue to argue for three states of involvement and orientations, only now they argue for two levels of task involvement! They introduce the term *task involvement–process*, which they define as "traditional" task involvement in which the individual perceives achievement in terms of effort expended "without any objective improvement in task execution or performance" (Harwood et al., 2008, p. 165). Then they introduce the term *task involvement–product* to reflect the state in which achievement is realized when mastery, improvement, and self-referenced performance are the end product. And they continue to argue for ego involvement and ego orientation.

As a rationale for their tripartite conceptualization of goal involvement states, Harwood and associates (2008) contend that athletes' failure to experience definite intraindividual improvement or mastery (task product) can be "motivationally crippling" (p. 165). Defining the source of achievement of task process as being simply self-referent task investment (e.g., effort) is, again, misrepresenting and misinterpreting achievement goal theory. Harwood and associates provide no conceptual (or empirical) insight into the antecedents and consequences of their proposed new goal and state of goal involvement. Harwood and colleagues argue that there is a major difference between defining task involvement as learning, working hard, and understanding (process) compared to defining it in terms such as mastery, improvement, and personal progress (product), which may be more relevant to sport. In the points raised by Harwood and associates, the interrelationships and interdependencies between these constructs are ignored. Indeed, how can a person experience mastery, improvement, and personal progress without learning, expending effort, and developing understanding? How can mastery or improvement occasion a sense of personal success if not coupled with effort and understanding (Treasure et al., 2001)? What needs to be crystal clear is that mastery, effort, learning, and personal progress are simply criteria that task-involved athletes use to evaluate whether they have been successful, the *why* of achievement striving (Roberts et al., 2007; see earlier). Adding a new state of goal involvement and a new goal orientation may be intuitively appealing when one is concerned with the *what* of achievement striving, but adding complexity without a concurrent surge in understanding and meaning confounds the theory: It is simply not conceptually coherent.

Harwood and colleagues (e.g., 2008) also argue that sport and education are fundamentally different. As their rationale, they imply that defining task involvement as learning, working hard, and understanding (process) is more appropriate in education but that defining task involvement in terms such as mastery, improvement, and personal progress (product) is more relevant to sport. Harwood and associates contend that elite performers cannot experience task involvement in competition and that recreational activities form the only setting where what they call pure task involvement (process) might be experienced. This is simply not the case! Empirical (e.g., Kristiansen & Roberts, 2010, in press; Kristiansen, Roberts, & Abrahamsen, 2008; Pensgaard & Roberts, 2002) and anecdotal evidence (e.g., Treasure et al., 2001) support this assertion. Researchers and practitioners must remember that athletes—junior, developing, and elite—in both training and competition may perceive success in terms of learning, mastery, and improvement. To use other research traditions, these are the athletes who get into the "zone" or experience "flow states." Although it is commendable that Harwood and colleagues question the relevance of certain aspects of achievement goal theory in sport, that they do not find direct evidence or compelling arguments to support their speculations is problematic. Meaningful differences may exist between achievement contexts such as education and sport, but it is also important to attend to features that are common to all achievement settings (Nicholls, 1992). I argue that the typical classroom is competitive, evaluative, public in nature, and colored by norms and tests of competence, just like sport. The classroom is not a utopian space where the focus is solely on intrinsic learning and mastery. The education context is as ego involving as the sport context (see Fry, 2001; Nicholls, 1989).

This argument raises an important issue about what the aim of the achievement goal framework is in the context of sport. The focus of achievement goal theory, as originally conceptualized (e.g., Nicholls, 1984), was to ascertain what features influence the quantity and quality of achievement striving over time. As discussed earlier, the heart of the achievement goal framework is the assumption that an examination of dispositional goal orientations and perceptions of the overriding motivational climate that surround athletes will help explain achievement patterns over time (i.e., effort exerted, persistence, developing mastery), as well as predict emotional responses, indices of psychological and physical well-being, moral reasoning, and multidimensional behavioral patterns. The aim of achievement goal theory is to further our understanding of motivation processes, not merely to predict variability in performance per se (Roberts, 2001).

The preceding discussion reflects a trend in achievement goal research, that of developing other achievement goals. In particular, there have been arguments in favor of recognizing different criteria of engagement in achievement striving and their distinct patterns of consequences. We have discussed the approach and avoid arguments of Elliot and colleagues that began this trend and the further suggestions that we may be able to bifurcate the current mastery (task) definitions of competence into separate categories for absolute (Did I perform this task as well as it can be performed?) and intrapersonal (Did I perform this task better than I did previously?) definitions of competence (Elliot, 1999; Elliot & Conroy, 2005) and into categories of task process (Did I try hard and learn?) and task product (Did I improve and learn this task well?) criteria of success (Harwood et al., 2008). The same may be argued for other goals, such as social goals and extrinsic goals (Dowson & McInerney, 2001). Thus, for example, social achievement goals may be to demonstrate competence to gain friends (If I play well, my friends will like me). Thus, the trend begun by Elliot continues. But Elliot and Conroy (2005) argue that any expansions of the achievement goal construct need to relate to existing dimensions of achievement goals (e.g., definitions of competence, valence of strivings, criteria of success and failure) or provide a rationale for incorporating new dimensions of competence. I could not agree more!

One other point about the proliferation of goal constructs that researchers seem to argue for is that these researchers may be focusing on goals from the content perspective and focus on what individuals are trying to achieve in a specific situation (Maehr & Zusho, 2009). This is precisely what Harwood and colleagues (e.g., Harwood et al., 2008) are doing, in my opinion. We may need to reconcile the varying operationalizations of the achievement goal construct as a necessary first step in clarifying achievement goal theory. Maehr and Zusho argue that by reconsidering the distinction between goal (purpose) and goal objective (target), we may facilitate a better understanding of achievement goal theory by renewing a focus on issues of goal hierarchy and multiple goal endorsement. But more than that, it would ensure that when we discuss achievement goals, we are discussing the goals at the same level of analysis, the *what* or the *why*, instead of talking across each other and discussing "apples and oranges"!

In the preceding section, I have attempted to present conceptual arguments against the penchant of some to add dimensions or new states and goals to the original achievement goal paradigm. With the hierarchical model, do we need to go back to the future by adding dimensions based on satisfying needs of approach and avoid, as we had in the 1960s? I believe not! With the arguments of Harwood and colleagues, is achievement goal theory pertinent to sport without adding so-called sport-relevant concepts? I think so! The criticisms are well taken, however, and as John Nicholls was wont to say, when people take your arguments seriously enough to criticize them and argue with you, it is a compliment and the ensuing debate helps to clarify the underpinning of the conceptual basis of achievement striving. And that has been a valuable debate in the motivation literature, in my mind. Although I believe that the arguments I have presented hold at the present time, one more argument is important to raise at this time. Maybe it is time to think about some fundamental attributes of science!

Parsimony, Elegance, and Conceptual Coherence in Sport Psychology

In 2008 I was asked to give the Coleman Griffith Lecture at the annual meeting of AASP in St. Louis, Missouri, which had the title, *Whatever Happened to Parsimony, Elegance, and Conceptual Coherence in Sport Psychology?* I decided to argue that forsaking some fundamental attributes of science was not in the best interests of scholars and practitioners in sport psychology. I believe that there is value in maintaining the attributes of parsimony, elegance, and conceptual coherence. Let me explain.

Parsimony

One of Einstein's famous quotes is that in science we should make everything as simple as possible, but not too simple! Parsimony in science simply means that we keep constructs as simple as possible. In my Coleman Griffith talk, I argued that there is a trend in sport psychology to make constructs more complex than they need to be. Some of this results from the natural desire to make constructs more applicable to the sport context, such as the efforts of Harwood and colleagues, but scholars often do not realize that by making things more "relevant" to sport they also make the constructs more complex and cause a subsequent loss of parsimony. McFee, a philosopher of science, is harshly critical of scholars in sport psychology because of their penchant for explaining phenomena with "boxes and arrows" and making things more complex than they should be (McFee, 2005). He argues that he is against the "boxes" mentality prevalent in sport psychology, where what is hoped for is a graphic model of *boxes* connected by *arrows*, as though sport psychologists knew what the boxes and arrows meant. In my address I gave several examples of complex multilevel theories (e.g., Vallerand, 2001; the hierarchical model of motivation derived from self-determination theory) of this trend toward complexity, in addition to the work of Elliot and colleagues (e.g., 1999) and Harwood and colleagues (e.g., 2008), which I criticized earlier. Is this trend toward complexity one that we should follow?

In her profile of Nobel Prize winners, Zuckerman (1977) gave several attributes of the typical prize winner, but one common attribute is particularly noteworthy: They see simplicity where other people see complexity. As an example, when Crick and Watson (1953) in their quest to discover the structure of the DNA molecule published their model of the double helix, Maurice Wilkins (a fellow scientist who was a rival in the quest) was surprised to see how simple the model was and is quoted to have said, "How simple, how elegant" (Watson, 1996). The quest for expanded frameworks might be valuable because we may be able to provide a better description of the complexity of motivation processes, but a cost is often present, and part of that cost is a loss of parsimony! It is well for sport scientists to remember the famous saying of William of Occam (1285–1347): "Entities are not to be multiplied beyond necessity." Known as *Occam's Razor*, it is a call for parsimony, which is sometimes ignored.

There are many examples of scientists in psychology "seeing simplicity" when others had noticed only complexity. These examples spur research into the phenomenon and allow us to understand it better. The example of the social facilitation paradigm is a case in point. Historically, scientists had noted that the presence of others sometimes facilitated and sometimes inhibited the performance of individuals on a variety of tasks (e.g., Triplett, 1897). But in his review of the findings, Zajonc (1965) saw simplicity when he realized that learning tasks were inhibited by the presence of others, whereas performance tasks or simple tasks were facilitated by the presence of others. Further, he argued, the presence of others creates arousal and arousal facilitates the dominant response. When learning, the dominant response was incorrect; when performing, the dominant response was correct. This simple insight suddenly made sense of the previous 70 years of conflicting research. This ability to see simplicity sometimes gives a conceptual insight into psychological (and other disciplinary) mechanisms.

Elegance

Again, Crick and Watson (1953) give a classic example of elegance, which is the attribute of being simple but profound in its implications. In their article in *Nature*, they concluded by stating that it had not escaped their notice that the specific pairing of the double helix they had postulated suggested a possible copying mechanism for the genetic material! As we now know, this was the most profound scientific finding of the 20th century. The double helix solution was elegant in that it gave clear theoretical and practical meaning and changed our understanding of biological systems. Indeed, it was the birth of modern biology.

We can find many examples in psychology, too. One elegant theory is the social facilitation paradigm (Zajonc, 1965), which I discussed earlier. Zajonc demonstrated his elegant conceptual explanation with an elegant experiment. He had two groups of participants learn a complex task over many trials. One group did it in the presence of others, and the control group learned the task alone. Zajonc demonstrated that performing in the presence of others inhibited learning but facilitated later performance when compared to the control group: A simple but elegant and profound experiment demonstrated his theory. This experiment, and the later research that it stimulated (e.g., Martens, 1969), gave us insight into the reasons arousal and evaluative anxiety inhibited learning on motor tasks.

Another example of a parsimonious and elegant construct is self-efficacy (e.g., Bandura, 1977b). Self-efficacy cognitions represent a person's convictions or beliefs that he or she can successfully execute a course of action to produce a certain outcome. It is likened to a situation-specific self-confidence. But in this context, it is a simple but elegant construct that has stimulated a great deal of research into the determinants of motivation in exercise and physical activity (see Gilson & Feltz, this volume). And, of course, as I have been trying to expound, achievement goal theory in its original form is a parsimonious and elegant theory, too.

Conceptual Coherence

Parsimony and elegance are valued attributes for a theory, but conceptual coherence is an essential attribute! As we all know, theory gives meaning to data. Having an empirical paradigm that is weak on coherent constructs is not a desirable paradigm. These empirical paradigms with weak constructs, or constructs that lack conceptual coherence, are what produce the random noise in the literature against which the true signal of advancement is difficult to discern (Roberts, 1989). I must confess that in my experience with doctoral students, I find that they generally become sophisticated in research methods and statistical analyses but often struggle with understanding the psychological constructs and mechanisms about how things work psychologically. My favorite question to students who are preparing a research agenda is to ask them how they know that they are asking the right questions, or even important ones? I am reminded of the adage, If it is not worth doing, it is not worth doing well! The most important task that we can do as mentors of doctoral students is to make certain they understand that theory gives meaning to data and that statistical and research sophistication are secondary and merely tools to demonstrate the meaningfulness of theory. But they must do more than use "just any theory." Is the theory coherent and meaningful to the question being asked? All of us have to make our own decisions about what constructs give meaning to the research that we are undertaking. My argument here is that the conceptual base should be coherent!

As an example, at the 2009 ISSP Congress in Marrakesh, Ed Deci was asked to react to some research papers, using self-determination theory as the conceptual base. When one researcher used self-determination theory to overlay his own theory to add impetus to his normal theoretical paradigm, Deci commented that it did not make much sense to do that because the theories were quite different in their conceptual base. His point was that it was better to build constructs within the conceptual paradigm used to capture the dynamics of the question being asked rather than bring in another theory and overlay the constructs of that theory over the original constructs. In other words, to give meaning to data, the theory must be conceptually coherent!

Achievement goal theory is a social-cognitive theory that was developed from the learned helplessness (mastery versus helplessness) research of Dweck (e.g., 1975), the cooperation–competition research of Ames (e.g., 1984a), the motivation research of Maehr (e.g., 1983) and the work of Nicholls (e.g., 1978) on the various conceptions of ability that children held. From this research, Nicholls saw simplicity where others had seen complexity and presented the parsimonious constructs that we all know today. Nicholls' unique contribution was to recognize that two understandings of ability existed and that previous theories had assumed one or the other. For example, self-efficacy (see Gilson & Feltz, this volume) assumes a task-involving conception of ability, whereas attribution theory (e.g., Weiner, 1972) assumes an ego-involving conception of ability. Nicholls, Maehr, Ames, and Dweck developed a theory (with their own interpretations) that recognized that both conceptions of ability need to be inherent in the theory. In addition, they recognized that individual difference variables (goal orientations) and contextual dynamics (motivational climate) were part of the same conceptual paradigm. That is the elegance of achievement goal theory. By recognizing that we each use task- or ego-involving conceptions of ability depending on the context, we have a conceptually coherent theory that encompasses both versions of the definition of success and embraces both individual difference variables (goal orientations) and the effect of the situation (motivational climate) on achievement striving.

And the Point Is?

As one of my friends, Bert Carron, is fond of asking, "And the point is?" Here we might ask this question: Does any of this matter? Are the preceding series of arguments merely the esoteric ramblings of professors who want to defend their pet theories and approaches to motivation and write more journal articles and chapters, or do these arguments matter to the people in the trenches—the teachers, coaches, parents, therapists, and so on? In my opinion, it matters a lot for one good reason: The important test of any motivation theory is its usefulness in informing teachers, coaches, parents, youth leaders, counselors, therapists, and indeed all those who make it their business to empower and encourage people to do "what needs to be done" (Kaplan & Maehr, 2002). In our case, within the applied sport and exercise psychology arena, we need parsimonious solutions to the task of enhancing motivation for achievement striving. And without question, the power of achievement goal theory is its parsimonious base, which has the ability to inform people whose job it is to use strategies that facilitate motivation. As Kaplan and Maehr (2007) stated, the parsimonious, elegant, and powerful framework of achievement goal theory has led researchers to use it as a guide for educational change that aims at facilitating students' adaptive motivation. The real contribution of achievement goal theory is simply that it has given practitioners the means to enhance adaptive motivation in the field of sport and physical activity in general.

Enhancing Adaptive Motivation

The question then becomes this: How do we use achievement goal theory to enhance motivation, especially the motivation of others? How can we empower and encourage people to do what needs to be done? We know from the evidence cited earlier that adopting a task-involved set of criteria leads to more adaptive motivation. How then can we encourage people to adopt such a set of criteria? We could focus on the individual to enhance the quality of motivation by effecting change in his or her dispositional goal orientation to a more adaptive mastery set of criteria. This approach would be effective, but it is not practical to have individual remediation for everyone, except for small groups such as elite athletes. But to concentrate on individual change may not be the most effective strategy from a motivational standpoint. As Maehr (1983) has stated, because the subjective meaning of the environment has been shown to be a critical factor in determining motivation, a more practical solution is to modify the extant criteria of success and failure in the achievement context to reflect mastery criteria, and this has been shown to be effective in the context of sport and physical activity (e.g., Balaguer et al., 1999; Brunel, 1999; Dunn, 2000; Pensgaard & Roberts, 2002; Pensgaard, Roberts, & Ursin, 1999; Treasure, 1997; Treasure & Roberts, 2001a). Researchers have suggested that time and effort be spent in developing strategies and instructional practices to help teachers of physical activity and coaches in children's, youth, and elite sport to create a mastery motivational climate (e.g., Ames, 1992b; Biddle, 2001; Duda, 2001, 2005; Newton & Duda, 1999; Roberts et al., 1997, 2007; Roberts, Abrahamsen, & Lemyre, 2009; Swain & Harwood, 1996; Treasure & Roberts, 1995, 2001a).

What we have advocated for some time now within the achievement goal tradition is to focus on creating a mastery set of criteria within achievement settings to enhance task-involved motivation. As encouraging as the results are from these studies, more research is needed to develop our understanding of how teachers, coaches, therapists, and others can go about structuring mastery-oriented achievement criteria for specific contexts. Epstein (1988, 1989) made one suggestion in the academic setting by arguing that various structural features of the achievement context have been consistently identified as influencing a wide range of motivational processes. These structural features are interdependent variables and when taken together define the motivational climate of a context. She coined the acronym TARGET to represent the task, authority, recognition, grouping, evaluation, and timing structures that she defined as the basic building blocks of motivation in an achievement setting (Epstein, 1988, p. 92). But it was Ames (1992b) who systematically examined past research (e.g., Brophy, 1987; Grolnick & Ryan, 1987; Marshall & Weinstein, 1984; Rosenholtz & Simpson, 1984) to determine how certain structures within the educational context make different goals salient. Ames took the important step of examining what it is about the cues emanating from the nature of the task, the autonomy given in acting, what recognition is given for, the grouping and evaluation procedures, and the time given to complete a task. The details of the dynamics that make a performance or mastery motivational climate salient have been discussed elsewhere (e.g., Ames, 1992b; Biddle, 2000; Duda & Whitehead, 1998; ; Treasure, 2001; Treasure & Roberts, 2001a) and earlier. I shall now briefly discuss the salient features of an adaptive mastery climate.

Task   The most important question here is what the person is asked to do and how important that task is to the person. Therefore, designing meaningful tasks that include variety, diversity, challenge, and control is crucial (Blumenfeld, 1992). Embedded in tasks is information that people use to make judgments about their ability, their willingness to apply effort, and feelings of satisfaction that are likely to facilitate an interest in learning and task involvement (e.g., Ames, 1992c; Kaplan & Maehr, 2007; Marshall & Weinstein, 1984; Nicholls, 1989; Rosenholtz & Simpson, 1984; Treasure, 2001). Individuals can develop a sense of their own ability that is not dependent on social comparison and find intrinsic motivation in the task.

Authority Structure   The question here is whether the person has the autonomy to decide when and how to do the task. Is the locus of responsibility in the learning situation a matter for the teacher or coach, or is the individual involved in decision making? Evidence suggests that in contexts that are autonomous (self-determined) in orientation (e.g., Ames, 1992a; Deci, 1992; Deci & Ryan, 1991; Ryan & Deci, 2000b; Vallerand, 2001), in which the person participates in decision making and has the authority to choose strategies to complete the task, then the individual perceives that her or his ability is higher and is more committed to the task. This is related to adaptive or positive motivation patterns. Note, however, that when individuals are given a choice, they must perceive the choice to be real. For a mastery-oriented climate to be salient, choices must be perceived as equal choices, set up, for example, by giving individuals a choice among a range of equally difficult tasks to ensure that their choice is guided by their interest and not by efforts to protect perceptions of ability or self-worth (Ames, 1992b; Kaplan & Maehr, 2007; Nicholls, 1989).

Recognition The question here is how outcomes and striving behaviors are recognized. The use of rewards and incentives is one of the more obvious aspects of sport during childhood and adolescence. It often seems that rewards and incentives are more important than the activity itself! But if the outcomes and behaviors that are recognized include applied effort, being creative, sharing ideas, and learning from mistakes, then recognition is mastery oriented. When rewards and recognition are perceived as bribes or as controlling (e.g., Ryan & Deci, 2000a), then the research evidence from varied contexts is considerable, demonstrating the undermining effects of rewards (Deci, 1992; Deci & Ryan, 1991; Treasure, 2001; Treasure & Roberts, 2001a; Vallerand, 2001).

Grouping The question here focuses on the criteria by which people are placed into groups. When people see that an individual can change groups relatively easily, that the criteria for grouping is based on domain of interest, and that differences between individuals are encouraged, then mastery motivation criteria are fostered (Ames, 1992b; Epstein, 1988). The extant evidence shows that when teachers and coaches treat groups differently by giving more instructional time, opportunities, encouragement, and attention to the brighter or more able groups, mastery criteria are undermined (e.g., Marshall & Weinstein, 1984; Treasure, 2001; Treasure & Roberts, 2001a; Weinstein, 1989). This practice often occurs in sport and physical activity contexts. Here the teacher or coach must accommodate people of widely differing levels of current ability, be they children or adults.

Evaluation How individuals are evaluated is one of the most salient features of any achievement context that can affect motivation. What is the meaning of the evaluation to the person? If one is evaluated privately for progress, mastery, creativity, and effort expended, then adaptive motivation is enhanced. Evaluation practices that are normatively based, public, and linked to ability assessments can have deleterious effects on motivation (e.g., Butler, 1987, 1988; Covington & Omelich, 1984; Jagacinski & Nicholls, 1984; Nicholls, 1989; Treasure, 1997; Treasure & Roberts, 2001a). But the mere availability of normative social comparison information is not problematic. Rather, it is when this information becomes emphasized (Cury, Biddle, et al., 1997; Hall, 1990; Jagacinski & Nicholls, 1987; Roberts et al., 2007; Treasure, 2001) that we see the demotivational effects. When evaluation is self-referenced and based on personal improvement, progress toward individual goals, participation, and effort, then the individual is more likely to experience adaptive motivation (Ames, 1992a; Cury, Biddle, et al., 1997; Hall, 1990; Treasure & Roberts, 2001a).

Timing Research in education has indicated that the pace of instruction and the time allotted for completing tasks significantly influence motivation

(Ames, 1992b; Epstein, 1988). The question here is how time is managed. The time dimension is closely related to the other TARGET areas, such as task (e.g., how much individuals are asked to accomplish within specific periods), authority (e.g., whether individuals are allowed to schedule the rate, order, or time of completion of tasks), grouping (e.g., whether quality of instructional time is equitable across groups), and evaluation (e.g., how much time pressure is placed on performance). In other words, can individuals work at their own pace? This attribute is important within learning environments, especially in sport and physical activity settings because some people need more time to develop the necessary skills to compete and participate actively.

Application Attempts

In 2001 Treasure was moved to state that very little research has applied and tested the contextual relevance of achievement goal theory in physical activity contexts. Since then, however, the research base and the application of achievement goal theory into sport and physical activity have grown. The earliest studies were by Lloyd and Fox (1992), Treasure (1993), Solmon (1996), and Theeboom and colleagues (1995). To illustrate this early research work, let us look at the Treasure approach.

Treasure's research (e.g., 1993; Treasure & Roberts, 2001a) demonstrated that by manipulating the TARGET structures, teachers within physical activity were able to affect the perceived motivational climate. The findings revealed that perceptions of the motivational climate were the most important predictors of the children's cognitive and affective responses during the intervention. By manipulating the TARGET structures of the context, the teacher was able to structure a motivational climate that fostered a mastery perspective. This finding is significant because the participants in the mastery treatment condition indicated that they preferred to engage in more challenging tasks, believed that success was the result of motivation and effort, and experienced more satisfaction with the activity than did participants in the performance treatment condition. The findings of Solmon (1996) confirmed the findings of Treasure in that the participants in the mastery-oriented condition demonstrated a greater willingness to persist on a difficult task than those in the performance-oriented condition. Simply put, motivation was enhanced!

Since then, we have had more attempts to manipulate the climate to determine its effect on behavioral, cognitive, and affective variables (e.g., Christodoulidis, Papaioannou, & Digelidis, 2001; Coudevylle et al., 2009; Cumming, Smoll, Smith, & Grossbard, 2007; Duda, 2010; Maro, Roberts, & Sørensen, 2009; Martin, Rudisill, & Hastie, 2009; Morgan & Kingston, 2008; Papaioannou, Tsigilis, Kosmidou, & Milosis, 2007; Smith, Cumming, & Smoll, 2008; Smith, Smoll, & Cumming, 2007; Smoll, Smith, & Cumming, 2007). As an example, when Smith and colleagues (2007) tested the effects of a mastery intervention based on the TARGET principles (although the use of TARGET is not explicitly acknowledged, perhaps because of the toothbrush syndrome?) over the course of a basketball season for both boys and girls, those who played for the trained coaches exhibited decreases on all scales of anxiety from preseason to late season when compared to the players for the untrained coaches. Similarly, Morgan and Kingston developed a mastery intervention program for PE teachers based explicitly on the TARGET principles. One of the most intriguing findings of this study was that the more disaffected pupils (those who disliked PE the most) significantly improved their motivational responses because of the intervention program. Another interesting finding in this study was that teacher feedback on effort and improvement when given publicly was perceived as performance involving rather than mastery involving. But the major conclusion of the study was that a mastery intervention program based on self-evaluation of teaching behaviors can increase mastery teaching behaviors and improve the motivation of the more disaffected pupils' motivation in PE, precisely those whom we need to motivate!

Martin et al. (2009) examined the influence of a mastery motivational climate intervention on children's motor skill performance in a naturalistic setting. Children exposed to the mastery motivational climate achieved greater improvement in motor skill development and improved significantly from pre- to postintervention for locomotor and object control skills when compared to the "normal" way of teaching. In addition, the children were more successful in maintaining high levels of intrinsic motivation. The final example is that of Maro and colleagues (e.g., 2009), who used a mastery intervention with peer teachers in a football program designed to teach HIV–AIDS prevention life skills to at-risk children in sub-Saharan Africa. Based in Dar es Salaam in Tanzania, the program has been in effect since 2001 and has used football skill practices as a means to teach the life skills. In 2007 Maro and colleagues (2009) conducted an evaluation research study into the effectiveness of the program. They introduced an additional intervention in which the peer coaches were taught TARGET mastery principles. The coaches then used the principles in the intervention program. Thus, the intervention had two groups, the normal life-skills program and one with specific mastery principles built into the football practice sessions. The research study also had two control groups, a group who received the normal HIV–AIDS education taught in classrooms through the school system and a group of children neither in school nor enrolled in the football program. When compared to the normal intervention program, the HIV–AIDS education using mastery principles was more effective for most variables, especially for variables related to condom use. Both interventions were clearly superior to the two control groups. In fact, an unexpected finding was that the group most at risk was the group in which the children in schools received the traditional classroom education about preventing HIV–AIDS, especially when condom-related variables were looked at!

One of the most impressive intervention research attempts into physical education contexts was conducted in Greece by Papaioannou and colleagues (e.g., Christodoulidis et al., 2001; Digelidis, Papaioannou, Laparidis, &

Christodoulidis, 2003; Digelidis & Papaioannou, 2006; Papaioannou & Milosis, 2009). Papaioannou and colleagues conducted interventions in physical education based on the TARGET principles and aimed at increasing a mastery climate and positive attitudes toward exercise and decreasing social evaluation and a performance climate. In his most recent work, Papaioannou integrated these curricula with life-skills programs aimed at teaching youngsters how to transfer adaptive self-regulatory strategies to other parts of their life, such as to academic subjects and home and peer contexts (Milosis & Papaioannou, 2007; Papaioannou & Milosis, 2009). Papaioannou asserts that the adoption of a mastery climate emphasizing personal improvement goals in life creates the appropriate substratum to promote life skills and healthy behaviors in childhood and adolescence (Papaioannou, Simou, Kosmidou, Milosis, & Tsigilis, 2009; Papaioannou, Sagovits, Ampatzoglou, Kalogiannis, & Skordala, in press).

In a similar vein, a large multisite trial in Europe investigating a mastery intervention strategy in sport is currently under way (Duda, 2010). Called the PAPA Project (Promoting Adolescent Physical Activity), the program is aimed at promoting an empowering motivational climate so that adolescents adopt adaptive motivational strategies that are assumed to promote physical activity in general. The program is predicated on the assumption that sport activity is essential for adolescents to develop active physical activity lifestyles. Begun in 2010, the trial is being conducted in sites in England, Spain, Greece, France, and Norway and is investigating whether the influence of a mastery climate within sport will promote continued engagement in physical activity for adolescents.

As we can appreciate, research into mastery intervention programs is increasing, and the evidence is accumulating that introducing mastery teaching and coaching strategies following the TARGET principles has an adaptive motivational effect and enhances desirable cognitive, behavioral, and affective responses. Such is the weight of the evidence that we are beginning to witness teaching and coaching programs that already advocate the introduction of mastery principles. A significant challenge facing researchers, however, is determining how to apply the burgeoning knowledge base with practitioners in a cost-effective, user-friendly, and scalable fashion. We shall briefly discuss some of these attempts next.

Applying the Evidence to Coaching and Teaching Programs

One strategy developed in the past few years, which has proven successful, is for researchers to provide insight to and collaborate with national sporting bodies that provide coach education to their membership. Treasure collaborated with the National Federation of State High School Associations (NFHS) in the creation of a coach education program targeting interscholastic coaches, which is delivered primarily online. The NFHS is the governing body of high school sport in the United States. It serves its 51 member state associations by providing a variety of program initiatives that reach the 18,500 high schools and over 8 million students involved in athletic programs. Although it is estimated that over 1 million coaches currently work with youth athletes in the interscholastic setting, a shocking statistic is that only 16% are believed to have received any formal coach education training.

Launched in January 2007, *Fundamentals of Coaching* (NFHS, 2007) is the signature course of the NFHS coach education program (see www.NFHS-Learn.com) and stresses a unique student-centered curriculum emphasizing the role of the teacher or coach in promoting learning and the creation of a healthy and developmentally appropriate athletic experience. Grounded in the fundamental tenets of achievement goal theory, the course provides coaches with the knowledge and strategies to create a mastery and autonomy supportive climate that will promote adaptive motivation and task involvement. The course also uses principles from self-determination theory (see Standage & Ryan, this volume) to facilitate student–athletes' basic psychological needs of autonomy, competence, and relatedness. In 2009 *Fundamentals of Coaching* became the first online program accredited by the National Council for the Accreditation of Coach Education (NCACE) for coaches working with athletes who compete in a structured, select, team, or sport setting. Successful accreditation demonstrated that the content met or exceeded the standards deemed essential to the preparation of well-qualified coaches as identified by over 100 national sporting organizations in the United States and published in the revised *National Standards for Sport Coaches* (National Association for Sports and Physical Education, 2006). To date over 200,000 interscholastic coaches have taken *Fundamentals of Coaching*, making it the most successful coach education program in the United States. The important point in this discussion, however, is that the program is based on evidence provided by researchers, as discussed earlier in this chapter, and offers a coaching program that complies with the knowledge base and is targeted toward providing mastery experiences for the athletes.

Another program has been developed by Smith and Smoll and colleagues (Cumming et al., 2007; Smith et al., 2007, 2008; Smoll et al., 2007; Smoll & Smith, 2010). Smith and Smoll have conducted both basic and applied research in youth sport since the early 1970s, and they have developed a system of categorizing coaching behaviors through the Coaching Behavior Assessment System (e.g., Smith, Smoll, & Curtis, 1978). Initially, their coaching intervention program was based on reinforcement principles. Of late, however, they have been promoting the Mastery Approach to Coaching Sports (MACS) (e.g., Smoll & Smith, 2010). The MACS approach is designed to help coaches and parents create a mastery climate that promotes adaptive motivation and healthy achievement. They advocate a classic mastery approach that uses most of the recommendations of the TARGET approach (e.g., Ames, 1992b; Treasure, 2001), although, surprisingly, they do not specifically refer to this body of evidence. Smith and Smoll argue that in such a climate people adopt adaptive achievement strategies such as selecting challenging tasks, giving maximum effort, persisting in the face of setbacks, and taking pride in personal improvement. In their research they have confirmed many of the findings reported earlier in this chapter. Smith and Smoll have developed a workshop for coaches and to date have conducted over 500 workshops in the United States and Canada. In the workshop they stress a positive approach to influencing athletes and emphasize the provision of mastery procedures along with the TARGET principles.

Another program that has used TARGET strategies is the HIV–AIDS prevention program (EMIMA) in Tanzania in sub-Saharan Africa (e.g., Maro et al., 2009). The EMIMA HIV–AIDS prevention program uses football as the means to provide life-skills strategies to at-risk adolescents in Tanzania. Following the research program in 2007 to determine whether the mastery strategies worked (e.g., Maro et al., 2009), the administrators of the program have built TARGET strategies into the ongoing education program for the peer coaches who deliver the life-skills strategies. The peer coaches undergo 6 months of training in delivering the coaching sessions, where the HIV–AIDS prevention strategies are taught to the adolescents in the practice sessions. Since 2008 the coaching program has deliberately used TARGET principles for its life-skills strategies. The program has been introduced at six sites in Tanzania, and more than 10,000 adolescents have participated in the life-skills intervention program. There are plans to introduce the program at more sites in sub-Saharan Africa, where 50% of all AIDS victims live and where one child in seven is an AIDS orphan. Clearly, such intervention programs are desperately needed.

Practical Applications

As we can readily appreciate from the previous discussion, strong research programs are continuing to build the conceptual and empirical base for interventions in sport and physical activity based on achievement goal theory. Coaching programs that use intervention strategies based on achievement goal theory principles are already in place and being used successfully. But where do we go from here? What is the future of achievement goal theory? Let me give you a personal appraisal of where I think we should go in the future, especially in our research endeavors.

First, although "traditional" achievement goal theory has been based on self-cognitions, the meaning of these cognitions, and personal theories of achievement for the ongoing stream of achievement behavior, several research traditions have embedded achievement goals in other constructs.

One approach has been to use the concept of value, in which goal orientations emerge from the value-laden attractiveness of an achievement context. Values are directed at desirable end states of behavior, but again, in these traditions, goals are seen as objectives (e.g., Bandura, 1986; Eccles & Harold,

1991; see Gilson & Feltz, this volume for self-efficacy research). As an example, Eccles and her colleagues (Eccles & Harold, 1991; Wigfield & Eccles, 1992) suggested that achievement goals emerge from values and expectancies. Thus, mastery goals emerge from intrinsic task values and a belief in one's competence to do the task, whereas performance goals emerge from the utility value of the task for success in an important domain and the expectancy of outperforming others. The research into task value and achievement goals is promising and increasing in sport (e.g., Weiss & Ferrer-Caja, 2002). The merit of the approach is that it is based on conceptual arguments on why these objective goals may energize achievement behavior, but more research is needed to develop the conceptual base of the approach in physical activity (Kaplan & Maehr, 2007). I would also argue that although the empirical evidence is impressive for these approaches, more concern needs to be directed to why these objective goals energize achievement behavior.

Goals have also been seen within the self-awareness paradigm, in which goals are seen as "self-primes," a form of heightened self-awareness (Kaplan & Maehr, 2002). Nicholls (1984) suggested that heightened self-awareness could make thoughts of competence salient. An ego goal (or performance goal) may well represent heightened awareness of the self because people may focus on who they are and what they can do within the achievement context (Kaplan & Maehr, 2007). Heightened self-awareness certainly may affect ego or performance goals, and Kaplan and Maehr suggested that exploratory behavior to discover oneself may be an extension of mastery orientation. But heightened self-awareness may also affect other thoughts about oneself. The research into self-awareness is meaningful to achievement goal theory and may propose a fruitful line of inquiry, but additional conceptual clarification and research are needed.

Given that achievement goal theory has always been based on self-cognitive schemas, it is interesting that few researchers have chosen to probe more deeply into the nature of cognitive processes and have used current models of cognitive processing to investigate the dynamic nature of goals. Questions such as the stability of goal orientations, the conditions under which they change, the process of pursuing multiple goals, and the way in which the environment affects goal adoption are interesting to pursue. Perhaps models that describe processes of schema construction and operation, such as production lines, activation patterns, and components, could provide useful hypotheses concerning schema development in achievement goal theory (Kaplan & Maehr, 2007). Pintrich (2000) argued that the use of parallel distributed processing could be useful in explaining cognitive processes that operate when a person is ego or task oriented. Such research is sparse, but in the future it may be useful in helping to understand the cognitive processes underpinning achievement goals.

In my mind, and this is where my bias shows, the most exciting research at the moment within the achievement goal theory perspective is the research that is using the weight of the evidence accumulated thus far to investigate intervention strategies to optimize adaptive motivation in sport and physical activity contexts. For example, the programs of Papaioannou and colleagues (e.g., Milosis & Papaioannou, 2007; Papaioannou & Milosis, 2009), Duda and colleagues (e.g., Duda, 2010), and Maro and colleagues (e.g., Maro et al., 2009;) are all based on the research evidence that demonstrates that mastery criteria within the coaching and teaching program enhance adaptive motivation. In addition, the intervention research is investigating whether other outcomes are also enhanced, such as developing general life skills, fostering an active lifestyle, or enhancing HIV–AIDS prevention life skills. These research directions are important, and the findings to date are promising. The findings reveal that changing teaching and coaching environments to increase emphasis on mastery goals has the potential to enhance not only the long-term outcome benefits but also the motivation, attitudes, self-esteem, well-being, and achievement of participants. But the research also reveals that changing the teaching and coaching environment is not easy and often flies in the face of teaching and coaching folklore! We need more evidence that the long-term effect of changing the environment has demonstrable value for the teachers and coaches who are in the trenches on an everyday basis. And, more important in the world of elite sport, we need evidence that changing the coaching environment has measurable benefits for elite athletes too.

Another important research direction is to examine what it is about the cues within the sport and physical activity context that make different goals salient to participants. Epstein (e.g., 1988) coined the acronym TARGET to represent the task, authority, recognition, grouping, evaluation, and timing structures that she defined as the "basic building blocks" of motivation in an achievement setting (Epstein, 1988, p. 92), but this idea was very generic. Ames (e.g., 1992a, 1992b, 1992c) systematically examined past research (e.g., Brophy, 1987) to determine how certain structures within the education context make different goals salient. As I stated earlier, Ames examined the cues emanating from the nature of the task, the autonomy given in acting, the outcomes and behaviors that are given recognition, the grouping and evaluation procedures, and the time given to complete a task in the educational context. What we have done in sport is to transfer these strategies into the sport context (e.g., Biddle, 2000; Christodoulidis et al., 2001; Coudevylle et al., 2009; Cumming et al., 2007; Duda, 2010; Duda & Whitehead, 1998; Maro et al., 2009; Martin, Rudisill, & Hastie, 2009; Morgan & Kingston, 2008; Papaioannou, Tsigilis, et al., 2007; Smith et al., 2008; Smith et al., 2007; Smoll et al., 2007; Treasure, 2001; Treasure & Roberts, 2001a). Perhaps the time has come to examine the most salient cues that may be unique to the sport or physical activity context. It could well be that some of the TARGET structures are more salient for mastery and performance criteria than others. I believe that this is another fruitful area for research. What moderating and mediating structural cues are the most powerful in determining whether the climate is perceived as fostering mastery criteria or performance criteria of success?

Related to the preceding, how are the TARGET structures related to each other and the consequent effects of their relationship on the effectiveness of intervention programs? Specifically, do the manipulations of the task, authority, recognition, grouping, evaluation, and timing structures operate in an additive or multiplicative fashion (Ames, 1992a; Krug, 1989; Treasure, 2001)? If they are additive, the structures are complementary and the inadequacies in one structure can be attenuated by strengths in another; if they are multiplicative, they cannot compensate for each other. Therefore, a coach who emphasizes performance criteria on one TARGET structure could not foster perceptions of a mastery-oriented motivational climate. This issue is important because it has considerable applied implications. Treasure argued that this issue is best addressed through laboratory-based interventions in which the various structures can be manipulated empirically to determine their effects.

One other line of research that would be valuable is that proposed by Harwood and colleagues when they argued that a goal pertinent to sport was what they called self-referenced ego involvement (Harwood et al., 2000, p. 244). They proposed that there were three goals and states of involvement called task involvement, self-referenced ego involvement, and norm-referenced ego involvement. In a later treatise (Harwood et al., 2008) they suggested that the three goal states and goal orientations are called task involvement–process, task involvement–product, and ego (p. 165). Harwood, Wilson, and Hardy (2002) have even suggested four goal orientations called self-directed task, self-directed ego, social approval task, and social approval ego. The basis of my criticisms is that there is no conceptual argument to support these contentions. Having disagreed with Harwood and colleagues over the introduction of other goals to task and ego (or mastery and performance, if people prefer that terminology), I can agree with them that there may be multiple states of involvement, and probably are!

It has always been argued that the state of involvement lies on a continuum from task to ego involvement: Goals are orthogonal; the state of involvement is not! So there may be many states of involvement, and we can label them with defining characteristics (e.g., self-referenced ego involvement, social approval ego, and so on). Researchers will have to determine their veracity and stability over time, as well as determine the antecedents of the states of involvement. But a critical point here is that, although there may be multiple states of involvement, we do not necessarily have multiple goal orientations. Each state of involvement does not inevitably have a corresponding goal orientation! I contend that, because goal orientations are orthogonal, the relative strength of each goal orientation may give rise to multiple states of involvement. As an example, we can appreciate that individuals with high task and low ego goal orientations would demonstrate task involvement and those with high ego and low task goal orientations would demonstrate ego involvement. But what if an individual has high task and high ego, as we have found with elite athletes, for example (Pensgaard & Roberts, 2000)? Where on the continuum between high task involvement and high ego involvement does that individual lie? And what are the defining characteristics that would allow us to label this state of involvement? Is this where we find the state of task involvement–product (or self-referenced ego involvement) suggested by Harwood and colleagues (2008)? This is where the continuum of state of goal involvement may be similar to the continuum of self-regulation within self-determination theory (see Standage & Deci; Ntoumanis, this volume). Multiple states of goal involvement are likely to be present. But we would need research to demonstrate that the variation in task and ego goal orientations does lead to identifiable states of involvement that can be described with the criteria pertinent to achievement goal theory.

Clearly, one of the important areas for future research and measurement development is to determine means to measure the states of involvement (Duda, 2001; Duda & Whitehead, 1998; Roberts et al., 2007). We use POSQ (Roberts et al., 1998) and TEOSQ (Duda & Whitehead, 1998) to measure whether people are prone to be task or ego involved in achievement tasks in sport. We assume that the scores reflect whether athletes are task or ego involved in the context. What most of us do not measure directly are states of involvement. This has been done (e.g., Hall & Kerr, 1997; Swain & Harwood, 1996; Williams, 1998), but we need to develop specific scales or procedures to measure these states. As Vallerand (2001) has argued, when we develop scales to measure states of involvement, we are able to determine the criteria that athletes use within the context rather than infer them. This has proved useful to Vallerand and colleagues in investigating intrinsic and extrinsic motivation from a self-determined theoretical point of view. But we need to develop state of involvement scales that are conceptually consistent with achievement goal theory if we wish to investigate multiple states of goal involvement.

The other area of research that would be beneficial is to pursue the interactionist approach, which looks to combine both dispositional goal orientations and perceptions of the extant motivational climate and which has the potential to lead to a far more complete understanding of the motivation process (Roberts et al., 2007; Treasure, 2001). As we read earlier, these two lines of research have been conducted in relative isolation, but as I have argued, they are part of the same dynamic process of achievement goal theory. Dweck and Leggett (1988) suggested that dispositional goal orientations should be seen as an individual variable that will determine the probability of adopting task or ego states of goal involvement, whereas perceptions of the motivational climate may be seen as potential moderators of the influence of the individual variables. As I and colleagues (Roberts et al., 1997) argued, when the situational criteria are vague or weak, an individual dispositional goal orientation is likely to determine the state of involvement. When the contextual criteria of success and failure are particularly salient, it is likely that the perceived motivational climate may override an individual's dispositional goal orientation and be a stronger predictor of the subsequent goal of action. It is also proposed that children and young adolescents, who have yet to firm up their personal theories of achievement, may be more susceptible to the influence of situational variables than are older adolescents and adults (Roberts & Treasure, 1992). But we need additional focused research on these important motivational questions!

The result of the limited research that has examined both individual and situational variables has shown that taking into account both of these variables enhances our understanding of the sport context (e.g., Kavussanu & Roberts, 1996; Seifriz et al., 1992). The limited evidence to date also provides support for Dweck and Leggett's (1988) contention that situational variables may moderate the influence of goal orientations (e.g., Swain & Harwood, 1996; Treasure & Roberts, 1998). When significant interaction effects emerged they did so in a manner consistent with a moderation model. Thus, this area of research would further our understanding of the process of motivation and is consistent with the fundamental tenets of achievement goal theory.

The achievement context of sport is characterized by greater evaluation and emphasis on performance outcomes as children progress through the competitive levels. Duda (1992) argued that this increase in the performance-oriented nature of the sport context should relate to a corresponding increase in ego orientation among sport participants. To date, no research has directly addressed this developmental process. Treasure (2001) speculated that the long-term effects of an intervention designed to enhance the mastery-oriented nature of the sport context would have an effect on the dispositional goal orientations across the same developmental time span. Individual differences in dispositional goal orientation may be the result of socialization through mastery or performance motivational climates in the home, school, or previous physical activity experiences. Longitudinal studies would provide some insight into how increased exposure of children to mastery-oriented situations might shape dispositional goal orientations (Treasure, 2001; Williams, 1998). Longitudinal research would allow us to investigate this important issue, as well as other key motivational variables. As an example, is the dropout rate higher for performance-oriented sport participants than for mastery-oriented sport participants, as the limited evidence suggests (e.g., Ewing, 1981)?

Directions for Future Research

As we can appreciate, many lines of research can be pursued to investigate further the influence of achievement goals on motivated cognitions, affect, and behavior. Much remains to be investigated to further our understanding of motivation from an achievement goal perspective. This research is exciting because what we are doing is basic research into motivational processes. We are fine-tuning the basic findings to further our understanding and improve our implementation of motivational enhancement strategies. Rather than being bored with our research into achievement goals or considering the research to be "old hat or flawed," we should be excited that, by standing on the shoulders of those who have gone before us and who have developed a reliable and consistent research base, we are extending our knowledge about what we need to do to make people do what needs to be done—the classic motivational dilemma! But more than that, we are also exhibiting that we understand the meaning and practice of good science by basing our research on a conceptually coherent theoretical framework instead of mixing, matching, or inventing constructs that are based on incompatible or nonexistent conceptual frameworks, which still seem to be attractive to the theoretically challenged among us.

In 1989 Csikszentmihalyi and Nakamura made the comment that the cognitive revolution in psychology in the 1970s and 1980s had given a new life to the study of motivation. The modest but profound findings of Bernie Weiner (e.g., 1972)—that people high or low in need achievement actually think differently about success and failure—transformed the focus of motivation research. Individual differences and the influence of the personality and needs waned in importance, and the situation and its meaning became the focus (Maehr & Braskamp, 1986). Motivation is now understood in terms of mediating cognitions not only in terms of control and competence but also in terms of purpose and meaning. For those of us who subscribe to the social-cognitive approach to understanding motivation, we accept that beliefs, thoughts, and perceptions are the basis of understanding the process of motivation. We do not need needs! We assume that cognitive schemas, the personal theory of what it takes to be successful, drive how a person sees the world and responds to the environmental cues extant with achievement striving. Whatever our conceptual stance, we must understand the process of motivation, have a clear notion of what motivation is, and recognize the constraints to our understanding. Clearly, we have much to do. There are some exciting questions to ask about motivational issues in the physical activity realm. The next few years can only add to our knowledge of the dynamics of motivation and achievement behavior in the sport, physical education, and exercise area.

As I have tried to make clear from the foregoing, where achievement goals come from, how they are operationalized, and how they are measured is an area with rich research traditions, both new and old. I have argued for an Ames–Nicholls approach to understanding the motivational equation. But other traditions are just as active, as this book clearly demonstrates. The reader may well ask, What are the key constructs underlying motivation? Of all the extant motivational paradigms, which of the constructs are central to understanding motivation? We have had calls for attempts to integrate some key constructs and untangle the motivation puzzle (e.g., Kaplan & Maehr, 2002; Maehr & Zusho, 2009). Are achievement goals the manifestation of needs, values, the valence of outcomes, or are they cognitive schemas driving how a person sees the world and responds to the environmental cues extant with achievement striving? The central question is this: What gives meaning to achievement striving? Within sport and physical activity, we need to address these questions and expand our conceptual understanding of motivational processes and achievement behaviors. As I argued in 2008, the challenge to all of us who investigate these issues is to enhance our knowledge so that we can intervene effectively to enhance motivation and make the sport and physical activity context enjoyable and satisfying for all. But, and for the last time, let me state that we in sport and exercise psychology need to be more thoughtful about the *why* of how things happen in our area. In my case, I have addressed motivation. But the principles that I have argued for regarding motivation are just as valid for other constructs and phenomena. In short, parsimonious, elegant, and conceptually coherent theories make us better practitioners! Nothing is so practical as a good theory!

Summary

In this chapter I have discussed the nature of achievement goals as being situated within the conceptual paradigm of the demonstration of competence and the avoidance of demonstrating incompetence. I discussed the fundamental conceptual infrastructure of achievement goals and reported the research evidence in support of achievement goal theory, from an individual difference perspective (goal orientations) and from the perspective of perception of the success criteria extant in achievement situations (the motivational climate). I demonstrated through the extensive literature review how being task or ego involved affects achievement cognitions, affect, and behavior. I discussed, and debated, the attempts to "extend" achievement goal theory in which affect-based incentives (at least partially) and the motivational surrogates of "needs" were argued to underpin motivation, and the arguments to extend the number and character of goals. I then discussed and argued that the powerful and parsimonious aspect of achievement goal theory lent itself to practical interventions to enhance adaptive motivation for both children and adults engaged in sport and physical activity. I concluded by identifying what I believe to be fruitful avenues for future research, but I cautioned that the research must be informed by theory.

Valle!

CHAPTER 2

The Place of Achievement Goals in the Social Context of Sport: A Comparison of Nicholls' and Elliot's Models

Athanasios G. Papaioannou, Professor
Nikos Zourbanos, PhD
Charalampos Krommidas, MSc
George Ampatzoglou, PhD
University of Thessaly

At the end of the 1980s research on motivation in physical education was either limited or virtually nonexistent. At that time Nicholls' (1981) achievement goal theory had an inherent appeal to motivational researchers (e.g., Roberts, 1984). There were three reasons for that appeal. First, the theory offered an important framework for the investigation of people's motivation in physical activity settings. Second, unlike some theories that focused primarily on the effects of situation on people's behaviors or others that focused primarily on dispositional differences, Nicholls' theory was a useful framework to investigate the motivational effects stemming from the interaction between person and environment. The third reason was an ethical one: Nicholls' theoretical framework was the first achievement motivation theory that seemed to provide effective answers about how to sustain optimum motivation for individuals of all levels of ability (Nicholls, 1979).

In 1980 Maehr and Nicholls suggested that in achievement settings three goals predominate, namely task, ego, and social approval. When a task-involving goal is adopted, success is defined in subjective terms, such as task mastery, skill development, and personal progress. When task involved, people focus on task mastery and task understanding, feel satisfaction from personal progress, and try hard to develop their competence and master the task. When an ego-involving goal is adopted, success is defined in normative terms, such as outperforming others or performing something that everyone considers difficult. When ego involved, individuals adopt normative criteria to evaluate their competence, feel satisfaction from looking superior relative to others, focus on normative outcomes, and try to exhibit high normative abilities by outperforming others or avoiding a task altogether to avoid looking incompetent. When Nicholls introduced his theory in 1981, he focused on these two goals and skipped the appeal of social approval goals, maybe because at that time social approval was supposed to be subsumed under ego involvement after the age of 12 years for children. Hence, we will not focus on social approval, although we consider this goal important (Kaplan & Maehr, 2002; Papaioannou, Tsigilis, Kosmidou, & Milosis, 2007; Papaioannou, Milosis, Kosmidou, & Tsigilis, 2007). In the beginning of the 1990s, the consensus was that task-involving, or mastery goals, are adaptive, whereas ego-involving, or performance goals, are maladaptive for youngsters' motivation in school (Ames, 1992a) and sport (e.g., Duda, 1993; Roberts, 1992) settings.

Unfortunately, Nicholls died early (1994). Almost immediately after Nicholls' death, many challenged his theory, notably researchers who introduced the concept of avoidance goals (e.g., Elliot & Harackiewitz, 1996; Skaalvik, 1997). These researchers first dissociated the definition of achievement goals from the concept of success and then split the two goals along the taxonomy approach–avoidance. Elliot and colleagues (e.g., 1996, 1997) termed the two goals performance (ego) and mastery (task). Initially, the ego, or performance, goal was split. Performance approach goals imply that individuals attempt to gain positive evaluations for their abilities, whereas performance avoidance goals suggest that individuals attempt to avoid negative evaluation of their abilities (Elliot & Church, 1997). This scheme is now known as the trichotomous model of achievement goals. Later, mastery goals were also split into mastery approach and mastery avoidance goals (Elliot & Thrash, 2001). Mastery approach goals represent strivings to attain task mastery and personal improvement, whereas mastery avoidance goals represent strivings not to fall short of task mastery or strivings not to lose one's mastery, abilities, and knowledge. In effect, Elliot suggested a two-by-two model of achievement goals (for a recent review in sport see, Roberts, Treasure, & Conroy, 2007).

In the last 15 years we have noticed a large production of research based on theories of achievement goals (Elliot, 2005) and a paradigm shift from the original achievement model to the trichotomous and two-by-two models. Nowadays, the original arguments of Nicholls about different conceptions of success are cited less often in mainstream psychology than they were in the late 1980s. On the other hand, Elliot shifted most motivational researchers' interest in the antecedents and consequences of approach and avoidance goals. After the demise of Nicholls some argued that we saw the beginning of the demise of some of his legacies, too. Although Nicholls favored the adoption of mastery goals and considered performance goals (ego-involving in Nicholls' terminology) deleterious for low-ability students and social harmony, Elliot and colleagues suggested that performance goals can be adaptive for both high- and low-ability individuals as long as they are connected with approach and not with avoidance tendencies (Elliot, 2005; Harackiewicz, Barron, Pintrich, Elliot, & Thrash, 2002). Here, however, we argue that the term *adaptive* should refer to the consequences of success for both the person and society.

Other researchers saw that in the trichotomous and two-by-two achievement goal models, the second and the third appeal of Nicholls' theory had vanished (e.g., Maehr & Zusho, 2009). Indeed, the following literature review revealed that studies focused on the interaction between the person and the environment. Later we suggest that this is not a coincidence but results from the difference between Elliot's and Nicholls' models. Elliot adopted a person-centered approach in the conceptualization of achievement goals by suggesting that their underlying cause is the individual's needs, moving away from Nicholls' suggestion that different definitions of competence stem from different definitions of success. As explained later the concept of success has important connotations in the social milieu that were not included in Elliot's model.

With regard to the third appeal of Nicholls' theory, Elliot's suggestions are straightforward. Only people with high perceived competence can adopt approach goals that exhibit adaptive motivational patterns. The fate for individuals with low perceived ability is the adoption of avoidance goals that give way to maladaptive motivational patterns. For Elliot (2005), Nicholls was an idealist. Other researchers believe that Nicholls' direction of research might have been shaped by his ideals, but that presents no problem as long as this line of research provides useful answers to practitioners who want to sustain equality and morality in education and sport contexts. We will discuss later that different findings on equality and morality stemming from Nicholls' and

Elliot's models are because of the adoption of a different measurement technology stemming from the two models. Elliot dissociated task accomplishment from reason to pursue the obtainment of major goals in life (i.e., success), and this trend is more evident in his latest measures (Elliot & Marayama, 2008). As explained later, this reduced the capacity of Elliot's measures to capture social-cognitive variables that are associated with different definitions of success, which are the core differences between task and ego goal adoption according to Nicholls (Roberts et al., 2007; Roberts, this volume).

Accordingly, the present chapter focuses on important differences between Nicholls' and Elliot's models. Although other important models of achievement goals exist (e.g., Dweck, 1998), we focused on Nicholls' and Elliot's models because they have been the most extensively applied in sport (Roberts et al., 2007). Moreover, a comparison among several models would increase the complexity and the length of this chapter. Readers can refer to other sources concerning various approaches in achievement goals research (e.g., Kaplan & Maehr, 2007; Maehr & Zusho, 2009; Nicholls, 1989; Roberts et al., 2007; Roberts, this volume). To realize the differences between the two lines of research we start with a summary of the main findings in sport based on the trichotomous and two-by-two models. These results are contrasted with findings stemming from the dichotomous model. Following the comparison of the two models an interpretation of our findings based on the trichotomous and two-by-two models is offered. This chapter finishes with examples indicating the various applications of the two models in sport and physical activity settings.

Review on Trichotomous and Two-by-Two Findings in Sport

The current review does not provide an extensive discussion of findings such as those of Roberts et al. (2007), but it is rather a summary of findings until the end of 2009. In total we identified 33 studies using the trichotomous and two-by-two models in sport and physical education settings. From them, 25 studies reported correlations between achievement goals and other constructs, 5 studies followed experimental manipulations, and 3 studies were longitudinal.

We separated the correlates of achievement goals as outcomes and antecedents. We considered antecedents those variables that are suggested by the theoretical frameworks of dichotomous, trichotomous, and two-by-two models: motivational climate, motive to achieve success, motive to avoid failure, fear of failure, and perceived competence. To have a general idea which achievement goals we should consider the most preferable, for reasons of simplicity we grouped most correlates of achievement goals under the general headline *outcomes*, although this classification is arbitrary given the lack of findings supporting the causal relationship between most of these variables and achievement goals. The associations of achievement goals with perfectionism were retained in a separate category (miscellaneous). When a relationship of achievement goals with a particular variable existed in more than one study, we conducted a meta-analysis, and instead of correlations we reported mean correlations and standard errors (Hunter & Schmidt, 1990). A summary of these findings follows.

Correlates of Achievement Goals in Sport and Physical Education

As noted earlier, concerning studies that were published until the end of 2009, correlations between achievement goals and other constructs as dependent variables were grouped under the general headline *outcomes*. Furthermore, outcomes based on the literature were further grouped and divided as adaptive and maladaptive. In general, adaptive outcomes included variables related to performance, satisfaction, intrinsic motivation, positive affect, enjoyment, and other positive related constructs in various sports or physical education settings. On the other hand, maladaptive outcomes focused on variables related to extrinsic motivation, anxiety, negative affect, boredom, and other negative related outcomes.

Adaptive Outcomes   Adaptive motivational patterns were positively related to (*a*) mastery approach goals in 21 studies (see table 2.1) and (*b*) performance approach goals in 11 studies. More specifically, mastery approach goals were positively related to race performance, shuttle run performance, academic performance, pacer test performance, fitness, intrinsic motivation, relatedness, relative autonomy, identified regulation, incremental theory, utility and intrinsic value, situational interest, initial interest, sport satisfaction, camp satisfaction, job satisfaction, involvement and participation in physical activity, positive teacher behavior, contribution to society and understanding science beliefs, perceptions that physical education should cultivate good citizens, self-reported tolerance and preference for strenuous exercise, locomotion, effort, metacognitive regulation, help seeking, self-esteem, pleasant affect in life, enjoyment, and positive affect.

Performance approach goals were positively related to race performance, pacer test performance, coach ratings, fitness, utility and intrinsic value, relatedness, sport satisfaction, self-esteem, effort, involvement and participation in physical activity, enjoyment, initial interest, metacognitive regulation, positive teacher behavior, and perceived purposes that physical education should cultivate good citizens.

Adaptive motivational patterns were mostly unrelated to (*a*) performance avoidance goals (in 19 studies) and (*b*) mastery avoidance goals (in 10 studies). More specifically, performance avoidance goals were unrelated to shuttle run performance, race performance, pacer test performance, academic performance, reading literature, effort, intrinsic motivation, relatedness, relative autonomy, interest, involvement in physical activity, help seeking, self-reported tolerance and preference for strenuous exercise, preparation for school,

TABLE 2.1

Correlates of Achievement Goals

	N	Mastery approach		Performance approach		Mastery avoidance		Performance avoidance	
		r	SE	r	SE	r	SE	r	SE
Athletic ability contrast[21]	51	—	—	Ns	—	—	—	Ns	—
Technical ability contrast[21]	51	—	—	Ns	—	—	—	Ns	—
Self-handicapping[4]	273	-.25***	—	-.15**	—	—	—	.23***	—
Metacognitive regulation[17]	273	.55***	—	.35***	—	—	—	Ns	—
Effort[10,3,17]	1,395	.51***	.02	.24***	.03	.18**	—	Ns	.03
Help seeking[17]	273	.40**	—	Ns	—	—	—	Ns	—
Self-esteem[12,19]	917	.43***	.06	Ns	.03	Ns	.03	Ns	.03
Negative affect[19,20]	796	Ns	.06	.16	.03	.27***	.03	.21***	.03
Unpleasant activation[32]	658	Ns	—	Ns	—	Ns	—	Ns	—
Unpleasant deactivation[32]	658	Ns	—	Ns	—	Ns	—	Ns	—
Test anxiety[3]	475	Ns	—	.15**	—	—	—	.51**	—
Positive affect[19,20]	796	.31***	.10	Ns	.04	Ns	.04	Ns	.04
Pleasant affect in life[32]	658	.23$_a$***	—	Ns	—	—	—	Ns	—
Contribution to society—beliefs[32]	658	.24$_a$***	—	-.16$_a$*	—	—	—	Ns	—
Good citizen—purposes[12]	493	.52**	—	.33**	—	.42**	—	.38**	—
Status and power—beliefs[32]	658	Ns	—	.19^a*	—	—	—	Ns	—
Social status—purposes[12]	493	.35**	—	.62**	—	.32**	—	.45**	—
Understand science—beliefs[32]	658	.28$_a$***	—	Ns	—	—	—	Ns	—
Locomotion[32]	658	.33$_a$***	—	Ns	—	—	—	Ns	—
Academic performance[9]	863	.12*	—	-.10*	—	Ns	—	Ns	—
Race performance[22]	112	.28**	—	.35***	—	Ns	—	Ns	—
Shuttle run performance[24]	155	.27**	—	Ns	—	.24**	—	Ns	—

	N	Mastery approach		Performance approach		Mastery avoidance		Performance avoidance	
		r	SE	r	SE	r	SE	r	SE
Pacer test performance[33]	204	.21**[a]	—	.33***[a]	—	Ns	—	Ns	—
Effort[33]	204	.53***[a]	—	Ns	—	Ns	—	Ns	—
Coach ratings[15]	237	Ns	—	.19*	—	—	—	—	—
Self-report strenuous exercise[24]	155	.37**	—	Ns	—	.21**	—	Ns	—
Fitness[12]	493	.55***	—	.19**	—	.33***	—	.26***	—
Tolerance[24]	155	.42***	—	Ns	—	.21**	—	Ns	—
Preference[24]	155	.25**	—	Ns	—	.27**	—	Ns	—
Boredom[10]	647	-.47***	—	Ns	—	Ns	—	-.09*	—
Physical activity participation[10]	647	.30***	—	.22**	—	.10*	—	.09*	—
Physical activity involvement[16]	231	.44***	—	.35***	—	—	—	Ns	—
Intrinsic motivation[3,7,26,29]	1,570	.53***	.06	.15	.10[n=1,120]	—	—	Ns	.02[n=1,120]
Relatedness[10,13]	1,250	.42***	.02	.18**	.03	.20**	—	Ns	.03
Relative autonomy[10,13]	1,033	.54***	.02	Ns	.00	.15	.03	Ns	.11
Identified regulation[3,7]	811	.41***	.03	Ns	.03	—	—	.19**	.03
Introjected regulation[3,7]	811	.21**	.03	.27***	.03	—	—	.30***	.03
External regulation[3,7]	811	Ns	.03	.20**	.03	—	—	.20**	.03
Extrinsic motivation[29]	450	Ns	—	.34**	—	Ns	—	Ns	—
Amotivation[3,7,10,29]	1,908	-.44***	.07	Ns	.03[n=1,458]	Ns	.03[n=1,097]	Ns	.02
Entity theory[23,26]	695	-.16	.04	Ns	.04	Ns	.04	.16	.04
Incremental theory[23,26]	695	.39***	.03	Ns	.04	Ns	.04	Ns	.04
Situational interest[25]	177	.40***	—	Ns	—	—	—	.30***	—
Individual interest[25]	177	Ns	—	Ns	—	—	—	Ns	—
Job satisfaction[8]	430	.38***	—	Ns	—	—	—	-.16**	—

continued ▶

▶ **Table 2.1** (continued)

	N	Mastery approach		Performance approach		Mastery avoidance		Performance avoidance	
		r	SE	r	SE	r	SE	r	SE
Sport satisfaction[9]	863	.35***	—	.09*	—	Ns	—	−.11**	—
Camp satisfaction[15]	237	.26*	—	Ns	—	—	—	—	—
Enjoyment[10,12]	1,140	*.65****	.00	*.29****	.03	*.29****	.03	*.26****	.01
Positive teacher behavior[12]	493	.47***	—	.12**	—	.33**	—	.17**	—
Negative teacher behavior[12]	493	−.21**	—	.17**	—	Ns	—	.15**	—
Initial interest[15]	237	.20*	—	.26*	—	—	—	—	—
Interest[13]	603	.53***	—	Ns	—	—	—	Ns	—
Intention to participate in sport[12]	493	.30***	—	.19**	—	.10*	—	.16**	—
Importance[13]	603	.46***	—	Ns	—	—	—	Ns	—
Usefulness[13]	603	.53***	—	Ns	—	—	—	Ns	—
Utility value[15]	237	.23**	—	.17*	—	—	—	—	—
Intrinsic value[15]	237	.17*	—	.18*	—	—	—	—	—

Note: r (coefficients not in italics) = Pearson product correlation; *r* (coefficients in italics) = mean correlation (reported when the correlation between two variables was found in more than one study); *SE* = standard error of the mean (reported when the correlation between two variables was found in more than one study);

[a] = standardized beta values; [n] = sample size for the specific mean correlation;

Ns = nonsignificant; *N* = sample; *$p < .05$; **$p < .01$; ***$p < .001$;

number in subscript indicates the number of the study in the list of references.

[3]Smith, M., Duda, J.L., Allen, J., & Hall, H. (2002); [4]Ommundsen, Y. (2004); [7]Barkoukis, V., Ntoumanis, N., & Nikitaras, N. (2007); [8]Papaioannou, A., & Christodoulidis, T. (2007); [9]Papaioannou, A.G., Ampatzoglou, G., Kalogiannis, P., & Sagovits, A. (2008); [10]Wang, C.K.J., Biddle, S.J.H., & Elliot, A.J. (2007); [12]Wang, C.K.J. et al. (2008); [13]Shen, B., McCaughtry, N., Martin, J.J., & Fahlman, M. (2009a); [15]Hulleman, C.S., Durik, A.M., Schweigert, S.A., & Harackiewicz, J.M. (2008); [16]Skjesol, K., & Halvari, H. (2005); [17]Ommundsen, Y. (2006); [19]Adie, J.W., Duda, J.L., & Ntoumanis, N. (2008); [20]Kaye, M.P., Conroy, D.E., & Fifer, A.M. (2008); [21]Chalabaev, A., Sarrazin, P., Stone, J., & Cury, F. (2008); [22]Stoeber, J., Uphill, M.A., & Hotham, S. (2009); [23]Stevenson, S.J., & Lochbaum, M.R. (2008); [24]Lochbaum, M.R., Stevenson, S., & Hilario, D. (2009); [25]Shen, B., Chen, A., & Guan, J. (2007); [26]Wang, C.K.J., Chia Liu, W., Lochbaum, M.R., & Stevenson, S.J. (2009); [29]Nien, C.L., & Duda, J.L. (2008); [32]Papaioannou, A., Simou, T., Kosmidou, E., Milosis, D., & Tsigilis, N. (2009); [33]Garn, A., & Sun, H. (2009).

self-esteem, beliefs about purposes in life (understand science, status and power, contribution to society), global self-regulation, locomotion, explanation of assessment, athletic and technical ability, importance, usefulness, incremental theory, positive affect, and affect in life. Mastery avoidance goals were unrelated to race performance, pacer test performance, academic performance, relative autonomy, incremental theory, effort, self-esteem, sport satisfaction, and positive affect.

In 18 studies performance approach goals were unrelated to adaptive outcomes, such as shuttle run performance, intrinsic motivation, relative autonomy, identified regulation, help seeking, situational and individual interest, self-reported tolerance and preference for strenuous exercise, job satisfaction, camp satisfaction, preparation for school, understand science, locomotion, reading literature, importance, usefulness, athletic and technical ability, effort, self-esteem, positive affect, and affect in life. Mastery approach goals were unrelated only to coach ratings and individual interest (2 studies).

Adaptive motivational patterns were negatively related to (*a*) performance approach goals in two studies, (*b*) mastery approach goals in no studies, (*c*) performance avoidance goals in two studies, and (*d*) mastery avoidance goals in no studies. More specifically, performance approach goals were negatively related to academic performance and contribution to society, whereas performance avoidance goals were negatively related to job satisfaction and sport satisfaction.

Maladaptive Outcomes   Maladaptive outcomes had a positive relationship with (*a*) performance approach goals in five studies, (*b*) mastery approach goals in no studies, (*c*) performance avoidance goals in eight studies, and (*d*) mastery avoidance goals in two studies (see table 2.1).

More specifically, performance approach goals were positively related to external regulation, extrinsic motivation, test anxiety, negative teacher behavior, and negative affect. Performance avoidance goals were positively related to external regulation, self-handicapping, test anxiety, entity theory, negative teacher behavior, and negative affect. Mastery avoidance goals were positively related to negative affect.

Mastery approach goals were negatively related to maladaptive outcomes such as amotivation, self-handicapping, entity theory, boredom, and negative teacher behavior in eight studies. Performance approach goals were negatively related to one maladaptive outcome, self-handicapping, in one study. In no study were performance avoidance and mastery avoidance goals negatively related to maladaptive outcomes.

Mastery approach goals were unrelated to maladaptive outcomes such as external regulation, extrinsic motivation, unpleasant activation and deactivation, negative affect, and test anxiety in six studies. Performance approach goal were unrelated to maladaptive outcomes such as amotivation, unpleasant activation and deactivation, boredom, and entity theory in six studies. Mastery avoidance goals were unrelated to maladaptive outcomes such as extrinsic motivation, amotivation, unpleasant activation and deactivation, boredom, entity theory, and teacher negative behavior in eight studies. Finally, performance avoidance goals were unrelated to maladaptive outcomes such as extrinsic motivation, amotivation, unpleasant activation, and deactivation in five studies.

Antecedents of Achievement Goals   Our literature search revealed 23 published studies that investigated the following antecedents: motive to achieve success and motive to avoid failure (2 studies), fear of failure (5 studies), perceived competence (9 studies), and mastery and performance climate (7 studies). The relationships between the aforementioned antecedents are presented in table 2.2. In general, the results from physical activity and sport are in line with Elliot and colleagues' research (Elliot, 1999; Elliot & McGregor, 2001).

More specifically, the results revealed that mastery approach goals were positively related to motive to achieve success, perceived competence, and mastery climate; negatively related to motive to avoid failure; and unrelated to performance climate. Performance approach goals were positively related to fear of failure, perceived competence, and performance climate; negatively related to motive to avoid failure; and unrelated to motive to achieve success and mastery climate. Mastery avoidance goals were positively related to fear of failure and mastery climate and unrelated to perceived competence and performance climate. Finally, performance avoidance goals were positively related to motive to avoid failure, fear of failure, and performance climate; negatively related to motive to achieve success; and unrelated to perceived competence and mastery climate.

TABLE 2.2

Corrected Mean Correlations Between Achievement Goals and Antecedents

	N	Mastery approach		Performance approach		Mastery avoidance		Performance avoidance	
		r	SE	r	SE	r	SE	r	SE
Motive to achieve success[18,28]	191	.45***	—	Ns	.07	—	—	−.47***	.04
Motive to avoid failure[18,28]	191	−.39***	—	−.16	.07	—	—	.51***	.05
Fear of failure[5,6,14,20,29]	1,974	Ns	.03 [n = 1,524]	.26***	.02	.47***	.02	.40***	.02
Perceived competence[3,4,10,12,13,16,23,26,29]	3,867	.38***	.04	.34***	.01	.15	.02 [n = 1,835]	Ns	.02 [n = 3,417]
Mastery climate[1,2,12,16,17,30,31]	2,825	.50***	.05	Ns	.05	.30***	.02 [n = 723]	Ns	.06
Performance climate[1,2,12,16,17,30,31]	2,825	Ns	.04	.41***	.04	Ns	.04 [n = 723]	.32***	.02

Note: r (coefficients not in italics) = Pearson product correlation; r (coefficients in italics) = mean correlation (reported when the correlation between two variables was found in more than one study); SE = standard error of the mean (reported when the correlation between two variables was found in more than one study);

[n] = sample size for the specific mean correlation; Ns = nonsignificant; N = sample; ***p < .001; number in subscript indicates the number of the study in the list of references.

[1]Cury, F., Da Fonséca, D., Rufo, M., & Sarrazin, P. (2002a); [2]Morris, R.L., & Kavussanu, M. (2008);[3]Smith, M., Duda, J.L., Allen, J., & Hall, H. (2002); [4]Ommundsen, Y. (2004);[5]Conroy, D.E., & Elliot, A.J. (2004); [6]Conroy, D.E. (2004); [10]Wang, C.K.J., Biddle, S.J.H., & Elliot, A.J. (2007); [12]Wang et al. (2008); [13]Shen, B., McCaughtry, N., Martin, J.J., & Fahlman, M. (2009a);[14]Conroy, D.E., Elliot, A.J., & Hofer, S.M. (2003);[16]Skjesol, K., & Halvari, H. (2005); [17]Ommundsen, Y. (2006);[18]Thomassen, T.O., & Halvari, H. (2007); [20]Kaye, M.P., Conroy, D.E., & Fifer, A.M. (2008); [23]Stevenson, S.J., & Lochbaum, M.R. (2008); [26]Wang, C.K.J., Chia Liu, W., Lochbaum, M.R., & Stevenson, S.J. (2009);[28]Halvari, H., & Kjormo, O. (1999); [29]Nien, C.L., & Duda, J.L. (2008); [30]Papaioannou, A., Milosis, D., Kosmidou, E., & Tsigilis, N. (2007); [31]Barkoukis, V., Thøgersen-Ntoumani, C., Ntoumanis, N., & Nikitaras, N. (2007).

Miscellaneous   Striving for perfection, imperfection, and other forms of perfectionism were identified in three studies (table 2.3). Striving for perfection and self-oriented perfectionism were positively related to performance approach and mastery approach goals and unrelated to mastery avoidance and performance avoidance goals. On the other hand, negative reactions to perfection and perfectionism concern over mistakes were positively related to performance approach and performance avoidance goals (three studies), mastery avoidance goals (two studies), and mastery approach goals (one study), whereas they were unrelated to mastery approach goals in two studies.

TABLE 2.3

Correlates Between Achievement Goals and Different Forms of Perfectionism

	N	Mastery approach		Performance approach		Mastery avoidance		Performance avoidance	
		r	SE	r	SE	r	SE	r	SE
Striving for perfection[11]	204	$.16_t$*	—	$.28_t$***	—	—	—	Ns	—
	204	$.32_c$***	—	$.19_c$**	—	—	—	Ns	—
	147	$.50_t$***	—	$.34_t$***	—	—	—	Ns	—
	147	$.49_c$***	—	$.35_c$***	—	$-.21_c$*	—	Ns	—
Negative reactions to imperfection[11]	204	Ns	—	$.26_t$***	—	—	—	$.38_t$***	—
	204	Ns	—	$.25_c$***	—	—	—	$.39_c$***	—
	147	$.29_t$***	—	$.37_t$***	—	$.27_t$***	—	Ns	—
	147	$.23_c$**	—	$.35_c$***	—	$.42_c$***	—	22_c**	—
Self-oriented perfectionism[20]	372	.36**	—	.38**	—	Ns	—	.14**	—
Other-oriented perfectionism[20]	372	Ns	—	.23**	—	Ns	—	Ns	—
Socially prescribed perfectionism[20]	372	Ns	—	.14**	—	.16**	—	.22**	—
Perfectionism personal standards[22]	112	.38***	—	.53***	—	.24*	—	Ns	—
Perfectionism concern over mistakes[22]	112	Ns	—	.49***	—	.46***	—	.47***	—

Note: r (coefficients not in italics) = Pearson product correlation; SE = standard error of the mean (reported when the correlation between two variables was found in more than one study); $_t$ = r in a training condition; $_c$ = r in a competition condition; Ns = nonsignificant; N = sample; * $p < .05$; ** $p < .01$; *** $p < .001$;

number in subscript indicates the number of the study in the list of references.

[11]Stoeber, J., Stoll, O., Pesheck, E., & Otto, K. (2008); [20]Kaye, M.P., Conroy, D.E., & Fifer, A.M. (2008); [22]Stoeber, J., Uphill, M.A., & Hotham, S. (2009).

Correlations Between Achievement Goals Our literature search revealed 25 published studies that reported correlation coefficients between achievement goals; 15 were based on the trichotomous model, and 10 were based on the two-by-two framework. The results revealed that mastery approach goals were positively related to performance approach goals and mastery avoidance goals and unrelated to performance avoidance goals (table 2.4). Performance approach goals were positively related to mastery avoidance goals and performance avoidance goals. Finally, mastery avoidance goals were positively related to performance avoidance goals.

Longitudinal Studies

We identified three longitudinal studies ranging in duration from 6 weeks to two terms (almost 6 months) in physical education (PE) and sport. Carr (2006) found that children who perceived a high-mastery and low-performance climate in PE over two terms maintained high levels of personal mastery goals while performance avoidance goals declined. Conroy, Kaye, and Coatsworth (2006) found that swimmers' mastery approach goals at the beginning of the season had positive effects on self-determined forms of situational motivation at the end of the season. Hulleman, Durik, Schweigert, and Harackiewicz (2008) examined the mediational role of task and utility values between initial interest, achievement goals and subsequent interest, camp satisfaction, and coach ratings in two learning contexts during a semester: a college classroom

TABLE 2.4

Mean Correlations Between Achievement Goals and Their Standard Errors

	N	Mastery approach		Performance approach		Mastery avoidance	
		r	SE	r	SE	r	SE
Pap[1,2,4,7,8,9,10,12,13,14,15,16,17,18,19,20,22,23,24,25,26,30,31]	8,957	*.26****	.01				
Mav[2,10,12,14,19,20,22,23,24,26]	3,963	*.30****	.01	*.28****	.01		
Pav[1,2,4,7,8,9,10,12,13,14,16,17,18,19,20,21,22,23,24,25,26,27,28,30,31]	8,957	*Ns*	.05	*.39****	.03[n = 9,182]	*.39****	.02[n = 3,963]

Note: r (coefficients in italics) = mean correlation (reported when the correlation between two variables was found in more than one study); *SE* = standard error of the mean (reported when the correlation between two variables was found in more than one study); [n] = sample size for the specific mean correlation; Pap = performance approach; Mav = mastery avoidance; Pav = performance avoidance; Ns = nonsignificant; *N* = sample; *** $p < .001$;

number in subscript indicates the number of the study in the list of references.

[1]Cury, F., Da Fonséca, D., Rufo, M., & Sarrazin, P. (2002a); [2]Morris, R.L., & Kavussanu, M. (2008); [4]Ommundsen, Y. (2004); [7]Barkoukis, V., Ntoumanis, N., & Nikitaras, N. (2007); [8]Papaioannou, A., & Christodoulidis, T. (2007); [9]Papaioannou, A.G., Ampatzoglou, G., Kalogiannis, P., & Sagovits, A. (2008); [10]Wang, C.K.J., Biddle, S.J.H., & Elliot, A.J. (2007); [12]Wang et al. (2008); [13]Shen, B., McCaughtry, N., Martin, J.J., & Fahlman, M. (2009a); [14]Conroy, D.E., Elliot, A.J., & Hofer, S.M. (2003); [15]Hulleman, C.S., Durik, A.M., Schweigert, S.A., & Harackiewicz, J.M. (2008); [16]Skjesol, K., & Halvari, H. (2005); [17]Ommundsen, Y. (2006); [18]Thomassen, T.O., & Halvari, H. (2007); [19]Adie, J.W., Duda, J.L., & Ntoumanis, N. (2008); [20]Kaye, M.P., Conroy, D.E., & Fifer, A.M. (2008); [21]Chalabaev, A., Sarrazin, P., Stone, J., & Cury, F. (2008); [22]Stoeber, J., Uphill, M.A., & Hotham, S. (2009); [23]Stevenson, S.J., & Lochbaum, M.R. (2008); [24]Lochbaum, M.R., Stevenson, S., & Hilario, D. (2009); [25]Shen, B., Chen, A., & Guan, J. (2007); [26]Wang, C.K.J., Chia Liu, W., Lochbaum, M.R., & Stevenson, S.J (2009); [27]Carr, S. (2006); [28]Halvari, H., & Kjormo, O. (1999); [30]Papaioannou, A., Milosis, D., Kosmidou, E., & Tsigilis, N. (2007); [31]Barkoukis, V., Thøgersen-Ntoumani, C., Ntoumanis, N., & Nikitaras, N. (2007).

(psychology, study 1) and a high school sports camp (football, study 2). The results for both studies revealed that initial mastery approach goals and interest predicted subsequent camp satisfaction and interest in the classroom and that this relationship was mediated by task values, whereas initial performance approach goals and utility values positively predicted coach ratings and course grade.

Experimental Studies

Cury, Elliot, Sarrazin, Da Fonseca, and Rufo (2002) found that performance approach and mastery conditions had similar effects on intrinsic motivation in a basketball dribbling activity, whereas performance avoidance conditions undermined intrinsic motivation. In a similar study using a basketball dribbling task, Cury, Da Fonséca, Rufo, Peres, and Sarrazin (2003) found that individuals in performance avoidance conditions reported higher state anxiety than those in the performance approach and mastery conditions. Furthermore, there were no significant differences in a short-term learning outcome between performance approach and mastery goal conditions. Elliot, Cury, Fryer, and Huguet (2006) examined the relationships between self-handicapping, achievement goals, and performance on dribbling activity. The object of the task was to dribble a basketball through a course of obstacles as quickly as possible in one timed trial under the conditions described in Cury and colleagues' experiments. The results supported the findings of Cury et al. (2003), and they revealed the mediating role of self-handicapping on the relationship between performance avoidance goals and performance.

Gernigon, d'Arripe-Longueville, Delignières, and Ninot (2004) explored how achievement goal involvement varied during a practice judo combat. The results revealed the dynamic nature of goal involvement states and their rapid change in the sport domain.

Field Experimental Intervention

Milosis and Papaioannou (2007) in a 6-month intervention study in physical education attempted to change students' goals in physical activity, academic subjects, and social settings through promoting a mastery climate and teaching interdisciplinary skills such as goal setting, self-monitoring, self-talk, and so on. Their results revealed a positive effect on all dimensions of self-concept, performance in an academic subject, satisfaction, and mastery approach goals in physical education and academic subjects, and a negative effect on performance approach and performance avoidance goals.

Summary of Findings From Literature Review

Based on our review we conclude that mastery approach goals are the most preferable goals. In support of Elliot's suggestions we found that the two avoidance goals have negative implications for people's motivation in physical activity settings. Findings concerning performance approach goals remain controversial. Performance approach goals were related to several adaptive outcomes but also some maladaptive outcomes. One might conclude that the adoption of a performance approach goal should be encouraged if a mastery approach goal is concurrently emphasized. But this argument is not based on research that investigates the effects of situations emphasizing performance approach goals on people's motivation in physical activity settings. Moreover, our review revealed few experimental studies and only one field experimental study aiming to affect youngsters' achievement goals. As we will point out later, we are somewhat skeptical about the findings of the existing experimental studies in labs because they do not provide true meaning of mastery, success, and failure.

Our review revealed no studies that investigated the possible effects of performance approach goal adoption on other achievement goals. Our meta-analysis implies that performance avoidance goals are positively related to performance approach goals. But no research has investigated the causal relationship of these goals in real life. Researchers such as Brophy (2005) argued that performance approach goals might turn to performance avoidance goals. This assumption can be examined with longitudinal or field experimental studies, but these have not been done.

Surprisingly, most studies adopted a narrow approach to the study of motivation, focusing solely on the goals of the person for the benefit of this person. The influence of society as a whole was almost absent in these studies. No study investigated the possible effects of different goal adoption on others. No study was truly developmental in investigating how achievement goals are shaped, at what age, why, how, whether achievement goals are undifferentiated in early childhood and split later in life, how they mutate over time because of environmental influences, and so on. No study investigated the interaction between individuals' achievement goals and major achievement goals in their environment. Apart from one intervention study, no other study investigated the effects of the environment on the formation of achievement goals. Even the investigation of the association of achievement goals with perceived motivational climate was limited in comparison with similar studies that were conducted based on the dichotomous model (Duda & Hall, 2001; Ntoumanis & Biddle, 1999b).

In conclusion, in comparison with applications of Nicholls' theory in sport (Duda & Hall, 2001; Duda, 2005; Roberts et al., 2007; Roberts, this volume), important lines of research are missing. No research has been done on the relation of mastery–performance and approach–avoidance goals to beliefs about effort and ability and the use of the more or less differentiated conception of ability for individuals who adopt different achievement goals. There is total absence of developmental research, and no study has been done on how nurture shapes achievement goals. Neither the two-by-two model nor the trichotomous model has been examined in relation to social outcomes such as moral behaviors and aggressiveness, social values, inequality, and equal opportunities for all. Scant information is available about the interaction of individuals' achievement goals with motivational climate (Elliot & Murayama, 2008), and there was no such information at all in physical activity at the time of the writing of this chapter. Our knowledge about how parenting, coaching, and teaching in physical activity settings facilitate the adoption of mastery approach goals is still based on assumptions, not on findings from field experimental research. We believe that the lack of research in some of the aforementioned issues is not a coincidence but results from different theoretical approaches in the conceptualization of achievement goals in Nicholls' and Elliot's models. Accordingly, we will attempt to draw lines between Nicholls' and Elliot's models.

A Comparison Between Elliot's and Nicholls' Models

In the first part of this section we explore the consequences of achievement goal adoption in the social milieu according to Nicholls' and Elliot's models. We reveal significant differences between the two models, which have important consequences in the research methodology that was followed based on the two models. These differences in methodological approaches are addressed in the second part of this section.

Achievement Goals in the Social Context

Nicholls (1989) and other researchers (e.g., Duda, Olson, & Templin, 1991; Kavussanu & Roberts, 2001; see also Roberts, this volume) were particularly interested in the consequences of achievement behaviors in the social milieu and the way in which social settings frame individuals' achievement goals. At the core of Nicholls' approach has been the meaning of success, the place of the individual within the social context, and the manner in which individuals' success can coincide with social progress and justice.

From Nicholls' writings we understand that he connected achievement goals with the concept of success for two reasons. First, in line with classic achievement motivation theory (Atkinson & Feather, 1966), achieving success has high value and the pursuit of success energizes a person's behavior and emits high levels of motivation. Being successful is highly valuable because success is not a piecemeal event but the favorable termination of many attempts and endeavors. Accomplishments in specific tasks when put together add up to a major obtainment in life known as success. In particular situations, high levels of motivation occur when task accomplishment conveys a meaning that is tied to a person's long-term major outcome in life, which is defined as success. Elliot and colleagues have not considered this. Indeed, as achievement goal researchers observed (Duda & Hall, 2001; Roberts et al., 2007; Roberts, this volume), although for Nicholls achievement goals energize the motivational process, for Elliot achievement goals are the manifestation of needs or the "motivational surrogates" of the needs of achievement motivation (Elliot & Church, 1997).

Second, success has different meanings for people who adopt different views about the desired consequences of their achievements for themselves and others. People can define success as the attainment of wealth, positions, honors, eminence, and the like. Individuals who endorse this definition view their career in life as a struggle to gain advantage over others. Other people are opponents in this battle. For high-ego-oriented individuals success is associated with pursuit of superiority and power (Nicholls, Patashnick, & Nolen, 1985; Nicholls, 1989). Individuals who have ego-oriented goals do not bother about social inequalities; in fact, a social context that sustains inequalities helps them derive gratification from being superior as long as they dominate. Success can be also defined as something desired such as equality, social welfare, social justice, ecological harmony, promotion of science, and so on. The attainment of these ideals has positive consequences for both the person and society (Nicholls et al., 1985; Nicholls, 1989). When priority is given to these kinds of ideals, people do not consider others as opponents but as partners in the ongoing realization of worthy outcomes that lead to success. These people try hard in life, school, sport, and work to achieve success, but their goals are not in conflict with others' goals. They focus on their personal progress, on improving their competence to help them achieve their ideals. These two different meanings of success have not been taken into account in Elliot's (2005) definition of achievement goals (Kaplan & Maehr, 2002).

The lack of developmental research based on the trichotomous and two-by-two models reflects the limitations of these models in theorization about the development of achievement goals in the social milieu. On the other hand, Nicholls suggested that the adoption of different conceptions of success and corresponding achievement goals is an outcome of nurture and one's involvement in social situations that emphasize different achievement goals and notions of success. Nicholls and Miller (1983, 1984b; Nicholls, 1978, 1989) investigated how different concepts of success, ability, and corresponding achievement goals develop in childhood. They found that although young children adopt subjective criteria to define success and ability, after entrance into elementary school they gradually realize the importance of normative criteria. A few years later they can understand that when different individuals attain equal performance, the most capable is the one who can achieve it with the least effort.

Proponents of the trichotomous and two-by-two models have not examined how the social context affects volition in the adoption of performance or mastery goals. On the contrary, for Nicholls (1989) the adoption of achievement goals is intentional and is the outcome of internalization of social influences about different conceptions of success. This internalization might take place early in life, but it is particularly important from late childhood until the end of adolescence. Adolescence is a time when individuals (a) are extremely interested in their position and their goals in relation to others, (b) intentionally prioritize their values about what is worthy to pursue in life, (c) explore ways to pursue their goals, and (d) have full understanding about the consequences of different goal pursuits in their and others' lives. Depending on their influences and how they are internalized, from late childhood onward some youngsters intentionally become prone to the use of normative definitions of success and the pursuit of normative goals. Others purposively continue thinking like young children by adopting subjective definitions of success and pursuing mastery goals. When they have the choice, both high-ego-oriented and high-task-oriented youngsters intentionally adopt either performance or mastery goals because goal adoption serves a major desired outcome in life, which is their subjective notion of success.

For Elliot achievement goals are framed by different perceptions of competence and different definitions of competence, but to date no one has investigated why people adopt these different definitions of competence. Using the dichotomous model, one could argue that those who consistently pursue positive evaluations of their abilities must have a reason for doing so. To understand the reasons, one has to examine the consequences of this behavior within the social context. In organizations that adopt meritocracy, such as schools and teams, the person who gets more benefits and tangible rewards is the one who gets the most favorable evaluations of his or her abilities. Hence, for individuals who adopt performance approach goals, what matters are the associated benefits that they get from exhibiting high competence. High-ego-oriented athletes envisage that these benefits will establish their superiority among their peers if they succeed. For that reason, many studies have found a positive relationship between ego orientation and extrinsic motivation (e.g., based on the dichotomous model: Brunel, 1999; Petherick & Weigand, 2002; based on the trichotomous and two-by-two models: Barkoukis, Ntoumanis, & Nikitaras, 2007; Nien & Duda, 2008; Smith, Duda, Allen, & Hall, 2002). On the other hand, individuals who give priority to mastery approach goals over other achievement goals envisage that the consequences of their success will benefit both themselves and others, and they try to integrate their interests with the interests of others. A student who pursues excellence and top marks in order to enter the best school of medicine might envisage benefits for both her- or himself and society (Nicholls et al., 1985).

Although the association of reason (e.g., to show others that I have ability) with aim (e.g., to do well relative to others) is central in the dichotomous model, for Elliot's aim should be separated from reason in the investigation of achievement goals. Elliot's argument implies that achievement goals are not dispositions because aim without reason cannot establish disposition. No rational person consistently seeks to achieve something without reason. Indeed, Mischel and Shoda (1998) argued that any given disposition is a network of cognitive-affective units that link goals with values, expectations, self-perceptions, affect, and self-regulation strategies. The stable network of these cognitive-affective units sustains cross-situational consistency in a person's behavior. As several researchers argued, achievement goals act as schemas that reflect the purposes underling achievement behavior and represent an integrated pattern of cognitions and emotions that underlie the various responses to achievement outcomes (Duda & Hall, 2001; Kaplan & Maehr, 1999; Roberts et al., 2007; Roberts, this volume).

Finally, the lack of research on the connection of beliefs about effort and ability with mastery–performance and approach–avoidance goals might not be coincidental. The exhibition of high effort or ability has social repercussions (Nicholls, 1976) that were not considered in the trichotomous and two-by-two models. In the dichotomous model, task-oriented youngsters continue to think like small children not because they are less cognitively mature but because they have realized that effort matters for the pursuit of their ideals. Moreover, high-task-oriented athletes try hard because they believe not only that competence is developed through high effort (Dweck, 1998) but also that the pursuit of their ideals is self-determined and does not depend on others' behaviors. They perceive that high effort leads them closer to the attainment of their ideals. High-task-oriented students ascribe high value to effort because effort is virtuous in society (Nicholls, 1976). High effort has positive consequences for the person without undermining others' positions, which coincides with task-oriented persons' view that success has positive consequences for both the person and others. On the other hand, high-ego-oriented individuals ascribe high value to normative ability because it establishes their superiority relative to others. High-ego-oriented persons expect that if they demonstrate high normative ability across several tasks, they will gain the common confession that they are superior to others, which is in line with their definition of success.

To conclude, proponents of the trichotomous and two-by-two models conceptualized achievement goals without considering that different definitions of competence reflect different views about the consequences of being competent for the person and others. They did not adopt Nicholls' suggestions that these different conceptions of competence reflect different views about (*a*) the consequences of achievement to society, (*b*) people's position and role in the social context, and (*c*) the way in which people perceive their interests in relation to the interests of others. In essence, Elliot and his colleagues disregarded the consequences of different conceptions of success (and their by-product, different definitions of competence; Duda & Hall, 2001; Roberts et al., 2007) for the person and others.

Measurement Issues

Differences between Elliot's and Nicholls' conceptualization are reflected in their measures. This might be a reason for some inconsistent findings between lines of research that are based on the two models.

Unlike Nicholls' (1989) measures, Elliot's measures do not capture different conceptions of success but different definitions of standards used to evaluate competence (i.e., intrapersonal or normative). Although different definitions of success are directly linked with different value systems and different worldviews (Nicholls et al., 1985; Nicholls, 1989), the association of worldviews with definitions of standards of competence is indirect and a by-product of the association of the latter with the definition of success (see also Roberts et al., 2007). Elliot's model has a narrower focus in the social milieu, and his measures might have weaker associations with several social constructs in comparison to Nicholls' model and measures. This is particularly true in investigations of the consequences of one's achievement behavior on others (e.g., studies that examine the consequences of mastery and performance goal adoption on sportspersonship, aggression, and so on).

Although almost from the beginning Elliot excluded the definition of success in the measurement of achievement goals (Elliot & Church, 1997), in his initial measures Elliot incorporated items connecting achievement goals with the perceived value of these goals (e.g., it is important for me to understand . . . ; it is important for me to do better than the other students; Elliot & Church, 1997). In his most recent work Elliot excluded all items connecting values and achievement goals (Elliot & Murayama, 2008) to keep "aim separate from reason," despite the importance of reason behind one's decision to select subjective or normative criteria of evaluation. As others have observed (Duda & Hall, 2001; Roberts at al., 2007), although Elliot moved the definition of achievement goals closer to the goal construct that is adopted by other goal literatures, such as goal-setting theory, his measures do not capture the breadth of goal orientations that were suggested by many achievement goal researchers. Elliot's argumentation to exclude values and beliefs about success from the definition of the achievement goals construct has been mainly based on construct validation arguments (e.g., Elliot & Thrash, 2001; Elliot & Murayama, 2008). This approach, however, does not acknowledge all the research findings suggesting that dispositional differences in the importance to pursue mastery and performance goals correspond to different worldviews, different definitions of success, and different definitions of standards of competence assessment. Moreover, Elliot's approach and measurement do not take into account that the interconnections among certain patterns of beliefs about success, standards used to evaluate competence, and values remain unchanged across situations (Duda & Nicholls, 1992; Papaioannou, 2006) and that it is this cross-situational stability in the adoption of different patterns of worldviews, beliefs about success, and standards of evaluation that shapes the two goal orientations. Questionnaires that exclude reason from the measurement of achievement goals, such as those of Elliot and Murayama (2008), can hardly assess dispositional differences in goal orientations, and they are at odds with contemporary social-cognitive theories of personality (Mischel & Shoda, 1998).

One might argue that Elliot and Murayama's (2008) instrument is situation specific. Still, it does not capture the whole range of differences between mastery–task and performance–ego goals as described in the dichotomous model. Even at the situational level of generality, achievement goal measures should incorporate reason with aim because as we have explained, high levels of motivation occur when the obtainment of desired outcomes in specific tasks conveys a meaning that is linked to one's major desired outcome in life. Hence, it is important to know the reason that determines a person's selection of a particular achievement goal in order to predict the person's emotions, self-regulation processes, and behaviors toward others who are involved in the same situation. To explain, let us consider an item including aim but not reason in Elliot and Murayama's questionnaire (2008) and a competitive game such as tennis. During the match even low-ego-oriented individuals "aim to perform better than the others" (Elliot & Murayama, 2008) because this is the ultimate goal of the game and they must pursue winning to enjoy the game, but this does not imply that they find winning important because the outcome of their behavior is not linked to their long-term desired outcome in life. On the contrary, for high-ego-oriented individuals who are playing competitive games, outperforming others is linked to their desire to establish superiority. This difference in the meaning of goal attainment has different consequences for high- and low-ego-oriented individuals. A low-ego-oriented person is less likely to become irritated and upset by a controversial decision than a high-ego-oriented person is.

Elliot's measures have additional limitations. Importantly, limitations in the measurement of mastery goals might explain why his mastery scales are not related to performance, whereas performance scales are. Across several mastery scales (e.g., Elliot & Murayama, 2008; Conroy, Elliot, & Hofer, 2003), the standards to evaluate mastery are not specific, goals are not easily measurable, and the wording is similar to the do-your-best goals approach that has been criticized in goal-setting research (e.g., My goal is to learn as much as possible; I want to perform as well as it is possible for me to perform) (see Roberts & Kristiansen, this volume). On the other hand, the standards to evaluate performance goals are specific, and goal attainment is easily and instantly measurable (e.g., My goal is to perform better than the other students). Taking into consideration that specific and measurable goals lead to better performance than do-your-best goals (e.g., Locke & Latham, 1990), we should not be surprised that in several studies achievement has a stronger connection with performance approach goals than with mastery approach goals.

We found similar and more crucial limitations in experimental conditions when manipulating mastery approach goals. In most of the existing manipulations of mastery conditions, the goals to be accomplished were not specific and personal improvement was hardly measurable. Even more striking, though, is the absence of meaningful reasons for participants' involvement in the so-called mastery approach conditions. For example, Cury, Elliot, et al. (2002) and Cury et al. (2003) manipulated mastery conditions by instructing participants that

> the intention (of this research) is to assess the teaching quality of the course in order to use it to teach dribbling in school. This course has been set up and used all over France. The aim of this session is to see if you can quickly improve your dribbling. There are two trials and the object is to go as fast as possible.

This do-your-best manipulation provides no specific measurable goals. More important, though, is how meaningful the "intention of this research" is to participants. Why should participants be intrinsically motivated in the 5 minutes following this manipulation, as the authors assumed they would be? In such experiments participants do not see why task accomplishment has any meaning to their important goals in life. The participants are doing the work for researchers, not for themselves. Yet, as Nicholls (1989, p. 83) argued, "The attempt to understand and predict cognition and action by way of empathy—by trying to put oneself in the shoes of our 'subjects'— . . . may advance us toward . . . predictions of actions and accomplishment." And he continued, "If a task is unimportant to a person, it is strange to describe such a person as task involved" (Nicholls, 1989, p. 88).

There is a contrasting difference between Nicholls and Elliot on the conceptualization of task involvement and task mastery goals. According to Nicholls, task-involved individuals have specific reasons to find a task important, and these exact reasons energize them to try hard to accomplish the task and improve their ability in the particular setting. Contrary to Elliot and Murayama's (2008) belief that mastery goals can be captured by separating aim from reason, conditions separating aim from reason convey no authentic meaning to participants and, as Nicholls suggested, describing them as task involving is strange.

Unfortunately, experiments conveying no authentic meaning to participants have been typical in the manipulation of mastery conditions. Elliot and his coworkers have made various experimental manipulations, but so far we have not seen manipulations of task accomplishment convey a sense of task importance and authentic meaning to participants. The equation of "puzzle solving without referring to normative comparison" with the adoption of mastery approach goals in manipulation checks (Elliot & Harackiewicz, 1996, p. 464) is arbitrary and unjustified unless the experimenters ensure that task accomplishment conveys meaning that is tied to participants' major desired outcomes in life. The same reasoning also applies to the unjustified use of the concepts of success and failure in these experiments. Researchers commonly assume that "the target task (i.e., puzzle solving) was described as diagnostic of success . . . or failure" (Elliot & Harackiewicz, 1996, p. 463). But success is not synonymous with the exhibition of high competence in unimportant tasks. The true notion of success and failure is lost in manipulations in which task accomplishment conveys no meaning to participants' important goals in life.

Ironically, although participants took part in most of these experiments to receive extra course credit (e.g., Elliot & Harackiewicz, 1996), experimenters assessed participants' intrinsic motivation during task accomplishment either by observing behavior during a "free-choice" (!) period or with self-reports that assessed enjoyment with the task. But positive feelings such as enjoyment and fun are manifestations of intrinsic motivation but are not synonymous with intrinsic motivation. Moreover, in these experiments participants did not go willingly to accomplish a meaningful task. Instead, they were tangibly rewarded to play for a few minutes with some puzzles. But playing with an unimportant task has nothing in common with intrinsic motivation during learning and involvement in important tasks in school and sport. Likewise, the measurement of task involvement with items such as "I was totally absorbed in the puzzles" and "I concentrated on finding the hidden Ninas" (Elliot & Harackiewicz, 1996) is totally irrelevant to the task involvement construct conceived by Nicholls, who has clearly stated that a task should be important in task involvement.

Thus, it is not peculiar to observe that the most consistent differences in these experiments are between avoidance and approach goals, which reflect different manipulations of participants' perceptions of competence. Proponents of the trichotomous and two-by-two models would have caused less confusion if they had clearly stated that their focus was the connection of perceived competence with approach and avoidance goals. The definition issue of competence should be investigated in connection with the definition of success; otherwise, we cannot expect activation of high levels of motivation, particularly in task-involving conditions.

Across all mastery and task orientation scales we can find additional shortcomings. In almost all of them the items do not capture task involvement (task absorption), which is important in Nicholls' theory. Although task absorption has a strong positive affective tone, the existing mastery items depict only cognitive involvement (e.g., I am striving to understand . . . ; my goal is to learn . . . ; Elliot & Murayama, 2008). Given the importance of affect in the determination of human behavior, this shortcoming in the measurement of mastery goals is another reason to find weaker relationships between mastery goals and achievement behaviors in existing studies than in real life.

Undoubtedly, proponents of the trichotomous and two-by-two models brought into the front line of research the importance of avoidance goals. On the other hand, researchers had already raised two major questions about avoidance goals. First, they questioned the very existence of mastery avoidance goals in sport and youth settings (Ciani & Sheldon, 2010; Sideridis & Mouratidis, 2008). It seems likely that if mastery avoidance goals exist in sport they should occur so rarely that their measurement is meaningless. The second concern is whether athletes or students understand avoidance goal items in the same way that researchers do. Analyzing interviews with students, Urdan and Mestas (2006) found that participants had difficulty distinguishing between "wanting to do better than others" and "not wanting to do worse" and that participants used approach explanations when they responded to performance avoidance items. Likewise, adopting the same methodology Ciani and Sheldon (2010) found that athletes who endorsed mastery avoidance goals used mastery approach explanations, such as "because I always want to be better" (p. 129). These findings imply that people, particularly youngsters, have difficulty understanding the items of performance or mastery avoidance scales.

Another positive effect of the research of Elliot and colleagues is their emphasis on the measurement of situational-specific goals. Achievement goal measures at the situational level of generality (i.e., at a particular moment) should not include items referring directly to success because success refers to major obtainments in life resulting from the accomplishment of many tasks. Items starting with the stem "I feel most successful in sport when," such as in the Task and Ego Orientation in Sport Questionnaire (TEOSQ) (Duda & Nicholls, 1992) and the Perception of Success Questionnaire (POSQ) (Roberts & Balague, 1989; Roberts, Treasure & Balague, 1998), are the most appropriate to capture dispositional goal orientations (Nicholls, 1989).

Interpretation of Findings Based on the Trichotomous and Two-by-Two Models

The aforementioned comments stem from self-reflection after several years of research using Nicholls' (1989) and Elliot and Church's (1997) measures (Papaioannou & Macdonald, 1993; Papaioannou, Tsigilis et al., 2007; Papaioannou, Kosmidou, Tsigilis, & Milosis, 2007). Later we present findings stemming from participants' responses to these measures that are in line with our assertions.

Dispositional Differences

In one of our studies (Pasxali, Kouli, Sidiropoulos, & Papaioannou, 2004) with 268 adolescent athletes from various sports, we compared the TEOSQ and POSQ with a measure (Papaioannou, Tsigilis, et al., 2007; Papaioannou, Kosmidou, et al., 2007) that is similar to Elliot and Church's (1997) measure. We examined the participants' relations with emotions, satisfaction in sport, intrinsic and extrinsic motivation, and normative expectations in sport. The latter was assessed with a self-efficacy scale that asked athletes how confident they were that at the end of the season their performance would be within the top 50 or 20 or 10 performances in their sport. Our results were consistent with others' findings that were summarized in the aforementioned review, although there were no between-measure differences in the relationships of achievement goals with other constructs. But a regression of normative expectation on ego orientation and perceived competence showed a significant interaction using the ego scales of the TEOSQ and POSQ, although this interaction was absent using the performance scale based on the trichotomous model. Using the TEOSQ (figure 2.1) and POSQ (figure 2.2), we found that, although expectation was considerably lower for low-perceived-competence athletes than for high-perceived-competence athletes when ego orientation was high, both high- and low-perceived-competence athletes had similar expectations when ego orientation was low. Nicholls' (1984) moderating hypothesis was supported when the concept of success was used to capture an ego (or performance) goal but not when the definition of competence was used to capture a

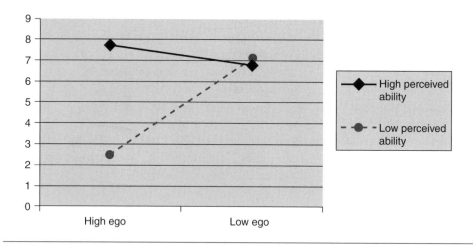

FIGURE 2.1 Self-efficacy for normative performance: interaction between perceived competence and ego orientation (TEOSQ).

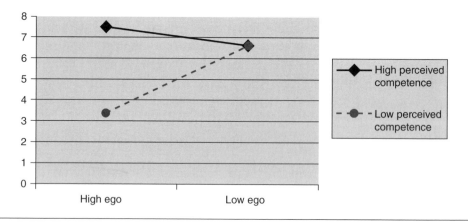

FIGURE 2.2 Self-efficacy for normative performance: interaction between perceived competence and ego orientation (POSQ).

performance goal (figure 2.3). These findings imply that, although measures similar to Elliot and Church's (1997) capture a lot of the cognitive-affective units that are associated with achievement goals, they probably have narrower focus and cannot perfectly discriminate individuals adopting the more and less differentiated conception of ability (Nicholls, 1984).

In the measure of Elliot and Church (1997), aim was associated with reason, and therefore the definition of competence was largely a by-product of the definition of success. Hence, in general, results based on this measure should be rather consistent with (but maybe weaker than) most of the previous findings based on Nicholls' model focusing on the effects of achievement goal adoption on others (e.g., Duda, 1989; Duda et al., 1991). Indeed, Papaioannou, Simou, Kosmidou, Milosis, and Tsigilis (2009) found that mastery approach goals

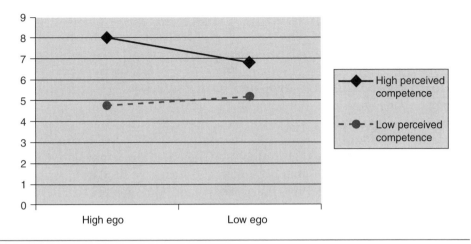

FIGURE 2.3   Self-efficacy for normative performance: interaction between perceived competence and performance approach goal (2 × 2 model).

were positively related to beliefs that the main purpose in life is to contribute to society and understand nature and science and that the purpose of physical education is to promote active lifestyles among students and cultivate good citizens. On the other hand, performance approach goals were positively related to beliefs that the main purpose in life is to acquire high status and power and that the purpose of physical education is to increase the competitiveness and status and career of students. These findings are in line with past results based on the dichotomous model (e.g., Duda, 1989; Nicholls et al., 1985; Papaioannou & Macdonald, 1993). Performance avoidance goals, however, were not related to any belief. To investigate further the possible differences between approach and avoidance goals, here we reanalyzed the findings of Papaioannou, Simou, et al. (2009) focusing on goal priorities.

We define goal priority as the relative importance of various goals to individuals. For example, a performance approach goal has higher priority for an individual scoring 4 in the performance approach goal scale but less than 4 in all other achievement goal scales than for an individual scoring 4 in the performance approach goal scale but also 4 or higher in other achievement goal scales. The larger the difference is between the most preferable goal and the mean rating of all achievement goals, the higher the priority that is given to the preferable goal. To investigate the association of goal priorities with other constructs, we followed a technique described by Schwartz (2008). We first made sure that all achievement goals ranged in the same scale, from 1 to 5. Next, we computed each individual's mean score across all achievement goals. Then, to investigate the association between goal priorities and their correlates, we computed partial correlations between achievement goals and other constructs, partialing on the mean rating.

As is shown in table 2.5, beliefs referring to competitiveness and acquisition of power in society corresponded positively to priority given to performance approach goals but negatively to priority given to performance avoidance goals. These findings go beyond Elliot's (1999) conceptualization that performance approach and avoidance goals are reflections of the needs for achievement and fear of failure, respectively. They reveal that the contrast between performance approach and performance avoidance goal profiles reflects different belief systems about important purposes in physical education and life. Although performance approach goal pursuit is connected with a major goal in life indicating high status and power, performance avoidance goal pursuit is rather disconnected from this major goal in life. The adoption of normative criteria of competence assessment does not reflect the pursuit of similar major goals in life. Elliot's (2005) two definitions of competence do not stem from Nicholls' conceptualization of task and ego goals because for Nicholls achievement goal pursuit in a particular task is connected with the accomplishment of a major life goal. Thus, Elliot did not just split the concept of ego (or performance) goals into approach and avoidance goals as many think; he actually created new constructs.

Although Elliot proposed that achievement goals emerge from unconscious needs, several authors have suggested that achievement goals might reflect values (Kaplan & Maehr, 2007; Roberts et al., 2007). Papaioannou and Karakanta (2010) investigated the association of achievement goals with two sets of Schwartz's (2008) universal values that have been found to

TABLE 2.5

Partial Correlations of Achievement Goals With Beliefs About Purpose of Life and Purpose of Physical Education, Controlling for Social Desirability

	Mastery approach		Performance approach		Performance avoidance	
	r_{sd}	r_{G-pr}	r_{sd}	r_{G-pr}	r_{sd}	r_{G-pr}
LIFE PURPOSE						
Contribution to society	.47***	.38***	.01	−.21***	−.10	−.14*
Status or power	−.04	−.05	.37***	.21***	.11	−.13*
Understanding nature or science	.33***	.29***	.00	−.11	−.12	−.16**
PURPOSE OF PHYSICAL EDUCATION						
Status or career	.10	.06	.23***	.00	.00	−.05
Active lifestyles	.40***	.43***	−.04	−.20***	−.05	−.20***
Competitiveness	.04	.02	.38***	.23***	.07	−.22***
Good citizens	.31***	.25***	.00	−.19**	−.11	−.06

r_{sd} = partial correlations controlling for social desirability;
r_{G-pr} = partial correlations controlling for the mean rating of three achievement goals and for social desirability;
*$p < .05$, **$p < .01$, ***$p < .001$.

lie opposite one another in the dimension "self-enhancement" versus "self-transcendence," that is, achievement (defined as personal success through demonstrating competence according to social standards) and power (social status and prestige, control or dominance over people and resources) versus benevolence (preserving and enhancing the welfare of those with whom one is in frequent personal contact) and universalism (understanding, appreciation, tolerance, and protection for the welfare of all people and nature). As shown in table 2.6, priority given to universalism and benevolence values corresponded positively to priority given to mastery goals, corresponded negatively to priority given to performance approach goals, and was unrelated to priority given to performance avoidance goals. On the other hand, priority given to power corresponded positively to priority given to performance approach goals, corresponded negatively to priority given to mastery goals, and was unrelated to priority given to performance avoidance goals.

These findings fit nicely with Butler and Ruzani's (1993). They found that cultures that emphasize cooperation, social interaction, and positive attitudes toward help seeking are likely to facilitate mastery goal adoption and inhibit performance goal adoption. Both studies support Nicholls' theorization that a mastery goal adoption is connected with an individual's concern for society and the interests and welfare of others, whereas a performance approach goal adoption is associated with prioritization of one's interests relative to others' and the pursuit of one's relative success and dominance over others. The latter worldview, however, is not shared by people who adopt performance avoidance goals. They might not even think about success; their goal pursuit is determined by low perceptions of ability and fear of failure. The present findings imply that socialization influences might be entirely different for people who espouse performance avoidance and performance approach goals. Individuals who espouse performance approach goals were probably

TABLE 2.6

Associations Between Achievement Goals and Universal Values

Values	Mastery approach		Performance approach		Performance avoidance		Mastery avoidance		
	r	$r_{VG\text{-}pr}$	r	$r_{VG\text{-}pr}$	r	$r_{VG\text{-}pr}$	r	$r_{VG\text{-}pr}$	alpha
Universalism	.32***	.14**	.00	−.24***	−.03	.01	.04	.13**	.70
Benevolence	.32***	.17***	−.06	−.25***	−.09*	−.09	.07	.21***	.63
Achievement	.20***	−.08	.49***	.36***	.07	−.12*	.04	−.21***	.65
Power	−.04	−.21***	.34***	.30***	.01	−.01	−.05	−.12*	.63

r = Pearson product moment correlations of values with achievement goals;

$r_{VG\text{-}pr}$ = partial correlations between value priorities and priorities given to achievement goals (i.e., controlling for the mean rating of 10 universal values and for the mean rating of four achievement goals);

*$p < .05$, **$p < .01$, ***$p < .001$.

raised in environments that encouraged them to pursue challenges and high performance so that they could dominate others and feel pride in achieving that notion of success. On the other hand, people who adopt performance avoidance goals were most likely shaped by social settings that focused on failure and inhibitions that made them afraid of negative evaluations of their ability. The only common element in these two environments is that in both settings individuals have difficulties integrating their goals with those of others. In both settings other people are presented as opponents or enemies. This setting is in direct contrast to the cooperative atmosphere that nurtures high-mastery-oriented and low-performance-oriented individuals (Butler & Ruzani, 1993) because in that setting people learn how to integrate their goals and benefits with others.

Indeed, Papaioannou, Doxakis, Van Stam, and Bakker (2009) presented evidence that, to resolve conflict, professional athletes espousing mastery approach goals were more likely to adopt an integrating style involving high concern for self and others and less likely to adopt an aggressive or a dominating style characterized by the implementation of tactics that push for one's goal at the expense of the other person's interest. Exactly the opposite pattern emerged for athletes prioritizing performance approach goals. They were more likely to adopt the aggressive and dominating styles and less likely to adopt the integrative style. Individuals prioritizing performance avoidance goals were also less likely to adopt the integrative style, which supports the argument that both performance-approach-oriented and performance-avoidance-oriented individuals have difficulties integrating the goals and interests of others with theirs. Although the adoption of a tolerating style corresponded negatively to priority given to performance approach goals, it was positively associated with priority given to performance avoidance goals. Obviously, athletes' goals to gain positive or negative evaluation of their athletic ability are irrelevant to these diverse social behaviors. Rather, the common element between strong performance approach goal adoption and low tolerance toward others in conflict resolution is the prioritization of one's own goals at the expense of the others' goals, which is caused by the same socialization process. On the other hand, the common element between strong performance avoidance goal adoption and high tolerance toward others in conflict resolution is the hesitance and fear to face others and pursue one's own goals, which also results from a particular socialization process. To sum up, although Nicholls' theorization can depict the social dynamics that shape particular patterns of interconnected achievement and social behaviors, Elliot's model cannot.

Several researchers (e.g., Duda & Hall, 2001; Kaplan & Maehr, 2007; Roberts et al., 2007) have conceived achievement goals in particular life contexts as malleable dispositions or midlevel variables between lower-order states (such as goal involvement, e.g., Gernigon et al., 2004) and higher-order goals (such as abstract goals in life to attain the desired or undesired self; Markus & Nurius, 1986) or long-term goals in life to serve people and society or to acquire status and power (Duda, 1989; Duda & Nicholls, 1992; Nicholls et al., 1985; Nicholls, 1989). Thus, achievement goals should be associated with behaviors that are regularly adopted in particular life settings such as sport and should be shaped by those environments. Indeed, Duda and Hall (2001) have summarized findings from several studies that document the association of achievement goals and persistence in sport. For example, results from a longitudinal study revealed that task orientation is a predictor of sport and exercise involvement in adolescence but that ego orientation is the outcome of the competitive nature of sport (Papaioannou, Bebetsos, Theodorakis, Christodoulidis, & Kouli, 2006). These and other findings, however, have been based on the dichotomous model.

In a recent three-wave, 3-year longitudinal study based on the trichotomous model, mastery approach goals were a positive predictor of future participation in sport from both year 1 to year 2 and year 2 to year 3, and performance approach goals were a positive predictor only from year 1 to year 2 (Papaioannou, Ampatzoglou, Kalogiannis, & Sagovits, 2008). On the other hand, performance avoidance was a negative predictor of future participation in adolescents' sport from both year 1 to year 2 and year 2 to year 3. These findings provide further support for the notion that achievement goal measures combining aim with reason assess dispositional differences because they unveil behaviors that are consistently adopted in a particular context (Elliot & Church, 1997). The study of Papaioannou, et al. (2008) also revealed that, although for low-perceived-ability adolescents, performance approach goals had positive effects on future performance avoidance goal adoption, this finding did not emerge for high-perceived-ability youngsters. This finding is in line with suggestions that performance approach goals might turn to performance avoidance goals (Brophy, 2005) that have negative consequences for future sport involvement.

Situational Goals and Experimental Studies

To convey meaning for high effort and achievement, mastery- or task-involving experimental conditions should preferably take place in the natural environments of participants where they exercise, learn, and perform. If the setting is physical education, participants should perceive a task-involving condition as something that serves their reasons for personal improvement in physical education. Accordingly, a task-involving condition in physical education should not be a piecemeal event of a few minutes that will be probably perceived as an experiment that serves the needs of researchers. Instead, it should be part of a task-involving process that takes place over a longer time. This process should assist participants in connecting the presence of researchers and experimental processes with their learning process and their reasons for task accomplishment in physical education. A longer process provides time for students' self-reflection, which helps them realize the benefits of task involvement and its significant effects on personal improvement over a longer time. In turn, this self-monitoring process increases further their commitment to adopt mastery goals in the immediate future. Indeed, investigating the effects of a 3-week intervention on perceived mastery climate and mastery goal adoption in the daily physical education lesson, we found small effects at the end of week 1, which increased at the end of week 2 and became even larger at the end of week 3 (Papaioannou, Milosis, et al., 2007). Similar findings emerged in a more recent study comparing two mastery-involving conditions against a control group (Papaioannou & Orfanidou, 2010). In this study the nonsignificant results between mastery and control conditions in lesson 1 were because participants had insufficient levels of task involvement in mastery conditions in their first contact with the experimental process. As students became acquainted with the experimental process they started to connect their accomplishments with their performances in the previous lessons. This helped them realize that by applying consistent effort they could show lasting improvement in physical education. This encouraged them to pursue even stronger mastery approach goals in the following lessons. To sum up, participants need time to internalize the goals that researchers want to promote in task-involving conditions.

Likewise, one-shot experimental conditions can hardly unveil the cognitive processes during task involvement. This contention might explain why no experimental study has found harmful effects of performance approach goals on mastery goal adoption. Indeed, the study of Papaioannou and Orfanidou (2010), which lasted four consecutive physical education lessons revealed that in comparison to mastery-involving conditions, a social evaluative condition that activated performance approach goals had no effect on mastery goal adoption in lesson 1 but had negative effects in lessons 2, 3, and 4. Importantly, the size of negative effects increased from lesson 2 to lesson 3 and from lesson 3 to lesson 4. Notably, in the mastery groups, although levels of task involvement increased from lesson 1 to lesson 4, performance approach and avoidance goal adoption steadily decreased. As students were becoming more task involved they were also becoming less interested in comparing themselves with others. None of these results occurred in the control group in which the same level of mastery approach and performance goal adoption emerged across the four lessons. Stronger negative effects of performance approach goals on mastery approach goal adoption can emerge only in conditions where students are strongly task involved. If they are not actually task involved, it is misleading to investigate effects on mastery goal adoption.

Practical Applications

We suggest that in comparison with Nicholls' model, the trichotomous and two-by-two models in their present versions have limited application in the social context of sport because they do not capture different concepts of success. To exemplify this suggestion, suppose that you are a sport psychology consultant and are asked to provide assistance in the following scenarios. In your intervention, incorporate the various concepts of success to promote mastery approach goals. Then investigate whether you can find a solution by using different definitions of standards of competence assessment but without mentioning the different definitions of success.

1. An outstanding athlete tells you that he is extremely stressed because he must decide whether to use anabolic steroids. One of the top coaches in his sport has told the athlete that he has the potential to achieve the best performance of the year but only if he takes anabolic steroids. A doctor of medicine who is a specialist in anabolic steroids has told the athlete that the antidoping controls have no possibility of identifying him and that there is no danger to his health. The athlete does not want to reveal the names of the coach and the specialist.

2. A professional basketball athlete who has been the top performer on his team during the regular season tells you that he is angry with the team's president because he was offered a low premium for the first critical match of the playoffs. The premium is the same for all players, and the president told the athletes that the team cannot afford to provide a higher premium. Your client believes that the president could have offered him a higher premium even at the cost of reducing the premium offered to his teammates, who have substantially lower performance. At the end, the reduction for each of his teammates would be small, but the benefit for him would be important. The athlete tells you that he has already complained to the president but got nowhere. Now he is thinking about reducing his effort in the first match to make his worth more evident. That tactic might press the president to increase the premium in the following matches. He is not afraid of conflict with the president because he has already arranged to change teams in the next season. On the other hand, the athlete tells you that a loss in the first match might demoralize his team-mates and cause them to lose the remaining matches. He asks your opinion about what he should do. Can you connect the consequences of the athlete's success with others?

3. A club that has some outstanding junior athletes hires a new coach of rhythmic gymnastics. The coach immediately realizes that some of the athletes go on diets that could result in eating disorders. The previous coach, who was promoted to the top category of the club, had told the new coach that he was aware of the junior athletes' diets and advised the new coach to continue the practice to ensure the athletes' success in competition. The new coach is uncertain about what to do and asks your advice.

4. A physical education teacher organizes a basketball game for students aged 13 years old. Students from both teams do not want to accept in their team one student who is far less skilled in basketball than the others. The teacher asks you how to respond to the situation next time.

Directions for Future Research

Following the comparison of the two models we conclude that the conceptualization of the two achievement goals should be based on different definitions of success. But this might leave unanswered some important questions that have been addressed by Elliot and his colleagues. Obviously, the greatest appeal of Elliot's model is the measurement of avoidance goals, which is absent in the tradition of dichotomous models. One solution to measure both approach and avoidance goals could be a combination of Nicholls' scales with Elliot's avoidance scales. This approach might solve some practical problems, but it is theoretically weak. The approach goals would stem from different worldviews and concepts of success, but the avoidance goals would stem from different needs. An alternative approach would be to conceptualize avoidance goals based on concepts of failure. This method might look appealing, but it is certainly challenging from a theoretical point of view.

The present instruments based on Nicholls' model do not directly capture intention, which is inherent in the goals construct (Elliot & Fryer, 2008). One might argue that this is not needed because they assess concepts of success that define integrated patterns of cognitive-affective units, including intentions in achievement contexts. Alternatively, one might try to rephrase items that were developed based on Nicholls' model to assess more directly the association of intention with concepts of success.

Summary

The current main message for coaches, teachers, and parents is not much different from the implications stemming from the dichotomous models (e.g., Duda & Hall, 2001). Coaches and parents should focus primarily on the promotion of mastery approach goals because this approach benefits both the person and society (e.g., other people participating in the same sport setting). On the other hand, although several studies imply that the adoption of performance approach goals might be adaptive for the person, research suggests that it is maladaptive for society. Avoidance goals are harmful, but we still need studies to unveil the parental and teaching behaviors that shape the adoption of avoidance goals. It seems likely that a focus on failure, inhibitions, and excessive negative feedback and punishment promotes the adoption of performance avoidance goals. Moreover, some studies (e.g., Papaioannou, Milosis, et al., 2007; Milosis & Papaioannou, 2007) imply that social evaluative conditions facilitate the activation of both performance approach and performance avoidance goals while they inhibit the adoption of mastery approach goals. Although youngsters who pursue performance approach goals in sport might sustain high motivation for some time, parents, coaches, and teachers should not emphasize interindividual competition and performance approach goals because this method disrupts task involvement, increases concerns about failure and avoidance tendencies, and might have negative consequences for the group and the larger society.

CHAPTER 3

A Self-Determination Theory Perspective on Motivation in Sport and Physical Education: Current Trends and Possible Future Research Directions

Nikos Ntoumanis, PhD
University of Birmingham

The primary aim of this chapter is to provide a critical evaluation of empirical work grounded in self-determination theory (SDT) that has been conducted in sport and school PE settings since the publication of the previous edition of this book in 2001. Concurrent with the discussion of available empirical evidence and its practical implications, gaps in current knowledge will be identified and suggestions for future research will be offered. The overview of the extant literature will focus largely on the sociocontextual motivational environment in sport and PE and in particular the interpersonal style adopted by coaches and PE teachers. Employing the tenets of SDT (Deci & Ryan, 2002a; Ryan & Deci, 2000b; Standage & Ryan, this volume), this chapter will also review evidence regarding the associations between basic psychological needs and various types of motivation using a plethora of psychological well-being, behavioral, and cognitive variables. The chapter does not aim to present evidence regarding the interplay of motivation variables at different levels of generality; interested readers are directed to Vallerand (2007) for an overview of the extant literature. Besides reviewing current empirical evidence, a secondary aim of this chapter is to discuss ways in which aspects of SDT can be integrated with other theoretical frameworks of human motivation and personal strivings. This important exercise facilitates the refinement of theoretical constructs or the reconsideration of the boundaries of their operational utility by including constructs from other theories and models. An overview of the main tenets of SDT and explanations of its key constructs and subtheories can be found in the chapter in this book written by Standage and Ryan, as well as in Ryan and Deci (2007). Note as well that, although measurement issues will be identified in this chapter, the psychometric properties of specific instruments will not be discussed.

Sociocontextual Environment

Early research in the sport context has used cognitive evaluation theory, a minitheory of SDT, to study the influence of rewards (e.g., athletic scholarships), competition, and success or failure feedback on intrinsic motivation (for overviews, see Frederick & Ryan, 1995; Vallerand & Losier, 1999). Recent research along these lines has been scarce. An exception to this trend is a study by Medic, Mack, Wilson, and Starkes (2007) that extended previous work on the effect of athletic scholarships on intrinsic motivation by incorporating multiple measures of motivation that reflect the full breadth of the self-determination continuum. The authors compared U.S. intercollegiate basketball players on scholarships with similar nonscholarship players from Canada. The results provided further support for earlier research that demonstrated the undermining effects of scholarships on athletes' motivation by showing that those on scholarships were more extrinsically motivated (in terms of external and introjected regulations) than those not on scholarships. Further, when presented with a hypothetical scenario of losing a scholarship or gaining one, those with no scholarship reported an increase in external regulation and both groups reported a decrease in intrinsic motivation. A conceptually similar pattern of results was reported by Kingston, Horrocks, and Hanton (2006), who found that college athletes on scholarships had significantly higher external and introjected regulations and lower intrinsic motivation than nonscholarship athletes. Given the extensive use of athletic scholarships in the United States and elsewhere, studies in this area are needed to examine over time the influence of these scholarships on athletes' performance, quality of sport engagement, and psychological well-being.

Most recent studies examining the role of sociocontextual variables in sport and PE settings have focused on the interpersonal style of coaches and teachers. The next section presents empirical evidence for an SDT-based multidimensional conceptualization of interpersonal styles.

Interpersonal Styles

Teachers' and coaches' behaviors and motivational styles can play a major role in shaping students' and athletes' performance and the quality of their psychological experiences in education and sport settings (Reeve, 2009; Vallerand & Losier, 1999). This section reviews early and recent SDT work on interpersonal styles in PE and sport that nurture rather than thwart the three basic psychological needs advanced by SDT.

Autonomy Support Most empirical work has focused on autonomy-supportive instructional behaviors. Such behaviors encourage initiative and autonomous self-regulation, allow participation in decision making, offer choices relevant to athletes' or students' goals and values, provide rationale for task engagement, acknowledge negative feelings associated with task engagement, are nonjudgmental, and attempt to understand athletes' or students' perspective before offering suggestions (Grolnick & Ryan, 1989; Mageau & Vallerand, 2003; Reeve, 2009). Despite the label, autonomy-supportive behaviors are theorized (Ryan & Deci, 2000b) and have often been empirically shown to predict the satisfaction of all basic psychological needs, not just that of autonomy. For example, Amorose and Anderson-Butcher (2007) found that all three psychological needs were positively predicted by perceptions of autonomy-supportive coaching. Further, the three needs mediated the direct effects of autonomy support on a composite index of athlete self-determination. This pattern of relationships, which was invariant across gender and competitive level (high school versus college athletes), has also been replicated in PE contexts (e.g., Standage, Duda, & Ntoumanis, 2006).

Hollembeak and Amorose (2005) found support for a similar predictive role of specific coaching behaviors (i.e., positive feedback, democratic style) taken from the Leadership Scale for Sports (Chelladurai & Saleh, 1980). These behaviors, however, do not encompass the broad spectrum of autonomy-supportive behaviors, as have been described in the SDT literature. Future research should examine whether and how (e.g., independently or jointly) specific autonomy-supportive behaviors are related to the satisfaction of each psychological need and indirectly related to autonomous motivation. The outcomes of such a research endeavor will have direct implications in terms of coaching and teaching training. Conroy and Coatsworth's (2007a) Autonomy-Supportive Coaching Questionnaire is a step in the right direction because it identifies two independent autonomy-supportive factors (i.e., "interest in athlete's input" and "praise for autonomous behavior"). Further, given that coaches and PE teachers are not the only significant social agents, it is imperative to examine autonomy-supportive behaviors employed by peers (e.g., see Hagger, Chatzisarantis, Hein, Pihu, Soós, & Karsai, 2007), as well as partners, and how these complement congruent coach, parent, and teacher behaviors in supporting athletes' or students' psychological needs and self-determination.

Research evidence is beginning to accumulate that shows that it is possible to train PE teachers and coaches to use autonomy-supportive strategies. The intervention studies described in the literature, however, vary significantly in terms of the facets of autonomy support targeted, the nature and length of training, and the evaluation procedures used. Some studies have focused exclusively on the role of choice. For example, Prusak, Treasure, Darst, and Pangrazi (2004) used a cluster randomized design with a PE class as the unit of analysis to assign 7th- and 8th-grade females into choice ($n = 21$) and no choice ($n = 21$) groups with respect to a walking program. The study lasted for 10 days and did not involve any specific training of teacher interpersonal style. Teachers were instructed to inform students in the choice group of the intervention that they could choose their walking partners and that they would have three options of the type of walking activities that they engaged in. The no-choice group was told that the teacher predetermined all walking activities. The same three activities were covered in both groups. The comparison of situational motivation scores between groups every 3 days during the program showed a consistent pattern of results across time points (because of the high within-group stability of mean scores), and classes in the choice group reported higher intrinsic motivation and identified regulation and less external regulation and amotivation. Within-group changes in contextual motivation toward PE from pre- to postintervention showed significant decreases, but only in amotivation and in the choice group. No significant between-group differences in contextual motivation were found. The lack of extensive differences in contextual motivation might be because walking activities are not activities typically covered by PE curricula or because of the limited time span of the intervention. It would be useful for similar future studies to use multilevel modeling analysis to examine the effects of a choice intervention at both the class and the student level. In the Prusak et al. study some students' contextual motivation might have been positively affected by the program, but this could not have been detected because of the aggregation of the data at the class level. More recently, in a survey study, Dupont, Carlier, Gérald, and

Delens (2009) showed that student choice, not only in terms of type of activity but also in relation to activity engagement (e.g., class organization, criteria for success, games rule modification), predicted autonomy and relatedness need satisfaction, and indirectly through autonomy, autonomous motivation (i.e., intrinsic motivation and identified regulation).

Ward, Wilkinson, Vincent-Graser, and Prusak (2008) extended the Prusak et al. (2004) study in an interesting way by examining the consequences of providing choice after a no-choice condition and withdrawing choice after a choice condition. Much of the design was similar to that employed by Prusak et al., but Ward et al. focused on high-intensity cardiovascular fitness activities (e.g., kickboxing and aerobics) and employed one teacher for both groups. The crucial difference in the design of the two studies is that Ward et al. created a counterbalanced design that had two classes experiencing choice first (over a 7-day period) followed by no choice over the same period, and two other classes experiencing choice in the reverse order. Mean comparisons indicated higher overall situational autonomous motivation in favor of choice, but surprisingly only at the end of the second period. More interesting, autonomous motivation increased for the classes that experienced choice after no-choice and decreased for the classes that experienced no-choice after choice. This effect was particularly pronounced in the latter condition, as indicated by the 64% decline in the autonomous motivation mean. Wilson et al. (2005) also documented the beneficial effects of providing choice in a 4-week multicomponent theory intervention in a small sample of underserved adolescents. Students in the experimental group reported greater increases in motivation for physical activity; positive self-concept; and objectively assessed moderate, moderate-to-vigorous, and vigorous physical activity from baseline to the end of the intervention compared to students in the control condition. A problem with the Wilson et al. study was that it did not measure which of its various components were associated with the obtained changes. Further, the control group did not have the opportunity to participate in after-school physical activity programs, unlike the experimental group, and this circumstance casts doubt on the credibility of the observed group differences.

The effects of choice provision and withdrawal on student self-determination are in accordance with the self-determination literature, because offering choice is considered an integral aspect of an autonomy-supportive style (Mageau & Vallerand, 2003; Reeve, 2009). Choice in PE is particularly important because, unlike out-of school sport, PE in most countries is a compulsory physical activity setting up to a certain age. Choice, however, is not always motivating. Research in educational contexts suggests that choice motivates when it is relevant to the students' personal interests and goals (Katz & Assor, 2007), that is, when it is true choice. Thus, it is not the act of choosing per se that is motivating, but the opportunity to choose activities that are personally meaningful and important, thus satisfying the need for autonomy. Choice is also motivating when available options are not too complex or numerous (particularly when instructing children) and when they provide optimal challenge, thus satisfying the need for competence (Katz & Assor, 2007). Lastly, Katz and Assor suggest that choice should be offered in a way that does not undermine relatedness, as may occur when the options offered alienate individuals from their peers or are inconsistent with their cultural values. Future research should examine how choice can satisfy or undermine psychological need satisfaction in PE and sport settings and how teachers and coaches can support need-satisfying choice within the time, resource, and curricula constraints and external pressures in which they have to operate (see Standage & Ryan, this volume, for an additional discussion on the role of choice).

Choice is not the only facet of autonomy support that has been experimentally manipulated in sport and PE settings. In a two-study paper, Mouratidis, Vansteenkiste, Lens, and Sideridis (2008) examined the effects of positive feedback (a facet of autonomy support, according to Reeve & Jang, 2006) on competence need satisfaction and motivation in PE (study 1) and sport (study 2). In the first study, after participating in a shuttle run task, PE students were offered either strong positive or mild positive feedback. After controlling for pretask perceived competence and competence valuation, the contrast between the two feedback conditions positively predicted competence need satisfaction, which in turn positively predicted autonomous motivation and negatively predicted amotivation. Note that strong positive feedback was beneficial even for students who reported that they did not much value doing well on the shuttle run task. Surprisingly, controlled motivation was not assessed in this paper. A similar pattern of results emerged in the second study in the same paper using a survey design with a sample of high-level sport students. Perceptions of coach positive feedback were positive predictors of competence need satisfaction and indirect predictors of autonomous motivation and amotivation (in a positive and negative direction, respectively). Further, positive feedback was a direct predictor of coach ratings of athlete interindividual and intraindividual performance levels. Conceptually similar findings were reported by Hein and Koka (2007) in a survey study in which perceived positive informational feedback by PE teachers predicted both student perceived competence and interest in PE, the latter being a proxy measure of student self-determination.

Choice and positive feedback are just two facets of an autonomy-supportive instructional style. Chatzisarantis and Hagger (2009) manipulated more aspects of autonomy support in a 5-week intervention study that compared two teaching styles that differed in the degree to which they were autonomy supportive (the study had no true control group). Based on Deci, Eghrari, Patrick, and Leone's (1994) work on facilitating the internalization of important but uninteresting activities, Chatzisarantis and Hagger trained PE teachers (over three workshops of 3 hours each) to implement either a more autonomy-supportive condition or a somewhat less autonomy-supportive one. In the former condition, teachers were trained to provide positive feedback and rationale for task engagement, acknowledge their students' difficulties and negative emotions, and enhance student choice. In the latter condition, teachers were instructed to employ only the first two facets of autonomy support. Use of a meaningful rationale (e.g., highlighting the health benefits of physical activity) is important in terms of full internalization because it can help students understand why certain activities are personally important even when they are not enjoyable. The teacher's acknowledgment of student difficulties (e.g., in terms of correct skill execution) and negative emotions enhances perceptions of empathy among students, particularly for activities that are not inherently interesting, and offers evidence of respect for the students' inclinations. According to Deci et al., internalization of extrinsic beliefs, goals, and behaviors is more likely to be fully integrated within the self if all facilitating factors of autonomy support are in operation. In contrast, when fewer or no facilitating factors are present, internalization is expected to be incomplete (i.e., introjected).

Chatzisarantis and Hagger (2009) showed that students in the more autonomy-supportive group had stronger intentions to participate in leisure-time physical activity and self-reported more frequent physical activity behavior 5 weeks later than did those assigned to the less autonomy-supportive group. Further, the effect of a contrast term representing the two groups on increased physical activity behavior was mediated by both intentions and increases in autonomous motivation. Thus, the group comparisons seem to indicate that providing positive feedback and rationale for activity engagement might not be sufficiently motivating unless those are communicated in a style that acknowledges personal difficulties and supports choice. A limitation of this study was that the students were asked at the end of the intervention to engage in leisure-time physical activity. Therefore, it is not known the extent to which social desirability might have influenced their responses regarding their intentions and physical activity behavior. Further, it was not possible to ascertain which manipulated aspects of autonomy support had the strongest effects on intentions and autonomous motivation. Although this problem is not limited to this study, it is important to emphasize it because, in assessing how an intervention works, the question of *how* it works is important. To this end, Michie and Abraham (2004) suggested the testing of specific theory-based components separately and in combination. These authors also suggested that intervention studies should describe the techniques that they employ in enough detail so that they can be replicated, a recommendation that should be taken up in future SDT-based intervention studies.

Another intervention on increasing student autonomy support was reported by Mandigo, Holt, Anderson, and Sheppard (2008). This four-lesson intervention used Reeve's (2002) conceptual work on the dimensions of teacher autonomy support in the classroom by focusing on PE teacher support (through the use of noncontrolling praise), responsiveness to students' requests, fostering student self-determination, avoiding controlling interactions, and allowing flexibility in terms of allocated time for learning. The results showed that girls reported higher ratings of optimal challenge, enjoyment, and autonomy support than boys, whereas boys reported higher perceived competence. Unfortunately, baseline values on these variables were not measured and therefore no within-person comparisons were possible. Further, there was no control group. Unlike aforementioned studies that have trained PE teachers to carry out the intervention, in the Mandigo et al. study, trained graduates or senior undergraduate students delivered the intervention. Although these university students were probably more familiar with SDT and therefore more likely to implement the autonomy-supportive strategies in accordance with SDT principles, a serious limitation of this approach is that it does not demonstrate whether PE teachers would be able to utilize these strategies to the same extent. Further, from an ecological validity perspective, the preferred approach is to train teachers to deliver the interventions themselves because they are the ones who typically instruct students in PE lessons.

A problem with experimental studies in this area is that the long-term effect of autonomy-supportive interventions is unknown. Further, these studies represent exploratory trials, not definitive randomized trials (cf. Craig et al., 2008). In addition, intervention studies should establish treatment fidelity. This term refers to the demonstration that instruction was offered in ways in which it was designed to be delivered. Establishing the fidelity of an intervention is a key methodological requirement of any sound trial (Dumas, Lynch, Laughlin, Smith, & Prinz, 2001). Such intervention fidelity checks are lacking in the PE literature.

To this end, a step in the right direction was a teacher training study conducted by Tessier, Sarrazin, and Ntoumanis (2008) in which observers, blind to the purposes of the experiment, were asked to rate teachers' behaviors according to the extent that they were autonomy supportive, not autonomy supportive (i.e., controlling), and neutral. Although the ratings on the observation grid were used as outcome variables and not with the explicit purpose of testing intervention fidelity, such grids can be useful monitoring tools in future intervention studies. Tessier et al.'s study was the most intensive intervention study reported in the PE literature to date. Its time span covered an 8-week gymnastics cycle in French schools. Teachers in the autonomy support group of the intervention were asked to participate in a workshop that aimed to present the features and consequences of an autonomy-supportive teaching style (based on work by Reeve, 1998, and Reeve, Jang, Carrell, Jeon, & Barch, 2004) through lectures and collaborative exercises. Following the workshop and throughout the cycle, an individualized guidance program was implemented for each teacher by using videotaped evidence of each teacher's existing interpersonal style and discussing ways of enhancing support for her or his students' psychological needs. The results of the study showed that teachers in the experimental group used more autonomy-supportive and neutral behaviors than did those in the control group, but no differences emerged in relation to controlling behaviors. Such intensive one-to-one intervention studies are more likely to be successful in training teachers to use autonomy-supportive strategies effectively. The trade-off is that it is difficult to recruit a large number of volunteer teachers to undergo extensive and lengthy training. In fact, only five teachers (two in the experimental and three in the control group) took part in the Tessier et al. intervention. Besides the small sample size, another limitation of this study was that the effects of intervention in terms of fostering student psychological need satisfaction, autonomous motivation, or engagement in the lesson were not assessed.

Intervention studies aiming to enhance perceptions of autonomy support in sport settings are rare. This scarcity is perhaps because of greater difficulties (compared to PE), particularly at a high completive level, to gain access and implement coach training programs that necessitate coach education, changes in coach practices and behaviors, and athlete monitoring over repeated occasions. Coatsworth and Conroy (2009) reported a rare study in this context. The authors used Smoll, Smith, Barnett, and Everett's (1993) Coach Effectiveness Training to educate, through a 2-hour workshop, a group of coaches of low competitive-level swimmers to employ adaptive coaching behaviors that were related, but not limited, to autonomy support. Surprisingly, when compared with a control sample of swimmers whose coaches did not take part in this training, the swimmers in the intervention group did not show greater increases in self-esteem over a 7-week period. The effects of the intervention were more pronounced for younger (age 11 or younger) than older swimmers and for females who had initial lower levels of self-esteem. Further intervention studies are needed in sport settings that target specific and multiple facets of autonomy support and examine their effects on various affective, cognitive, and behavioral outcomes.

Despite the beneficial effects of autonomy support, many coaches and PE teachers more generally engage in behaviors that do not foster autonomy or need satisfaction. Such behaviors have been labeled controlling and are examined next.

Controlling Behaviors   Controlling behaviors undermine athletes' or students' psychological needs because they pressure them to think, feel, or behave in specific ways (Reeve, Deci, & Ryan, 2004). According to cognitive evaluation theory, autonomy support and control lie at the opposite ends of a bipolar continuum (Deci, Schwartz, Sheinman, Ryan, 1981; Reeve, 2009). For example, coaches can either dismiss or actively encourage their athletes' thoughts or feelings. In practice, however, initial empirical evidence and anecdotal experience indicate that coaches and teachers use a combination of different autonomy-supportive and controlling behaviors. Thus, assessing both is important. For example, a PE teacher might use pressure-inducing language but also offer explanatory rationales for task engagement. Extensive observations of PE teachers by Tessier et al. (2008) showed that during lessons they engaged in both autonomy-supportive and controlling behaviors. Similar findings have been reported in classroom-based research and in the parental literature (e.g., Assor, Kaplan, & Roth, 2002; Barber, 1996; Silk, Morris, Kanaya, & Steinberg, 2003).

Controlling coaching environments are, unfortunately, not rare in educational or sport settings (Conroy & Coatsworth, 2007a). Many teachers report that autonomy is an unfamiliar, even foreign, concept to them (e.g., Boggiano, Barrett, Weiher, McClelland, & Lusk, 1987). Most of them spontaneously use controlling strategies (Newby, 1991); the same often holds true for PE teachers (Sarrazin, Tessier, Pelletier, Trouilloud, & Chanal, 2006). In sport, controlling coaching environments are frequently in the media spotlight. For example, before the 2008 Beijing Olympic Games, reports in the press claimed that Chinese athletes were subjected to "authoritarian" training regimes. In other countries, stories about coaches abusing (verbally or physically) their athletes or interfering with their lives are not uncommon. This issue is particularly worrisome because coaching behaviors, particularly in youth sport, can have a significant influence on the psychological experiences of young athletes (Smoll & Smith, 2002). Controlling behaviors often induce a change in individuals' perceived locus of causality from internal to external (Ryan & Deci, 2002). When controlled, individuals engage in requested behaviors, not because of personal endorsement, interest, or valuing of the behavior, but because of coercive demands and reward contingencies or a sense of guilt and obligation. Thus, the ensuing behaviors have little or no self-determination, resulting, as will be explained in detail later in the chapter, in negative consequences for psychological well-being and performance.

Only a limited number of studies have examined controlling strategies of coaches. A common problem in these studies is that the assessment of controlling strategies has not been the product of a systematic scale development process, and, thus, the assessment has focused on only some aspects of coach control. Pelletier, Fortier, Vallerand, and Brière (2001) used a four-item scale to tap coach coercive behaviors and the extent to which these, alongside autonomy-supportive behaviors, could predict different forms of behavioral regulation and, prospectively, sport participation in a sample of swimmers. Mean comparisons indicated that perceptions of coach control were greater in dropouts than in persistent swimmers. Structural equation modeling analysis indicated that perceptions of coach control predicted amotivation and non-self-determined forms of extrinsic motivation (i.e., external and introjected), whereas perceptions of autonomy support were predictors of primarily autonomous motivation (i.e., intrinsic and identified) and, to a much lesser extent, introjected regulation. These findings are in line with Deci and Ryan's (1985a) theorizing. Interestingly, the two types of coach interpersonal style were only moderately intercorrelated (latent factor $r = -.36$), and this finding prompted Pelletier et al. to suggest that autonomy support and control might not be the exact opposites of each other.

Blanchard, Amiot, Perreault, Vallerand, and Provencher (2009) used three items to measure the extent to which a sample of basketball players perceived their coach as controlling. Using structural equation modeling analysis, the authors showed that perceptions of coach control negatively predicted autonomy but not relatedness or competence need satisfaction. From a conceptual viewpoint, controlling environments are more likely to thwart than to satisfy psychological needs. As will be argued later in the chapter, measures of psychological need thwarting (as opposed to need satisfaction) might be more suitable to demonstrate how coach control undermines athletes' functioning and development.

Conroy and Coatsworth (2007b) went a step further than previous research by assessing two aspects of controlling behaviors by coaches. The first was labeled *control* and referred to forceful coach actions (e.g., "The coaches forced me to act in a particular way"), and the second factor was labeled *blame* (e.g., "The coaches blamed me for what I did"). Blaming aims to induce guilt and ultimately control behavior (Soenens, Vansteenkiste, & Sierens, 2009). Conroy and Coatsworth assessed how the control and blame factors, alongside perceptions of coach affiliation, could predict changes in self-talk and fear of failure over a relatively short period (6 weeks) in a sample of young swimmers from a summer league. Latent growth modeling analysis indicated that coach control and blame were predictors of initial levels of fear of failure but that only changes in perceptions of blame behaviors were predictive of changes in fear of failure over the 6 weeks. Perceptions of coach affiliation were predictive of increases in all three psychological needs and indirectly (through autonomy only) predictive of decreases in fear of failure. Further, coach control and blame predicted increases in internally controlling self-talk and self-blame self-talk, respectively. In another study from the same data set, Conroy and Coatsworth (2007a) reported that perceptions of coach affiliation were unrelated to coach control and blame scores. Further, the two maladaptive coach behaviors were either unrelated or weakly related (in a negative fashion) with the two-factor Autonomy-Supportive Coaching Questionnaire (i.e., "interest in athlete's input" and "praise for autonomous behavior"), providing further evidence that autonomy-supportive and coach-controlling behaviors are probably independent from a measurement perspective.

A systematic attempt to identify controlling strategies that coaches might employ in sport was undertaken by Bartholomew, Ntoumanis, and Thøgersen-Ntoumani (2009). The authors reviewed the parental and educational literatures on psychological control, as well as the limited sport literature, and presented a parsimonious set of controlling strategies (and the diverse behaviors associated with each) that have direct relevance to coaching. The authors offered examples of the behaviors associated with each strategy in the context of sport coaching and argued that although these controlling strategies can sometimes evoke desired athlete behaviors in the short term, they will ultimately forestall athletes' psychological needs, capacity for self-regulation, and well-being. The identified strategies referred to the use of (*a*) tangible rewards (e.g., for task engagement and task completion), (*b*) controlling feedback (e.g., praise to reinforce expected or desired athlete behaviors), (*c*) excessive personal control (e.g., surveillance, overintrusive behaviors), (*d*) intimidation behaviors (e.g., humiliation, punishment), (*e*) ego involvement (e.g., public evaluation), and (*f*) conditional regard (e.g., positive regard following success and negative regard following failure). Bartholomew et al. stated that future research should explore the antecedents of controlling coaching strategies (e.g., situational pressures, coach personality, experience, and perceptions of athlete motivation and behavior) and their consequences in terms of athletes' motivation and psychological and physical health (e.g., feelings of overtraining and burnout, body-image concerns, and disordered eating).

Such research endeavors can be facilitated by the development of a multidimensional measure of controlling coach behaviors, presented by Bartholomew, Ntoumanis, and Thøgersen-Ntoumani (2010). Unlike previous coach control scales used in sport, this scale was the outcome of a systematic process involving, over a series of four studies, item development (based on past literature, focus group interviews with coaches and athletes, and feedback from SDT experts) and factor structure validation through a series of exploratory and confirmatory factor analyses. The scale taps four separate controlling motivational strategies salient in the context of sport: the controlling use of rewards, negative conditional regard, intimidation, and excessive personal control. This multidimensional approach to measurement of coach control can be useful both in empirical and applied work with regard to identifying specific maladaptive aspects of a coach's style.

Are controlling behaviors also maladaptive for those who use them? No empirical evidence directly addresses this question. However, research outside the sport context shows that autonomy support is beneficial for psychological need satisfaction, well-being, and quality of close relationships not only for those who receive it but also for those who offer it (Deci, La Guardia, Moller, Scheiner, & Ryan, 2006). It is possible that a controlling style might be maladaptive for coaches' and teachers' own psychological functioning. Future research should address this interesting issue. If a controlling style is maladaptive, why do many coaches and PE teachers adopt it? Reeve (2009) identified seven reasons teachers engage in controlling behaviors: (1) there is a power differential between teachers and students, (2) teachers are increasingly accountable for student behaviors and outcomes, (3) from a Western, and in particular American, perspective teachers who use controlling strategies are considered more competent than those who use autonomy-supportive ones, (4) controlling strategies are mistakenly deemed as the only means by which to create a structured learning environment, (5) teachers become more controlling when faced with students who have low motivation, (6) teachers believe (or have been educated to believe) that controlling strategies are more effective in terms of student learning than autonomy-supportive ones, and (7) some teachers have a personality disposition toward a controlling style. Virtually no research has examined antecedents of a controlling style in sport settings, which is surprising given that many of the factors identified by Reeve could explain the use of controlling coaching behaviors. Nevertheless, some of these antecedents have been investigated in PE settings, and the relevant SDT-based evidence will be reviewed later in this chapter. The PE literature has also examined additional facets of an interpersonal style, besides autonomy support and control, and these facets are reviewed next.

Beyond Autonomy Support and Control: Structure and Interpersonal Involvement Researchers in the educational psychology and parental literatures (Connell & Wellborn, 1991; Grolnick & Ryan, 1989; Skinner & Belmont, 1993) have extended the autonomy support versus control SDT-based work on interpersonal styles by suggesting that it is important to consider the degree to which people in positions of authority offer structure and interpersonal involvement. Structure (as opposed to chaos; Skinner & Edge, 2002) refers to the extent to which significant others provide clear, contingent, and consistent guidelines; optimal challenges; and timely and informative feedback that can facilitate the achievement of desirable outcomes (Connell & Wellborn, 1991; Grolnick & Ryan, 1989). An example of a structured coaching environment is one in which at the beginning of a training session the coach clearly outlines the aims of the session, sets optimal challenges for all athletes, and offers pertinent instructions that will help the athletes achieve their goals for that session.

A structured environment promotes competence need satisfaction (Connell & Wellborn, 1991; Skinner & Edge, 2002), but it does not necessarily promote autonomy. Structure and autonomy support are independent dimensions (Connell & Wellborn, 1991). A structured teaching or coaching environment can be either autonomy supportive or controlling; individuals' motivation will be optimal when they operate in a structured environment that sets expectations and guidelines but at the same time encourages personal volition and self-regulation within established boundaries (Reeve, 2002). In other words, optimal motivation necessitates a synergistic interaction between structure and autonomy support. This proposition, empirically demonstrated by Sierens, Vansteenkiste, Goossens, Soenens, and Dochy (2009) in the classroom, represents an interesting avenue for future work in sport and PE settings. When some young children lack relevant experience in certain sports or skills, some coaches or PE teachers erroneously think that these children prefer to be told what to do and do not value choice and personal volition. Although in such situations the learning environment should be highly structured to offer the appropriate guidance and support, personal autonomy and exploration should be encouraged as well.

Besides structure, Connell and Wellborn (1991), Grolnick and Ryan (1989), and Skinner and Belmont (1993) identified interpersonal involvement as another important contextual determinant of individual motivation. Interpersonal involvement or warmth (as opposed to hostility; Skinner & Edge, 2002) refers to the extent to which coaches and teachers show a genuine interest in their athletes or students, are knowledgeable about them, are emotionally available, and express affection and care (Grolnick & Ryan, 1989). Interpersonal involvement can facilitate feelings of relatedness (Connell & Wellborn, 1991) and the internalization of important behaviors and values. Cox and Williams (2008) provided support for these arguments in the context of PE by showing that perceptions of teacher interpersonal support were positive predictors of relatedness (and to a much lesser degree of the other two psychological needs) and autonomous motivation. In a subsequent study, Cox, Ducheon, and McDavid (2009) showed that, although teacher support was the strongest predictor, peer acceptance and quality of friendship also contributed to the prediction of perceived relatedness and autonomous motivation in PE classes. Taylor and Ntoumanis (2007) examined student perceptions of teacher interpersonal involvement, as well as structure and autonomy support, in PE classes. Their results showed that perceptions of all three contextual factors predicted student autonomous motivation, and this effect was mediated by competence and autonomy need satisfaction. Unfortunately, the interaction between structure and autonomy support was not tested. Future research should examine how peers can enhance feelings of need satisfaction and self-determination by also engaging in interpersonally involving behaviors. In sum, there is preliminary evidence in PE, but not yet in sport, to indicate that the provision of structure and interpersonal involvement can be motivationally beneficial to students.

In the Taylor and Ntoumanis (2007) study, teachers' own reports of their interpersonal style (i.e., provision of autonomy support, structure, and involvement) did not correlate as strongly with student self-determination and need satisfaction as student perceptions of teacher interpersonal style did. In fact, teacher perceptions of autonomy support and structure were not significantly related to student perceptions of the corresponding variables, whereas reports of teacher involvement were only weakly correlated. This lack of congruence between teacher and student perceptions is problematic. Intervention programs are often aimed at teachers, but the outcomes of interest are student focused (e.g., student motivation and achievement). However, students may not always recognize an increase in teachers' use of adaptive motivational strategies. Consequently, such interventions should also focus on how students code and interpret teacher motivational strategies. The low congruence between teacher and student reports might also result from the possibility that teachers are unaware or excessively positive about the degree to which they use adaptive motivational strategies. Thus, objective measures (e.g., use of independent observers, such as those employed by Tessier et al., 2008) of the different facets of a teacher's interpersonal style might be useful when evaluating teacher reports. In conclusion, the research evidence to date indicates that promoting an adaptive interpersonal teaching or coaching style requires the provision of autonomy support in a structured environment, interpersonal involvement, and minimization of controlling behaviors and vocalizations. Comprehensive intervention studies describing in detail how each of the aforementioned facets has been operationalized and monitored are needed in the literature.

What factors determine the extent to which PE teachers or coaches use motivationally adaptive or maladaptive behaviors in their interactions with students or athletes? This important question has received some, albeit rather limited, research attention in the PE literature.

Antecedents of PE Teachers' Interpersonal Style

Extending previous work in classroom settings (Pelletier, Séguin-Lévesque, & Legault, 2002; Skinner & Belmont, 1993), Taylor and Ntoumanis (2007) showed that the extent to which PE teachers used autonomy support, structure, and interpersonal involvement was positively predicted by their perceptions of their classes' autonomous motivation (the latter represented aggregated teacher ratings of each student's motivation within a class). This finding is consonant with the behavioral confirmation hypothesis (Snyder, 1984) and suggests that classes perceived by their teacher as low in self-determination may receive less adaptive motivational strategies. Further, teachers' perception of class self-determination positively predicted their own self-determination to teach that class. In turn, the more self-determined the teachers were, the higher the level of autonomy support and involvement they provided. Teachers' autonomous motivation mediated the effects of teachers' perceptions of class motivation to the degree to which they used autonomy support and involvement. As discussed earlier, in the same study Taylor and Ntoumanis showed that student perceptions of teacher use of autonomy support, structure, and involvement were positive predictors of student autonomous motivation. Thus, although the study was not longitudinal, the findings from it suggest that when teachers perceive their classes to be low in self-determination, they are less likely to employ adaptive motivational strategies, which might further reduce student self-determination.

Similar results were reported by Sarrazin et al. (2006), who videotaped interactions during lessons between students and PE teachers. Their analysis showed that teachers interacted less frequently with students whom they expected to be more motivated (a composite measure of effort and autonomy) and were more controlling toward students whom they believed to be less motivated. Ironically, as discussed in the previous paragraph, controlling interactions make students less, and not more, self-determined (see also Reeve, 2009), and over time such interactions can reinforce initial teacher expectations (see Trouilloud, Sarrazin, Bressoux, & Bois, 2006). A recent study by Radel, Sarrazin, Legrain, and Wild (in press) replicated and extended the links between teacher and student motivation by adding a second teaching and learning situation. Based on the social contagion of the motivational orientations model (Wild & Enzle, 2002), Radel et al. showed that motivation cues can be implicitly spread from instructors to students and then to fellow students in consecutive learning sessions. Specifically, PE students who were taught a novel sport activity by an allegedly paid invited instructor reported lower interest in learning and showed less free-choice persistence than did students taught by a supposedly volunteer instructor, despite the fact that students in both conditions received the same standardized lesson. Subsequently, the students were asked to teach the same activity to peers who were not present in the first lesson. Interestingly, the students in the second lesson reported lower interest and persistence when they were instructed by students who were in the "paid" condition in the first lesson.

Structural equation modeling analysis showed that the intrinsic motivation of the students in the second lesson was influenced by their perceptions of the intrinsic motivation of their peer tutors. Such perceptions were shaped by the degree to which peer tutors were autonomy supportive (as rated by independent observations) and the degree to which they experienced positive affect while teaching (as self-reported by the peer tutors). These results are interesting and important from an applied perspective because they demonstrate that students can make inferences about their instructors' motivation based on implicit motivational cues and that such inferences can affect subsequent student motivation, both directly and indirectly.

If teachers' perceptions or expectations of student self-determination partly determine the motivational strategies that the former use, then an important issue is how compatible teachers' perceptions of student motivation are with student reports of their own motivation. Taylor and Ntoumanis (2007) addressed this question with multilevel modeling and showed that, with the exception of external regulation, teacher and student perceptions of student individual motivational regulations and overall self-determination were somewhat congruent with each other. The beta coefficients, however, were small to moderate. Although a variety of methodological and conceptual factors can account for the small overlap in teachers' and students' perceptions, Skinner and Belmont (1993) have reported similar findings in the classroom. Taken together, the results of the two studies indicate the need for teachers to be trained so that they can more accurately identify behavioral and affective indices of the different types of student motivation.

Taylor, Ntoumanis, and Standage (2008) extended Taylor and Ntoumanis' (2007) findings by examining a variety of antecedents of teacher use of three specific adaptive motivational behaviors: gaining understanding of students (reflecting interpersonal involvement), providing instrumental help and support (a component of structure), and offering meaningful rationale (a facet of autonomy support). Structural equation modeling analysis supported a model in which perceived job pressures (negatively) and perceptions of student self-determination and teacher autonomous orientation (positively) predicted teacher psychological need satisfaction, which, in turn positively related to teacher self-determination. The latter positively predicted the use of all three aforementioned teacher strategies. Direct positive effects of teachers' psychological need satisfaction on the strategies of gaining an understanding of students and instrumental help and support were also found. Significant indirect effects on the three strategies through perceived job pressure, autonomous orientation, and perceptions of student autonomous motivation were reported. Taken together, the results emphasize the importance of understanding the diversity of factors (i.e., school system, teacher personality, student motivation) that could affect teacher autonomous motivation. These factors will have important consequences not only for the teacher but also, as demonstrated on previous pages, for students through the teachers' degree of use of motivationally adaptive strategies.

A limitation of Taylor, Ntoumanis, and Standage's (2008) study was that it did not investigate antecedents of maladaptive motivational strategies. This issue was addressed in a subsequent study in which Taylor, Ntoumanis, & Smith (2009) carried out in-depth interviews of 22 PE teachers. The teachers reported that overemphasis on student assessment by the school culture, their own performance evaluations by school authorities, cultural norms regarding the teacher–student relationship, and time constraints during lessons contributed to their engaging in more controlling interactions with their students. Some teachers reported an inner conflict between their own beliefs about effective teaching and the behaviors that they felt compelled to adopt. Their perceptions of their students' motivation, ability, and discipline; perceived pressure to conform to their colleagues' teaching methods; and various student characteristics (e.g., body size, age, and gender) also affected, in multiple ways, the teachers' chosen motivational strategies.

Surprisingly, antecedents of coaches' use of adaptive and maladaptive motivational strategies have not been researched in the literature. Many antecedents in the educational domain might be pertinent to the coaching context, although unique predictors might be present (e.g., short-term renewable coaching contracts). Developing validated measures of psychological need satisfaction and multidimensional motivation specific to coaching is a first step in addressing this significant gap in the literature.

Satisfaction and Thwarting of Psychological Needs

One of the minitheories of SDT is basic needs theory, which outlines the relationship between the degree of satisfaction of the basic psychological needs for autonomy, competence, and relatedness with psychological health and well-being (see Standage & Ryan, this volume, and Deci & Ryan, 2000, for a more detailed description of these needs and the way in which the concept of needs as advanced by SDT differs from that of other need theories). Research in sport and PE settings has examined how the three needs are related to different types of motivation and various indices of well-being or ill-being, behavior, and cognition. This evidence is reviewed in this section. Studies looking at the mediatory role or indirect effects of motivation on the relationship between psychological needs and motivation-related outcomes will be presented later in the chapter when we review the empirical evidence on the various types of behavioral regulations.

Psychological Needs as Predictors of Motivational Regulations

Deci and Ryan (2000) discussed the relationship of the satisfaction of each psychological need with intrinsic motivation and internalized extrinsic motivation. They proposed that intrinsically motivated behavior requires the satisfaction of both autonomy and competence; relatedness satisfaction is not always important in this relationship because some activities can be carried out in isolation. In the context of sport or PE, however, few activities are carried out in isolation. Deci and Ryan also argued that relatedness and competence satisfaction without autonomy need satisfaction can result in introjected or identified regulations. Full internalization (i.e., integrated regulation of behavior) requires satisfaction of the need for autonomy as well. Koestner and Losier (2002) have put forth somewhat similar propositions regarding the relationships between psychological needs and motivation.

In the context of sport and PE, researchers have examined how the three psychological needs, individually or in combination, predict intrinsic motivation, multiple motivational regulations reflecting the self-determination continuum, or a composite self-determination index that signifies the presence or absence of self-determination in one's behavioral engagement. Unfortunately, no experimental studies have been carried out in which individual needs are satisfied or thwarted, thus directly testing Deci and Ryan's (2000) propositions. Such studies could make an important contribution to current knowledge because in survey-based studies (which predominate in the literature) the three psychological needs are often moderately to highly correlated. Occasionally, such correlations result in some needs not having a unique predictive role when pitted against other needs (such as in regression analysis or structural equation modeling). But a common pattern of results across studies in PE settings is that competence need satisfaction makes a stronger contribution to the prediction of autonomous motivation compared to the other two psychological needs (e.g., Dupont et al., 2009; Ntoumanis, 2001a; Standage, Duda, & Ntoumanis, 2006), occasionally alongside relatedness (Cox & Williams, 2008). In contrast, in sport the need for autonomy has been demonstrated to have the strongest predictive effects (Amorose & Anderson-Butcher, 2007; Blanchard et al., 2009; Hollembeak & Amorose, 2005; Ntoumanis & Standage, 2009; Sarrazin, Vallerand, Guillet, Pelletier, & Cury, 2002), although the odd exception exists (Kowal & Fortier, 2000, found stronger effects for the other two needs).

Deci and Ryan (1985a) argued that the relative influence of each psychological need varies depending on the functional significance of the situation. In PE the role of perceived competence is crucial because some students do not have experience with some of the sport or motor activities undertaken (Papaioannou, 1994); thus, interindividual variations in competence are probably wider in PE than in sport. Consequently, those who feel and are physically competent are more likely to find PE interesting and fun, and they will want to participate in it to develop their sport skills further (i.e., they have high autonomous motivation). In sport, perceptions of autonomy are more important, perhaps because participation is optional (unlike in school PE), and thus athletes need to feel volitional in the various aspects of their sport engagement.

A limitation of the studies that examine the relationship between psychological needs and motivational regulations is that they have employed cross-sectional designs that fail to capture the dynamic interplay between the constructs under investigation. A rare exception is a study by Ntoumanis, Barkoukis, and Thøgersen-Ntoumani (2009) that examined changes in motivation-related variables in Greek secondary school PE at the beginning and end of the school year over a period of 3 years. Multilevel analysis showed significant decreases in relatedness need satisfaction, identified regulation, and intrinsic motivation over the 3 years. In contrast, significant increases in amotivation occurred. No significant changes were observed in competence need satisfaction and extrinsic and introjected regulations. The authors found substantial between-student variability in the intercepts and growth trajectories of most variables and therefore tested a number of predictors to account for such variations. The results indicated that decrements in adaptive motivation in PE over time were not uniform across all students and could be partly tackled by facilitating competence need satisfaction.

Psychological Needs as Predictors of Psychological Health and Physical Functioning

Autonomy, competences, and relatedness need satisfaction have been examined as antecedents of a variety of indices of optimal (versus problematic) functioning, primarily in sport. A number of studies have investigated burnout as an outcome, predominantly using the Athlete Burnout Questionnaire (ABQ; Raedeke & Smith, 2001), which includes three subscales: Emotional or Physical Exhaustion, Devaluation, and Reduced Sense of Accomplishment. In a cross-sectional study of elite rugby players, Hodge, Lonsdale, and Ng (2008) reported that competence and autonomy, and to a lesser extent relatedness, were negative predictors of burnout, primarily of sport devaluation and reduced sense of accomplishment. Similar results were reported by Lonsdale, Hodge, and Rose (2009), who examined the effects of need satisfaction on burnout in a sample of elite Canadian athletes. These findings provide indirect support for Deci and Ryan's (2000) argument that psychological need satisfaction is essential for psychological and physical health.

Perreault, Gaudreau, Lapointe, and Lacroix (2007) explored the relationship between psychological need satisfaction and burnout in a sample of student–athletes who attended a sports high school. The authors offered the first test in a sport context of Sheldon and Niemiec's (2006) proposition that the degree to which the three needs are balanced can predict psychological well-being over and above the individual effects of the three needs. Perreault et al. found some, albeit weak, support for this argument. Although incremental contributions of a balanced need satisfaction score were significant when predicting some ABQ subscales, the amount of additional variance explained by this score ranged from 0% to 2%; similar low percentages were also reported by Sheldon and Niemiec. Although the evidence is still preliminary, findings so far are not promising regarding the unique predictive ability of balanced need satisfaction. From a conceptual viewpoint, such balanced scores might be of some importance when satisfaction of all needs is moderate or high; it is difficult to imagine how low satisfaction scores across all needs would be beneficial. Perreault et al. recommended that future research examine the differential degree to which needs are satisfied in sport and other life contexts (e.g., school) when investigating burnout in sport. This extension of the need balance idea is interesting because potential buffering and synergistic effects of need satisfaction across domains on sport burnout could be tested. No research has examined this issue in sport. Milyavskaya, Gingras, Mageau, Koestner, and Gagnon (2009) found that balanced need satisfaction across three life domains (i.e., home, friendships, and part-time jobs) predicted well-being and school adjustment over and above individual balanced satisfaction scores within domains. The amount of incremental variance predicted, however, was again minimal.

Amorose, Anderson-Butcher, and Cooper (2009) expanded on previous studies by adopting a longitudinal approach and hypothesizing that changes in psychological need satisfaction would predict changes in burnout symptoms in a sample of adolescent female players. The results supported their hypothesis by showing significant predictions made by changes in all three psychological needs. Whether the differential predictive effect of relatedness in the Amorose et al. study compared with those reported by Hodge et al. (2008) and Lonsdale et al. (2009) is because of the different scales employed to measure this psychological need is unknown. From a conceptual and applied perspective, it would be interesting for future research to ascertain whether feelings of relatedness need satisfaction emerging from interactions with teammates compared with interactions with the coach have equal predictive effects. Research on relationship functioning outside sport (e.g. Patrick, Knee, Canavello, & Lonsbary, 2007) has shown that satisfaction of relatedness, and to a lesser extent autonomy and competence, is an important determinant of relationship quality and well-being. Similar research in sport is required to examine how the quality of athletes' relationships with their coaches, teammates, parents, or other important individuals predicts and is predicted by psychological need satisfaction. This question should be explored from the perspective of both parties in a relationship, ideally using longitudinal (e.g., diary) approaches.

Schaufeli and Salanova (2007) proposed the concept of engagement as the opposite of burnout. Based on this premise, Hodge, Lonsdale, and Jackson (2009) used a cross-sectional design to test the effects of psychological need satisfaction on a composite athlete engagement score in the same sample of elite athletes reported by Lonsdale, Hodge, et al. (2009). Structural equation modeling analysis showed significant direct effects on athlete engagement and flow from competence and autonomy. The effects of relatedness were not significant, as in Lonsdale, Hodge, et al. (2009). Further, indirect effects from competence and autonomy on flow through engagement were also found. These findings provide direct support to Deci and Ryan's (2000) proposition that psychological need satisfaction can predict behavioral investment and quality of experience in various life domains.

Reinboth, Duda, and Ntoumanis (2004) adopted a broader perspective regarding athletes' welfare by examining whether the three psychological needs can predict athletes' physical symptoms (e.g., runny nose, headaches, and stomachache in the past two weeks), subjective vitality, and intrinsic satisfaction or interest with their sport. Structural equation modeling analysis showed that competence was the strongest predictor of all indices of psychological and physical well-being. Autonomy predicted only subjective vitality and intrinsic satisfaction or interest, whereas, surprisingly, relatedness did not have any unique predictive effects, although correlation analysis showed significant positive relationships between this need and both indices of psychological well-being. In a related study, Adie, Duda, and Ntoumanis (2008) found that all three needs had unique predictive effects with respect to subjective vitality, although the effect of relatedness was smaller than the effects of the other two psychological needs. Further, perception of emotional and physical exhaustion (an indicator of burnout) was predicted in a negative direction by autonomy only. Podlog, Lochbaum, and Stevens (2010) also examined the relationship between need satisfaction and psychological well-being in a sample of high-level athletes who had experienced an injury that required prolonged sport absence and, for half of them, surgical intervention. Psychological need satisfaction was measured in relation to athletes' perceptions of need satisfaction over the course of their injury rehabilitation using a retrospective recall design. Results showed that each need variable predicted most or all assessed indices of well-being or ill-being (positive affect, negative affect, self-esteem, and vitality) in the expected direction. Mediation analyses also showed that competence and autonomy need satisfaction positively predicted a renewed perspective on sport after returning to action (e.g., "My appreciation of sport has been greater") through positive affect, whereas relatedness need satisfaction negatively predicted concerns (e.g., "My fear of reinjury has interfered with performances") through negative affect, self-esteem, and vitality. The mediation results indicate that the satisfaction of different psychological needs during injury is associated with distinct postinjury outcomes by facilitating psychological well-being.

Future research examining the relationship between psychological need satisfaction and athletes' welfare might benefit from including biological markers of well-being (e.g., cortisol responses or other indicators of immune functioning). Further, longitudinal research is needed to examine how need satisfaction is related to changes in affect and well-being over time. In a rare study on this issue, Gaudreau, Amiot, and Vallerand (2009) followed a sample of elite hockey players over a period of 11 weeks and identified three distinct trajectories of positive affect and three trajectories of negative affect, using latent class growth modeling. Their analysis indicated that a composite psychological need satisfaction score was a positive predictor of the most adaptive trajectory of change for each type of affect.

Two longitudinal studies have examined the role of psychological needs in predicting self-esteem in young athletes. Coatsworth and Conroy (2009), using a sample of swimmers in a 7-week summer league, showed that initial levels of competence need satisfaction in the swimmers' relationships with their coaches predicted changes in self-esteem over the summer league through increases in swimmers' perceived swimming competence. Amorose et al. (2009), using a longer time frame (competitive volleyball season), showed that increases in competence and autonomy, but not relatedness, predicted increases in self-esteem. Another longitudinal study on the role of need satisfaction in sport was a qualitative investigation by Podlog and Eklund (2009) of high-level athletes' perceptions of success in returning to sport following injury, which required, on average, a 7-month absence. A strength of this study was that the athletes were interviewed over a period of 6 to 8 months, once before their return to competition and two or three times following their comeback. Several key aspects of a successful return from injury were identified in the interviews, most of which involved issues of competence (e.g., achieving a variety of goals), relatedness (e.g., feelings that they are contributing to and are accepted as members of their team), and autonomy (e.g., negotiating internal and external pressures and expectations). It would have been interesting in this study if stress appraisals, coping resources, and coping responses had been measured to offer an integrative analysis of stress, coping, and motivational issues associated with returning from injury. As will be suggested later in this chapter, an important future direction for motivation researchers is to attempt to combine motivational constructs from theories, such as SDT, with other important psychological constructs related to human strivings and adaptations.

Psychological Need Thwarting

The empirical research conducted to date (e.g., Adie et al., 2008; Hodge et al., 2008; Reinboth et al., 2004) that has looked at the relationship between psychological need satisfaction and ill-being (primarily in terms of indices of burnout and physical symptoms) has not provided a direct test for Deci and Ryan's (2000) argument that psychological need thwarting will lead to psychological accommodations that can undermine health and well-being. According to Bartholomew, Ntoumanis, Ryan, and Thøgersen-Ntoumani (2011), low scores on a need satisfaction scale may not necessarily indicate that an athlete's needs are being thwarted; such scores may merely suggest that an athlete feels unsatisfied with the degree to which his or her needs are currently being met. For example, if a coach is indifferent toward an athlete, the athlete's psychological needs are likely to be unsatisfied. But if a coach engages in behaviors that pressure the athlete into changing her or his own thoughts, feelings, and behaviors to make them more concordant with the coach's expectations, the athlete's psychological needs are likely to be thwarted.

According to Ryan and Deci (2000c), "SDT has historically dealt not only with growth and well-being, but equally with the undermining, alienating, and pathogenic effects of need thwarting social environments" (p. 319). Ryan and Deci argued that the thwarting of psychological needs can promote the development of controlling regulatory styles, compensatory motives or need substitutes, and rigid behavior patterns that may over time lead to further need thwarting. Aligned with Vallerand, Pelletier, and Koestner's (2008) call for empirical work on need thwarting in the SDT literature, Bartholomew et al. (2011) presented a systematic attempt to develop and validate a measure of psychological need thwarting in the sport context. Surprisingly, there is no such measure in any life domain. In a series of three studies that involved coaches, athletes, and SDT experts, Bartholomew et al. developed and validated a three-factor model with good content, factorial, and predictive validity, as well as internal consistency and invariance across gender and type of sport (individual versus team). The authors claimed that, although athletes' perceptions of both need satisfaction and need thwarting can be helpful in understanding their psychological experiences in sport, when ill-being and other maladaptive outcomes are the focus of investigation, psychological need thwarting should predict a larger amount of variance when compared to measures of psychological need satisfaction. Indeed, the authors showed that psychological need thwarting scores were more strongly predictive of emotional and physical exhaustion when compared to need satisfaction scores.

Future research should investigate the role that the thwarting of one or more psychological needs plays in predicting various maladaptive outcomes such as body-image concerns and disordered eating in competitive sport. Further, longitudinal research could examine whether need thwarting increases the motivation for identifying need-satisfying experiences within the same context or in other contexts (cf. Sheldon & Gunz, 2009). The concept of need thwarting is also relevant to the context of PE. For example, it would be interesting to identify the extent to which need thwarting predicts the use of self-worth protection strategies, such as self-handicapping.

Motivational Regulations and the Self-Determination Continuum

The theoretical foundation for the empirical work on motivational regulations is provided by the organismic integration theory, another subtheory of SDT. Organismic integration theory provides the basis for understanding the processes of internalization and integration, which are reflected in the multidimensional conceptualization of extrinsic motivation. According to Ryan and Deci (2007), organismic integration theory classifies the quality of motivation along a perceived locus of causality continuum ranging from highly autonomous to highly controlling (see Standage and Ryan, this volume, for more information and definitions of each type of motivation). Extensive research evidence has provided support for the theoretical proposition (e.g., Deci & Ryan, 2000) that the different types of motivation form a somewhat simple model according to which each regulation correlates stronger with regulations closer to it on the continuum than with regulations farther apart (e.g., see the meta-analysis by Chatzisarantis, Hagger, Biddle, Smith, & Wang, 2003).

A large volume of empirical evidence has documented the interrelationships between the various types of motivation and the manner in which these types are linked to a wide variety of well-being, cognition, and behavior-related indices in sport and PE. This body of evidence will be reviewed in this section.

Relationships Between Motivation Regulations, Psychological Well-Being, Cognition, and Behavior

Studies in this area have modeled motivation in various ways. Some have tested the unique predictive utility of each type of motivation, providing a strong test of SDT. However, because occasionally some motivational regulations are highly correlated or because researchers have tested complex models with structural equation modeling, the various types of motivation have at times been reduced into autonomous (intrinsic and identified) and controlled (introjected and external) motivation composite scores or have been combined into a self-determination index (SDI), in which higher scores reflect higher self-determination (see Vallerand, 2007). Further, based on Vallerand's hierarchical model of intrinsic and extrinsic motivation, some studies have examined whether motivation mediates the effects of psychological needs on cognition, behavior, and affect.

One topic of empirical investigation has been the relationship between athletes' motivation and symptoms of burnout, as assessed by the ABQ. Lonsdale, Hodge, and Rose (2008) explored the cross-sectional relationships between individual motivational regulations (measured with three questionnaires) and the three subscales of the ABQ. As theoretically expected, amotivation and external and introjected regulations were negatively related to an overall burnout score. Further, intrinsic motivation and identified and integrated regulations were negatively related or unrelated to indices of burnout. The relationship between athletes' motivation and burnout has also been examined longitudinally. Lemyre et al. (2007) showed in a sample of elite winter athletes that SDI at the beginning of the season could prospectively predict symptoms of burnout at the end of the season (six months later), over and above the effects of overtraining (measured at the end of season). A limitation of this study was that it did not examine how changes in motivation were related to changes in burnout symptoms and whether such a relationship was reciprocal. This limitation was partly addressed by Lemyre et al. (2006) in a season-long investigation, over a period of 5 to 7 months, of situational motivation, affect, and burnout in elite swimmers. The authors showed that athletes who experienced shifts in the quality of their situational motivation (measured every 3 weeks) from more to less self-determined reported stronger symptoms of burnout (measured with the ABQ at the end of the season only) than those who reported opposite trends in their situational motivation.

In a related study, Cresswell and Eklund (2005b) examined cross-sectionally three competing models that offered different explanations for the relationship between motivation and burnout. Specifically, the models tested whether the relationship between burnout symptoms and three types of motivation (intrinsic motivation, external regulation, and amotivation) is bidirectional, whether burnout predicts motivation, or whether motivation predicts burnout. The authors found support for all three possible associations between motivation and burnout. Within each tested model, amotivation had large positive associations with burnout, external regulation had nonsignificant relationships, and intrinsic motivation exhibited significant negative associations. A better discrimination among the competing models could have possibly been achieved if the authors had examined the relationship between burnout and motivation over time. Such a study is currently missing from the literature.

Motivation has also been examined as a predictor of other affective and cognitive variables. In brief, autonomous motivation (as an SDI, autonomous composite score, or separate intrinsic motivation and identified regulation scores) has been found to be a positive predictor of positive emotions experienced and satisfaction with sport, as well as dispositional flow (Blanchard et al., 2009; Lonsdale et al., 2008; Mouratidis et al., 2008). Autonomous motivation has also been reported as a positive predictor of general self-esteem (Hein & Hagger, 2007; Standage & Gillison, 2007), a positive predictor of vitality and positive affect (Dupont et al., 2009; Standage, Duda, & Ntoumanis, 2005; Zhang, 2009), and a negative predictor of negative affect in PE (Ntoumanis, 2005; Standage et al., 2005). Amiot, Gaudreau, and Blanchard (2004) and Gaudreau and Antl (2008) reported that autonomous motivation predicted coping efforts that are usually adaptive (i.e., task oriented). Perceptions of learning (Dupont et al., 2009) and self-reported levels of concentration and task challenge (Ntoumanis, 2005; Standage et al., 2005) have also been positively associated with autonomous motivation in PE. In contrast, amotivation, composite controlling motivation scores, or corresponding regulations (i.e., external and introjected) have been associated with negative affect in PE and sport (Ntoumanis, 2001a; Mouratidis et al., 2008), coping responses that are often nonoptimal (i.e., disengagement and distraction-oriented coping; Amiot et al., 2004; Gaudreau & Antl, 2008), and low levels of dispositional flow in sport (Lonsdale et al., 2008). Note that when studies examined the predictive ability of individual motivational regulations, although many findings consistent with SDT emerged, null findings also appeared partly because of high intercorrelations among the regulations.

Longitudinal studies investigating the association between motivational regulations and affect or well-being indices are sparse. Gaudreau et al. (2009), in an 11-week investigation of affect trajectories in adolescent elite hockey players, reported that low SDI was a significant predictor of undesirable trajectories of positive affect, but it did not discriminate among different trajectories of negative affect. Gagné, Ryan, and Bargmann (2003) demonstrated the usefulness of a diary-based approach in examining within-person associations between motivation, psychological need satisfaction, and well-being. In that study female gymnasts were asked to complete diaries before and after practice sessions over a period of four weeks. Using multilevel modeling analysis, Gagné et al. showed that prepractice well-being (positive and negative affect, vitality, and self-esteem) was predicted by the gymnasts' situational intrinsic and identified motivation. Changes in well-being from before to after practice, however, were not predicted by any of the motivational regulations; instead, such changes were accounted for by the degree of satisfaction of the three psychological needs during practice. This study exemplifies particularly well the useful contribution that longitudinal designs can make in advancing our understanding of psychological well-being in sport. As Gagné et al. concluded, it was what happened during practice (in terms of need-satisfying interactions with the coach and teammates) that predicted gymnasts' changes in well-being, not their incoming situational motivation.

Some studies have examined the relationship between motivation and indices of morality. Donahue et al. (2006) and Ntoumanis and Standage (2009) found positive associations between autonomous motivation and sportspersonship, and negative associations between controlling motivation and sportspersonship. Donahue et al. also showed that sportspersonship mediated the effects of both autonomous and controlling motivation composite scores on self-reported performance-enhancing substance use. Lastly, self-reported aggression and cheating have been positively related to controlling motivation (Chantal, Robin, Vernat, & Bernache-Assollant, 2005; Ntoumanis & Standage, 2009).

Relatively few studies have examined the prediction of indices of behavior by motivation. Gillet, Berjot, and Gobancé (2010) showed in a sample of young tennis players that the self-determination index was positively, albeit weakly, related to objective performance scores (as obtained by the French Tennis Federation) at the beginning of a season, as well as 2 years later. Changes in self-determination, however, did not significantly predict changes in performance scores. Sarrazin et al. (2002) investigated dropout decisions in female athletes over a 21-month period. Their analysis indicated that SDI was a negative predictor of intentions to drop out, which in turn prospectively predicted actual dropout behavior. Pelletier et al. (2001) sampled competitive swimmers and measured persistence (operationalized as the opposite of dropout) 10 and 22 months later. Structural equation modeling analysis indicated that intrinsic motivation and identified regulation were positive predictors of persistence at both time points. Amotivation was a negative predictor at both time points, whereas external regulation was a nonsignificant predictor at 10 months and a negative predictor at 22 months. Interestingly, whereas at 10 months introjected regulation was a positive predictor of persistence, subsequently it became unrelated. The pattern of results pertaining to introjected regulation could be explained by Ryan, Koestner, and Deci's (1991) work on ego-involved persistence. Ryan et al. showed that introjected regulation could activate behavioral persistence under conditions of nonpositive feedback. However, persistence based on introjection is qualitatively inferior in terms of affect experienced and less likely to remain strong in the long term compared to persistence-based or self-determined reasons. The findings of Pelletier et al. point to the same conclusion. A limitation of both the Pelletier et al. study and the Sarrazin et al. study is that the reasons the athletes dropped out from the registered sports club were not established. This information would have been useful in terms of excluding cases in which athletes dropped out because of factors irrelevant to motivation (e.g., serious injuries, home relocation). Nevertheless, consistent findings emerged across both studies in support of SDT.

Studies that examine behavioral persistence in PE are limited, probably because PE is a compulsory context. Ntoumanis (2005) examined the transition from compulsory to optional PE at the age of 16 years in a sample of British students. Consonant with aforementioned related findings in sport, Ntoumanis reported that SDI was a positive predictor of intentions to participate in optional PE classes, which in turn predicted actual participation status in the following school year. Further, SDI was positively associated with teacher ratings of individual student effort. Those who participated in the optional programs were rated higher by their teachers in terms of their effort, and they reported higher intrinsic motivation and identified regulation, and lower amotivation a year earlier. No differences were found in terms of external and introjected regulations. A limitation of this study was that it did not establish whether the children who did not participate in optional PE programs remained physically active. However, students who report high levels of amotivation in PE are not likely to be physically active out of school (Ntoumanis, Pensgaard, Martin, & Pipe, 2004).

Some SDT-based studies have examined the role of motivation in PE as a vehicle for exercise or leisure-time physical activity participation. The transcontextual model proposes and has offered empirical support (e.g., Hagger et al., 2009) for a motivational sequence according to which autonomous motivation in PE predicts autonomous motivation in a leisure-time context, which in turn indirectly predicts leisure-time physical activity behavior through the theory of planned behavior variables (Ajzen, 1985; attitudes, subjective norms, and perceived behavioral control). Other studies have explored and found direct links between autonomous motivation in PE and self-reported leisure-time physical activity using cross-sectional (e.g., Zhang, 2009) and longitudinal designs (e.g., Taylor, Ntoumanis, Standage, & Spray, 2010). Autonomous motivation has also been linked with objectively assessed physical activity behavior and fitness. For example, Shen, McCaughtry, Martin, and Fahlman (2009) have reported that changes in autonomous motivation across a school semester (i.e., 4-month period) were positively associated with changes in cardiorespiratory fitness. Vierling, Standage, and Treasure (2007) have found a significant, albeit weak, relationship between autonomous motivation in PE and 4-day physical activity (during school days) assessed by pedometers.

Alternative and Unexplored Approaches to Researching the Role of Personal Motivation

Following Vallerand's (1997) suggestion that researchers should examine how different types of motivation combine into diverse motivational profiles, a number of studies in sport and PE have used cluster analysis to identify distinct profiles of motivational regulations and subsequently investigate which of these profiles relate to adaptive and maladaptive variables. This person-based approach explores how different motivational regulations are combined within individuals. In contrast, the variable-based approach used by most statistical tests (e.g., SEM, regression analysis) investigates each regulation independently from the others. The person-based approach has a lot of intuitive appeal because, within a particular context, individuals are usually motivated by a variety of reasons, although the relative salience of each will vary from person to person. For example, a female student might engage in PE activities not only because they are interesting and personally useful but also because she wants to please her teachers and parents and attain a good grade. Such within-person diversity in the reasons for motivational engagement cannot be captured by the variable-based approach.

Some of the authors who have employed the cluster analytic approach were interested in examining whether there is an additive effect between self-determined and controlling regulations, or whether it is the combination of high self-determined motivation with low controlling motivation that is associated with the most adaptive outcomes (cf. Vallerand & Fortier, 1998). No consistent answer to this question has been found, possibly because of methodological reasons. Despite available guidelines, cluster analysis involves a certain degree of subjectivity in terms of determining the number of clusters in a data set and defining what constitutes a high, moderate, or low mean score for a cluster. Studies have reported different numbers of clusters (usually ranging from two to five), and similarly labeled clusters have not always produced equivalent scores. Differences in the scales employed to measure motivational regulations, in the set of variables used for cluster analysis, and the age and the context under examination (sport versus PE) could potentially account for such variable results. For example, with regard to the composition of the clusters, some studies have created clusters using only motivational regulation scores (e.g., Vlachopoulos, Karageorghis, & Terry, 2000; Yli-Piipari, Watt, Jaakkola, Liukkonen, & Nurmi, 2009), whereas others have included both regulations and related antecedent and outcome variables (e.g., Ntoumanis, 2002) or motivation variables from other theories (e.g., Spray & Wang, 2001, and McNeill & Wang, 2005, also included task and ego achievement goals). With regard to context-related differences, a low self-determined or high controlling profile has more often emerged in PE (e.g., Boiché, Sarrazin, Grouzet, Pelletier, & Chanal, 2008; Ntoumanis, 2002) than in sport (e.g., Gillet, Vallerand, & Rosnet, 2009; Vlachopoulos et al., 2000), which is not surprising given that PE is a compulsory physical activity context.

A finding that has emerged across all studies that use the cluster analytic method is that a high self-determined profile, in conjunction with either a low controlling (e.g., Boiché et al., 2008) or a high controlling motivation profile (e.g., Vlachopoulos et al., 2000), or irrespective of controlling motivation levels (e.g., Gillet et al., 2009; Ullrich-French & Cox, 2009), reported the most adaptive outcomes in terms of effort, affect, discipline, attitude toward sport, performance, and grades. In this respect, the findings of both person- and variable-centered approaches point to the importance of having high levels of autonomous motivation.

A different approach to studying the role of individual motivation was taken by Smith, Ntoumanis, and Duda (2007). Based on Sheldon and Elliot's (1999) self-concordance model, Smith et al. examined motives underlying personal goal striving, the influences of goal motives on goal attainment, and the consequences for psychological well-being. Specifically, athletes were asked to nominate four goals that they were pursuing during the competitive season. To assess the motives underlying each of their goals, participants were asked to rate why they were striving for each goal in terms of four reasons relating to intrinsic, identified, introjected, and external regulations. For each participant, composite autonomous and controlled goal motives scores were created and aggregated across the four goals. Structural equation modeling analysis showed that autonomous goal motives positively predicted effort, which in turn predicted goal attainment. Goal attainment was positively linked to need satisfaction, which in turn predicted psychological well-being. In contrast, controlled motives directly and negatively predicted psychological well-being. Interestingly, the relationship between autonomous motives and effort remained significant after controlling for goal difficulty, goal specificity, and goal efficacy. Similar findings were reported by Smith, Ntoumanis, Duda, and Vansteenkiste (2011) in a season-long investigation of goal striving in sport. From an applied perspective, these findings emphasize the importance of encouraging athletes to set and strive for goals that are congruent with their values and interests, and training coaches to aid athletes in doing so. Even when coaches establish some goals, as is often the case in sport, they can still aid athletes in fully internalizing the importance of such goals through autonomy-supportive behaviors. Smith et al. found such a link between autonomy support and autonomous goal striving.

Whereas measures of motivational regulations tap the extent to which one is generally autonomously or nonautonomously motivated within sport or PE, goal motives assess motivation specific to salient goals pursued at a particular point in time. This distinction is important. For example, a male swimmer might generally be highly self-determined in his sport involvement, but during a sport season he might not pursue a particular goal for internalized reasons (e.g., improve strength by weight training in the gym). Given the significance of goal setting in sport, it is useful to know that athletes are striving for important goals for the right reasons. A limitation of the Smith, Ntoumanis, et al. (2007, 2011) studies was that they followed the example of previous research on goal motives in the social psychology literature (e.g., Sheldon & Elliot, 1998, 1999) and aggregated the motive ratings across the four goals identified by the athletes. As different goals can be pursued for different motives, it would be interesting for future research to look at performance and well-being consequences when the motives for important goals conflict. In addition, Smith et al. examined personal goals only; in team contexts it is important and pertinent to consider autonomous versus controlled motives for pursuing team goals as well (cf. Gore & Cross, 2006). Further, future studies could examine goal content (intrinsic versus extrinsic; Kasser & Ryan, 1996) in conjunction with goal motives. Goal content refers to the *what* as opposed to the *why* of goal pursuit (see Standage & Ryan, this volume). In the only study to date testing goal content in a PE context, Vansteenkiste, Simons, Soenens, and Lens (2004) showed that framing a new activity in a PE class in terms of future intrinsic goal attainment (health and fitness) had a positive effect on effort, autonomous motivation, and performance, whereas framing the same activity in relation to future extrinsic goal attainment (physical appearance and attractiveness) undermined these outcomes compared to a no-future-goal control group. In addition to work in exercise and PE settings, future research about the relative importance and functioning of intrinsic and extrinsic goal content in competitive sport would be useful.

The empirical evidence to date confirms theoretical propositions regarding the adaptive role of self-determined regulations. Both intrinsic and high self-determined extrinsic types of motivation are important given that some behaviors might not be inherently enjoyable (e.g., repetitive drills during training) but could have high instrumental value (cf. Koestner & Losier, 2002). Future research might consider using "think aloud" protocols to elicit different reasons individuals value an activity (i.e., high identified regulation) and whether some reasons might in fact be not self-determined in nature. Introjected regulation, although representing a relatively controlling type of motivation, has often but not always been associated with negative outcomes (e.g., Ntoumanis, 2005). Assor, Vansteenkiste, and Kaplan (2009) have proposed an interesting distinction between approach (e.g., "I participate in sport because I want to prove to myself that I am able to persist") and avoidance (e.g., "I participate in sport because I would feel ashamed if I quit") introjection. In two studies across academic and sport domains, Assor et al. showed that introjected avoidance motivation, compared to introjected approach, was associated with a more negative pattern of affective and performance-related variables. This distinction between approach and avoidance components might explain some unexpected findings regarding introjected regulation in the sport and PE domain and is worthy of future research attention. But note that Assor et al. found that identified regulation when compared to introjected approach motivation had a more positive pattern of correlates.

External regulation and amotivation have been frequently related to negative outcomes, as theorized by SDT. As far as external regulation is concerned, a more differentiated approach could occasionally be useful. For example, motivation to obtain contingent extrinsic rewards, to avoid punishment, or to please others might have unique consequences. Further, a differentiated approach might also be beneficial in terms of studying amotivation, in particular in PE contexts, where it is relatively often encountered (Ntoumanis et al., 2004). For example, researchers could adapt and use Vlachopoulos and Gigoudi's (2008) four-factor amotivation scale for exercise.

A limitation of many of the studies reviewed in this section is that motivation and its correlates have been examined largely through self-reports. Research designs could be improved by including alternative measurement approaches (e.g., biomedical indicators of well-being and immune functioning, physiological, neuropsychological, and behavioral indices of motivation; see Fulmer & Frijters, 2009), which could be used alongside self-reports. Qualitative studies in this area of literature are rare. Exceptions are studies by Hassandra, Goudas, and Chroni (2003) and Ntoumanis et al. (2004), which provided rich information about antecedents and consequences of intrinsic motivation and amotivation in PE, respectively. More such studies and other qualitative methodologies (e.g., case studies, observations) are needed to explore in detail various motivational regulations in varying contexts and populations (e.g., see initial quantitative work by Hodge, Allen, & Smellie, 2008, and Perreault & Vallerand, 2007, on masters sport and disabled athletes, respectively). Moreover, future studies should extend their focus beyond athlete and student populations and investigate motivational regulations, as well as psychological needs, in relation to coaching, teaching PE, or officiating (see initial work by Allen & Shaw, 2009; Gray & Wilson, 2008).

Practical Applications

SDT offers a number of concrete suggestions about how to build and sustain adaptive motivational environments and promote psychological need satisfaction, autonomous motivation, personal growth, well-being, and adaptive behaviors. Despite differences between the sport and the PE contexts in terms of the type of provision, skill level of participants, and objectives of participation, a fundamental principle of SDT that cuts across both contexts is that motivational environments are optimal when structured in ways that facilitate the satisfaction of the three basic psychological needs, support intrinsic motivation, and actively promote the internalization process.

Reviews by Reeve (2009) and Mageau and Vallerand (2003) and empirical studies by Deci, Eghrari, Patrick, and Leone (1994) and Reeve et al. (2004) offer numerous examples of how to build adaptive motivational environments. Examples of applying SDT propositions in sport and PE settings are discussed in this section of the chapter. Although some intervention strategies might be operationalized differently across the two contexts, the basic principles behind these strategies are the same. One such strategy is to offer choices of activities, while obviously being cognizant of existing constraints created by curricula guidelines, practical considerations, or other limiting external factors. Choices should have specific rules and boundaries (i.e., should be structured), be meaningful to the students or athletes, and, as discussed earlier in this chapter, should meet the latter's basic psychological needs (Katz & Assor, 2007). For example, a coach should (*a*) offer his or her soccer players a choice of drills that will help the development of a particular skill (e.g., awareness of opponents' off-the-ball movements) that is highly relevant to the athletes' goals and interests, (*b*) ensure that the offered choices are not too numerous or complex for the players' development levels, and (*c*) will not result in intrateam conflict. Although choice can be motivating, it is also important (some argue even more important; Assor et al., 2002) that meaningful rationales are offered, particularly for uninteresting behaviors or for behaviors that have to be repeatedly performed to achieve expert performance (Ericsson, 2006). For instance, a young swimmer will more fully internalize the importance of unexciting weight-training sessions if her or his coach can clearly demonstrate the direct benefits of such activities for swimming performance. In a broader sense, rationales should clearly explain how a particular activity serves broader goals and priorities. Rationales are also useful to explain the purpose of existing restrictions and rules (e.g., why discipline is important). Athletes are more likely to be motivated when they are offered explanations that are clear, truthful, and meaningful, as opposed to when they are treated with a "It's my way or the highway" attitude.

Coaches and PE teachers should also be empathetic and acknowledge the difficulties, negative feelings, or objections that their athletes or students might have in relation to particular tasks, goals, or rules. For example, a PE teacher should be receptive to his or her students' complaints that certain activities during a lesson are too boring or too difficult; such complaints are common in PE classes because of large variability in physical ability levels. Expressions of dissatisfaction should be welcomed or even invited because they give athletes and students the message that their voices are heard and respected (Reeve, 2009). Further, such objections can result in better rationales being provided or in structural changes (e.g., more choices) that could address criticisms.

Coaches and PE teachers should also provide feedback that is constructive, detailed, informative in terms of competence development (e.g., "Your defensive skills have really improved this season because you are now able to . . ."), and positive where appropriate. Further, they should take time to listen first and then respond to athletes' and students' ideas and goals, be patient with their progress, offer them nonconditional praise, try to develop an understanding of how their athletes or students think and feel about certain things, and give them sufficient time and encouragement to take initiative and develop independently (Mageau & Vallerand, 2003; Reeve, 2009). A basic premise of SDT is that a need supportive environment is evident when people take ownership of their behaviors and display volitional engagement. For example, in terms of goal setting, in a motivational environment of this sort athletes should be encouraged to set and strive for goals that are congruent with their values and interests. Obviously, for inexperienced students and athletes such initiatives must be undertaken in a highly structured environment that offers guidance and clear expectations. To facilitate competence need satisfaction in particular, lessons or training regimes should provide optimally challenging opportunities that are matched with students' and athletes' levels of skill development and experience (Treasure, Lemyre, Kuczka, & Standage, 2007). Further, in terms of facilitating relatedness need satisfaction, team-building exercises (Martin, Carron, & Burke, 2009) and one-to-one meetings to discuss both individual and team goals should be scheduled. When required, such meetings should also aim to help athletes fully internalize and volitionally engage in team goals and activities that serve the greater good, sometimes at the expense of individual goals (e.g., prioritize team success over an individual accolade). In brief, an interpersonally involving coach or PE teacher who makes an athlete or student feel valued, appreciated, and respected will facilitate feelings of relatedness.

Given that the empirical evidence reviewed in this chapter indicates that coaches and teachers use a combination of adaptive and maladaptive instructional behaviors, interventions in sport and PE settings must aim at addressing both. With regard to the latter type of behaviors, a coach should not use language that is verbally abusive (e.g., name calling), threatens, humiliates, or forces (through fear, guilt inducement, conditional regard, or evaluative statements) athletes to accept rules, limits, or activities (e.g., "You don't wanna see me angry," "Don't let me down," "Don't talk, just do it"). Other controlling instructional behaviors that should be avoided (with varying degrees of applicability to sport and PE) are monopolizing conversations and discouraging questions or alternative opinions; issuing deadlines; uttering directives and commands; asking controlling questions (e.g., "Can you do this the way I want it?"); using praising as a contingent reward (e.g., "You did exactly what I asked you to do during the game"); telling others how they ought to feel; offering only predetermined goals, choices, values, and opinions; and using surveillance and other intrusive behaviors to influence athletes' lives outside sport (see Bartholomew et al., 2009; Reeve, 2009; Reeve & Jang, 2006, for illustrations of these behaviors in sport and education).

Besides teachers and coaches, influential peers (e.g., team captains) and parents (primarily in competitive sport) can foster or undermine psychological need satisfaction and self-determined motivation by engaging in some of the aforementioned behaviors. For example, team captains can exhibit intimating behaviors, and parents of a talented athlete might use excessive surveillance to monitor their son's or daughter's life outside sport (e.g., see the case of the father of Jelena Dokić, a world-class tennis player). Equally, adaptive behaviors can be exhibited from both sides. For instance, experienced teammates can offer meaningful rationales for activity engagement, and parents can communicate perspective-taking statements (e.g., "We fully understand that it is difficult for you to balance sport and school work"). Thus, where possible, SDT interventions should target multiple significant others because they can independently influence athlete and student motivation. In the context of competitive sport, individuals should also be aware of the potentially debilitating effects of various rewards offered for task engagement or completion. Rewards are inextricably linked with sport participation, especially at a high competitive level. They should be used carefully, however, particularly with young athletes. Interviews in the media of famous sportspeople often portray athletes as predominantly motivated for intrinsic reasons (e.g., "for the love of the game"). Nevertheless, some athletes, when offered large sums of money, often make poor decisions that can undermine their careers (e.g., consider David Beckham's move from Real Madrid, voted by FIFA as the most successful soccer club of the 20th century, to the relative obscurity of the Major League Soccer club Los Angeles Galaxy). But it should be emphasized that the role of rewards in high-level sport has not been systematically examined (apart from the effects of athletic scholarships) and is not well understood.

Research reviewed in this chapter indicates that students can make inferences about their instructors' motivation based on implicit motivational cues and that such inferences can affect subsequent student motivation. Further, although teachers are not often good judges of the extent to which their students are self-determined in their engagement, their judgments subsequently influence the instructional style that they use. Both sets of results have implications for future intervention work because they indicate the need to increase awareness of PE teachers (and probably coaches) about factors that enhance or undermine student motivation other than direct communications (e.g., nonverbal language). These findings also underscore the importance of helping teachers and coaches develop more accurate assessments of the various behavioral and affective manifestations of autonomous and controlling motivational regulations. Further, raising mindfulness in terms of how teacher or coach motivation is reciprocally linked with student or athlete motivation and achievement can be beneficial to both sets of parties.

The empirical evidence reviewed in this chapter demonstrates the diversity of factors (i.e., organizational structures and pressures, personality dispositions, perceptions of subordinates' motivation) that can affect the use of SDT-based instruction. Implementing coach and PE teacher training programs structured on SDT principles requires not only access (which can be difficult, especially at a high competitive level in sport) but also willingness to change established practices and behaviors at the individual and organizational level. At the individual level, coaches and PE teachers need to be convinced that adopting a SDT-based instructional style will improve not only the quality and effectiveness of their instruction and psychological well-being but also the quality of athlete or student motivation, well-being, and performance. In essence, a first step in intervention work is to facilitate the internalization and volitional endorsement of an SDT-based instructional style to foster a more autonomous motivation to implement such a style.

The work of Reeve (2009) and Taylor et al. (2009) on the antecedents of teachers' instructional styles, presented in earlier sections of this chapter, offers a number of findings that should be carefully considered when attempting to recruit PE teachers (and coaches) to SDT-based interventions. For example, beliefs that controlling strategies are the most effective (or that those who use them are the most competent instructors) in terms of creating organized and productive instructional environments should be tackled with available empirical evidence. Also, distinctions between autonomy support and a laissez-faire or permissive instructional style should be clearly made to reassure that offering autonomy does not mean that teachers' and coaches' perspectives, experiences, and values are put aside. In a similar vein, distinctions should be made between offering structure and being controlling (Reeve, 2009). Cultural norms regarding power relations between the teacher or coach and the student or athlete should be challenged. Also, practical examples should be offered of how time, resources, and other external constraints and pressures (e.g., from colleagues) that are not conducive to SDT-based instruction could be overcome. Such examples are imperative to demonstrate the viability of the recommended instructional style.

Even if coaches and PE teachers are willing to adopt an SDT-based instructional style, their clubs and schools also need to be convinced regarding the merits of a student- or athlete-centered approach versus the more traditional teacher- or coach-centered approach. This task might not be easy given that these organizations operate under various constraints (e.g., pressure from parents, media, fans, or curricula targets) or traditional modus operandi (e.g., short-term contracts) that are not conducive to the application of many instructional strategies described in this chapter. Some of the suggestions offered in the previous paragraph (e.g., challenging notions of what is an effective instructional style) are also applicable in terms of attempting to change philosophy and practice at a wider organizational level. Schools and sport clubs should be educated that the pressure they put on teachers and coaches, although it sometimes might produce quick results, will inevitably bring about maladaptive instructional practices, which in turn will lead to negative consequences for the psychological welfare of the instructors and those instructed.

Directions for Future Research

A risk for researchers who routinely use any one particular theoretical framework in their work is that they may develop a rather myopic focus and overlook opportunities to combine their chosen framework with complementary theoretical approaches or models. Although a complete integration of different theoretical perspectives is probably impossible or undesirable for various reasons, few would argue against refining or expanding theoretical constructs or reconsidering the boundaries of their operational utility by including constructs from other theories and models. This section will briefly offer some illustrative examples by referring to the rather scarce work that has been conducted in exploring potential links between constructs from SDT and those from other theoretical frameworks. An extensive discussion of the potential scope, benefits, and pitfalls of exploring such links is beyond the scope of this chapter.

One line of work has examined how SDT research could benefit from incorporating constructs from achievement goal theory (AGT; see Roberts, this volume, for definitions of key constructs from this theory), both the classic (Nicholls, 1989) and the revised (Elliot & McGregor, 2001). Standage, Duda, and Ntoumanis (2003a) measured student perceptions of PE teacher motivational climate by examining, besides autonomy-supportive behaviors, reports of teacher task- and ego-involving climate. The latter constructs include in their description perceptions of contextual influences not captured by autonomy support or control, such as the use of heterogeneous versus homogeneous ability groupings and self-referenced versus normative criteria for judging success and failure (Ames, 1992c). Spray, Wang, Biddle, and Chatzisarantis (2006) went a step further by experimentally creating conditions in PE classes that crossed autonomous and controlling with task- and ego-involving instructions. Further, Nien and Duda (2008) investigated how motivational regulations in sport are predicted not by athletes' psychological needs, as has often been the case in the SDT literature, but by their approach and avoidance achievement goals (Elliot & McGregor, 2001). Both SDT and AGT underline the role of perceived competence in guiding achievement behavior. AGT, however, distinguishes between a differentiated and a less differentiated conception of ability (Nicholls, 1989; Roberts, this volume). In contrast, SDT views competence as a unitary human need, the satisfaction of which promotes autonomous motivation. It would be interesting for future studies to examine how social contexts influence psychological need satisfaction and autonomous motivation by promoting the satisfaction of one conception of competence rather than another (Ntoumanis, 2001b).

Some SDT researchers (e.g., Amiot et al., 2004; Gaudreau & Antl, 2008) have examined how self-determined and controlled motivational regulations are related to adaptive and maladaptive coping efforts. In his 1991 book Lazarus emphasized that coping efforts should never be examined in isolation from motivation because the latter is essential for proper understanding of cognitive appraisals and coping responses in troubled person–environment relationships. Although perceptions of stress, appraisals, and coping responses are highly relevant to the competitive context of sport, to date no study in this context has attempted to test the relationships between sociocontextual factors, need satisfaction or thwarting, motivational regulations, stress appraisals, associated emotional and coping efforts and performance, well-being, and cognitive outcomes. Future studies that examine such links might benefit from integrative models of coping and motivation (from an SDT perspective) proposed by Ntoumanis, Edmunds, and Duda (2009) and Skinner and Edge (2002).

Another fruitful avenue for future research would be to examine how SDT could be related to other frameworks of self-regulation or self-control. Studies in social psychology have shown that why someone exerts self-control (i.e., inhibiting habitual behaviors, urges, or emotions that interfere with goal-directed behavior; Muraven, Gagné, & Rosman, 2008) can influence how the extent to which self-control can deplete energy resources. For example, based on Muraven and Baumeister's (2000) assertion that exertions of self-control deplete an individual's energy levels, Muraven (2008) and Muraven et al. (2008) showed that when people are autonomously motivated or in an autonomy-supportive environment, their self-control strength is less depleting than when they are nonautonomous in their motivation or under a controlling environment. Importantly, such differences were mediated by feelings of vitality associated with autonomy. No such links have been explored in the sport domain. This circumstance is surprising given that in sport high levels of self-control are required to operate within written (and often unwritten) rules and to avoid temptations that interfere with an athlete's dedication to training and development. Personal goal striving (e.g., see the control process model of goal pursuit by Carver & Scheier, 1998) can offer another potential interface between self-regulation and SDT research. As an illustration, Wrosch, Scheier, Miller, Schulz, and Carver (2003) suggested that when faced with unattainable goals, individuals' psychological well-being will benefit from goal disengagement and reengagement with alternative goals. Athletes heavily invest in some long-term goals, and anecdotal evidence suggests that they often find it difficult to disengage when faced with failure or uncontrollable factors (e.g., long-term injuries). The role of autonomous and controlled goal motives in predicting goal flexibility or rigidity is an interesting area of inquiry. Additionally, following the lead of Smith, Ntoumanis, et al. (2007) and Smith et al. (2011), it is important to explore further the role of goal motives in adaptive goal-setting pursuit. Locke and Latham's (1990) goal-setting theory is a widely applied motivational framework in sport, but it addresses only the *how* and not the *why* of goal pursuit; both aspects are essential for understanding effective goal striving.

Another exciting avenue for future work would be to examine nonconscious processes in the activation and direction of motivated behavior. According to the auto model put forward by Bargh (1997), goals are mental representations of motivational states that can be activated automatically by relevant environmental stimuli. Initial evidence in the SDT literature (e.g., Levesque & Pelletier, 2003; Ratelle, Baldwin, & Vallerand, 2005) suggests that motivational regulations and autonomy versus controlling environments can be nonconsciously primed and then can influence behavior and affective states in similar ways to conscious motivational processes. This approach is an interesting diversion from the position taken by most SDT researchers, who maintain that motivational states are outcomes of deliberate and conscious processes. In sport and PE numerous autonomous and controlling primes (e.g., see the aforementioned discussion of the Radel et al., in press, findings on motivational contagion) deserve research attention. Radel, Sarrazin, and Pelletier (2009) have recently shown that motivation for a new motor task in a lab situation could be triggered unconsciously by subliminal words corresponding to autonomous, neutral, or controlled motivation. As expected, the priming of autonomous motivation led to more positive outcomes than the priming of controlling motivation. This research report was the first SDT study that tested unconscious motivation processes with a motor task; more research is needed, ideally in more naturalistic settings using subliminal primes (e.g. words, music, or images that can be associated with various motivational states). Radel et al. (2009) offered an interesting direction for future research, which is the comparison of self-reported and nonconscious motivational states. Such a comparison could be useful when individuals are, whether intentionally or not (e.g., because of self-deception; see Hirschfeld, Thomas, & McNatt, 2008), inaccurate in their self-reports of how self-determined or controlled their motivation is.

In terms of examining the role of nonconscious processes on the activation of motivation, it is also worth considering the findings of Schüler, Sheldon, and Fröhlich (2010). These authors attempted to integrate the SDT view on needs with the motive disposition approach on needs (McClelland, 1987). In two studies (cross-sectional and longitudinal) using university sport athletes, Schüler et al. showed that individuals high in the need or motive for achievement reported greater levels of flow and intrinsic motivation when they experienced competence need satisfaction compared to those who did not experience competence satisfaction and those low in the need for achievement irrespective of competence satisfaction levels. Note that the moderation between competence and achievement was found with an implicit (nonconscious) measure of achievement but not with an explicit measure. These findings indicate that individual difference factors, perhaps because of developmental experiences, might moderate the degree of effects of the three SDT-proposed psychological needs on motivation. This argument, however, has yet to be tested with regard to autonomy and relatedness need satisfaction.

Summary

SDT has nearly 40 years of presence in the psychology literature and about 25 years in the sport and physical education domains. The widespread application of SDT in sport and PE contexts, especially since the mid- to late 1990s, is not surprising. Contextual influences, primarily in terms of the interpersonal style of the coach and the PE teacher, have been shown to shape the degree of active engagement and the quality of psychological experiences of athletes and students alike. Autonomy support, structure, and involvement encompass a number of concrete examples of how people in positions of authority can support the basic psychological needs of those they interact with (e.g., see Jang, 2008; Reeve & Jang, 2006) and indirectly promote self-determined reasons for engagement and psychological well-being. The research evidence reviewed in this chapter offers strong support for the usefulness of the SDT approach for understanding and promoting adaptive motivation in sport and PE. A number of future research directions were identified that could be valuable in further testing some of its constructs, pushing its boundaries, and facilitating its evolution over time.

CHAPTER 4

Perfectionism: A Foundation for Sporting Excellence or an Uneasy Pathway Toward Purgatory?

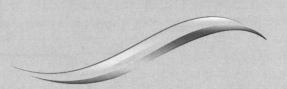

Howard K. Hall, PhD
York St. John University

Andrew P. Hill, PhD
York St. John University

Paul R. Appleton, PhD
University of Birmingham

In the last decade, research into perfectionism has developed rapidly in social, educational, and clinical psychology (Beiling, Israeli, Smith, & Antony, 2003; Flett & Hewitt, 2002, 2006; Owens & Slade, 2008; Parker, 1997; Rice, Vergera, & Aldea, 2006; Shafran, Cooper, & Fairburn, 2002; Stoeber & Otto, 2006). During the same period, research on the influence of perfectionism in sport has begun to emerge (e.g. Anshel & Eom, 2002; Appleton, Hall, & Hill, 2009; Dunn, Gotwals, & Causgrove Dunn, 2005; Flett & Hewitt, 2005; Hall, Kerr, & Matthews, 1998; Hill, Hall, Appleton, & Kozub, 2008; McArdle & Duda, 2008; Ommundsen, Roberts, Lemyre, & Miller, 2005; Stoeber, Stoll, Pescheck, & Otto, 2008). A review of research in the area of sport by Hall (2006) concluded that perfectionism appeared to be an inherently debilitating personality characteristic that undermines the fulfillment of athletic potential in all but the most exceptional circumstances. He concurred with a position put forward by Greenspon (2000) that questioned whether perfectionism could ever be considered a fundamentally beneficial quality, and he concluded that little evidence supported the view that perfectionism of any type was synonymous with adaptive achievement striving in sport. Since the review, a growing body of empirical evidence has accrued that appears to demonstrate that some dimensions of perfectionism are not only associated with positive outcomes but may also underpin adaptive patterns of motivation and enhance athletic performance (Stoeber, Otto, Pescheck, Becker, & Stoll, 2007; Stoeber, Stoll, Pescheck, & Otto, 2008; Stoeber, Uphill, & Hotham, 2009; Stoll, Lau, & Stoeber, 2008; and colleagues' multiple studies). This evidence clearly challenges the position put forward by Hall (2006) and warrants scrutiny.

The purpose of this chapter is to establish whether perfectionism affords a motivational foundation for sporting excellence or whether it provides a framework for performance appraisal that condemns many achievement-obsessed athletes to a life of purgatory because their accomplishments are seldom sufficient to meet their exacting standards. The chapter draws on evidence from extant literature to provide a clear understanding of the meaning and significance of perfectionism in sport. The chapter also revisits questions that have puzzled both sport psychologists and coaches for some time. These include whether striving for perfection can ever be considered to reflect a truly adaptive form of motivation and whether the term *perfectionism* can describe anything other than a fundamentally maladaptive pattern of achievement activity. Two seemingly polarized views on perfectionism have emerged from research in this area (Stoeber & Otto, 2006; Owens & Slade, 2008; Flett & Hewitt, 2005, 2006). One prevailing view considers that because perfectionism reflects a broad array of personal qualities, it may assume multiple forms that can range from motivationally enabling to psychologically debilitating.

Those adhering to this perspective believe that in its most positive guise, perfectionism may depict a largely beneficial personality characteristic that underpins both adaptive and sustained motivation and thereby facilitates an athlete's quest for sporting excellence. In contrast, others endorse the belief that despite the apparent benefits that perfectionism may bring, it is best considered a potentially debilitating attribute because the style of achievement striving that it engenders is fundamentally maladaptive. Over time, this type of achievement striving will not only inhibit athletic performance but also undermine an athlete's psychological well-being. Although these two perspectives may appear to be incompatible, the chapter will provide evidence to suggest that this apparent contradiction may be more about the terminology adopted and the manner in which multidimensional measures have been used than about a fundamental disagreement regarding the underlying psychological processes associated with the construct.

The chapter first describes a number of high-profile athletes to illustrate the influence that perfectionism may have on those performing at the highest level of sport. Beyond achievement striving, the examples reveal a wide range of behavioral and psychological effects that have the potential to lead to both impairment and distress. But because these detrimental outcomes often occur in combination with unrivaled sporting achievement, those interested in performance excellence tend to limit their focus to the energizing features of the disposition. They suggest that perfectionism constrained in this manner might be considered a hallmark quality of elite performance rather than a broadly debilitating personality characteristic (Anshel & Eom, 2002; Dunn, Causgrove Dunn, & Syrotuik, 2002; Hardy, Jones, & Gould, 1996; Henschen, 2000). We believe that the accounts of these elite athletes illustrate that debilitating consequences of perfectionism arise from the same psychological processes that energize high levels of achievement striving.

To evaluate the degree to which the features of perfectionism may be responsible for performance excellence, the chapter then examines how perfectionism has been defined. Various definitions are considered, and, through a synthesis of the literature, we identify the core cognitive and behavioral features of the construct. This synthesis draws attention to the fact that when perfectionism is defined in a constrained manner, using isolated features such as heightened goal striving, it may describe something other than perfectionism. The chapter then considers how, in some instances, perfectionism has been defined by its measures rather than by its core features, and that through the disaggregation of its defining qualities empirical evidence has been accrued to support the notion that certain forms of perfectionism may be universally positive or healthy. Evidence is presented to demonstrate that in the absence of the core defining features of perfectionism, the concept of positive perfectionism bears such a strong resemblance to various adaptive motivational constructs that it makes neither conceptual nor empirical sense to refer to this form of achievement striving as perfectionism.

The chapter reviews empirical literature that has examined perfectionism in sport to illustrate that when perfectionism is measured in a manner that captures its core features simultaneously, it has few positive psychological and performance consequences. This literature challenges notions that perfectionism can be positive and demonstrates that the outcomes are more detrimental when the construct is viewed in its broadest sense. Finally, because little work has been done to develop effective interventions to manage perfectionism in sport, the chapter builds upon ideas proffered by Flett and Hewitt (2005) that suggest various options for reframing and moderating the cognitions associated with perfectionism to help athletes manage the deleterious consequences.

Perfectionism in Elite Sport Performers

A number of prominent sport psychology practitioners and coaches have noted that at an elite level, many athletes appear to exhibit distinct qualities of perfectionism in their achievement striving (Gould, Dieffenbach, & Moffett, 2002; Stoeber, Uphill, & Hotham, 2009). Some have suggested that these qualities may play a significant role in helping athletes to achieve and maintain performance excellence, leading to a belief that perfectionism is a positive characteristic that should not be discouraged (Hardy, Jones, & Gould, 1996; Henschen, 2000). Mallet and Hanrahan (2004) argue that this pattern of achievement striving may enable some elite athletes to fulfill fundamental needs because it allows them to demonstrate competence, prove their worth to others, and gain a high degree of recognition, all of which contribute to positive self-perceptions. Others have taken a more guarded approach (e.g., Flett & Hewitt, 2005; Hall, 2006). They suggest that although perfectionism may appear to be influential in enabling some athletes to perform at the highest level, this particular type of striving may bring with it significant psychological and personal costs. Growing evidence suggests that this occurs because the beliefs that energize heightened achievement striving also appear to activate a range of debilitating cognitive, affective, and behavioral processes. These processes may ultimately prevent potentially talented athletes from fulfilling their athletic potential and may undermine their psychological well-being. Accounts of elite athletes who are described by themselves or others as perfectionists are not uncommon. But the experiences of athletes who exhibit the core characteristics of perfectionism are rarely positive when one considers the consequences beyond achievement behavior and on their lives more broadly.

The case of Johnny Wilkinson, an England rugby player, is illuminating. Hall (2006) highlighted that during coverage of the 2003 Rugby World Cup, a competition in which Wilkinson kicked the winning drop goal and was the leading points scorer in the tournament, the perfectionistic tendencies that he reported were revered as the source of his exceptional talent. But his perfectionism also appeared to be the source of a number of psychological problems, including relaxation difficulties, worry, and stress. At the time, these issues were consigned to being inconsequential, and perhaps necessary, costs of his success. Wilkinson has since provided vivid accounts of his experiences during this period (Wilkinson, 2004, 2008). According to his recollection, a fear of failure, feelings of guilt associated with even minor deviations from his strict training regimen, and an extreme desire for control over performance outcomes characterized this period of his career. At the time, his response to this intense internal pressure was to practice obsessively, especially his kicking. Wilkinson described this behavior as both exhausting and destructive, in part because it led to numerous back, groin, and leg muscle injuries.

Other top athletes have encountered similar experiences because of their perfectionism. One of these is Victoria Pendleton, currently a six-time world champion, Commonwealth champion, and Olympic champion in track sprint cycling. She is also the current Commonwealth and Olympic record holder in the 200-meter time trial event and the U.K. national record holder in the 200-meter and 500-meter time trial events. When commenting on her successes in 2008, a year in which she won two world championships and an Olympic gold medal (McRae, 2008), she described herself as unsatisfied and under pressure. Despite achieving at the highest level, she recounted being profoundly dissatisfied and unable to take pleasure in her accomplishments. In her words, she described feeling that "she is nowhere near as good as she should be." Pendleton still considers herself "a self-critical perfectionist." She believes that she is striving for something that she will never achieve and consequently often finds herself in a state of emotional turmoil. Given her considerable accomplishments to date, it is unlikely that future achievements will satisfy her desire for perfection.

In the case of Ronnie O'Sullivan, a world-class snooker player, the consequences of failing to cope with perfectionism continue to be debilitating and pathological. Like Pendleton, O'Sullivan experienced major success in sport. He is a four-time world snooker champion, masters champion, and the winner of 22 ranking events. He attributes these successes to a commitment to perfection that he considers instrumental to maintaining his motivation. But O'Sullivan also has a history of drug addiction and depression. This, too, he attributes to his perfectionism. Again, despite his sporting achievements, O'Sullivan has described an inability to derive a sense of satisfaction from his achievements. Moreover, he describes experiencing "a constant sense of failure" because of being unable to achieve the perfectionistic standards that he holds for himself (O'Sullivan, 2004).

Although perfectionism can clearly have a profound personal effect, in team sports it may also have a disruptive influence on the interpersonal dynamics of the group. The behavior of former Irish international footballer and Manchester United F.C. captain Roy Keane illustrates how perfectionism can detrimentally influence team dynamics. As the Irish team prepared for the 2002 World Cup tournament in Japan and Korea, Keane's perfectionism and intense motivation for success was clearly evident through the high expectations that he maintained for himself, his teammates, and the coaching staff. But his incessant demands seemed to undermine cohesion and disrupt team unity because others were perceived as being unable to meet his expectations. Keane's overall dissatisfaction with preparations and complaints about training facilities and the poor professional standards exhibited by others led to arguments, team disunity, and interpersonal conflict, which eventually resulted in Keane's being ejected from the team's training camp before the World Cup tournament (O'Hagan, 2002).

Although the motivational qualities of perfectionism are evident in all the preceding examples, this pattern of achievement striving clearly contributes to numerous aversive psychological consequences and may ultimately lead to debilitation. But because it encourages a commitment to the pursuit of high standards, some consider it a valued quality for athletes to exhibit and a possible route to sporting success (Stoeber & Otto, 2006; Stoll et al. 2008). The label *perfectionist* is often used loosely to describe athletes who demonstrate this type of commitment, and this labeling contributes to uncertainty among coaches and sport psychologists about its genuine influence. Many find it difficult to see beyond the beneficial performance effects associated with striving to achieve (Hall, 2006). In our view, however, the term *perfectionism* refers to individuals who exhibit more than a commitment to high standards. To understand why perfectionism may energize heightened achievement striving, bring about positive outcomes, but ultimately carry the potential for psychological debilitation, we must consider how the core features of this personality characteristic give rise to psychological processes underpinning this form of achievement behavior.

Definition

The overall uncertainty about the influence of perfectionism on athletes may be attributed, in part, to the absence of a clear definition of the construct. This lack of definitional clarity has been noted by Flett and Hewitt (2002), who identified as many as 21 separate terms that purported to describe perfectionism. These terms have been gleaned from a variety of approaches that differ both in their perspective and in their assumptions about the nature of the construct. Although each holds that distinguishing qualities are at the heart of the disposition, there appears to be little overall agreement about the precise defining characteristics. Similarly, opinion is divided about which of these characteristics must be exhibited for a person to be labeled a perfectionist (e.g., Frost, Marten, Lahart, & Rosenblate, 1990; Shafran & Mansell, 2001). The inability to agree on these issues has effectively blurred the distinction between perfectionism and other forms of achievement behavior that involve striving to excel. Ultimately, some have argued that perfectionism can exist in both adaptive and maladaptive forms (e.g., Enns, Cox, Sareen, & Freeman, 2001; Rice & Lapsley, 2001; Slaney & Ashby, 1996; Slade & Owens, 1998). But when we look beyond the act of perfectionistic striving to identify the core defining qualities of this characteristic, we contend that perfectionism represents a unique disposition whose essential features are distinct from other forms of achievement motivation that may share some, but not all, of the fundamental characteristics of perfectionism.

Although most people accepted that the pursuit of high standards is an important quality of perfectionism, when considered in isolation, this behavior is insufficient to accurately define the construct (Flett & Hewitt, 2002; Frost et al. 1990). Many believe that perfectionism involves much more than the act of striving (Burns, 1980; Greenspon, 2000; Hamachek, 1978; Hollander, 1965; Flett & Hewitt, 2002). Rather, perfectionism is a psychological commitment to exceedingly high standards that is believed to reflect an extreme way of thinking in which the meaning of achievement becomes distorted by irrational beliefs and dysfunctional attitudes (Ellis, 1962; Hamachek, 1978; Jones, 1968; Weissman & Beck, 1978). When committed to the pursuit of high standards, radical beliefs that consider that success and failure exist as dichotomous extremes and that self-worth is contingent on achievement distort the perceived criteria against which performance is appraised.

When accomplishment is assigned such irrational importance and the margin between success and failure is considered so narrow, anything that is perceived to fall short will evoke self-censure (Flett & Hewitt, 2002). This tendency to engage in excessively harsh self-evaluation while in the pursuit of exceedingly high standards is purported to be a further key distinguishing feature of perfectionism, and it is this tendency that gives rise to many of the cognitive and behavioral patterns that are considered to define the construct (Greenspon, 2000; Hamachek, 1978; Hewitt & Flett, 1991). The use of dichotomous evaluative processes results in the condemnation of anything less than flawlessness, and this circumstance provides perfectionists with little scope for error (Burns, 1980; Hollander, 1965). As a result, perfectionists are extraordinarily concerned about making mistakes and tend to overgeneralize failure experiences beyond any single event (Burns, 1980; Frost et al., 1990; Hamachek, 1978). They also exhibit selective attention to, and a preoccupation with, personal shortcomings. When this is combined with concerns about the potential impact of failure, perfectionists frequently exhibit vague doubts about whether the quality of their performance, their preparation, or their effort will be sufficient to meet extreme standards (Frost et al., 1990). They have difficulty making an independent evaluation about whether they have completed any task satisfactorily, and they may strive obsessively as a compensatory strategy (Frost et al., 1990).

We propose, therefore, that perfectionism does not simply reflect the pursuit of high standards but rather appears to be a multifaceted personality characteristic that encompasses a particular constellation of achievement-related cognition and behavior associated with a commitment to flawlessness in contexts that hold personal relevance (Campbell & Di Paula, 2002; Flett & Hewitt, 2002). The framework on which this pattern of cognition is based pertains to a belief that self-acceptance is inextricably tied to accomplishment. This conditional self-acceptance fosters an overdependence on personal attainment and causes goal striving to become compulsive (Greenspon, 2000; Lundh, 2004; Lundh, Saboonchi, & Wangby, 2008). Although this mindset has the potential to bring about positive outcomes through heightened achievement striving, these beliefs may also provide the basis for psychological difficulties. For some, these negative consequences may go unnoticed, and their achievement striving leads to personal attainment. Inevitably, however, the harsh self-evaluation that follows perceived failure to meet internalized ideal standards underpins the development of a wide range of debilitating consequences (see Dunkley, Zuroff, & Blankstein, 2006).

When defined in this manner, perfectionism cannot be considered an adaptive motivational pattern. It is thus intriguing that many consider perfectionism a positive characteristic (Stoeber & Otto, 2006; Slade & Owens, 1998; Slaney & Ashby, 1996). The notion that perfectionism may be a constructive quality seems to have originated from the early writings of Adler (1956) and Hollander (1965). The idea was given significant impetus, however, by Hamachek (1978), who coined the terms *normal perfectionism* and *neurotic perfectionism* in an attempt to differentiate between the adaptive and maladaptive psychological processes that underpin striving to reach excessively high standards. Hamachek (1978) considered normal perfectionism an adaptive characteristic because it reflected an appetitive pattern of achievement behavior. This idea implied that individuals sought opportunities to achieve and were able to gain pleasure from the process of striving to meet personally challenging goals, to derive intrinsic satisfaction from task mastery, and to attain self-esteem from goal accomplishment. Hamachek believed that neurotic perfectionism, in contrast, was fundamentally maladaptive because it reflected a failure avoidance pattern in which the threshold for avoidance is the accomplishment of excessive personal demands. The process of striving leads neurotic perfectionists to focus on their deficiencies because it induces incessant worry that any outcomes that fall short of demanding standards will be insufficient to gain either approval or acceptance from significant others (Hamachek, 1978).

Note that in Hamachek's description, the goals toward which neurotic perfectionists strive and the process by which their goals are evaluated are qualitatively different from those of normal perfectionists. The goals of neurotic perfectionists will typically offer a level of challenge that lies beyond the individual's capability. Furthermore, the inflexibility within the appraisal process in comparison to that of normal perfectionists means that the neurotic perfectionist rarely experiences any sense of accomplishment. Normal perfectionists seek goals that are challenging yet flexible, and their self-expectations are realistic, so appraisal tends to be a reflective task-focused process, as opposed to the ruminative self-focused process employed by neurotic perfectionists.

Although Hamachek's description of neurotic perfectionism has informed the conceptual development of some contemporary approaches to perfectionism (Hewitt & Flett, 1991; Frost et al., 1990; Slaney, Ashby, & Trippi, 1995), the notion of normal perfectionism has not always been readily accepted. This has occurred, in part, because some consider this concept to lack many of the core characteristics of perfectionism. Consequently, normal perfectionism demonstrates a large degree of conceptual overlap with other adaptive forms of achievement behavior (Greenspon, 2000, 2008; Flett & Hewitt, 2006; Hall, 2006). For example, normal perfectionism seems to depict what Dweck

(2006) has referred to as a growth mind-set in which a person can develop basic qualities through challenge and effort. As a result, it is never clear how normal perfectionism is conceptually and empirically distinct from adaptive forms of achievement behavior in which highly motivated people are simply striving to meet challenging goals. Noting this, Hall (2006) has argued that if it is not possible to make such a distinction, using the term *normal* when referring to perfectionism will do little more than create conceptual confusion.

The notion that perfectionism could be described in any sense as normal has been challenged at a conceptual level by a number of other authors (Greenspon, 2000; Flett & Hewitt, 2006). For example, Flett and Hewitt (2006) question whether the behavioral characteristics exhibited by normal perfectionists are sufficient to be defined as a perfectionist. They argue that striving for perfection by definition goes beyond the pursuit of excellence. That is, when striving for perfection, individuals not only place irrational importance on flawlessness but also retain an inflexible commitment to their goals and hold firmly to a belief that achievement will come about only when they adhere to these rigid, exacting principles. Greenspon (2000, 2008) was especially scathing in his criticism, suggesting that it was inappropriate to attach the label *normal* to perfectionism because perfection was largely an illusory and irrational concept. For this reason he thought it questionable to consider the behavior of individuals who pursue perfection as either normal or psychologically healthy, and he suggested that the term *normal perfectionism* might be regarded as an oxymoron. Greenspon (2000) further claimed that there was neither a valid conceptual reason nor an empirically based argument to support the existence of a construct labeled normal, or healthy, perfectionism and that its existence has been based on uncritical acceptance of Hamachek's ideas rather than on any credible empirical evidence.

Since Greenspon's (2000) initial critique, empirical evidence has emerged that some believe provides support for Hamachek's (1978) original contentions that perfectionism may manifest in either an adaptive or a maladaptive form (e.g., Owens & Slade, 2008; Stoeber & Otto, 2006). The evidence has been drawn from studies that have examined the consequences of various perfectionism dimensions on psychological health, the results of factor analytical studies, and investigations that have examined the consequences of perfectionism after controlling for any relationship between perfectionism dimensions. A critical examination of these strategies highlights a number of concerns about the quality of the evidence that has been generated by available measures.

Disaggregation of Multidimensional Measures of Perfectionism

Only after the development of multidimensional measures have researchers been able to claim empirical support for the existence of positive forms of perfectionism. Multidimensional measures made it possible to capture the broad range of defining qualities, which reflected the personal and social nature of the construct, as well as the source and direction of perfectionistic behavior (Cox, Enns, & Clara, 2002; Hewitt & Flett, 1991; Frost et al., 1990). Multidimensional measures have also allowed researchers to examine dimensions of perfectionism that reflect a commitment to exceedingly high standards and evaluative concerns independently. The finding that specific subdimensions of perfectionism are associated with various positive outcomes has led some to argue that it is possible to determine the effects of normal or positive perfectionism by disaggregating these dimensions from others that are typically associated with debilitating consequences (Parker & Adkins, 1995; Rice, Ashby, & Slaney, 1998; Rice, Bair, Castro, Cohen, & Hood, 2003). Although it may be convenient to isolate specific dimensions, this approach seems counterintuitive to an argument that perfectionism is best understood as a broad multidimensional construct. Furthermore, the disaggregation strategy is methodologically problematic for a number of reasons. In particular, individual dimensions of perfectionism are not inclusive of all the core features of perfectionism. In fact, in some instances the constructs being examined will bear little resemblance to what theorists would consider perfectionism. Therefore, perfectionism becomes defined by its measures rather than by a clear conceptual basis and agreement on its core qualities.

One scale that has frequently been subjected to this type of disaggregation is Frost's Multidimensional Perfectionism Scale (F-MPS) (Frost et al., 1990). MPS lends itself to this strategy because two subscales reflect generally adaptive behaviors (the pursuit of exceedingly high personal standards and an emphasis on precision and order) and the remaining four subscales reflect more critical and evaluative cognitions (a preoccupation with avoiding mistakes, overall doubt about the quality of one's performance and preparation, perceived parental expectations, and perceived evaluation by parents). But to suggest that the subscales reflecting the pursuit of high standards and organization together constitute a measure of positive perfectionism is conceptually problematic. Frost et al. (1990) argued that the pursuit of high personal standards is not the central defining quality of perfectionism and that the organization dimension is largely peripheral. Therefore, before any judgment about perfectionism can be made, the pursuit of high personal standards must be considered in conjunction with concern about mistakes that Frost et al. (1990) considered the fundamental defining quality. When the individual dimensions of the F-MPS are considered in isolation, they may misrepresent the broader construct of perfectionism and lead to errors of inclusion because a person who obtains a high score on any one dimension may be mislabeled as a perfectionist. Clearly, therefore, disaggregation of the subscales on the F-MPS is a problematic strategy because it fails to recognize the complex multidimensional nature of the construct and obfuscates the meaning of the term *perfectionism*.

Factor Analysis of Multidimensional Perfectionism Scales

A second approach that has provided empirical support for a distinction between normal and neurotic perfectionism is the factor analysis of existing multidimensional perfectionism measures. Factor analyzing the subscales from

Hewitt and Flett's (1991) Multidimensional Perfectionism Scale (H-MPS) and the F-MPS to create composite measures is one strategy that attempts to ensure that the self-critical element of perfectionism is not lost through disaggregation. The H-MPS comprises three subscales that measure essential components of perfectionistic behavior that are thought to be associated with varying levels of psychological impairment and distress. Self-oriented perfectionism reflects a process by which people set exceedingly high personal standards and employ a harsh, self-critical style in response to attempts to meet those standards. Socially prescribed perfectionism describes a slightly different process whereby people strive to meet internalized high standards, which they believe others expect of them. Other-oriented perfectionism is considered to have a similar basis to self-oriented perfectionism, but the behavior is interpersonal in nature. In other words, those high in other-oriented perfectionism direct their unrealistic expectations toward other people and respond to others' attempts to meet expectations in a harsh, critical manner (Flett & Hewitt, 2002; Hewitt & Flett, 1991).

In a number of studies, factor analysis of the various H-MPS and F-MPS subscales (e.g., Frost, Heimberg, Holt, Mattia, & Neubauer, 1993; Rice, Ashby, & Slaney, 1998; Stumpf & Parker, 2000) has revealed two higher-order latent factors. The first, labeled personal standards perfectionism, comprises the self- and other-oriented perfectionism scales from the H-MPS, as well as the personal standards and organization scales from the F-MPS. The second, labeled evaluative concerns perfectionism, comprises concern about mistakes, doubts about action, parental expectations, and parental criticism from the F-MPS and socially prescribed perfectionism from the H-MPS. The emergence of these two higher-order factors are purported to be indicative of the normal and neurotic distinction highlighted by Hamachek. A review by Stoeber and Otto (2006) of 15 studies adopting this approach found evidence that a single factor reflecting positive dimensions of perfectionism such as striving for high personal standards, organization, and self-oriented perfectionism was positively associated with adaptive correlates. A second approach has employed either cluster analysis or cutoff scores on various perfectionism measures to derive groups of healthy and unhealthy perfectionists (Stoeber & Otto, 2006). The evidence from 12 out of 20 studies reviewed by Stoeber and Otto (2006) suggests that individuals labeled healthy perfectionists have higher scores on perfectionism subscales that reflect adaptive functioning and lower scores on those that represent maladaptive functioning. After classifying individuals in this manner, it was found that people in the healthy perfectionism cluster groups reported more positive outcomes than did those in the unhealthy or nonperfectionist groups.

Although Stoeber and Otto (2006) concluded that these approaches provided strong support for the existence of two distinct forms of perfectionism, methodological concerns have been raised, which suggest that caution may be warranted before any firm conclusions can be drawn (Flett & Hewitt, 2006; Greenspon, 2000). As with the disaggregation approach, the principal concern in employing either factor analysis or cluster analysis to define the perfectionism construct is that core elements of perfectionism may be omitted from each identified form. Subsequently, it is possible that neither form provides an adequate conceptual representation of the perfectionism construct. For example, it can be argued that the pursuit of high personal standards should be a core feature of both forms of perfectionism, but in this approach it emerges only as a dimension of positive perfectionism. Again, perfectionism becomes a function of the measures rather than a construct that encompasses all necessary defining qualities.

Partialing the Effects of Dimensions of Perfectionism

Some researchers (e.g., Stoeber, Stoll, Pescheck, & Otto, 2008; Stoll, Lau, & Stoeber, 2008) have examined the consequences of dimensions of perfectionism after partialing out the effects of negative perfectionism (e.g., negative reactions to imperfection) from positive perfectionism (i.e., perfectionistic striving). Predictably, this strategy offers statistical verification of the adaptive consequences of positive perfectionism. But it is again questionable whether it makes conceptual sense to partial out important components that contribute to the broad multidimensional nature of the construct and then make inferences about the construct as a whole. Dimensions of perfectionism typically regarded as maladaptive and adaptive are often positively correlated (Flett and Hewitt, 2006). Indeed, the shared variance between adaptive and maladaptive qualities of perfectionism may represent important, and defining, characteristics of maladaptive forms of perfectionism (see Campbell & Di Paula, 2002). It is at least indicative of the relationship between the commitment to high standards and core debilitating features described by early theorists. Consequently, this strategy creates a further artificial distinction between two core features of perfectionism.

A perusal of the extant literature on perfectionism makes it clear not only that there is little consensus on a definition of perfectionism but also that researchers do not agree on how to measure the construct. Examination of the emerging body of literature concerned with perfectionism in sport reveals that the disaggregation of perfectionism subscales from established measures does not provide a satisfactory approach to the assessment of perfectionism. Employment of this strategy has led researchers to conclude that some forms of perfectionism are uniformly positive whereas others are consistently debilitating. We contend, however, that inferences about the consequences of perfectionism can be made only when the core components are considered together. The following section draws on a body of research that has assessed perfectionism as a broad multidimensional construct. It uses these studies to provide an analysis of the association between perfectionism and various sport-related outcomes and to illustrate that the influence of perfectionism is qualitatively different from the act of striving to achieve perfection.

Empirical Evidence of Perfectionism in Sport

Sport has been identified as an ideal context to examine perfectionism (Flett & Hewitt, 2005; Hall, 2006). This notion is not simply because the highest levels of achievement require individuals to strive for demanding goals, invest considerable effort, and engage in sustained striving (Ericsson, 1996; Hall & Kerr, 2001; Starkes, 2000); rather, it is because for many people, sport is a meaningful context in which identity, self-definition, and self-worth can be established (Hall, 2006). Moreover, because the achievement outcomes and psychological processes associated with striving to achieve in sport are perhaps more transparent than in other contexts, the effect of perfectionism may be more visible. Since Hall's (2006) review, research in sport has demonstrated that perfectionism is associated with a wide variety of cognitive, affective, and behavioral outcomes (e.g., Gaudreau & Antl, 2008; Hall, Hill, Appleton, & Kozub, 2009; Kaye, Conroy, & Fifer, 2008; Lemyre, Hall, & Roberts, 2008; Stoeber, Uphill, & Hotham, 2009). Research has also confirmed that perfectionism may reflect a domain-specific quality rather than a global personality characteristic (Dunn, Gotwals, & Causgrove Dunn, 2005; Dunn, Craft, Causgrove Dunn, & Gotwals, in press; McArdle, 2010). Consequently, sport may elicit perfectionistic behavior in some individuals who consider this domain to be one in which achievement is vital.

Although the volume of research on perfectionism in sport has grown considerably in recent years, the inconsistent use of perfectionism measures hinders a clear interpretation of the available findings. Even though sporting research has broadly endorsed the use of multidimensional measures of perfectionism, a significant number of studies have employed methodologies that we argue are problematic. That is, many have chosen to disaggregate multidimensional perfectionism measures and examine the influence of individual components, thereby overlooking the effects of the broader perfectionism construct on cognitive, affective, and behavioral outcomes. Based on the findings of some of these studies, claims have been made that certain forms of perfectionism are associated with broadly adaptive qualities (Anshel & Eom, 2002; Dunn et al., 2002; Stoeber, Stoll, Salmi, & Tiikkaja, 2009). Some clinical psychologists may therefore be premature in arguing that perfectionism is a fundamentally maladaptive characteristic (e.g. Flett & Hewitt, 2002; Shafran & Mansell, 2001). But to recognize the genuine effect that perfectionism may have on sport-related outcomes, it is necessary to consider the composite influence of multidimensional measures rather than the separate effects of individual dimensions. By employing this strategy researchers will be able to differentiate between striving (for high standards) that is regulated by a desire for improvement or personal growth and striving that has the added dimension of a harsh, self-critical style, which reflects the broad fundamental characteristics of the perfectionism construct. The following review emphasizes studies in sport that have adopted a multidimensional approach to examine the combined effects of the core dimensions of perfectionism on key outcomes. The review also challenges whether studies that have adopted a narrow or single-dimension approach to the measurement of the construct are genuinely assessing perfectionism in athletes. Finally, the review emphasizes studies that have employed the H-MPS, because this instrument is not subject to the same criticism over disaggregation as others (Hall, 2006). The separate dimensions of self-oriented and socially prescribed perfectionism of the H-MPS appear to capture the broad characteristics of perfectionism, including the pursuit of high standards and self-critical concerns.

Perfectionism and Achievement Goals

In a previous review of perfectionism in sport, Hall (2006) proposed that the underlying differences between perfectionism and adaptive forms of striving may be a function of the motivational goals that regulate achievement cognition and behavior. He argued that unlike adaptive achievement striving, perfectionism may be underpinned by potentially debilitating patterns of achievement goals that energize perfectionistic striving. These patterns impart a particular narrow meaning to success and failure and thus provide little scope for error and the avoidance of failure. Within the perfectionism literature scant attention has been devoted to the motivational processes underpinning perfectionistic achievement striving, although considerable speculation focuses on why an individual may feel compelled to pursue excessively demanding goals (Hewitt & Flett, 1991; Flett & Hewitt, 2006; Slade & Owens, 1998, Owens & Slade, 2008). Clearly, however, contemporary theories of achievement motivation may help to provide much needed insight into the motivational processes that are thought to underpin variations in goal pursuit. For example, it has been argued that when perfectionism is considered to reflect an adaptive form of achievement behavior, striving will be underpinned by a pattern of approach motives (Stoeber, Stoll, et al., 2008). In contrast, it is believed that when perfectionism incorporates a harsh, self-critical style, it will be regulated by a combination of approach and avoidance tendencies and will be governed largely by fear of failure (Flett & Hewitt, 2006; Hall, 2006; Hewitt & Flett, 1991; Hewitt, Flett, Besser, Sherry, McGee, 2003). For those who exhibit this latter form of perfectionism, the primary reason for striving hard to reach exceedingly high standards is to avoid any judgment of failure, incompetence, or inadequacy.

In educational contexts Covington and colleagues (Covington, 1992; Covington & Mueller, 2001) have referred to those who exhibit strong approach and avoidance tendencies as overstrivers. This term describes an extreme way of thinking whereby individuals appear simultaneously attracted to and repelled by thoughts about achievement. That is, they are motivated by a combination of hope that they can meet their exceedingly high standards and constant worry about the consequences of failing. It is easy to see how this particular combination of approach and avoidance motives might underpin perfectionism in sport. This pattern of motives elicits not only a strong desire to demonstrate ability but also an equally strong desire to avoid failure. With this mind-set, the act of striving may lead to positive outcomes, but it will provide only temporary respite from the potentially aversive consequences of failure. Regardless of accomplishment, satisfaction will tend to be fleeting because self-worth can be maintained only through sustained achievement. Therefore, self-imposed demands to avoid failure will remain unyielding (Hall et al., 1998; Hall, 2006; Hill, Hall, & Appleton, 2010). Although various authors have demonstrated that fear of failure is a key motivational mechanism underlying self-critical forms of perfectionism in sport (Conroy, Willow, & Metzler, 2002; Conroy, Kaye, & Fifer, 2007; Kaye, Conroy, & Fifer, 2008; Sagar & Stoeber, 2009), a combination of both approach and avoidance goals appears to regulate the achievement striving of those who exhibit perfectionism in its broadest sense. The strategy to pursue perfection as a means of failure avoidance seems, therefore, to be reflective of those who demonstrate both a strong commitment to excellence and a belief that self-worth can be established only through achievement.

A number of studies have attempted to explore the degree to which perfectionism in athletes is underpinned by distinct motivational patterns. Based on Covington's (1992) conceptualization, Hall, Kerr, and Matthews (1998) hypothesized that dimensions of perfectionism measured on Frost's MPS would be associated with a combination of high task and high ego orientations. They believed that athletes' exhibiting elevated scores on all dimensions of perfectionism would give meaning to achievement by endorsing a combination of goals whereby competence could be evaluated through both personal improvement and the demonstration of ability. Hall et al. (1998) found that a combination of perfectionism dimensions, including high personal standards, concern over mistakes, doubts about action, parental criticism, and parental expectancies, was positively associated with a combination of high ego and moderate task goals, thereby providing support for their hypothesis. Hall et al. (1998) concluded that even in combination with a strong task orientation, a potent ego orientation may provide the motivational foundation for perfectionistic striving because it heightens self-awareness and encourages a preoccupation with self-validation (Duda & Hall, 2001).

A more recent study by Dunn, Causgrove Dunn, and Syrotuik (2002) sought to extend the work of Hall et al. through the use of a modified version of Frost's MPS. Their findings were in partial agreement with those of Hall et al. and suggested that rather than a constellation of task and ego goals underpinning perfectionism, only a strong ego orientation was associated with a combination of high personal standards, concern about mistakes, and perceived coach and parental pressure. Dunn et al. (2002) did not find that a task orientation was positively related to a combination of perfectionism dimensions. Instead, they found that a task orientation by itself was positively associated with a combination of high personal standards and negatively related with all other dimensions of perfectionism. This finding seems to confirm that when individuals focus on the pursuit of high standards, are not worried about making mistakes, and perceive no pressure from external sources, their achievement striving exhibits an adaptive motivational pattern, not one that necessarily reflects perfectionism.

Although the previous studies measured perfectionism using Frost's MPS, Appleton, Hall, and Hill (2009) recently examined whether patterns of task and ego goals underpinned self-oriented and socially prescribed perfectionism. Appleton et al. (2009) found evidence that both task and ego goals were associated with self-oriented perfectionism but that neither goal was related to socially prescribed perfectionism. Although unexpected, these findings are not dissimilar from those reported by Flett and Hewitt (2006). Flett and Hewitt explain that although self-oriented perfectionism tends to be associated with a combination of approach and avoidance tendencies, socially prescribed perfectionism is largely underpinned by failure avoidance. Using the findings from Appleton and colleagues' study, we might speculate that self-oriented perfectionism is characterized by overstriving. In contrast, failure avoidance rather than overstriving may be responsible for regulating achievement striving in athletes high in socially prescribed perfectionism. Unfortunately, testing this hypothesis by using a dichotomous goal framework is not possible because this conceptualization of achievement goals does not permit discrimination between approach and avoidance tendencies.

Because most previous investigations had concentrated on testing the relationship between perfectionism and dichotomous goals, Stoeber, Stoll, Pescheck, and Otto (2008) sought to examine whether perfectionism was related to a combination of approach and avoidance goals. They first adopted a trichotomous goal framework (Elliot & Harackiewicz, 1996) and then subsequently a two-by-two goal framework whereby achievement goals could be clearly differentiated into approach or avoidance motives (Elliot, 2005; Elliot & McGregor, 2001). In one study with high school athletes, Stoeber, Stoll, et al. (2008) found that an adaptive dimension of perfectionism, which they labeled striving for perfection, was positively related to both mastery and performance approach goals. A second, self-critical dimension of perfectionism, labeled negative reactions to imperfection, was found to be positively associated with a combination of performance approach and avoidance goals and negatively related to mastery goals. In a follow-up study with sport science students, Stoeber, Stoll, et al. (2008) reported that striving for perfection was again positively related to mastery and performance approach goals, whereas negative reactions to imperfection were related to a combination of mastery avoidance, performance approach, and performance avoidance goals.

The findings from these two studies confirm that a self-critical form of perfectionism appears to be regulated by failure avoidance and worries about not living up to expectations. Moreover, this form of perfectionism appears to be further regulated by a strong desire to demonstrate ability and gain the approval of others, thereby providing support for the notion of overstriving in sport. Conversely, striving for perfection, which comprises none of the self-critical elements of perfectionism, appears to be largely synonymous with adaptive achievement striving. This idea becomes even more apparent when the shared variance with negative reactions to imperfection is removed. After controlling for shared variance, Stoeber, Stoll, et al. (2008) found that the association between negative reactions to imperfection and performance approach goals was significantly reduced, leaving mastery approach goals to account for the largest proportion of variance in striving for perfection.

Although the findings support a view that the act of striving for perfection is largely adaptive, we might question whether this behavior is genuinely indicative of perfectionism because many of the core characteristics of the perfectionism disposition are absent. Similarly, when Campbell and Di Paula (2002) attempted to disaggregate Hewitt and Flett's (1991) Multidimensional Perfectionism Scale, they found that striving for perfection, a component of self-oriented perfectionism, was associated with conscientiousness and did not contribute to adjustment difficulties. But they found that the desire to be perfect was the component of self-oriented perfectionism that was associated with debilitation. Campell and Di Paula (2002) argued that when the primary concerns of the individual are with achieving success rather than avoiding failure, the act of striving for perfection is not likely to be debilitating. Only when failure avoidance becomes the primary motive does striving for perfection become problematic and lead to adjustment problems. Similarly, it may be ill advised to consider that either striving for perfection or negative reactions to imperfection will independently reflect the core characteristics of perfectionism. Both are rather narrow components of a broader construct, so avoiding their disaggregation would make better conceptual sense.

Considering that Stoeber and colleagues' (Stoeber, Stoll, et al., 2008) findings were largely exploratory and took into account only two dimensions of perfectionism, Stoeber, Uphill, et al. (2009) conducted a follow-up study that examined whether this same pattern would hold up when additional dimensions of perfectionism were considered. Stoeber, Uphill, et al. (2009) constructed composite measures of perfectionistic striving by combining measures of personal standards and striving for perfection. They also constructed a composite measure of perfectionistic concerns by combining the concern about mistakes and negative reactions to imperfection subscales. Subsequent structural equation modeling indicated that the composite measure of perfectionistic striving was associated with a seemingly adaptive pattern of mastery and performance approach goals. In contrast, the measure of perfectionistic concerns was unrelated to mastery approach goals but positively associated with a combination of performance approach goals and mastery and performance avoidance goals.

Stoeber, Uphill, et al. (2009) claimed that the findings provide support for Slade and Owens' (1998) dual-process model that considers perfectionism to be either positively or negatively reinforced by the individual's approach or avoidance behavior. They found that perfectionistic striving was underpinned by a pattern of approach goals, whereas both approach and avoidance goals regulated the achievement striving of those with perfectionistic concerns. But one must be cautious in concluding support for a dual-process model when the shared variance between the two different forms of perfectionism is almost 48%. Because of this overlap, it is not possible to ascertain whether distinct regulatory patterns underpin striving for perfection and negative reactions to imperfection that act positively or negatively to reinforce perfectionistic behavior. Furthermore, when bivariate correlations indicate that all dimensions of perfectionism are positively associated with all two-by-two goal forms, a strong case can be made that multidimensional perfectionism is associated with a constellation of both approach and avoidance goals and that Covington's notion of overstriving remains a distinct possibility.

Some further empirical evidence to support Covington's (1992) notion of overstriving has been reported in two recent studies. Hall, Hill, and Appleton (2009) found that self-oriented perfectionism was positively associated with mastery and performance approach goals, as well as performance avoidance goals in junior elite swimmers. More recently, in a study of junior elite athletes, Hall, Hill & Jowett (2010) found that self-oriented perfectionism was positively associated with a combination of mastery approach and avoidance goals, as well as with performance approach and avoidance goals. In contrast, socially prescribed perfectionism was positively associated with a combination of performance approach goals, as well as mastery and performance avoidance goals.

In considering the research conducted to date on this issue, the evidence indicates that when perfectionism is considered to involve more than striving to achieve high standards and incorporates a self-critical style, striving to achieve is regulated by a pattern of goals that reflects a combination of approach and avoidance tendencies that resembles overstriving. In contrast, when measures of perfectionism are disaggregated, individual components such as striving for perfection and pursuing high personal standards may appear broadly adaptive because the primary motive with which they are associated is to approach success. Our view, however, is that athletes whose behavior is regulated by this adaptive pattern of achievement striving and who eschew failure avoidance goals do not exhibit the core characteristics of perfectionism.

Perfectionism and Anxiety

One of the fundamental characteristics of perfectionism is that it induces worry. In meaningful achievement contexts where self-worth is threatened, worry manifests as elevated state anxiety (Flett, Hewitt, Endler, & Tassone, 1995; Frost & Marten, 1990). A number of empirical studies have examined the degree to which perfectionism influences achievement-related anxiety in sport. Although some studies have examined how separate dimensions of perfectionism are associated with anxiety, most of these studies have considered perfectionism in its widest multidimensional form. One of the first studies to examine the relationship between perfectionism and anxiety in athletes was undertaken by Frost and Henderson (1991). Using Frost's multidimensional scale, they found that overall perfectionism, incorporating a composite measure of all 35 items, was associated with elevated levels of trait anxiety. This initial finding confirms that perfectionism may predispose athletes to experience anxiety in competitive situations because these individuals perceive most sporting environments to be high in evaluative threat.

Basing their hypotheses on a theoretical approach to emotion forwarded by Lazarus and Folkman (1984) and Smith's (1986) model of sport performance anxiety, Hall, Kerr, and Matthews (1998) proposed that perfectionism would be a critical antecedent of state anxiety in young distance runners. They argued that perfectionism gave meaning to the appraisal of achievement information and that those unable to employ adequate coping strategies would experience elevated state anxiety. They found that overall perfectionism predicted cognitive anxiety at regular intervals in the lead-up to a competitive event and that concern over mistakes and doubts about action were critical dimensions that contributed to heightened anxiety.

In a novel study that examined various perfectionism profiles exhibited by athletes, Koivula, Hassmen, and Fallby (2002) found that a group of athletes who were high in personal standards, in concern about mistakes, and in doubts about action reported greater levels of cognitive anxiety than a group who were high in personal standards and low in both concern about mistakes and doubts about action, as well those who were low on all three dimensions of perfectionism. The only group that reported higher levels of cognitive anxiety than this group was athletes who were low on the personal standards dimension and high on both concern about mistakes and doubts about action. The findings of Koivula et al. provide further evidence that when high standards and self-critical forms of perfectionism are considered together, the outcomes are potentially debilitating.

Because they believe that some forms of perfectionism can be motivationally adaptive, Stoeber, Otto, Pescheck, Becker, and Stoll (2007) have attempted to counter claims that perfectionism is an inherently debilitating characteristic. They assert that perfectionism does not automatically predispose athletes to experience anxiety, and they explain that when perfectionism is differentiated into adaptive and maladaptive components, only in its maladaptive form does perfectionism demonstrate a positive association with competitive anxiety. They further suggest that athletes who simply strive for perfection are unlikely to experience anxiety. In an empirical test of their assertions, Stoeber et al. (2007) measured overall perfectionism, striving for perfection, negative reactions to imperfection, and state anxiety in four samples of athletes. Although their findings revealed that overall perfectionism was positively associated with cognitive and somatic anxiety in all samples, disaggregation of the perfectionism scales suggested that only negative reactions to imperfection were responsible for a positive association with competitive state anxiety. Calculating partial correlations to remove shared variance between perfectionism dimensions further revealed that striving for perfection had a negative association with cognitive and somatic anxiety. Stoeber at al. argued that these findings provide support for the idea that perfectionism is not inherently maladaptive and that it may even be considered adaptive if negative reactions to imperfection can be managed.

An alternative perspective on Stoeber and colleagues' findings is that the act of striving for perfection reflects little more than a person's aspirations and an indication of goal-directed behavior. Disaggregating this facet of perfectionism from other self-critical components removes any reference to the cognitive processes that inform the appraisal of achievement information. Because it is not possible to capture these processes in the measurement of the perfectionism construct, there is no conceptual reason for the act of striving for perfection to be systematically associated with achievement-related anxiety or any other emotion. Therefore, the more appropriate conclusion may be that the lack of association between striving for perfection and competitive anxiety reflects the absence of any systematic pattern in the data rather than striving for perfection being an adaptive quality that does not engender achievement anxiety in athletes.

To overcome this limitation, we believe that striving for perfection must be considered in conjunction with negative reactions to imperfection and other self-critical dimensions of perfectionism. The negative reaction to imperfection subscale is the one that reflects the consequences of a cognitive appraisal process in which existential threat is a common outcome. It therefore provides insight into whether striving for perfection will be anxiety producing. When striving for perfection is accompanied by negative self-evaluation, a sense of personal inadequacy, and self-doubt, threat to self-worth will be appraised and achievement anxiety will become elevated. Without negative self-appraisal, perceived threats to self will be unlikely and emotional responses that are more positive will be observed.

Perfectionism and Anger

A further potentially debilitating emotion that has been found to be associated with perfectionism in sport is anger. In the same way that perfectionism is a critical antecedent of anxiety, it may predispose athletes to exhibit anger because it heightens vulnerability to stress and increases the degree to which stressors are considered aversive (Hewitt, Caelian, Flett, Sherry, Collins, & Flynn, 2002). Anger is thought to result when an action has been appraised as unjust, unfair, or demeaning (Averill, 1982; Deffenbacher, 1999; Lazarus, 1991). Thus, in sport, perfectionism may contribute to an elevated sense of injustice or a perception that an outcome is personally demeaning when goals are blocked, failure is perceived, or contingent reinforcement is not forthcoming. Moreover, because perfectionists believe that they should achieve flawlessness, anger may be directed inward because of self-blame (Hamachek,

1978; Horney, 1950) or outward because others are blamed for thwarting goal achievement (Burns, 1980; Hamachek, 1978). A small body of research in social psychology has reported evidence to support the notion that perfectionism may predispose individuals to experience both trait and state anger (Dunkley & Blankstein, 2000; Hewitt & Flett, 1991; Hewitt, Caelian, Flett, Sherry, Collins, & Flynn, 2002; Saboonchi & Lundh, 2003). Recently, research has also begun to explore this association in sporting contexts.

In a sample of Canadian football players, Dunn, Gotwals, Causgrove Dunn, and Syrotuik (2006) found that a combination of high personal standards, concern over mistakes, and perceived coach pressure was associated with two dimensions of trait anger (Spielberger, 1999). These included the disposition to experience anger without provocation and angry feelings that involve frustration and negative evaluations. Clearly, the characteristic pursuit of high standards in combination with a self-critical style and perceived pressure to excel from the coaching staff may underpin a general disposition toward anger, and this tendency might lead to angry outbursts in competitive contexts. Dunn et al. (2006) confirmed this, finding that the same perfectionism dimensions were associated with a combination of angry reactions to mistakes. Thus, the harsh, self-critical tendencies in perfectionists appear to manifest in state anger when mistakes occur. Although some degree of state anger may have an energizing effect for athletes (Lazarus, 1991), it is equally likely to undermine task-focused attention and interfere with sport performance (Abrams & Hale, 2005; Botterill & Brown, 2002; Nideffer, 1989), promote aggressive behavior (Isberg, 2000) and lead to interpersonal conflict (Hall, Hill, & Appleton, 2009).

A follow-up study by Vallance, Dunn, and Causgrove Dunn (2006) again found that trait anger in youth ice hockey players was underpinned by a combination of high personal standards, concern over mistakes, perceived coach pressure, and perceived parental pressure. Furthermore, when Vallance et al. (2006) examined clusters of athletes who had been identified as high, moderate, or low in perfectionism, those who were high in personal standards, concern about mistakes, perceived coach pressure, and perceived parental pressure expressed the highest levels of anger irrespective of the criticality of the situation that they were facing.

A more recent study by Hall, Hill, Appleton, and Ariano (2009) examined whether a similar relationship between perfectionism and anger would be identified when self-oriented, socially prescribed, and other-oriented perfectionism were used. Previous work by Hewitt et al. (2002) indicated that children who perceive that others have exceedingly high expectations of them often respond to these pressures with externally directed expressions of anger and hostility. As in previous sporting studies (Dunn et al., 2006; Vallance et al., 2006), Hall et al. found that a combination of all three dimensions of perfectionism was positively associated with trait anger. Moreover, the combined measures of perfectionism were associated with feeling angry and verbally expressing anger when athletes made mistakes.

Because any outward expression of anger resulting from perfectionism may have a detrimental effect on interpersonal relationships (Hill, Zrull, & Turlington, 1997), Hall, Hill, et al. (2009) further examined whether multidimensional perfectionism was associated with feelings of displaced aggression toward other athletes. Displaced aggression (Denson, Pederson, & Miller, 2006) is a construct that comprises three subdimensions. These have been labeled anger rumination, revenge planning, and displaced aggression. Anger rumination reflects a cognitive preoccupation with the events that caused an individual to feel angry. Revenge planning involves thoughts about how to get back at those who are perceived to be the source of some demeaning offense, and displaced aggression reflects the venting of anger toward others who may not be the cause of the emotion. Hall et al. found that only socially prescribed perfectionism was positively associated with the three dimensions of displaced aggression. A combination of fear of failure, a perception that one must meet the standards of others to gain recognition, and a perceived lack of control over outcomes may be responsible for this relationship. This combination may not only precipitate feelings of rivalry but also generate feelings of interpersonal hostility toward others who may have little to do with circumstances that give rise to the emotion. These feelings may be heightened by the influence that socially prescribed perfectionism has on the appraisal of achievement information so that undesirable sporting outcomes are seen to be unjust or personally demeaning. In sum, the results from this small but emerging body of research add further weight to the suggestion that perfectionism underpins negative emotions in sport.

Perfectionism and Burnout

Because perfectionism carries the potential to underpin chronic debilitating effects in sport, research has recently begun to explore the relationship between perfectionism and athlete burnout (e.g. Appleton, Hall, & Hill, 2009; Hill, Hall, Appleton, & Kozub, 2008; Lemyre, Hall, & Roberts, 2008). It has been argued that perfectionism may be a critical antecedent of burnout because it confers specific meaning to the appraisal of achievement information (Hall, 2006; Hall, Kerr, & Cawthra, 1997; Lemyre et al., 2008) and leads to a process whereby athletes feel entrapped (Raedeke, 1997; Schmidt & Stein, 1991). Although perfectionism may energize heightened achievement striving and lead to recognized accomplishment, personal improvement, and tangible sporting success in the short term, over time the self-critical style used to appraise achievement information means that perfectionistic standards are rarely achieved and performance satisfaction is intermittent at best. For most people, continued disaffection resulting from achievement striving may cause sporting attrition. For many perfectionists, however, dropping out to protect self-worth is not a viable option. Those overstrivers who are serious about their sport and have reached a high standard will have invested considerable resources to reach their current status. Moreover, because identity and self-worth are often inextricably linked with achievement for these individuals, they cannot easily extricate themselves from the sporting context without seriously undermining their own self-definition (Appleton et al., 2009; Hall, 2006; Hall, Kerr, & Matthews, 1998; Hill, Hall, Appleton, & Murray, 2010). Consequently, the burden of obligation to maintain investment ultimately precipitates a sense of emotional exhaustion, a perception of reduced accomplishment, and an eventual devaluation of the sport. The perfectionistic athlete experiences a growing aversion to sport as a direct consequence of sustaining this pattern of achievement striving.

Recognizing this process, Gould (1996) suggested that burnout might be viewed as "motivation gone awry." He argued that burned-out athletes begin their sporting careers striving to achieve and tend to demonstrate a seemingly adaptive pattern of achievement-related cognition, affect, and behavior as they develop and experience relative success. But he argued that athletes' motivation may become increasingly maladaptive later in their careers because of chronic stress. Believing that perfectionism could be a cause of this stress, Gould and his colleagues (Gould, Udry, Tuffey, & Loehr, 1996; Gould, Tuffey, Udry, & Loehr, 1996) compared a group of active junior elite tennis players to a group of burned-out former players to try to determine whether perfectionism was an important discriminating characteristic. They found that burned-out players reported higher scores on a number of perfectionism dimensions. Specifically, these former athletes were higher in concern about mistakes, parental expectations, and parental pressure. Although they reported being lower on the high personal standards dimension than players who remained active, the burned-out players still reported pursuing high standards.

The notion that various dimensions of perfectionism give rise to athlete burnout informed subsequent research by Lemyre, Hall, and Roberts (2008). They measured multidimensional perfectionism, achievement goals, and the perceived motivational climate in a sample of Norwegian elite winter sport athletes at the beginning of a season and athlete burnout at season's end. Cluster analysis of the predictor variables was used to create two athlete profiles. A maladaptive motivational profile reflected individuals who were higher in all dimensions of perfectionism, questioned their ability, had low task goals and high ego goals, and perceived their training environment as being strongly performance oriented. Athletes with this motivational profile scored significantly higher on burnout dimensions at season's end than athletes whose motivational profile appeared more adaptive.

We might speculate that the self-critical nature of these perfectionistic athletes renders them vulnerable to burnout. Repeated exposure of perfectionists to a performance climate not only gives rise to self-focused attention but also ensures that the establishment and maintenance of self-worth through athletic performance remains a salient concern. It has been demonstrated that contingent self-worth is a feature of self-critical forms of perfectionism (e.g., Flett, Besser, Davis, & Hewitt; 2003; Stoeber, Kempe, & Keogh, 2008; Sturman,

Flett, Hewitt, & Rudolph, 2009), and it is likely that as perfectionistic athletes strive to achieve in sport, their self-worth is gradually eroded by a perceived failure to meet personal standards or the expectations of others. This process leads athletes who exhibit perfectionistic qualities to experience burnout.

Hill, Hall, Appleton, and Kozub (2008) set out to explore this line of reasoning. They examined whether contingent self-worth mediated the relationship between dimensions of perfectionism and burnout in a group of elite junior football players. Structural equation modeling revealed that unconditional self-acceptance partially mediated the relationship between multidimensional perfectionism and burnout, suggesting that when self-worth is contingent on achievement, both self-oriented and socially prescribed perfectionism may give rise to burnout. The findings also suggest that when self-worth is not perceived to be contingent on achievement, self-oriented perfectionism may be motivationally benign and or even have constructive consequences. But because self-oriented perfectionism and perceived goal progress were positively correlated, any debilitating effects of self-oriented perfectionism may be masked until athletes experience a systematic struggle with goal achievement.

This evidence from the research by Lemyre et al. (2008) and Hill et al. (2008) has highlighted that particular forms of perfectionism may engender a need for some athletes to repeatedly validate a sense of self through their achievements. Moreover, this pattern of striving may prevent athletes from extricating themselves from the sporting environment when the perceived demands of practice and performance become a source of chronic stress. Dykman (1998) has claimed that the pursuit of self-validation might reflect an active vulnerability factor that underpins motivational difficulties because achievement striving is constantly focused on proving basic worth, competence, or likability. For those focused on validation seeking, self-critical forms of perfectionism will increase the likelihood of perceived failure. Consequently, attempts to validate a sense of self will be undermined, making burnout an inevitable consequence of this process. Using this conceptual reasoning, Hill, Hall, Appleton, and Murray (2010) tested whether both validation seeking and growth seeking had a mediating effect on the relationship between multidimensional forms of perfectionism and athlete burnout. The principal finding from a structural equation model was conceptually consistent with the theoretical premises being tested. The model revealed that validation seeking partially mediated the relationship between socially prescribed perfectionism and burnout. This finding suggests that the failure to fulfill a desire for basic worth, competence, or likability will lead athletes who are high in socially prescribed perfectionism to experience symptoms of burnout.

The same psychological processes that influence patterns of achievement striving may affect the adoption of distinct coping strategies in those who exhibit self-oriented and socially prescribed perfectionism (Hill, Hall, & Appleton, 2010). Thus, coping strategies may be viewed as important mediators of the relationship between perfectionism and burnout. Based on research by

Dunkley and colleagues (Dunkley & Blankstein, 2000; Dunkley, Blankstein, Halsall, Williams, & Winkworth, 2000; Dunkley, Zuroff, & Blankstein, 2003), Hill, Hall, and Appleton (2010) hypothesized that socially prescribed perfectionism would be associated with coping strategies that attempt to avoid sources of stress. In contrast, self-oriented perfectionism would be associated with coping strategies that attempt to confront and remove those sources. Hewitt and Flett (1991) earlier argued that such differential patterns of coping emanate from the source and level of perceived control that is associated with different forms of perfectionism. That is, because those high in socially prescribed perfectionism believe that control over achievement lies with others, the use of problem-focused coping strategies that implement personal control is unlikely. Problem-focused strategies are perceived to be ineffective and may simply heighten the threat when athletes reengage with the source of stress (Dunkley et al., 2003; Hill et al., 2010). The use of avoidance strategies is likely to have an immediate effect in reducing the source of stress for those high in socially prescribed perfectionism. But because these strategies will not remove the underlying source of the stress or the belief that achievement is necessary to validate self-worth, burnout is likely when athletes choose to cope in this manner.

Hill et al. (2010) found support for this perspective in a sample of elite junior athletes from a variety of sports. As predicted, avoidance coping was found to mediate the relationship between socially prescribed perfectionism and athlete burnout, and both problem-focused coping and avoidance coping mediated the relationship between self-oriented perfectionism and burnout. But a tendency to spurn avoidance coping contributed more to the inverse relationship between self-oriented perfectionism and burnout than did the use of problem-focused coping.

Moderation of the Perfectionism–Burnout Relationship

Not all athletes characterized by self-critical forms of perfectionism will experience debilitating outcomes. Flett and Hewitt (2005) argued that the perils of perfectionism may be moderated by other important qualities of character or features of the environment. Appleton, Hall, and Hill (2009) considered that some degree of protection against athlete burnout may be achieved by endorsing high-task and low-ego goals and by the experience of high perceived goal satisfaction. But in a sample of elite sport participants, they found no evidence to suggest that athletes' achievement goals moderated the effects of self-oriented or socially prescribed perfectionism on burnout. Further analysis indicated that regardless of the form of perfectionism, greater perceptions of athlete and coach satisfaction with goal progress were associated with lower levels of burnout in the form of reduced accomplishment. The fact that goals did not emerge as moderators of the perfectionism–burnout relationship might be explained by the fact that different patterns of achievement goals are inextricably tied to various forms of perfectionism, as suggested earlier, and are therefore unlikely to moderate its debilitating qualities. Other goal-related variables, however, may act as key moderators. One of these is the perceived achievement climate. When coaches promote a strong mastery environment and eschew a performance climate, the environment may be perceived as less threatening by those high in self-critical forms of perfectionism (Flett, Hewitt, Endler, & Tassone, 1995; Frost & Marten, 1990). Consequently, the achievement climate may act to moderate any potentially debilitating effects that perfectionism might have.

Appleton, Hall, and Hill (2006) discovered some support for this hypothesis with a sample of junior elite cricketers. First, they found that socially prescribed perfectionism was associated with all three dimensions of burnout, whereas self-oriented perfectionism was inversely related to reduced accomplishment and devaluation of the activity. Moreover, they found that higher perceptions of a performance climate and lower perceptions of a mastery climate were associated with higher reported burnout scores. Finally, in support of moderation, they found that when socially prescribed perfectionism was high and the performance climate was perceived to be low, athletes scored lower on sport devaluation. Because numerous studies have shown that socially prescribed perfectionism has greater potential to cause debilitation, the finding that the achievement climate can help to moderate its debilitating effects is important. Although it might be argued that self-oriented perfectionism does not appear to hold the same potential for debilitation and subsequent athlete burnout, Appleton and colleagues' findings revealed that self-oriented perfectionism was associated with perceived satisfaction regarding goal progress. Clearly, it would be interesting to discover how self-oriented perfectionism influences athletes when they begin to experience repeated failure or encounter difficulties that lead to dissatisfaction with goal progress.

Some evidence of this emerged in a qualitative investigation by Gustaffson, Hassmen, Kentta, and Johansson (2008). They describe the burnout experience of 10 former elite Swedish athletes who had left their sports because of burnout. Most of these athletes described themselves as exhibiting debilitating characteristics of perfectionism, endorsing a strong ego orientation, and having a narrowly defined identity whereby they could establish self-worth only through accomplishment. Toward the latter stages of their careers, these athletes felt entrapped by their level of investment, by perceived social constraints, and by inflexible sporting organizations. But psychological process variables appeared to contribute significantly to a change in motivation and an increase in burnout over the course of a career. Although they experienced initial success and felt self-determined because their competence needs were being fulfilled, these athletes began to experience negative affect, frustration, and irritability associated with their perceived failure to demonstrate requisite ability, as well as significant worry about inadequate performance. They were also striving to achieve in an environment where they perceived excessive performance demands from coaches, low autonomy support, and little social support, and they commonly exhibited avoidance coping strategies when faced with challenge. Collectively, these factors contributed to the onset of burnout. We might speculate, however, that perfectionism provided the overarching framework that underpinned the debilitating pattern of cognition, affect, and behavior that over time led to these athletes' decision to quit their sport.

Perfectionism and Exercise Dependence

The research reviewed earlier demonstrates that self-critical forms of perfectionism contribute to patterns of achievement behavior that may not only heighten perceptions of entrapment but also foster an obligation to maintain investment in sport despite the chronic disaffection that it brings. Perfectionism may also have an influential effect on exercise behavior and cause people to experience other debilitative motivational patterns. One of the first to examine this notion was Coen and Ogles (1993), who tested whether a sample of marathon runners who had been categorized as either high or low in obligatory exercise behavior differed in perfectionism. They found that obligatory exercisers were higher than nonobligatory exercisers on personal standards, concern about mistakes, doubts about action, and organization. Although they argued that perfectionistic qualities did not seem to cause impairment in this sample of marathon runners, Coen and Ogles noted that the obligatory athletes exhibited some of the characteristic symptoms of exercise dependence. These indications included feeling compelled to run, experiencing anxiety when prevented from running, and continually pushing to achieve greater personal goals. Research by Hagan and Hausenblas (2003) more recently provided empirical evidence to support Coen and Ogles' observations, and this evidence has linked perfectionism directly to exercise dependence. They found that in a group of university students, those exhibiting strong symptoms of exercise dependence were significantly higher in overall perfectionism than those who were low in exercise dependence. In a follow-up study, Symons Downs, Hausenblas, and Nigg (2004) demonstrated that students "at risk" of experiencing exercise dependence scored significantly higher in concern about mistakes, personal standards, and doubts about action than did those who were nondependent and asymptomatic.

Although these early studies implicated perfectionism as one possible antecedent of problematic exercise behavior, Hall, Kerr, Kozub, and Finnie (2007) were among the first to examine the degree to which these variables predicted obligatory exercise. They found that a combination of task and ego goals, high perceived ability, high personal standards, and concerns about mistakes accounted for 31% of the variance in obligatory exercise. The dimensions of perfectionism had the strongest predictive influence. These findings provide further evidence that the pursuit of high personal standards may not be an adaptive strategy when it is accompanied by self-critical tendencies.

A more recent study by Hall, Hill, Appleton, & Kozub (2009) has demonstrated that although both socially prescribed and self-oriented forms of perfectionism are important antecedents of exercise dependence, the association may be a function of different psychological processes. Hall, Hill, et al. (2009) found that in a sample of recreational distance runners both forms of perfectionism were indirectly associated with exercise dependence through their effects on unconditional self-acceptance and labile self-esteem. But only self-oriented perfectionism exhibited a direct relationship with exercise dependence. Using these findings, Hall et al. (2009) argued that when exercise is considered an important domain in which to establish self-worth, both self-oriented and socially prescribed perfectionism may elevate the risk for dependence because individuals feel obligated to exercise to validate self-worth. Fluctuations in self-esteem may also occur when people perceive that they are failing to reach desired standards. This circumstance may influence exercise dependence because individuals find it difficult to revise goals or disengage from an activity that brings about self-validation, even when the action appears to be dysfunctional. In explaining the direct relationship between self-oriented perfectionism and exercise dependence, Hall et al. speculated that disaffection with the outcomes of goal striving may have triggered compulsive bouts of exercise for those high in self-oriented perfectionism. But because successful accomplishment of desired standards is rarely achieved, heightened symptoms of exercise dependence may be the consequence.

A further study by Hall, Hill, and Appleton (2008), which extended this line of research, revealed that the relationships between self-oriented and socially prescribed perfectionism with exercise dependence were mediated by contingent self-worth and rumination. Hall et al. (2008) explained that because perfectionism encourages contingent self-worth, perceived failures lead to rumination, a process that increases the risk of exercise dependence. The findings offer support for claims made by Hausenblas and Symons Downs (2002) that exercise dependence may be a function of both maladaptive cognition and dysfunctional coping associated with perfectionism. The findings further highlight why it is particularly difficult for those high in perfectionism to disengage themselves from potentially debilitating contexts. Specifically, when achievement in exercise is inextricably tied to identity and self-worth, goal disengagement becomes difficult because doing so means rejecting the behaviors and strategies that may bring about self-validation (Pyszczynski & Greenberg, 1987). Clearly, the same psychological processes that contribute to potentially debilitating outcomes in sport manifest in exercise contexts and underpin exercise dependence.

Perfectionism and Athletic Performance

Although evidence suggests that broad self-critical forms of perfectionism contribute to a pattern of achievement-related cognition, affect, and behavior that may have detrimental effects on athletic performance, research on the relationship between perfectionism and sporting performance is in its infancy.

Conceptually, it follows that when athletes manage self-critical appraisal and are able to maintain the act of striving for perfection, perfectionism may have an indirect positive association with performance. This positive association occurs through the athletes' pursuit of high personal standards, the specific goals that they set, and the achievement goals that they endorse, which subsequently regulate the quality of motivation. This further governs the psychological and behavioral strategies that perfectionists adopt as they pursue desired outcomes. Clearly, because sport represents a meaningful context in which athletes can achieve, we would expect that perfectionism would have performance effects because of its motivational energizing qualities. Regardless of how achievement striving is regulated we might expect gains in performance when perfectionistic athletes are in the early stage of their athletic careers, when they are required to perform novel activities, or when they set fresh challenges for themselves. But the association between perfectionism and performance is not straightforward. Over time, we might expect self-critical processes to begin to undermine performance because characteristic dissatisfaction with anything less than flawlessness induces a debilitating pattern of cognition, leads to poor coping behaviors, and causes the use of inappropriate behavioral strategies. This process, although intended to protect self-worth, will ultimately undermine performance.

To date, the relationship between perfectionism and athletic performance has received little empirical attention. Only four studies have included performance as an outcome variable (Anshel & Mansouri, 2005; Hill, Hall, Duda, & Appleton, in press; Stoll, Lau, & Stoeber, 2008; Stoeber, Uphill, & Hotham, 2009). Although the findings from these studies have been mixed, they are conceptually consistent with motivational research in other contexts. For example, Stoeber, Uphill, and Hotham (2009) found that in two studies examining the influence of perfectionism on triathlete performance, only Frost's dimension of high personal standards had significant performance effects. As previously stated, this dimension appears compatible with adaptive achievement striving, and this assertion was confirmed by analyses that revealed that a performance approach–avoidance contrast mediated the relationship between personal standards and performance in both studies. Furthermore, in the second study the act of goal setting also mediated the relationship between performance approach goals and performance. In sum, the findings suggest that elite triathletes who strive to achieve high personal standards, demonstrate performance approach goals, and set themselves challenging goals for competition achieve superior performance. But because performance approach goals have been found to be underpinned by high ability (Harackiewicz, Barron, Elliot, Carter, & Lehto; 1997) the long-term performance effects of striving for perfection may not become clear until research has examined this association over time and under conditions in which athletes experience considerable challenge and difficulty.

One study that has attempted to look at the relationship between perfectionism and performance over time involved athletes who performed a novel basketball training task. Stoll, Lau, and Stoeber (2008) found that in a sample of student–athletes, striving for perfection was positively related to performance on multiple trial blocks. In contrast, negative reaction to mistakes was inversely associated with performance at the beginning of the task but was not in evidence on subsequent trials. We might speculate that for athletes who are experiencing self-critical forms of perfectionism, the performance of a novel task may be threatening, which could undermine initial performance. In the same study, Stoll et al. also found that when average task performance was considered, the largest performance increments were found in those athletes who exhibited the highest levels of both perfectionistic striving and negative reactions to mistakes. This finding suggests that on novel activities, perfectionism may have initial performance effects. But research needs to examine whether these effects can be maintained after athletes begin to experience prolonged dissatisfaction with performance or begin to experience repeated failure.

The experience of receiving failure information was tested by Anshel and Mansouri (2005), who examined how the interaction between dimensions of perfectionism and feedback conditions (negative versus control) affected performance. They found that, with the exception of the need for organization, all dimensions from Frost's MPS and total perfectionism led to performance deterioration on a simple motor task following the provision of negative feedback. Although it confirmed that perfectionism may undermine performance following aversive feedback, this research gave no indication about the psychological processes that are responsible for performance deterioration.

A recent study by Hill, Hall, Duda, & Appleton (in press) has attempted to examine these processes in a laboratory study using student–athletes. Hill et al. compared the cognitive, affective, and behavioral responses of athletes who reported higher and lower levels of self-oriented perfectionism after experiencing two successive manipulated failures on a cycling endurance task. The performance of all participants decreased significantly after the first failure, but no performance differences were found between those higher and lower in self-oriented perfectionism on the two experimental trials. Nor were differences found in terms of reported affect or thoughts of escape because of the two failures. But the analyses did indicate that following failure on the first trial, those higher in self-oriented perfectionism experienced a more pronounced increase in threat, reported significantly greater reduction in effort from the subsequent trial, and reported a decrease in satisfaction. Moreover, the effects on threat and effort remained statistically significant when controlling for differences between the two groups in level of socially prescribed perfectionism. Consequently, there is at least some indication that beyond the documented benefits of pursuing exceptionally high standards, perfectionism may have a number of negative psychological consequences that may act to undermine performance in some circumstances.

Note, however, that empirical evidence is currently insufficient to draw any firm conclusions about the effect of perfectionism on performance. We might speculate that because achievement striving and personal performance outcomes tend to carry irrational importance for perfectionists (Besser et al., 2004; Hewitt et al., 1989) and because failure is associated with a number of negative consequences that include shame and embarrassment (Conroy, Kaye, et al., 2007; Flett, Blankstein, Hewitt, & Koledin, 1992), performance contexts provide perfectionists with an interesting dilemma. Extremely high levels of effort are required to attain flawless standards so immediate performance improvements may occur. But by exerting effort, people may fail, thus exposing themselves to perceptions of inadequacy (Covington, 1992; Thompson, 1993). Consequently, perfectionists are more likely to use various defensive strategies to protect themselves from negative self-perceptions (Covington, 1992; Crocker & Park, 2004). Over time, these strategies are likely to lead to learning and performance deficits that may undermine the fulfillment of athletic potential (Crocker & Park, 2004; Kernis, 2003). Although little research in sport is available to draw on, some evidence outside sport suggests that this may be the case. For example, people higher in self-oriented perfectionism have been found to use self-handicapping behaviors when they perceive a lack of control over successful outcomes (Hobden & Pliner, 1995) and experience failure (Doebler, Schnick, Beck, & Astor-Stetson, 2000). Further empirical research of a longitudinal nature is clearly necessary to begin to test these contentions in sport.

Perfectionism and Psychological Well-Being in Sport Participants

One area in which little research has been done to date in sport concerns how perfectionism might affect the psychological well-being of athletes. Research in this area is required because high-profile examples such as Johnny Wilkinson and Victoria Pendleton have suggested that although perfectionism may have been the energizing force behind their unprecedented sporting achievements, they also experienced emotional turmoil because of their self-critical personality characteristics. From the research conducted to date, two studies have reported that self-critical dimensions of perfectionism are associated with lower self-esteem (Gotwals, Dunn, & Wayment, 2002) and higher, labile self-esteem (McArdle & Duda, 2008) in athletes. A further study by Gaudreau and Antl (2008) examined the process by which perfectionism might affect life satisfaction. They found that a self-critical form of perfectionism, labeled evaluative concerns perfectionism, was negatively related to life satisfaction. Moreover, this relationship was mediated by non-self-determined motivation, disengagement coping strategies, and perceived failure to achieve sporting goals. In contrast, perfectionism that included high personal standards and self-oriented perfectionism was unrelated to life satisfaction, but it appeared to encourage the use of self-determined forms of motivation and task-oriented coping, which resulted in strong perceptions of goal attainment. Gaudreau and

Antl (2008) suggested that because personal standards perfectionism included a measure of self-oriented perfectionism that is known to be underpinned by both approach and avoidance goals, it may be subject to antagonist mediation processes that both promote and thwart feelings of life satisfaction. Clearly, this area is an important one to explore to gain better understanding of the processes that lead to variations in psychological well-being in perfectionistic athletes.

Another area of research that sport psychologists should consider developing further concerns the influence that perfectionism might have on interpersonal relationships in sport. Habke and Flynn (2002) have proposed that intense self-focus is an important mechanism that may begin to undermine interpersonal relations. They suggest that perfectionists' preoccupation with their own achievement standards and their hypersensitivity toward criticism adversely affect their interpersonal relationships. These contentions have received some initial indirect confirmation in the social psychology literature (Blatt & Zuroff, 1992; Hill, Zrull, & Turlington, 1997; Hewitt & Flett, 1991; Flett, Hewitt, Blankstein, & Dynin; 1994; Nielson et al.; 1997). Taken together, the findings suggest that perfectionism may underpin the development of an aversive interpersonal style. This style may stimulate negative responses from those with whom perfectionists interact in the social environment and directly affect the appraisal of interpersonal interactions by perfectionistic individuals. To date, only one study has examined the influence of perfectionism on interpersonal relations in sporting contexts (Ommundsen, Roberts, Lemyre, & Miller, 2005). This research found that heightened perfectionism was associated with lower peer acceptance, poorer quality of peer relations, and greater conflict with friends who played on the same soccer team. In light of their findings, Ommundsen et al. proposed that examining the effects of perfectionism on interpersonal dynamics may be a productive avenue for future sport research.

Research Evidence Summary

The analysis provided in this review has concentrated largely on studies that examined perfectionism as a multidimensional construct and simultaneously considered various core dimensions. This body of research indicates that when considered in this manner, perfectionism does not appear to be either adaptive or healthy. Although perfectionism may lead to heightened achievement striving and bring about various positive outcomes, it also induces a psychological process that underpins potentially debilitating cognition, affect, and behavior that may undermine psychological well-being. It might therefore be argued that when perfectionism governs an athletes' achievement striving, performances will rarely be considered sufficient to meet exacting standards, and when the underlying cognitive processes give rise to a state of chronic disaffection, further sustained achievement striving is more likely to contribute to motivational debilitation than to a sense of performance excellence and accomplishment.

Practical Applications

In a formalized treatment setting, perfectionism has a reputation for being difficult to treat (e.g., Greenspon, 2008; Sorotzkin, 1998; Ramsey & Ramsey, 2002). Psychologists with counseling experience of perfectionism have identified a number of reasons this is the case. The beliefs that encapsulate perfectionism are deeply entrenched in one's sense of identity, so bringing about substantive structural change is difficult. In addition, because people often attribute successes to their commitment to perfection, they may be reluctant to relinquish their belief in its efficacy, despite any negative concomitants. Some psychologists have also argued that perfectionists may resist change because doing so requires them to acknowledge that their dedication to their domain of interest (e.g., sport, exercise, dance) and their achievements in that domain may reflect an unhealthy commitment to high standards rather than a genuine interest, love, or enthusiasm for the activity as an end in itself. Finally, some dimensions of perfectionism are thought to undermine the therapeutic process by engendering negative attitudes toward treatment (Ey, Henning, & Shaw, 2000; Oliver, Hart, Ross, & Katz, 2001) and corroding the therapeutic alliance required for effective treatment (Blatt, Zuroff, Hawley, & Auerbach, 2010).

The most common approach adopted in the treatment of perfectionism is cognitive-behavioral therapy (CBT). There is, however, currently some disagreement about the focus of this treatment when aimed at reducing perfectionism. Flett and Hewitt (2008) and Hewitt, Flett, Besser, Sherry, and McGee, 2003 argue that perfectionism should be treated as a multidimensional trait because it requires long-term treatment that addresses the need for perfection and a conditional sense of acceptance associated with its etiology. In other words, substantial structural change to beliefs embedded in the self-schema is required. In contrast, Shafran and colleagues (Riley, Lee, Cooper, Fairburn, & Shafran, 2007; Glover, Brown, Fairburn, & Shafran, 2007) have argued that when perfectionism is considered more narrowly as psychopathology that is maintained by maladaptive cognitions and behaviors rather than a personality trait, relatively shorter treatments focused on the mechanisms that sustain perfectionism (e.g., irrational self-evaluative processes) may also be effective.

Given the potential pathological consequences of higher levels of perfectionism, those responsible for safeguarding the welfare of athletes should be mindful of the level of the perfectionism reported by athletes. Norms are available for some measures of perfectionism (e.g., H-MPS, Hewitt & Flett, 2004; APS-R, Rice & Slaney, 2007). Although it is not yet clear whether the norms developed in community and clinical samples are applicable to athletes, they provide a point of comparison and guidance for referring athletes for counseling. Obviously, the role of coaches, parents, and other figures in the sport context is limited to helping athletes manage subclinical perfectionism and its negative consequences. But because those in this domain heavily influence and can change patterns of cognition and behavior exhibited by athletes, their role may be considerable.

To date, little research has examined variables that may ameliorate the aversive effects of perfectionism for athletes (e.g., Appleton et al., 2009; Dunn et al., 2002; Hall et al., 1998; Vallance, Courneya, Jones, & Reiman, 2006). Flett and Hewitt (2005) and others (e.g., Dunn et al., 2002; Hall et al., 1998) have speculated that a number of factors may provide resiliency to the perils of perfectionism for athletes. These include the adoption of adaptive strategies for dealing with excessive demands and setbacks, the development of heightened control beliefs, greater levels of task focus, and positive perceptions of meeting standards. Some of these possibilities are explored in the next section.

Perfectionism and Coping

One potential strategy for managing perfectionism is to teach athletes to become more adept at coping with the inevitable achievement difficulties that will arise when striving unremittingly for increasingly more difficult goals. For example, the promotion of problem-focused coping tendencies, as opposed to avoidance coping, may have a number of beneficial consequences. Hill, Hall, and Appleton (2010) have recently found that the relationship between self-oriented and socially prescribed dimensions of perfectionism and athlete burnout is mediated by coping tendencies so that dealing with achievement difficulties using problem-focused coping, and eschewing avoidant coping, may help to manage the potentially debilitating consequences of perfectionism. Gaudreau and Antl (2008) have also demonstrated similar findings with respect to goal attainment and life satisfaction reported by athletes. The consequences of problem-focused coping are likely to extend to other salutogenic outcomes such as positive emotional adjustment when dealing with stress (Dunkley, Zuroff, & Blankstein, 2003). Consequently, promoting problem-focused strategies when dealing with achievement difficulties may have a number of benefits for athletes who exhibit higher levels of perfectionism.

But for a number of reasons, coping tendencies may be unlikely to be an effective long-term strategy. In particular, there is mixed support for the moderating role of coping in the perfectionism–distress relationship. Some studies outside sport have found support for the moderating role of coping variables (e.g., O'Connor & O'Connor, 2003; Dunkley, Blankstein, Halsall, Williams, & Winkworth, 2000), whereas others have not (e.g., Rice & Lapsley, 2001; Blankstein, Lumley, & Crawford, 2007). Dunkley, Zuroff, and Blankstein (2003) have found evidence that suggests that problem-focused coping may be ineffective in mitigating stress when individuals exhibit higher levels of socially prescribed perfectionism. Differences in coping variables, however, do appear to distinguish dimensions of perfectionism. For example, self-oriented and socially prescribed perfectionism can be distinguished based on their relationship with variables associated with the coping process (e.g., problem-solving confidence, constructive thinking, learned resourcefulness; Flett, Hewitt, Blankstein, & O'Brien, 1991; Flett et al., 1996; Flett, Russo, & Hewitt, 1994), as well as coping strategies (Hewitt, Flett, & Endler, 1995). Similarly, Dunkley and colleagues (Dunkley & Blankstein, 2000; Dunkley,

Blankstein, et al., 2000; Dunkley, Sanislow, Grilo, & McGlashan, 2006; Dunkley, Zuroff, & Blankstein, 2003) have found that higher-order factors of perfectionism (evaluative concerns perfectionism and personal standards perfectionism) encourage different coping strategies (e.g., problem-focused versus avoidance) and that coping is an important partial mediator of the relationship between these dimensions of perfectionism and psychological distress (e.g., anxiety, negative affect, anger, and depression). Overall, further research appears to be needed to clarify the relationship between dimensions of perfectionism and coping in athletes before coping can be recommended as the basis for effective interventions to manage perfectionism in the sport domain.

Basic Psychological Skills Training

The management of perfectionism may be built in to the psychological skills training aimed at maximizing psychological performance. This training could include attempts to educate athletes about the difference between perfectionism and more adaptive achievement striving, as well as effective strategies for dealing with the negative cognition and affect that arise because of perfectionism. In an educational context some evidence suggests that basic cognitive restructuring can be effective when attempting to attenuate the immediate negative cognitions and emotions evoked by evaluative tasks. DiBartolo and colleagues (DiBartolo, Frost, Dixon, & Almodovar, 2001), for example, found that a short bout of cognitive restructuring focused on ameliorating the overestimation of the probability of negative events, decatastrophizing feared outcomes, and enhancing perceived coping efficacy reduced levels of anxiety and negative appraisals associated with a public speaking task. Kearns, Forbes, and Gardiner (2007) have also described cognitive behavioral coaching (CBC) that is specifically aimed at nonclinical populations. This coaching includes goal-setting exercises whereby individuals identify obstacles and patterns of behavior that may prevent the attainment of the goal, as well as the costs associated with the patterns identified. Basic psychological skills such as relaxation, mental rehearsal, and self-talk may also have the potential to moderate the perfectionism–distress relationship.

The use of effective goal setting is an especially intuitive strategy when considering the management of perfectionism. The benefits of flexible and optimally challenging goals are well documented. Many of the intervention strategies that have led to decreases in perfectionism outside sport have entailed large goal-setting components (e.g., Egan & Hine, 2008; Kearns, Forbes, & Gardiner, 2007; Kutlesa & Arthur, 2008). But it is noteworthy that empirical evidence suggests that striving for perfection is not in itself problematic, even when standards are perceived to be imposed by others (Campbell & Di Paula, 2002). In terms of goal setting, the focus should therefore be on goal flexibility and evaluation rather than on reducing standards. The negative reactions to mistakes and the meaning given to personal failure is what lead to difficulties for perfectionists. To address these issues, fundamental change to the beliefs associated with perfectionism is required.

Perfectionism, Achievement Goals, and the Achievement Climate

A number of sport psychologists have suggested that promoting task involvement and reducing ego involvement may ameliorate some of the negative consequences of perfectionism for athletes (Appleton et al., 2009; Dunn et al., 2002; Hall et al., 1998). Consequently, the promotion of a task orientation may be another means of managing perfectionism. Hall et al. (1998) and Appleton et al. (2009) have examined the possibility that dispositional achievement goals moderate the relationship between perfectionism and anxiety and burnout for athletes. To date, however, no support has been found for the moderating role of dispositional achievement goals. Rather, dispositional achievement goals appear to be relatively stable and defining characteristics of perfectionism. Achievement goals may therefore be better considered regulators of the achievement striving associated with perfectionism rather than moderating variables (Appleton et al., 2009)

It remains possible, and in fact may be likely, that perceptions of the achievement climate moderate the relationship between perfectionism and its negative consequences. The achievement climate is presumed to influence the immediate goal involvement adopted by athletes, and over time it may influence dispositional achievement goals (Ames, 1992c; Dweck & Leggett, 1988). Consequently, perceptions of the achievement climate may have the potential to promote task involvement directly, as well as indirectly, through their influence on dispositional achievement goals. In support of this possibility, empirical examination of the influence of perceptions of the achievement climate has found that the motivational climate moderates the relationship between dispositional achievement goals and achievement-related outcomes (e.g., Swain & Harwood, 1996; Treasure & Roberts, 1998; Newton & Duda, 1999) and contributes to achievement-related outcomes above the variance accounted for by dispositional goals (e.g., Seifriz, Duda, & Chi, 1992; Treasure & Roberts, 1998, 2001). In terms of perfectionism, as a short-term strategy, promoting a mastery climate may have the potential to temper any immediate negative consequences of perfectionism in achievement settings. In the long-term, manipulating the achievement climate to promote mastery goals may be a strategy for bringing about fundamental change by socializing more adaptive beliefs about the purpose of sport and the causes of success (Dunn et al., 2002; Hall et al., 1998).

Autonomy-Supportive Environments

Other models suggest that similar strategies may provide an opportunity to address the debilitating beliefs that underpin perfectionism. Models of self-worth offer a number of possible means of mitigating the effects of perfectionism by directly addressing the sense of conditional acceptance that underpins perfectionism. Alternatives to the pursuit of contingent self-worth include the development of unconditional self-acceptance (Ellis, 2003), unconditional positive regard (Rogers, 1959), authenticity (Kernis, 2003), and true self-esteem

(Deci & Ryan, 1995). According to self-determination theory (Ryan & Deci, 2002), true self-esteem is developed through the fulfillment of the psychological needs for competence, autonomy, and relatedness. This is achieved by providing social contexts in which an individual can act autonomously and experience a sense of efficacy within the context of authentic relationships. Autonomy-supportive environments in the context of sport include providing choice in tasks, offering rationales for decisions, acknowledging and valuing athletes' feelings, and avoiding controlling behaviors such as self-criticism and controlling competence (Mageau & Vallerand, 2003). The explicit focus on creating a social context in which people are able to feel accepted by others and eventually themselves (Deci & Ryan, 1995) has the potential to alter contingencies of self-worth associated with perfectionism and bring about substantial change in the motives associated with perfectionism (see Adie, Duda, & Ntoumanis, 2008; Alvarez, Balaguer, Castillo, & Duda, 2009). Future empirical research is required to examine this possibility.

Perfectionistic Cognitions

It is possible that perfectionism may be managed by focusing on the cognitive components of perfectionism. Flett and colleagues have also argued that in addition to trait dimensions, perfectionism entails a number of cognitive components that include a ruminative response style and the experience of automatic thoughts that reflect the need to be perfect (Flett, Hewitt, Blankstein, & Gray, 1998). Perfectionistic cognitions are frequent automatic thoughts and images that involve the need to be perfect. They indicate a preoccupation with the attainment of perfection and the regularity with which individuals engage in self-evaluation against an ideal, perfect self (Flett et al., 1998; Hewitt & Genest, 1990). Research has found that individual differences in the frequency of these perfectionistic cognitions explain additional unique variance in the psychological distress reported by perfectionists (Ferrari, 1995; Flett, Madorsky, Hewitt, & Heisel, 2002; Flett et al., 1998; Flett, Greene, & Hewitt, 2004; Rudolph, Flett, & Hewitt, 2007) beyond trait perfectionism dimensions. Consequently, the experience of ruminative cognition is an important target for the management of perfectionism (Flett et al., 1998). Moreover, in comparison to trait perfectionism, the experience of perfectionistic cognition may be more amenable to change (Moore & Barrow, 1986; Flett et al., 2007). Therefore, targeting athletes' experience of these cognitions may provide an opportunity to ameliorate the negative effects of trait perfectionism, at least in the short term. In the long term, because of the unique predictive ability of trait dimensions of perfectionism and perfectionistic cognitions, both must be the focus of interventions (Flett et al., 2007).

Any attempt to manage subclinical perfectionism in athletes is likely to create a significant dilemma for coaches and sport psychologists when there is widespread disagreement on both its definition and long-term consequences. Because perfectionism is a characteristic that reflects a strong commitment to high standards and may stimulate fervent achievement striving, it seems to have become a socially valued quality to many in the world of sport, where both achievement and excellence are highly prized. Interventions aimed at managing perfectionism are clearly unnecessary for people who strive to achieve high personal standards, endorse mastery approach goals, eschew avoidance goals, and engage in reflective performance appraisal rather than self-critical derision. We agree with Stoeber, Uphill, and Hotham (2009) that this motivational pattern appears adaptive. Unlike Stoeber et al., however, we do not believe that this pattern of achievement striving reflects perfectionism. Targeted interventions are therefore clearly warranted for athletes who exhibit the core characteristics of perfectionism described earlier. The achievement striving of these athletes may occasionally result in positive performance outcomes. Coaches and sport psychologists need to understand, however, that the same mind-set that energizes achievement striving also gives rise to an array of debilitating psychological processes that may ultimately lead to considerable impairment and distress.

Directions for Future Research

Research into perfectionism in sport is still in its infancy, and thus there is considerable scope to advance knowledge about the nature and influence of this personality characteristic in sporting contexts. Although advances have occurred in the measurement of multidimensional perfectionism, the assessment of perfectionism in sport has been hindered by the fact that the dispositional measures used in clinical and social psychology contexts do not transfer easily. There is an obvious need to develop and validate measures that better reflect the core characteristics of the disposition as it manifests in sport. New measures must enable users to differentiate between the construct of perfectionism and behavior that is reflective of adaptive achievement striving.

Another area that sport researchers must consider is how perfectionism develops in athletes. Shafran, Egan, and Wade (2010) suggested that between 24% and 49% of perfectionism may be inherited. Of course, that means that our social environment plays a considerable role in the development of this personality construct. Parents are thought to play a significant role (Flett, Hewitt, Oliver, & McDonald, 2002; Frost, Laharte, & Rosenblate, 1991; Spiers Neumeister, Williams, & Cross, 2009), but little is known about whether sport might be a vehicle through which perfectionistic beliefs and attitudes are transmitted from parents to their children. Appleton, Hall, & Hill (2010) have recently begun to examine the role played by family members in this development of perfectionism, and further research must explore the psychological mechanisms by which parents transmit perfectionistic behavior to their children. Additionally, research should address the process by which coaches might influence perfectionistic achievement striving through the environment that they create.

Research in sport must also begin to consider the mechanisms by which perfectionistic achievement striving becomes destructive. Little research of a longitudinal nature has been conducted to date. Research of this type might specifically begin to examine the degree to which self-oriented perfectionism is a vulnerability factor rather than a dimension of "adaptive perfectionism." Cleverly designed diary studies may allow researchers to understand more about the dynamics of perfectionism. The data generated would provide more detail about the cognitive and affective processes experienced by athletes as they strive to reach perfectionistic standards. Future research might also consider how different forms of perfectionism exhibited by both athletes and coaches might influence the interpersonal dynamics within teams because interpersonal factors may indirectly influence various outcome measures ranging from performance to enjoyment.

Summary

The productivity of a number of research groups has advanced our understanding of perfectionism in sport. For example, both Stoeber and colleagues (Stoeber & Becker, 2008; Stoeber & Otto, 2006; Stoeber, Otto, Pescheck, Becker, & Stoll, 2007; Stoeber, Stoll, Pescheck, & Otto, 2008; Stoeber, Uphill, & Hotham, 2009; Stoll, Lau, & Stoeber, 2008) and Dunn and colleagues (Dunn, Causgrove Dunn, & Syrotuik, 2002; Dunn, Craft, Causgrove Dunn, & Gotwals, in press; Dunn, Gotwals, & Causgrove Dunn, 2005; Dunn, Causgrove Dunn, Gotwals, Vallance, Craft, & Syrotuik, 2006; Dunn, Gotwals, Causgrove Dunn, & Syrotuik, 2006; Gotwals & Dunn, 2009; Vallance, Dunn, & Causgrove Dunn, 2006) have made substantial contributions to the conceptual understanding and measurement of perfectionism in sport. At a recent gathering of perfectionism researchers hosted by Joachim Stoeber at the University of Kent, one of the delegates expressed the view that those researching in this area should be more accepting of the diverse approaches to the study of perfectionism, many of which differ markedly from one another both conceptually and methodologically. Our position is that it behooves researchers to reflect on areas of disagreement and engage in critical discourse that will help to develop and refine ideas and bring about greater understanding of the subject. Our aim in writing this chapter was not to discredit the invaluable contribution of colleagues who help shape our thinking or others who do not share our viewpoint. The purpose was to explain the arguments that inform our beliefs surrounding the influence of perfectionism in sport and to outline why we are not convinced by either the conceptual or empirical evidence offered in support of the notion that perfectionism contributes to adaptive motivation and sporting excellence.

What we have challenged within the chapter is the idea that an individual can be defined as a perfectionist without exhibiting the core characteristics of this personality disposition. We have also challenged the value of disaggregating multidimensional measures and the notion of adaptive perfectionism. Our views are not wholly incongruent with those of other groups who are examining perfectionism in sport because we believe that self-critical forms of perfectionism are fundamentally debilitating, and we believe, like others (e.g. Greenspon, 2000, Flett & Hewitt, 2006), that what has been labeled positive perfectionism is simply adaptive achievement striving. Moreover, the empirical evidence points clearly to the fact that, although adaptive achievement striving provides a sustainable route to fulfilling a person's sporting potential, perfectionism is not a foundation for excellence. Rather, it is an uneasy pathway toward purgatory because it gives rise to an array of debilitating processes that athletes will encounter as they strive to reach the unattainable.

CHAPTER 5

The Dualistic Model of Passion in Sport and Exercise

Robert J. Vallerand, PhD
Université du Québec à Montréal

Author's Note

Robert J. Vallerand, PhD, Laboratoire de Recherche sur le Comportement Social, Université du Québec à Montréal, Montréal, Québec, Canada. This research program was supported by grants from the Fonds Québécois pour la Recherche sur la Société et la Culture (FQRSC) and the Social Sciences Humanities Research Council of Canada (SSHRC). Correspondence concerning this article should be addressed to Robert J. Vallerand, Laboratoire de Recherche sur le Comportement Social, Département de psychologie, Université du Québec à Montréal, C.P. 8888, succursale Centre-ville, Montréal, Québec, Canada, H3C 3P8. Electronic mail may be sent to vallerand.bob@gmail.com. Additional information on this program of research can be obtained by visiting www.psycho.uqam.ca/lrcs.

port is a collection of activities that people love, deeply care about, and engage in on a prolonged basis. Indeed, some people have been involved in a given sport for a lifetime. For instance, Penn State's former football team coach Joe Paterno (84 years of age in December 2010) coached football for over 60 years, and NBA referee Dick Bavetta (71 years of age in December 2010) is still refereeing in the NBA after more than 35 years on the job. Similarly, regular exercisers often surmount significant obstacles to remain active and train for many years on their favorite activity, be it swimming, cycling, or jogging. For example, Jenny Wood-Allen completed the London Marathon at the age of 90 years in 2002!

What is it that leads these people to remain engaged in an activity for so long? I submit that the passion that individuals experience toward their sport or exercise activity is a key answer to this question. Indeed, I believe that passion provides the sustained energy required to remain involved in the activity in the face of obstacles. Most people seem to agree. Passion is one of the most important explanations for athletes' high-level performance and sustained engagement. At the same time, passion may explain athletes and exercisers' ill-advised decisions to continue participation, thereby leading to unsuccessful attempts to come out of retirement, chronic injuries, and sometimes worse. For instance, Jim Goodman died of a heart attack in June 2008 at the age of 46 during the swimming leg in the U.S. Olympic Triathlon Trials. But is it the case? Is passion responsible for both the positive and negative outcomes that athletes and exercisers experience? Given the prevalence of the use of the passion construct in sport and exercise, it is ironic that little scientific information has existed until recently on its role in outcomes and on the psychological processes through which such outcomes take place.

The purpose of this chapter is to present the dualistic model of passion (DMP; Vallerand, 2008, 2010; Vallerand et al., 2003) and conduct a review of research on the model. Although much research on passion has recently been carried out in a number of real-life contexts, including gaming (e.g., Wang & Chu, 2007; Lafrenière, Vallerand, Donahue, & Lavigne, 2009), online shopping addiction (e.g., Wang & Yang, 2007), leisure (Stenseng, 2008), the Internet (Tosun & Lajunen, 2009), work (Burke & Fiksenbaum, 2009; Carbonneau, Vallerand, Fernet, & Guay, 2008), and gambling (e.g., MacKillop, Anderson, Castelda, Mattson, & Donovick, 2006; Mageau, Vallerand, Rosseau, Ratelle, & Provencher, 2005; Philippe & Vallerand, 2007; Ratelle, Vallerand, Mageau, Rousseau, & Provencher, 2004; Rousseau, Vallerand, Ratelle, Mageau, & Provencher, 2002), the emphasis in this chapter is on sport and exercise research. Research has been conducted on all types of sport participants (athletes, coaches, referees, and fans) and exercisers. Following a theoretical discussion on the concept of passion and a presentation of the DMP, research on passion is reviewed in six major sections. In the first section, I review the results of initial research (i.e., Vallerand et al., 2003, Study 1) as it pertains to the validation of the concept of passion. Next, I address research on the development of passion. In the following sections, the role of passion is addressed as it pertains to intrapersonal consequences (cognition, affect, psychological well-being, physical health, and performance), as well as interpersonal and intergroup outcomes. Then, research on the role of the situation as a moderator of the effects of passion on outcomes is reviewed. It will be seen that passion permeates the fabric of everyday life and does make a difference in people's lives. Finally, I conclude with suggestions for future research and applications.

Psychology of Passion

Passion has a rich history in philosophy but has received much less attention in psychology. In fact, although passion can be seen as related to a number of psychological constructs, until recently no research has focused on passion for activities. In this vein, my colleagues and I have proposed a model to account for the important role that passion for activities plays in people's lives. These various issues are addressed next.

A Brief History of Passion

Passion has received much attention from philosophers (although their focus has been more on the emotional aspect of passion than on its motivational dimension). Two distinct perspectives have emerged (Rony, 1990). The first posits that passion entails a loss of reason and control. For instance, for Plato (429–347 BC), reason moves people upward toward the divine, whereas passions take people downward toward animal instincts and the flesh. Similarly, Spinoza (1632–1677) proposed that acceptable thoughts originated from reason, whereas unacceptable thoughts derived from passion. People afflicted with passion were seen as experiencing a kind of suffering, in line with the etymology of the word *passion* (from the Latin *passio*, meaning "suffering"). According to this perspective, individuals with a passion are seen as passive, as slaves to their passion, because it comes to control them.

The second perspective portrays passions in a more positive light. For instance, Aristotle proposed that people should not be ashamed of their passions because they reflect human qualities, or what it is to be human. Aristotle nevertheless recommended that passions be controlled by reason to prevent negative outcomes from taking place. Similarly, in *The Passions of the Soul* (1649/1972), Descartes (1596–1650) defined passions as strong emotions with inherent behavioral tendencies that can be positive as long as reason underlies the behavior. Rousseau (1712–1778) went further and even suggested that passion can lead to knowledge and truth. Hegel (1770–1831) further argued that passions are highly energetic and, in fact, are necessary to reach the highest levels of achievement. Thus, this second view of passion not only sees people as more active in relation to their passion but also suggests that adaptive benefits will accrue when people are in control of their passion.

Little has been written on the psychology of passion. The few psychologists who have looked at the concept have underscored its motivational aspect. For instance, Frijda, Mesquita, Sonnemans, and Van Goozen (1991) posited, "Passions are defined as high-priority goals with emotionally important outcomes" (p. 218). According to these authors, people spend large amounts of time and effort to reach their passionate goals. Other researchers have proposed that passion (or love) for work as an entrepreneur plays a major role in how one's vision is accepted in the organization and how the company performs (Baum & Locke, 2004). Nearly all empirical work on passion has been conducted in the area of close relationships under the rubric of passionate love (e.g., Hatfield & Walster, 1978; Sternberg, 1986). Although such research is important, it does not deal with the main topic at hand, namely passion toward activities.

Other psychologists have focused on related concepts such as positive addiction (Glasser, 1976) for activities that people enjoy (such as running). For instance, in line with perspectives from philosophers such as Rousseau (1712–1778), who proposed that to control a passion a person needs to replace it with another passion, Glasser suggested that positive addiction entails replacing a negative activity (e.g., gambling) with a more positive one (e.g., running). But it is not clear from Glasser's position how an addiction can truly be positive because it is merely suggested that one addiction replaces another. Further, this position has been largely atheoretical and to the best of my knowledge has led to no empirical research. Other authors (Duckworth, Peterson, Matthews, & Kelly, 2007) have started to look at how a concept that they call grit (defined as perseverance and passion for long-term goals) can predict performance. Although grit has indeed been found to predict performance, this concept implies that passion always leads to persistence. As will become obvious in this chapter, under some conditions passion (and especially harmonious passion) may not lead to persistence.

Passion and Other Constructs

Note that constructs related to that of passion have been proposed in sport psychology. Thus, constructs have been proposed such as running addiction (e.g., Morgan, 1979; Sachs, 1981), sport commitment (e.g., Carmac & Martens, 1979), exercise dependence, and obligatory running (for a review see Hausenblas & Symons Downs, 2002). Although these constructs may appear closely related to that of passion, such a link may not be as straightforward as first anticipated. Let's take commitment. Although people who are heavily committed to exercise can be passionate, it is possible for such people not to be passionate toward exercise because they may not necessarily like it. Thus, people may be highly committed to jogging not because they love it but because they desperately need to lose weight. Thus, the concept of commitment is not equivalent to that of passion. A second point is that it is not clear how concepts dealing with dependence and obligatory running and the like can be adaptive. Finally, these constructs do not address the issue of the duality of passion in which both adaptive and maladaptive outcomes can be experienced as a function of passion.

Perhaps passion is most closely linked to intrinsic motivation. Intrinsic motivation shares some conceptual similarity with passion because both involve interest and liking toward the activity. But intrinsically motivated activities are typically not seen as being internalized in the person's identity and are best seen as emerging from the person–task interaction at the short-term level (Koestner & Losier, 2002). Furthermore, intrinsic motivation does not address the duality of passion in which both adaptive and maladaptive outcomes are experienced. Intrinsic motivation is hypothesized to lead only to adaptive outcomes (Deci & Ryan, 2000). On the other hand, extrinsic motivation entails performing the activity not out of enjoyment but for external reasons (i.e., for reasons other than for the activity itself, such as external or internal pressure). Therefore, although some forms of extrinsic motivation, such as identified and integrated regulation, entail some internalization of an activity that one does not like in itself, a fundamental difference between extrinsic motivation and passion is the relative lack of liking (or loving) for the activity that is present with extrinsic motivation. Research empirically supports these distinctions between passion and intrinsic and extrinsic motivation and even shows that controlling for intrinsic and extrinsic motivation does not change the role of harmonious and obsessive passion in the prediction of positive and negative affect (Vallerand et al., 2003, Study 2).

In sum, although the concept of passion does have conceptual similarities with other motivational constructs, it also differs from them in significant ways. Of major importance is the fact that no other concept seems to convey the duality of effects associated with passion.

The Dualistic Model of Passion

Vallerand and his colleagues (Vallerand, 2008, 2010; Vallerand et al., 2003; Vallerand & Houlfort, 2003) have recently developed a model of passion that addresses the dualism inherent in passion. In line with self-determination theory (Deci & Ryan, 2000; see Ntoumanis, this volume and Standage & Ryan, this volume), the dualistic model of passion (DMP) proposes that people engage in various activities throughout life in hope of satisfying the basic psychological needs of autonomy (a desire to feel a sense of personal initiative), competence (a desire to interact effectively with the environment), and relatedness (a desire to feel connected to significant others). Eventually, after a period of trial and error, most people eventually start to show preference for some activities, especially those that are enjoyable and allow the satisfaction of the psychological needs of competence, autonomy, and relatedness (Ryan & Deci, 2003). Of these activities, a limited few will be perceived as particularly enjoyable and important and will have some resonance with how we see ourselves. These activities become passionate activities.

So, what is passion? The DMP defines passion as a strong inclination toward a self-defining activity that one likes (or even loves), finds important (or highly values), and invests time and energy in. These activities come to be so self-defining that they represent central features of a person's identity. For instance, those who have a passion for playing basketball or jogging do not merely engage in these activities. They *are* basketball players and joggers.

Thus, a passion is much more than experiencing "love" for an activity; it entails making it one of the central aspects of one's identity, valuing the activity to a high degree, and devoting ample time to it.

Research has shown that values and regulations concerning uninteresting activities can be internalized in either a controlled or an autonomous fashion (Deci, Eghrari, Patrick, & Leone, 1994; Sheldon, 2002; Vallerand, 1997; Vallerand & Ratelle, 2002). Similarly, the DMP posits that activities that people like will also be internalized in the person's identity to the extent that these are highly valued and meaningful for the person. Furthermore, the DMP proposes that there are two types of passion, obsessive and harmonious, that can be distinguished in terms of how the passionate activity has been internalized into one's identity. Obsessive passion results from a controlled internalization of the activity into one's identity. Such an internalization process not only causes the activity representation to be part of the person's identity but also leads to values and regulations associated with the activity to be partially internalized at best and to be internalized completely outside the integrating self (Deci & Ryan, 2000) at worst, leading to a phenomenological experience of relative lack of control over the activity. A controlled internalization originates from intra- or interpersonal pressure, typically because certain contingencies are attached to the activity, such as feelings of social acceptance or self-esteem or because the sense of excitement derived from activity engagement is uncontrollable. People with an obsessive passion can thus find themselves in the position of experiencing an uncontrollable urge to partake in the activity that they view as important and enjoyable. They cannot help but to engage in the passionate activity. The passion must run its course because it controls the person. Consequently, people risk experiencing conflicts and other negative affective, cognitive, and behavioral consequences during and after activity engagement. For instance, a student–athlete with an obsessive passion for basketball might not be able to resist an invitation to a scrimmage from his friends the night before an important final exam that he still needs to study for. During the game, the athlete might be upset with himself for playing basketball instead of studying for his exam. He might therefore have difficulties focusing on the task at hand (playing basketball) and may not experience as much positive affect and flow as he should while playing. Moreover, he may experience anxiety for not being ready for the exam, and his grades may suffer as well.

As seen from the preceding, obsessive passion leads people to display a rigid persistence toward the activity because often they cannot help but engage in the passionate activity (as was the case for the student–basketball player). This occurs because internally controlling self-processes rather than integrative ones (Hodgins & Knee, 2002) are at play. Obsessive passion leads the person to engage in the activity with a fragile and contingent sense of self-esteem (e.g., Crocker, 2002; Kernis, 2003), and he eventually becomes defensive rather than open to new experiences and information. Clearly, self-esteem and social recognition contingencies can lead the individual to become dependent on the passionate activity and to suffer emotionally in the face of failure. Furthermore, although the dependence and rigid persistence that obsessive passion creates may lead to some benefits (e.g., improved health and performance at the activity), it may also come at a cost for the individual. Indeed, depending on the situation and the type of task, the lack of flexibility that obsessive passion entails may potentially lead to less than optimal functioning within the confines of the passionate activity, such as less creativity. Furthermore, such a rigid persistence toward the passionate activity may lead the person to experience conflict with other aspects of his or her life when engaging in the activity, as well as to frustration and rumination about the activity when prevented from engaging in it. Thus, to return to our example, if the obsessively passionate athlete manages to say no to his friends and the basketball scrimmage, he still may end up suffering because he may have difficulties concentrating on preparing for the exam because of ruminations about the lost opportunity to play basketball.

Conversely, harmonious passion results from an autonomous internalization of the activity into the person's identity. An autonomous internalization occurs when individuals have freely accepted the activity as important for them without any contingencies attached to it. This type of internalization emanates from the intrinsic and integrative tendencies of the self (Deci & Ryan, 2000; Ryan & Deci, 2003), produces a motivational force to engage in the activity willingly, and engenders a sense of volition and personal endorsement about pursuing the activity. When harmonious passion is at play, people do not experience an uncontrollable urge to engage in the passionate activity but rather freely choose to do so. The circumstance is reminiscent of the second, more positive, philosophical perspective on passion described earlier, whereby the person remains in control of the passionate activity or object. With this type of passion, the activity is in harmony with other aspects of the person's identity and life. With harmonious passion the authentic integrating self (Deci & Ryan, 2000) is at play, allowing the person to partake fully in the activity that she or he is passionate about with a secure sense of self-esteem, as well as an openness to experience the world in a nondefensive (Hodgins & Knee, 2002) and mindful manner (Brown & Ryan, 2003). Consequently, people with a harmonious passion should be able to focus fully on the task at hand and experience positive outcomes both during task engagement (e.g., situational positive affect, concentration, flow) and after task engagement (general positive affect, life satisfaction). Thus, little or no conflict should occur between the person's passionate activity and his or her other life activities. Furthermore, when prevented from engaging in their passionate activity, people with a harmonious passion should be able to adapt well to the situation and focus their attention and energy on other life tasks. Finally, with harmonious passion, the person is in control of the activity and can decide when and when not to engage in the activity. Thus, when confronted with the possibility of playing basketball with his friends or preparing for the next day's exam, the student–athlete with a harmonious passion toward basketball can readily tell his friends that he'll take the night off and can then proceed to immerse himself in preparing for the exam without thinking about the basketball scrimmage. People with a harmonious passion are able to decide not to play on a given day or even to disengage from the activity permanently if they determine that it has become a permanent negative factor in their lives. Thus, behavioral engagement in the passionate activity can be seen as flexible when harmonious passion is at play.

Initial Research on the Concept of Passion

The initial study (Vallerand et al., 2003, Study 1) had two major purposes: to develop the Passion Scale and to test the validity of the passion definition. To that end, over 500 university students completed the Passion Scale with respect to an activity that they loved, that they valued, and in which they invested time and energy (i.e., the passion definition), as well as other scales, allowing us to test predictions derived from the passion model. A large variety of passionate activities were reported, ranging from physical activity and sports to watching movies and reading. Of interest is that more than 60% of participants reported that they were passionate about an activity that pertained to sport or physical activity. Thus, the results from this initial study are highly relevant to the sport and exercise domain. Participants reported engaging in their passionate activity for an average of 8.5 hours per week and had been engaging in that activity for almost 6 years (see also Stenseng, 2008, for similar results). Thus, passionate activities are clearly meaningful to people and do not simply reflect a fleeting interest. Interestingly, 84% of our participants indicated that they had at least a moderate level of passion for a given activity in their lives (they scored at least 4 out of 7 on a question asking them whether their favorite activity was a "passion" for them). Thus, the prevalence of passion appears to be rather high, at least in the province of Quebec.

Research from Vallerand et al. (2003, Study 1), as well as from other authors, has provided empirical support for several aspects of the passion conceptualization. First, Vallerand et al. (2003, Study 1) randomly split their sample of over 500 participants into two subsamples. After conducting an exploratory factor analysis supporting the presence of two factors corresponding to the two types of passion with the first sample, they confirmed the bifactorial structure with the second sample using confirmatory factor analysis. These findings on the factor validity of the Passion Scale have been replicated in a number of studies conducted in the realm of both sport and physical activity (e.g., Lafrenière, Jowett, Vallerand, Donahue, & Lorimer, 2008, Studies 1 and 2; Philippe, Vallerand, Adrianarisoa, & Brunel, 2009, Studies 1 and 2; Rousseau & Vallerand, 2008; Vallerand, Mageau, et al., 2008, Studies 1 and 2; Vallerand, Ntoumanis, et al., 2008, Studies 1, 2, and 3; Vallerand, Rousseau, Grouzet, Dumais, & Grenier, 2006, Studies 1, 2, and 3), as well as outside it (e.g., Carbonneau, Vallerand, Fernet, & Guay, 2008; Castelda, Mattson, MacKillop, Anderson, & Donovick, 2007; Rousseau, Vallerand, Ratelle, Mageau, & Provencher, 2002; Vallerand & Houlfort, 2003).

The original Passion Scale (available from Vallerand et al., 2003) consisted of two seven-item subscales. A slightly revised scale consisting of two six-item scales is now used. These subscales correlate highly with their respective original subscale (r = .80 and above) and yield the same findings with determinants and outcomes. In addition, we have used a three-item version (Vallerand et al., 2007) and even a one-item version (Philippe & Vallerand, 2007) of each subscale with much success.

The Passion Scale presents two six-item subscales, namely the Obsessive subscale (e.g., "I almost have an obsessive feeling toward this activity") and Harmonious Passion subscale (e.g., "This activity is in harmony with other activities in my life"). Furthermore, internal consistency analyses have shown that both subscales are reliable (typically .75 and above). Finally, test–retest correlations over periods ranging from 4 to 6 weeks revealed moderately high stability values (in the .80s, Rousseau et al., 2002), thereby supporting the hypothesis that although the two subscales are relatively stable (and thus that there seems to be a predominant form of passion for each individual), temporary fluctuations can still occur.

Finally, note that there is a third subscale in the Passion Scale. This subscale serves to assess the passion criteria of activity valuation, degree of involvement (time and energy expenditure) and love for the activity, as well as the participant's perception of his or her activity as being a passion. This subscale is useful in allowing researchers to determine whether someone is passionate or not. The subscale has rarely been used in sport because most athletes are highly passionate for their sport.

A second series of critical findings pertaining to the results from partial correlations (controlling for the correlation between the two types of passion) showed that both harmonious and obsessive passions are positively associated with the passion criteria and measures of the activity being perceived as a passion, thereby providing support for the definition of passion (e.g., see Vallerand, 2010; Vallerand et al., 2003, Study 1). In addition, although both types of passion have been found to relate to a person's identity (e.g., Vallerand et al., 2003, Study 1; Vallerand, Noutmanis, et al., 2008, Study 1), obsessive passion has been found to relate more strongly to measures of both identity and conflict with other life activities than harmonious passion does (e.g., Vallerand et al., 2003, Study 1; Vallerand, Noutmanis, et al., 2008, Study 3). Thus, overall, these findings support the view that both harmonious passion and obsessive passion are indeed "passions" because each reflects the definition of the passion construct. Finally, additional research has also shown that obsessive (but not harmonious) passion leads to rigid persistence in ill-advised activities, such as cycling over ice and snow in winter (Vallerand et al., 2003, Study 3), and pursuing one's engagement in activities that have become negative for the person, such as pathological gambling (Vallerand et al., 2003, Study 4).

In sum, initial research provided support for the concept of harmonious and obsessive passion. I now turn to research that has explored some of the determinants and outcomes associated with the passion construct.

Development of Passion

The DMP posits that three processes influence the initial development of passion toward an activity: activity selection, activity valuation, and the internalization of the activity representation in a person's identity. Activity selection refers to the person's preference for the activity over other activities. To the extent that the person feels that such selection reflects true choice and interests and is consonant with her or his identity, it should promote the development of passion toward that activity. Activity valuation (or the subjective importance given to the activity by the person) is expected to play an important role in the internalization of the activity in identity. Research has indeed shown that when the object of interest is highly valued and meaningful, one is inclined to internalize the valued object, to make it part of him- or herself (Aron, Aron, & Smollan, 1992; Deci et al., 1994). The more important (or valued) the activity is, then the more the activity will be internalized in the person's identity and the more passionate the person will be toward the activity.

The DMP further posits that after an interesting activity becomes highly valued, the type of passion that will ensue is determined by the type of internalization that takes place. In line with self-determination theory (Deci & Ryan, 2000), two internalization processes are hypothesized to be involved: the autonomous and the controlled internalization processes. An autonomous internalization of the activity representation is expected to lead to the development of harmonious passion, whereas a controlled internalization is hypothesized to lead to an obsessive passion. The DMP further proposes that one important determinant of the internalization process is the extent to which the social environment promotes a person's autonomy (Deci & Ryan, 1987) toward activity selection and activity valuation. Much research has shown that autonomy support (or promoting choice and self-initiation of another person's behavior) from parents and teachers facilitates children's autonomous internalization of values and regulations of relatively uninteresting activities such as school (see Grolnick & Ryan, 1989; Vallerand, Fortier, & Guay, 1997). Similarly, the DMP proposes that autonomy support facilitates the autonomous internalization of an interesting activity in one's identity, thereby leading to harmonious passion. Conversely, after an individual selects a given activity and values it highly, a controlling environment should facilitate a controlled internalization of the activity in the person's identity, thereby leading to an obsessive passion for the activity.

My colleagues and I have tested some of the preceding hypotheses in a recent study with new music students (Mageau, Vallerand, Charest, et al., 2009, Study 3). First-year high school students who had never played a musical instrument completed a series of questionnaires early in the term assessing activity selection (both perceived parental and children activity specialization) and valuation (perceived parental activity valuation) and perceived autonomy support from parents and music teachers, as well as the extent to which students perceived music as potentially part of their identity. By following participants who were registered in their first music class over the course of their first semester, we could predict who would develop a passion for music at the end of the term and, among those who did, predict those who would develop a harmonious passion or an obsessive passion. Based on the passion criteria (see the third subscale in table 5.1), we could identify that 36% of the sample was at least moderately passionate for music at the end of the term (having obtained an average of 4 or above on the four passion criteria). These numbers suggest that people do not develop a passion for any or all activities that they engage in.

Results of a discriminant analysis revealed that students who ended up being passionate for music (36% of the sample) at the end of the term had reported higher levels of activity selection (specialization) and valuation, identity processes, and parental and teacher autonomy support earlier in the term than those students who did not turn out to be passionate. Furthermore, high levels of autonomy support from close adults (parents and music teachers) were conducive to the development of harmonious passion. But high levels of parental perceived valuation for music (probably experienced as external pressure) and lack of autonomy support (or its opposite, controlling behavior from close adults) predicted the development of obsessive passion. In sum, these results provided support for the role of activity selection and valuation, identity processes, and autonomy support from significant adults in the development of a passion for music in general and harmonious and obsessive passion in particular. Clearly, future research is needed to replicate these findings in the realm of sport and physical activity using longitudinal design.

The DMP also posits that personal factors (i.e., individual differences and personality processes) constitute a second important determinant of the internalization process, and thus indirectly, of the type of passion that initially develops. The DMP posits that personal factors that orient the individual toward autonomy will facilitate the autonomous internalization process and thus lead to the initial development of harmonious passion. Conversely, personal factors that lead the person to feel controlled while engaging in the activity will trigger the controlled internalization process and lead to the development of obsessive passion.

Past research (for reviews, see Vallerand, 1997; Vallerand & Ratelle, 2002) has shown that an autonomous personality orientation (having a tendency to do things out of pleasure or choice) leads to the autonomous internalization of uninteresting activities, whereas a controlled personality orientation (a tendency to do things out of external or inner pressure) leads to the controlled internalization of uninteresting activities (Guay, Mageau, & Vallerand, 2003; see also Vallerand, 1997, 2001). It thus appears that an autonomous personality is associated with the autonomous internalization process, whereas a controlled personality is associated with a controlled internalization style. In light of the preceding, to the extent that people highly value an enjoyable activity, those with an autonomous personality should be more likely to facilitate the development and maintenance of a harmonious passion. On the other hand, a controlled personality should be more conducive to obsessive passion. Recent research by Vallerand et al. (2006) conducted with athletes supported the hypotheses. Specifically, Vallerand et al. (2006, Study 1) reported the results of a structural equation modeling analysis that showed that valuation of the sport activity and an autonomous personality (as assessed by the Global Motivation Scale; Guay et al., 2003) both predicted harmonious passion. On the other hand, a controlled personality and valuation of the activity both predicted obsessive passion. These findings appear in figure 5.1. These findings were replicated in a second study (Vallerand et al., 2006, Study 3) using a short longitudinal design.

The DMP further posits that after a passion for a given activity has initially developed, its development continues as it is ongoing. Thus, increases and decreases in activity valuation will lead to similar modulation in the intensity of passion. Further, the presence or absence of social and personal factors that pertain to the autonomous versus controlled internalization process will influence the ongoing development of passion in a corresponding fashion. Of course, the internalization process is not an all or none process. Although the internalization process leads to the initial development of a predominant type of passion, both types of passion are nevertheless present within the individual to different degrees depending on the social and personal factors at play. The fact that both types of passion are internalized in identity makes it possible to facilitate one or the other by making salient certain social or personal factors. Thus, although the predominant type of passion is usually in operation, it is possible to reinforce the predominant passion or to make the other type

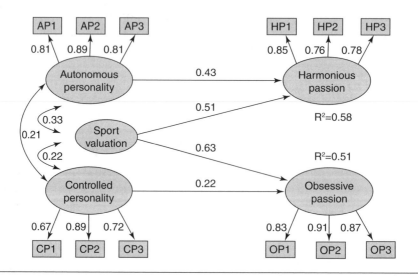

FIGURE 5.1 Results of the structural equation modeling analyses on the role of activity valuation and personality processes in the prediction of passion. From Vallerand et al. (2006, Study 1). For sake of clarity, the disturbances and the covariances are not presented.

Reprinted, by permission, from R.J. Vallerand et al., 2006, "Passion in sport: A look at determinants and affective experiences," *Journal of Sport & Exercise Psychology* 28: 454-478.

of passion operative depending on which type of social or personal factors is made salient. Preliminary research has been successfully conducted to test some of the elements dealing with the ongoing development of passion toward nonsport studies (see Vallerand, 2010). No research in the realm of sport or exercise has been conducted on the ongoing development of passion. Such research is clearly needed.

In sum, results presented in this section provide support for the DMP as it pertains to the development of passion. Research is needed to determine more clearly how passion develops, as well how the newly developed passion varies as a function of prevalent social and personal factors in sport and exercise.

Passion and Intrapersonal Outcomes

In this section, I review research on the role of passion in a number of outcomes. These include cognitive and affective processes, psychological well-being, physical health, and performance.

Passion and Cognitive Processes

Based on the DMP, it would be expected that harmonious passion facilitates adaptive cognitive processes, whereas obsessive passion should not, or at least should have less effect. This expectation is so because with harmonious passion, integrative self-processes are at play, leading the person to partake fully in the passion activity with an openness that is conducive to mindful attention, concentration, and flow. The situation is different when obsessive passion is at play because ego-invested processes are involved (Hodgins & Knee, 2002), thereby leading people to adopt a defensive orientation that permits only partial investment in the activity. Thus, less than full attention, concentration, and flow should be experienced in the process. Research provides support for this hypothesis. For instance, in research with soccer referees (including professional ones) by Philippe, Vallerand, Andrianarisoa, & Brunel (2009, Study 1), participants were asked to complete the Passion Scale, as well as indicate to what extent they typically experience high levels of concentration while they engage in the passionate activity. The results of partial correlations revealed that compared with obsessive passion, harmonious passion correlated more strongly with concentration on the passionate activity. Vallerand et al. (2003, Study 1) had found similar results.

Another form of concentration was empirically scrutinized in research with English soccer fans (Vallerand, Ntoumanis, et al., 2008, Study 1). In that study, the researchers found that obsessive passion for soccer prevented full concentration on other life activities taking place on the same (game) day, whereas that was not the case for fans with harmonious passion. Thus although harmonious passion facilitates concentration during engagement in the passionate activity, it does not appear to detract from full engagement in other life activities that take place while waiting to engage in the passionate activity (watching the soccer game). Obsessive passion, however, detracts from fully concentrating both during engagement in the passionate activity and in other life activities while waiting to partake in the passionate one.

Another cognitive concept of interest is flow (Csikszentmihalyi, 1978; Csikszentmihalyi, Rathunde, & Whalen, 1993). Flow refers to a desirable state that people experience when they feel completely immersed in the activity (e.g., "I have a feeling of total control"). Because harmonious passion allows the person to partake fully in the passionate activity with a secure sense of self-esteem, flexibility, and an openness to experience the world in a nondefensive, mindful manner, it should be conducive to focusing on the task at hand and consequently to experiencing flow. Conversely, with obsessive passion, internally controlling rather than integrative self-processes are at play, leading the person to engage in the activity with a fragile and contingent sense of self-esteem (e.g., Crocker, 2002; Kernis, 2003) and eventually to become defensive rather than open to experience. Such a state should not be conducive to the experience of flow. In the Philippe, Vallerand, Andrianarisoa, & Brunel (2009, Study 1), we had French soccer referees complete various flow indices (including the challenge and control dimensions of flow; Jackson & Marsh, 1996), as well as the Passion Scale. The results revealed that harmonious passion facilitates the experience of flow, whereas obsessive passion does not. These results have also been obtained in the Vallerand et al. (2003, Study 1) initial study, as well as in the work domain (Forest, Mageau, Sarrazin, & Morin, 2010).

A final cognitive process that has been examined is decision making. One area where decision making is important is with referees. Such decision making is crucial because the outcome of the game may depend on appropriate decisions by referees. Of interest is that referees' decision making may be particularly affected after they have made a mistake. In fact, their reactions and strategies to deal with their mistakes may lead some to engage in makeup calls (i.e., favoring the party or team that has been unjustly penalized by the poor call; Wolfson & Neave, 2007). Makeup calls are particularly interesting because they amount to making a second poor decision deliberately, after the first error. Makeup calls are a decision-making process that referees should avoid at all costs because they can potentially entrap themselves in a vicious circle of unending poor decisions.

Using the DMP, we can hypothesize that passion might account for the different ways in which referees react after having committed an important error. Because harmonious passion emanates from the integrating self, a referee might accept making an error without experiencing a self-threat that needs to be removed through an immediate correction (i.e., a makeup call). Consequently, with harmonious passion, it should prove possible to deal with the situation without engaging in making makeup calls to repair the first mistake. Conversely, with obsessive passion, the person's identity is attached contingently to the activity such that doing well in the passionate activity becomes important to self-esteem. Therefore, making an error becomes highly self-threatening, leading the person to seek removal of the threat by making a makeup call. Philippe, Vallerand, Andrianarisoa, and Brunel (2009, Study 2) conducted a study to test these hypotheses. European soccer referees completed the Passion Scale, as well as their tendency to engage in makeup calls after having made an important mistake. Results revealed, as expected, that subsequent to an important error obsessive passion was positively associated with engaging in makeup calls. Conversely, harmonious passion was negatively associated with makeup calls. Thus, as hypothesized, obsessive passion was found to undermine optimal cognitive functioning and decision making, whereas harmonious passion was found to facilitate such processes.

Clearly, the two types of passion lead to different cognitive functioning. Harmonious passion leads to the most adaptive types of cognitive processes, and obsessive passion leads to the least adaptive types. Future research on the role of coping strategies as mediators of the relationship between passion and cognitive functioning would appear important, especially under pressure situations.

Passion and Affect

Given that task valuation increases affect (Brown & Weiner, 1984), being passionate for an activity should also increase affect. Such affect, however, should differ as a function of the type of predominant passion held by the person. Thus, with harmonious passion, people volitionally engage in the passionate activity with an openness and a mindfulness that allow them to partake fully in the activity and thus experience positive affective experiences (Hodgins & Knee, 2002) during task engagement (e.g., positive affect). Furthermore, the lack of conflict with other life activities that harmonious passion entails should maximize the duration of the positive affect experienced during activity engagement and lead people to experience positive affect after task engagement. Finally, because task engagement is volitional, people are unlikely to experience negative affect when unable to engage in the passionate activity (such as feelings of dependence).

Conversely, with obsessive passion, people engage in the activity with a defensive, rather than an open, orientation, preventing them from fully experiencing the positive emotions that they should derive from engaging in their favorite activity. Moreover, because engagement is often out of their control and may be performed at ill-advised times, some conflict may be experienced with other life activities, thereby preventing them from fully enjoying participation in the passionate activity and leading them to experience negative affect following task engagement (e.g., guilt, shame, anxiety). Finally, they are likely to experience high levels of negative affect when prevented from engaging in the passionate activity because they experience engagement in the passionate activity out of obsessive passion as an uncontrollable desire to partake in the activity. Consequently, being prevented from engaging in the passionate activity should lead to some sense of suffering.

In a number of studies, results from partial correlations between the two types of passion and affective variables have supported these hypotheses. For instance, Vallerand et al. (2003, Study 1) asked college students who were passionate toward an activity to complete the Passion Scale and report the positive and negative emotions that they typically experience during and after task engagement, as well as when they are prevented from engaging in their passionate activity. Results from partial correlations (controlling for obsessive passion) revealed that harmonious passion was positively associated with positive experiences such as positive emotions during activity engagement. In addition, harmonious passion was positively related to positive emotions and the absence of negative affect following task engagement, and the absence of negative emotions when prevented from engaging in the passionate activity. On the other hand, when controlling for harmonious passion, obsessive passion was positively associated with negative emotions (especially shame) and unrelated to positive emotions both during and following activity engagement. Furthermore, obsessive passion was strongly related to negative affect when a person is prevented from engaging in the activity. These results have been replicated in how athletes (e.g., Vallerand et al., 2006, Studies 2 and 3) and referees (e.g., Philippe, Vallerand, Andrianarisoa, & Brunel, 2009, Study 1) typically feel when engaged in their sport.

Research seen so far reveals that obsessive passion rarely predicts positive affect. This finding may seem surprising given the high level of activity involvement that obsessive passion entails. As such, we may predict that obsessive passion should be conducive to some forms of positive affect at least sometimes or in certain situations. For instance, given that the passionate activity is internalized in a person's identity, we might expect that affect related to the self (e.g., feeling proud, confident, competent, and so forth) is positively related to both obsessive and harmonious passion. This hypothesis was tested in a recent study with sport fans (Vallerand, Ntoumanis, et al., 2008, Study 2). In this study, Canadian fans of the two finalist countries (France and Italy) in the 2006 World Soccer Cup Finals completed the Passion Scale and both general and positive self-related emotions experienced up to that point in the tournament. Results revealed that harmonious passion positively predicted both types of positive affect. On the other hand, obsessive passion correlated positively only with positive self-related affect. These findings are important because they show that, in addition to negative affect, some types of positive affective experiences (i.e., self-related affect) can be derived from activity engagement fueled by obsessive passion.

If passion contributes to situational affective experiences, can it also influence a person's general affect in life (i.e., outside the purview of the passionate activity)? Indeed, it could be hypothesized that because the passionate activity is highly valued, affect experienced as a function of engagement in the passionate activity should spill over into life in general. To test this hypothesis,

Vallerand et al. (2003, Study 2) followed collegiate football players over the course of an entire football season and assessed passion and general positive and negative affect before and after the end of the season. Results revealed that harmonious passion predicted an increase in general positive affect, whereas obsessive passion predicted an increase in general negative affect, in a player's life over the course of an entire football season. Furthermore, these findings were obtained while controlling for intrinsic and extrinsic motivation toward football. Thus, passion matters not only with respect to situational affect experienced within the purview of the passionate activity but also as it pertains to general affect in life. Similar findings were obtained by Mageau and Vallerand (2007) using a 14-day diary study with positive affect and a variety of passionate activities.

Passion and Psychological Well-Being

If harmonious and obsessive passion are respectively conducive to increases in general positive and negative affect over time as shown in research presented previously (Mageau & Vallerand, 2007; Vallerand et al., 2003, Study 2), is it possible that they also affect psychological well-being? Research supports this hypothesis. For instance, research with athletes using different measures of psychological well-being, such as life satisfaction, has indeed shown that harmonious passion positively predicts well-being, whereas obsessive passion does not (Vallerand, Mageau, et al., 2008, Study 2).

Additional research has attempted to answer the question, What are some of the personal factors likely to trigger the passion–outcomes relation? Research by Vallerand et al. (2006, Study 1) showed that having an autonomous versus controlled personality represents such a factor. Specifically, to the extent that people highly value an enjoyable activity, those with an autonomous personality orientation are more likely to develop and maintain a harmonious passion. On the other hand, a controlled personality orientation is more conducive to obsessive passion. In a subsequent study, Vallerand et al. (2006, Study 3) tested the same sequence of personal determinants but also included subjective well-being at time 2 as an outcome. It was predicted that only harmonious passion would predict well-being at time 2. Elite athletes completed questionnaires assessing activity (sport) valuation, personality orientations, and passion at time 1 and well-being at time 2 (4 months later). The hypothesized model posited that the more athletes value their sport and display an autonomous personality, the more harmonious their passion would become. On the other hand, highly valuing their sport and holding a controlled personality should lead athletes to develop an obsessive passion for their sport. In turn, it was hypothesized that harmonious passion would lead to higher levels of well-being in sport, whereas obsessive passion was expected to be unrelated to well-being. Results of structural equation modeling analyses provided support for the model.

A final issue assessed in the relationship between passion and psychological well-being deals with the nature of the processes mediating such a relationship. Although several processes may be at play, one that appears particularly important deals with the repeated experience of situational (or state) positive affect during the course of engagement of the passionate activity. Much research has focused on the adaptive role of positive affect in a variety of outcomes, including psychological well-being (Lyubomirsky, King, & Diener, 2005; Sedikides, Wildschut, Arndt, & Routledge, 2008). In one important line of research, Fredrickson (2001) proposed and found support for a broaden-and-build theory that posits that positive emotions are adaptive because they broaden people's thought–action repertoires and self, leading to better decision making and higher levels of psychological well-being. Thus, considering the fact that harmonious passion positively contributes to the experience of positive affect during activity engagement (e.g., Mageau et al., 2005; Vallerand et al., 2003, Study 1; Vallerand et al., 2006, Study 2) and that such positive affect seems to endure for a substantial period (Mageau & Vallerand, 2007), it would appear that harmonious passion can lead people to experience a significant amount of additional cumulative positive affect each week (at least an additional 10% on top of what may be experienced in other life domains). Such cumulative experience of positive affect may facilitate psychological well-being.

A recent study by Rousseau and Vallerand (2008) tested this hypothesis with senior individuals who had a passion for physical activity. At time 1, participants completed the Passion Scale with respect to physical activity, as well as a measure of psychological well-being using the French form (Blais, Vallerand, Pelletier, & Brière, 1989) of the Satisfaction With Life Scale (Diener, Emmons, Larsen, & Griffin, 1985). Five weeks later, at time 2, immediately following an exercise session, they completed situational measures of general positive and negative affect experienced while exercising (e.g., feeling happy, joyful). Finally, 3 weeks later, at time 3, participants completed measures of psychological well-being again. Results from a path analysis using structural equation modeling revealed that harmonious passion positively predicted positive affect that led to increases in psychological well-being from time 1 to time 3. On the other hand, obsessive passion was unrelated to positive affect but positively predicted negative affect. The latter did not predict psychological well-being. These findings are illustrated in figure 5.2.

As a closing note to this section, it should be underscored that the research conducted on passion and outcomes has been largely correlational in nature. Thus, a caveat is in order regarding causality issues. But the results of a recent study (Carbonneau et al., 2008) using a cross-lagged panel design with 500 teachers revealed that passion predicted changes in outcomes over a 3-month period, whereas outcomes did not predict changes in passion. Passion, then, appears to be involved in producing changes in psychological outcomes, whereas the reverse may not be true. Clearly, however, future longitudinal research is needed to replicate these findings within the realm of sport and physical activity.

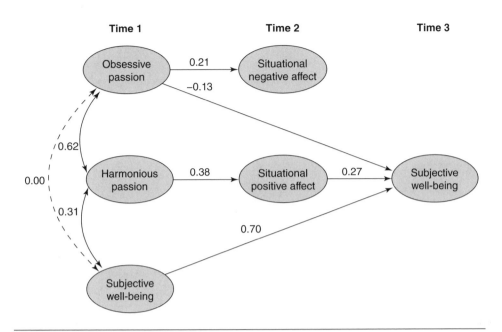

FIGURE 5.2   Results of the path analysis on the role of passion and affect in subjective well-being. For sake of clarity, the disturbances and the covariances are not presented.

Reprinted, by permission, from F.L. Rousseau and R.J. Vallerand, 2008, "An examination of the relationship between passion and subjective well-being in older adults," *International Journal of Aging and Human Development* 66: 195-211.

Passion and Physical Health

Passion may affect physical health in a number of ways, including some positive ones. For instance, by leading people to engage regularly in physical activity, passion may positively contribute to their health. At the same time, passion can also lead to excess because people may engage in fitness behavior when they should not, thereby putting their health at risk. Take cycling. In spring, summer, and fall this activity can be a lot of fun and can promote health. But the reality in winter can be very different (at least in the province of Quebec). The icy, snow-filled roads make cycling a hazardous affair that may lead to falls and injuries. Clearly, cycling under such conditions is not advisable. If our hypothesis on the rigid persistence induced by obsessive passion is correct, then obsessive passion should lead people to engage in risky behaviors such as winter cycling. On the other hand, if harmonious passion induces flexible persistence, then it should not lead to risky behavior. Indeed, with harmonious passion, people are mindful of changing situations and can adapt accordingly. Thus, they should be able to refrain from cycling outside in winter.

Vallerand et al. (2003, Study 3) have tested these very hypotheses with cyclists. Regular cyclists completed the Passion Scale in August with respect to cycling. Six months later, they were contacted again through e-mail to determine who was still cycling in February. Results showed that only 30% of participants were still cycling outside in winter. It was found that those persistent cyclists had reported higher levels of obsessive passion 6 months earlier than those who did not cycle in the winter. No differences were found with respect to harmonious passion. Results from a discriminant analysis further revealed that obsessive passion was able to predict group membership correctly in 79% of cases. Thus, obsessive passion may potentially affect people's health by leading them to engage in certain risky activities (such as cycling under dangerous conditions). Such is not the case for harmonious passion.

The preceding results suggest that obsessive passion can lead people to put themselves at risk of experiencing injuries when engaging in the passionate activity. But injuries were not assessed in that study (Vallerand et al., 2003, Study 3). Does obsessive passion indeed represent a risk factor for injuries? This question has been recently addressed in a study by Stephan, Deroche, Brewer, Caudroit, and Le Scanff (2009). In their study with competitive long-distance runners, the authors showed that obsessive passion positively predicted perceived susceptibility to injury while controlling for a number of variables, including the number of weekly training sessions and years of experience in running. Harmonious passion was negatively related to susceptibility to injury. Of additional interest, Stephan et al. reported that obsessive (but not harmonious) passion was positively related to the number of past injuries. Thus, it would appear that obsessive passion is a risk factor for sport injuries.

Research by Rip, Fortin, and Vallerand (2006) with modern and jazz dance students went one step further and examined the passion–injury relationship by distinguishing between acute and chronic injuries. As suggested previously, because both types of passion encourage persistence, being passionate should lead a person to train regularly, to remain in great shape, and thus to reduce the number of acute injuries. But when injured, obsessive passion should lead people to continue dancing, because it leads dancers to adopt a rigid persistence toward dancing, thereby leading to chronic injuries. On the other hand, with harmonious passion, the person is in control of the activity. Thus, persistence is expected to be flexible, as was seen in the cycling study. As such, the harmoniously passionate dancers can decide to stop dancing for a while when injured if risk of developing a chronic injury is present.

In the Rip et al. (2006) study, dancers (n = 80) completed the Passion Scale, as well as questions pertaining to injuries incurred over the past year. Results from partial correlations revealed that both types of passion were negatively related to the number of weeks missed because of acute injuries. This result was expected because the more passionate the dancers are, the more likely they are to dance, to keep fit, and thus to prevent acute injuries. Results with chronic injuries revealed that obsessive passion was positively related to the number of weeks missed, whereas harmonious passion was unrelated to chronic injuries. These findings are illustrated in figure 5.3. Thus, the Rip et al. research suggests that obsessive passion is a risk factor for chronic injuries.

In sum, harmonious and obsessive passion can lead to positive and negative effects on health, respectively, through the different mediating processes that are triggered, such as rigid persistence and engagement in risky behavior. Future research is needed to replicate the present findings with more objective measures of injuries and health, such as medical records and informant reports (e.g., coaches, physiotherapists).

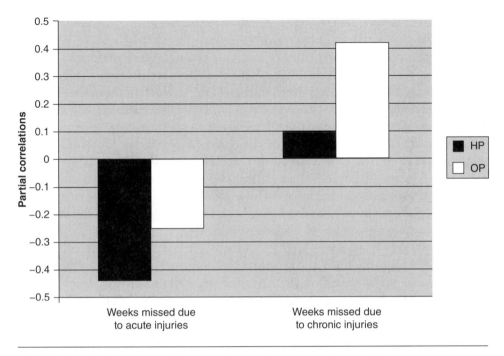

FIGURE 5.3   On the role of harmonious and obsessive passion in the prediction of acute and chronic injuries (partial correlations).

Based on Rip, Fortin, & Vallerand (2006).

Passion and Performance

Over the years, much effort has been deployed to identify the nature of processes involved in expert performance (see Ericsson, 1996; Starkes & Ericsson, 2003). Some authors have suggested that natural talent is one of the key elements (see Gagné, 2007). Although some "natural" talent is indeed necessary, it surely does not explain all because some top athletes such as Michael Jordan initially failed at their craft. Indeed, it is well known that Jordan was cut from his varsity high school basketball team when he first tried out for the team. Research with outstanding athletes reveals that they do not have faster reaction times than the normal population on nonsport tasks! What they do have is a sport-specific cognitive (knowledge), rather than physical, advantage that has developed over time with practice in their respective sport (see Moran, 2009).

So if natural talent is not the key element in performance, then what is it that matters with respect to performance? Although it is hard to dispute that some talent is necessary to reach high levels of performance and that special circumstances (Gladwell, 2008) may give an athlete an edge on the competition, I suggest that passion for the activity is the fundamental ingredient. Indeed, if a person is to engage in the activity for long hours over several years and sometimes a lifetime, he or she must love the activity dearly and have the desire to pursue engagement, especially when times are rough. For instance, although he failed initially, Jordan did not give up. Rather, he worked harder at his craft each day for long hours. His passion was not a fleeting interest, and it helped him overcome obstacles, practice regularly, and eventually become perhaps the best basketball player of all time.

Research on expert performance reveals that high-level performers spend several years of considerable engagement in deliberate practice (i.e., engagement in the activity with clear goals of improving on certain task components) to reach excellence in their chosen field of expertise (see Ericsson & Charness, 1994). For instance, reaching the Olympics or the professional levels requires 10,000 hours of deliberate practice (Ericsson & Charness, 1994). This time expenditure amounts to 4 hours a day, 6 days a week, 48 weeks a year, for roughly 10 years. Vallerand et al. (2007) proposed that passion is needed to go through such training regimens. Thus, it is hypothesized that the two types of passion (harmonious and obsessive) both lead to engagement in deliberate practice that, in turn, leads to improved performance.

This first basic model was tested in a study with college basketball players (Vallerand, Mageau, et al., 2008, Study 1). Male and female basketball players completed scales assessing their passion, as well as deliberate practice, in basketball (based on Ericsson & Charness, 1994). Then, later, coaches independently rated the athletes' performance over the season. A path analysis using structural equation modeling provided support for the basic model. Both types of passion led to engagement in deliberate practice that, in turn, led to objective performance. These findings were replicated in a study with dramatic arts performers (Vallerand et al., 2007, Study 1). Also of interest is the finding that in the study with dramatic arts students, harmonious passion was positively and significantly related to life satisfaction, whereas obsessive passion was unrelated to it. This result is in line with research discussed previously on the positive role of harmonious passion in psychological well-being.

An additional study (Vallerand, Mageau, et al., 2008, Study 2) was conducted to examine the psychological processes through which passion contributes to deliberate practice and indirectly contributes to performance. It was proposed that achievement goals should represent important mediators between passion and deliberate practice. Elliot and colleagues (Elliot, 1997; Elliot & Church, 1997; Elliot & Harackiewicz, 1996) have distinguished between three types of achievement goals: mastery goals (which focus on the development of personal competence and task mastery), performance approach goals (which focus on the attainment of personal competence relative to others), and performance avoidance goals (which focus on avoiding incompetence relative to others). Passion has been found to relate to affective and cognitive investment in an activity, thereby implying that the individual is committed to engaging in that activity in a competent manner. Harmonious passion, being an autonomous form of regulation, is predicted to be positively related to mastery goals but not to performance goals of either type. On the other hand, obsessive passion, being a more pressured, internally controlling form of regulation, is likely to lead the individual to feel compelled to seek any and all forms of success at the activity. As such, obsessive passion should be positively related to mastery and performance approach goals, as well as to performance avoidance goals.

A study with men and women water polo and synchronized swimmers (including some who were part of the junior national teams) was conducted over an entire season to test the preceding model (Vallerand, Mageau, et al., 2008, Study 2). At time 1, individuals completed the Passion Scale, the Achievement Goals Scale (see Elliot & Church, 1997), and scales assessing psychological well-being. At time 2, they completed the Deliberate Practice Scale. Finally, at time 3, coaches assessed players' performance over the entire season. A path analysis tested the proposed model. The results are illustrated in figure 5.4. As can be seen, harmonious passion positively predicted mastery goals that, in turn, led to deliberate practice that positively predicted objective performance. On the other hand, obsessive passion was positively related to all three goals. Although performance approach goals did not predict any variables in the model, performance avoidance goals negatively predicted

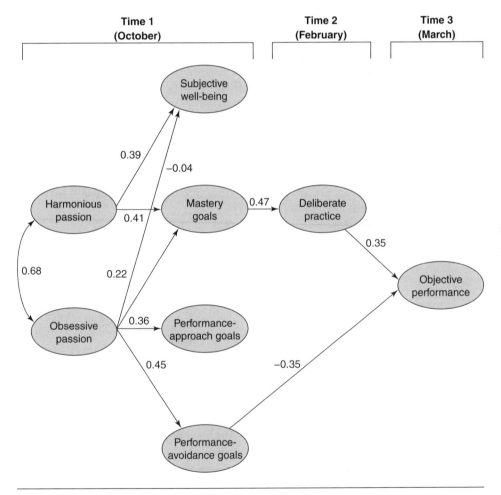

FIGURE 5.4   Results from the path analysis of the passion performance model in sport. (Note: All coefficients were significant (p <.05), except the link between obsessive passion and subjective well-being). For sake of clarity, the disturbances and the covariances are not presented.

Adapted from *Psychology of Sport and Exercise*, Vol. 9, R.J. Vallerand et al., "Passion and performance attainment in sport," pgs, 373-392, copyright 2008, with permission from Elsevier.

performance. Finally, as in the Vallerand et al. (2007, Study 1) study with the dramatic arts performers, harmonious passion was positively associated with psychological well-being, whereas obsessive passion was unrelated to it. This basic model was replicated in a study with students who had a passion toward studying psychology as their future profession using objective exam scores in a psychology course as a measure of performance (Vallerand et al., 2007, Study 2) and in another study with national and world-class classical musicians (Bonneville-Roussy, Lavigne, & Vallerand, 2010).

Overall, the preceding research on passion and performance suggests the existence of two roads leading to performance attainment. The first road originates from harmonious passion and exclusively promotes a mastery focus that leads the person to engage in activities specifically aimed at skill improvement. Such deliberate practice eventually leads to high levels of performance. Of additional interest is that this harmonious engagement process also facilitates psychological well-being. The second road leading to performance attainment emanates from obsessive passion. Such a road is more complex than the first because it involves the adoption of both adaptive (mastery goals) and maladaptive (performance avoidance) achievement goals. This second road to performance thus appears to be less than optimal for the individual. Indeed, besides leading to mixed performance through the adoption of mastery and performance avoidance goals, it does not facilitate psychological well-being. Thus, contrary to what is typically believed, a person can be a high-level performer and lead a relatively balanced, happy life at the same time, to the extent that harmonious passion underlies engagement in the field of excellence. These findings should be replicated with other activities and participants (e.g., coaches, referees, fitness instructors, and so on).

Passion and Interpersonal and Intergroup Outcomes

Research presented so far has focused on intrapersonal outcomes. In this section, I focus on outcomes with implications for other people and groups.

Passion and Quality of Interpersonal Relationships

Parents and coaches often ask this important question: "Does passion affect the quality of a person's relationships in sport?" A complete answer to this question must consider the object (or activity) of the person's passion, the type of passion underlying engagement in the passionate activity, and the context within which the relationships take place. In this section, I discuss two contexts where passion affects relationships.

A first context where a person's passion can affect the quality of relationships takes place within the purview of the passionate activity. It is reasonable to suggest that being passionate for an activity may influence the quality of relationships that people develop in this area. Indeed, passionate people are typically seen as highly engaging and as such should be popular and able to make friends easily. But if that is the case, what is the process through which they make friends? Further, does it make a difference whether the person is harmoniously or obsessively passionate? Again, in line with the work of Fredrickson (2001), the DMP posits that the experience of situational positive affect is also conducive to high-quality relationships. This is so because positive affect opens up people's thought–action repertoires and selves, leading them to experience the world more fully, thereby facilitating smiles, positive sharing of the activity, and connection and openness toward others all of which are conducive to positive relationships (see Waugh & Fredrickson, 2006). Because harmonious passion leads people to experience positive affect during engagement in the passionate activity, it can be hypothesized that it should indirectly lead to high-quality relationships within the passionate activity. Conversely, because obsessive passion is typically unrelated to positive affect and at times is correlated with negative affect, it would be expected to have a negative effect on the quality of relationships that develop within the purview of the passionate activity.

Initial research conducted on this issue in a field setting (Lafrenière, Jowett, Vallerand, Donahue, & Lorimer, 2008, Study 1) revealed that athletes' harmonious passion toward their sport was positively related to various indices of relationship satisfaction with their coach, whereas obsessive passion was either unrelated or negatively related to those relationships. Subsequent research (Lafrenière et al., 2008, Study 2) with coaches confirmed the role of positive affect, generally experienced by coaches while coaching, as a mediator of the relation between harmonious passion toward coaching and perceived relationship quality with their players. Obsessive passion was unrelated to affect or relationship quality.

Although this research (i.e., Lafrenière et al., 2008, Studies 1 and 2) provided preliminary support for the hypothesized sequence of harmonious passion → positive affect → interpersonal relationship, such research had some limitations. First, it relied exclusively on self-reports. Second, because coaches and athletes knew each other at the time that they completed the questionnaire, it is possible that the quality of relationships influenced passion rather than the other way around. Third, these studies took place at one point in time, thereby precluding examination of the development of relationships as such. Finally, these studies did not identify a potential mediator of the influence of obsessive passion on relationship quality. Recent research conducted in a variety of settings, including sport, has addressed these issues (Philippe, Vallerand, Houlfort, Lavigne, & Donahue, 2010). In one study dealing with basketball players in a 1-week summer basketball camp (Philippe et al., 2010, Study 3), 200 athletes who did not know each other at the beginning of the week completed the Passion Scale toward basketball. Then, toward the end of the week they indicated the (general) positive and negative emotions experienced during the camp, as well as the quality of relationships developed during the camp. Furthermore, coaches were asked to rate their perceptions of each of their athletes' quality of interpersonal relationships developed with the other players at the camp. It was hypothesized that harmonious passion would positively predict positive affect experienced but negatively predict negative affect experienced, whereas obsessive passion would only positively predict negative affect. In turn, it was hypothesized that positive and negative affect experienced during the week would positively and negatively predict athletes' and coaches' relationship assessments, respectively. Results from structural equation modeling analyses provided support for the hypotheses. These findings were also obtained in three studies in other settings with both subjective and informant assessments (Philippe et al., 2010).

Overall, the findings from the Philippe et al. (2010) studies are important for at least three reasons. First, they show that passion does affect the quality of relationships that people develop in the passionate activity, from day 1. Second, these studies also reveal the nature of the processes, namely positive and negative affect, through which harmonious and obsessive passion differentially affect relationships, respectively. Finally, these affective processes are not only experienced by the passionate performers but also are being picked up by the people with whom they engage in the activity, thereby affecting their relationship with the passionate individuals as well.

The second relevant context where passion affects relationships takes place outside the purview of the passionate activity. Specifically, it pertains to the role of passion for a given activity (e.g., sport) on the quality of relationships outside the passionate activity (e.g., relationship with a spouse). The DMP posits that having an obsessive passion toward an activity should lead to conflict with other life activities because with obsessive passion, a person cannot let go of the passionate activity, whereas this should not be the case for harmonious passion. Recall that results from the Vallerand et al. (2003, Study 1) study provided preliminary evidence for this hypothesis on the role of obsessive (but not harmonious) passion in conflict between the passionate activity and other life domains. This basic hypothesis has important implications for the quality of interpersonal relationships that people experience outside the realm of the passionate activity. For instance, people with a passion for the Manchester United Football (soccer) Club may watch, read, listen to, and search the net for information on this team. If obsessive passion underlies such activity engagement, people may neglect other aspects of their lives, including their love lives. If done on a repeated basis, such behavior may have severe detrimental effects on a couple's relationship. Such should not be the case with harmonious passion because the person can let go of the passionate activity when needed and thus will not experience conflict between pursuing engagement in the passionate activity and spending time with the loved one.

A recent research with 150 English soccer fans (Vallerand, Ntoumanis, et al., 2008, Study 3) tested more directly the hypothesized sequence. English soccer fans were contacted at the soccer stadium of a large metropolitan city and asked to complete a questionnaire assessing passion toward soccer, perceptions of conflict between soccer and the loved one (adapted from Séguin-Lévesque, Laliberté, Pelletier, Blanchard, & Vallerand, 2003), and the satisfaction with their intimate relationship using the Perceived Relationship Quality Components Inventory (Fletcher, Simpson, & Thomas, 2000). Structural equation modeling analyses were conducted. As can be seen in figure 5.5, the results

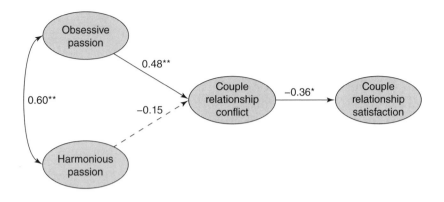

FIGURE 5.5 Results from the passion–conflict–couple relationship satisfaction model. For sake of clarity, the disturbances and the covariances are not presented.

Reprinted, by permission, from R.J. Vallerand et al., 2008, "On passion and sports fans: A look at football," *Journal of Sport Sciences* 26: 1279-1293.

revealed that an obsessive passion for a soccer team predicted conflict between soccer and the loved one. Conflict, in turn, negatively predicted satisfaction with the relationship. Harmonious passion was unrelated to these variables.

In sum, findings from the preceding research reveal that passion does make a difference with respect to relationships that people develop within the purview of the passionate activity, as well as relationships outside the realm of the passionate activity. Future research is needed to explore the role of passion in other types of relationships (e.g., friends, parents, siblings, and so on), as well as identify the actual behaviors at play in such relationships.

Passion and Intergroup Outcomes

International sport events are fascinating to study from the fans' perspective. Perhaps because passionate fans have internalized both the sport and their country, activity valuation is extremely high. Soccer fans, for instance, display high levels of support for their national teams, ranging from flag waving to singing national anthems, and even to having their bodies painted in their country's colors. Such sport events are often the display of pride in team achievement, as well as frustration after a team's defeat. Such events can lead to antagonistic and, at times, aggressive, behavior (Stott, Hutchison, & Drury, 2001). Why would fans engage in such negative behavior? Of course, frustration (e.g., Dollard & Miller, 1941) following a loss provides one answer. But frustration does not explain all because people can engage in violent behavior even following a victory by their team. For example, fans of the winning team can celebrate their team victory peacefully, or they can mock fans from the losing team, thereby triggering escalation and violence between the two groups of fans. What are some of the psychological processes underlying such diametrically opposed behavior following team victory?

It is hypothesized that the type of passion that people hold and the emotions that it triggers can help explain these different behaviors. Two relevant emotions are pride and hate. Pride is closely linked to a person's identity. Therefore, it should lead people to want to express this emotion publicly, such as peacefully celebrating, especially following a win by their team. On the other hand, hate is a negative emotion specifically oriented at someone. It can lead to outward behavior aimed at others, such as mocking fans of the losing team. Both harmonious and obsessive passion are expected to be positively related to the emotion of pride, especially after success, because for both types of passion the team that a person is rooting for is part of identity. On the other hand, the two types of passion should differentially predict the hatred directed toward opponents. Because harmonious passion takes root in the authentic integrating self (Deci & Ryan, 2000; Hodgins & Knee, 2002), it should cause the person's identity to be secure, and thus the fans of the other team should be perceived not as obstacles or enemies but merely as opponents. Therefore, harmonious passion should not lead to the experience of hate toward supporters of other teams. Conversely, because it originates from ego-invested self-structures (Hodgins & Knee, 2002), obsessive passion may lead to the perception that fans of other teams are obstacles in the way of the team's victory or even as a symbolic threat to the self (Steele, 1988). Thus, obsessive passion would be expected to lead to the experience of hate toward opposing teams. In turn, the emotions of pride and hate should have different effects on the two types of behavior discussed previously. Specifically, hating supporters of other teams should primarily lead people to go into the streets to mock them (or worse!), whereas the emotion of pride is expected to lead primarily to celebrating peacefully in the streets.

My colleagues and I have recently conducted research to explore these issues (Vallerand, Ntoumanis, et al., 2008, Study 2). In that study, conducted in Montreal just a few hours before the start of the 2006 World Soccer Cup Finals, we asked fans of the two finalist countries (France and Italy) to complete a questionnaire assessing their passion for soccer and various emotions experienced during the tournament up to that point, including those of pride and hate toward the teams that they faced. Finally, we asked them the extent to which they engaged in peaceful celebration and in mocking the fans of the other team following their team's victory during the tournament. Because both teams had won all their games up to the finals, this study allowed us to provide some answers to the question posed earlier with respect to acceptable and unacceptable behavior following team victory. Results from structural equation modeling provided support for the hypothesized model. Specifically, both types of passion predicted the emotion of pride that, in turn, predicted peaceful celebration of the team's victory. But as expected, only obsessive passion predicted the emotion of hate, which in turn was found to lead to mocking the fans of the losing team.

In sum the present research supports the view from the DMP that harmonious and obsessive passions predict different emotions (pride and hate) that in turn lead to different behaviors (including some that can lead to violence) toward fans of other teams. Future research is needed on this issue because it may lead to an increased understanding of some of the roots of hooliganism (e.g., Stott et al., 2001). Furthermore, additional research is needed on the role of passion in intergroup behavior that takes place with other participants, such as competing athletes and exercisers.

Passionate Functioning Under Various Situations

The DMP makes more refined predictions regarding the behavior of highly involved individuals, such as passionate ones, in specific situations. This is especially the case when situations (e.g., success or failure) have implications for a person's sense of identity (Sedikides & Gregg, 2003; Sedikides & Strube, 1997). When finding themselves in such situations, passionate people should react differently as a function of the predominant type of passion that they hold toward the passionate activity. At least two situations seem relevant: (1) failure prevention by aggressively removing interpersonal obstacles and (2) irremediable success and failure and their influence on psychological well-being. These situations and relevant research are discussed in the following sections.

Failure Prevention by Attacking the Threat Source

My colleagues and I have recently conducted a series of studies to gain a better understanding of the conditions under which aggressive behavior is likely to occur in various real-life situations, including those that pertain to sport. The basic relation between passion and aggression was tested in two studies with basketball players (Donahue, Rip, & Vallerand, 2009). Results of Study 1 confirmed that college basketball players with a predominant obsessive passion generally report being more aggressive when they play than those with a predominant harmonious passion. The goal of Study 2 was to determine under which circumstances obsessively passionate athletes are more likely to display aggressive behavior. Furthermore, these aggressive behaviors are more likely to take place when their sense of competence and identity has been threatened. Indeed, research has shown that aggressive behavior can result from threatened egotism (i.e., highly favorable views of the self that are disputed by others; Baumeister, Bushman, & Campbell, 2000). When their self-views are threatened, people are motivated to act aggressively to restore positive self-views, especially if such aggression leads to success in the situation at hand. Thus, under conditions in which identity is threatened or diminished, people would be likely to react aggressively toward others to restore their positive self-views (Steele, 1988). Finally, such an effect should be even more important for obsessively passionate individuals because their defensive mode of functioning leads them to be highly motivated to defend against any threat that is targeted at the self (see Hodgins, Yacko, & Gottlieb, 2006). Such is not the case for harmoniously passionate individuals, who can face threatening information nondefensively.

Of additional importance is the fact that research has shown that when people have the opportunity to self-affirm (Steele, 1988) or to focus on some of their competent personal skills or abilities before having their identity threatened, then they become less defensive about the threatening information. We would then predict that people would be much less aggressive under self-affirming conditions. In fact, under conditions of self-affirmation, differences between the two types of passionate individuals should be much less pronounced because obsessively passionate individuals' sense of identity has been secured before receiving the threatening information.

In Study 2, Donahue et al. (2009) tested those hypotheses. College basketball players first completed the passion scale toward basketball and were then randomly assigned to one of two conditions: identity threat or self-affirmation. In line with research on self-affirmation (e.g., Steele, 1988), identity threat was induced by asking participants to reflect on some of their weaknesses as a basketball player, whereas participants in the self-affirmation conditions were asked to reflect on their strengths. Finally, participants read three hypothetical situations and for each one responded to four items that measured the athletes' intention to use aggression in that situation. For instance, the first situation read this way:

> There are 2 seconds left in an important game. Your team is winning by 1 point. The other team shot the ball, and there is a rebound. An opponent is just about to make a tip-in and win the game. You are under the basket and nobody is looking at you (not even the referees) because all eyes are turned toward the opposing player. What do you do to the opposing player?

Participants then indicated on a 7-point scale the extent to which they would behave aggressively on each of four items that reflected a linear increase in aggression: (1) "I let him (her) shoot"; (2) "I try to break his (her) concentration by screaming"; (3) "I touch him (her) slightly and hope that it will be enough to make him (her) miss"; and (4) "I clip his (her) legs and act as if it was a box out." A composite score reflecting the linear increase in aggression from items 1 to 4 was computed.

In line with the preceding reasoning, it was expected that obsessively passionate players in the identity threat condition would display higher levels of situational aggression compared to harmoniously passionate players. Conversely, it was expected that no difference would be found in the situational aggression between obsessively and harmoniously passionate players under the self-affirming condition. A two-by-two (passion types by identity threat versus self-affirmation) ANOVA was conducted on the behavioral intentions of aggression. The results revealed the presence of a main effect for passion where obsessive passion led to higher levels of aggression than did harmonious passion. These findings replicated those of Study 1. More important, the results also revealed the presence of an interaction that supported the hypotheses. Specifically, although no difference took place between the two types of passionate groups under conditions of self-affirmation, significant differences appeared under identity threat conditions where obsessively passionate athletes were found to be more aggressive than harmoniously passionate ones. Note as well that the findings were replicated in another series of studies on passion and aggression (road rage) by Philippe, Vallerand, Richer, Vallieres, and Bergeron (2009), including research under controlled laboratory conditions and with an objective assessment of aggression (observers' measure).

Overall, research reviewed in this section revealed that aggression is especially likely to take place for obsessively passionate individuals following identity threat and when aggression is likely to help remove the obstacle (or threat) that prevents achieving success. Research is needed to determine under which conditions, if any, harmonious passion leads to aggression.

Subjective Well-Being Following Irremediable Success and Failure

Playing poorly in the last game of the season and consequently failing to make the playoffs or failing to make the national team for the Olympics are situations that connote clear success or failure that cannot be changed (at least not in the near future). Thus, people have to deal affectively with these situations (Campbell & Sedikides, 1999; Sedikides & Gregg, 2008). How should people with a predominant obsessive or harmonious passion react psychologically to such situations? To the extent that the event is highly significant and irremediable, then failing should lead to similar effects for individuals with a predominant harmonious and obsessive passion.

Amiot, Vallerand, and Blanchard (2006) tested this hypothesis. Male adolescent and young adult hockey players (n = 233) who had been playing competitive hockey for several years and who presented themselves at a tryout camp for a team playing in a highly competitive league participated in this study. Making the most competitive league was important for them because it significantly increased the likelihood that they would be drafted by a professional team. Failing to make this league seriously jeopardized their chances. Athletes then completed a questionnaire at time 1 that assessed their level of passion toward hockey as well as their subjective well-being (the French form of the Satisfaction With Life Scale by Blais et al., 1989; the PANAS Scale of Watson, Clark, & Tellegan, 1988; and the Center for Epidemiological Studies Depression Scale, Radloff, 1977, reverse scored). Two weeks later, at time 2, athletes completed a second questionnaire that assessed well-being immediately after finding out whether they had made the team. We created two groups of harmoniously and obsessively passionate hockey players using the same procedures as those reported earlier (e.g., Philippe, Vallerand, & Lavigne, 2009; Vallerand & Houlfort, 2003). Then a two-by-two (passion type by success or failure) ANCOVA was conducted on time 2 well-being, controlling for time 1 well-being. Results showed that participants who did not make a team from a highly competitive league (and thus whose future career in hockey was seriously jeopardized) experienced significantly lower levels of psychological well-being than those who made that team (i.e., those who were selected by a more competitive league), irrespective of their type of passion. Harmoniously passionate people, then, can suffer psychologically following failure just as obsessively passionate people do, especially when the negative event is a highly negative one and is irreversible.

The Amiot et al. study had a second purpose. Specifically, in line with a P–E fit perspective, we sought to determine whether there were different situations or contexts wherein each type of passionate individual would thrive psychologically and experience high levels of well-being. A P–E fit is achieved when there is a match between personal characteristics of the person and characteristics of the environment. Past research has shown that a P–E fit is positively associated with various indices of psychological well-being (see Harackiewicz, Sansone, Blair, Epstein, & Manderlink, 1987; O'Connor & Vallerand, 1994; Tauer & Harackiewicz, 1999). It was hypothesized that highly competitive environments that require people to be highly involved in the activity at the expense of other life domains can be seen as fitting well with an obsessive type of passion. Conversely, less demanding competitive environments that do not require an inordinate investment of time in the activity should fit better with those holding a harmonious passion who may have more diversified interests (Vallerand et al., 2003; Vallerand & Houlfort, 2003). It was thus hypothesized that a match between the passion type and the environment (obsessive versus harmonious league) would lead to higher levels of subjective well-being.

To provide a test of the preceding hypotheses, the hockey players of the Amiot et al. study were followed 2 months after team selection (i.e., after approximately one-third of the regular hockey season had elapsed). This interval allowed players ample time to get used to their environment. Participants completed the same well-being measures at that time (time 3). In line with the P–E fit perspective, results from the ANCOVA revealed the presence of an interaction at time 3, controlling for time 1 well-being. More specifically, it was found that among those who were playing in the highly competitive leagues, obsessively passionate individuals displayed higher levels of well-being compared to harmoniously passionate athletes. Conversely, among the athletes who ended up playing in the less competitive leagues, harmoniously passionate athletes reported higher levels of well-being than did obsessively passionate ones.

In sum, it appears that when the outcome is supremely important, no differences take place between the two types of passionate individuals, at least as pertain to psychological well-being (Amiot et al., 2006). Furthermore, it appears that a P–E fit process is at play where environments that match a person's type of passion are conducive to higher levels of subjective well-being. Future research is needed to increase understanding of the psychological processes at play for passionate individuals in various situations and the ways in which those processes affect their sense of well-being and other outcomes.

Practical Applications

Although some nuances were found, research reviewed in this chapter has shown that harmonious passion is generally associated with more positive consequences than obsessive passion is. It would therefore seem appropriate to propose ways of facilitating harmonious passion. To promote harmonious passion, the three-step process at the core of the development of passion (see Mageau, Vallerand, Charest, et al., 2009) can be used. The three steps are, respectively, (1) activity selection, (2) activity valuation, and (3) the internalization of the activity representation in a person's identity. As seen previously, the role of the social environment at each of the three stages is crucial. Adults are in a prime position to promote children's harmonious passion, especially if they nurture children's need for autonomy and relatedness. With respect to the first step of activity selection, parents and physical educators should encourage children to perform a variety of sport activities, especially at a relatively young age (3–6 years). Later on (age 7–10 years), parents can register their children for a different activity each term. When they have tried a variety of activities and have developed sufficient knowledge to make decisions (perhaps around age 10 to 13 years), children can be encouraged to decide for themselves which activity they would like to engage in for the season. Such a variety of experiences may translate into a greater likelihood of selecting an activity that is a good fit with the child's identity and will thus later become a passion (see Mageau et al., 2009). Enjoyable experiences devoid of pressure and coercion in which children are provided with autonomy support and have the opportunity to choose by themselves their sport activity should set the stage for harmonious passion to blossom. In contrast, pressure or coercion to engage in sport or physical activity is likely to lead to the development of either amotivation (or the loss of motivation) or an obsessive passion toward the sport.

Autonomy support is also recommended for the other two stages of passion development. For instance, with respect to the second step in the passion development process, namely valuation of the selected sport activity, noncontrolling and supportive parents, physical educators, and coaches who preach by example and serve as models (e.g., Bandura, 1977a) may provide the necessary impetus to lead the young athletes to invest further in the sport activity and value it even more. The role of peers should not be underestimated because friends' influence becomes increasingly important as children move toward puberty (Damon, 1988). It should not be surprising that players on the same team have similar levels and types of passion in part because of the coach's influence but also because of the modeling influence that teammates provide. Such influence may lead to the internalization of the prevalent type of passion in that particular team environment. Similarly, a harmonious passion is likely to develop if the internalization process takes place in social environments (e.g., parents, friends, and especially coaches) that promote children's sense of autonomy (Deci & Ryan, 1987, 2000) by providing opportunities for choices, ownership, or "voice" regarding decisions and behaviors. For example, athletes who have recently started cross country running would be more likely to develop a harmonious passion toward this sport if their coach clearly explains to them why it is important to practice daily and gives them opportunities to choose among various practice regimens. Conversely, chances are that the same athletes would either lose their motivation for running or develop an obsessive passion if their coach pressures or coerces them to practice more or fails to explain the purpose of various training exercises.

Finally, practitioners and coaches who work with elite athletes should keep in mind that providing autonomy support is also important with high-level athletes. Indeed, by helping athletes feel autonomous by allowing them to provide input in game decisions (perhaps in the manner of Phil Jackson of the Los Angeles Lakers), the coach is likely to help maintain athletes' harmonious passion, facilitate a high level of performance, and create positive coach–athlete relationships. Coaches and consultants may believe that it is appropriate to be controlling toward high elite and professional athletes because such practices may enhance performance. Although the evidence presented in this chapter does not indicate that being controlling necessarily undermines performance, it does indicate that such behavior is likely to lead to obsessive passion and thus to some negative outcomes, such as lower levels of psychological, health, and relational well-being in athletes. In turn, negative coach–athlete relationships may have ill effects on cohesion, indirectly and negatively affect performance, and even cost the coach her or his job. Thus, creating an autonomy supportive environment may go a long way in providing positive outcomes for both athletes and coaches.

Directions for Future Research

So far in this chapter, I have reviewed several studies that provide strong support for the DMP. Although the research conducted to date is indeed encouraging, additional research is needed to probe further the role of passion in sport and exercise. In the following section, I present certain directions for future research that appear particularly exciting.

Passion Development

Research seen earlier reveals that a number of processes are important for the development of passion (i.e., activity selection and valuation, identity, and internalization processes; Mageau, Vallerand, Charest, et al., 2009). But other important issues should also be considered in the development of passion. The first pertains to the level of passion that a significant adult such as a coach or a parent may transmit to children. For instance, a basketball coach who is dynamic, energetic, and enthusiastic may be more likely to transmit his or her passion for basketball to athletes than a coach who is boring. Does such a phenomenon exist? Can others transmit passion? Although some authors think so (Cardon, 2008), research is needed to answer this question. And if so, what processes are involved in passion transmission?

A second issue of interest pertaining to the development of passion deals with the potential existence of stages of passion. People often assume that some form of universal sequence exists with respect to the development of passion (e.g., people initially experience an obsessive passion for the activity and then the passion becomes progressively more harmonious). No direct empirical evidence currently exists on this issue. Nevertheless, preliminary evidence seems to indicate that such is not the case. Vallerand and colleagues (2003, Study 1) did not find any relationship between length of involvement and the two types of passion. Furthermore, additional research that has reanalyzed the developmental study of Mageau, Vallerand, Charest, et al. (2009, Study 3) did not find evidence of stages (see Vallerand, 2010). These findings, however, are limited in scope, and future research is needed to address the stage hypothesis more directly using longitudinal designs.

A third fruitful area for future research deals with the potential role that perceptions of progression toward the activity may play in the ongoing development of the passion. Individuals who expect a bright future in the passionate activity might be more likely to develop and maintain a passion for the activity. Perceptions of progression would appear different from those of competence. For instance, a person may feel competent now but see that progression will no longer continue. Such perceptions of lack of progression might curtail the development of passion, especially if people believe that their desired "future self" (Markus & Nurius, 1986) or future identity as an athlete (or coach or referee) is no longer attainable. Furthermore, it might prove important to determine whether progression has the same influence on the two types of passion. Because of the rigid persistence that it creates, obsessive passion may lead people to persist in the activity no matter what the progression is likely to be. But perceptions of progression should influence harmonious passion because they lead people to engage in the passionate activity with choice and flexibility. Persistence in the activity in this case represents a continued reflective choice to pursue task engagement, and perceptions of progression may represent one of the determinants of such choice. Thus, we might hypothesize that perceptions of progression are more important for the maintenance of harmonious passion than for obsessive passion. Future research on these issues would be useful to predict long-term passionate activity engagement that is needed to reach the highest levels of excellence.

A final research issue pertains to the potential changes in passion that may take place over time. For example, can an obsessive passion be changed into a harmonious one? Given that the activity is already passionate, the activity is sufficiently important to have been internalized into the person's identity. Thus, based on the DMP, one way to induce changes from an obsessive passion to a harmonious passion would be to replace the controlled internalization process by the autonomous internalization process. This could be done by having the person reflect on the variety of ways through which the activity is consonant with her or his intrinsic values (Kasser, 2002) or by identifying the various autonomous reasons the activity is important for the person (e.g., fun aspect of it, positive feelings experienced when engaging in the activity, perceptions of competence and creativity, sense of choice in deciding when and how to do the activity, and so on). Over time, changes in the type of predominant passion should take place.

Long-Term Sport Performance

Research so far on passion and performance (Bonneville-Roussy et al., 2010; Vallerand, Salvy, et al., 2007; Vallerand, Mageau, et al., 2008) is limited in scope because it has spanned only 6 months at the most. What do we know about athletes who train to reach the Olympics or the professional levels? Such performance levels may take up to 10 years to be attained (Ericsson & Charness, 1994). What type of passion may most benefit the athlete? Our research on persistence (e.g., Vallerand et al., 2003, Studies 3 and 4) tends to suggest that athletes with an obsessive passion should persist more, especially if conditions are difficult. Given similar levels of time involvement and quality of deliberate practice, increased persistence in sport should be conducive to higher levels of performance. Thus, on the one hand, it might be predicted that obsessive passion is conducive to higher levels of performance in the long run. On the other hand, because it facilitates high levels of SWB, Subjective Well-Being, in the process (Vallerand, 2010), harmonious passion may lead athletes to persist more in sport and eventually reach the highest performance levels. Clearly, future research is needed to test these competing hypotheses on the long-term effects of passion on sport performance.

Optimal Conditions for Harmonious and Obsessive Passion

The research reviewed in this chapter overwhelmingly revealed that, overall, harmonious passion leads to adaptive outcomes, whereas obsessive passion leads to less adaptive and at times clearly maladaptive outcomes. Yet I hasten to add that this does not mean that harmonious passion is always "good" and obsessive passion is always "bad." Indeed, we have seen that under certain conditions obsessive passion is more conducive to positive effects than harmonious passion is (e.g., Amiot et al., 2006). For instance, it appears that "obsessive" and "harmonious" environments (like the different leagues in the Amiot et al., 2006, study) lead to different levels of psychological well-being in the two types of passionate individuals. Clearly, future research is needed to identify what adaptive processes are triggered by these situations in each type of passionate individual. By identifying the adaptive mind-set developed by each type of passionate individual, it might be possible to teach it to the other type of passionate individual, thereby leading to positive outcomes in both harmoniously and obsessively passionate people. Future research on this issue should thus lead to both theoretical and applied benefits.

End of Engagement in the Passionate Activity

One interesting question that the DMP raises deals with the consequences of permanently stopping activity engagement. Who is likely to adjust better psychologically after such "retirement" from the activity—harmoniously passionate or obsessively passionate individuals? We could hypothesize that harmoniously passionate people should fare better because harmonious passion is characterized by a flexible engagement toward the activity (Vallerand et al., 2003). Thus, it should be easier for those individuals to disengage from the activity (see Wrosch et al., 2003) and move on to (or reinvest in) something else. On the other hand, because obsessive passion is characterized by rigid persistence toward the activity and given that contingencies such as self-esteem are attached to the activity, people with an obsessive passion should have a difficult time letting go of their passionate activity. They therefore should not adjust well after retirement. Thus, athletes with a predominant obsessive passion may be more likely to come out of retirement à la Michael Jordan, and sometimes more than once.

A study of ours within the work domain (see Vallerand & Houlfort, 2003) has addressed some of these issues. Workers who had recently retired were asked to report their level of passion toward work retrospectively and their current subjective well-being. Results revealed that harmonious passion for work was associated with enhanced subjective well-being, whereas obsessive passion was negatively related to well-being, following retirement. Because of the obvious limitations of retrospective designs, prospective and longitudinal research is needed to demonstrate more clearly the psychological processes involved in letting go of the passionate activity and determine whether different processes are at play for the harmoniously and obsessively passionate workers. Longitudinal research is needed to establish the role of passion in the decision to disengage permanently from an activity that people have been involved with for a lifetime, such as sport or exercise, and the implications that such a decision may have on subjective well-being.

Summary

The purpose of the present chapter was to present the DMP (e.g., Vallerand, 2008, 2010; Vallerand et al., 2003; Vallerand & Houlfort, 2003) and review some of the relevant research in sport and exercise. Passion is defined as a strong inclination toward a self-defining activity that one loves, values (finds important), and devotes a significant amount of time and energy to. Furthermore, two types of passion are proposed. Harmonious passion originates from an autonomous internalization in identity and entails control over the activity and a harmonious coexistence of the passionate activity with other activities. On the other hand, obsessive passion follows a controlled internalization and entails a relative lack of control over the passionate activity, rigid persistence, and conflict with other activities in the person's life. Furthermore, a number of social and personal determinants are hypothesized to determine the initial and ongoing development of passion for a given activity. Finally, in general, more adaptive outcomes are hypothesized to follow from harmonious passion than from obsessive passion.

The review of evidence provides strong support for the model. Specifically, a Passion Scale was developed to assess harmonious and obsessive passion. In addition, research on the development of passion provided support for the processes proposed by the DMP. Furthermore, research has shown that harmonious passion promotes adaptive outcomes to a greater extent than obsessive passion does on a number of cognitive, affective, behavioral, psychological and physical health; interpersonal and intergroup; and performance outcomes using self-report, as well as informant reports and objective data. It was also found that, under certain specific situations, obsessive passion can lead to some positive outcomes and harmonious passion can lead to less adaptive ones. Although much of the research conducted to date is correlational in nature, several studies using prospective and longitudinal designs showed that passion leads to changes in outcomes over time. In addition, an increasing number of studies use experimental designs to test the processes and conditions through which passion leads to different outcomes. Finally, directions for future research and applications were proposed.

The use of the word *passion* permeates the world of sport and exercise, yet until recently little theory and research have focused on this concept. I submit that the DMP represents a useful blueprint that can help us better understand the passion construct and its diverse ramifications, eventually leading to both conceptual and applied advances for the realm of sport and exercise.

CHAPTER 6

Goal Setting to Enhance Motivation in Sport

Glyn C. Roberts, PhD
Elsa Kristiansen, PhD
Norwegian School of Sport Sciences

Goal setting is the most utilized motivational enhancement technique in sport psychology. Every applied sport psychology textbook has a chapter explaining that goal setting is a useful tool to enhance motivation and self-confidence (e.g., Williams, 2010). Research in the area have proliferated with the growth of sport psychology as a field. Just over 30 years has passed since the first goal-setting study specifically in the physical activity area was conducted (Barnett, 1977), but since then the research field has grown exponentially. Originally given impetus in sport psychology by Weinberg and colleagues (e.g., Weinberg, Bruya, & Jackson, 1985), it is now one of the most active research areas in applied sport psychology (see Burton & Weiss, 2008). Recent reviews have clearly shown that goal setting consistently works in enhancing performance in sport, that it is effective across a wide array of athletic events and athletic experience, and that more concern is being paid to the processes underpinning goal setting (e.g., Burton & Weiss, 2008; Gould, 2010; Kingston & Wilson, 2009). Despite this increased activity and concern for how goal setting works, there is still confusion in the literature about what goals people should set, what psychological processes are involved in goal setting, and how people go about setting goals for either themselves or others (Roberts & Kristiansen, 2010).

The purpose of this chapter is to examine the conceptual underpinning of goal setting by reviewing the existing theory and research on goal setting. The intention is to gain better understanding of the motivational process of goal setting. This will not be a definitive review of the goal setting literature; for that we refer you to Burton and Weiss (2008) and their excellent review of the 88 (to date) studies that met their inclusion criteria on goal setting in sport and physical activity and to Kingston and Wilson (2009) for their thoughtful insight into goal-setting mechanisms. Rather, we attempt here to clarify what we believe to be a conceptual confusion in the literature and to place goal-setting research more firmly into a coherent theoretical motivational framework. Specifically, we discuss the conceptual arguments and counterarguments that have separated achievement goals in goal-setting research from the achievement goals in contemporary motivation theory and research.

Goal Setting

Goal setting is a mental technique that has been used sporadically since the end of the 19th century (Latham & Locke, 2007), especially in organizational psychology. The goal-setting literature is impressive and extensive, and it has a long and distinguished history. Initiated by Locke and colleagues (e.g., Locke & Latham, 1990; Locke, Shaw, Saari, & Latham, 1981), goal setting has been applied to various laboratory, field, and real-world settings using a myriad of tasks. Individuals who set specific and challenging goals perform better than people who set no goals or who are simply told to do their best. Goal setting is a popular basic sport psychology technique, and it is often the one first introduced when implementing mental training because it is claimed to be fundamental to maximizing athletic potential (Hardy, Jones, & Gould, 1996). In fact, goal setting has been claimed to be the single most used psychological intervention of sport psychologists working with Olympic athletes as long ago as 1989 (Gould, Tammen, Murphy, & May, 1989), and its popularity continues to the present day (Burton, Pickering, Weinberg, Yukelson, & Weigand, 2010; Gould, 2010). Goal setting works, and it is apparently easy to employ. It is little wonder that goal setting became a staple of mental skills coaching in sport.

However, no theoretical framework was in place to guide these early studies, nor was it discovered why goal setting affected performance in the work setting. The field became more theoretical with the seminal work of Locke and Latham in presenting their goal-setting theory (1990). It may be argued, however, that goal setting has not been informed by theory per se but is simply the investigation of the strong functional relationship between the setting of goals and performance on a sport task or skill (Hall & Kerr, 2001). Therefore, a pertinent question may be, What is the conceptual base of goal setting? Locke and colleagues (Locke et al., 1981) defined a goal as "what an individual is trying to accomplish; it is the object or aim of an action" (p. 126). Later, a goal was defined as attaining "a specific standard of proficiency at a task" (Locke & Latham, 2002). As Gould (2010) specified, goals focus on achieving some standard of excellence or reaching some performance criterion in sport. It may be argued that goals within the goal-setting milieu are what we would describe as achievement goals in the motivation literature.

Goals are assumed to enhance performance primarily through enhancing motivation. Locke and Latham (1990) argue that goals affect performance by focusing attention to the task, encouraging persistence, increasing effort and performance intensity, and promoting new performance strategies. These are precisely the attributes that motivation theories purport to affect (e.g., see Roberts, this volume; Roberts, Treasure, & Conroy, 2007). Goals affect performance through both the content of the goal (i.e., the nature of what is to be accomplished) and the intensity with which the goal will be pursued (i.e., the perceived resource requirements to attain the performance goal) (Hall & Kerr, 2001). These ideas led to the fundamental findings of goal-setting research, a research that has mostly concerned goal-setting techniques to enhance performance. As a result we know that difficult goals lead to higher performance than easy goals and that specific goals lead to higher performance than "do your best" goals or no goals (Haslam, Wegge, & Postmes, 2009; Kingston & Wilson, 2009).

But goal setting is a "double-edged sword" according to Hall and Kerr (2001), and Burton and Naylor (2002) say that it has a "Jekyll and Hyde nature." Goal setting is now universally known. Athletes know that goal setting is good, but they struggle with how best to set goals that will maximize their performance. Because of the general knowledge and understanding about how goals should be implemented and what type of goals to use, coaches and athletes often forget that many factors can affect the goal-setting process. Although practitioners continue to use and recommend it, researchers continue to argue about why and how well it works.

Within organizational psychology, the basic findings just mentioned have been replicated consistently, and Locke and Latham (1985) argued that it should be replicated in sport. But the findings have not been replicated with the same consistency within the sport context (e.g., Burton, 1992; Hall & Byrne, 1988; Weinberg & Weigand, 1993). Many have been troubled by the inconsistency in the findings within sport psychology (see e.g., Gould, 2010; Hall & Kerr, 2001; Kingston & Wilson, 2009), and some have proffered explanations to account for these differences (e.g., Burton, Naylor, & Holliday, 2001). In a more recent comprehensive review, Burton and Weiss (2008) argue that the weight of the extant evidence is now so overwhelming that the findings confirm "that goal setting is also an effective performance enhancement technique in the physical activity domain" (p. 344). On the other hand, Hall and Kerr argue that it is "not so much a flawed methodology that renders goal-setting research in sport problematic but rather a conceptual narrowness that encourages a preoccupation with performance effects while largely ignoring how athletes who are striving for goals process performance information" (Hall & Kerr, 2001, p. 185).

A Search for Theory

Most of the research in sport psychology has been atheoretical in that the studies have applied specific goal-setting techniques (e.g., setting short-term, specific, discrete, or challenging goals) to sport tasks (see Burton et al., 2001). But not all researchers are concerned solely in *whether* goal setting works; some are also interested in *why* it works (e.g., Burton & Weiss, 2008; Hall & Kerr, 2001; Kingston & Wilson, 2009; Roberts & Kristiansen, 2010). One of the first studies in sport on goal setting (Burton, 1984) is also important because it is one of the first studies to apply theory to goal setting. Because goal setting is assumed to promote performance through enhancing motivation to perform, Burton applied motivation theory to the goal-setting phenomenon. Burton looked at the effect of a goal-setting program on performance and certain cognitions of intercollegiate swimmers, male and female. Burton applied his interpretation of achievement goal theory (e.g., Nicholls, 1984, 1989) and found that when the swimmers focused on what he termed *performance goals* rather than on what he termed *outcome goals*, then they had better performance and more positive cognitions (lower in anxiety, higher in self-confidence). Achievement goal theory informed the intervention successfully. But rather than continuing with achievement goal theory, Burton and colleagues (e.g., Burton & Naylor, 2002; Burton & Weiss, 2008) developed a competitive goal model (CGS) that advances a fundamental goal concept in sport that integrates "discrete and global conceptions of goals, and accounts for personality influences on the goal-setting process" (p. 355).

Burton and colleagues (e.g., Burton & Weiss, 2008) advocate that the fundamental goal concept in sport is "perhaps the most important concept in all of sport psychology" (Burton & Weiss, 2008, p. 355). In their CGS model, Burton and colleagues adopt the notion of others in advocating outcome, performance, and process goals within the goal-setting phenomenon (e.g., Hardy & Nelson, 1988). Process goals refer to improving form, technique, and strategy; performance goals refer to improving personal performance; and outcome goals emphasize outperforming others and achieving objective outcomes (e.g., Gould, 2010; Kingston & Wilson, 2009). According to Burton and colleagues, focusing on process and performance goals rather than outcome goals is the basis of the fundamental goal concept. They argue that we should emphasize process and performance goals because these form the basis to realize outcome goals. They advocate that the three goals lie on a continuum that has process goals on one end of the continuum, outcome goals on the other end, and performance goals midway between the two. To enhance motivation and performance, practitioners should stress process and performance goals so that they can achieve outcome goals (Burton & Weiss, 2008). The whole chapter is devoted to demonstrating the efficacy of CGS. But their arguments of a correspondence between goal-setting styles (process, performance, and outcome goals) and dispositional goal orientations was considered "difficult to substantiate at either a conceptual or an empirical level" (Hall & Kerr, 2001, p. 225).

Another attempt to understand why goal setting works was by Kingston and Wilson (2009) and their colleagues (e.g., Kingston, Harwood, & Spray, 2006). They argue that it is "limiting not to consider the potential underlying factors that may well influence (*a*) the discrete moment to moment goals that individuals set; and (*b*) the cognitive, affective, and behavioral responses to setting and striving towards those goals" (p. 77). Kingston and Wilson used achievement goal theory (e.g., Nicholls, 1989), in which goals are the cognitive drivers of both involvement and achievement behavior in sport. They are congruent with achievement goal theory in sport when they stated that people are motivated to demonstrate competence and adopt achievement goals that are meaningful for them within the context. Individuals develop a personal theory about how things work in the achievement setting and then set goals that are consistent with their personal theory of what it takes to demonstrate competence within the context (e.g., Nicholls, 1989; Roberts, 2001; Roberts et al., 2007). Kingston and Wilson concurred with achievement goal theory evidence in sport (e.g., Roberts, this volume; Roberts et al., 2007) that two basic goals exist in which individuals who are focused on demonstrating competence through mastery and learning of tasks are termed *task involved* and individuals who are focused on demonstrating competence through outperforming others and in demonstrating superiority are termed *ego involved*. Again consistent with achievement goal theory, Kingston and Wilson embrace the argument of Nicholls that individuals are predisposed to be task or ego involved and termed these predispositions task orientation and ego orientation. But Kingston and

Wilson begin to deviate from achievement goal theory when they argue that the goals are not orthogonal. They argue that even Nicholls (1989) believed that the orientations were not orthogonal all the time, and they cite Nicholls' suggestion that "one cannot be both task and ego involved at the same moment in time" (p. 240). The work of Harwood and colleagues (e.g., Harwood, Hardy, & Swain, 2000) is cited to confirm that the moment-to-moment fluctuation of goal states is an entirely plausible state of affairs. We do not argue with Kingston and Wilson about changing goal involvement, and strong evidence shows that goal involvement does change over time (e.g., Gernigon, d'Arripe-Longueville, Delignières, & Ninot, 2004; Pensgaard & Roberts, 2002). But Kingston and Wilson, in concert with others (e.g., Harwood et al., 2000), confuse goal involvement with goal orientations! To explain, we must briefly review the substance of achievement goal theory. To understand and be able to enhance motivation in the context of sport, we must attempt to understand the process of motivation, the constructs that drive the process, and the way in which goal setting becomes an integral part of the process. We will not discuss achievement goal theory in detail but instead refer the reader to Roberts (this volume) for a comprehensive explanation. Nevertheless, we need to discuss the process briefly to set later arguments into perspective.

Achievement Goal Theory

Motivational processes can be defined by the psychological constructs that energize, direct, and regulate achievement behavior (cf. Roberts, 2001, this volume). First, motivation processes are qualities of the person and refer to how the person assesses what is needed to succeed. Second, motivation processes are future oriented because they help people anticipate and predict future events and consequences that are meaningful to them. Motivation prepares the individual to move forward to reach desired goals or produce desired outcomes. Third, motivation processes are evaluative in character. These evaluations may be self-referenced or may involve pertinent others as criteria of reference. Motivation involves the person assessing whether to increase or decrease behavioral striving to achieve success and avoid failure.

People become motivated, or demotivated, through assessments of their competencies within the achievement context and the meaning of the context to themselves. The individual develops personal goals (e.g., by being exposed to them by family and friends or by being exposed to institutional agents such as teachers or coaches) within any achievement context, and these personal goals give meaning to achievement striving and energize subsequent action. Personal goals reside in the person, but they may be derived from context cues or through instructions given by significant others. The personal goals may also be culturally or socially defined, but they will be useful as a part of a motivational process only if the person adopts them. Within achievement goal theory, it is these personal or socially valued goals that energize achievement striving.

Individuals give meaning to their achievement behavior through the goals that they adopt. These goals reflect the purposes of achievement striving. Once adopted, the achievement goal determines the integrated pattern of beliefs that undergird approach and avoid strategies, the differing engagement levels, and the differing responses to achievement outcomes. Thus, variation of achievement behavior may not be the manifestation of high or low motivation per se but the expression of different perceptions of appropriate goals with their attendant constellation of cognitions.

The overall goal of action in achievement goal theory is assumed to be the desire to develop and demonstrate competence and to avoid demonstrating incompetence. One of Nicholls' (1984) conceptual contributions was to argue that more than one conception of ability exists and that achievement goals and behavior may differ depending on the conception of ability held by the person. Nicholls argued that two conceptions of ability (at least) manifest themselves in achievement contexts, namely an undifferentiated concept of ability, in which ability and effort are not differentiated by the individual, and a differentiated concept of ability, in which ability and effort are differentiated (Nicholls, 1984, 1989).

Following a series of experiments, Nicholls (e.g., 1978; Nicholls & Miller, 1983, 1984b) determined that young children are typically task involved because they are incapable of differentiating ability from effort and often define ability as effort expended (Nicholls, 1978). But adolescents and adults are able to differentiate effort from ability and are thus capable of being ego involved. Adolescents and adults can therefore choose to be task or ego involved, depending on their interpretation of what it takes to be successful in the context.

People will approach a task or activity with certain goals of action reflecting their personal perceptions and beliefs about the particular achievement activity in which they are engaged. The conception of ability that they employ and the ways in which they interpret their performance can be understood in terms of these perceptions and beliefs. These perceptions and beliefs form a personal theory of achievement for the activity (Nicholls, 1989; Roberts, this volume) that reflects the individual's perception of how things work in achievement situations. The adopted personal theory of achievement affects the person's beliefs about how to achieve success and avoid failure at the activity. Therefore, people differ in which conceptions of ability and criteria of success and failure they use, and in how they use them, based on their personal theory of achievement.

Goal Involvement

The two conceptions of ability thereby become the source of the criteria by which individuals assess success and failure. Nicholls identifies achievement behavior utilizing the undifferentiated conception of ability as task involvement and achievement behavior utilizing the differentiated conception of ability as ego involvement. In this chapter we are consistent with Nicholls' use of the terms when we refer to the motivated state of involvement of the individual. Nicholls argued that a person's state of involvement lies on a continuum from task involvement to ego involvement. As Roberts (this volume) argues, when a person is task involved, the goal of action is to develop mastery, improvement, or learning, and the demonstration of ability is self-referenced. Success is realized by attaining mastery or improvement. The goal of action for an ego-involved individual, on the other hand, is to demonstrate ability relative to others or to outperform others, making ability other-referenced. Success is realized by exceeding the performance of others, especially when expending less effort than others (Nicholls, 1984, 1989).

The important matter here is that the state of involvement for a person is dynamic. It may change from moment to moment as demonstrated by Gernigon and colleagues (2004). Athletes may switch from one goal state to another as they evaluate the ongoing stream of events within the context. As an example, an athlete may be task involved, but an incident can suddenly cause the athlete to become ego involved, such as when a teammate or another athlete challenges the person to a competitive event. Within achievement goal theory, the athlete's state of motivational involvement is subject to change, even rapid change, as the athlete evaluates the unfolding events. This element is a central tenet of the theory. The question then becomes, What makes an individual task or ego involved?

Achievement Goal Orientations

When we refer to the individual differences between people (e.g., self-schemas, personal theories of achievement, dispositions) to be task or ego involved, we use the terms *task orientation* and *ego orientation*. It is assumed that individuals are predisposed (e.g., by their personal theory of achievement) to act in an ego- or task-involved manner; these predispositions are called achievement goal orientations. As argued in a previous chapter (Roberts, this volume), goal orientations are cognitive schemas that are relatively enduring. Thus, being task or ego oriented refers to the inclination of the individual to be task or ego involved, respectively.

The most important attribute of achievement goal orientations is that they are orthogonal! That is, task and ego goal orientations are independent, which means that a person can be high or low in each or both orientations at the same time. In the sport and exercise literature, this orthogonality has been supported (e.g., Duda, 1988; Lemyre, Roberts, & Ommundsen, 2000; Pensgaard & Roberts, 2000; Roberts, Treasure, & Kavussanu, 1996; Walling & Duda, 1995). For reviews see Duda and Whitehead (1998) and Roberts and colleagues (Roberts, Treasure, & Kavussanu, 1997, Roberts et al., 2007; Roberts, this volume). The avenue of research related to achievement goals in the context of physical activity has demonstrated that individual differences in goal orientation are associated with different motivational processes and different achievement behaviors.

Motivational Climate

When we refer to the situational determinants of motivation, the achievement cues inherent within the context, and the schemas emerging from achievement situations, we will be consistent with Ames (1984a, 1992b) and refer to the task-involving aspect of the context as mastery criteria and the ego involving aspect of the context as performance criteria. This research has examined how the structure of the environment by the coach, teacher, or parent, referred to as the motivational climate (Ames, 1992b), makes inducement of an ego or task state of involvement in the individual in the context more or less likely.

A performance climate is created when the criteria of success and failure are other-referenced and ego involving (Ames, 1992b). A mastery climate is created when the criteria of success and failure are self-referenced and task involving (Ames, 1992b). This is assumed to affect an individual's interpretation of the criteria of success and failure extant in the context and to affect achievement behavior. The individual will adopt adaptive achievement strategies (namely to work hard, seek challenging tasks, and persist in the face of difficulty) in the climate in which he or she feels comfortable. For most people, especially children, this occurs in the climate that emphasizes mastery (e.g., Biddle, 2001; Roberts et al., 1997, 2007; Treasure, 2001). But we must not forget that some people function well in a performance climate. Within achievement goal theory, these people are assumed to be those who are high in perceived competence at the activity and who wish to demonstrate their competence and superiority to others.

For the purposes of the present discussion, it is good to realize that dispositional goal orientations and perceptions of the climate are two independent dimensions of motivation that interact to affect the state of involvement of the person, and consequentially their motivated behavior (Nicholls, 1989). The powerful and parsimonious aspect of achievement goal theory is that both the individual dispositions and the perception of the motivational climate are encompassed by the theory (for a more detailed discussion, see Roberts, this volume).

Achievement Goal Theory and Goal Setting

The preceding discussion is an attempt to summarize the conceptual arguments behind achievement goal theory to place into perspective the arguments of Kingston and Wilson (2009) and Burton and colleagues (e.g., 2008). Burton and colleagues and Kingston and Wilson argue that there are three goal orientations. They term them, as we discussed earlier, process, performance, and outcome goals. Burton goes as far as to say that the goals are on a continuum and that process and performance goals make up the heart of the fundamental goal concept. In any case, all the authors use these goals as part of goal setting in sport.

All the researchers based their original arguments on achievement goal theory, and Kingston and Wilson (2009) retained the basic fundamental concepts. But we do have a misuse of terms. Burton and colleagues (e.g., Burton, 1984; Burton et al., 2001) used the term *performance goals* to refer to mastery goals (as defined by achievement goal theory) and the term *outcome goals* to refer to performance goals. Although Burton used achievement goal theory in his early work (e.g., 1984), he termed them *performance goals* and *outcome goals*. Nicholls in his early work (e.g., Nicholls, 1978, 1984) on achievement goals was at pains to reject the concept of outcome goals. His argument was that outcomes were subjectively defined as success and failure based on the goal of the participant. Thus, it is conceptually more coherent to define goals in terms of the criteria of success and failure held by the participant. However, we have witnessed consistent use of the terms *process goals*, *performance goals*, and *outcome goals* even though they are not consistent with the arguments of Nicholls (e.g., 1989), Ames (e.g., 1992b), Maehr (e.g., Maehr & Nicholls, 1980), or Dweck (e.g., Dweck & Legget, 1988), who are the major theorists behind achievement goals. We can only assume that the "toothbrush syndrome" (Frese, 2006) applied: That is, researchers would rather use another scientist's toothbrush than their theory and terms!

But researchers with a background in goal-setting theory who have begun to integrate goal-setting theory with achievement goal theory (e.g., Latham & Locke, 2007; Sejits, Latham, Tasa, & Latham, 2004) have termed them *learning goals* and *performance goals*, consistent with Dweck (e.g., 1999). Because these terms are completely consistent with the meaning of performance and mastery goals, this terminology is acceptable conceptually, but the use of the same term for different goals is confusing to the naive reader. We argue that it is more appropriate to use the terms *mastery* for performance goals and *performance* for outcome goals. This approach recognizes the heritage of these goals and makes the use of terms consistent with contemporary motivation theories.

As a result, in the contemporary goal-setting motivational literature in sport, we read extensively about outcome, performance, and process goals (e.g., Burton et al., 2001; Burton & Weiss, 2008; Gould, 2010; Hardy et al., 1996; Harwood et al., 2008; Kingston & Wilson, 2009; Martens, 1987; Wilson & Brookfield, 2009). Process goals are defined (e.g., Gould, 2006) as procedures that the performer engages in during performance (e.g., a skier focusing on keeping the hands in front of him or her while skiing). However, process goals are inherent in both performance and mastery goals (e.g., an athlete with a performance goal who tries to win without apparently trying hard because that approach demonstrates even greater competence or an athlete with a mastery goal who concentrates on the dynamics of the skill because doing so will assist learning). Wilson, Hardy, and Harwood (2006) found that what they defined as process goals had positive correlations with both ego and task orientations and that ego-oriented athletes set process goals. Therefore, to be consistent with motivation theory, we simply make the distinction between mastery and performance goals and recognize that process goals are embedded within both mastery and performance goals. In addition, by doing this we remain conceptually coherent with achievement goal theory, which has the potential to inform goals and goal setting in sport and other achievement contexts (e.g., Hall & Kerr, 2001). In particular, the greatest conceptual weakness of the work of researchers who use process, performance, and outcome goals is the rejection of the concept of the orthogonality of goals and their attendant behavioral, affective, and cognitive concomitants (see Treasure, 2001).

Why Goal Setting Works

The most impressive attempt to understand the how and why of goal setting is the work of Hall and Kerr (2001). Drawing on achievement goal theory, Hall and Kerr review the past literature and attempt to reconcile the various differences within it. They acknowledge that attempting to merge two very different research traditions will not be successful until we clarify conceptual details (such as what the goals are). But Hall and Kerr argue that there are beneficial aspects to understanding goal setting within a conceptually coherent achievement goal theory perspective.

First, researchers and practitioners would be able to understand better why athletes make the motivational choices that they do. As Hall and Kerr (2001) stated, this will "enable us to go beyond noting that an athlete is energized to achieve discrete goals, to explain why the athlete is energized and what the accompanying cognitions might be" (p. 231). Second, motivation theory can help researchers understand some of the idiosyncratic findings within the sport context. Athletes asked to "do their best" often do as well as athletes given discrete goals, which is contrary to the findings of Locke et al. (1981). This result makes sense if the athletes asked to do their best are mastery oriented and already have the goal of doing their best. In other words, the meaning of achievement within the context needs to be taken into account to understand goal setting. Lastly, the "traditional" goal-setting literature is preoccupied with performance effects and fails to appreciate that the athlete's achievement goals give meaning to the context so that any feedback may have adaptive and maladaptive motivational effects. As an example, the literature suggests that performance goals and public goals are more effective for performance (e.g., Kyllo & Landers, 1995) than are mastery goals. In fact, public goals may be a problem if they are broadcast by the athlete. It has been stated that being performance oriented is preferable for competent athletes (e.g., Hanton & Jones, 1999), but we should add that athletes should be careful about stating their performance goals in public to opponents or the media. Making your goals public means that people can evaluate your progress, so by definition these goals then become performance goals. This circumstance puts unnecessary performance pressure on the athlete (Kristiansen & Roberts, 2010). In addition, this is part of the "double-edged sword" syndrome in that it is known that performance goals are "fragile" over the long term (e.g., Roberts et al., 2007). When a person's perception of ability is high, then performance goals are motivational. But perception of ability is subject to change for many reasons (e.g., an aging athlete, injury, moving to a higher competitive level). When a person's perception of ability declines for some reason, performance goals may be demotivational. When the meaning and value of the context are considered, then the ultimate effect of performance goals can be demotivational, especially when perceived relative competence of the athlete is low. Therefore, only when we consider goal-setting strategies with an understanding of what success and failure mean to the athlete within that context will we be able to attain full understanding of goal-setting strategies. Without this understanding, practitioners cannot be aware of the motivational and cognitive effect that various performance outcomes may have for the athlete and will not be able to optimize the goal-setting strategies for that athlete.

Having stated that applying goal achievement theory to goal-setting strategies will aid us in both understanding and applying goal setting to the sport context, let us now examine how this may be the case. When considering goal setting for motivation, we have two facets of the equation. First, how can we help sport psychologists assist coaches, teachers, and even parents to give motivational succor to the athlete in his or her endeavors? This process is what we call managing the motivation of others versus aiding athletes to manage their own motivation. The latter topic is what the majority of the goal-setting literature addresses. We will begin by looking how we can help coaches manage the motivation of their athletes and then address how we can help people set effective goals that feed motivational processes.

Managing the Motivation of Others

Individual goal setting is a way to structure and organize the athlete, the daily training, and the goals to attend to over the entire competitive season because goal setting provides focus and direction (Locke, 1968; Weinberg, Butt, Knight, & Perritt, 2001). However, goal-setting procedures need to be effective, and several guidelines are useful for goal-setting techniques. One of the best is the chapter by Gould (2010), who uses the goal staircase as a model to structure goal setting. The starting point is the present ability of the athlete. The staircase has a long-term mastery goal, and to reach the long-term goal, the athlete follows several short-term mastery goals that increase in competence demands. This goal staircase is a coherent way of approaching goal setting for performance and for motivation. The short-term goals are for immediate improvement and motivation to work harder for their long-term goals, and the long-term goals give meaning for the athlete. Goal setting can become complicated because it is pertinent to have performance goals as part of a goal-setting staircase. The important point is that the performance goals are not to be considered ends in themselves but are a means by which the athlete can observe progress relative to others. A coach or sport psychologist must help the athlete interpret the performance goals as steps in the process. Target days for reaching the various short- and long-term goals may be advantageous, and goals for training and competition should be set and implemented together.

As a result, goal setting should be a coach–athlete project. Strategies to reach the goals need to be worked out together, and this involves skill development and creative problem solving (Locke et al., 1981). How coaches choose to use goal setting with their teams or individual athletes will vary, but it is recommended to introduce a system and routines within a mastery climate. Weinberg and colleagues found that most college coaches set predominantly individual and team short-term goals not only to focus attention on immediate practices and games but also because the short-term goals provide feedback toward achievement of long-term goals (Weinberg et al., 2001). When goals are established, the work of training should be related to those goals. Further, the focus on mastery as success is more likely to develop a perception that effort and self-referenced accomplishment are valued and important. In turn, a focus on mastery is more likely to lead to positive outcomes such as intrinsically regulated motivation and autonomy, in that the intrinsic value of the task is highlighted.

Hall and Kerr (2001) have identified two moderators of goal-setting performance in sport, namely feedback and commitment. Both the coach and the team or athlete have to be committed to the goals and work hard to reach them regardless of the age of the athlete. No matter how well designed the planning process, if the coach and athlete are not committed to the goals and fail to evaluate progress, or lack of progress, then the likelihood of success declines. Provision of feedback has been emphasized by Burton et al. (2001, 2008), and the feedback should be given in ways that will make the athlete stick to the task and show performance in relation to her or his mastery goals. The efficacy of specific reinforcement techniques in relation to achievement and goal-related behavior modification has previously been documented (e.g., Galvan & Ward, 1998). Consequently, the same points behind the setting of goals should be considered when giving feedback. In addition, goal acceptance has been shown to moderate the goal performance relationship (Erez & Zidon, 1984; Hardy, Maiden, & Sherry, 1986; O'Brien, Mallalieu, & Hanton, 2009). Extremely difficult goals may be committed to as long as the athletes accept them (Erez & Zidon, 1984), and enhancing ownership and empowerment in the goal-setting process is important (O'Brien et al., 2009): These are your goals, and you can do them! Lastly, a commitment to goals and to the goal-setting program takes time, which the athlete needs to understand. But by keeping the coaching climate mastery oriented and supportive, the coach may facilitate progress when implementing a goal-setting program (O'Brien et al., 2009).

Mastery goals are not only to be set at the beginning of a season but also to be sustained throughout the season. We all have anecdotal experience with coaches "losing it" in a game (e.g., Bobby Knight, the former Indiana coach, who threw a chair onto the basketball court during a game). What coaches sometimes do not understand is how athletes perceive their actions. This issue is particularly true for young athletes, as a recent research article illustrates (Kristiansen & Roberts, 2011). In this study, the researchers interviewed young athletes immediately after a major youth competition (the European Youth Olympics). In one of the interviews, a young athlete demonstrated the influence of a coach who apparently changed his goal focus at the event:

> My coach totally changed focus as soon as we arrived in Belgrade. He told me that I had to reach the finals. I had to prove that I deserved to be in [the event], and he told me, "You must win." That totally blew it for me; usually he is such a good coach, always focusing on the task ahead. But in major competitions he becomes another person, he takes off. His comments affected my results, everything went wrong, and it was hard to concentrate. It took me a few days to get the right task focus back. (p. 357)

Normally, the coach was mastery goal oriented, but at the competitive venue, he suddenly became performance oriented. As it happened, the national governing body (NGB) of his event had told the coach that future funding was dependent on the results of the competition. What the coach did was transfer the performance goals given by the NGB to the coach onto the athlete. The coach shifted the perceived motivational climate from mastery-based criteria of success to performance-based criteria of success. With young and inexperienced athletes, this action may create serious problems of focus. With more mature athletes, this issue is less severe, but it can still be a problem. The state of involvement of athletes may change quickly (Gernigon et al., 2004) depending on the athlete's reading of the ebb and flow of the coach's criteria of success in a competitive context. One example may be a coach who has mastery criteria of success in practice but suddenly emphasizes performance criteria when the competitive event begins. Unfortunately, this happens all the time:

> Every player wants to win; you don't need to tell him. You should focus on your task, on how to win the game. . . . Leaders and coaches make these types of mistakes all the time, I don't know why. Maybe it is because they don't know better; it is easier just to tell the players to win. (Kristiansen & Roberts, 2011, interviewing a professional soccer player)

As Pensgaard and Roberts (2002) found, even elite athletes prefer their coaches to have a mastery approach to performance because it alleviates stress, although some suggest that under certain conditions (e.g., debilitative anxiety interpretation, low self-confidence) setting goals may be inappropriate and dysfunctional for some sport performers (e.g., Hardy et al., 1996). But as we elaborate later, for some elite athletes who are extremely secure in their perception of competence, being performance oriented is acceptable, and even preferred, if the coach ensures that the athlete is able to cope effectively with the demands of the goal (Hanton & Jones, 1999). Clearly, the bottom line of managing the motivation of others is to create a mastery motivational climate for the athletes. This point is especially relevant to practice sessions but is also true of elite athletes in major competitive events, as demonstrated earlier.

Goal Setting as a Motivational Strategy for Injuries and Rehabilitation

Goal setting may be an important tool when helping athletes regain their motivation and get back into sport following an injury, because we know that injury will affect performance regardless of age and ability (Gould, 2010). But this topic has received scant attention in the literature. The coping strategy often used when an athlete is injured or disabled is imagery (Hanrahan, 2007). Numerous cognitive factors have been linked to sport injury rehabilitation outcomes. Wiese and Weiss (1987) argued that goal setting to assist motivation, together with imagery, relaxation, and communication skills, helps athletes recuperate from injury. Gould and colleagues (Gould, Udry, Bridges, & Beck, 1997) and Ievleva and Orlick (1991) have also documented the positive effect of goal setting for injured athletes. But the conceptual framework behind goal setting is not always stated in these studies. Much of the literature has been eclectic and fragmented, and a more focused and unified research agenda is needed (Williams & Andersen, 2007). In addition, this group is highly hetero-geneous, and the needs of the specific patient or athlete must be acknowledged (Playford et al., 2000). Strategies used with athletes with mild injuries or burnout are hard to compare to strategies used for those with acute onset of severe permanent disabilities or those with chronic or progressive disabilities.

Burnout is often described as something that is easier to observe than to define (Gould, Tuffey, et al., 1997), but little research has been done on inter-ventions to help athletes to recover from burnout. Burnout research (e.g., Lemyre, Hall, & Roberts, 2008) addresses both athletes and coaches, and burnout has been examined as an individual psychological phenomenon. Most of the research addresses conceptualization, measurement, and correlates of burnout (e.g., Goodger, Gorely, Lavallee, & Harwood, 2007), and as a result "research focusing on interventions, however, remains largely unexplored, with no published studies of this nature to date" (p. 146).

When an athlete has burned out, recovery is a long-term process. The coop-eration of the coach and family members—they need to be educated too—is crucial to creating the appropriate climate for recovery. Lemyre and colleagues (e.g., 2008) recommended that we adopt a mastery focus for the recuperation period. The support team needs to recognize that the entire recovery process when setting goals following injury or other health-compromising aspects needs to be colored by the principles of keeping the athlete task involved. Involving the athletes in decision making about the short-term goals is often recommended. But when the athlete is an adolescent, even small decisions may be experienced as stressful and too much to cope with. As a result, we recom-mend that the coach and the athlete agree on the small steps necessary in the goal-setting process and that parents be involved in the process. Recovery from burnout takes time; goals need to be set in a long-term time frame to bring the athlete back to full fitness and competence following rehabilitation. The important point is that athletes need help and support when implementing a goal-setting strategy to recuperate from being burned out, and the process may be gradual and time consuming (even over several years).

Conceptual confusion is present in the rehabilitation literature as well. The principles mentioned earlier should also guide the support person working with rehabilitation. Locke and Latham (1990) are used as a reference within the rehabilitation goal-setting literature, but the use of terms is inconsistent. Terms such as goal planning, goal setting, aim, objective, target, and goal achievement are used (Wade, 1998). There is evidence that goal setting works because it promotes behavioral change and improves interventions and patient involvement (Wade, 1998). Further, Wade argued that "there is little or no evidence to guide clinicians on the most appropriate method to undertake goal planning" (p. 275).

Within rehabilitation, goal setting is used with patients who suffer from long-standing or permanent impairment, such as spinal cord injury (SCI). Although goal setting is considered a cornerstone in rehabilitation practice (Duff, Evans, & Kennedy, 2004; Kennedy, Evans, Berry, & Mullin, 2003), limited evidence about the process and its effectiveness is available. One popular way of implementing a goal-setting procedure is to use motivational principles. The tool often used is the Needs Assessment Checklist (NAC; Kennedy & Hamilton, 1999), a clinical tool developed to "increase positive patient engagement" (Kennedy et al., 2003, p. 46). This clinical tool helps to ensure that rehabilitation programs are geared toward each patient's individual needs and improves the communication between patient and rehabilitation professionals (Duff et al., 2004; Kennedy et al., 2003). Duff and colleagues admit, however, that a more systematic investigation of the psychological processes involved in SCI rehabilitation is required.

This recommendation has been put into action in a recent study by Lannem and colleagues (Lannem, Sorensen, Lidal, & Hjeltnes, in press). Goal setting has been argued to be a help for SCI patients to cope with their daily lives and help them become as independent and responsible for their own lives as possible. The subsequent goal-setting program reflects individual needs in terms of neurological level of injury and the use of care pathways to allow the identification of the specific components for physical rehabilitation. Lannem and colleagues state that the goal-setting process works better when using a mastery focus, but it is important for the health professionals guiding and advising patients to make the goal-setting process realistic during both early and later rehabilitation. But in a qualitative follow-up survey, when the research team interviewed six SCI-patients (Lannem & Sorensen, in review), one finding noted was that the age of the patient and time since injury were important variables to consider. One of the interviewees was almost burned out 40 years postinjury after working hard to achieve his goals for an independent and active life. As his capacity diminished over time, this interviewee worked harder to maintain his capacity and became at risk for burning out because he could not meet his goals. The understanding of age as an intervening variable when tailoring goal setting to age-related capacities for maintaining and not increasing performance is a radical departure from the typical goal-setting program. In a similar vein, a recent study with people with visual impairment on the disengagement from unattainable goals and the setting of goals to reengage in alternative, meaningful goals (Garnefski, Kraaij, De Graaf, & Karels, 2010) found that coping with reengagement to alternative goals was an adaptive strategy and that goal adjustment had beneficial effects on mental health.

Naturally, when the goal becomes focused on maintaining capacity because of a reduction in capacity as a result of injury, age, or illness, goal setting in a mastery climate becomes pivotal to avoiding any perception of failure. As motivation prepares the individual to move forward to reach desired goals or produce desired outcomes (Roberts, 2001), knowledge about motivation processes helps the support team set appropriate goals that are focused on maintaining the diminishing capacity of the person. The content, intensity, frequency, or duration of the mastery goals would need to be continually revised as the resources required to attain the level of performance diminish.

Goal setting for Paralympic athletes is also important. This group might need even more support and help with their goal-setting process than do their able-bodied counterparts. In a recent study of sources of strain experienced during the 2010 Vancouver Paralympics (Kristiansen, Sørensen, Lannem, & Abrahamsen, 2011), one of the elite athletes with a progressive disability talked about his goal-setting process:

> I make goals for six months at a time, like now I have made a goal for the next World Championship. I make realistic goals, and to reach the goal for the season I have to do the required work every day. [...] However, I also think a lot about what will happen if I suddenly got worse, maybe I will be in a wheelchair only able to move my head in two years? The development might happen very sudden, and I also worry a little that I push my body too hard with the training. So for me it is impossible to talk about the Sochi 2014 Paralympics, even though people say that I will be a participant there as well. I cannot relate to a goal like that, I just say that: *I will be a skier as long as I can do what I am doing.*

Goal setting must be used with caution, and coaches and sport psychologists need to be aware of the consequences of the goals made in the context, especially when the athlete is injured or suffers from acute, chronic, or degenerative disabilities. The previous examples reinforce that goal setting is more complex than it appears, in that it may help athletes recover from burnout, for example, but might lead others to become burned out. Therefore, knowledge of the theoretical underpinnings and consequences of goals made is crucial. When a person's perception of competence declines through a reduction in capacity, the normal goal-setting program with its attendant evaluation, feedback, and reassessment may be interpreted as a performance criterion because the diminished capacity of the athlete does not allow him or her to attain what was once possible. This circumstance may directly affect the athlete's self-worth (Hall & Kerr, 2001). We need sensitivity toward the athlete's perception of success and failure with the present capacity. Here we need to have a mastery climate to help the athlete adjust to new realities with realistic goals within the achievement context.

Managing Individual Motivation

One characteristic of highly successful athletes is their practice of setting clear daily practice goals and using goal setting among several other strategies (e.g., Burton et al., 2010; Gould, Guinan, Greenleaf, Medberty, & Peterson, 1999; Gould & Maynard, 2009; Orlick & Partington, 1988; Williams & Krane, 2001). Elite athletes are probably the most dedicated group of goal setters. Burton and colleagues (2010) confirmed this point when they found that 40% of their sample was highly committed to goal-setting procedures.

Many eminent athletes have used goal setting to give themselves structure for a training regime to accomplish a long-term goal. Jones and Hardy in an early study (1990) noted a variety of approaches when interviewing British elite athletes about their use of this strategy. For them it was one way of enhancing motivation: "Having a long-term goal keeps you going through the difficult times" (1990, p. 259). In addition, the importance of short-term goals was underlined, both personal and team goals. Burton and colleagues' (2010) recent study on prospective Olympic athletes supports this use of goal setting. The athletes had implemented strategies to enhance goal effectiveness. The use of long-term goals for successful Olympic and World Championship athletes was supported by Jones and colleagues when identifying the possible reasons for successful performance (Jones, Hanton, & Connaughton, 2007). Long-term goals functioned as a source of motivation.

The positive effects of the consistent application of goal-setting techniques in a mastery motivational setting was noted in a recent study on elite wrestling (Kristiansen et al., 2008). The Olympic winners in that study argued that the ability to work with details, have daily goals, and stay focused on the goals for practice through each practice were factors behind their success. Further, the wrestlers stressed that they sought to stay task focused and not think too much about winning in the daily technique practice sessions. The link between AGT and goal setting was underlined several times in the interviews. But one study participant noted, "You must think of both. Every move you make takes you one step closer to winning. Every point is one step closer to winning" (2008, p. 532). From this perspective, to win means being motivated to continue the daily training at a high performance level (see also Jones & Hardy, 1990). An important point to make here is that choosing a mastery approach is not about not wanting to win; it is simply the best way of setting practice goals that may culminate in achieving a dream goal (or performance goal). Motivation over the long term is better served with mastery-based short-term and long-term goals. The extant evidence is relatively clear: When setting short-term goals to achieve long-term goals, coaches should set the goals within a mastery framework (e.g., Pensgaard & Roberts, 2002). Pensgaard and Roberts found that even successful Olympic athletes prefer their coaches to set mental skill strategies within a mastery framework.

Finally, when writing their biographies, elite athletes always dwell on their use of goal setting in achieving their ultimate goals. Seven-time winner of the Tour de France (1999–2005) Lance Armstrong was no exception. He has made himself into an almost mythical hero with his story of being the underdog who first fought cancer and then became a historic winner through hard training (Sparkes, 2004). When preparing for his first long-term goal to win the 1999 tour after recovering from the cancer, he sacrificed an entire season to prepare for the specific challenges of the course for the 1999 race. Feedback came mostly through heart rate, times, and the strength that he regained, but he did not focus on winning or losing. During the race itself, he forced himself to focus on every little detail in front of him. The team manager was important because he broke down the race into "wattages and split times, and gave me precise instructions" (Armstrong & Jenkins, 2001, p. 225). The instructions also included heart rates. In his biography, Armstrong wrote that cancer forced him to develop a plan for living "and in turn, taught me how to develop a plan for smaller goals such as each stage of the tour" (p. 284). In response to what he thought about during 6 or 7 hours on the bike in a competition stage of the Tour de France, Armstrong stated:

> My mind didn't wander. I didn't daydream. I thought about techniques of the various stages. I told myself over and over that this was the kind of race in which I had to always push if I wanted to stay ahead. I worried about my lead. I kept a close watch on my competitors, in case one of them tried a breakaway. I stayed alert to what was around me, and wary of crashing. (2001, p. 244)

This quotation underlines Armstrong's total focus on mastery goals during the race. The stories of elite athletes are excellent examples of accepting and committing to an extremely difficult goal and setting mastery goals to achieve this long-term goal (Erez & Zidon, 1984; O'Brien et al., 2009). In addition, the athletes always refer to an important support person, such as the coach, a team leader, or a family member. It is interesting to speculate about how important the support people are in the process of managing the motivation of others. Coaches, and others, may be more important as support people in maintaining goal focus during an important competitive event. It has often been noted that continued support and evaluation of progress is essential to facilitating self-confidence (e.g., Burton et al., 2001) because developing the competencies to become an elite athlete is a long-term process that involves a strong support system (Gould & Maynard, 2009).

Practical Applications

As has been evident throughout this chapter, goal setting is a way to structure and organize the athlete, the daily training, and the goals to attend to over the entire competitive season because goal setting provides focus and direction. We recommended that the reader consult the how-to guidelines for goal-setting techniques, in particular the chapter by Gould (2010), who uses the goal staircase as a model to structure goal setting. The starting point is the present ability of the athlete. The staircase has a long-term mastery goal, and to attain the long-term goal, the athlete strives for several short-term mastery goals that increase in competence demands. This goal staircase to organize goal setting is a coherent way of approaching goal setting for performance. The short-term goals are for immediate improvement and motivation to work harder for the long-term goals, and the long-term goals give direction to the athlete about the ultimate goal of the training program. Target days for reaching the various short- and long-term goals may be helpful, and goals for training and competition should be set and implemented together.

Goal setting is a project for the coach and the athlete. How coaches choose to use goal setting with their teams or individual athletes will depend on personal preferences, but we recommend introducing goal setting within a mastery climate. The focus on mastery as success will highlight that effort, and self-referenced accomplishments are important for achieving long-term goals.

Goal-setting procedures are not just for elite athletes. Goal setting can be introduced early to child and adolescent athletes. The important issue is how to adapt the procedure to make sport training more effective without taking out the fun element. Coaches can make young athletes interested in what they do at training and train them to structure and take charge of their own training. Some coaches intuitively use this means to enhance performance, but they have to help all young athletes develop their talents. As Gould and Maynard recently concluded when reviewing how to prepare for excellent performance, "Mental preparation, then, starts when Olympians enter the sport system, not when they are at the pinnacles of their careers" (2009, p. 1399). With young athletes, coaches must take the long view and set goal-setting programs to keep all the athletes interested and developing at their optimal rates. To do this, coaches must take a developmental stance, adopt a mastery climate, and set mastery goals within the coaching program that is aimed at keeping all the athletes within the program until they develop physiologically.

Directions for Future Research

Usually, reviews of goal setting in sport and physical activity end with advice on ways to improve goal-setting techniques (e.g., Burton & Naylor, 2002; Gould, 2010) or a quest for a more coherent theoretical framework (e.g., Hall & Kerr, 2001; Kingston & Wilson, 2009). Kingston and Wilson conclude that they regret the "lack of adequate theoretical models to guide researchers and aid practitioners when applying goals within sport" (2009, p. 115). In contrast, Latham and Locke (2007) simply state that goal setting is "an open theory" (p. 298), a theory built through induction. As scientists, however, we have a responsibility to seek a better understanding of the motivational process behind goal setting and to ask questions about why goal setting works.

We need to be more thoughtful about the conceptual underpinning of goal setting. A prime example of a thoughtful insight into the mechanisms of goal setting is the work of Hall and Kerr (2001). Using achievement goal theory, they argue that recognizing both the individual orientations of being task and ego involved and the influence of the perceived criteria of success and failure in the extant motivational climate will "enable us to go beyond noting that an athlete is energized to achieve discrete goals, to explain why the athlete is energized and what the accompanying cognitions might be" (p. 231). The future direction for goal-setting theorists should be to integrate the current empirical knowledge base with conceptual anchors to understand why goal setting works and to fine-tune the practical guidelines. But we want to be on record in stating that achievement goal theory may not be the only theory that can help us understand and implement goal-setting procedures in a more efficacious way. It is up to us as researchers and practitioners in sport psychology to be thoughtful about why goal setting works and how we can implement that insight to make goal setting more effective!

Summary

In this chapter we examined the extant evidence and the conceptual explanations of goal setting, used achievement goal theory to provide a conceptual structure to explain why goal setting may work, and suggested ways to enhance the effectiveness of goal setting in sport. We argued that motivation is better served with mastery-based short- and long-term goals.

Understanding the Psychological Determinants and Mediators of Physical Activity Behavior

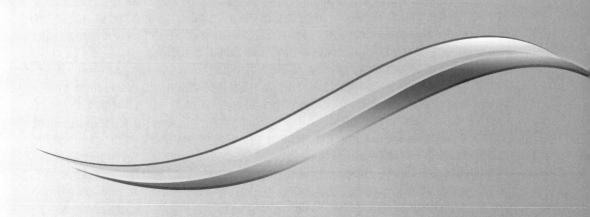

In the past 20 years, the last decade in particular, there has been an explosion in the amount of research focused on understanding why people are, or more commonly are not, physically active. Research into the possible determinants and mediators of physical activity has become critically important as the overwhelming amount of evidence now demonstrates the many physiological and psychological health benefits that result from a physically active lifestyle (ACSM, 2009; WHO, 2003). In contrast, physical inactivity has been shown to be an independent health risk factor for chronic disease and negative mental health. As highlighted by Standage and Ryan in this volume, the WHO (2003) has estimated that approximately 60% of the world's population is insufficiently active to acquire any benefit. Moreover, globally there are now over 1 billion people who are overweight, with 300 million individuals who are obese. In light of these statistics, it is not surprising that a great deal of attention is now focused on factors that might motivate individuals to engage and persist in physical activity and reduce sedentary behaviors.

To this end, the second section of this volume focuses on the multiple personal and environmental factors that are possible determinants and mediators of physical activity behavior. Although each of the chapters deals with a different aspect of the motivation question, with different populations, and in different settings, they all place an emphasis on theory and the need for a deeper understanding of the role psychology may play in the design and implementation of interventions that promote physical activity behavior change. As evidenced by the chapters in this section, the work has really only just begun, with numerous critical questions of motivation and physical activity behavior still needing to be addressed.

The first chapter of this section by Standage and Ryan offers a thorough description of the macro theory, as well as the mini-theories that make up the complex conceptual infrastructure of Deci and Ryan's self-determination theory (Deci & Ryan, 2000; Ryan & Deci, 2000a, 2008). They review recent research that has examined the important questions of physical activity behavior, physical health, and psychological well-being from an SDT perspective. Standage and Ryan conclude by highlighting suggestions for future exercise-related research grounded in SDT.

The second chapter in this section by Gilson and Feltz examines the self-efficacy aspect of Bandura's (1997) social-cognitive theory applied to sport and exercise. The chapter reviews self-efficacy at both the individual and group levels and examines the relationship to performance and other behavioral outcomes.

Vallance and Courneya next review the extant literature that has examined social-cognitive approaches to understanding exercise motivation and behavior in cancer survivors. The research clearly shows that physical activity has a positive influence on health-related quality of life in cancer survivors; however, a small number of these individuals are meeting the minimal amounts of exercise that are required for the accrual of health benefits. Vallance and Courneya contend that motivation and adherence are clearly important issues when considering exercise programs, and they report promising research that may help in the development of physical activity programs designed to improve health-related quality of life in cancer survivors.

The fourth chapter in this section by Martin Ginis and Mack examines exercise behavior from a self-presentational perspective. Specifically, the authors document the pervasiveness and potency of self-presentational motives in physical activity settings. The authors conclude by suggesting ways self-presentation influences exercise motivation. However, they also state that the evidence is far from complete in this regard and challenge researchers to provide a stronger theoretical and empirical basis for motivational interventions.

The final chapter of this section is ambitious and far reaching as Biddle and his colleagues approach the physical activity motivation question from a broad public health perspective. Specifically, they contend that there is a clear and immediate need to develop and implement effective physical activity behavior change programs not only at the individual but also community and societal levels. Biddle and colleagues strongly assert that researchers in the area of physical activity for health have a real opportunity to contribute to and recommend the adoption of an ecological framework that examines multiple influences, such as individual psychology, social circumstances, the surrounding physical environment, and wider sociopolitical influences (e.g., policy) that may affect physical activity and sedentary behaviors. It is perhaps wise to acknowledge in a volume devoted to a social cognitive approach to understanding physical activity that, while motivation is important, it is not the only influence on human behavior.

CHAPTER 7

Self-Determination Theory and Exercise Motivation: Facilitating Self-Regulatory Processes to Support and Maintain Health and Well-Being

Martyn Standage, PhD
University of Bath

Richard M. Ryan, PhD
University of Rochester

he issue of physical inactivity has become a focus of public health concern across nations, particularly modern industrialized societies and countries undergoing accelerated economic growth and increased urbanization (i.e., those that have populations that are physically slowing down even as the pace of life speeds up). The so-called modern Western lifestyle entails epidemiological transition (i.e., lower energy requirements at work and for procurement of food, increased dependence on the automobile, greater exposure to sedentary leisure-time activities, and so on) (cf. Katzmarzyk & Mason, 2009). For many people, this lifestyle is accompanied by the intake of high-fat fast foods that are amplifying the negative effects of lower physical output.

These shifts are occurring even as increasing empirical evidence documents the many physiological and psychological health benefits conferred by a physically active lifestyle (cf. American College of Sports Medicine [ACSM], 2009; World Health Organization [WHO], 2003). To accrue the health benefits associated with physical activity behavior, the ACSM and the American Heart Association (AHA) recommend that adults engage in 30 minutes or more of moderate-intensity (i.e., between 3 and 6 METs) activity a minimum of 5 days each week (Haskell et al., 2007). Recent accelerometer data suggest that less than 5% of American adults meet such recommendations (Troiano et al., 2008).

Although the benefits of an active lifestyle are well known, physical inactivity has been reported to be an independent health risk factor for chronic disease, causing around 1.9 million deaths worldwide each year (WHO, 2003). The economic and social implications associated with physical inactivity are also high (see Biddle et al., this volume). In the United States, for example, if 10% of adults were to begin and maintain participation in a regular walking program, savings of $5.6 billion in heart disease costs would be achieved (Centers for Disease Control and Prevention, 2008). Despite the known health, social, and economic benefits associated with physical activity behavior, approximately 60% of the world's population is insufficiently active to acquire benefit. Moreover, globally there are now over one billion people who are overweight, including 300 million who are obese (WHO, 2003).

In view of such statistics it is not surprising that researchers, health professionals, policy makers, and practitioners have been increasingly focused on factors that might motivate people to engage and persist in physical activity or regular exercise.[1] Yet motivation is more complex than many have imagined. In the past many researchers have seen motivation as a unitary phenomenon, varying mainly in quantity (e.g., Bandura, 1997). More recently, however,

Footnote

[1]Physical activity encompasses all movement produced by skeletal muscles that confer energy expenditure above rest. The term *exercise* is often used interchangeably with *physical activity*. Within this chapter, however, when we discuss exercise we are doing so as a subcomponent of physical activity that is "planned, structured, repetitive, and purposive in the sense that improvement or maintenance of one or more components of physical fitness is an objective" (Caspersen, Powell, & Christenson, 1985, p. 128). In considering exercise as a type of physical activity that is planned, structured, repetitive, and purposeful, it appropriately delineates exercise from physical activities of daily living and captures exercise as a behavioral enactment that is sufficiently purposeful to require cognitive processes (e.g., Edmunds, Ntoumanis, & Duda, 2006a) pertaining to the psychology of motivation.

researchers and practitioners alike are discovering that fostering optimal and sustained engagement also depends on the quality of motivation. That is, much can be gleaned from distinguishing between distinct types (or kinds) of motivation that vary in their inherent qualities and regulatory processes. Indeed, an abundance of experimental and field studies across a wide array of life domains supports the veracity of focusing on the quality of a person's motivation when predicting differential responses in important outcomes, such as psychological well-being, performance, personal experience, behavioral persistence, and learning (see Deci & Ryan, 2008).

A general theory of human motivation, personality, and emotion that addresses the quality of motivation, as well as the conditions that promote, as opposed to forestall, optimal engagement, growth, and development, is self-determination theory (SDT; Deci & Ryan, 2000; Ryan & Deci, 2000a, 2008). Developed over the past five decades, SDT is the product of a comprehensive and systematic program of inductive research. In using an empirically driven approach to the development and refinement of SDT, a high level of internal consistency has been maintained (Vansteenkiste, Niemiec, & Soenens, 2010).

Although SDT is far from being a new theory in physical activity literatures (e.g., see Deci & Ryan, 1985a; Ntoumanis, this volume; Vallerand, Deci, & Ryan, 1987), a considerable increase in basic research using the theory has occurred within such settings since the last edition of this text (i.e., Roberts, 2001). Indeed, the past decade has witnessed exponential growth in empirical research framed within SDT, exemplified by a recent textbook (i.e., Hagger & Chatzisarantis, 2007) comprising 19 chapters focused on the theoretical and applied contributions of the theory within sport and exercise settings. In addition to rising public health concerns associated with sedentary lifestyles yielding more motivation-related work, the rapid increase in research attention given to SDT may, in part, be because of the breadth of motivational phenomena addressed within this macro theory of motivation, as well as its ready applicability to interventions aimed at well-being and health. With such issues in mind, it is worth noting that theories that previously dominated the sport and exercise science literature have been social-cognitive perspectives centered largely on competence-related issues (e.g., achievement goal theory, Nicholls, 1989; social-cognitive theory, Bandura, 1986). Although SDT is not unique in recognizing the importance of competence to motivated behavior, the theory also posits the needs for autonomy (or choicefulness) and relatedness (or connectedness and belonging) as germane to high-quality forms of motivation, effective functioning, enhanced performance, and well-being.

When applied to physical activity settings, the extant research typically falls into two overarching categories. First, researchers have investigated the association between distinct types of motivation that vary in their experience and performance characteristics and the way in which acting through these differing motives has important implications for behavioral engagement, persistence, exercise-related cognitions, and physical and psychological well-being in physical activity settings. Second, attention has been given to the conditions and processes that support, rather than forestall, an individual's innate organizational tendency toward growth- and health-oriented processes (see Hagger & Chatzisarantis, 2007, for reviews).

In this chapter we present the central components and motivational phenomena researched within SDT. Specifically, we draw from five interrelated minitheories that have evolved in an inductive manner to form the building blocks for the overall SDT framework (see Ryan & Deci, 2002, 2008; Vansteen-kiste et al., 2010, for discussions of each minitheory). We then review specific phenomena and hypotheses stemming from each minitheory and critique extant work addressing these within the exercise domain. Attention is then given to SDT's theory of vitality (i.e., subjective energy) as a process integral to effective functioning and wellness. Suggestions for practical applications grounded in the tenets of SDT are made. Finally, we conclude by highlighting a number of future research directions.

Basic Components of SDT and Mapping of Minitheories

Self-determination theory is a macro theory of human motivation that comprises both organismic and dialectical elements to address motivated behavior in all life domains. With respect to the organismic proposition, SDT considers humans to be growth-oriented organisms who actively seek optimal challenges and new experiences to master and integrate (Ryan & Deci, 2002). Within SDT the exemplar of human growth tendencies is termed *intrinsic motivation*, a construct that is held to be inseparably intertwined with the notion of active and spontaneous activity (Deci & Ryan, 1991). Building and extending on the work of White (1959), who conceptualized effectance motivation to reflect an innate motive to develop competencies (or feelings of effectance), and the writings of deCharms (1968) pertaining to individuals' propensity to experience internal personal causation (i.e., being the origin as opposed to a pawn of one's action), intrinsic motivation represented the initial basis for the SDT framework. People who are intrinsically motivated are fully self-regulated, engage in activities out of interest, experience a sense of volition, and function without the aid of external rewards or constraints (Deci & Ryan, 1985a, 2000). Put more simply, intrinsically motivated individuals take part in activities for their own sake because such behaviors in and of themselves offer rewarding consequences (Deci & Ryan, 1991). Indeed, the first SDT minitheory, cognitive evaluation theory (CET; Deci, 1975; Deci & Ryan, 1980) was specifically developed to identify and synthesize empirical findings regarding how various external events (and later internal events; Ryan, 1982) enhance or diminish intrinsic motivation. The theory considers factors such as rewards, feedback, evaluations, and ways of communicating as they affect the actor's interest, enjoyment, and free persistence in activities.

Despite the importance of intrinsic motivation as a prototype of human growth tendencies, a fundamental principle of SDT is that behaviors, including sport and exercise activities, can be intrinsically or extrinsically motivated (see Ntoumanis, this volume; Ryan, Williams, Patrick, & Deci, 2009). In contrast to intrinsic motivation, in which behaviors are engaged in for inherent satisfaction, extrinsic motivation refers to behaviors that are characterized by an individual's goal of action being governed by some separable outcome (e.g., seeking approval, obtaining a tangible reward or outcome, avoiding punishment). Rather than viewing extrinsic motivation as antithetical to intrinsic motivation, as considered by previous approaches (e.g., deCharms, 1968; Harter, 1981), SDT identifies four types of extrinsic motive that are quantified as being more, or less, reflective of oneself (i.e., the degree to which they are autonomously pursued). This differentiated perspective on extrinsic motivation is specified within a second minitheory, organismic integration theory (OIT; Deci & Ryan, 1985a).

OIT assumes that extrinsic motivation varies in the degree to which it has been internalized and integrated (Ryan & Deci, 2000a). The term *internalization* describes how people, within appropriate social conditions, take in and accept values and norms that regulate and guide behavior. Through internalization, behaviors that were previously carried out by external prompts become increasingly self-regulated, or integrated. Simply stated, internalization and integration represent the processes through which controlled (or externally regulated) motives for uninteresting, yet potentially important, tasks become increasingly autonomous. Greater discussion and application of internalization will be offered when we consider the differing types of extrinsic motivation and their relations with exercise and health-related outcomes.

Given that a person's engagement in activities does not exist in isolation, the dialectical component embraced within SDT addresses the interaction between the active self and various forces (external and internal) in social contexts that either support or impede an individual's active engagement, personal growth, and development (Deci & Ryan, 1991). According to SDT, growth, development, and well-being are most readily achieved through social contexts that are supportive and satisfying of three innate and basic psychological needs (Deci & Vansteenkiste, 2004; Ryan, 1995). Addressed within a third minitheory, basic psychological needs theory (BPNT; Ryan & Deci, 2000a), three psychological needs are argued to be essential nutriments for growth and healthy functioning: the need for autonomy (i.e., the need to experience activities as self-endorsed and choicefully enacted), the need for competence (i.e., the need to interact effectively within the environment), and the need for relatedness (i.e., the need to feel close, connected, and cared for with important others) (Ryan & Deci, 2002). When these psychological needs are satisfied, more integrated and volitional forms of motivation, greater effective functioning, and increased well-being are expected, whereas if the social context frustrates these needs, ill-being, passive engagement, and restricted development are predicted (Deci & Ryan, 2000). According to SDT, these basic needs for autonomy, competence, and relatedness are universal, meaning that rather than being learned or accrued through value systems, they have a functional influence irrespective of issues such as culture, gender, developmental stages, and context (Deci & Vansteenkiste, 2004; Ryan, 1995).

Empirical support for the veracity and universality of the basic needs as an invariant process has been shown across various cultures (e.g., Deci et al., 2001), across both genders (e.g., Ryan, Bernstein, & Brown, 2010; Standage, Duda, & Ntoumanis, 2005), throughout stages of the lifespan (e.g., Deci, Driver, Hotchkiss, Robbins, & Wilson, 1993; Kasser & Ryan, 1999), and within numerous life contexts (see Ryan & Deci, 2008).

One line of research that was initially examined under the BPNT umbrella pertains to the study of individuals' goal pursuits (or the content of their goals). Now articulated as a separate minitheory, titled goal contents theory (GCT; Ryan et al., 2009; Vansteenkiste et al., 2010), research from this perspective holds that "all goals are not created equal" and that valuing goals with different foci will be differentially associated with well-being and adjustment outcomes (see Ryan, Sheldon, Kasser, & Deci, 1996; Vansteenkiste, Lens, & Deci, 2006). GCT originates from the work of Kasser and Ryan (1993, 1996), who classified individuals' general life goals (or aspirations) as a function of their capacity to satisfy basic psychological needs. Specifically, Kasser and Ryan labeled goals with an internal foci as being intrinsic (viz., growth, affiliation, community contribution, and maintenance of physical health) and those with an outward orientation as being extrinsic (e.g., financial success, social recognition, and image or attractiveness). Intrinsic goals are those focused on developing personal interests, values, and potentials and are inherently satisfying to pursue (i.e., they reflect a "being" orientation; Fromm, 1976). These characteristics align with the organismic foundations of the self within SDT and are thus conducive to basic psychological need satisfaction. In contrast, extrinsic goals are primarily characterized by having an "outward" orientation (Williams, Cox, Hedberg, & Deci, 2000), and pursuits are directed toward external indicators of worth such as wealth, fame, and appealing image (Kasser & Ryan, 1993, 1996; Vansteenkiste et al., 2006). Unlike intrinsic goal pursuits, extrinsic goal pursuits are less supportive, or even thwarting, of basic psychological needs, and consequently they are considered to hinder optimal human development (Deci & Ryan, 2000; Kasser, 2002). Empirical studies have provided support for the stability of the distinction between intrinsic and extrinsic goals across cultures (e.g., Grouzet et al., 2005) and its usefulness in differentially predicting numerous indicators of well-being (see Kasser 2002; Ryan et al., 1996).

Although CET, OIT, and BPNT draw heavily on the effects of social contexts (i.e., their influence on intrinsic motivation, internalization of extrinsic motivation, and supports for basic needs, respectively), an individual's inner resources have also been central to the development of SDT (Ryan & Deci, 2002). A further minitheory within SDT, labeled causality orientations theory (COT; Deci & Ryan, 1985a, 1985b), was developed, which posits that everyone, to some degree, has varying levels of autonomy orientation (i.e., a disposition to orient toward intrinsic motivation and well-integrated extrinsic motivation), controlled orientation (viz., an orientation toward being motivated by internal or external controls, constraints, and directives), and impersonal orientation (i.e., a tendency for people to consider themselves as incompetent and to act without intentionality). These causality orientations are viewed as developmental outcomes that result from repeated interactions between the active, developing individual and his or her social world. As opposed to operating at the domain-specific or activity level (as do the motives or social contexts discussed thus far), causality orientations operate at a more global level (or life domain), referring to an individual's stable and consistent pattern of thinking as it relates to seeking out, selecting, and interpreting the initiation and regulation of her or his behavior (Deci & Ryan, 1985b). These distinct aspects of a person's orientation may be more or less chronically salient, but each can also be nonconsciously primed, making it more functionally salient in a given setting (e.g., Weinstein & Ryan, 2010). According to COT, understanding a person's level of these motivational orientations permits researchers and practitioners to make important predictions about psychological, health, and behavioral outcomes. Specifically, the endorsement of an autonomous orientation is hypothesized to positively predict effective functioning, adaptive behavior, and psychological health. Numerous studies have supported the tenets of COT by showing autonomous orientation to be positively associated with adaptive outcomes such as better self-esteem, greater ego development, and a tendency to support autonomy in others, whereas control and impersonal orientations show distinct associations with various maladaptive styles and negative outcomes (see Deci & Ryan, 1985a, 2000).

Self-Determination Theory in Exercise Science Research

Understanding the reasons individuals are moved to act, that is, the sources of people's motivation, is critical to the promotion of engagement and persistence in exercise activities. Whether individuals are taking part in jogging, cycling, swimming, or rowing for prolonged durations, they are exerting and expending much effort in their motivated endeavors. Although the quantity of engagement may not differ (at least in the short term), the nature and focus of motivation giving rise to action can vary greatly among individuals. For example, some people may exercise for the enjoyment that comes from exercise activities, others because they want to improve their energy and health, and still others because friends or family say that they should. Clearly, the reasons for engagement can differ in terms of the level of self-regulation. According to SDT, the differing reasons for engagement are conceptualized on a continuum of relative autonomy encompassing intrinsic motivation and various forms of extrinsic motivation.

Intrinsic Motivation, Extrinsic Motivation, and Amotivation

As previously noted, intrinsic motivation is the prototype of autonomous regulation within SDT and refers to partaking in an activity for its inherent satisfaction as opposed to doing it to obtain separable consequence (Ryan & Deci, 2000a). That is, when people are intrinsically motivated, they freely take part in activities for the interest and spontaneous enjoyment that participation brings. This active engagement with tasks promotes growth (Deci & Ryan, 1985a, 2000). To provide a better understanding of intrinsic motivation as conceptualized within SDT, much can be gleaned from four characteristics identified by Deci and Ryan (1991). First, intrinsically motivated behaviors can occur in the absence of any apparent external reward. Second, individuals take part in intrinsically motivated behaviors out of interest because such curious engagement is fundamental to understanding one's self-development. Third, intrinsically motivated behaviors can be challenging but not so difficult that the person cannot experience progress and mastery. Finally, intrinsically motivated behaviors are couched within innate psychological needs. In particular, according to CET, intrinsic motivation is enhanced and maintained when the needs for autonomy and competence are supported and experienced. If not accompanied by autonomy, even mastery experiences will not foster intrinsic motivation. Finally, note that, although the need for relatedness is considered to be more distal in supporting intrinsic motivation (Deci & Moller, 2005), SDT holds that intrinsically motivated behaviors are more likely to occur and thrive in contexts supportive of a sense of connectedness and belonging.

Research stemming back to descriptive accounts of youth participation in sport (e.g., Gill, Gross, & Huddleston, 1983; Gould, Feltz, & Weiss, 1985) attests to the fact that participation in sport is largely underpinned by intrinsic motives such as fun, challenge, and learning. Although participation in sport across the lifespan is for many people intrinsically motivating, the motives underpinning exercise engagement are often more extrinsic or instrumental in nature. A study that illustrates this point was conducted by Frederick and Ryan (1993), who surveyed 376 adults to ascertain their primary reasons for partaking in either an individual sport or a fitness-oriented activity. Although intrinsic motives were common reasons for participants in both settings, results showed that individual sport participants endorsed intrinsic reasons (viz., higher levels of interest or enjoyment and competence motivation) more than those in the fitness group did. In contrast, fitness group participants reported higher levels of body-related motivations that were instrumental (or extrinsic) in nature (e.g., to lose or maintain weight, to improve appearance, to be attractive to others, and so on). With exercise participation in mind, Ryan, Frederick, Lepes, Rubio, and Sheldon (1997) reported on the adaptive concomitants of intrinsic motives in their work with first-time fitness center members. Specifically, they reported that intrinsic motives (i.e., enjoyment, competence, and social interaction) were positively correlated with class attendance, workout enjoyment, and exercise adherence, whereas extrinsic motives (viz., for fitness or appearance) were unrelated to those factors. The findings reported by Ryan et al. (1997) also provided support for the premise that, although people may initially partake in exercise for extrinsic reasons (e.g., to improve their health, enhance their appearance, or increase their fitness), intrinsic motives are central to sustained persistence. Collectively, findings from these early studies on intrinsic and extrinsic exercise motives provide insight into the role that divergent motives have in driving participation.

That intrinsic and extrinsic motivations have been implicated in predicting a person's exercise engagement is akin to the theoretical tenets of OIT, which hold that people typically have multiple motives (both intrinsic and extrinsic) that operate simultaneously to determine the overall quality of motivation (Ryan & Connell, 1989). As we have discussed, many people participate in exercise for instrumental reasons such as improving their health and fitness, losing weight, and enhancing their appearance. Moreover, because certain exercise activities (e.g., running on a treadmill, exercising on a step machine) can sometimes be construed as being boring, participation in such activities is driven by what can be obtained from it (e.g., health gains) as opposed to being underpinned by inherent interest (i.e., intrinsic motivation). For such reasons, any complete theory of motivation must also address and explain aspects of exercise engagement that are not intrinsically motivated. Within SDT two categories of nonintrinsic motivation are outlined. The first is extrinsic motivation, which refers to behaviors that are characterized as instrumental, or done to attain separable outcomes, or that comply with contingencies out of fear of threat or punishment. The second is labeled amotivation, which refers to a lack of intentionality to act (Ryan & Deci, 2000a).

Although SDT adopts a relatively unified view of intrinsic motivation, the category of extrinsic motivation is more complex. Indeed, rather than considering motivation in terms of a dichotomy (e.g., internal versus external motivation; deCharms, 1968, Harter, 1981), OIT was developed to distinguish between unique types of extrinsic motivation that vary in the degree to which they are experienced as being autonomous (versus controlled). Built around the concept of internalization (cf. Deci & Ryan, 2000), the different types of extrinsic motivation outlined in OIT are hypothesized to form a quasi-simplex pattern that reflects a continuum of self-determination. From most to least autonomous, these are labeled integrated regulation, identified regulation, introjected regulation, and external regulation (Deci & Ryan, 1985a; Ryan & Connell, 1989). A simplex-like (or ordered correlation) pattern of associations whereby regulations more proximal to one another on the continuum (e.g., external regulation and introjected regulation) are more highly correlated than regulations more distal on the continuum (e.g., external regulation and identified regulation) has been supported in exercise settings (e.g., Li & Harmer, 1996; Markland & Tobin, 2004). Moreover, a meta-analysis encompassing 21 published papers from sport, exercise, and PE settings has provided support for the existence of a self-determination continuum from external regulation to introjected regulation and identified regulation (Chatzisarantis, Hagger, Biddle, Smith, & Wang, 2003). Note at this juncture, however, that the self-determination continuum is not a developmental structure but rather an organizational representation of the motivational regulations. Depending on the social context, an individual can adopt a regulation at any stage of the continuum (Ryan & Deci, 2002).

Figure 7.1 provides a schematic overview of the types of motivation embraced within OIT, their regulatory processes, and the defining features of each distinct regulation. As shown, the four regulations pertinent to OIT's multidimensional perspective of extrinsic motivation are located between the extremities of inaction and action as defined with SDT. These unique types of extrinsic motivation are anchored between amotivation (a state of lacking intention to act) and intrinsic motivation (the prototype of autonomous regulation).

Type of motivation	Amotivation	Extrinsic motivation				Intrinsic motivation
Type of regulation	Nonregulation	External	Introjection	Identified	Integration	Intrinsic
Perceived locus of causality	Impersonal	External	Somewhat external	Somewhat internal	Internal	Internal
Internalization	No	No	Partial	Almost full	Full	Not required
Position on the autonomy continuum		Controlled motivation		Autonomous motivation		
Defining features	Lack of intention to act and personal causation	Action to obtain reward, to avoid punishment, or to meet external expectations	Action to avoid guilt and shame and to attain ego enhancements and feelings of worth	Action is personally valued and important	Action is identified and aligned with other aspects of the self	Action is based in interest and inherent satisfaction

FIGURE 7.1 Schematic overview of the self-determination continuum outlining the types of motivation advanced within SDT and related processes.

Based on Ryan and Deci 2000, "Intrinsic and extrinsic motivations."

External regulation represents the least autonomous (or most controlling) type of extrinsic motivation and refers to actions that are carried out to gain an external reward, comply with social pressure, or avoid punishment. This type of extrinsic motivation is defined and used in the traditional lab studies and dichotomized discussions of extrinsic versus intrinsic motivation (e.g., deCharms, 1968; Lepper, Greene, & Nisbett, 1973). Actions that are externally regulated are intentional but are dependent on, and directed by, separable contingencies (i.e., because the regulation is not internalized, if the contingency is removed, the behavior ceases) (Deci & Ryan, 1985a). The exerciser who goes to the gym because he feels pressured and controlled by his family and friends' desire for him to attend would be acting out of external regulation.

The next three types of extrinsic motivation are characterized by the internalization process (Ryan & Deci, 2000a). The first and least autonomous of these regulations is introjected regulation. This type of extrinsic motivation is characterized by an individual's partial internalization of an external regulation. With this type of regulation, the engagement in an activity is still relatively controlled, but the source of control is internal. That is, rather than external contingencies directing a person's actions (e.g., rewards, punishment), the impetus for introjected regulated behavior comes through self-imposed intrapersonal sanctions and rewards, such as shame, guilt, ego enhancement, and pride. Introjected behaviors are couched within self-esteem-related contingencies and are carried out because an individual feels that she or he should act. Although a relatively unstable form of regulation, introjected regulations have been partially internalized, and as such they are more likely than external regulations to be maintained (Deci & Ryan, 2000). An exerciser who would feel ashamed or guilty if she or he were to miss an aerobics session would be acting out of introjected regulation.

Next on the continuum is identified regulation. This regulation is relatively self-determined and refers to behaviors that stem from the conscious valuing of an activity. When identified regulation is manifested, the individual is identifying with an activity as being important to his or her aims or goals (Ryan & Deci, 2000a). That is, rather than feeling that he or she should partake in a behavior, the person willingly performs actions with the view of obtaining some desired and valued consequence. With identified regulation, the person's behavior is still instrumental because it is the usefulness of the activity rather than the activity's inherent interest that guides participation (Ryan & Deci, 2000a). An exerciser who chooses (i.e., volitionally engages) to partake in aerobic-based gym sessions such as jogging on a treadmill because it feels personally valuable for health would be behaving for identified reasons.

Integrated regulation, the most self-determined extrinsic motivation, occurs when identified regulations have been coordinated and made concordant with other identifications and well-internalized life goals. Specifically, it reflects the stage in which identifications have been assessed and brought into congruence with the individual's other values, goals, and needs (Ryan & Deci, 2000a).

Through integrated regulation, previous external regulations will have been fully transformed into self-regulation, resulting in self-determined extrinsic motivation (Deci & Ryan, 2000). Note at this point, however, that although integrated regulation shares many attributes with intrinsic motivation (e.g., it is autonomous), it is still considered extrinsic because the action is performed to achieve a separable outcome (Ryan & Deci, 2002). People who exercise as part of a healthy lifestyle and align exercise with their other valued life goals would be participating in exercise out of integrated regulation.

Although intrinsic motivation and the various types of extrinsic motivation refer to intentional (or motivated) and energized behavior, amotivation occurs when an individual lacks motivation to act or passively performs activities (Ryan & Deci, 2000a). Accordingly, when people are amotivated in their actions they have a complete lack of self-determination toward undertaking a given behavior. Amotivation can result when the person lacks competence, believes that an activity is unimportant, or does not perceive contingencies between his or her behavior and the desired outcomes (Ryan & Deci, 2000a; Vallerand, 1997). An individual who has joined a gym but has concluded that exercising is a waste of time because he or she is not going to achieve the ideal body would be considered amotivated.

Autonomous and Controlled Motivation

In view of the differentiation of extrinsic forms of motivational regulation, coupled with the concept of internalization, the primary distinction of comparison has shifted from a focus of intrinsic versus extrinsic motivation to one of autonomous versus controlled motivation (Deci & Ryan, 2008). When autonomously motivated, people endorse their own actions and act with a full sense of volition because they find the activity to hold inherent interest or personal value (Ryan & Deci, 2006). In this approach, identified regulation, integrated regulations, and intrinsic motivation are forms of autonomous motivation. Controlled motivation is characterized by an individual's behavior being governed by external or internal pressures, such as being coerced, persuaded, or seduced (Moller, Deci, & Ryan, 2006). The behavioral regulations that are classed as being controlled are introjected regulation and external regulation.

Exercise Motivation and Outcome Variables

The arrangement of the motivational types along the self-determination continuum is helpful in hypothesizing their associations with outcome variables (Deci & Ryan, 1991; Ryan & Connell 1989). Indeed, the taxonomy of regulations advanced within OIT not only provides a schematic representation of how internalized and integrated a motive is but also provides a sound conceptual basis to understand and define motivation from a quality perspective. That is, moving from left to right in figure 7.1, the regulation of behavior becomes more autonomous, internalized, and integrated, and the inherent quality and defining features of motivation become increasingly enriched, thus promoting and supporting adaptive engagement and effective functioning in activities.

According to SDT, intrinsic and integrated motivations lead to the most positive consequences, followed by identified regulation. In contrast, external regulation and amotivation are hypothesized to be associated with negative consequences. Introjected regulation is hypothesized to lead to consequences that lie between external regulation and identified regulation. Because introjected regulations are within the person, yet still relatively external to the self, this regulatory style is particularly interesting (Deci & Ryan, 2000).

In considering the shift of focus within contemporary SDT literature to distinguishing motivation based on it being autonomous or controlled, note that within SDT it is held that autonomous motivation (relative to controlled motivation) will lead to, or correlate with, more adaptive consequences. To this end, an abundance of empirical studies (both experimental and field based) across many life domains has shown the advantages of being autonomously motivated for adaptive motivational consequences such as long-term persistence, better psychological well-being, enhanced performance, increased creativity, and healthier lifestyles (Deci & Ryan, 2008).

To enable researchers to assess the strength to which they endorse distinct and qualitatively different reasons for engaging in exercise behaviors, initial research efforts aimed at applying SDT to the exercise domain focused on exercise-specific measures. Drawing from existing scales (viz., Academic Motivation Scale, Vallerand et al., 1992; Self-Regulation Questionnaire, Ryan & Connell, 1989) and adapting the items to tap reasons for engaging in exercise, Mullan, Markland, and Ingledew (1997) developed the Behavioural Regulation in Exercise Questionnaire (BREQ). Responding to the stem "Why do you exercise?" the BREQ comprises 15 items that assess intrinsic, identified, introjected, and external motivational regulations. Although removed from the original BREQ model because of high levels of skewness (suggesting amotivation to be irrelevant for freely chosen exercise behavior), a 4-item amotivation scale was added to the BREQ, a modification that resulted in the BREQ-2 (Markland & Tobin, 2004). The addition of these items to the scale when a more motivationally diverse sample was surveyed (i.e., 194 former exercise referral scheme participants) led to a measurement model (assessed by confirmatory factor analysis, or CFA) that had an excellent fit to the study data. Support for the BREQ–BREQ-2 as a theoretically based and psychometrically sound tool with which to assess exercise motivation from the perspective of SDT is accumulating (e.g., Wilson, Rodgers, & Fraser, 2002; Wilson & Rogers, 2008). Further, research has also shown that the addition of items to assess integrated regulation does not compromise responses to the BREQ—either from items developed to supplement the BREQ (Wilson, Rodgers, Loitz, & Scime, 2006) or from employing the integrated regulation subscale of the Exercise Motivation Scale (EMS; Li, 1999) (e.g., Edmunds, Ntoumanis, & Duda, 2008). With the latter items in mind, note that other measures of exercise motivation such as the EMS have been developed and are aligned with the theoretical tenets of SDT, but we will not elaborate on such scales further here, because to date they have been used sparingly in exercise-based research (see Wininger, 2007, for discussion of the psychometric properties of the EMS).

Predominantly employing the BREQ or BREQ-2 (or adapted versions), numerous exercise-based studies have examined the differential effects that various types of motivation have on important outcomes such as effortful engagement, exercise persistence, adaptive exercise cognitions, indices of positive psychological well-being, and physical self-perceptions. In the following section we review a number of empirical investigations grounded within SDT that report on the associations between the different motivation types and a number of key exercise-related outcome variables.

Exercise Behavior In view of growing concern that many people are not accruing enough physical activity needed for health benefit (e.g., ACSM, 2009), one avenue of research has focused on gaining a better understanding of the association between the quality of a person's motivation and her or his level of health-enhancing exercise behavior. From the perspective of SDT, the adaptive behavioral concomitants of motivation such as effortful and sustained behavioral engagement in activities of moderate to vigorous intensity are most likely to occur when an individual partakes in the activity for autonomous reasons (i.e., acts through intrinsic motivation and well-internalized extrinsic motivation) (Ryan & Deci, 2007).

Initial attempts to examine the relationship between an individual's exercise motivation and his or her behavioral engagement relied on self-reported measures (e.g., Edmunds, Ntoumanis, & Duda, 2006a, 2006b; Gillison, Standage, & Skevington, 2006; Wilson, Rodgers, Fraser, & Murray, 2004; Wilson et al., 2002). For the most part, researchers investigating motivation from SDT's differentiated perspective have used the Leisure Time Exercise Questionnaire (LTEQ; Godin & Shepard, 1985) to gain, and quantify, a self-reported assessment of the frequency of mild, moderate, and strenuous exercise behavior (for a minimum of 15 minutes during a typical week). Consistent with the tenets of SDT, results from several correlational studies have shown that autonomous types of motivation positively predict higher levels of reported moderate- or strenuous-intensity exercise behavior (e.g., Brunet & Sabiston, 2009; Edmunds et al., 2006a; Gillison et al., 2006; Wilson et al., 2002).

Although self-reports of exercise behavior have a number of merits (e.g., they are cost effective, entail low participant burden, are feasible for use in research with large samples, and so on), they are also vulnerable to issues such as social desirability and recall biases (Dale, Welk, & Matthews, 2002). Recent work has also shown that although the LTEQ provides an approximation of exercise behavior at a population level, the measure does not inform whether a given individual is participating in the type, intensity, and amount of physical activity advocated in current public health recommendations (Loney,

Standage, Thompson, Sebire, & Cumming, 2011). A further issue pertains to a systematic source of error (viz., common-method variance) in which the observed relationships between scores may be influenced by the similarity of measurement methods (e.g., in this case BREQ and LTEQ) rather than the constructs represented by the measures (Podsakoff, MacKenzie, Lee, & Podsakoff, 2003). Such issues have led researchers interested in examining the association between different types of motivational regulation and exercise behavior to call for the use of more objective assessments (e.g., Standage et al., 2005; Standage & Vallerand, 2008).

A study by Vierling, Standage, and Treasure (2007) was one of the first to examine the association between autonomous motivation and an objective marker of activity (i.e., through the use of pedometer step counts). The authors sampled 237 predominantly low socioeconomic Hispanic students classified as being at risk (i.e., for disparities that will inversely affect their health and well-being) to examine a model of motivational processes couched within SDT. After controlling for the possible confounding effects of age and gender, a combined variable consisting of the intrinsic motivation and identified regulation subscales (viz., labeled autonomous motivation toward physical activity) was shown, albeit weakly, to positively predict pedometer step counts over a 4-day period.

Although the use of pedometers in SDT research (e.g., Lonsdale, Sabiston, Raedeke, Ha, & Sum, 2009; Vierling et al., 2007) provides an estimate of behavior through the number of steps per day, pedometers are unable to differentiate between activities of varying intensity (i.e., this information cannot be derived from step counts) (Bassett & Strath, 2002). Considering these limitations, Standage, Sebire, and Loney (2008) examined whether the positive relationship shown between autonomous exercise motivation and (a) self-reported exercise behavior and (b) pedometer step counts would hold when behavior was objectively quantified in terms of intensity and duration. Specifically, to assess moderate-intensity exercise bouts of greater than (or equal to) to 10 minutes, 20 minutes, and an accumulation of activity needed to meet the ACSM–AHA guidelines, the authors employed a unit (viz., Actiheart; Cambridge Neurotechnology, U.K.) that uses a synchronized branched equation to predict energy expenditure above rest from simultaneously recorded heart rate and accelerometry data. After controlling for the potential confounding effects of gender and a marker of body composition (i.e., a combined index of BMI and waist circumference), results showed that autonomous motivation positively predicted the amount of time spent in moderate bouts of exercise behavior for 10 or more minutes and 20 or more minutes over a 7-day period and an accumulation of activity needed to meet the ACSM–AHA guidelines. In this work, controlled motivation was unrelated to time spent in bouts of exercise behavior. The findings reported by Standage et al. advanced the exercise motivation literature by showing the autonomous versus controlled distinction to be useful in predicting objectively assessed engagement in exercise at levels that are deemed health enhancing (cf. Haskell et al., 2007).

In line with SDT predictions, past work using self-reported and objective assessments of activity have shown autonomous motivation (relative to controlled motivation) to predict exercise behavior. Although such findings are consonant with SDT, a number of interesting results have emerged when researchers have examined the independent utility of each distinct motivational regulation.

The first of these findings pertains to identified regulation, which has been shown to be a better positive predictor, relative to intrinsic motivation, of self-reported exercise behavior (e.g., Edmunds et al., 2006a), to share a greater association with objectively assessed exercise bouts of moderate-intensity exercise (Standage et al., 2008) and to distinguish between those who report exercising infrequently as opposed to those exercising regularly for a period of less than 6 months (Thørgensen-Ntoumani & Ntoumanis, 2006). Moreover, in certain studies researchers have failed to find relationships between intrinsic motivation and exercise behavior when controlling for the other regulation types (e.g., Edmunds et al., 2006a). To this end, because many people participate in exercise for instrumental reasons, such as improving their health and fitness, losing weight, and enhancing their appearance, coupled with the fact that certain exercise activities (e.g., running on a treadmill, exercising on a step machine) can sometimes be construed as being boring, mundane, or not inherently enjoyable, these findings are completely explicable at a cross-sectional level (i.e., when the target activity is valued but not inherently self-rewarding, well-externalized extrinsic motivation may be as useful to understanding behavioral regulation as intrinsic motivation; see Ryan, 1995). That said, and although identified regulation has been advanced as a key variable when predicting proximal measures of exercise behavior, past work has shown that when exercising for intrinsic factors people are more likely to persist (e.g., Ryan et al., 1997). Moreover, and using discriminant function analysis, Mullan and Markland (1997) found that intrinsic motivation, in combination with identified regulation, distinguished between participants who were in the action and maintenance stages of change as opposed to being in the prepreparation and preparation stages (see Prochaska & DiClemente, 1984, for a discussion of the stages of change model). Similar findings were reported by Thøgersen-Ntoumani and Ntoumanis (2006) in their work with exercisers from nine health clubs. Specifically, they found meaningful effect sizes to exist when comparing the reported level of intrinsic motivation and identified regulation for those categorized as being in the maintenance stage to those classed as being in the preparation (d values = 1.10 and 1.12, respectively) and action stages (d values = .66 and .53, respectively). Collectively, such findings seem to support Deci and Ryan's (1985a) view that the integration of extrinsic motivation can occur concurrently alongside the development of intrinsic motivation, or sometimes independently of it.

Another finding that warrants discussion pertains to the role of introjected regulation in the prediction of exercise behavior. That is, although past work has generally supported the positive role of autonomous motivation (relative to controlled motivation) in predicting exercise behavior, a number of studies have shown positive associations between introjected regulation and (*a*) self-reported activity (e.g., Edmunds et al., 2006a; Wilson et al., 2004), (*b*) behavioral persistence based on changes in LTEQ scores (i.e., over a duration of 10 months; a finding in adolescent boys but not adolescent girls) (Gillison, Standage, & Skevington, 2011), and (*c*) categorizations of exercise behavior (e.g., Thøgersen-Ntoumani & Ntoumanis, 2006). For example, and with the latter in mind, Thøgersen-Ntoumani and Ntoumanis (2006) found that exercisers classified as being in the maintenance stage (i.e., those who have exercised regularly for greater than 6 months) reported higher introjection than individuals in the preparation and action stages. Within SDT, introjected regulation is considered a controlling form of behavioral regulation manifested by self-imposed sanctions, such as guilt, shame, and pride. But it may be that in view of the omnipresent messages and health campaigns regarding the benefits that physical activity holds for health, acting because of introjects in the short term (i.e., because of feelings of guilt or socially relevant criteria or ego enhancements) may play a role in helping a person stave off anxiety pertaining to the health-related implications or social stigma associated with a sedentary lifestyle. Such an approach would make intuitive sense within terror management theory (Greenberg, Pyszczynski, & Solomon, 1986), but SDT also suggests that healthy development is more about the unfolding of intrinsic growth tendencies than about flights from anxiety (Ryan & Deci, 2004). Akin to SDT's focus on the natural, innate, and constructive tendency for growth and development, it is likely that an individual's exercise experience will be of low quality and that behavioral persistence will be fragile unless such introjects are internalized. As with work in the sporting domain (e.g., Pelletier, Fortier, Vallerand, & Brière, 2001), it may be that exercising through self-imposed pressure provides immediate impetus for prompting a behavior but over time such internal sanctions (which are quite energy depleting) have negative implications for long-term behavioral engagement. To this end, the weak positive prediction reported by Gillison et al. (2011) for persistence at 10 months is consistent with the findings of Pelletier et al., who found introjected regulation to predict persistence at 10 months ($b = .23$) but then became a nonsignificant predictor of persistence at 22 months ($b = -.04$), whereas more autonomous motives continued to predict persistence. Clearly, longer-term measures of behavioral persistence in the future exercise-related work would be particularly insightful.

Intention and Effort-Related Outcomes   In addition to studies that have focused on exercise behavior as a correlate of exercise motivation, numerous studies have used intention or effort-related outcomes as dependent variables. Collectively, this line of empirical inquiry supports the manifold behavior-related advantages associated with autonomous reasons for exercise.

For example, studies have shown autonomous forms of exercise behavioral regulation to positively predict behavior-related variables, such as self-rated exercise effort (Vansteenkiste, Simons, Soenens, & Lens, 2004; Wilson et al., 2004), exercise intentions (Hagger, Chatzisarantis, & Harris, 2006; Thøgersen-Ntoumani & Ntoumanis, 2006; Wilson & Rodgers, 2004; Wilson et al., 2004), club membership (i.e., tai-bo; Vansteenkiste, Simons, Soenens, et al., 2004), lower self-reported frequency of exercise relapse (Thøgersen-Ntoumani & Ntoumanis, 2006), and reported persistence in exercise (i.e., at 3 and 6 weeks) following competition of a cardiac rehabilitation program (Russell & Bray, 2009).

Exercise-Related Well-Being, Physical Self-Evaluations, and Cognitions Beyond predicting indicators of behavioral quality, SDT posits that intrinsic motivation and well-internalized or autonomously regulated extrinsic motivation will positively predict greater psychological well-being, as indexed by affect, adaptive cognitions, more adaptive self-perceptions, and enhanced mental health. Indeed, and increasingly over the past 10 years, researchers interested in the subjective experiences, mental health, cognitive, and well-being responses of those engaged in exercise contexts have explored how autonomous (relative to controlled) motivation differentially predicts important outcome variables. The positive outcomes found to be associated with autonomous forms of exercise motivation include greater psychological well-being (Sebire, Standage, & Vansteenkiste, 2009), enhanced perceptions of physical self-esteem or self-worth (Sebire et al., 2009; Thøgersen-Ntoumani & Ntoumanis, 2006; Wilson & Rodgers, 2002), more positive attitudes toward exercising (Vierling et al., 2007; Wilson, Rodgers, Blanchard, & Gessell, 2003), better quality of life (Gillison et al., 2006), improved body satisfaction (Gillison et al., 2011), and increased self-efficacy to overcome barriers to regular exercise (Thøgersen-Ntoumani & Ntoumanis, 2006). Further, negative associations have been reported between autonomous motivation and exercise anxiety (Sebire et al., 2009), as well as reported levels of social physique anxiety (Brunet & Sabiston, 2009; Gillison et al., 2011; Thøgersen-Ntoumani & Ntoumanis, 2006).

In contrast, controlled forms of extrinsic motivation (viz., introjected and external regulation) or amotivation have been shown to be associated with maladaptive exercise-related outcomes. For example, Thøgersen-Ntoumani and Ntoumanis (2006) reported that amotivation, external regulation, and introjected regulation were positively related to social physique anxiety, whereas amotivation and external regulation were shown to be negatively associated with the participants' reported levels of physical self-worth and their self-efficacy to overcome barriers to regular exercise. In this work, introjected regulation shared a positive association with barriers of self-efficacy.

A point that warrants further discussion is the pattern of findings as they relate to introjected regulation. As we have alluded to earlier in this chapter, a number of studies have shown positive associations between introjected regulation and behavior-related outcomes (e.g., Edmunds et al., 2006a; Thøgersen-Ntoumani & Ntoumanis, 2006). But despite sometimes predicting the quantity of a person's exercise behavior, at least in the short-term, research also shows that introjected regulation has negative implications for the quality of the experience (viz., more anxiety, guilt, and contingent self-worth). In fact, introjected regulation has been shown to be associated with maladaptive outcomes, such as social physique anxiety, body dissatisfaction, perceived pressure to lose weight, and lower subjective vitality (e.g., Edmunds et al., 2006a; Gillison et al., 2011 Thøgersen-Ntoumani & Ntoumanis, 2006). That introjected regulation appears to predict short-term behavioral outcomes (albeit through intrapersonal sanctions) but also corresponds to maladaptive cognitive and affective outcomes is akin to data from other life domains such as academia (e.g., Ryan & Connell, 1989) and religion (e.g., Neyrinck, Vansteenkiste, Lens, Duriez, & Hutsebaut, 2006) where strong internal pressures motivate individuals but not always in a way conducive to positive engagement or experience. Such evidence provides credence to SDT's approach to distinguishing between the quantity and quality of motivational engagement.

Promoting Intrinsic Motivation and Well-Internalized Extrinsic Motivation

In view of the many positive concomitants of acting through more autonomous forms of motivation, an important strand of work within SDT has been to identify and test the social conditions and processes that support, as opposed to forestall, such volitional engagement. According to SDT, all people have an innate need to feel autonomous, competent, and related to others (Deci & Ryan, 2000). Social environments that are conducive to the satisfaction of these basic needs will facilitate optimal motivation and well-being (cf. Deci & Ryan, 2008). In this section we review the social conditions that are conducive to supporting intrinsic motivation and well-internalized extrinsic motivation.

Supporting Intrinsic Motivation   Within the broader SDT framework, the minitheory of CET provides the theoretical basis for examining the conditions that facilitate rather than diminish or undermine intrinsic motivation. Stemming from the question of how social inputs affect intrinsic motivation and related processes, numerous experimental and field studies have examined the functional significance (or meaning) of events as they affect intrinsic motivation. CET specifies two types of inputs: informational events (which are noncontrolling and provide effectance-relevant information) and controlling events (which represent pressure to feel, behave, or think in specific ways) (see Deci & Ryan, 1980, 1985a). CET holds that informational events facilitate intrinsic motivation by supporting needs for competence and autonomy. In contrast, controlling events undermine or frustrate an individual's experience of autonomy and diminish intrinsic motivation even when people are competent. Much empirical support for these propositions has accumulated (see, e.g., Ryan & Deci, 2000a). For example, in a sample of adult exercisers Markland and Hardy (1997) found that perceived locus of causality (or relative autonomy) mediated the effects of competence on intrinsic motivation (as indexed by greater interest and enjoyment, greater effort and importance, and lower pressure and tension).

Numerous empirical studies have supported the tenets of CET by showing that events deemed as controlling or lacking in support for competence undermine intrinsic motivation. External events that have been shown to undermine intrinsic motivation include deadlines (Amabile, Dejong, & Lepper, 1976), rewards (Deci, Koestner, & Ryan, 1999), surveillance (Plant & Ryan, 1985), and imposed goals (Mossholder, 1980). In contrast, events that provide provision for choice (Patall, Cooper, & Robinson, 2008), provide optimal challenge (Shapira, 1976), and offer effectance-affirmative feedback (Ryan, 1982; Vallerand & Reid, 1984) have been shown to enhance intrinsic motivation. CET extends this formulation to intrapersonal processes as well (Ryan, 1982). Ego involvement, which is controlling in nature and pressures the individual to specific outcomes, is theorized and has been shown to undermine intrinsic motivation (Ryan, Koestner, & Deci, 1991). Moreover, and consonant with CET tenets, some evidence also exists to support the mediational role of perceived competence and autonomy in the relationship between elements of the social context (viz., competence evaluation, competitive outcome, and controlling versus noncontrolling interpersonal contexts) and intrinsic motivation (Reeve & Deci, 1996).

The majority of research that tests the informational or controlling properties of situations and the way in which these affect intrinsic motivation has been conducted in laboratory settings. To date, little field-based work has extended the study of tangible elements within real-world exercise settings. A topical area of debate that transcends directly into the exercise domain relates to the question, Can you pay people to be healthy? (see Wilkinson, 2008). Recently, Standage, Gillison, and Verplanken (2010) conducted a cluster randomized control trial to test whether rewards, as chosen by the target age group (viz. £10 cell phone vouchers or £10 driving lesson vouchers), could provide the incentive to encourage young people leaving school for work to engage in an initiative aimed at improving health behaviors (i.e., exercise behavior and healthy diet). Following recruitment, stratified sampling was used to allocate participants to three groups (i.e., a control group, a behavioral support group, and a behavioral support group with incentives). Although the number of participants attending their first appointment was higher for those gaining the reward (43% as opposed to 28% and 8% for the behavioral support and control groups, respectively), of the 171 participants allocated to the group receiving incentives, only 74 attended their first intervention appointment, and this figure decreased to only 18 at follow-up (about 11%). These findings speak to the weak motivational role that such rewards play in the short-term enactment of even specific behaviors (e.g., attending a session), let alone the potential contribution that they may make to changes in complex behaviors (e.g., exercise and diet). Moreover, and more important from a health perspective, the findings support the premise that "financial incentives also seem to be pretty useless in the long term unless they are linked to some sort of skills based programme" (Wilkinson, 2008, p. 1325). From a CET perspective, the incentive used in the Standage et al. work was engagement contingent (i.e., being offered in exchange for task participation, without any specific standard to meet), and as such it is likely that it primarily communicated control and offered little, if anything, in the way of providing feedback to the participant regarding his or her competence (viz., there was no competence affirmation in the incentive to counteract the negative effects of feeling controlled to attend). Such findings provide support for the ecological validity of CET and support the meta-analytical findings of Deci et al. (1999), which revealed that tangible rewards that involved engaging in a target activity undermined intrinsic motivation. Future work considering the use of incentives in real-world settings would do well to test the utility of informational rather than controlled rewards to support, as opposed to frustrate, the participants' experience of autonomy and competence.

Keep in mind that people will be intrinsically motivated only for activities that hold intrinsic interest for them (Ryan & Deci, 2000a). As we have previously mentioned, motivation toward exercise (relative to sport) is often engaged in for more extrinsic reasons (although without some enjoyment or appreciation for the activity, sustained involvement is unlikely). Fortunately, exercise settings can be made more autonomously motivating, enjoyable, and valued through the provision of optimally supportive social environments. Indeed, the factors that facilitate people to internalize and integrate extrinsic motivation are similar to those that maintain intrinsic motivation. Specifically, the social conditions that are created by significant others (e.g., exercise instructors, friends, teachers, parents) serve a central role in supporting the internalization and integration of activities enacted for extrinsic reasons. As outlined previously (e.g., Deci & Ryan, 1991; Ryan & Deci, 2000a), although autonomy and competence have been shown to be highly salient supports for intrinsic motivation, the need for relatedness, which may play a more distal role in supporting the maintenance of intrinsic motivation, is to a large extent the impetus for internalizing values and regulatory processes. In short, within OIT it is held that people will accept and internalize a new behavioral regulation or value to the extent to which their needs for autonomy, competence, and relatedness are met within that context. It is to such social environments that our attention now turns.

Autonomy Support   A line of empirical enquiry that has received some attention by exercise psychologists is the role that the interpersonal context plays in supporting the experience and persistence of exercise participants. Within SDT, it is hypothesized that autonomy-supportive environments (i.e., social contexts that support choice, initiation, and understanding and minimize the need to perform and act in a prescribed manner) facilitate autonomous motivation, greater engagement, better internalization and integration, and optimal psychological functioning (see Deci & Ryan, 2008). In contrast, controlling contexts (e.g., pressuring, evaluative, or authoritarian) undermine many of these positive outcomes. According to SDT, the manifold benefits offered to people interacting with autonomy-supportive instructors, peers, teachers, and others is as a function of such environments' provision of the necessary support for the satisfaction of people's basic psychological needs. Supporting such reasoning, research in exercise settings has shown perceptions of autonomy support to positively predict levels of autonomous motivation, both directly (e.g., Hagger et al., 2007; Russell & Bray, 2010; Wilson & Rodgers, 2004) and through the satisfaction of autonomy, competence, and relatedness (e.g., Edmunds et al., 2006a; Vierling et al., 2007). Moreover, perceptions of autonomy support have also been shown to positively predict positive attitudes or intentions as they relate to physical activity (e.g., Chatzisarantis, Hagger, & Smith, 2007; Vierling et al., 2007).

Some experimental support also exists regarding the positive effect that autonomy-supportive contexts have on motivation-related outcomes. For example, in a study of students who were introduced to a new exercise activity (viz., tai-bo), Vansteenkiste, Simons, Soenens, et al. (2004) found that the provision of an autonomy-supportive context linked to increased effort, more autonomous forms of behavioral regulation, greater persistence (of up to 4 months), and future enrollment in a tai-bo club. In an exercise context, Edmunds et al. (2008) examined the effects of instructional styles based on SDT (viz., autonomy support, structure, and involvement) and participants' affect, psychological need satisfaction, motivational regulations, behavioral intentions, and attendance. Female exercisers at a university were exposed to either an SDT-based (n = 22) or typical (n = 31) teaching style class for 10 weeks. Analyses revealed that participants in the SDT-based condition reported a significantly greater linear increase in interpersonal involvement, perceived competence, relatedness, and positive affect. Moreover, attendance rates were greater in the SDT-based intervention group.

Facilitating Optimal Motivation and Well-Being: The Role of Basic Psychological Needs

As previously noted, a fundamental postulate within SDT is that for individuals to be optimally motivated, satisfy their growth tendencies, function effectively, and experience psychological well-being within and across life domains, they must satisfy three basic psychological needs (viz., for autonomy, competence, and relatedness). At this juncture it seems appropriate to clarify a point of confusion sometimes observed in the exercise science literature. That is, and often based on cross-sectional data, researchers have on occasion highlighted a particular basic need as being more germane than others to exercise settings.

Although such assertions are explicable when considering specific behaviors or given situations, the basic needs are defined as essential nutriments for ongoing growth, integrated functioning, and well-being (Deci & Ryan, 1991). If any of the needs are frustrated or thwarted, an individual will experience diminished motivation and well-being (see Ryan & Deci, 2008). Accordingly, for ongoing and maintained optimal functioning in exercise settings, supports for the satisfaction of all three needs are required.

Although much empirical support for the tenets of BPNT has emerged in the broader literature (see Ryan & Deci, 2008), the application of the basic need constructs within exercise settings is still in its relative infancy. To aid researchers in this line of work, Wilson, Rogers, Rodgers, and Wild (2006) developed and validated the Psychological Need Satisfaction in Exercise Scale (PNSE), a multidimensional instrument by which to assess and analyze psychological need satisfaction within the exercise domain. A similar measure was developed by Vlachopoulos and Michailidou (2006) for use with Greek samples (viz., Basic Psychological Needs in Exercise Scale [BPNES]), and preliminary support for a translated English version has recently been provided (Vlachopoulos, Ntoumanis, & Smith, in press).

These measures, along with other psychological need satisfaction scales adapted to exercise from various contexts, have been used to examine the consequences of experiencing need satisfaction in exercise settings. A number of studies have provided empirical support for the premise that the satisfaction of the three needs provides the nutriments for healthy physical, psychological, and social functioning. For example, in their cross-cultural validation study, Vlachopoulos et al. (2010) collected need satisfaction data using both the PNSE and BPNES from 346 British exercise participants. Results from both measures showed positive associations between the need satisfaction variables and subjective vitality, autonomous forms of motivation, and self-reported exercise behavior. Similarly, in a sample of 261 British university students, Hagger et al. (2006) found that exercise-based psychological need satisfaction predicted, both directly and indirectly (through autonomous motivation), exercise-based attitude and perceived behavioral control constructs from the theory of planned behavior (Ajzen, 1991), as well as yielding a direct effect on the subjective norm facet.

In another illustrative study, Sebire et al. (2009) found, through structural equation modeling, that a latent composite index of need satisfaction was positively associated with physical self-worth and psychological well-being and negatively with exercise anxiety. With the latter variable in mind, need satisfaction within exercise as reported by 350 Greek adolescent girls has been shown to be a negative direct predictor of other maladaptive indices, such as body-image concerns (indexed by a drive for thinness and body dissatisfaction), and to have negative indirect effects on unhealthy weight control behaviors, such as taking diet pills, skipping meals, fasting (for a day or more), and inducing vomiting (Thøgersen-Ntoumani, Ntoumanis, & Nikitaras, 2010).

As previously reviewed, a further line of exercise-based work has examined how differing social forces and interpersonal contexts affect the basic needs to mediate a person's motivation, well-being, and effective functioning. In general, empirical research addressing this question provides support for the tenets of BPNT by showing that need satisfaction partially mediates the positive effects conveyed from experiencing autonomy-supportive exercise contexts (e.g., Edmunds et al., 2006a; also see Wilson, Mack, & Grattan, 2008).

Exercise Goal Contents

Although studies from the early 1990s onward supported the premise that the pursuit of intrinsic (relative to extrinsic) life goals is associated with numerous indicators of positive psychological health and adjustment (see Kasser, 2002), the lack of a valid and reliable assessment of exercise-based goal content precluded initial studies from exploring the concomitants of individuals' reported goals for exercise. That said, a number of goal-framing studies were conducted (see Vansteenkiste, Soenens, & Lens, 2007). For example, in a sample of Belgian high school participants Vansteenkiste, Simons, Lens, Sheldon, and Deci (2004, Study 3) used written scripts to frame tai-bo exercises as being for the attainment of either intrinsic (viz., physical health) or extrinsic (viz., appearing attractive to others) goals. Results showed that participants randomized into the intrinsic goal-framing group displayed greater behavioral persistence and graded performance on the tai-bo exercise.

To aid in the assessment and study of goal contents within exercise settings, Sebire, Standage, and Vansteenkiste (2008) developed the Goal Content for Exercise Questionnaire (GCEQ), a 20-item measure that aligns categories akin to past work (e.g., Kasser & Ryan, 1996). In this measure, goals for health management, skill development, and social affiliation are classified as intrinsic, whereas exercise goals for image and social recognition are categorized as extrinsic. In their development and validation paper, Sebire et al. provided evidence for adequate factorial validity (both higher and lower order), as well as for conventionally acceptable scores for external validity, temporal stability, invariance across gender, and internal consistency. Having provided support for the psychometric properties of the GCEQ, Sebire and colleagues (2009) conducted a subsequent study in which they studied the responses of 410 British adults to (a) examine the associations between goal content and cognitive, affective, and behavioral outcomes and (b) test the mediating role of the basic needs in the "goal content–outcomes" relationship. After controlling for the participants' age and gender, results showed that relative intrinsic goal content (indexed by subtracting the mean of intrinsic goals from the mean of extrinsic goal subscales) positively predicted psychological need satisfaction in exercise, physical self-worth, psychological well-being, and self-reported exercise behavior and negatively predicted exercise-based anxiety. With the exception of self-reported exercise behavior, relative intrinsic goals remained a significant predictor of the cognitive and affective outcomes after controlling for the participants' relative autonomous motivation toward exercise. Using structural equation modeling analyses, the authors found that exercise-based psychological need satisfaction partially mediated the effect of relative intrinsic goal content on physical self-worth, psychological well-being, and exercise anxiety.

Interestingly, although the work of Sebire et al. showed that goal content played a crucial role in supporting the quality of the participants' exercise experiences, holding relative intrinsic goals did not contribute to the prediction of self-reported exercise behavior (i.e., after relative autonomous motivation was added to the regression equation). To explore this issue further, Sebire, Standage, and Vansteenkiste (in press) examined the effects of the content and regulation of adults' exercise goals on moderate to vigorous physical activity and objectively assessed bouts of exercise behavior. Specifically, a week after reporting the content and regulation of their exercise goals, 101 adult participants wore an accelerometer (viz., ActiGraph GT1M) for 7 consecutive days. A bootstrapping analytic approach as presented in Preacher and Hayes (2008) was used to test a single-step multiple mediation model. Results showed that relative intrinsic exercise goals had a positive indirect effect on average daily moderate to vigorous physical activity, average daily moderate to vigorous activity accumulated in exercise bouts of 10 minutes, and the number of days on which participants performed 30 or more minutes of moderate to vigorous activity (i.e., achieved the ACSM–AHA guidelines) through autonomous motivation. Because no direct independent effect of goal content on behavior was found, the findings were akin to other observations in the exercise science literature (e.g., Ingledew & Markland, 2008; Sebire et al., 2009) and support a motivational sequence in which intrinsic goal content supports autonomous motivation, which in turn positively predicts physical activity and bouts of exercise behavior.

Consistent with research in other life domains (see Vansteenkiste, Soenens, & Duriez, 2008), the data presented on goal content within the exercise domain provide support for the tenets of GCT. That is, intrinsic exercise goals have been shown to be conducive to the satisfaction of basic needs and facilitative of indices of well-being and adaptive cognitions (through direct effects and indirectly through need satisfaction). Moreover, that the effect of relative intrinsic goals has been shown to be mediated by autonomous motivation does not reduce the import of fostering intrinsic goals. It may be that the assessment of goals as captured by the GCEQ (i.e., rated importance of the extent to which the goals are for exercising) taps a goal focus in which the individual's aspiration is cognitively too distal (e.g., to be slim to look attractive to others, to improve overall health, and so on). Thus, it may be the case that when seeking to predict recently enacted behaviors, the more proximal motivation for action has better predictive utility. Irrespective of whether this is a measurement issue or that goals predict exercise-related cognitive and affective outcomes (but not behavior), within SDT both autonomous motivation and intrinsic goal constructs are inherently supportive of a person's growth-oriented tendencies through his or her ability to satisfy basic needs, and both have been shown repeatedly and uniquely to support a high-quality exercise experience.

Causality Orientations

Individual differences within SDT are often studied using causality orientations theory (COT). To date, however, little attention has been given to the study and application of COT within exercise settings. This lack of attention is most likely because of the conceptualization of causality orientations residing and operating across domains (i.e., a general level) as opposed to being domain specific (e.g., toward exercise, sport, education, and so on).

An exception is work carried out by Rose, Markland, and Parfitt (2001), who developed the Exercise Causality Orientations Scale (ECOS) to assess causality orientations salient within exercise settings. Having provided some evidence for acceptable psychometric properties, Rose, Parfitt, and Williams (2005) used the ECOS with 184 adults to (a) examine the relationships between exercise causality orientations and stages of change and (b) explore the relative importance of exercise causality orientations and motivational regulations in discriminating stage of change. Results showed that the level of endorsement for autonomy orientation increased across the stages of change, whereas reported levels of control orientation remained stable. In examining the ECOS and BREQ scores in combination, the only variables that emerged in the discriminant functional analysis to distinguish between stages of change were indentified and introjected regulations. Rose et al. (2005) concluded their paper by pointing out that behavioral regulations predicted stage of change better than causality orientations, yet the causal relationship between the two constructs warrants further investigation. Work pursuing such lines of enquiry would do well to consider how such domain-specific orientations fit within COT's developmental and growth-oriented approach to personality.

Theory of Vitality

SDT has developed in an inductive manner over the past five decades to form the macro theory of motivation as it is today. Just as the other components and motivational phenomena studied within SDT have evolved through academic discourse and empirical investigation, new directions and possible extensions to the framework continue to evolve. One applicable offshoot within exercise and health fields pertains to the study of vitality.

The energization of individuals' psychological processes and behaviors is an important aspect of motivation (see Ryan & Deci, 2008, for a discussion). As a concept that aligns with the energy required for engaging and persisting in exercise behavior, vitality has received increasing attention within the SDT literature. Vitality refers to a dynamic aspect of well-being indexed by the subjective experience of energy and positive aliveness (Ryan & Frederick, 1997). From the SDT perspective, events or social conditions that satisfy the basic needs provide the energy to maintain or enhance vitality, whereas those that frustrate needs drain the person's available energy resources. Moreover, the vigor and invigorating energy derived from the satisfaction of basic needs serve to support people in their volitional and persistent engagement in important activities. In their work on exercise and sport motivation, Frederick and Ryan (1993) found that many participants referred to vitality as a prime motivator of their engagement, stating that participation in exercise did not drain their subjective energy but rather made them feel more alive and vital. According to SDT, whereas controlled regulations are energy depleting, autonomous motives are vitalizing. Empirical support for such postulations has emerged in the extant literature (e.g., Moller et al., 2006; Nix, Ryan, Manly, & Deci, 1999).

Ryan and Deci (2007) have highlighted a number of important reasons for work in exercise domains to address the role of vitality. First, vitality is in and of itself a positive psychological state. Second, vitality holds particular import for activities requiring prolonged investment and expenditure of effort. Third, vitality could serve as a marker of health and may positively relate to immunological status and capacity for psychological well-being and coping, as well as provide a protective physical function (i.e., physical resilience).

Some evidence for the role that vitality may play in physical resilience emerged from a study conducted by Richman et al. (2009), who examined the association between vitality and their participants' cardiovascular health over a period of 2 years. Specifically, a sample of 1,041 patients (M age = 61.8 years; 44.8% male) was randomly selected from 5,500 patients who attended a multispecialty medical practice. Data (viz., mental and physical health indices) were obtained from their medical records and responses to a questionnaire pack including the vitality measure. After controlling for age and gender, the findings showed that vitality was associated with reduced odds (or likelihood) of several negative cardiovascular outcomes (i.e., CHD and CVD prevalence, hypertension, high cholesterol). Moreover, prospective analyses suggested that vitality might serve a protective function in the development of cardiovascular disease.

Practical Applications

Vansteenkiste et al. (2010) recently likened the theoretical development of SDT to the construction of a puzzle. This same systematic research-driven approach to the development of SDT has provided a number of explicit avenues for intervention. The applied implications of SDT can be best illustrated by the use of the basic psychological needs as a core basis for integrating and organizing the motivational phenomena stemming from a broad and rich body of empirical work. Indeed, research conducted across a broad array of life domains has shown that social conditions supportive of the needs serve to maintain or enhance intrinsic motivation, support the internalization and integration of extrinsic motivation, provide support for intrinsic goals (or aspirations), and directly affect an individual's well-being and health. Thus, from the perspective of SDT a thorough understanding of the qualities and nature of environments that are supportive of autonomy, competence, and relatedness holds particular import to practitioners.

Practitioners in exercise settings are encouraged to focus on the intrinsic aspects of the activity when and where possible (e.g., stress the inherent fun and enjoyment of activities). Such an endeavor would seemingly be best achieved through the provision of need-satisfying activities. But because many people do not perceive exercise-based activities that are desirable for health gain as being intrinsically interesting, the concepts of internalization and integration espoused within OIT bear particular practical relevance. That is, these constructs provide valuable insight into how practitioners can help to foster persistent and high-quality engagement in nonintrinsically motivated activities. As previously mentioned, internalization denotes a progressive and natural process in which people attempt to transform externally requested or prescribed regulations (e.g., socially sanctioned requests from significant others such as peers, parents, teachers, and instructors) into personally endorsed values that are taken in and internally endorsed, valued, and autonomously regulated (see figure 7.1) (Ryan & Deci, 2000a). Numerous studies have supported the tenets of OIT by showing that greater internalization yields better behavioral, affective, and cognitive outcomes (for exercise-related reviews see Hagger & Chatzisarantis, 2007). Accordingly, when attempting to foster sustained and high-quality exercise engagement, it is important to consider the factors that help individuals achieve organismic integration. For practitioners interested in helping people to accept values or new behavioral regulations as they pertain to exercise, OIT holds that social conditions that are supportive of autonomy, competence, and relatedness provide the basis for people to internalize and integrate aspects of their social world so as to develop healthy self-endorsed extrinsic motivation (Deci & Ryan, 2000). Many field studies (e.g., Niemiec et al., 2006, Ntoumanis, 2005; Standage et al., 2005) and a number of experimental investigations (e.g., Sheldon & Filak, 2008) provide credence to the notion that need supports are central to internalization. Moreover, health care intervention studies, including a number of randomized clinical trials grounded in the SDT model of health behavior change, have shown that when patients experience need satisfaction in their treatment they experience greater volitional engagement in their treatment and demonstrate greater maintenance of desirable health behaviors (Ryan, Patrick, Deci, & Williams, 2008; Williams et al., 2002). Interventions based on the SDT framework to the exercise domain have been less numerous, but some support exists for the motivational benefits of exercise instructors' use of autonomy-supportive teaching styles (e.g., Edmunds et al., 2008; Vansteenkiste, Simons, Soenens, et al., 2004).

Although applications to the exercise domain are in their infancy, numerous recommendations of how to transfer the tenets of SDT to practice can be gleaned from an impressive body of empirical contributions, coupled with past work that has outlined a number of preconditions for supporting intrinsic motivation, effective functioning, and the internalization and integration of values across several life domains (e.g., Deci, Eghrari, Patrick, & Leone, 1994; Deci, Ryan, & Williams, 1996; Deci & Vansteenkiste, 2004). We now turn our focus to the applied implications of SDT within the exercise domain.

Much of the work that has focused on supports for the basic needs has come under the banner of autonomy support. Autonomy-supportive contexts actually enhance the likelihood that an individual will satisfy all three needs, including competence and relatedness (Baard, Deci, & Ryan, 2004; Ryan & Deci, 2000a). That is, when a person's autonomy is supported, the supporter is likely to be attuned to other needs and the individual will, when experiencing autonomy, be more empowered and free to fulfill other needs. Practitioners who are autonomy supportive thus refrain from the use of pressure or contingencies to motivate, and they relate to motivates in a manner in which they take interest in their perspective, are responsive to their thoughts and feelings, offer opportunities for choice and initiation, communicate the value of uninteresting tasks, and provide an empathic approach to concerns (or negative feelings) related to partaking in a requested task. Dozens of studies across an array of life domains attest to the benefits of these elements of autonomy support for optimal motivation and effective functioning (see Deci & Ryan, 2008; Reeve & Halusic, 2009). In the section that follows, we consider the situational components that provide supports for each basic need in turn as they might be applied in exercise and physical activity settings.

Supports for Autonomy

In exercise settings, practitioners (e.g., exercise instructors, health counselors) may enhance individuals' perceptions of autonomy by using a number of empirically supported techniques. These components include maximizing opportunity for choice (e.g., Zuckerman, Porac, Lathin, Smith, & Deci, 1978), acknowledging people's feelings (e.g., Koestner, Ryan, Bernieri, & Holt, 1984), providing meaningful rationales (e.g., Deci et al., 1994), minimizing ego involvement (Ryan, 1982), reducing controlling self-talk (Oliver, Markland, Hardy, & Petherick, 2008), and vocalizing messages in an appropriate manner (e.g., Ryan, Mims, & Koestner, 1983).

Provision of choice can be achieved by maximizing the options available to people about what exercise activities they wish to partake in (e.g., encourage active exploration of different and new tasks), where they perform their chosen activities (e.g., gym or more natural settings), and when they decide to participate in exercise (i.e., choice about which days and segments of the day work best). Because it is key that choice be self-endorsed (i.e., true and without implicit control; cf. Ryan & Deci, 2006), it is important to ensure that available options are meaningful and personally important. Thus, practitioners should listen to clients rather than impose their views (i.e., avoid a controlling approach such as by saying, "This is what you should do"), involve them in the decision-making process rather than simply prescribe activities (e.g., ask them what they want to do and achieve), be responsive to input (i.e., be flexible to change rather than rigid in their approach, e.g., "What would you like to change?"), and avoid being judgmental. With the latter in mind, those working with people in exercise settings can express empathy or acknowledgment of the concerns that people face with regard to requested behaviors, lapses, obstacles, or relapses. This issue is particularly salient for those who are in the early stages of a program because the benefits offered by exercise are not instantaneous (e.g., weight loss or strength gains require many weeks of regular workouts) and instead may evoke negative repercussions (e.g., fatigue, muscle soreness, breathlessness). Thus, practitioners are advised to provide nonjudgmental support to legitimize their clients' perceptions of concern, thus ensuring that they feel understood and accepted.

An overarching objective of interventions couched within SDT is to raise an individual's awareness and involvement in activities. Central to such an endeavor is the provision of meaningful rationales that provide a basis for people to understand why a target behavior is important. For example, the health benefits of an activity (e.g., circuit training) may be conveyed to help the person understand why participation is personally useful (e.g., "Circuit training will improve your fitness, strength, and overall health"). A lab study conducted by Deci et al. (1994) showed that the provision of a meaningful rationale for an uninteresting activity (along with acknowledgment of feelings and minimizing control) promoted internalization and integration. Thus, to be effective, meaningful rationales should be presented in a noncontrolling way, while providing some form of choice and acknowledging the person's feelings (Deci et al., 1994).

SDT also stresses the role task and ego involvement. When individuals become ego involved in an activity and the outcome, they put pressure on themselves such that their feelings of self-worth hinge on performing well and proving themselves as individuals (Ryan, 1982). In contrast, when people are task involved the focus is on self-referenced gains, the putting forth of effort, and becoming more involved with the task. To this effect, previous research grounded in CET has shown that when participants feel pressured to perform well (ego involved) as opposed to being told just to try their best (task involved), their intrinsic motivation toward the task decreases (Reeve & Deci, 1996; Ryan, 1982; Ryan et al., 1991). Based on such evidence, exercise instructors can foster a more task-involved orientation in their clients by focusing on the mastering of the inherent qualities of tasks, helping individuals focus on self-referenced and progressive improvement, and supporting ongoing effortful but autonomous engagement with exercise endeavors. They can also be attuned to and intervene in the controlling self-talk (see Oliver et al., 2008) that so often accompanies ego involvement.

The way in which instructors phrase messages that convey a sense of choice, meaningful rationales, and acknowledgment of empathy to their clients can differ greatly. Specifically, the use of language rich in controlling content (e.g.,

"You must," "You have to," "You should") can readily undermine autonomy. Rather, vocalizations portraying choice and support (e.g., "You may want to," "You can try to") are more likely to support autonomy (cf. Deci et al., 1994; Ryan et al., 1983), along with a responsive attitude in which the exerciser's frame of reference with respect to tasks, challenges, and barriers is always being considered.

A randomized control trial examining the efficacy of an SDT-informed intervention for weight management provides support for a number of these intervention strategies (e.g., autonomous interpersonal language, choice and initiation, clear and meaningful rationales). Specifically, Silva et al. (2010) examined the efficacy of a 1-year intervention based on SDT (compared to a general health program) on female participants' physical activity, body weight and composition, and a number of theory-based psychosocial mediating variables. Results showed the intervention group to report higher levels of reported physical activity and weight loss when compared to the control (or standard care) group. Further, those in the intervention group reported higher levels of autonomous motivation (for treatment and for exercise), greater levels of locus of causality for exercise, high endorsement of intrinsic exercise motives (or goals), and exercise intrinsic motivation facets (i.e., as indexed by the IMI).

Supports for Competence

As we have previously mentioned, SDT is not exclusive in recognizing the importance of competence for motivated behavior. A basic tenet of both CET and OIT is that feelings of competence are essential for any intentional behavior, irrespective of whether the action is motivated by external, introjected, indentified, integrated, or intrinsic regulations. That is, without competence or a sense of effectance one would be amotivated. Moreover, as a basic need underpinning healthy development, well-being, and optimal functioning, supports for competence are essential for people in exercise settings. Research couched within SDT has provided support for a number of competence supports that can readily be applied to exercise, including provision for optimal challenge (e.g., Deci, 1975; Harter, 1974), ample administration of positive feedback (e.g., Ryan, 1982; Vallerand & Reid, 1984), and the fostering of task involvement in activities (e.g., Ryan, 1982; Ryan et al., 1991).

Essential within SDT to the growth of competence is the provision of structure (Grolnick & Seal, 2008; Markland, Ryan, Tobin, & Rollnick, 2005). Structure, which consists of the guidance and goal setting that provide scaffolding for developing competencies and discipline, aids motivation insofar as it is implemented in autonomy-supportive ways. Unfortunately, all too many practitioners confuse structure with control.

Based on past work (see Deci & Ryan, 1985a), exercise practitioners who work in collaboration with their clients should ensure that they engage in tasks and activities that are optimally challenging. Activities and tasks should be carefully defined and well suited to the individuals' competencies. That is, people will feel most competent when they can test and expand their capabilities (viz., they feel optimally challenged) and achieve success with concerted effort (i.e., tasks that are too easy would engender boredom, whereas tasks that are too difficult would be provoke anxiety; Deci & Ryan, 2002b). In working to achieve these objectives, the instructor should carefully assist in realistic goal setting and monitor the individual's progress to support the ongoing provision of challenging, yet attainable, tasks. Such an objective would be best achieved through providing support for structure so that the client understands the behavior–outcome contingencies, has clear expectations, and receives feedback.

As already noted, a tenet of CET is that to experience and maintain intrinsic motivation, people must satisfy their competence in the context of autonomy. Past work has shown that positive feedback (as opposed to negative feedback; Vallerand & Reid, 1984) supports perceptions of competence when provided in an autonomy-supportive way (viz., informational; Deci & Ryan, 1985a) but not when conveyed in a controlling manner (Ryan, 1982). As such, practitioners would do well to use positive, meaningful (e.g., task related and personally relevant) feedback to enhance perceptions of competence, autonomy, and subsequently autonomous engagement (e.g., "It is good that you managed to increase your minutes on the exercise bike. I particularly like the fact that you decided to do this"). Lastly, critical or negative feedback related to abilities should be avoided because such information is likely to diminish feelings of competence and discourage active or sustained involvement.

Supports for Relatedness

Although CET identified autonomy and competence to be the central nutriments to intrinsic motivation (with relatedness playing a more distal role), within SDT, relatedness provides a fundamental motivational basis for internalization (Deci & Ryan, 2000). Indeed, research with children in the education domain has supported the proposition that people are more likely to accept and internalize the values, norms, and guidelines espoused by socializing agents (viz., in this case parents) for whom they feel a sense of connection and belonging (Grolnick & Ryan, 1989; Roth, Assor, Niemiec, Ryan, & Deci, 2009). Moreover, in exercise settings feelings of relatedness have been shown to positively predict internalized forms of motivation, indices of well-being, and overall attitude and interest toward physical activity (including a marker of importance) (e.g., Vierling et al., 2007; Wilson, Longley, Muon, Rodgers, & Murray, 2006).

As key social agents introducing the values of exercise to clients, those working in exercise settings should seek to engage in close, caring, warm, and respectful interactions with their clients. To facilitate such secure attachments and perceptions of belonging, exercise professionals should express an authentic interest in the individual and interact with him or her in a caring and warm manner. Moreover, and as we noted in the section "Supports for Autonomy," practitioners who express empathy, avoid blaming or being judgmental, and acknowledge their clients' perspective, feelings, and values in their interactions are more likely to foster a sense of relatedness (LaGuardia & Patrick, 2008).

Because relatedness entails a sense of being significant and cared for by others, one element of exercise settings that can foster relatedness is involvement. Within SDT, involvement has been defined as the degree to which significant others devote time, energy, and interest to others (Grolnick & Ryan, 1989; Markland et al., 2005). When parents, coaches and trainers show interest and dedication, their involvement is more likely to facilitate relatedness and, in turn, the internalization of exercise-related values and behavioral regulations. As with structure, involvement must be characterized by autonomy support, rather than pressure and control, to promote integration and true self-regulation.

Yet another means of attempting to develop a sense of connection and belonging with others within the exercise domain may stem from supporting an "exercise buddy" scheme. Indeed, when and where possible, practitioners may support connections among members of exercise groups to assist them in finding an exercise buddy who has similar aims, objectives, and ability. Such an approach would provide cooperation and relational support. Further, we suspect that such an approach would also promote structure as individuals work together to develop and stick to mutually beneficial exercise-related schedules and goals.

Exercise Goal Inducements

Similar to the values interview (viz., an initial meeting in which a practitioner asks the clients about their life aspirations and goals) approach outlined by Fortier, Williams, Sweet, and Patrick (2009), a discussion with clients about their exercise goals may represent a point of intervention. For example, such an approach used at an initial meeting would entail the exercise practitioner discussing the content of the client's goals and asking the client to reflect on how best to achieve those aspirations. Using past research showing a positive relationship between intrinsic goals and an adaptive exercise experience (e.g., Sebire et al., 2009), practitioners may want to bring attention to goals such as physical health, social affiliation, and development of skills as opposed to extrinsic goals (e.g., social recognition or appearance augmentation). But in keeping with the dictum to provide empathy, if an exerciser has developed extrinsic goals those goals should not be judged negatively. Rather, the practitioner should acknowledge and support the client's perspective and values while normalizing extrinsic goal pursuit as entirely understandable and common to many individuals (Ingledew & Markland, 2008). Encouraging exercisers to reflect on whether they would be able to achieve their extrinsic goal strivings and whether such goals would realistically be associated with the expected positive benefits would be a meaningful discussion between practitioner and client.

Couched within GCT, a possible means for cost-effective intervention in the exercise domain pertains to the use of goal-framing inducements. Research has shown marked benefits for participants' effortful engagement and behavioral persistence when they receive a written description framing the benefits of a novel activity (viz., tai-bo) as being for intrinsic (fitness and health) goals as opposed to extrinsic (attractiveness) goals (e.g., Vansteenkiste, Simons, Soenens, et al., 2004). But a recent attempt to use this approach in a more ecologically valid manner (i.e., using traditional PE activities) with similar aged students failed to induce similar adaptive effects (Gillison, 2007). In part, such incongruity may be because the participants in Gillison's study held preexisting goals and motives toward the target activity. Thus, goal inducements employed in real-world settings may need to be adapted to hold more relevance and be of greater saliency (i.e., to overcome preexisting motives and goals). Goal-based interventions, that is, may need to be processed and assimilated to be effective. Given that theory and past research (see Vansteenkiste et al., 2007) have shown the effects of promoting intrinsic goals to be conducive to basic need satisfaction, further work addressing how best to translate goal-framing techniques to naturally occurring exercise contexts would seem to hold much practical import.

Unconscious Motivational Orientations

Drawing from COT, recent investigations have sought to prime automatic and unconscious motivational orientations (viz., autonomy, control, and interpersonal) to examine whether these implicit states affect behavior, performance, and well-being in a parallel fashion to SDT-based work using explicit measures such as the General Causality Orientations Scale (Deci & Ryan, 1985b). Results from several investigations (e.g., Hodgins, Yacko, & Gottlieb, 2006; Levesque & Pelletier, 2003) have provided support for theoretically aligned propositions in which those receiving a primed autonomy orientation have reported greater levels of enjoyment, perceived choice, free-choice behavior, and better performance than those activated with control and, to a greater extent, interpersonal orientations, who have reported more self-handicapping claims, enhanced self-serving bias, and worse performance. Although extremely interesting, in real-world exercise contexts perhaps the most feasible route for intervention is through goal-directed behavior that is automatically triggered by simply watching the behavior of others. To this end, two experiments conducted by Friedman, Deci, Elliot, Moller, and Aarts (2010) used live confederates to test whether simply observing others' motivational orientation (viz., implying intrinsic or extrinsic) can prime the motivational orientation of an observer. Results supported a motivational synchronicity hypothesis by showing that exposure to an intrinsically motivated target (as opposed to an extrinsically controlled target) led observers to engage in greater levels of free-choice behavior (study 1) and performance (study 2). Future research would do well to test whether such implicit inducements may be extended to ecological exercise settings, as well as by audiovisual materials (e.g., short clips showing examples of targets autonomously engaged in exercise activities).

Directions for Future Research

Future exercise-related research grounded in SDT may take many directions, far too many to be comprehensively captured within this section. A number of these directions we have alluded to during the course of this chapter, and herein we highlight just a few avenues of work that we consider important for future SDT work.

Researchers would do well to examine the dynamic interplay between key exercise-related SDT constructs (e.g., goal contents, need satisfaction, and behavioral regulations) at various levels (viz., person level and day level) alongside ongoing assessments of wellness and objectively assessed exercise behavior. Within SDT, individuals have multiple motives and goals that constitute the overall quality of motivation (i.e., the degree to which they satisfy the basic needs). Thus, similar to past research examining the relation between basic need satisfaction and indices of well-being using within- and between-person designs (e.g., Reis, Sheldon, Gable, Roscoe, & Ryan, 2000; Ryan et al., 2010), such work would be particularly insightful in providing an understanding of how fluctuations in motives and goals interact with need satisfaction to support temporal changes in the quality of the exercise experience, as well as effortful and health-enhancing engagement.

Another line of future investigation pertains to the role of SDT constructs in predicting and supporting positive indices of physical health and well-being. Preliminary work has shown relative intrinsic content for exercise and basic psychological needs toward health to be negatively associated with a marker of liver disease (i.e., alanine transaminase, or ALT) and higher concentrations of "bad cholesterol" (viz., low-density lipoprotein, or LDL) and positively related with lower levels of body fat (i.e., as assessed by dual-energy X-ray absorptiometry, or DXA) (Standage, 2009). The mechanisms underpinning these findings warrant further research investigation. Drawing from SDT, two mechanisms are likely to contribute to such relations. First, the biomedical outcomes are likely to be expressive of a relation between a satisfaction of basic needs, the holding of intrinsic goals, and a life well lived over numerous years (e.g., including regular exercise participation, healthy diet, and so on). Second, physical ill-being is also likely to result from negative psychological (e.g., anxiety, depression, distress, negative emotions, and so on) and physiological responses (e.g., cortisol and alpha-amylase levels, cardiovascular responses, and so on) that people experience because of daily pressures and strains that undermine basic needs and growth-oriented tendencies (see Ryan & Deci, 2000b, for a discussion of the darker and brighter sides of human existence). Exercise as a vehicle for need satisfaction to induce vitality, happiness, and energy to assist with coping with the demands of everyday life and ameliorating the symptoms of stress warrants further consideration. Recent research (e.g., Ryan, Weinstein, et al., 2010) also suggests that contact with nature is associated with increased vitality; thus, exploring whether exercising in natural environments (surrounded by trees, plants, water, and so forth) contributes to enhanced overall wellness is an intriguing line of work for future investigation.

Continuing with the theme of interaction with the physical environment, social ecological models have received increased attention (cf. Sallis, Owen, & Fisher, 2008). Such models are characterized by multiple levels of influence (e.g., policy factors, social norms, health status, and others), but particular import is given to the role that built and physical environments have on enhancing versus diminishing opportunities for exercise and physical activity. In contemporary societies, built environments (design of communities and living spaces) coupled with modern lifestyles often engineer out the opportunity for active and natural engagement in physical activities. For example, auto-dependent suburbs have led to reduced access for children to facilities and playgrounds (and thus less interaction with playmates), resulting in decreased opportunities for them to experience natural and spontaneous engagement in unstructured sport and play. Rather, such activities have been replaced by adult-organized sessions or events. Such reliance on structured planning for activities that were once enacted with friends in playing fields or streets would seem to diminish children's autonomous and active exploration of activities. But these issues are not confined to children. We are increasingly seeing physical activity across the lifespan being crowded out by issues such as computer-centric work environments, longer working hours, improved leisure-time technologies, and greater urbanization. A particular challenge, therefore, is to gain better understanding of how people can be motivated to engage and persist in activities when faced with such obstacles. As researchers continue to examine these complex issues, we believe that it is crucial that researchers, policy makers, and practitioners remember that within social ecological models it is still the *meaning* of built and physical environments that will serve to increase or diminish our effortful and sustained engagement. To this effect, the basic needs approach espoused within SDT would seem particularly useful because it provides a sound theoretical basis to understand the functional significance of how and why aspects of our physical environment and surroundings affect our health and well-being (i.e., those that are need satisfying as opposed to need thwarting).

Empirical work that tests and elaborates on the various phenomena embraced within SDT has expanded rapidly in recent years. In addition to being large in quantity, a striking richness to SDT contributions has appeared within physical activity settings. Indeed, basic and applied research studies in these settings have made marked contributions to our knowledge about motivational processes, mechanisms, and applications. That said, we concur with recent calls (e.g., Hagger & Chatzisarantis, 2008; Wilson et al., 2008) for SDT-related work in physical activity settings to consider a broader range of methodologies and move toward more carefully designed studies that also give greater consideration to sampling (i.e., going beyond convenience). Methodologies suitable for use in future SDT work include between-person (individual differences) and within-person (i.e., daily fluctuation) designs to examine temporal changes in SDT variables (i.e., through multilevel modeling), increased application of longitudinal designs to understand the processes underpinning exercise maintenance, augmented use of objective indicators (i.e., of behavior, wellness, health, and performance), additional qualitative work to elicit insight into the motivational experiences of exercisers, more experimental work (e.g., priming and mindfulness studies), and increased application of SDT as a basis for exercise intervention.

In considering the application of SDT, before proceeding to full randomized control trials (RCTs) researchers must focus systematically on key elements of intervention development. That is, to ensure the best translation of SDT principles to practice, close attention should be paid to the piloting and implementation (i.e., several studies may be required to refine the design and procedures before an RCT), appreciation should be paid to the fact that complex interventions may work best if they are tailored to local contexts, and process and outcome evaluations should be nested in the work to help identify why interventions were successful or failed (e.g., assessments of fidelity, quality of implementation, contextual variables related to outcomes, and so on) (see Craig et al., 2008). Lastly, the use of simultaneous mixed-method approaches would represent an insightful addition to intervention trials grounded in SDT. Such an approach would glean in-depth accounts of the differing motivational experiences of particular groupings (i.e., those for whom an intervention was effective, those who gained little, if any, change, and those for whom an intervention had inverse effects).

Summary

Physical activity is a part of our human nature, but for many in the world of new economics our activity is shifting from our bodies to our heads. With this shift comes an increasing need for planned insertion of activity into our lives in the form of regular exercise. Although exercise is instrumentally important to health it is not always fun or done willingly, and thus motivation becomes a key issue in the initiation and maintenance of physical activity. It is this issue to which SDT research has been widely applied.

SDT views motivation not as a unitary construct or single quantity but as a complex phenomena fed by multiple sources. Some sources are experienced as controlling and acting on the self, whereas others stem from within the self and represent volition and growth. SDT research shows multiple advantages of these later, more autonomous, motivations in advancing persistent and beneficial physical activity. SDT also distinguishes the goals of exercise, such as goals for health versus attractiveness, as bearing on exercise outcomes and well-being. Finally, SDT specifies practices in social contexts that facilitate versus undermine autonomous engagement, detailing how communications, feedback, rewards and structure, and relational supports contribute to or derail volition in this important life domain.

Despite rapid progress in this area of research, much remains to do. In particular, SDT researchers have already accomplished successful randomized clinical trials in health-related areas such as smoking, weight loss, and hygiene, and the time is ripe for similar projects in the exercise domain. Such trials depend on careful study and implementation of components and practices. The stakes are high because people are battling not only themselves but also social forces tilted away from meaningfully active lifestyles and the health and vitality that derive from them.

CHAPTER 8

Self-Efficacy and Motivation in Physical Activity and Sport: Mediating Processes and Outcomes

Todd A. Gilson, PhD
Northern Illinois University

Deborah L. Feltz, PhD
Michigan State University

When examining the choices that people make regarding exercise and sport activities, beliefs that they hold about their perceived capabilities to be successful at the endeavor can play an important motivational role. These beliefs, called self-efficacy beliefs, are dynamic in nature and can affect activity choice, effort, and persistence in the face of unplanned setbacks. Specifically, the cognitive calculations that individuals make regarding impending goal-striving decisions and behavior can determine the levels of stress and depression that they experience, as well as how adaptively they cope with the imminent demands of a task or environmental situation (Bandura, 1997). In exercise, for instance, these efficacy beliefs are relevant because participants often face challenges in beginning an exercise routine when they have previously lived a sedentary life. Later, they face the challenge of maintaining exercise adherence for the long term to experience health-related benefits. In either of these cases, self-efficacy has been shown to be especially salient (Ewart, Taylor, Reese, & DeBusk, 1983; McAuley, Lox, & Duncan, 1993), which is important because the attrition rate in exercise programs has been found to be approximately 50% within the first 6 months (Dishman, 1982). In the sporting world, building a strong sense of self-efficacy about what one can successfully execute has been shown to increase an individual's motivation and athletic skill set in a variety of sports, from tennis to power lifting (Feltz, Short, & Sullivan, 2008). Additionally, after the requisite skills have been learned in a specific sport, the person's level of perceived efficacy is one of the most important psychological factors that differentiates successful elite athletes from less successful ones (Burke & Jin, 1996) because unstable efficacy beliefs are likely to set up an individual for failure when faced with a pressure-filled situation (Bandura, 1997). Although the beliefs that individuals base their motivation on in exercise and sport are important, what is vital to understand is that people's perceived self-efficacy affects motivation based on what they believe to be true rather than what is objectively factual in their environment (Bandura, 1997).

But debate still occurs about the effectiveness of self-efficacy in mastering tasks. For example, starting in 2001, a series of studies by Vancouver and his colleagues suggested that a high sense of self-efficacy can actually impede a person's performance over a period of time, although, when compared with others, a stronger sense of self-efficacy elicited a better performance on a task (Vancouver & Kendall, 2006; Vancouver, Thompson, Tischner, & Putka, 2002; Vancouver, Thompson, & Williams, 2001). Although the work of Vancouver and his colleagues remains suspect (Bandura, 2009), the idea that high self-efficacy leads to low performance in athletes has received little empirical attention. In addition, the decision-making processes that athletes use during competition remains largely unstudied. Specifically, when faced with a problem, people rely on their first heuristic (or solution) 60 to 70% of the time (Hepler, 2008). Questions remain about why this figure is not 100%, when the first heuristic is often a correct decision in the realm of sport. Perhaps pressure that individuals feel, in conjunction with self-efficacy levels, affects the problem-solving strategies that people use (Beilock & DeCaro, 2007). These examples serve as a reminder that, although much is known about self-efficacy in the realms of exercise and sport, researchers and practitioners must continue to work so that they can better understand how people, according to Bandura (1977b), process, weigh, and integrate diverse sources of information concerning their capability and then regulate their choice of behavior and motivation accordingly.

This chapter is divided into five major sections. We begin by discussing the theoretical principles that form the framework of self-efficacy within social-cognitive theory and the manner in which self-efficacy is distinguished from other psychological constructs related to the self (Bandura, 1986, 1997). Additionally, in this section we highlight the sources of efficacy information that are salient to individuals, the varying cross-cultural perspectives of self-efficacy, and how efficacy beliefs can best be measured. Second, we focus on efficacy research at the individual level in both exercise and sport. Specifically, we discuss the mediating mechanisms that influence behavior. We then present relevant research for exercise and sport environments, illustrating the effects of efficacy beliefs on motivational outcomes (e.g., adherence and effort) and performance. The third section focuses on collective efficacy. In this segment, exercise group, sport team, and coach efficacy are discussed in relation to the traditional self-efficacy definition and research findings. The fourth section of this chapter discusses new lines of research within efficacy-belief theory. In particular, we explore the topics of efficacy beliefs related to decision making, within-team dispersion, and the divergent views of self-efficacy within social-cognitive theory and perceptual control theory (Powers, 1973, 1978, 1991). Finally, we conclude with a section related to the application of efficacy beliefs for exercise and sport professionals and summary remarks.

Theoretical Overview of Self-Efficacy

Self-efficacy is uniquely different from the use of abundant skills that a world-champion tennis player possesses or the global self-image that a person has toward his or her body after exercising for several months. In particular, Bandura defines a person's perceived self-efficacy as "beliefs in one's capabilities to organize and execute the courses of action required to produce given attainments" (Bandura, 1997, p. 3). Thus, self-efficacy is not concerned with the abilities that one has; rather it is the belief in executing the skills that one already possesses that makes up an individual's efficacy beliefs. In addition, self-efficacy is a situation-specific construct that fluctuates as the demands of a particular task change or as individuals cognitively interpret their ability to produce a desired behavior or achieve a specific level of proficiency. For example, as a person learns how to use a new piece of exercise equipment at a local health club, the person's efficacy for working out using that specific piece of equipment increases. Because efficacy beliefs are dynamic (especially during the early stages of learning a new task or skill), they are frequently being altered by one of four main sources of information: mastery experiences, vicarious experiences, verbal persuasion, and physiological and affective states (Bandura, 1997).

Sources of Self-Efficacy

A first-person mastery experience is the most influential source of efficacy information because it provides an "authentic experience," revealing whether the skills or behaviors that the person possesses or displays will result in success (Bandura, 1997). As we would expect, past successes generally increase an individual's self-efficacy regardless of the domain in which the person is acting (e.g., Kane, Marks, Zaccaro, & Blair, 1996; McAuley, 1985; Watkins, Garcia, & Turek, 1994). But as Bandura (1997) notes, past performance successes are not the direct cause of increased self-efficacy. Instead, the changes in a person's self-efficacy result from the cognitive processing of a performance, which then conveys information about the capability that the person possesses. Additionally, this type of efficacy information is most significant during early trials, when future performances remain in doubt (Feltz, 1982, 1988). Thus, although failure generally undermines self-efficacy, a highly resilient source of self-efficacy requires perseverance in overcoming obstacles using persistence and effort (Bandura, 1997).

A vicarious experience, or comparing the capabilities that one has with another, is the second source of self-efficacy that is salient because in many activities an absolute measure of excellence may not be available (Bandura, 1997). For example, Weinberg, Gould, and Jackson (1979) found that efficacy expectations were altered for participants based on their perceptions of another's physical status. Specifically, participants who were told that their competitor in a muscular leg endurance task was recovering from an injury had higher self-efficacy beliefs and subsequent performances when compared to participants who believed that their competitor was a varsity track athlete. Although this source of efficacy is generally not as potent as mastery experiences, it benefits individuals by providing a model on how best to accomplish a skill or task and can strengthen the capability of one's beliefs, especially when the model being observed is assumed to be similar to oneself (Bandura, 1997).

Furthermore, Bandura (1997) includes cognitive self-modeling (or cognitive enactment) as a form of modeling influence. For instance, imagining oneself or others behaving successfully or unsuccessfully in upcoming performance situations can be a source of positive efficacy information. Feltz and Riessinger (1990) showed that imagining oneself winning against an opponent could raise efficacy judgments and endurance performance.

A third way to increase a person's self-efficacy is through direct statements (including self-statements) or social persuasion from significant others. As Bandura (1997) states, "It is easier to sustain a sense of efficacy, especially when struggling with difficulties, if significant others express faith in one's capabilities than if they convey doubts" (p. 101). But this source of self-efficacy has many caveats that need to be considered. For example, a personal trainer attempting to persuade an exerciser by telling her that she can succeed with just more effort may actually undermine self-efficacy in the long run. This occurs because being repeatedly told that the cause of failure was the lack of effort could result in her questioning her talents when she provides great effort and still fails (Bandura, 1997). In addition, the perceptions of credibility, expertise, and trustworthiness can affect the ability of social persuaders because people are more apt to trust those who are also skilled in the activity (Bandura, 1997; Feltz & Lirgg, 2001). Finally, the debilitating effects of verbal persuasion are stronger than the enhancing effects; therefore, a coach, for instance, must be cautious when attempting to motivate his or her players with the use of negative statements relating to ability.

Perhaps the most diverse source of efficacy, physiological and affective states, makes up the last component. Specifically, Bandura (1997) argues that these somatic indicators are especially relevant in the domains of physical accomplishments and health functioning, such as exercise and sport. Again, the important factor for this source of self-efficacy is not the fact that a person's hands become sweaty before the big game or that a person experiences a gut-wrenching feeling before his or her first 5K road race; instead, the important point is how these reactions are perceived and then interpreted. As Bandura (1997) notes, high achievers perceive these somatic responses as energizing factors, whereas low achievers view them as hindrances for their upcoming performance. Furthermore, an individual's mood state can have an effect on perceived self-efficacy because people are more apt to make positive evaluations about why things occurred when they are in a good mood and negative evaluations when they are in a bad mood. Finally, physiological and affective states can also encompass individuals' perceptions about their fitness, fatigue, or injury (Feltz, 1988).

Social-Cognitive Theory

People's efficacy beliefs do not operate devoid of a higher order set of theorized rules. To the contrary, self-efficacy beliefs are believed to have a positive or negative influence on motivation, affect, and behavior through social-cognitive theory (Bandura, 1986). On the "theoretical scale," social-cognitive theory is unique because it claims that behavior is neither driven by strictly internal forces nor controlled by external stimuli. In other words, people do not come programmed with an inherent trait or desire to execute a behavior based on experiences. Instead, social-cognitive theory proposes a triadic reciprocal causation. In this relationship, cognition, behavior, and the external environment all act and are acted upon by each other, although not always equally (Bandura, 1986). Further, individuals are viewed as proactive agents in this relationship in which they regulate their cognition, behavior, and environment rather than passively react.

Let's examine these theoretical principles in a real-life sporting scenario. A hockey goalie is charged with being the last line of defense for a team to prevent opposing players from scoring a goal. According to social-cognitive theory, this goalie's behavior in preventing a goal on a breakaway late in the game may be influenced by personal cognitions such as his or her cognitive worry about giving up a goal that may cost the team the game, efficacy belief about being capable of preventing the goal, and environmental factors such as the skill level of the opponent who is skating in to take the shot. The goalie who is unsuccessful over time may even change the environment (e.g., switch to club hockey) to feel less pressure and achieve more success.

Within social-cognitive theory, self-efficacy is concerned primarily with the cognitive aspect of triadic reciprocal process (Maddux, 1995). As such, self-efficacy beliefs influence behavior, affect, and selection of environments and are influenced by behavior, affect, and environmental events. Thus, according to Bandura (1997), self-efficacy beliefs represent the core agentic factor that determines people's goal-directed behavior.

Self-Efficacy-Related Constructs

Many concepts have caused confusion with respect to self-efficacy. For example, a person's self-esteem and self-efficacy have been used interchangeably, although they represent different constructs. Specifically, an individual's self-esteem is related to judgments about self-worth, whereas self-efficacy is concerned with judgments about personal capability (Bandura, 1997). Although self-esteem is considered a vital part of psychological health and well-being (Rosenberg, 1979), this concept is relatively stable and does not match the capacity of self-efficacy to fluctuate as perceptions of ability change over time. Additionally, as Bandura (1997) argued, a person's self-liking does not always correlate with performance attainment. For example, an individual may perceive his or her self-efficacy in a skill or task to be quite high yet take little or no pride when engaging in the specified skill or task.

Outcome expectancy is another concept that is sometimes confused with self-efficacy. This line of thinking argues that behaviors are influenced by expectancies and then actual outcomes are brought to fruition by either one's actions or forces outside one's control (i.e., generally viewed as chance factors). According to Feltz, Short, and Sullivan (2008), in exercise and sport settings, outcome expectancies have often been confused with a person's final position or winning a competition. These "outcomes" are, in fact, performance markers that individuals use to evaluate the consequence of their performance, whereas true outcome expectancies may be the self-satisfaction of exercising or gaining approval from a coach about a recent performance (Bandura, 1997). Thus, outcome expectancies rely largely on self-efficacy beliefs, which have been shown to be a good predictor of diverse forms of behavior, whereas an individual's beliefs about whether actions affect outcomes has been generally shown as a weak or inconsistent predictor (Bandura, 1997). But both Bandura (1997) and Maddux agree that outcome expectancies can influence behavior; nevertheless, explaining human actions and affective states may be best accomplished by a combination of efficacy beliefs and types of performance outcomes in social situations.

Finally, Vealey (1986) conceptualized the notion of sport confidence, which is the degree of certainty that people possess about their ability to achieve success in sport. Although sport confidence does have commonalities with self-efficacy (Feltz & Chase, 1998), one of the biggest differences is that the former is more broadly defined to encompass a confidence that varies on a continuum of state and trait, whereas the scope of self-efficacy is narrower and more state specific (Feltz, Short, & Sullivan, 2008). In particular, the revision of sport confidence by Vealey and colleagues lists antecedents of confidence that include the organizational culture of the program (e.g., type of sport, competitive level, and motivational climate), as well as characteristics of the athlete (e.g., age, gender, and personality) (Vealey, Hayashi, Garner-Holman, & Giacobbi, 1998). When comparing, in a meta-analytic review, the predictive power related to performance, the state version of sport confidence (which would align with the statelike nature of self-efficacy) was found to be a subpar measurement instrument when compared to task-specific efficacy scales (Moritz, Feltz, Fahrback, & Mack, 2000).

Cross-Cultural Perspective of Self-Efficacy

Recently, the question has arisen as to how self-efficacy manifests itself in cultures that are more collectivist (e.g., Asian, South American, and Eastern European) when compared to Western nations (e.g., United States, Western Europe, Australia) that emphasize individualism. Bandura (1997, 2002) contends that self-efficacy plays a vital role regardless of individualistic or collective cultural characteristics because people in any society do not live their lives completely separately or codependently, and furthermore, codependence does not eliminate the importance of the personal self. But in a meta-analytic review comparing achievement of students from these different cultures, self-efficacy beliefs were typically stronger for individuals from Western, individualistic cultures than they were for individuals from Asian, collectivist societies (see Klassen, 2004, for a complete review). Thus, the work of Klassen definitively supports the notion that self-efficacy beliefs operate differently in Western and non-Western cultures. Nevertheless, the evidence also supports the premise that efficacy beliefs play an important role in motivation and prediction of performance regardless of culture because, although efficacy beliefs are typically lower in collectivist societies, these perceived beliefs are "equally or even more predictive of performance, and . . . calibration of their efficacy beliefs and subsequent functioning may be more accurate than among individualists" (Klassen, 2004, p. 225).

Measuring Efficacy Beliefs

Because efficacy beliefs are not a global, static construct, they should be measured under different levels of task demands and situational circumstances (Bandura, 1997). The specific guidelines and protocols for measuring efficacy beliefs have been thoroughly discussed in many other works to date; thus, we will provide only an overview of key points when gathering efficacy information from individuals, teams, and coaches. For a complete review of this topic we recommend that readers examine the works of Bandura (2006), Feltz, Short, and Sullivan (2008), or Dithurbide and Feltz (in press).

The first important point related to efficacy measurement is that efficacy beliefs vary on three main dimensions: generality, level, and strength (Bandura, 1997). Generality is concerned with the number of domains in which individuals judge themselves to be confident. For example, one might feel highly efficacious across various tasks that have similar subskills or across sports that share general categories of actions (e.g., strategy, goal setting, or teamwork). An efficacy level (or magnitude) refers to perceived capability measured against varying degrees of challenge or task demands. For example, an athlete who runs 5K races could have her self-efficacy level measured by assessing her perceptions about how fast she thinks she can run the race in a sequence of decreasing times. Finally, perceived efficacy can also be measured by strength. In this method, individuals' certainties of their beliefs are the focus by presenting a series of different-level task demands and then rating their beliefs in their ability against said demands. Using the same runner as an example in this dimension, she would answer a series of questions on a scale (most commonly from 0 to 10), and each question would again ask her perception about completing the upcoming 5K race in progressively faster times.

When measuring efficacy beliefs at the individual level, researchers should first determine the dimensions of efficacy to be included in the questionnaire. Although incorporating both efficacy level and strength in one questionnaire may be viewed as attractive, because individuals would first rate whether they believe that they can accomplish the task at hand and then rate their efficacy for each task demand, a single judgment measure (using the person's efficacy strength) provides essentially the same information (Bandura, 1997). Because of this fact, Maddux (1995) notes that most studies incorporating measures of self-efficacy choose a format that most resembles the strength dimension. Questionnaire items should also be phrased in terms of "can do" statements for respondents, and instructions should be clear so that people rate their capabilities in the present and not at some future time (Bandura, 1997, 2006). After the questionnaires are completed, they should be reviewed using the chosen conceptual analysis, expert guidance, and pilot testing to ensure that the measure and the skills or behaviors being tested are concordant. Easily attainable questionnaire items within the test population should be discarded for data collection so that differences among respondents can be detected (Bandura, 2006; Feltz, Chow, and Hepler, 2008; Moritz et al., 2000). Finally, researchers should attempt to deliver the developed questionnaire to participants within 24 hours of a performance test or behavior measurement to limit the number of yet unknown factors that may alter the respondent's observed self-efficacy, performance, or behavior (Feltz & Lirgg, 2001).

A group or team's collective efficacy also has methodological considerations that need to be implemented to measure it effectively. Primarily, how collective efficacy is defined serves as the basis for how the measures are constructed. Briefly, Bandura (1997) defined collective efficacy as "a group's shared belief in its conjoint capabilities to organize and execute the courses of action required to produce given levels of attainment" (p. 477). Alternatively, Zaccaro, Blair, Peterson, and Zazanis (1995) defined collective efficacy as "a sense of collective competence shared among individuals when allocating, coordinating, and integrating their resources in a successful concerted response to specific situational demands" (p. 309). As Chow and Feltz (2008) noted, the detailed description of the interacting components required among members of a team signifies the subtle difference between the Zaccaro et al. and Bandura definitions. These different definitions have led to different assessment methods. For example, some questionnaire stems read, "Rate your confidence in your team's ability to . . ." based on the Bandura definition, whereas others ask participants to rate "Our team's confidence in . . ." based on the Zaccaro et al. definition. Maddux (1995) has contended that the latter assessment method is superior because it allows individuals to act as informants related to the collective efficacy of the group by cognitively considering what the team believes in terms of its interacting tasks. Both approaches to measuring collective efficacy rely on individual-level beliefs that are then aggregated to a group level, but Myers and Feltz (2007) recommend using Bandura's approach, "Rate your confidence in your team's ability to . . . ," because they argue that people have better access to their own beliefs about a group's capabilities than they do to a group's beliefs about its capabilities. This approach conforms to how Bandura's original conceptualization of collective efficacy was constructed. (see Myers & Feltz, 2007, for a complete review).

In addition, Bandura (1997) has described another method of assessing collective efficacy based on aggregating team members' individual perceptions of their own capabilities to perform within the team. The phrasing of the stem of items in this method would be, "Rate your confidence that *you* can. . . ." Bandura hypothesized that aggregated perceptions of individual efficacy beliefs of performance may be sufficient to predict team performance in tasks that are additive in nature (e.g., bowling, golf, swimming), but aggregated perceptions of beliefs in the team would be more predictive of team performance when the tasks are more interdependent.

Finally, in addition to measuring individuals and teams in athletic functioning, efficacy beliefs of coaches also have been assessed. Pioneered by Feltz, Chase, Moritz, & Sullivan (1999), coaching efficacy is defined as the extent to which coaches believe that they have the capacity to affect the learning and performance of their athletes. Composing this efficacy measure are four dimensions: (*a*) the confidence that coaches have in their ability to affect psychological mood and skill, (*b*) the confidence that coaches have in their ability to influence personal development and attitude, (*c*) the confidence that coaches have in their ability to lead during competition, and (*d*) the confidence that coaches have in their instructional and diagnostic skills. Feltz et al. (1999) developed the Coaching Efficacy Scale (CES), which asks coaches to answer questions with the stem, "How confident are you in your ability to . . ." on a scale from 0 being not at all confident to 9 being extremely confident. Confirmatory factor analyses have shown that the CES either approached or met acceptable levels of fit with youth sport, high school, and college coaches (Feltz et al., 1999; Feltz, Hepler, Roman, & Paiement, 2009; Sullivan & Kent, 2003) and that measures produced by the CES have consistently related to theoretically relevant external variables (Myers, Wolfe, & Feltz, 2005). More recently, Myers, Feltz, Chase, Reckase, and Hancock (2008) developed the Coaching Efficacy Scale II–High School Teams (CES II–HST) and added a fifth dimension of training and conditioning to improve the precision of the measure and narrow its scope to high school coaches. The CES II has also shown acceptable fit levels. These two measures are to date the only published instruments designed to measure coaching efficacy.

Individual-Level Self-Efficacy Research

Without question, the level in which most self-efficacy research has taken place for over 30 years has been with individuals. In both exercise and sport, individuals have been studied with a variety of methods to gain better understanding of the link between this construct and behavior. In the next section we review the findings in both environments, discuss the mediating mechanisms that affect self-efficacy, and show results related to dependent variables of interest.

Exercise

It has long been documented that self-efficacy is related to the adoption and adherence of exercise by individuals. Perhaps most well known are a series of large community studies by Sallis and colleagues in which self-efficacy was shown to predict adoption of vigorous physical activity, maintenance of moderate physical activity, and exercise behavior over time (Sallis et al., 1986; Sallis et al., 1989). Sallis, Hovell, Hofstetter, and Barrington (1992) repeated much of their work but included factors that were perceived to change over time (i.e., social, cognitive, and environmental variables). Results again showed that changes in self-efficacy were the best predictors of corresponding changes in exercise behavior.

Research by McAuley and associates has focused on how self-efficacy may play different roles during exercise progression by individuals (Hu, Motl,

McAuley, & Konopack, 2007; Katula & McAuley, 2001; McAuley, 1992, 1993; McAuley et al., 1993; McAuley & Courneya, 1992, 1994; McAuley, Blissmer, Katula, & Duncan, 2000; McAuley, Courneya, Rudolph, & Cox, 1994; Poag & McAuley, 1992; Rodgers, Hall, Blanchard, McAuley, & Munroe, 2002; Rogers, McAuley, Courneya, Humphries, & Gutin, 2007). For instance, self-efficacy has been found to be predictive of exercise frequency and intensity for older adults when measured during the halfway point of a 5-month exercise program (McAuley, 1992). Furthermore, when examining the exercise habits of individuals after program cessation, self-efficacy was the only significant individual predictor of exercise behavior, accounting for 12.5% of the unique variance related to the continuation of exercise and an additional 14% of the variance with $\dot{V}O_2$max and behavioral parameters included (McAuley, 1993). In an attempt to understand causation with these previous results, McAuley et al. (1994) used a randomized trials design. Results again showed that the intervention group (who received such efficacy-boosting treatments as videotapes of people becoming healthy through exercise, monitored progress with physiological adaption perceptions, and participation in exercise using a buddy system) adhered to exercise at a significantly higher level over the 5-month period.

Recent work in the area of self-efficacy and exercise has incorporated participant self-evaluation and the unique differences associated with exercise as variables of interest. Jerome et al. (2002) examined women assigned to either a low- or high-efficacy condition and found that participants in the high-efficacy condition had more energy, reported a more positive well-being, and perceived less psychological distress. Furthermore, research has shown that improving self-efficacy and the affective states can also be accomplished by having people exercise in social (or group) environments (McAuley et al., 2000). Note, however, that research has also demonstrated that in some conditions exercise had no effect on subsequent enjoyment levels. In particular, participants who exercised at moderate intensity, regardless of how self-efficacy was manipulated, did not differ in enjoyment levels. On the other hand, when individuals performed maximum exercise tests, higher self-efficacy significantly influenced enjoyment; thus, the intensity of exercise should also be a consideration for exercise practitioners (Hu et al., 2007). Finally, in perhaps one of the most interesting studies, Katula and McAuley (2001) demonstrated that a person's exercise self-efficacy could be enhanced by exercising in front of a mirror. Specifically, Katula and McAuley had participants exercise both in front of and in the absence of full-length mirrors. Results indicated that self-efficacy, assessed postexercise, increased when participants performed aerobic exercises in front of a mirror, showing that self-evaluation following mirrored exercise increased both perceptions and capabilities.

Research examining self-efficacy and exercise has also been studied from a transtheoretical viewpoint (Prochaska & DiClimente, 1983), which postulates that people progress through stages of change in a cyclic fashion and can both advance and retract through stages. Specifically, individuals can advance through five stages of change; the first two (precontemplation and contemplation) focus on intentions that the person has to exhibit for a measured behavior, the third (preparation) represents a stronger intention to display the behavior in question, and the final two stages (action and maintenance) are concerned with the lengths of time that the individual has been able to achieve consistent behavior results. Research findings from multiple studies have shown that as people progress through the stages of change, self-efficacy typically shows a corresponding increase (Cardinal, 1997; Gorley & Gordon, 1995; Marcus & Owen, 1992). Practitioners should understand, however, that simple increases in self-efficacy may not be the uniform answer because each stage has specific intervention strategies and when intervention strategy and actual stage of change are not aligned attrition is greatest (see Berger, Pargman, & Weinberg, 2007, for a more complete discussion). Although Bandura (1997) has questioned the legitimacy of the transtheoretical model as a true stage theory, this research is important because it incorporates a model that examines physical activity behavior over time.

Self-efficacy is not limited to having a positive effect on exercise; research has shown that acute, as well as chronic exercise, can act as a source for feelings of efficacy. As we might expect, exposure to an exercise session can serve as a mastery experience and improve quality of life (McAuley, 1991; Motl, McAuley, Snook, & Gliottoni, 2009), both of which can help alter cognitions for future experiences (Bandura, 1997). Furthermore, exercise allows efficacy perceptions to rebound after a program has ended. Specifically, McAuley et al. (1993) found that after 9 months, efficacy perceptions of participants that had fallen off were brought up to the same statistical level as those of participants who had just completed an exercise program by the first group's participation in an acute session of cycle ergometry and assessment of abdominal strength. Chronic exercise has been shown to have similar effects. For instance, when older individuals suffering from chronic obstructive pulmonary disease engaged in a treadmill endurance program, self-efficacy levels were higher than those in a control group at a 6-month follow-up (Toshima, Kaplan, & Ries, 1990). Later work reexamined this same data set and found that perceived efficacy was a significant predictor of survival (Kaplan, Ries, Prewitt, & Eakin, 1994), further validating the importance of self-efficacy not only to psychological function but also to physical health and survival.

As mentioned earlier, however, self-efficacy operates within the confines of social-cognitive theory, which postulates that a triad of behavior, personal factors, and the external environment constantly influence each other with respect to confidence. Thus, efficacy beliefs need to be discussed in relation to the processes in which their effects are produced. Although Bandura (1997) argued that self-efficacy beliefs operate mainly through four major processes (i.e., cognitive processes, motivational processes, affective processes, and selection processes), for the purposes of this chapter we will specifically focus on some of the motivational variables important in the realm of exercise.

Goal setting is an important mediating variable for self-efficacy because efficacy beliefs will partially affect what challenges people undertake (i.e., what goals they set), how much effort they will put forth in achieving those goals, and how long they will persevere when difficulties arise (Bandura, 1986). In addition, after accomplishing a difficult task, those who maintain their high level of self-efficacy are more likely to set further challenging goals, whereas those who accomplish the task at hand yet doubt their ability in the future will suffer a decline in motivation (Bandura, 1997). In the exercise and physical rehabilitation realm, research has documented these effects. For instance, Theodorakis, Malliou, Papaioannou, Beneca, and Filactakidou (1996) used both injured and noninjured women (along with a control group) on a knee extension task. Results showed that when experimental groups set personal goals, performance improvement resulted. Furthermore, the relationship between self-efficacy, self-satisfaction, goal setting, and performance was statistically significant. This relationship was also documented over a 5-week goal intervention study in which a goal-setting group showed significantly better adherence to a rehabilitation program and reported the highest level of self-efficacy compared to a social support control and general control group (Evans & Hardy, 2002). Bandura (1997) phrased it best when he stated, "Motivation is perhaps best maintained by a strong sense of efficacy to withstand failure, coupled with some uncertainty that is ascribed to the challenge of the task rather than fundamental doubts in one's abilities" (p. 130). Thus, goal setting for challenging tasks will enhance efficacy and produce corresponding changes in motivation because, when individuals set a goal, they then act for the sake of realizing it.

Another mediating variable related to self-efficacy is perception of effort. Previous research has shown that people who believed that they expended more effort also had increased negative affect responses in exercise (Hardy & Rejeski, 1989) and that greater exercise-related efficacy is linked with lower perceptions of effort and fatigue (Rudolph & McAuley, 1996). Recently, Hutchinson, Sherman, Martinovic, and Tenenbaum (2008) conducted a repeated measures experimental design focused on determining the function of self-efficacy in perceived and sustained effort. Results confirmed earlier notions by showing that the high-efficacy group found the exercise task of an isometric handgrip exercise to be more enjoyable and displayed greater tolerance when compared to the low-efficacy or control group. Important to note is that effort attributions and efficacy beliefs do not share a uniform relationship. Specifically, individuals who belief that ability is acquired by hard work will exhibit a positive relationship between effort and self-efficacy, whereas those who regard ability as a stable attribute that cannot be changed will show evidence of the opposite (Bandura, 1997). This relationship was found in a physical activity setting. Chase (2001) discovered that high self-efficacy children held the belief that failure resulted from a lack of effort, not ability, and chose to participate more in the future.

Sport

In sport, in which the goal is a combination of learning, improving, and winning, self-efficacy is vital because athletes must manage ever-changing situations that are usually unpredictable and stressful. Although ability may be paramount to competent functioning in this environment, self-doubt can seriously impair motivation and performance. Thus, self-efficacy and sport have a permanent marriage because "where everyone is highly skilled, small variations in adeptness of execution can spell the difference between triumph and defeat" (Bandura, 1990, p. 152).

Early work related to sport functioning was heavily researched by Feltz and her associates and by Weinberg and his colleagues. Feltz's work tended to focus on the causal relationship between self-efficacy and performance in tasks that required participants to partake in some level of risk taking to be successful, and Weinberg and colleagues' approach to studying self-efficacy in sport was to use experimental designs in competitive sport situations. Results from Feltz's work demonstrated that self-efficacy was enhanced by participant modeling; furthermore, self-efficacy was more important than arousal, state anxiety, and past performance for diving and gymnastics (Feltz, 1982; Feltz, Landers, & Raeder, 1979; Feltz & Mugno, 1983; McAuley, 1985). Weinberg and colleagues' findings, in studies from 1979 through 1985, showed that self-efficacy levels were related to performance on muscular endurance tasks. In separate studies, individuals "competed" against a hypothetical track athlete, competed against another individual, and measured self-efficacy's relationship with an objective failure (Weinberg, 1985; Weinberg et al., 1979; Weinberg, Gould, Yukelson, & Jackson, 1981; Weinberg, Yukelson, & Jackson, 1980). In all the works by Feltz and Weinberg, results showed that higher levels of self-efficacy led to more adaptive behaviors and performances. Researchers examining self-efficacy within the sport domain have predominately focused on the dependent variable of performance, although they have defined performance in a multitude of ways. Although this relationship is not the focus of this chapter, the enormity of this line of research deserves a brief discussion. Past notable works include Kane et al. (1996), in which results revealed that self-efficacy was the sole determinant of success during overtime for wrestlers who were evenly matched. In addition, in the sports of baseball, strength training, crew, and diving, higher self-efficacy predicted greater individual performances by athletes (Feltz, 1982; Feltz, Chow, & Hepler, 2008; George, 1994; Magyar, Feltz, & Simpson, 2004; Wells, Collins, & Hale, 1993). Thus, taken together, research from experimental to path analytic designs has shown self-efficacy to be consistently and positively related to athletic performance (Moritz et al., 2000). In recent years, self-efficacy research has branched into exciting new avenues. One of the most notable is the effect of hypnosis on self-efficacy and performance. The impetus beyond this line of research started with Barker and Jones (2008) and a football player suffering from low self-efficacy and negative mood states. As a result of hypnosis sessions, the athlete reported increases in self-efficacy, mood state, and performance. Barker, Jones, and Greenlees (2010) then conducted a laboratory experiment in which football players were randomly assigned to hypnosis or control groups. Results again confirmed that players who underwent hypnosis benefited from increased self-efficacy and performance in a wall volley task; in addition, the same results were found after a follow-up period of 4 weeks had elapsed.

Self-efficacy has also been shown to be related to more traditional concepts. For instance, self-talk and verbal persuasion from coaches can increase self-efficacy levels of athletes playing football and tennis (Hatzigeorgiadis, Zourbanos, Goltsios, & Theordorakis, 2008; Vargas-Tonsing, 2009). As already mentioned, these increases should allow athletes to perform better in their chosen discipline (Bandura, 1997). But in sport the path that a person takes to the goal is not always progressive and smooth, because one person or team must be unsuccessful. Self-efficacy can also have a positive effect in these situations. Specifically, the ability of participants to cope with extraordinary demands in sport can help stave off both somatic and cognitive anxiety (Nicholls, Polman, & Levy, 2010). Finally, when failure in sport does occur, Brown and Malouff (2005) demonstrated that having participants reflect back on their performances, while incorporating the tenants of self-efficacy, resulted in greater positive affect when compared to a control group. Thus, continuing to value self-efficacy, even when performances or conditions are not ideal, can be a useful strategy to develop desirable attributions for the future (Allen, Jones, & Sheffield, 2010).

As with exercise, in the sporting environment mediating mechanisms affect how self-efficacy outcomes are realized. Although many of these variables are the same as in exercise, their application to this specific realm sets them apart. For example, goal setting is highly applicable to motivation in the sporting world because personal goals rather than the standards set by others regulate behavior (Bandura, 1997). Research examining this mediating variable has shown that goals are partially set based on the perceived efficacy beliefs that people hold (Bueno, Weinberg, Fernandez-Castro, & Capdevila, 2008; Kane et al., 1996; Lerner & Locke, 1995). For example, keeping all other variables equal, a track and field 200-meter sprinter who has a stronger sense of self-efficacy than her competitors will set more challenging goals for herself, because of her beliefs.

Bandura (1997) asserted that the importance of goals is relevant not only for athletes with high self-efficacy who experience success (a topic that has been predominately researched in the past) but also for individuals during times of difficulty. As we would expect, it is challenging for athletes to remain motivated when they encounter failures, setbacks, and long stretches of minimal improvement. During these grueling times, the efficacy beliefs that athletes hold can sustain the motivating power of goals, an assertion supported by findings with competitive chess athletes (Okurame, 2006). Thus, when the same 200-meter sprinter competes and loses in her first national-level meet, her strong sense of personal efficacy can continue to motivate her toward achieving her previously set goals.

The role of self-efficacy in athletic functioning is also mediated by the variables of activity choice and effort displayed at any given point in time and through overall persistence. For each of these variables, the relationship with self-efficacy is hypothesized to be positive and research has confirmed these notions. For instance, both Escarti and Guzman (1999) and Chase (2001) found that individuals who held higher self-efficacy beliefs would choose to attempt more difficult skills when presented with increasing levels of a task. In relation to effort, Weinberg and colleagues' work during the early to mid-1980s highlighted how efficacy beliefs affect individuals' performance on endurance tasks (i.e., overall persistence), but this same relationship has also been found for activities that take place in a matter of seconds. Specifically, in the sport of baseball, perceptions of higher self-efficacy have been related to increased effort using path analysis techniques (George, 1994). These studies confirm the hypotheses of Bandura (1986) in that people will avoid situations that they do not believe they can cope with and, for activities that people engage in, high self-efficacy will result in vigorous and persistent effort.

Collective Efficacy Research

In addition to beliefs that people hold about their own abilities, efficacy perceptions can be measured at an aggregated or collective level for a group or team. This collective efficacy is the group's shared belief in its capabilities to organize, execute, and achieve levels of proficiency (Bandura, 1997). The consequences of collective efficacy are similar to those of self-efficacy, but they extend to the group level, affecting the amount of effort that teams will exert, the degree to which teams will remain task oriented when members are not performing well, and the resiliency of teams following a difficult defeat. As discussed in the measurement section of this chapter, in highly interactive sports (e.g., basketball, hockey, volleyball), collective efficacy is best represented by the sum of individual team members' perceived efficacy beliefs in their team's capabilities. Consider the case of two outside midfielders on a football (soccer) team who believe that their own abilities are lacking in comparison to their teammates and other outside midfielders in the same league. Although these two athletes' perceived individual-level efficacy will be lower than that of many other athletes, their collective efficacy regarding what their team can accomplish may be extremely high because the strategy for this team is to play the ball directly up through the middle of the field whenever possible and not put the outside midfielders in one-on-one situations with the players whom they are matched against. Thus, if all or most members agree with this perception, the collective efficacy of this team (which has strong players up the middle of the field) should allow them to achieve at a higher level (Bandura, 1997). Collective efficacy can also be influenced by significant others (specifically, the coach or coaches) and through similar sources of self-efficacy applied to teams (e.g., past performance, vicarious experience, and perceived physical condition).

Although researchers have sometimes defined collective efficacy using slight alterations in the definition originally developed by Bandura or by employing the term *group potency* (see Shea & Guzzo, 1987), what is important is that all definitions related to this construct incorporate judgments by group members about the overall ability of the collective group to act effectively (Zaccaro et al., 1995). In the following section, we highlight how collectively efficacy is evident in exercise and sport.

Exercise

In the realm of exercise, increases in collective efficacy have resulted in corresponding increases in goals and performance. For example, Greenlees, Graydon, and Maynard (2000) found that finishing time and group position goals for teams on a cycle ergometer task were maintained by high collective efficacy groups over trials, whereas groups whose collective efficacy was manipulated downward suffered a decline in the variables measured.

In motivating people to exercise, however, the central problem often lies with the initiation or infrequency of exercise, not the performance after exercise is undertaken. There is a paucity of research on the influence of collective efficacy on the initiation and frequency of exercise. In one study that explored collective efficacy for couples in which one of the partners suffered from type 2 diabetes, Beverly and Wray (2008) found that the collective efficacy of couples encompassed collective support related to exercise, collective motivation to engage in exercise, and collective responsibility toward exercise. In particular, couples who believed that they were "in this together" and had a high level of spousal support were more likely to adopt and maintain an exercise program than those individuals or couples who displayed low levels of collective efficacy related to exercise. Thus, the perceived collective efficacy for couples to work together to maintain their adherence to an exercise program may help with individuals who have weak motivation to engage in physical activity. Although little research has been conducted on collective efficacy in exercise groups, future research might explore collective efficacy and the variance in personal and group exercise goals, along with how exercise groups attribute success or failure. As Biddle and Mutrie (2001) explain, these avenues for future research have great potential but to date have not been explored.

Collective efficacy has also been examined using a community, social coherence approach. Specifically, Sampson, Raudenbush, and Earls (1997) developed a collective efficacy scale that they defined as social cohesion among neighbors, combined with their willingness to intervene on behalf of the common good (i.e., how likely it is that neighbors would help each other for the benefit of everyone in the community). Although the measure does not align itself with the guidelines put forth by Bandura (1997), it has been used as a sense of confidence in one's neighborhood to be able to work together to improve the community living environment. The budding research in this area has shown significantly positive relationships between this "neighborhood efficacy" and recreational walking (Sugiyama, Leslie, Giles-Corti, & Owen, 2008).

Sport

As with research on self-efficacy at the individual level, collective efficacy has been more frequently studied in sport when compared to exercise, and results again show that teams with stronger senses of collective efficacy experience greater cohesiveness, group processes, and performance attainments (Feltz & Lirgg, 1998; Magyar et al., 2004; Myers, Payment, & Feltz, 2004; Spink, 1990).

In a laboratory setting, Bray (2004) studied groups using a muscular endurance task. In this study, participants, in groups, developed group goals and were measured in their collective efficacy related to accomplishing these goals. Results highlighted the fact that collective efficacy explained variations in performance at time 2 (after initial performance was controlled). Furthermore, as occurred with the mediating effects of goals on self-efficacy at the individual level, a group's goal level (e.g., high or low) significantly mediated the relationship between collective efficacy and performance. Another important work, in which conditions were manipulated, revealed that when people were assigned to low collective efficacy groups and failed at a task, they responded by continuing to suffer from performance deterioration (Greenlees, Graydon, & Maynard, 1999). Additionally, in a follow-up study to the 1999 work, Greenlees, Graydon, and Maynard (2000) also found goals to be an important factor in mediating collective efficacy and performance. Specifically, when both the low collective efficacy and high collective efficacy groups experienced failure, only the former group lowered their goals to be more easily attainable, whereas the latter group continued to leave goals unchanged for future trials.

Collective efficacy in sport has also been studied in field settings, and although these studies may not be as efficient as the previously described laboratory works in supporting theoretical links between collective efficacy and measured outcomes, their importance is vital because simply grouping participants together to perform a task does not meet the true definition of a sport team (Feltz et al., 2008). In the sports of hockey and American football, research has shown that prior performance outcomes (i.e., winning or losing) had effects on impending collective efficacy (Feltz & Lirgg, 1998; Myers, Feltz, & Short, 2004; Myers, Payment, et al., 2004). For instance, in men's collegiate hockey, before playing a game on a Friday teams showed no difference in collective efficacy, but the winners of Friday night's hockey games had significantly higher collective efficacy going into competition on Saturdays when compared to teams that lost on Friday nights (Feltz & Lirgg, 1998). One methodological problem in researching sport teams in regard to collective efficacy is the fact that measures should ideally be completed during competition to increase understanding of this phenomenon, although many coaches are reluctant to subject their players to questionnaires during the course of play (Feltz et al., 2008). In one of the few studies to solve this dilemma, Edmonds, Tenenbaum, Kamata, and Johnson (2009) assessed collective efficacy of adventure racing teams before competition and during various stages. As hypothesized by Bandura (1997), collective efficacy was significantly related to performance and differentiated between higher- and lower-ranked teams throughout the race.

Finally, collective efficacy relates to much more than performance of groups. Bandura (1997) reasoned that collective efficacy is related to perseverance and collective effort at a task. But Carron, Hausenblas, and Eys (2005) noted in their book that if an individual has more confidence in the team's ability than in his or her ability, social loafing may result because the individual in question assumes that other team members are better qualified. On the other hand, Feltz et al. (2008) contended that reduced effort in a team setting may actually be the result of a combination of low motivation and low confidence in the team. The work of Lichacz and Partington (1996) may support this claim. In this study the authors found that teams with low collective efficacy (which was derived by negative feedback performances) were less interested in a rowing performance task and loafed more in comparison to groups that had high collective efficacy. But note that this relationship did not hold true for already intact rowing teams. Thus, the authors hypothesized that when team members view a task as important, low collective efficacy is much less likely to induce social loafing.

Coaching Efficacy Research

As mentioned previously, Feltz and associates (Feltz et al., 1999) proposed a conceptual model of coaching efficacy, based on Bandura's (1986, 1997) writings, in which the four dimensions of coaching efficacy beliefs are influenced by their past performance and experience (e.g., coaching experience, coaching preparation, previous win–loss record), the perceived ability of the coaches' athletes, and perceived social support (e.g., faculty, student, administrative, community, and parental support). Coaching efficacy beliefs are, in turn, proposed to influence coaches' behavior (e.g., type of feedback used, management strategies, coaching style) and athletes' performance, motivation, and satisfaction with the coach.

In general, results have shown support for the predictive strength of the proposed sources of coaching efficacy (Feltz et al., 2008). But as Feltz et al. noted, the specific sources of coaching efficacy appear to influence the coaching efficacy dimensions differentially, depending on the level of coaches involved (e.g., youth, high school, or collegiate), organizational factors (e.g., local versus travel leagues, competition divisions, size of school), and, to a certain extent, gender of the coach. For instance, at the collegiate level of competition, Myers, Vargas-Tonsing, and Feltz (2005) reported that perceived team ability level was the strongest predictor of coaching efficacy. The most robust dimensions were motivation and character building. Additionally, gender differences were noted in this work. Female coaches believed that social support from the surrounding community was a stronger source of character-building efficacy when compared to males. In other words, female coaches who perceived support from the community had more confidence in their ability to teach and instill character-building lessons of fair play and respect for others compared to male coaches. At the volunteer youth coach level, Feltz, Hepler, Roman, and Paiement (2009) found that years of playing experience was the strongest predictor of coaching efficacy, and technique and game strategy were the most robust dimensions.

In terms of the influence of coaching efficacy beliefs on behavioral outcomes and attitudes, research has supported that higher-efficacy coaches, as compared to lower-efficacy coaches, use more positive coaching behaviors, have more athletes who are satisfied with them as coaches, and have better performing teams in terms of winning percentage (Feltz et al., 1999; Myers et al., 2005). Although the concept of coaching efficacy is relatively new and only a handful of studies have been published on this paradigm to date, in this chapter we do not have enough space to describe the conceptual model and research studies in detail. For a comprehensive look at this topic, we recommend that the reader examine chapter 5 of Feltz et al. (2008).

Practical Applications

In this segment of the chapter, we focus on how practitioners (e.g., fitness trainers, athletes, coaches, and sport and exercise psychologists) can implement the theoretical components and research suggestions from previous sections. In applying Bandura's (1997) theory of self-efficacy, we focus on his four main sources of efficacy information: mastery experiences, vicarious experiences, social persuasion, and physiological and emotional states. The most effective way of creating a strong sense of efficacy is through mastery experiences (Bandura, 1997), but vicarious experiences provided by social models can also be effective (George, Feltz, & Chase, 1992). Consequently, most of the research aimed at raising self-efficacy beliefs has used mastery experience and vicarious experience (e.g., participant modeling) interventions. In this section space does not allow a detailed presentation of all efficacy-enhancing strategies. Thus, the interested reader should consult Feltz et al. (2008), chapters 6, 7, and 8, for an in-depth review. Finally, because the strategies for exercisers, athletes, and teams are based on the same approaches, we combine examples for these populations.

Mastery-Based Strategies

When individuals, teams, and coaches achieve success in tasks in which they have had difficulty, they feel more efficacious. One way of facilitating performance success is through instructional techniques to enhance mastery.

Note here that mastery should not be confused with mastery climates and the work of Ames (1992a, 1992b). Although mastery climates can enhance self-efficacy and technical execution in physical exertion tasks (Barkouis, Koidou, & Tsorbatzoudis, 2010), these climate structures are not a prerequisite for efficacy improvement. Generally, instructional strategies include providing a progressive sequence of modified activities, breaking complex skills or challenging behaviors into parts, providing performance aids or physical guidance, or offering a combination of these strategies. The idea is to build success based on relevant and realistic progressions and to remove physical guidance and performance aids as soon as possible to allow exercisers, athletes, or teams to engage in self-directed mastery (Feltz, 1994). For instance, in working with cardiac rehabilitation patients, the instructor can start with the performance aid of continuous ECG monitoring and supervised exercise sessions and then design progressive activities to challenge improving skill and reduce ECG-monitored sessions to build a sense of independent mastery (Feltz & Payment, 2005).

Helping participants set realistic and relevant goals is another means of facilitating success. Setting goals helps people define realistic performance standards toward which they can strive (see Roberts & Kristiansen, this volume). For instance, a group of individuals will have increased levels of motivation to continue exercising together if they have all set goals concerning the amount of weight that they wish to lose. Additionally, with those goals in place, if the individuals in question suffer a setback of increased soreness after exercising, their goals will help prevent the deterioration of self-efficacy levels and result in the adaptive behaviors of continued persistence and effort in future exercise sessions (Bandura, 1997). Finally, people must understand that it is acceptable, and even appropriate, to adjust goals up or down based on ever-changing conditions. But even if goals are adjusted downward, individuals must take something positive home with them after each competition or exercise bout (Feltz et al., 2008). This outcome is important because, when people attain their goals, efficacy increases (Bandura, 1997).

Another performance-based technique that is especially suited to athletes and teams is to create environments that simulate as closely as possible their performance contests so that athletes can practice their skills. The most popular implementation of this strategy is with field simulations (e.g., where loud noise is pumped into a stadium for a team preparing to play in a hostile environment), but technological simulations may also serve to increase efficacy (Bandura, 1997; Feltz et al., 2008; Hepler, 2008). The main benefit of this tactic is that when competition day arrives, athletes will have already practiced their anticipated performance responses (Orlick, 2000). Finally, when simulating anticipated events, practitioners should include events that may cause a lapse in concentration, such as a poor officiating call, to help athletes' efficacy levels because they will have already coped with a potentially negative situation (Feltz et al., 2008).

Vicarious-Based Strategies

Observing similar others has been a source of increased efficacy beliefs when a person has no experience with a task. Similarity of personal characteristics (e.g., age, race, sex) is important, but skill set is the most important factor in modeling (George, Feltz, & Chase, 1992) because models can provide information and strategies about how to perform an exercise or skill successfully (Feltz et al., 2008). Specifically, novice athletes may more quickly learn how to perform a task correctly if they view a proficient modeler (Feltz & Lirgg, 2001). But coping models, who may initially exhibit difficulty in a task but successfully overcome their difficulties, may be especially helpful to those who have fear and anxiety about a particular challenge. Observing another cope with a threatening situation reduces the uncertainty for the observer and therefore increases the predictability of the challenge and the observer's preparedness. For example, observing another athlete coping with the discomfort of physical rehabilitation can reduce inhibitions and anxiety in an athlete who is just beginning physical rehabilitation (Scorniaechi & Feltz, 2009). Thus, the selection of a modeler's skill level is of great consequence because a modeler with far greater skill level may cause an unwanted evaluative effect and a corresponding reduction in self-efficacy (Bandura, 1997).

Persuasion-Based Strategies

Persuasion and communication strategies are best used in conjunction with performance-based techniques. For instance, a personal trainer can help beginning exercisers take small risks by using persuasory information that is slightly exaggerated beyond their current capabilities to help them mount the extra effort needed to succeed (Bandura, 1997). But as Feltz and Payment (2005) note, excessive exaggeration that leads to repeated failures can undermine the professional's credibility, which will then negatively affect the power of this source of efficacy information.

A simple step that practitioners can implement in the category of persuasion is focusing on positive feedback. Besides being believable, feedback should also be noncomparative for individuals still acquiring the necessary skill sets. Specifically, practitioners should focus their feedback on how each person is progressing without regard to others. Failure to use this strategy may lower the efficacy beliefs of some individuals (Short & Vadocz, 2002). In addition to framing feedback in a positive light, practitioners should also make it performance contingent (Feltz, 1994). For instance, consider the following two comments by a coach in the sport of basketball: "Good try, you can do it next time" as compared to "Great effort on that play, all you have to do is rub shoulder to shoulder coming off the screen and you will be open for your shot." Both comments include positive feedback, but the second one also acknowledges a mistake and informs the athlete how to correct it. The use of noncontingent, positive feedback for the first athlete implies lower expectations and suggests that the coach values the performance of the second athlete more.

Verbal encouragement can also take place before an event or competition and serve as a reminder related to strategies and skill sets that people possess and thus strengthen efficacy beliefs. In particular, a coach's "pep talk" can enhance efficacy beliefs in the team. Vargas-Tonsing and Bartholomew (2006) showed that athletes' confidence in their team increased after listening to a motivational talk from the coach. In a follow-up study, the amount of perceived informational content in pregame speeches increased athletes' self-efficacy beliefs and positive emotions (Vargas-Tonsing, 2009). Practitioners should also note that goals and persuasion are related (Bandura & Cervone, 1983; Locke & Latham, 1990). Specifically, for persuasion to be most effective it should be conveyed in relation to the defined goals or standards previously set (Bandura, 1997).

Finally, persuasion does not have to take place immediately before or after a skill is attempted; efficacy by proxy, workshops, and media campaigns is also considered a form of social persuasion. In efficacy by proxy, self-efficacy is hypothesized to be enhanced when individuals are surrounded by people who believe in them and convey that belief. Although the topic is relatively new in the fields of exercise and sport, initial studies have validated a questionnaire for exercisers in a group setting and found that proxy efficacy is related to the amount of physical activity that middle school children engage in (Bray, Gyurcsik, Martin Ginis, & Culos-Reed, 2004; Dzewaltowski, Karteroliotis, Welk, Johnston, Nyaronga, & Estabrooks, 2007; see also Martin Ginis & Mack, this volume). In the latter, research has shown that when people attend workshops about how to engage in exercise, their decision to undertake a program may rest with their beliefs about the probability and value of possible benefits (Rodgers & Brawley, 1993). Thus, Bandura (1997) contends that the more that media and other social outlets enhance people's efficacy beliefs, the more likely they will be to adopt the proposed practices.

Physiology-Based Strategies

A number of physiological based strategies can also be employed to help build efficacy. Practitioners must remember, however, that mastery experiences are the most salient source for building self-efficacy; thus, physiology-based techniques should not be used exclusively.

The first way that people can alter their perceptions of physiological symptoms is through controlling negative self-talk and blocking out distractions. This type of strategy may be necessary for an exercise participant who notices an individual seemingly staring at her or him from across the room. This behavior may trigger thoughts about why that individual is looking in her or his direction and can result in skills that are seemingly well learned becoming harder to produce because more attention is paid to previously automated skills (Beilock & Carr, 2001). To counteract the numerous distractions that may exist in exercise and sport settings, people should follow a prescribed routine because doing so will help maintain confidence and focus when a distraction is detected (Chase, 2006). But as Feltz et al. (2008) note, the fact that a person's thoughts begin to wander may signify that the current routine has lost its purpose and may need to be revised.

Additionally, people have the ability to control their efficacy levels better when they reduce the number of negative thoughts (Bandura, 1997). To accomplish this, individuals must examine the intensity and frequency of negative thoughts that they experience in a set period. After completing this examination, they should reconstruct thoughts that are phrased in a negative way so that positive outcomes become the focus of the thought, thus producing adaptive behavior changes (Feltz et al., 2008). As Bandura (1997) noted, it is the interpretations of the physiological states that can affect efficacy; therefore, rephrasing negative thoughts into positive ones should have an equally positive effect on future self-efficacy levels.

Finally, individuals can use imagery, or the practicing of skills without external stimuli, to foster a sense of relaxation, competence, and control (Feltz et al., 2008). Recent research has shown that imagery is effective in building golf and soccer participants' self-efficacy and developing adaptive attributions (Allen et al., 2010; Munroe-Chandler, Hall, & Fishburne, 2008). When setting up an imagery program with an exercise client or athlete, practitioners should work to keep the imagery session simple and easy to replicate at the start and involve all five senses to facilitate resemblance to the event or skill being rehearsed (Vealey & Greenleaf, 2010).

Directions for Future Research

Up to this point in the chapter there has been little debate about how self-efficacy beliefs form and the directional effects of self-efficacy on motivation and performance regardless of the domain and the level in which efficacy beliefs are measured. But new avenues of research have resulted in reexamination of the uniform beliefs of the effects of self-efficacy. In this section, we briefly describe three budding future research topics: self-efficacy and decision making, dispersion of efficacy beliefs in teams, and the contradictions between social-cognitive theory and perceptual control theory.

Self-Efficacy and Decision Making

Decision making, a process by which people select one action from a host of alternative choices for a specific situation (Tenenbaum, 2004), can often determine victory or defeat in sporting contests. In these same sporting events, however, athletes usually do not have the luxury of contemplating a decision by assessing the situation, listing all possible choices and their outcomes, and then choosing the best one from the options generated. Thus, Johnson and Raab (2003) proposed a take-the-first heuristic, which asserts that, when a person is presented with familiar yet ill-defined tasks, the best course of action is to select one of the first solutions that comes to mind instead of spending time to generate and evaluate all possible outcomes. Furthermore, this heuristic assumes that because options are generated in a pattern in which early options represent better decisions than later ones, the first solution to a problem will usually produce the best result to the current problem.

Hepler (2008) examined the take-the-first heuristic and self-efficacy in simulated basketball tasks to explore how efficacy beliefs would be related to the number of options generated, the quality of decisions made, and the speed at which options were produced. Results revealed that participants reported higher efficacy beliefs in their decisions when they generated only one option, although self-efficacy did not continue to decrease as more options were generated (e.g., there was no statistical difference in confidence when participants produced three solutions or six solutions). Furthermore, when controlling for years of competitive basketball experience and basketball knowledge, self-efficacy significantly predicted decision quality but exhibited no relationship with the speed at which solutions were generated. Taken as a whole, this work showed that participants in basketball simulation tasks employed the take-the-first heuristic when presented with challenging game scenarios, but in the 252 trials in which participants did not employ the take-the-first heuristic, changing their answer proved beneficial on 161 occasions. To increase understanding of this phenomenon, real-world examination of the take-the-first heuristic should be studied to investigate whether it generalizes to real-life decision making (Hepler, 2008).

Dispersion of Efficacy Beliefs in Teams

The discussion of collective efficacy in this chapter has thus far focused on aggregated beliefs of team members to represent a single team efficacy belief. But athletes who participate in team sports can differ in their beliefs about the team's capabilities, and some authors believe that this within-team variability in beliefs is not simply a methodological concern and a statistical prerequisite but may provide interesting and explanatory information about team effectiveness (DeRue, Hollenbeck, Ilgen, & Feltz, 2010; Moritz & Watson, 1998). DeRue et al. proposed the concept of efficacy dispersion as the team-level variability in the magnitude of collective efficacy perceptions within the team. As Feltz et al. (2008) noted, efficacy dispersion may be thought of as the inverse of efficacy consensus.

DeRue and colleagues (2010) propose that in the preparatory phase of performance when teams are preparing for an upcoming competition, the greater the dispersion that exists within a team, the greater the team's capacity and effort at performance will be. They reason that dispersion in efficacy beliefs of the team leads team members to reappraise the team's strategies and enhances their cognitive and behavioral processing. Furthermore, DeRue et al. argue that consensus in efficacy beliefs, especially when beliefs are high, hinders reappraisal motivation and could contribute to maladaptive behaviors. No published research has investigated any of the tenets of the model proposed by DeRue and colleagues, but a first step might be to investigate whether, for a given level of collective efficacy, teams with high consensus in their collective beliefs put forth more effort in practice than teams with dispersed perceptions in their efficacy judgments.

Perceptual Control Theory

First presented in 1978 by Powers, perceptual control theory asserts that behavior is a direct result of the cognitive perceptions that people develop from input received. This input can take the form of sore muscles from an exercise session, negative feedback from a coach, or achieving a goal in a marathon. Thus, perceptual control theory contends that when the input is altered, future output is affected. Specifically, a person's actions are driven by a discrepancy between the current situation, as assessed, and the perception of skills that one has to meet the demands of said situation (Powers, 1991). Thus, output behavior is explained by the concept of dynamic stability, whereby an individual works to reverse the effects of disturbances that push perceptions away from a goal or level of accomplishment. For example, an athlete who has the goal of making the local rugby team but perceives that he is weaker than other candidates will spend extra time lifting weights to change his perception and achieve his overall goal.

When utilizing self-efficacy from a perceptual control theory framework, results have been reported that appear to contradict some of the previous work described in this chapter. Vancouver and colleagues (2001, 2002, 2006, 2008) and Yeo and Neal (2006) reported that self-efficacy was negatively related to performance at the within-person level over time (level 1) but was positively related to performance when examining data at the between-person level (level 2) when participants performed computer analytical games and had academic performance measured. To explain these findings, Vancouver and associates argued that if individuals have a great performance, self-efficacy will be enhanced, which could result in complacency on future trials. On the contrary, individuals who do not achieve their goals will suffer from a reduction in self-efficacy, which will then lead to more studying or practice to improve future performances.

Bandura (1997) has long been aware of the contentions that perceptual control theory makes regarding self-efficacy and has, together with colleagues, taken exception to these studies' results by pointing to their methodological flaws (Bandura & Locke, 2003; Stajkovic & Bandura, 2009). Specifically, the two theoretical bases differ on how past performance should be controlled. Perceptual control theory favors controlling raw past performance, whereas Bandura and Wood (1989) contend that the psychosocial aspects embedded in a performance score should also be statistically partialled out (i.e., residualizing past performance). Failure to perform this additional step provides a performance measure that includes a mix of psychosocial factors unmeasured at that time point (Bandura & Locke, 2003). Additionally, Yeo and Neal's negative relationship in their within-person analysis accounted for less than 1% of the variance in subsequent performance and when reanalyzed was found to have methodological flaws (Stajkovic & Bandura, 2009).

Only one study to date has examined this issue at the within-person level in a sport context and implemented the research suggestion of Vancouver et al. (2002) calling for future work to use tasks that require less cognitive processing. Gilson, Chow, and Feltz (in press) tracked collegiate American football athletes during strength training over 8 months and found that self-efficacy (both within-person and between-person) was positively and significantly related to lifting performance. Thus, the suggestion that a coach or other person should undermine the efficacy beliefs of athletes to motivate them to practice may be ill advised. To understand the effects of self-efficacy on performance, other researchers argue that ambiguity of the task may be an important factor (Schmidt & DeShon, 2010). Although the methodology was a computer simulation, Schmidt and DeShon found that when task ambiguity was low, the relationship between self-efficacy and performance was positive; conversely, when task ambiguity was high, the relationship between self-efficacy and performance was negative. Thus, more work along these lines is needed to determine the generalizability of these findings.

Summary

Self-efficacy, rooted within social-cognitive theory, can offer valuable insights into people's motivational tendencies in both exercise and sport. Research has consistently shown efficacy beliefs to be strong predictors of future activity choices, behaviors, and perseverance during difficult times. These conclusions exist not only at the individual level but also for a group or team acting within an environment, all striving to meet a common goal, and for the coach of the individuals related to his or her coaching efficacy. In addition, perceived outcomes from activities that people engage in can strengthen or contribute to a degree of uncertainty in future self-efficacy. Thus, the practitioner (be it a fitness trainer, physical therapist, coach, or sport and exercise psychologist) can assess and then apply efficacy-building techniques to improve the self-confidence of exercisers, athletes, teams, and even coaches. Self-efficacy is an imperative psychological construct because quite simply, in both exercise and sport, the capacity for self-motivation and purposeful behavior is found within a person's cognitions. Projections of the future are not the cause of current motivation; instead, behaviors exhibited are a result of the future being brought into the present by forethought and combined with current efficacy beliefs (Bandura, 1997).

CHAPTER 9

Social-Cognitive Approaches to Understanding Exercise Motivation and Behavior in Cancer Survivors

Jeff K. Vallance, PhD
Athabasca University

Kerry S. Courneya, PhD
University of Alberta

Author's Note

Jeff Vallance is supported by a Population Health Investigator Salary Award from Alberta Innovates—Health Solutions and a New Investigator Award from the Canadian Institutes of Health Research. Kerry Courneya is supported by the Canada Research Chairs Program.

In the United States alone, approximately 1.5 million new cases of cancer (excluding skin cancer) were expected to be diagnosed in 2009, and just over 560,000 Americans were expected to die from their cancer (American Cancer Society, 2010). Cancer is the second most common cause of death in the United States after heart disease. The four most common cancers—prostate, breast, colorectal, and lung—account for over 55% of all new cancer cases and over 50% of all new cancer deaths each year (American Cancer Society, 2010).

Further, it was estimated that the overall costs of cancer in the United States in 2008 were just over $228 billion (American Cancer Society, 2010). Cancer has established itself as a major public health burden not just in the United States but worldwide. Despite the high death rates, more individuals are surviving their cancer. The 5-year relative survival rate in the United States across all cancers and disease stages is 66% (American Cancer Society), although this survival rate varies substantially by cancer type and stage. For example, the 5-year relative survival rate for breast cancer is now 89% (98% if the cancer is local and has not spread to other parts of the body outside the breast). In contrast, the 5-year relative survival rate for lung cancer that is still local (i.e., early stage) is 50% but only 15% when all stages are considered.

Although several definitions have been proposed, the National Cancer Institute Office of Cancer Survivorship (2009) states that an individual is considered a cancer survivor from the time of diagnosis through the balance of his or her life. The high incidence and good survival rates mean that over 10 million cancer survivors are currently living in the United States. Consequently, there is a growing population of cancer survivors.

Cancer Treatments

Cancers grow at different rates and respond to different treatments. People with cancer require treatment that is aimed at their specific kind of cancer (e.g., breast, lung, colorectal). Therefore, treatment protocols for breast cancer are different from treatment protocols for prostate or lung cancer. The most common treatment modalities for cancer are surgery, systemic therapy (i.e., chemotherapy, hormone replacement therapy), and radiation therapy. Surgery is the primary treatment for most solid tumors and can oftentimes result in a cure all by itself. Systemic therapies (i.e., drugs) are often needed to track down and destroy the cancer cells wherever they may be. One of the most common systemic therapies is chemotherapy. Chemotherapy usually involves a combination of two to four active drugs (or agents) given four to six times every 2 or 3 weeks to treat a given cancer by killing the rapidly proliferating cancerous cells. Chemotherapy is often given in the adjuvant context, that is, it is often administered after surgery when the tumor has been removed (thus the term *adjuvant chemotherapy*). Approximately 60% of people with cancer will receive radiation therapy at some point during their treatments (Maher, 2000). External beam radiation therapy is the most common method of delivering radiation to a localized tumor to maximize the killing of cancer cells and minimize the damage to normal cells. Some tumors are dependent on hormones in the body. Hormone therapy is used to reduce sex hormones, such as estrogen or testosterone, that can facilitate the growth of some cancers. These drugs can be administered orally (continuously or intermittently) for many years.

Cancer and its extensive treatments can take a significant toll on the physical and psychosocial health and well-being of cancer survivors. Although these treatments have been shown to improve survival rates, cancer survivors are also at increased risk for many acute, chronic, and late effects of their disease and treatments, including a recurrence of another type of cancer, second cancers, cardiac dysfunction, weight gain, bone loss, lymphedema, arthralgias, cognitive dysfunction, menopausal symptoms, reduced health-related quality of life (HRQoL), fatigue, and psychosocial distress (Shapiro & Recht, 2001). The adverse side effects of treatments associated with cancer have spurred a major research effort into strategies to alleviate and minimize treatment effects; hasten recovery after treatments; improve long-term HRQoL; and reduce the risk of disease recurrence, other chronic diseases, and premature death. Given these consequences, cancer survivors represent an important target population for health promotion interventions.

Exercise and Cancer Survivorship

One intervention that has been found to enhance HRQoL in cancer survivors is exercise (Markes, Brockow, & Resch, 2006; McNeely et al., 2006; Schmitz et al., 2005; Speck, Courneya, Masse, Duval, & Schmitz, 2010). Traditionally, cancer survivors are offered informational and educational nonbehavioral counseling, psychotherapy, social support, and other nontraditional therapies such as music or art therapy (Meyer & Mark, 1995). It has recently been suggested that no evidence-based guidelines exist to inform and guide psychosocial interventions to improve HRQoL in cancer survivors (Galway, Black, Cantwell, Cardwell, Mills, & Donnelly, 2008). A meta-analysis by Meyer and Mark (1995) reported that randomized interventions with psychosocial dependent outcomes were generally small. For instance, effect sizes ranged from .19 (functional adjustment) to .26 (treatment-related symptoms). Although somewhat effective in a limited number of psychosocial domains (e.g., emotional, coping), these therapies are largely psychological in nature and less likely to address the physical and functional problems encountered by cancer survivors (e.g., fatigue, physical functioning, nausea).

Recent meta-analyses and systematic reviews suggest that exercise can improve multiple physical and psychosocial health outcomes both during and after cancer treatments (Markes et al., 2006; McNeely et al., 2006; Schmitz et al., 2005; Speck et al., 2010). One of the most recent systematic reviews identified 64 randomized controlled trials (RCT) postdiagnosis (i.e., both during and after treatments) across various cancer groups (Speck et al., 2010). Properly conducted and well-designed RCTs provide the best evidence of the efficacy of a treatment or health care intervention (Altman, Schulz, Moher, Egger, Davidoff, Elbourne, et al. 2001). Significant weighted effect sizes from controlled studies conducted during treatment were observed for aerobic fitness, upper-body strength, lower-body strength, body weight, body fat percentage, HRQoL, mood, anxiety, and self-esteem. Significant weighted effect sizes from controlled studies conducted posttreatment were observed for exercise level, aerobic fitness, upper-body strength, lower-body strength, body weight, body fat percentage, BMI, HRQoL, fatigue, and general symptoms and side effects. This systematic review corroborates previously conducted reviews in that exercise has facilitative effects on various health outcomes both during and after cancer treatments (Markes et al., 2006; McNeely et al., 2006; Schmitz et al., 2005).

Since these reviews, clinically relevant and exciting evidence continues to emerge that supports the role of exercise as a safe and effective intervention to facilitate favorable physical and psychosocial health outcomes among various cancer survivor groups. For breast cancer survivors, perhaps the most clinically relevant information to emerge is related to exercise and breast cancer-related lymphedema (i.e., limb swelling because of surgical resection of lymph nodes). Traditionally, breast cancer survivors were instructed to avoid lifting heavy objects with their affecting arm, and as a result upper-body weightlifting (i.e., resistance training) was contraindicated. But a recently published randomized controlled trial reported that breast cancer survivors who engaged in progressive weightlifting had no significant limb swelling, decreased incidence of lymphedema exacerbations, reduced symptoms, and increased strength (Schmitz et al., 2009). Furthermore, other quality randomized controlled trials that explored resistance training in the breast cancer survivor population have reported clinically relevant benefits such as improved chemotherapy completion rates, muscular strength, and lean body mass (Courneya et al., 2007; Segal et al., 2003). Although most RCTs conducted evaluated the efficacy of aerobic training (e.g., cycle ergometer, walking), the trials evaluating resistance training are suggesting that different modes of exercise are associated with unique health outcomes.

Recent prospective observational research is suggesting that cancer survivors who exercise after their treatments are less likely to have a cancer recurrence, less likely to die from their cancer, and more likely to live longer than survivors who do not exercise. One prospective cohort study of almost 3,000 women found that higher levels of posttreatment exercise were associated with reduced risks of breast cancer recurrence, breast-cancer-specific mortality, and all-cause mortality (Holmes, Chen, Feskanich, Kroenke, & Colditz, 2005). The most interesting finding from this study was that exercising at a higher dose (i.e., higher frequency and intensity) was not associated with any additional benefits beyond brisk walking for 3 hours per week. Other studies with breast cancer survivors are consistently showing that 2 to 3 hours per week of exercise at the equivalent of walking at a brisk pace (i.e., as would be done when late for an appointment) is associated with better breast-cancer-free survival

(Friedenreich, Gregory, Kopciuk, Mackey, & Courneya, 2009; Holick et al., 2008; Irwin et al., 2008). That is, breast cancer survivors who walk only 3 hours per week were more likely to live longer without a breast cancer recurrence than survivors who are not walking. This research supports starting exercise even after being diagnosed. Unfortunately, women who decreased their exercise level after they were diagnosed with breast cancer had a four times greater risk of dying when compared to women who started exercising after their diagnosis (Irwin et al., 2008).

Similar data are emerging in colon cancer survivors. In the CALGB 89803 cohort, researchers found that exercise may also reduce the risk of colon cancer recurrence (Meyerhardt, Heseltine, et al., 2006). It was found that survivors who walked as little as 6 hours per week at a moderate intensity had a 47% improvement in disease-free survival when compared to colon cancer survivors who did not exercise. These studies also found that the amount of exercise done before being diagnosed with colon cancer was not nearly as important as the amount of exercise performed after diagnosis and treatment. In another prospective study, researchers followed almost 600 women who had been diagnosed with colorectal cancer (Meyerhardt, Giovannucci, et al., 2006). Data indicated that colorectal cancer survivors who increased their exercise after their diagnosis had a 52% lower chance of dying from the disease compared to those who did not change their exercise involvement. Also, those who decreased their exercise after their diagnosis had a 32% increase in their risk of dying from their colorectal cancer. The same study found that colon cancer survivors who did more than 18 metabolic equivalents of exercise per week (approximately 6 hours of walking per week) were more likely to live longer than colon cancer survivors who engaged in little or no activity.

The mechanisms responsible for these outcomes are unclear. But there are explanations by which exercise behavior may influence these disease and survival outcomes. Exercise may improve survival through acute and chronic improvements in insulin resistance, C-peptide (a marker of insulin secretion), insulin-like growth factor (Meyerhardt, Giovannucci, et al., 2006), a reduction in hyperinsulinemia (Holmes et al., 2005), and changes in sex hormones and reduced inflammation markers (Irwin, 2009). It has also been suggested that the biologic mechanisms of exercise on breast cancer risk may be applicable to breast cancer survival (Friedenreich & Cust, 2008). That is, decreasing endogenous estrogens, facilitating long-term energy balance, and decreasing body fat levels may also be responsible for increasing overall survival and reducing the risk of recurrence (Friedenreich & Cust, 2008).

In summary, the existing literature has demonstrated that higher levels of postdiagnosis exercise are associated with disease-free outcomes in breast and colon cancer survivors. Furthermore, it appears that survivors who were relatively inactive before their diagnosis can modify their relapse risk by increasing their exercise behavior after being diagnosed. Given these promising findings, there clearly is a need to develop and evaluate methods of facilitating exercise behavior among the population of cancer survivors.

Exercise Prevalence in Cancer Survivors

Unfortunately, the majority of cancer survivors will not realize these afore-mentioned health benefits and potential survival advantages. Despite the accumulating evidence documenting the associated benefits of exercise after a cancer diagnosis (See figure 9.1), most cancer survivors are not meeting the minimal amounts of exercise required for the accrual of health benefits (Blanchard, Courneya, & Stein, 2008; Coups & Ostroff, 2005; Courneya, Katzmarzyk, & Bacon, 2008; Irwin et al., 2004). As shown in figure 9.2, this evidence suggests that exercise behavior substantially decreases as an individual moves through the cancer trajectory. These changes in exercise behavior are most prominent after diagnosis relative to prediagnosis levels. The most recognizable change in exercise behavior occurs during treatment (Courneya & Friedenreich, 1997b, 1997c; Jones, Courneya, Vallance, et al., 2004; Jones, Guill, et al., 2006; Karvinen, Courneya, North, & Venner, 2007; Stevinson, Steed, et al., 2009; Vallance, Courneya, Jones, & Reiman, 2005). These studies consistently indicate that total exercise, moderate-intensity exercise, vigorous-intensity exercise, and sports or recreational exercise substantially decrease from prediagnosis, on to treatment, and through to postdiagnosis.

The American Cancer Society's Study of Cancer Survivors-II (ACS SCS-II) provides the most recent evidence that only a minority of cancer survivors are meeting exercise guidelines (Blanchard et al., 2008). In particular, a minority of breast (37.1%), prostate (43.2%), colorectal (35.0%), bladder (36%), and uterine (29.6%) cancer survivors were meeting exercise guidelines published by the American Cancer Society (i.e., accumulate at least 150 minutes of moderate to strenuous exercise or 60 minutes of strenuous exercise per week) (Doyle, Kushi, et al., 2006). Data from a Canadian sample of cancer survivors yielded similar results. Courneya and colleagues (Courneya, Katzmarzyk, et al., 2008) obtained data from the Canadian Community Health Survey and reported that a minority of prostate (23.9%), breast (16.6%), and colorectal (17.1%) cancer survivors were achieving exercise behavior levels consistent with public health recommendations. Among a large sample of mixed cancer survivors, the 2000 National Health Interview Survey indicated that 25.2% of cancer survivors between the ages of 40 and 64 years were engaging in either 20 minutes (or more) of vigorous exercise, three or more times per week, or 30 minutes (or more) of light or moderate exercise, five or more times per week (Coups & Ostroff, 2005). Only 20.6% of survivors over the age of 65 years were achieving these guidelines. Results from these studies provide consistent evidence that the majority of cancer survivors are not achieving desirable exercise behavior levels that are consistent with the recommended public health guidelines.

Similar results have been reported by our research group across a range of cancer survivors (e.g., breast, colorectal, non-Hodgkin's lymphoma, multiple myeloma, endometrial, bladder, colorectal) using population-based provincial cancer registry data from Alberta, Canada (Courneya & Friedenreich, 1997b, 1997c; Jones, Courneya, Vallance, et al., 2004; Karvinen, Courneya,

North, et al., 2007; Peddle, Au, & Courneya, 2008; Stevinson, Steed, et al., 2009; Vallance et al., 2005). Besides being asked about current exercise rates in these studies, survivors were asked to recall their exercise behavior during treatments. The results of these studies have shown that approximately 20% to 30% of cancer survivors report meeting public health exercise guidelines posttreatment but only 5% to 10% report meeting the guidelines during treatment. Data suggest, however, that some tumor groups report higher exercise prevalence rates. For example, Jones, Guill, et al. (2006) reported that 38% and 41% of brain tumor patients, respectively, met national exercise prescription guidelines during adjuvant treatment and after the completion of treatment. Although some survivor groups report higher exercise prevalence, some sub-populations of cancer survivors report lower exercise prevalence rates. For example, Rogers and colleagues reported that only 19% of rural breast cancer survivors reported meeting exercise guidelines (Rogers, Markwell, Verhulst, McAuley, & Courneya, 2009).

Strong evidence suggests that the decrease in exercise across the cancer trajectory may be a function of treatment factors. For example, Irwin and colleagues (2003) found that breast cancer survivors who received a combination of surgery, chemotherapy, and radiation therapy had more substantial decreases in exercise behavior than did surgery-only patients and patients who had surgery combined with radiation. To quantify the amount of exercise loss, Irwin and colleagues further estimated that the time spent engaging in exercise decreased on average 2 hours per week from prediagnosis to post-treatment. In all these aforementioned studies, cancer survivors reported that their exercise behavior levels increased after their treatment. But of concern here is that exercise behavior levels typically did not recover to their (higher) prediagnosis levels. Promoting exercise after treatment is important given that increasing exercise after diagnosis may minimize the negative physical and psychosocial sequela that are associated with the posttreatment phase of the cancer trajectory. These consistent trends in declining exercise behavior provide a strong rationale to encourage and facilitate exercise behavior among the population of cancer survivors (Irwin et al., 2004).

Although the exercise patterns and prevalence data appear to be consistent across various tumor groups, important limitations in the research deserve mention. The first limitation is that studies have relied on self-report data. Given the tendency of participants to overestimate their exercise behavior patterns, it is reasonable to suggest that the prevalence rates reported may be higher than the actual rates. Second, given the transparent nature of the studies, a resulting selection bias may also lead to an overestimation in the data. Third, many of the studies are retrospective, which can create problems of memory and recall bias. Fourth, few studies consist of a nationally representative sample, and few have made comparisons with appropriately matched controls. Finally, it is not clear what the exercise guidelines are for cancer survivors, especially during treatments, and these guidelines may vary by cancer survivor group, symptoms, and prognosis.

Exercise Motivation in Cancer Survivors

Given the challenges that cancer survivors face in their exercise pursuits (e.g., treatment side effects, physical and psychological side effects), coupled with the evidence of exercise behavior decline across the cancer trajectory, motivation and adherence are important issues when considering exercise programs for cancer survivors. These factors also make the cancer survivor population a unique area of inquiry in which to study exercise. For example, researchers have contended that cancer survivors from several different tumor groups may be motivated for health behavior change by embracing and participating in efforts aimed at facilitating exercise behavior. For example, the published studies indicate that about 70% of survivors (including breast, prostate, head and neck, brain, bladder, endometrial, NHL, and ovarian cancer) were interested in participating in an exercise program at some point during their diagnosis (Jones, Guill, et al., 2007a; Karvinen, Courneya, Venner, & North, 2007; Rogers, Malone, et al., 2009; Stevinson, Capstick, et al., 2009; Vallance, Courneya, Jones, & Reiman, 2006). What is more telling is that in most of these studies over 80% of survivors indicated that they felt able to participate in an exercise program (Jones, Guill, et al., 2007a; Karvinen, Courneya, Venner, et al., 2007; Stevinson, Capstick, et al., 2009; Vallance et al., 2006). Overall, this evidence suggests that the cancer survivor population may be receptive to exercise behavior change efforts because of a documented high level of interest. This evidence corroborates the contention that a cancer diagnosis might be a teachable moment in which survivors may feel more likely to make healthy lifestyle changes (Demark-Wahnefried, Morey, et al., 2003).

Exercise Behavior in Cancer Survivors

Given the low exercise prevalence in many cancer survivor groups, researchers and practitioners have started to explore the factors that affect a cancer survivor's participating in, or refraining from participating in, exercise (i.e., determinants of exercise). By starting to understand the determinants of exercise in cancer survivors, researchers and practitioners can develop and implement relevant exercise behavior change programs and strategies to facilitate exercise behavior in this population. In our efforts to understand exercise behavior in the cancer context, research has applied one of the currently validated social-cognitive models of human motivation and behavior to facilitate understanding. Application of social-cognitive models can assist researchers and practitioners in understanding the mechanisms through which cancer survivors change (or do not change) their exercise behavior. The two models that have been applied most often to exercise in cancer survivors have been the theory of planned behavior (TPB) (Ajzen, 1991) and social-cognitive theory (SCT) (Bandura, 2000). Recently, emerging evidence suggests that self-determination theory (SDT) also appears promising for understanding exercise motivation and behavior in cancer survivors (Deci & Ryan, 2002a). Although not intended to be an exhaustive review, the next sections of this chapter focus on these three theories as they relate to understanding the determinants of exercise behavior in cancer survivors. A summary of the theoretical studies examining social-cognitive determinants of exercise in cancer survivors is presented in table 9.1.

TABLE 9.1

Summary of Theoretical Studies Examining Social-Cognitive Determinants of Exercise in Cancer Survivors

Authors	Sample	Design	Results
THEORY OF PLANNED BEHAVIOR			
Courneya & Friedenreich, 1997a	110 colorectal cancer survivors receiving treatment	Retrospective	Intention and perceived behavioral control were independent correlates of behavior ($R^2 = .22$), and attitude was an independent correlate of intention ($R^2 = .31$).
Courneya & Friedenreich, 1999	164 breast cancer survivors receiving treatment	Retrospective	Intention and perceived behavioral control were independent correlates of behavior ($R^2 = .14$), and attitude and subjective norm were independent correlates of intention ($R^2 = .23$).
Courneya et al., 1999	66 colorectal cancer survivors of which 73% were receiving treatment	Prospective	Intention was an independent predictor of behavior ($R^2 = .30$), and attitude was an independent correlate of intention ($R^2 = .23$).
Courneya et al., 2000	37 mixed cancer survivors receiving high-dose treatment	Prospective	Intention was an independent predictor of behavior ($R^2 = .14$), and attitude and perceived behavioral control were independent correlates of intention ($R^2 = .68$).
Courneya et al., 2001	24 posttreatment breast cancer survivors training for dragon boat racing	Prospective	Intention was an independent predictor of behavior ($R^2 = .35$), and subjective norm was an independent correlate of intention ($R^2 = .49$).
Blanchard et al., 2002	83 posttreatment breast cancer survivors and 46 posttreatment prostate cancer survivors	Cross-sectional	In breast cancer survivors, intention was an independent correlate of behavior ($R^2 = .32$), and attitude and perceived behavioral control were independent correlates of intention ($R^2 = .45$). In prostate cancer survivors, intention was an independent correlate of behavior ($R^2 = .37$), and perceived behavioral control was an independent correlate of intention ($R^2 = .36$).
Courneya et al., 2002	51 mixed cancer survivors randomized to a 10-week home-based exercise program	Prospective as part of an RCT	Independent predictors of exercise adherence were sex (male), extraversion, normative beliefs (–), and perceived behavioral control ($R^2 = .42$).

continued ▶

Authors	Sample	Design	Results
THEORY OF PLANNED BEHAVIOR (continued)			
Rhodes & Courneya, 2003	272 posttreatment mixed cancer survivors	Cross-sectional	Intention and perceived behavioral control were independent correlates of behavior (R^2 = .34), and affective attitude, subjective norm, and perceived behavioral control were independent correlates of intention (R^2 = .46).
Courneya et al., 2004	62 colorectal cancer survivors randomized to a 16-week home-based exercise program	Prospective as part of an RCT	Independent predictors of exercise adherences were exercise stage of change, employment status, treatment protocol, and perceived behavioral control (R^2 = .40).
Courneya et al., 2004	82 prostate cancer survivors randomized to a 12-week supervised exercise program	Prospective as part of an RCT	Independent predictors of exercise adherence were exercise stage of change, age (−), and intention (R^2 = .20).
Courneya et al., 2005	399 posttreatment non-Hodgkin's lymphoma survivors	Cross-sectional	Affective attitude, subjective norm, and perceived behavioral control were independent correlates of intention (R^2 = .55).
Jones, Courneya, et al., 2006	70 posttreatment multiple myeloma survivors	Cross-sectional	Affective attitude, instrumental attitude, and perceived behavioral control were independent correlates of intention (R^2 = .43).
Andrykowski et al., 2006	130 postdiagnosis breast cancer survivors	Cross-sectional	Subjective norm, attitude, and intention were independent correlates of behavior (R^2 = .42).
Karvinen, Courneya, Campbell, et al., 2007	354 posttreatment endometrial cancer survivors	Cross-sectional	Intention was an independent correlate of behavior (R^2 = .24), and affective attitude and self-efficacy were independent correlates of intention (R^2 = .38).
Keats et al., 2007	118 adolescent cancer survivors	Cross-sectional	Intention and self-efficacy were independent correlates of behavior (R^2 = .29), and affective attitude and instrumental attitude were independent correlates of intention (R^2 = .34).
Jones, Guill, et al., 2006	100 brain tumor survivors receiving treatment	Prospective	Affective attitude and perceived behavioral control were independent correlates of intentions (R^2 = .32).
Karvinen et al., 2009	397 posttreatment bladder cancer survivors	Cross-sectional	Intentions, perceived behavioral control, and planning were independent correlates of behavior (R^2 = .21), and affective attitude, perceived behavioral control, instrumental attitude, and descriptive norms were independent correlates of intentions (R^2 = .39).
Stevinson, Tonkin, et al., 2009	359 posttreatment ovarian cancer survivors	Cross-sectional	Instrumental attitude, affective attitude, and perceived behavioral control were independent correlates of intention (R^2 = .39), and intention was an independent correlate of behavior (R^2 = .36).

Authors	Sample	Design	Results
SOCIAL-COGNITIVE THEORY			
Rogers et al., 2005	21 breast cancer survivors undergoing treatment	Retrospective	Higher average of steps per day was significantly associated with having a breast cancer exercise role model (r = .56) and higher annual income (r = .61). Higher daily energy expenditure was significantly associated with higher barrier self-efficacy (r = .62), higher task self-efficacy (r = .77), having an exercise partner (r = .71), and having a breast cancer exercise role model (r = .74).
Rogers, Courneya, et al., 2008	59 head and neck cancer survivors	Cross-sectional	Strongest correlates of behavior were task self-efficacy (r = .33) and perceived barriers (r = −.27).
Rogers, McAuley, et al., 2008	192 posttreatment breast cancer survivors	Cross-sectional	Behavior was correlated with barrier self-efficacy (r = .27), task self-efficacy (r = .36), perceived barriers (r = −.24), and social support (r = .38).
Coups et al., 2009	175 early stage lung cancer survivors	Cross-sectional	SCT variables explained 38% of the variance in self-report PA and 19% of the variance in leisurely walking. In particular, significant predictors that emerged in both the PA and walking models were outcome expectations.
SELF-DETERMINATION THEORY			
Milne et al., 2008	558 posttreatment breast cancer survivors	Cross-sectional	Identified regulation, competence, and autonomy support were independent predictors of behavior (R^2 = .20). Survivors meeting exercise guidelines reported more identified regulations and intrinsic motivation, autonomy support, and competence.
Wilson, Blanchard, et al., 2006	220 mixed cancer survivors	Cross-sectional	Autonomous motives and controlled motives were independent predictors of behavior (R^2 = .07).
Peddle, Plotnikoff et al., 2008	414 posttreatment colorectal cancer survivors	Cross-sectional	Identified regulation and introjected regulation were independent predictors of behavior (R^2 = .16).

Theory of Planned Behavior

The theory of planned behavior (TPB) (Ajzen, 1991) (see figure 9.3) is a widely used and validated model for predicting and explaining exercise motivation and behavior in cancer survivors. The traditional TPB model postulates that intention is the most important determinant of behavior. Intention is, in turn, determined by subjective norm, attitude, and perceived behavioral control. Recently, TPB theorists have suggested that each TPB component is better represented by two specific subcomponents (Rhodes & Courneya, 2003). Subjective norm measures the perceptions of social pressure to perform the behavior and includes the more traditionally measured injunctive component (e.g., whether important others approve of the person performing the behavior) and a descriptive component (e.g., whether important others perform the behavior themselves). Attitude reflects the individual's overall evaluations of performing the behavior and is composed of instrumental (e.g., harmful or beneficial) and affective (e.g., unenjoyable or enjoyable) components. Perceived behavioral control reflects the degree of personal control that the individual has over performing the behavior and is composed of self-efficacy (e.g., ease or difficulty, confidence) and controllability (e.g., personal control over behavior).

The TPB also proposes that attitude, subjective norm, and PBC are composed of underlying accessible beliefs in an expectancy-value formulation (Ajzen, 1991). Subjective norm is influenced by normative beliefs, which refer to the specific individuals who may approve or disapprove of the behavior and perform or not perform the behavior themselves. Attitude is determined by behavioral beliefs, which consist of perceived advantages and disadvantages of participating in the behavior and the factors that make the behavior enjoyable or unenjoyable. Finally, perceived behavioral control is a function

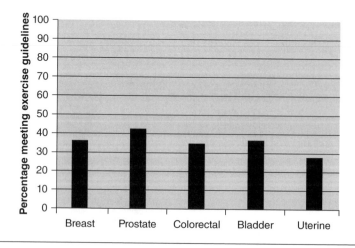

FIGURE 9.1 Percentage of various cancer survivor groups (N = 8,344) meeting public health exercise guidelines.

Data are from Blanchard, Courneya, Stein. 2008.

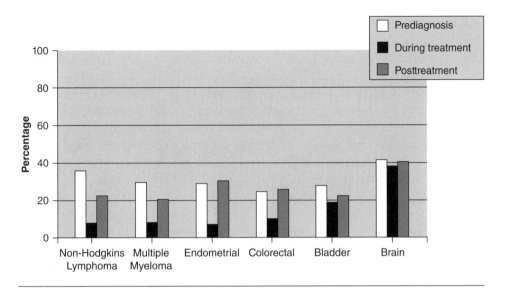

FIGURE 9.2   Percentage of various cancer survivor groups (N = 1,310) meeting public health exercise guidelines.

Data from Vallance et al. 2005; Jones et al. 2004; Courneya et al. 2005; Peddle, Au and Courneya 2005; Jones et al. 2006.

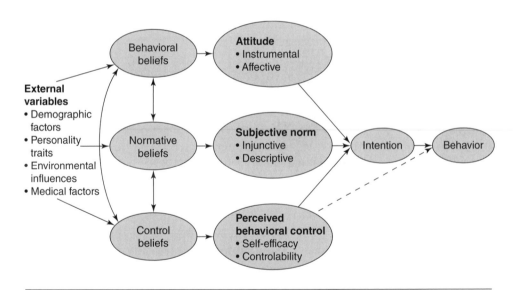

FIGURE 9.3   Two-component model of the theory of planned behavior.

of control beliefs, which refer to the degree of perceived opportunities and resources that the individual has for performing the behavior.

Several cross-sectional studies have demonstrated support for using the TPB as a model for understanding the determinants of exercise motivation and behavior in a variety of cancer groups. Cancer survivor groups that have been studied include breast (both during and posttreatment), colorectal, non-Hodgkin's lymphoma, multiple myeloma, brain, pediatric, endometrial, bladder, ovarian, and prostate cancers (Blanchard, Courneya, Rodgers, & Murnaghan, 2002; Courneya & Friedenreich, 1997a, 1999; Courneya, Vallance, Jones, & Reiman, 2005; Jones, Courneya, et al., 2006; Jones, Guill, et al., 2007b; Karvinen, Courneya, Campbell, et al., 2007; Karvinen et al., 2009; Keats, Culos-Reed, Courneya, & McBride, 2007; Stevinson, Tonkin, et al., 2009). Although earlier studies focused on breast and colorectal cancer survivors, more recent studies are exploring lesser studied survivor groups such as pediatric, ovarian, and bladder cancer survivors. In one of the earlier published studies, Courneya and Friedenreich (1999) examined the utility of the TPB in understanding breast cancer survivors' motivation to exercise during treatment for breast cancer. Survivors (N = 164) retrospectively recalled their beliefs and exercise behavior while they were on treatment. Results indicated that the TPB variables (i.e., attitude, subjective norm, perceived behavioral control) explained 23% of the variance in intention (i.e., exercise motivation). Further, intention to exercise explained 10% of the variance in exercise behavior, and significant contributions came from attitude (β = .29) and subjective norm (β = .30).

It appears, however, that the strength of the TPB variables with respect to predicting exercise intentions and behavior varies across tumor groups. For example, Courneya, Vallance, et al. (2005) found the TPB to explain 55% of the variance in intentions in a large sample (N = 399) of non-Hodgkin's lymphoma survivors. The most important predictors that emerged in this model were perceived behavioral control (β = .47), affective attitude (β = .23), and subjective norm (β =.15). Across the aforementioned published studies, the percentage of variance in exercise intentions explained by the TPB model ranged between 23% and 55%. The TPB has also been shown to be useful in explaining exercise behavior in cancer survivors because the percentage of explained variance ranged from 29% to 34%.

Perhaps it is most interesting to note that unique determinants emerge across the different tumor groups, leading to the argument that a person surviving one type of cancer (e.g., non-Hodgkin's lymphoma) may have different attitudes and beliefs about exercise than a person surviving a different type of cancer (e.g., endometrial cancer). For example, subjective norm (perceptions of social pressure to perform the behavior) emerges as a significant predictor of exercise intentions (i.e., exercise motivation) in the breast cancer (β = .30) (Courneya, Friedenreich, Arthur, & Bobick, 1999), bladder cancer (β = .10) (Karvinen et al., 2009), and non-Hodgkin's lymphoma (β = .15) (Courneya, Vallance, et al., 2005) survivor populations. The subjective norm component does not emerge as a significant predictor of exercise intentions in any of the other cancer survivor groups. But the attitude component (i.e., affective or instrumental attitude) emerges as a significant predictor of exercise intentions across all cancer survivor groups studied. These studies provide some confirmation that the TPB may be an effective model for examining the cognitive antecedents of exercise behavior in cancer survivors. But the constructs that made the most important contributions to predicting exercise intentions and behavior do appear to vary by cancer survivor group. These results provide a strong rationale for developing exercise programs and resources for specific cancer survivor groups that are relevant and targeted to the unique determinants observed in each survivor population.

When applying the TPB to understanding exercise behavior, most studies report that both perceived behavioral control (self-efficacy) and exercise intentions were significant predictors of exercise behavior (see table 9.1). But one study also found that planning (β =.12) was a significant predictor of exercise behavior (Karvinen et al., 2009). A criticism of the TPB is its failure to account for how motivational intentions (volitional phase) can translate into actual behavior (deliberative phase) (i.e., "the intention–behavior gap"). TPB theorists propose that intentions to perform a behavior will more likely translate into behavior when implementation intentions are garnered (Gollwitzer, 1999; Sheeran, Webb, & Gollwitzer, 2005). Implementation intentions (such as planning) propose that successful behavior change is facilitated by furnishing the intention with an if-then plan specifying when, where, how, and how often the individual will perform the behavior (Sheeran et al., 2005). Previous research has demonstrated the beneficial effects of formulating an implementation intention by action planning on exercise behavior change in various populations (Luszczynska, 2006; Milne, Orbell, & Sheeran, 2002; Walsh, da Fonseca, & Banta, 2005).

It is well known that the health benefits of exercise can be attained only by engaging in regular and sustained exercise (i.e., maintenance). Adhering to exercise during adjuvant therapy, as well as into survivorship, is difficult because of the stresses of a cancer diagnosis and the well-known side effects of the various treatments that cancer survivors may receive (e.g., surgery, chemotherapy) (Courneya, Segal, et al., 2008). To facilitate an understanding of factors affecting exercise adherence and maintenance, exercise oncology researchers have started to implement the TPB framework to determine the predictors of adherence to exercise behavior both during and after randomized trials examining the effects of exercise in various cancer survivor groups. For example, Courneya and colleagues examined the predictors of exercise adherence in (*a*) a randomized controlled trial (RCT) of home-based exercise in colorectal cancer survivors (Courneya et al., 2004) and (*b*) an RCT of exercise in a mixed group of cancer survivors participating in group psychotherapy classes (Courneya, Friedenreich, Sela, Quinney, & Rhodes, 2002). In both studies, perceived behavioral control emerged as significant independent predictors of exercise adherence during the trials. These findings suggest that exercisers in an RCT have a new and uniform intention to follow, which may allow PBC to influence their exercise behavior (Courneya et al., 2004).

Although research has explored the role of exercise across all phases of the cancer trajectory (e.g., prediagnosis, during treatment, posttreatment, survival, palliation), only recently have investigations explored the effect of pretreatment (presurgery) exercise training on posttreatment health outcomes

(Jones, Peddle, et al., 2007). In the first study to examine social-cognitive correlates of exercise adherence before surgical resection (i.e., pretreatment) in a sample of cancer survivors, Peddle and colleagues (2009) found that lung cancer survivors with greater than 80% exercise adherence to the exercise intervention (during their surgical wait time) reported significantly higher PBC than did survivors with less than 80% exercise adherence. Although components of the TPB appear to lend understanding to exercise behavior during RCTs before the initiation of treatment, as well as after treatments are completed, motivational constructs from the TPB appear to have a minimal predictive ability when applied to exercise behavior during chemotherapy. For example, Courneya, Segal, and colleagues (2008) reported that exercise adherence during a randomized trial of aerobic and resistance training during adjuvant chemotherapy for breast cancer was predicted by disease stage, aerobic fitness, and depression but not social-cognitive variables (i.e., TPB constructs). Adherence to exercise during chemotherapy may be more affected by uncontrollable factors such as treatment toxicities or psychological distress that is associated with the chemotherapy trajectory (Courneya et al., 2009). Nonetheless, introducing strategies to facilitate cancer survivors PBC (i.e., self-efficacy, controllability, confidence) may lead to enhanced adherence to the exercise program. Ultimately, maximizing exercise adherence may facilitate the realization and accrual of the associated health outcomes associated with regular and sustained exercise.

Social-Cognitive Theory

Studies are emerging in the exercise and cancer literature providing support for Bandura's social-cognitive theory (SCT) (Bandura, 2000) as another social-cognitive model that can be used to explain exercise behavior in cancer survivors. SCT is based on the concept of reciprocal determinism among behavior, the person, and the environment. Self-efficacy is considered the key organizing construct within SCT and is defined as "beliefs in one's capabilities to organize and execute the courses of action required to produce given levels of attainment" (Bandura, 2000, p. 300). Self-efficacy is theorized to influence the activities that people choose to approach, the effort expended on such activities, and the degree of persistence in the face of failure or obstacles (Bandura, 1986). Self-efficacy is often composed of barrier self-efficacy and task self-efficacy (Maddux, 1995). Barrier self-efficacy is defined as confidence in the ability to overcome barriers to behavior performance. Task self-efficacy is defined as confidence in the ability to perform the constituent components of the task.

Another important construct in SCT is outcome expectation, which refers to the expected outcomes associated with the performance of a behavior. Outcome expectations serve as incentives or disincentives, depending on whether the anticipated outcomes are positive or negative. Bandura described three main categories of outcomes expectations labeled physical, social, and self-evaluative (Bandura, 2000). Physical outcome expectations include the physical effects of a behavior such as pain, injury, and disease risk. Social outcomes include anticipated social reactions toward the behavior such as disapproval. Self-evaluative outcome expectations focus on a person's own reaction to performing a given behavior (e.g., guilty, proud, embarrassed).

Most studies to date have implemented the SCT framework with samples of breast cancer survivors both on and off treatment (Pinto et al., 2002; Rogers et al., 2005, 2006; Rogers, McAuley, Courneya, & Verhulst, 2008). These studies all report positive associations between exercise behavior and barrier and task self-efficacy, self-efficacy, outcome expectations, and social support. Single studies have also explored the SCT framework in samples of head and neck cancer survivors (Coups et al., 2009; Rogers, Courneya, et al., 2008) and lung cancer survivors. In a sample of 59 head and neck cancer survivors, Rogers, Courneya, et al. (2008) found an independent association between exercise behavior and task self-efficacy. And in the most rigorous test of SCT to date in a cancer survivor population, Coups and colleagues (2009) surveyed 175 lung cancer survivors and reported that SCT variables explained 38% of the variance in self-report PA and 19% of the variance in leisurely walking. In particular, significant predictors emerging in both the PA and walking models were outcome expectations and self-efficacy. These studies provide support for some of the SCT variables, most notably self-efficacy. Given this evidence, researchers developing exercise interventions and programs based on SCT clearly need to target self-efficacy given the consistent relationship with exercise behavior across the studies. Similar to what is seen in the aforementioned TPB literature, the relative contribution of each SCT construct appears to be inconsistent, although this may be a function of the cancer type, treatments, age, or other health indicators (e.g., BMI, comorbidities). Regardless, more studies are needed that provide an evaluation of the complete SCT framework as opposed to single SCT constructs.

Self-Determination Theory

Our ability to comprehend and understand the factors that facilitate or impede cancer survivors in their exercise pursuits is limited (Wilson, Blanchard, Nehl, & Baker, 2006). In response, a growing body of literature in the exercise oncology field has started to explore the utility of other theoretical frameworks to provide a more complete understanding of exercise behavior in this population. One theoretical framework that is garnering attention is self-determination theory (SDT) (Deci & Ryan, 2002a). SDT is a theory of human motivation that postulates that an individual's motivation to engage in activities (e.g., exercise, healthy eating, smoking) lies along a continuum ranging from the activity being completely controlled by external forces (e.g., other people, incentives) to activities that are fully self-determined (e.g., done for enjoyment of the activity, personal importance). Furthermore, SDT theorizes that people have three fundamental needs, including (*a*) competence (an individual's ability to experience mastery at challenging tasks), (*b*) relatedness (degree to which an individual feels connected to others in his or her environment), and (*c*) autonomy (i.e., self-determination) (how controlled an individual perceives his or her choices to be) (Deci & Ryan, 2002a; see also Standage & Ryan, this volume; Ntoumanis, this volume).

To date, three studies have explored the utility of the SDT framework in explaining exercise behavior in cancer survivors (H.M. Milne, Wallman, Guilfoyle, Gordon, & Courneya, 2008; Peddle, Plotnikoff, Wild, Au, & Courneya, 2008; Wilson, Blanchard et al., 2006). The largest study to date examined the constructs of autonomy support and competence and their role in understanding exercise behavior in a sample of 558 breast cancer survivors (H.M. Milne et al., 2008). Data from this study indicated that breast cancer survivors who regularly exercised reported more intrinsic motivation, autonomy support, and competence. Overall, the SDT constructs explained 20.2% of the variance in exercise behavior, and significant independent predictors included identified regulation (e.g., behavior is motivated by personal goals) ($\beta = .14$), competence ($\beta = .23$), and autonomy ($\beta = .09$). In the most recent application of the SDT framework to cancer survivors' exercise behavior, Peddle, Plotnikoff, and colleagues (2008) examined correlates of exercise behavior in a sample of 414 colorectal cancer survivors and reported that 28% of the variance in exercise behavior was explained by the SDT constructs. Specifically, introjected regulation (e.g., behavior is done out of self-imposed pressure) ($\beta = .15$) and identified regulation ($\beta = .17$) demonstrated independent associations with exercise behavior. Finally, in a sample of mixed cancer survivors (N = 220), Wilson and colleagues (Wilson, Blanchard, et al. 2006) found that the SDT framework accounted for only a small portion of the variance in exercise behavior.

Given the relatively small number of studies exploring the SDT framework in the cancer and exercise context, conclusions regarding the utility of the SDT framework are tentative. Intuitively, it is reasonable to speculate that progressing cancer survivors along the motivational continuum toward more self-determined directives may cause more cancer survivors to engage in regular and sustained exercise behavior, thus realizing the health benefits associated with such activity. To date, no published studies have evaluated this contention.

Exercise Beliefs Among Cancer Survivors

Several studies have elicited the beliefs and barriers regarding exercise behavior across a variety of cancer survivor groups. Eliciting underlying beliefs about exercise behavior is critical in the development of any exercise behavior change intervention. According to Ajzen (2009a, p. 2), behavioral interventions must try to change the beliefs that ultimately guide performance of the behavior.

Fishbein further advocates identifying salient beliefs from the intended population, developing persuasive messages around the beliefs, and then developing suitable and appropriate materials based on and developed around the elicited beliefs (Fishbein, von Haeften, & Appleyard, 2001). For this reason, identifying the salient beliefs and barriers from different cancer survivor groups has practical utility in the effort to facilitate exercise behavior change.

Although earlier research focused on common cancers such as breast and colorectal (Courneya & Friedenreich, 1997b, 1997c), more recent research has examined larger and less-studied cancer survivor groups (Courneya, Vallance, et al., 2005; Karvinen, Courneya, Campbell, et al., 2007; Stevinson, Tonkin, et al., 2009). For example, Stevinson and colleagues surveyed 359 ovarian cancer survivors and asked them to recall the major benefits and barriers to exercise during their treatments. The main benefits of exercise that were reported were (*a*) improved physical health, (*b*) better control of body weight, (*c*) increased energy, (*d*) increased aerobic fitness, (*e*) felt better, (*f*) increased muscle tone and strength, and (*g*) improved psychological well-being. The main exercise barriers in this group were (*a*) lack of time, (*b*) lack of motivation, (*c*) fatigue, (*d*) arthritis or bad joints, (*e*) health problems, (*f*) lack of facilities, and (*g*) too sick. These results indicate many unique exercise motives and barriers that are based on the cancer experience. In a similar study design, Courneya and colleagues surveyed 399 non-Hodgkin's lymphoma survivors (Courneya, Vallance, et al., 2005). Survivors were asked to list what they believed were the main advantages of exercise after their cancer diagnosis and the main factors that made it easier or more difficult for them to exercise during their cancer care. The most common perceived advantages of exercise were that it leads to (*a*) a positive mental attitude, (*b*) better muscular strength and tone, (*c*) improved aerobic fitness and endurance, (*d*) a sense of well-being, (*e*) increased energy, (*f*) improved circulation, and (*g*) stress relief. The seven most common perceived barriers to exercise in this population were (*a*) a lack of energy or fatigue, (*b*) being too deconditioned or too weak, (*c*) nausea, (*d*) pain, (*e*) feeling ill, (*f*) a lack of motivation or laziness, and (*g*) depression.

Although several of the exercise beliefs and barriers are consistent across tumor groups (e.g., physical and psychological health benefits), several beliefs and barriers appear to be unique to specific cancer survivor groups. For example, the finding that weight loss is the most commonly reported benefit of exercise in the endometrial cancer population is consistent with the high obesity rate in this population. Further, the finding that deconditioning or weakness was the second most commonly identified barrier in non-Hodgkin's lymphoma survivors is consistent with common clinical observations of this population. The rationale for eliciting beliefs and barriers to each tumor group is strengthened when considering less prevalent cancers given the unique treatments and side effects that cancer survivors from these groups may experience. For example, Rogers and colleagues (Rogers, Courneya, et al., 2008) reported that head and neck cancer survivors' most common barriers to exercise included (*a*) dry mouth or throat, (*b*) drainage in mouth or throat, (*c*) pain, (*d*) difficulty swallowing, (*e*) difficulty breathing, (*f*) shoulder weakness, and (*g*) cough. In a pediatric and adolescent cancer survivor sample, Keats and colleagues (2007) found that the most common perceived advantages of exercise were (*a*) keeping physically fit, (*b*) looking good, (*c*) having fun, (*d*) recovering from treatment, (*e*) staying connected with friends, and (*f*) feeling normal. Clearly, an exercise behavior change intervention for ovarian cancer survivors should be different from an intervention for head and neck survivors. For any exercise behavior change intervention for these survivor groups, it would be prudent to elicit, consider, and incorporate the unique exercise beliefs and barriers salient to each survivor population.

Not surprisingly, exercise motives and barriers also vary by treatment status. Barriers to exercise during treatment often reflect the well-known side effects of treatments (e.g., nausea, diarrhea, fatigue, depression), whereas barriers to exercise after treatments tend to realign with barriers in the general population (e.g., lack of time, too busy). For example, Courneya and Friedenreich (1997a; Courneya et al., 1999) asked breast and colorectal cancer survivors to recall the major benefits and barriers to exercise during their treatments. The main benefits of exercise that were reported were (*a*) getting mind off cancer and treatment, (*b*) feeling better and improving well-being, (*c*) maintaining a normal lifestyle, (*d*) coping with the stress of cancer and treatment, (*e*) gaining control over cancer and life, (*f*) recovering from surgery and treatment, and (*g*) controlling weight. The main exercise barriers in this group were (*a*) nausea, (*b*) fatigue or tiredness, (*c*) no time to exercise, (*d*) no support for exercise, (*e*) pain or soreness, (*f*) no counseling for exercise, and (*g*) working at a regular job. Behavior change efforts must be targeted not only to the specific tumor group but also to the survivor's status along the cancer trajectory (e.g., pretreatment, treatment, posttreatment, palliation).

Overall, these studies indicate that cancer survivors have diverse motives and barriers to exercise, some of which are unique to the cancer experience and some of which are common to other populations. It is also apparent that exercise motives and barriers vary by cancer survivor group, reflecting the unique profile of the particular disease. Understanding the beliefs and barriers in various cancer survivor populations can lead to the development of targeted and relevant exercise behavior change interventions for cancer survivors. Ultimately, these interventions must consider the unique factors that may affect exercise behavior in the cancer survivor population under study.

Practical Applications

Research implementing social-cognitive frameworks to understand exercise behavior in cancer survivors provides strong evidence that using some of these frameworks may be an effective strategy for developing practical interventions aimed at promoting PA after a cancer diagnosis. Although research to support this contention is still sparse, exercise behavior change interventions using social-cognitive frameworks within the cancer survivor context are now emerging. There are multiple advantages to developing and evaluating theoretically framed exercise behavior change interventions. Theory can be used not only to inform the behavioral intervention but also to facilitate identification of the active ingredients of the intervention (Pinto & Floyd, 2008). In other words, application of behavioral theories can assist researchers in understanding the mechanisms through which people change (or do not change) their behavior. Theory-based mediating variables in randomized controlled trials may potentially play an important role in understanding the pathways to behavior change (Rejeski, Brawley, McAuley, & Rapp, 2000).

To date, only a few published studies have examined the effects of theoretically based exercise behavior change strategies in cancer survivors. The Oncologist Recommendation to Exercise (ONCORE) Trial was a trial that examined the effects of two oncologist-centered interventions on self-reported exercise behavior in breast cancer survivors beginning treatment (Jones, Courneya, Fairey, & Mackey, 2004). Developed within the theoretical tenets of the TPB, newly diagnosed breast cancer survivors were randomized to receive either (*a*) an oncologist's recommendation to exercise, (*b*) an oncologist's recommendation to exercise plus a referral to a kinesiologist, and (*c*) usual care (i.e., no recommendation). Results of this study indicated that participants who received an exercise recommendation reported more exercise than those who received usual care. Follow-up analysis exploring the effects of the TPB constructs on exercise behavior indicated that perceived behavioral control had a direct effect on exercise behavior. Furthermore, attitude, subjective norm, and perceived behavioral control had direct effects on intention. The authors noted, however, that the initial treatment consultation may not be the opportune time to recommend exercise given the amount of information dispensed during this time and the stress level of the cancer survivor. Nonetheless, this trial suggests that advocating exercise behavior through an oncologist's recommendation framed around the theoretical tenets of the TPB may be an efficient and practical mode of promoting exercise in cancer survivors.

We recently explored the effects of a TPB-based intervention resource on exercise behavior and health outcomes in a large sample of breast cancer survivors by developing a 62-page theoretically based exercise guidebook designed exclusively for breast cancer survivors, titled *Exercise for Health: An Exercise Guide for Breast Cancer Survivors* (Vallance, Courneya, Taylor, Plotnikoff, & Mackey, 2008). This guidebook is based on the theoretical components of the TPB. The information in the exercise guidebook was formulated and written based on the varying theoretical beliefs that have been elicited from breast cancer survivors in previous research (Courneya, Blanchard, & Laing, 2001; Courneya, Jones, Mackey, & Fairey, 2006). The guidebook was also based on previous research examining the exercise preferences of breast cancer survivors (Jones & Courneya, 2002). The guidebook consisted of 10 chapters and includes participant-centered activities designed to enhance attitude (i.e., instrumental and affective attitudes), subjective norm (i.e., injunctive and descriptive norms), perceived behavioral control (i.e., self-efficacy and controllability), and implementation intentions (e.g., goal setting, planning) pertaining to PA. Before implementation, we rigorously evaluated our guidebook for its theoretical merit, suitability, and readability. We previously reported empirical evidence that our guidebook indeed targeted the TPB components and was suitable and appropriate for use in the breast cancer survivor population (Vallance, Courneya, Taylor, et al., 2008).

The *Exercise for Health* guidebook was then part of an intervention designed to increase exercise behavior in breast cancer survivors (Vallance, Courneya, Plotnikoff, Yasui, & Mackey, 2007). The Activity Promotion (ACTION) Trial was a randomized controlled trial designed to determine the effects of the theoretically based exercise guidebook (PM) (i.e., *Exercise for Health: An Exercise Guide for Breast Cancer Survivors*), a step pedometer (PED), or their combination (COM) on exercise behavior, HRQoL, and fatigue in breast cancer survivors compared to a group receiving a standard verbal public health recommendation for exercise (SR). At the 3-month postintervention assessment, the theoretically based exercise print materials and step pedometers were effective strategies for increasing exercise behavior (both individually and in combination), enhancing HRQoL, and reducing fatigue symptoms in breast cancer survivors. Specifically, moderate- to vigorous-intensity exercise increased by about 40 to 60 minutes per week in the intervention groups compared to the SR group, and brisk walking increased by about 60 to 90 minutes per week. The COM group also reported significantly better HRQoL and reduced fatigue compared with the SR group. In terms of long-term maintenance, the intervention groups reported 30 to 60 minutes per week more exercise and 35 to 50 minutes per week more brisk walking compared to the SR group (Vallance, Courneya, Plotnikoff, Dinu, & Mackey, 2008). This difference of 30 to 60 minutes per week of exercise is equivalent to 1 to 2 extra days of exercise per week.

In examining the possible theoretical mechanisms of our exercise behavior change findings (Vallance, Courneya, Plotnikoff, & Mackey, 2008), we noted that survivors receiving the TPB-based interventions (i.e., exercise guidebook) generally reported positive changes in the TPB constructs and beliefs compared to the SR group. Several of these effects were significant or borderline significant, including changes in instrumental attitude, injunctive norm, intention, and several specific behavioral and control beliefs. Changes in the TPB mediated the effects of our interventions on changes in exercise behavior. Overall, these results provided support for the use of the TPB as a framework for developing, implementing, and evaluating exercise behavior change interventions in breast cancer survivors.

Although researchers often state that their respective intervention materials are developed around a particular theory of behavior change, typically little or no evidence to support the theoretical basis of the intervention is provided. The ACTION Trial is the first exercise intervention trial to (*a*) document the development of the intervention material and evaluate its theoretical merit, (*b*) provide evidence of its effectiveness in facilitating behavior change and positive health outcomes, and (*c*) attempt to explain the underlying theoretical mechanisms of the PA behavior change.

Given that recent observational studies have shown that exercising after a colon cancer diagnosis is associated with a significant reduction in cancer recurrence and overall mortality, we recently reported the development and assessment of an exercise guidebook for colon cancer survivors called *Step Up to the Challenge* (Vallance, Lesniak, et al., 2010). This resource is being used to support a comprehensive TPB-based behavior change intervention in the Colon Health and Life Long Exercise Change Trial (CHALLENGE Trial) (Courneya, Booth, et al., 2008). The CHALLENGE trial is a randomized controlled trial examining exercise behavior and disease-free survival in colon cancer survivors.

Step Up to the Challenge was formulated and written based on salient PA beliefs (i.e., control, normative, and behavioral beliefs) that were elicited from colon cancer survivors in previous research (Courneya & Friedenreich, 1997a; Courneya, Friedenreich, et al., 2005). To be consistent with guidelines for developing TPB-based interventions, we used these salient beliefs and developed persuasive messages around those beliefs (Fishebein et al., 2001). The guidebook is one of the core resources in the behavioral intervention that includes (*a*) an emphasis on the unique benefits of PA for colon cancer survivors, (*b*) strategies for making PA enjoyable, (*c*) strategies for overcoming barriers, (*d*) ideas for securing support from family and friends, (*e*) techniques for identifying PA opportunities, (*f*) time management training, (*g*) goal-setting training, and (*h*) self-regulation (Courneya, Booth, et al., 2008). This guidebook will be provided to all colon cancer survivors randomized to the exercise intervention arm of the CHALLENGE trial. It is generally believed that exercise behavior change resources are most effective if they conform to the highest standards of suitability and appropriateness for the target population (Coulter, 1998). By rigorously evaluating the suitability and theoretical merit of our intervention guidebook (and making appropriate revisions), the likelihood is greater that the intervention guidebook is not only suitable for colon cancer survivors but also has high fidelity with the TPB framework based on the empirical evaluations of expert judges. Overall, results suggested that the exercise guidebook was suitable, appropriate, and theoretically faithful to the TPB. Given the theoretical basis of our guidebook (as in the ACTION Trial), we may be able to gain insight into the reasons colon cancer survivors change (or do not change) their exercise behavior. Ultimately, exercise behavior change resources (e.g., intervention or program resources) that are purported to be based on a theoretical framework need to be appropriately evaluated before implementation (and distribution) to (*a*) provide some assurance that the tools are indeed framed within the theoretical framework being used and (*b*) enhance the likelihood that the information in the resource can be applied to have a positive effect on health behavior (Vallance, Lesniak, et al., 2010).

In one of the lesser-studied cancer survivor groups, Keats and Culos-Reed (2009) recently examined the efficacy of a TPB-based intervention designed to facilitate exercise behavior in a group of pediatric cancer survivors. The TPB intervention was based on findings from a previously conducted elicitation study conducted by the authors (Keats et al., 2007). One component of the exercise intervention consisted of educational sessions targeted to the TPB variables of attitude, perceived behavioral control, subjective norm, and intentions. In brief, survivors met on a weekly basis for 16 weeks and participated in educational sessions, aerobic training, resistance training, and flexibility training. In analyzing the TPB variables, the authors reported that the intervention had a small yet meaningful effect on the TPB constructs, particularly behavioral intentions. Although both the Keats study (Keats & Culos-Reed, 2009) and the Vallance study (Vallance, Courneya, Plotnikoff, & Mackey, 2008) reported relatively high positive baseline values for all of the TPB constructs, it is important to recognize that the interventions were still able to influence these components. To expect substantial changes in these cognitive variables as a function of a minimal contact intervention using educational sessions or printed material as the primary modes of information delivery may be unrealistic. Ultimately, evaluating these interventions in a sample of less motivated survivors may provide a more thorough and robust test of the theoretical intervention.

Two randomized controlled trials conducted by Demark-Wahnefried and her colleagues (2006, 2007) using the SCT framework have recently been published. These trials were designed to test whether various health behavior counseling methods affect exercise behavior and fruit and vegetable consumption in breast and prostate cancer survivors. The first trial, Project LEAD (Project Leading the Way in Education Against Disease) (Demark-Wahnefried et al., 2006; Demark-Wahnefried, Morey, et al., 2003) was the first trial to test whether a 6-month personally tailored telephone-counseling program was effective in improving diet and exercise behaviors in early stage breast and prostate cancer survivors. The experimental group received a mailed workbook and telephone counseling (tailored to stage of readiness) pertaining to overall diet and exercise behaviors. Intervention group participants received telephone-counseling calls of up to 30 minutes every 2 weeks for 6 months. The transtheoretical model and the SCT framework provided the behavioral framework for each counseling session (Demark-Wahnefried, Morey, et al., 2003). Survivors in the intervention arm of the trial reported significant changes in self-efficacy for exercise and exercise frequency. Although not statistically significant, the intervention arm also showed improvements in physical functioning.

Demark-Wahnefried et al. (2007) also recently completed and published results from the FRESH START trial (a randomized trial of activity and diet among cancer survivors). The FRESH START trial was designed to evaluate the efficacy and effectiveness of personally tailored print materials in promoting lifestyle changes in breast and prostate cancer survivors. Survivors in the intervention group received the FRESH START intervention program, which consisted of a series of workbooks, newsletters, and update cards that were tailored based on information collected during a baseline interview. Similar to Project LEAD, the FRESH START trial intervention was also framed within the SCT framework (Demark-Wahnefried, Clipp, et al., 2003). In keeping with the SCT, survivors were encouraged to set small incremental goals. Achievement of these goals provided reinforcement to build self-efficacy. Survivors receiving the FRESH START intervention reported increases in goal-setting behavior and exercise minutes per week. These aforementioned studies will provide important initial information pertaining to the efficacy of exercise behavior interventions that are framed within the SCT framework.

More recently, Rogers and colleagues determined the feasibility and preliminary effectiveness of an SCT-based exercise behavior change intervention in 41 breast cancer survivors receiving hormonal therapy (Rogers, Hopkins-Price, Vicari, Markwell, et al., 2009). The exercise behavior change intervention consisted of group and individual sessions. Survivors attended multiple discussion group sessions with a clinical psychologist, who encouraged social support, provided breast cancer survivor exercise role models, and covered the following topics: journaling, time management, stress management, dealing with exercise barriers, and behavior modification. The specific SCT constructs addressed by the group sessions included self-efficacy, emotional coping, reciprocal determinism, perceived barriers, outcome expectations, behavioral capability, goal setting, environment, observational learning, and self-control. A series of individual face-to-face sessions targeted self-efficacy, outcome expectations, behavioral capability, perceived barriers, and goal setting with self-monitoring. Differences favoring the intervention group were reported for accelerometer exercise counts (i.e., objective exercise behavior measure) and aerobic fitness. The effects of the intervention on exercise behavior were maintained at 3 months postintervention (Rogers, Hopkins-Price, Vicari, Markwell, et al., 2009). In a sample of endometrial cancer survivors, von Gruenigen et al. (2009) also found that individual and group exercise counseling based on self-efficacy and building short-term goals were effective in facilitating exercise behavior. But the potential mediating role of the SCT components in these intervention effects needs to be explored. A more thorough understanding of the SCT constructs that may be responsible for these effects on exercise behavior would enable researchers and practitioners to develop targeted behavior change interventions aimed at enhancing exercise behavior in the cancer survivor population.

In summary, these trial results indicate that the TPB and SCT provide reasonable theoretical frameworks on which to base exercise behavior change interventions (e.g., print, physician-delivered, lifestyle) in cancer survivors and further explain their effectiveness. But further evaluative inquiry is needed to establish stronger support for the use of the TPB as a framework for developing, implementing, and evaluating exercise behavior change interventions in cancer survivors. Research into factors that help cancer survivors become lifelong exercisers may ultimately result in better HRQoL, reduced risk of recurrence, and longer survival for millions of cancer survivors. Staging these efforts within a theoretical framework appears to be one effective way to encourage and facilitate the adoption and maintenance of exercise behavior in various cancer survivor groups.

Directions for Future Research

Research into exercise motivation and behavior change in cancer survivors is just beginning, and we still need answers to many basic questions. Therefore, in terms of descriptive behavioral epidemiology, we need more studies documenting the exercise patterns and prevalence rates of cancer survivors from different tumor groups. These studies should include the type, frequency, duration, and intensity of the exercises. There is also growing interest in the study of sedentary behavior as a behavioral risk factor. Future studies should include sedentary behavior to gain a more complete and comprehensive activity and behavior profile of the individual. Consequently, studies can then explore the primary determinants of sedentary behavior in the cancer survivor population. Ultimately, a more complete evaluation of social-cognitive-based interventions that includes survivors who have less favorable beliefs than the already motivated samples may result in larger cognitive and behavior changes. Future trials should be more proactive at recruiting less motivated survivors to avoid these possible ceiling effects and to provide a deeper understanding regarding the utility of theoretical models in facilitating exercise behavior change in the cancer context. As another example, we need research on the determinants of walking for exercise because walking is the most popular form of exercise for cancer survivors. We also need research on resistance exercise, which has largely been neglected in the exercise oncology domain but is gaining support as a critical component of exercise for health and function in breast and prostate cancer survivors (Courneya et al., 2007; Schmitz et al., 2009; Segal et al., 2003).

Determinants research is also needed for all the various cancer-related periods (e.g., pretreatment, on various treatments, posttreatment, long-term survivors). In particular, given that we are starting to see specific exercise interventions targeted at particular time points across the cancer trajectory (e.g., postsurgery, during adjuvant chemotherapy, long-term survivorship), understanding the determinants of exercise behavior will facilitate the development of more targeted, appropriate, and relevant interventions and programs for these time points.

Future research exploring exercise determinants across the cancer context should examine a wider spectrum of exercise determinants that includes medical, demographic, and behavioral variables, as well as other factors such as the physical environment, culture, personality, and policy. The social ecological approach may be one such framework within which to study the multiple factors that may affect a survivor's exercise behavior. The social ecological approach provides a framework to examine the multiple effects and interrelatedness of various factors (e.g., social, biological, personal, environmental) at all levels of influence (i.e., individual, interpersonal, organizational, community, and society). Given that most research to date has applied the TPB as a framework for understanding social-cognitive components of exercise in cancer survivors, researchers should more rigorously examine other theories of health behavior to discover what theoretical frameworks are the most effective to use with cancer survivors. If deemed suitable, these determinants should be used as the basis for exercise and health promotion strategies. Only after these variables are explored and considered will we have a more thorough understanding of (*a*) the determinants of exercise in cancer survivors and (*b*) best practice for assisting cancer survivors in achieving the adequate dose of exercise necessary for health benefits.

With respect to theoretically based exercise behavior change interventions, researchers must rigorously evaluate the theoretical merit of their behavior change strategies before implementing evaluative efforts such as randomized controlled trials. Exercise behavior change research in cancer survivors needs to be informed by exercise determinants research. Given that exercise determinants research should be guided by theory, exercise behavior change interventions should also be guided by theory. Beyond the utility of a theory for the development of a behavior change intervention, the assessment of a theoretical model during an intervention also allows the determination of why a particular behavior change intervention either worked or did not work for a given cancer survivor group in a given context. This information can then be used in further refinement of the intervention.

We encourage researchers in the area of exercise behavior change across the cancer trajectory to publish empirical evidence providing adequate description and detail pertaining to the theoretical relevance and merit of the theoretically based intervention that they are implementing. In this chapter, we provide two examples of how we have incorporated theory into our intervention resources (Vallance, Courneya, Taylor, et al., 2008; Vallance, Lesniak, et al., 2010). Researchers need to continue to explore and evaluate the utility of the TPB, as well as other social-cognitive theories, in the development and evaluation of such materials. Although most research to date has explored the TPB as a framework in which to understand and facilitate exercise behavior, there clearly is a role for the implementation of other social-cognitive theories. For more complete understanding of exercise behavior in cancer survivors, researchers need to continue the consideration of these theories in their research pursuits.

Summary

The rising number of cancer survivors has led to a need for exercise behavior change strategies and interventions that can potentially improve HRQoL and disease-free outcomes (e.g., survival, recurrence) in this population. With this has come increasing interest in the area of exercise as a possible means of alleviating some of the physical, functional, biological, and psychological impairments associated with the cancer experience. But the effectiveness of exercise as a supportive care intervention for cancer survivors depends largely on the motivation and adherence of participants to such a program. Based on the current evidence, cancer care professionals can expect that less than 10% of cancer survivors will exercise during treatments and between 20% and 30% will exercise after their treatments. These data indicate that unless exercise behavior change interventions are provided, most cancer survivors will not benefit from regular exercise. Strategies to assist cancer survivors in adopting and maintaining exercise can be developed based on current knowledge of the determinants of exercise in this population. The key point for cancer care and fitness professionals is that cancer survivors have unique incentives, barriers, and preferences for exercise that will need to be taken into account when developing creative intervention strategies for this population.

CHAPTER 10

Understanding Exercise Behavior: A Self-Presentational Perspective

Kathleen A. Martin Ginis, PhD
McMaster University

Diane Mack, PhD
Brock University

The impressions that we make on others have important implications for how we see ourselves, how other people treat us, and how successful we are at obtaining valued social and material outcomes (Leary & Kowalski, 1990). Consequently, people are often motivated to behave in ways that will create desired impressions in other people's eyes. The processes by which people monitor and control how they are perceived and evaluated by others are referred to as self-presentation, or impression management (Schlenker, 1980). These processes have been identified as a potential influence on motivation to engage in a wide variety of health-related behaviors (e.g., smoking, drug use, cancer screening, sunscreen use; for reviews see Leary, Tchividjian, & Kraxberger, 1994; Martin Ginis & Leary, 2004). In this chapter, we explore the role of self-presentation in motivation to exercise.

Background

Social psychologist Mark Leary sparked interest in self-presentation among exercise psychologists with an NASPSPA (North American Society for the Psychology of Sport & Physical Activity) address and companion paper that highlighted the pervasiveness and potency of self-presentational motives in physical activity settings (Leary, 1992). Leary argued that self-presentational processes could affect several aspects of physical activity, including exercise motivation. Before Leary's paper appeared, the self-presentational perspective was applied in only a few exercise studies. But since then, the self-presentational approach has been applied in dozens of studies to explain an array of exercise-related phenomena, such as exercise setting and attire preferences, adherence, and affective responses to acute exercise.

In 2004 the *Journal of Applied Sport Psychology* recognized the growing interest in this research area with a special issue on self-presentation in sport and exercise (Prapavessis, 2004). The special issue included narrative reviews of the literature on self-presentation and exercise participation and avoidance (Hausenblas et al., 2004; Martin Ginis & Leary, 2004). Consistent with Leary's (1992) perspective, both reviews concluded that self-presentation processes play a role in exercise motivation.

Subsequently, Martin Ginis and colleagues (Martin Ginis, Lindwall, & Prapavessis, 2007) used a generational approach (Zanna & Fazio, 1982) to review and categorize the physical activity and self-presentation literature. They classified studies according to whether they addressed first-, second-, or third-generation research questions (i.e., descriptive studies, studies of moderators, or studies of mediators, respectively) or measurement research questions. From their review, the authors concluded that the self-presentation and exercise research was predominately first generational. They also reported that most studies lacked any type of guiding theoretical framework, were one-offs that did not build on one another, and were contributing little to the development of theory. Characterizing the literature as "chaos in the brickyard" (Forscher,

1963), Martin Ginis and colleagues urged researchers to begin taking stock of "the bricks" by synthesizing the existing data to determine the nature of the relationships between self-presentational and physical activity variables (e.g., the relationship between social physique anxiety and exercise participation). A clearer understanding of these relationships would allow investigators to begin establishing much-needed, basic theoretical principles regarding the role of self-presentation in exercise motivation. As such, the first objective of our chapter is to synthesize what is known about the role of self-presentation in exercise motivation from both empirical and theoretical perspectives. A second purpose is to provide a framework for advancing theory-driven research and evidence-informed practical strategies for using self-presentation to enhance exercise motivation.

To address these objectives, we begin by reviewing the research on self-presentation and exercise motivation. Exercise motivation is generally conceptualized as persistence, effort, and choice. Persistence, the most common measure of motivation in the exercise psychology literature, is typically operationalized in terms of how much people exercise (e.g., average number of days per week of exercise, number of exercise classes attended). To a lesser extent, effort and choice have also been used as indices of exercise motivation. Effort is typically defined in terms of the intensity of exercise (e.g., heart rate during a workout, ratings of perceived exertion [RPE]), and choice is reflected in the types of exercise-related goals and activities that people choose to pursue (e.g., trying a new exercise class, joining a gym).

In this chapter, we summarize what is known about the relationship between self-presentation and each of these indices of motivation by drawing from previous narrative reviews (Hausenblas et al., 2004; Martin Ginis & Leary, 2004; Martin Ginis et al., 2007) and conducting our own qualitative syntheses of the literature. In addition, for topics with a substantive number of published studies, we conduct meta-analyses. Next, we review the theoretical frameworks that have been used to couch the study of self-presentation and exercise. The information and limitations gleaned from our literature and theory reviews are then used as the basis for developing a framework for guiding better theory-driven research on self-presentation and exercise motivation. Finally, we provide practical guidance for using what we know about self-presentation to enhance motivation.

Evidence

In their 2007 review, Martin Ginis et al. conducted comprehensive literature searches to identify published, English-language studies that addressed self-presentational phenomena within a physical activity context or that used a self-presentational approach or measures of self-presentational constructs to study physical activity phenomena. The studies were then grouped according to common themes and topics. The most frequently studied self-presentational variable in physical activity contexts was social physique anxiety (41% of retrieved studies), followed by impression motivation and construction (16% of studies) and self-presentational efficacy and confidence (8% of studies). As these topics capture the majority of the exercise and self-presentation literature, they are the focus of our review.

Social Physique Anxiety

Social physique anxiety (SPA) is anxiety experienced in response to the real or imagined evaluation of one's body by others (Hart, Leary, & Rejeski, 1989). SPA was originally conceptualized and measured as a dispositional characteristic. Consequently, most studies have looked at whether people's dispositional tendencies to experience SPA are associated with their exercise behavior. Although preliminary data indicate that SPA can also have situational manifestations and fluctuations, such that people experience varying levels of SPA across different situations (e.g., Carron & Prapavessis, 1997; Kruissel-brink et al., 2004), only a handful of studies have examined the relationship between state SPA and exercise.

SPA is, by far, the most studied self-presentational concept in exercise psychology. This trend can likely be attributed to the publication of Hart et al.'s (1989) seminal SPA paper in the *Journal of Sport & Exercise Psychology*. With the SPA concept and the accompanying Social Physique Anxiety Scale (Hart et al., 1989) rooted in the exercise psychology literature, exercise behavioral scientists enthusiastically embraced SPA as a variable of interest. Indeed, since 1989, dozens of studies have examined the relationship between SPA and exercise-related variables.

Persistence   Virtually all studies of SPA and exercise motivation have been cross-sectional investigations of the relationship between SPA and usual exercise behavior. Two narrative reviews have been conducted on this body of literature (Hausenblas et al., 2004; Martin Ginis et al., 2007), along with a meta-analysis comparing SPA in exercisers versus nonexercisers (Mack, Wilson, Waddell, & Gasparotto, 2008).

In the first review, Hausenblas et al. (2004) noted that researchers have generally found a small, negative association between SPA and exercise participation, such that people with greater SPA tend to exercise less. Consistent with this perspective, Mack and colleagues (2008) found that nonexercisers tended to have higher SPA than exercisers ($d = -.10$). The effect size was small, however, and the confidence intervals spanned zero, suggesting no statistically significant between-group differences. In the second narrative review, Martin Ginis et al. (2007) emphasized the inconsistency in the data. Some studies have found a positive relationship between SPA and physical activity, some have found a negative relationship, and others have found no relationship. Based on these findings, Martin Ginis et al. (2007) concluded that the SPA–exercise relationship is likely a moderated, rather than a direct, relationship. Depending on characteristics of the study sample (e.g., participants' sex, age, exercise experience) and the exercise itself (e.g., home based versus group based, health focused versus appearance focused), the strength and direction of the relationship could vary. For example, Treasure and colleagues (1998) found a strong, statistically significant negative relationship between SPA and exercise adherence in younger women but essentially no relationship among older women. Accordingly, Martin Ginis and colleagues (2007) urged researchers to focus efforts on exploring individual and situational moderators of this potentially complex relationship.

To explore the nature of the SPA–exercise relationship further, we conducted a meta-analysis of observational studies. The results of the individual studies (see figure 10.1) reflected the inconsistencies highlighted by Martin Ginis et al. (2007). Specifically, more than half (10 of 18) of the studies had confidence intervals spanning zero, which suggests that the SPA–physical activity behavior relationship could be positive, negative, or null. The overall effect size across studies was $r = -.10$, indicating that, on average, SPA accounts for about 1% of the variance in physical activity participation. Although very small, this relationship was statistically significant ($p = .001$, 95% confidence interval ranging from -0.06 to -0.15).

There was also some indication of the presence of moderators. In particular, the value for the I^2 statistic was 63.55%. I^2 serves as a marker of real (as

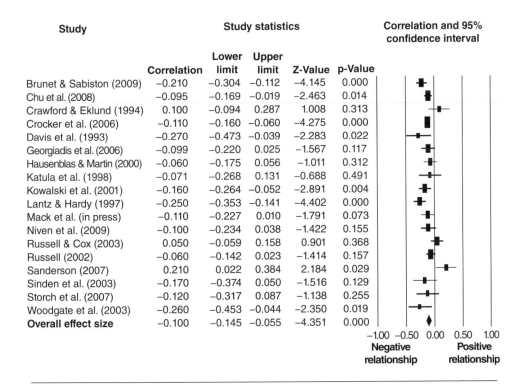

Study	Correlation	Lower limit	Upper limit	Z-Value	p-Value
Brunet & Sabiston (2009)	−0.210	−0.304	−0.112	−4.145	0.000
Chu et al. (2008)	−0.095	−0.169	−0.019	−2.463	0.014
Crawford & Eklund (1994)	0.100	−0.094	0.287	1.008	0.313
Crocker et al. (2006)	−0.110	−0.160	−0.060	−4.275	0.000
Davis et al. (1993)	−0.270	−0.473	−0.039	−2.283	0.022
Georgiadis et al. (2006)	−0.099	−0.220	0.025	−1.567	0.117
Hausenblas & Martin (2000)	−0.060	−0.175	0.056	−1.011	0.312
Katula et al. (1998)	−0.071	−0.268	0.131	−0.688	0.491
Kowalski et al. (2001)	−0.160	−0.264	−0.052	−2.891	0.004
Lantz & Hardy (1997)	−0.250	−0.353	−0.141	−4.402	0.000
Mack et al. (in press)	−0.110	−0.227	0.010	−1.791	0.073
Niven et al. (2009)	−0.100	−0.234	0.038	−1.422	0.155
Russell & Cox (2003)	0.050	−0.059	0.158	0.901	0.368
Russell (2002)	−0.060	−0.142	0.023	−1.414	0.157
Sanderson (2007)	0.210	0.022	0.384	2.184	0.029
Sinden et al. (2003)	−0.170	−0.374	0.050	−1.516	0.129
Storch et al. (2007)	−0.120	−0.317	0.087	−1.138	0.255
Woodgate et al. (2003)	−0.260	−0.453	−0.044	−2.350	0.019
Overall effect size	−0.100	−0.145	−0.055	−4.351	0.000

FIGURE 10.1 Forest plot of effect sizes (random-effects model) for studies of the relationship between social physique anxiety and exercise. Larger squares indicate larger samples.

opposed to spurious) dispersion. A value of this magnitude suggests moderate to large variance (Higgins, Thompson, Deeks, & Altman, 2003) and the likelihood that moderators influence the SPA–exercise behavior relationship. Although the relatively small number of studies available precluded further analyses, we strongly suspect that study design, participant, and exercise characteristics moderate the strength of the SPA–exercise relationship.

Effort We might expect SPA to be positively correlated with exercise intensity, such that people with high SPA work out harder to maximize changes in their appearance (i.e., reduce weight, increase muscle mass) and ultimately alleviate physique anxiety. Research suggests, however, that exercise is not typically used as a strategy to manage SPA and other body-image-related concerns (Kowalski, Mack, Crocker, Niefer, & Fleming, 2006). Alternatively, SPA could be expected to correlate negatively with exercise intensity such that physique anxious people avoid working out at high intensity for fear of huffing, puffing, and sweating in front of others. Consistent with this reasoning, Katula and colleagues (Katula, McAuley, Mihalko, & Bane, 1998) found a modest negative relationship ($r = -.35$) between SPA and ratings of perceived exertion (RPE) among people running on a treadmill such that those with high SPA exerted themselves less than those with low SPA. Although Katula's is the only study of SPA and exercise intensity, we suspect that like the relationship observed between SPA and exercise participation, SPA accounts for negligible variance in exercise effort.

Choice SPA has been examined in relation to choices of exercise settings, primarily among women. One study found that women with high SPA prefer to exercise with one partner rather than alone or in a group (Diehl, Brewer, VanRaalte, Shaw, Fiero, & Sorensen, 2001). Another study (Burke, Carron, & Eys, 2006) found that women's preferences for exercising alone versus with others were unrelated to SPA such that most women preferred to exercise in groups regardless of their level of physique anxiety. These studies of exercise preferences contrast with the results of a study of exercise practices. Spink (1992) showed that women with higher SPA are more likely to exercise alone than their low-SPA counterparts are. Thus, women with high SPA might want to exercise with others, but their body anxiety can prevent them from doing so.

When women with high SPA do exercise with others, they may be more likely than women with low SPA to choose to exercise in all-female environments (Yin, 2001; Eklund & Crawford, 1994) and in classes in which participants wear modest, as opposed to revealing, exercise attire (Eklund & Crawford, 1994; Sinden, Martin Ginis, & Angove 2003). Women with high SPA may also be more likely to choose to exercise at the back rather than at the front of a fitness class (Brewer et al., 2004). Overall, the relationship between SPA and these indicators of exercise choice tend to be modest. Nevertheless, the evidence converges on the finding that when women with high SPA exercise, they choose environments that minimize the likelihood of physique evaluation.

Impression Motivation and Construction

Self-presentation involves two discrete processes: impression motivation and construction (Leary & Kowalski, 1990). Impression motivation reflects the general desire to create impressions. Impression construction involves putting impression motivation into action, that is, choosing a particular impression to create and then using tactics to convey it. Several studies have examined the role of these processes in exercise motivation. Note that although impression motivation and construction are considered conceptually distinct, teasing them apart in both real-world situations and experimental designs is often difficult (Leary & Kowalski, 1990). This conundrum is reflected in our review whereby the two processes are treated unitarily.

Persistence Persistence has been examined in relation to trait measures of attributes associated with impression motivation and construction, exercise-specific measures of impression motivation and construction, and the strength of self-presentational motives for exercise. Attributes associated with impression motivation include traits such as public self-consciousness, fear of negative evaluation, and self-monitoring. Mixed findings have emerged from cross-sectional studies examining the relationship between these traits and exercise participation. For example, a study of adult cosmetic surgery patients showed that frequent exercisers scored lower on public self-consciousness than did nonexercisers and infrequent exercisers (Culos-Reed, Brawley, Martin, & Leary, 2002). In contrast, a study of high school students found exercise to be unrelated to public self-consciousness (Martin, Leary, & O'Brien, 2001) but negatively related to fear of negative evaluation.

Exercise-specific measures of impression motivation and construction have also been examined in relation to exercise participation. Conroy, Motl, and Hall (2000) developed the Self-Presentation in Exercise Questionnaire (SPEQ) to assess people's motivation to create the impression of being an exerciser (i.e., a fit, healthy, active person) and their use of strategies to construct an exercise impression. The authors found a weak albeit statistically significant positive correlation between number of days per week of exercise and impression motivation ($r = .16$) but not impression construction. Subsequent research using different versions of the SPEQ has failed to provide consistent support for the hypothesis that exercise impression motivation and construction are positively correlated with exercise behavior (Gammage, Hall, & Martin Ginis, 2004; Lindwall, 2005). However, concerns about the face and construct validity of the SPEQ (for a review, see Martin Ginis et al., 2007) make it impossible to determine whether the inconsistent findings are the result of the psychometric properties of the scale or a true lack of association between these variables.

The extent to which people endorse self-presentational motives for exercise is another exercise-specific measure of impression motivation. Self-presentational exercise motives include exercising to look more physically attractive, to lose or maintain weight, to improve muscularity, and to develop a fit and athletic social image (Hausenblas et al., 2004; Strong, Martin Ginis, Mack, & Wilson, 2006). Non-self-presentational motives include exercising to have fun, to reduce stress, and to improve health and fitness (Hausenblas & Martin, 2000; Prichard & Tiggemann, 2008). Study results have been consistent in showing that people who exercise for self-presentational reasons exercise less than people who work out for health and fitness reasons (Hausenblas et al., 2004). For instance, Culos-Reed et al.'s (2002) study of cosmetic surgery patients found that low-frequency exercisers were exercising primarily to change their appearance, whereas higher-frequency exercisers were working out primarily for health-related reasons. In a similar vein, Ingledew and colleagues (1998) reported that the long-term maintenance of exercise is associated with exercising more for mood-enhancing reasons than for self-presentational reasons.

Self-presentational reasons for avoiding exercise have also been studied. Although the desire to avoid making negative impressions, such as being uncoordinated, overweight, or unfit, can deter exercise (Hausenblas et al., 2004; Martin Ginis & Leary, 2004; Martin Ginis et al., 2007), the effect of these motives on exercise avoidance probably varies across populations and exercise settings. For example, two studies of adolescent nonexercisers (Martin, Leary, & O'Brien, 2001; Martin Ginis, O'Brien, & Watson, 2003) found that impression motivation and construction concerns were only slightly important reasons for avoiding exercise. In contrast, obese women have cited fear of negative evaluation of their bodies as the primary reason for avoiding public exercise settings (Bain, Wilson, & Chaikind, 1989).

Unfortunately, conducting a meta-analysis on the studies of impression motivation and construction was not possible because of the disparate measures used in these investigations. Nevertheless, narrative reviews make it clear that people who are motivated to exercise primarily for self-presentational reasons do less exercise than people who are motivated to work out for non-self-presentational reasons. There is little evidence to suggest that dispositional concerns with impression motivation and construction are related to exercise participation.

Effort   In his seminal paper on self-presentation processes in exercise and sport, Leary (1992) contended that "people work harder at things, including exercise, when they think that effort or exertion will create desired impressions in others' eyes" (p. 344). Several studies have tested this proposition by manipulating aspects of the exercise environment that could prompt impression motivation and construction, such as the presence of other exercisers and observers. For example, in one study, researchers compared the amount of weight that participants bench-pressed both with and without an audience present (Rhea, Landers, Alvar, & Arent, 2003). On average, participants lifted 12 kilograms more in the presence of an audience. Although other processes could mediate the effects of audience presence on effort and exertion when performing exercise tasks (for reviews of the social facilitation literature with regard to performance of motor tasks, see Strauss, 2002), the desire to make a good impression is certainly one of them (Leary, 1992).

The exercise literature is consistent in showing that people tend to exercise harder when they know that other people are watching them and, presumably, when they believe that their effort will lead to the desired impression (Hausenblas et al., 2004; Martin Ginis et al., 2007). This pattern of results is most consistent when effort is objectively measured (e.g., distance run, weight lifted). In contrast, in studies where effort has been measured as self-reported exertion (i.e., ratings of perceived exertion [RPE]), participants assigned to a condition designed to prompt impression motivation and construction have sometimes reported *less* exercise effort than participants did in a control condition (Boutcher, Fleischer-Curtian, & Gines, 1988; Hardy, Hall, & Prestholdt, 1986). Reporting low levels of exertion during an objectively strenuous workout could be used as a tactic to convey the impression of being physically fit. Conversely, reporting high levels of exertion during less (objectively) strenuous exercise could be a strategy to convey the impression of being a hard-working exerciser, willing to push oneself and give 110%.

We conducted a meta-analysis of published English-language studies that manipulated impression management or construction in either an exercise-testing situation or a naturalistic exercise setting. Only studies that used an objective measure of effort (e.g., weight lifted, distance walked) were included because of the potential difficulties associated with interpreting the results of studies that used RPE as an outcome (i.e., as noted earlier, impression motivation could prompt both high and low RPEs). Five studies met our inclusion criteria.

Overall, impression motivation and construction manipulations had small to moderate effects on effort (overall effect size: $r = 0.28$; 95% confidence interval ranging from 0.12 to 0.42, $p = .001$). Examination of the effects reported in the individual studies and their confidence intervals indicated considerable variability in the effects (see figure 10.2). Between-study differences in design characteristics (e.g., samples, protocols) probably account for much of this variability.

Study name	Correlation	Lower limit	Upper limit	Z-Value	p-Value
		Statistics for each study			
Grindrod et al. (2006)	0.530	0.047	0.812	2.128	0.033
Olmos et al. (2008)	0.080	−0.402	0.527	0.311	0.756
Rhea et al. (2003)	0.130	−0.229	0.458	0.704	0.481
Strube et al. (1981)	0.340	0.127	0.523	3.067	0.002
Worringham & Messick (1983)	0.130	−0.480	0.655	0.392	0.695
Overall effect size	0.279	0.121	0.423	3.402	0.001

Correlation and 95% CI

−1.00 −0.50 0.00 0.50 1.00
Lower effort   Higher effort

FIGURE 10.2 Forest plot of effect sizes (random-effects model) for studies of the effects of impression motivation or construction manipulations on exercise effort. Larger squares indicate larger samples.

Choice   We are aware of only one study that has examined whether impression motivation and construction are associated with choice of exercise activities. Prichard and Tiggemann (2008) conducted a study of 571 female fitness center members. They found that endorsement of self-presentational (i.e., appearance-based) motives for exercise was weakly albeit significantly positively correlated with time spent in cardio-based aerobics classes ($r = .09$) and on cardio-based individual workouts ($r = .16$). In contrast, self-presentational motives were negatively correlated with time spent in yoga classes ($r = -.12$) and unrelated to time spent resistance training. Cardiovascular activities are essential ingredients of weight loss regimens. Thus, it makes sense that women who are strongly motivated to exercise for self-presentational reasons would choose to spend more time on activities that they perceive as conducive to appearance change and less time on activities (i.e., yoga) that will not help them reach their self-presentational goals. Note, however, that self-presentational motives accounted for only about 1% of the variance in participation in these activities.

Self-Presentational Efficacy and Confidence

In situations that prompt impression management, people hold an expectancy regarding their ability to convey desired impressions to others (Leary & Kowalski, 1995). For instance, an exerciser who wants to impress a new running group will have a sense of the likelihood of presenting himself as a fit, well-conditioned runner. Perceptions of one's ability to create desired impressions have been defined as both self-presentation confidence (Ryckman, Robbins, Thornton, & Cantrell, 1982) and self-presentational efficacy (Leary & Kowalski, 1995). In the exercise domain, self-presentation confidence has been conceptualized as a trait construct that reflects a person's level of confidence in displaying physical skills and having these skills evaluated by others (i.e., physical self-presentation confidence [PSPC]; Ryckman et al., 1982). Self-presentational efficacy is considered situation specific and refers to expectations about one's ability to perform the behaviors or present the images that lead to desired outcomes (Maddux, Norton, & Leary, 1988). In the exercise domain, self-presentational efficacy has been typically conceptualized as confidence in the ability to convey images of oneself as a fit and competent exerciser (Gammage, Martin Ginis, & Hall, 2004).

Persistence   All the published studies examining the relationship between self-presentation confidence or efficacy and exercise have been cross-sectional. Two narrative reviews conducted on this literature (Hausenblas et al., 2004; Martin Ginis et al. 2007) led to the conclusion that active people are more confident in their abilities to present themselves as physically fit and competent compared to less active or inactive people. This relationship holds for measures of both self-presentational efficacy (Gammage et al., 2004) and PSPC (Yeung & Hemsley, 1997).

We conducted a meta-analysis of this evidence (see figure 10.3). Overall, self-presentational efficacy and confidence had a small- to medium-sized (Cohen,

1982) association with exercise (overall effect size: $r = 0.26$; 95% confidence interval ranging from 0.09 to 0.41, $p = .003$). These findings reinforce the observations made in the narrative reviews; active people are more confident than less active people regarding their physical self-presentation abilities.

Effort   We are aware of only two published papers that have examined the relationship between self-presentational confidence or efficacy and exercise effort. The first paper (Tenenbaum, Lidor, Lavyan, Morrow, Tonnel, & Gershgoren, 2005) consisted of three studies examining the multivariate relationships between various psychosocial variables, including PSPC, and the amount of effort that men put forth across a series of running trials. In four out of eight trials, PSPC was a significant, positive predictor of the amount of time that participants were willing to continue running at 90% of their maximum (Studies 1 and 2). In three out of eight trials, PSPC was a significant, negative predictor of time to run a 2.2-kilometer course (Study 3). In the second publication, participants completed the PSPC, along with a questionnaire assessing the amount of effort that they typically put forth during their workouts (Wright, Ding, & Li, 2005). There was a significant correlation ($r = .25$) between these variables. One possible interpretation of these studies' findings is that people with high PSPC push themselves harder during exercise because they are more confident in their ability to perform the exercise-related behaviors (i.e., running faster) that will lead to self-presentational success.

Choice   We are unaware of any studies examining self-presentational efficacy or confidence and exercise choice. We would hypothesize, however, that self-presentationally efficacious or confident people would be more willing to try different exercise activities than their less confident counterparts. Presumably, people with high levels of self-presentational efficacy or confidence would be less worried about embarrassing themselves in unfamiliar exercise settings.

Study name	Correlation	Lower limit	Upper limit	Z-Value	p-Value
Woodgate et al. (2003)	−0.120	−0.330	0.101	−1.065	0.287
Fleming & Martin Ginis (2004)	0.340	0.154	0.503	3.487	0.000
Gammage et al. (2004)	0.320	0.200	0.430	5.051	0.000
Yeung & Hemsley (1997)	0.210	0.089	0.325	3.364	0.001
Wright et al. (2005)	0.530	0.283	0.711	3.870	0.000
Overall effect size	0.257	0.090	0.409	2.993	0.003

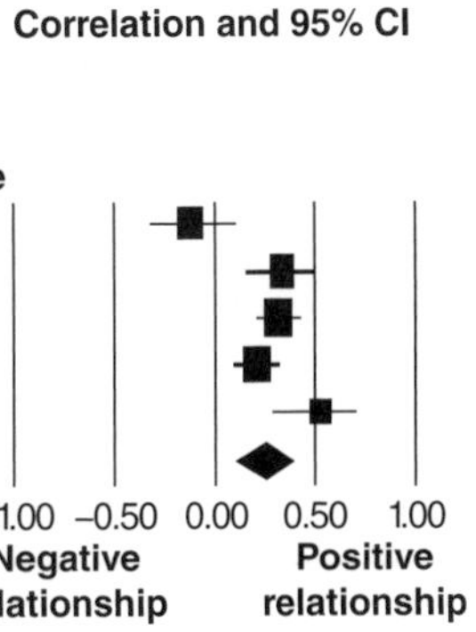

Statistics for each study — Correlation and 95% CI

−1.00 −0.50 0.00 0.50 1.00

Negative relationship — Positive relationship

FIGURE 10.3   Forest plot of effect sizes (random-effects model) for studies of the relationship between physical self-presentation confidence or self-efficacy and exercise. Larger squares indicate larger samples.

Summary

In summary, research on self-presentation and exercise motivation has focused primarily on determining whether direct relationships exist between dispositional measures of self-presentational constructs (e.g., SPA, attributes associated with impression motivation and construction, endorsement of self-presentational motives for exercise) and exercise participation. SPA and dispositional attributes associated with impression motivation and construction tend to have inconsistent albeit very weak negative associations with exercise. In fact, the SPA–exercise relationship is virtually zero. In contrast, the evidence is remarkably consistent that self-presentational motives for exercise are negatively related to exercise persistence. Given the variety of ways that motives have been operationalized, measured, and analyzed, it is not possible to comment on the magnitude of this relationship. Finally, self-presentational efficacy and confidence tend to be positively correlated with exercise participation, although the magnitude of this correlation is typically small to medium sized (Cohen, 1982).

Few studies have operationalized motivation in terms of exercise effort or choice. In studies that have measured these types of behavior, greater effort has been associated with greater self-presentational confidence and observed in situations that elicit impression motivation and construction. Women's choice of exercise activities and settings has shown an association with SPA. Again, these effects are generally small (Cohen, 1982).

Based on these findings, we conclude that there are small to medium-sized direct associations between self-presentation and exercise motivation. The associations are more consistent when exercise-specific measures of self-presentational variables are used (e.g., self-presentational efficacy, self-presentational exercise motives) as opposed to generic measures of self-presentational variables (e.g., SPA, fear of negative evaluation). Exercise effort and choice have been understudied in the self-presentation literature but may prove to be more strongly related to self-presentation than measures of persistence.

Theoretical Perspectives on Self-Presentation and Exercise Motivation

In this section we look at theoretical perspectives that have been used to examine the role of self-presentation in exercise. Although some authors have referred to the use of "self-presentational theory" to guide their exercise studies, there is, in fact, no comprehensive theory of self-presentation per se. Rather, the self-presentational approach has been characterized as a "metatheoretical framework within which one can formulate and seek answers to questions on the causes and consequences of human social behavior" (Tetlock & Manstead, 1985, p. 62). One such self-presentational framework is the two-component model of impression management.

Two-Component Model of Impression Management

This model delineates factors underlying the self-presentation processes of impression motivation and construction. Impression motivation is influenced by the importance of creating a particular impression to achieve one's goals, the value placed on those goals, and the discrepancy between one's existing and desired images. Impression construction is influenced by one's current or potential social image, the types of impressions preferred by significant others, role constraints, desired and undesired images, and self-concept.

Within the exercise motivation literature, the two-component model has been used primarily in studies of impression formation and construction to generate hypotheses regarding the relationship between the desire to create the image of being physically fit and active and exercise participation (Conroy et al., 2000; Gammage, Martin Ginis, & Hall, 2004; Lindwall, 2005). Essentially, these studies have conceptualized exercise as an impression construction strategy that is directly influenced by impression motivation. As noted in our literature review, support for this notion has been mixed.

The two-component model elegantly captures and organizes the many processes involved in impression-relevant behavior. Nevertheless, a couple of features limit its potential applicability to the study and explanation of exercise motivation. First, the model was formulated primarily by drawing on the results of lab-based studies examining single episodes of self-presentation during interpersonal exchanges (e.g., first-time interactions with a potential romantic partner or employer). Although the model might help to explain acute manifestations of self-presentationally motivated exercise behavior (e.g., putting forth more effort at the gym when an attractive observer is nearby), the factors that predict one-off, self-presentationally motivated interpersonal behaviors may be different from the factors that explain ongoing behaviors, such as exercise, that do not always have an interpersonal element (e.g., exercise that is performed alone). A second limitation is that the model does not possess (nor does it claim to possess) the predictive and explanatory powers associated with more fully developed and delineated social psychological theories of interpersonal behavior. Of particular relevance to exercise psychologists, the model does not specify the mechanisms by which, or the conditions when, an increase in the desire to convey a particular impression (e.g., lean, fit exerciser) leads to the use of strategies to convey that impression (e.g., exercise). These limitations may explain why the two-component model has not been used more in exercise research.

Social-Cognitive Theories

Some investigators have incorporated self-presentational variables into social-cognitive theories of motivated behavior and used these integrative frameworks to study self-presentation and exercise. Bandura's (1999, 1997) social-cognitive theory, the theory of planned behavior (Ajzen, 1985), and self-determination theory (Deci & Ryan, 1985a, 2002a) have each been used in studies of self-presentation and exercise.

Social-cognitive theory (SCT) has been used primarily in studies of the relationship between self-presentational efficacy or confidence and exercise. According to SCT, self-efficacy expectancies (i.e., confidence in one's abilities to perform the behaviors necessary to produce a particular outcome), outcome expectancies, and the value placed on those outcomes can each influence motivated behavior (Bandura, 1999, 1997). Likewise, the self-presentational efficacy construct, which is firmly rooted in SCT (Leary, 1983; Maddux, Norton, & Leary, 1988), also incorporates self-presentational efficacy expectancies, outcomes, and values.

Within the exercise motivation and self-presentation literature, SCT has been used to generate and test hypotheses regarding the direct relationship between exercise and self-presentational efficacy or confidence (e.g., Gammage, Martin Ginis, & Hall, 2004; Wright et al., 2005). That is, exercise should be greater among people who have greater confidence in their physical self-presentation (i.e., greater efficacy expectancies), who believe that exercise will maintain this impression (i.e., high outcome expectancies), and who place greater value on making such impressions (i.e., high outcome value). As shown in figure 10.2, this hypothesis has been generally supported. Also consistent with SCT, the self-presentational efficacy construct has been hypothesized to function as a situation-specific moderator of trait influences on physical activity (Martin Ginis et al., 2007). In support of this notion, Woodgate et al. (2003) found that self-presentational efficacy moderated the relationship between SPA and physical activity. SPA was unrelated to exercise frequency among women with low self-presentational efficacy and negatively associated with frequency among those with high self-presentational efficacy.

Although not explicitly framed in SCT, a few exercise studies have looked at the relationship between self-presentation and self-efficacy variables. One study demonstrated that higher SPA was significantly associated ($r = -0.18$) with lower self-efficacy to overcome barriers to exercise (Thøgersen-Ntoumani & Ntoumanis, 2006). This finding is consistent with the SCT prediction that negative affect and arousal (i.e., SPA) can be detrimental to self-efficacy. Other studies have shown that higher self-presentational efficacy is associated with higher exercise task self-efficacy (rs ranged from .43 to .63, Fleming & Martin Ginis, 2004; Martin & Brawley, 2002), suggesting that these two forms of self-efficacy draw on some similar sources.

The theory of planned behavior (TPB; Ajzen, 1985) has also been applied in the self-presentation and exercise motivation literature. According to the TPB, intentions to perform a particular behavior are the most proximal determinant of that behavior. Intentions are influenced by the person's attitude toward the behavior, perceived social pressure (i.e., subjective norms) to perform it, and perceptions of control (i.e., perceived behavioral control). Perceived behavioral control also has a direct influence on behavior.

The TPB was used as the framework in a study examining the moderated, indirect effects of self-presentation on exercise motivation (Latimer & Martin Ginis, 2005). This study revealed that the relationship between social pressure to exercise and exercise intentions is stronger among people who score high on the trait of fear of negative evaluation than among those who score low on this trait. The direct effects of fear of negative evaluation on exercise intentions were not significant. Similar to Woodgate et al.'s (2003) findings, this pattern of results suggests that dispositional self-presentational variables may interact with exercise-specific social cognitions that underlie exercise motivation.

We are not aware of any other studies of self-presentation and motivation that were explicitly couched within the TPB, although some studies have looked at the relationship between self-presentation and constructs captured by the TPB. For instance, a couple of investigations have shown that SPA is associated with women's beliefs about, and attitudes toward, exercise classes in which participants wear revealing versus conservative exercise attire (Crawford & Eklund, 1994; Eklund & Crawford, 1994). Not surprisingly, compared to women with low SPA, those with high SPA have more negative attitudes toward classes in which revealing exercise attire is the norm. Another study (Raedeke, Focht, & Scales, 2007) found that among women with high SPA, an exercise class that draws attention away from the physique (i.e., a health-focused exercise class) leads to greater enjoyment and ultimately greater intention to participate in future classes than a class focused on physique change does. Considering enjoyment as an affective dimension of attitudes, these findings are consistent with the TPB prediction that attitudes toward a specific behavior are a significant predictor of intentions to engage in that behavior.

Self-determination theory (SDT; Deci & Ryan, 1985a, 2002a) is the third social-cognitive approach that has been used to study self-presentation in exercise. Fundamental to SDT is the notion that the quality of a person's motivation is more important than the quantity when it comes to understanding volitional behavior, human growth, and well-being. SDT is composed of five minitheories, and research on self-presentation and exercise has been framed in three of these: organismic integration theory, basic needs theory, and causality orientations theory. SPA is the only self-presentational construct that has been examined in the SDT-framed studies.

Organismic integration theory (OIT) reflects the distinction between controlled (i.e., external and introjected) and autonomous (or self-determined) regulations (i.e., identified, integrated, and intrinsic) that shape participatory behavior. Although both controlling and autonomous motives can regulate exercise behavior, exercise for more self-determined reasons is associated with better long-term adherence. Two studies have examined the relationship between SPA and endorsement of controlling and autonomous forms of motivation.

The first study (Thøgersen-Ntoumani & Ntoumanis, 2006) showed that greater SPA was associated with greater endorsement of introjected forms of regulation (i.e., exercising out of guilt or anxiety) and weaker endorsement of intrinsic forms of regulation (i.e., exercising for the self-rewarding nature of the activity) among male and female exercisers. The second study (Thøgersen-Ntoumani & Ntoumanis, 2007) showed that in a regression model, introjected regulation was a positive predictor of SPA among aerobic instructors. These findings are consistent with the results of other (non-SDT based) studies indicating that SPA is positively correlated with the extent to which people endorse self-presentational exercise motives (for reviews, see Hausenblas et al., 2004; Martin Ginis et al., 2007). Together, the results suggest that exercisers with higher SPA may feel pressure to engage in physical activity for reasons linked to social contingent feelings of self-worth and to avoid unpleasant psychological states, such as physique-related guilt or anxiety. People who exercise for these reasons may be poor adherers because their reasons for exercising can be experienced as controlling (Deci & Ryan, 1985a, 2002a).

Basic needs theory proposes that people have innate psychological needs that, when fulfilled, promote personal growth, psychosocial adjustment, and well-being (Deci & Ryan, 1985a, 2002a; Ryan & Deci, 2001). Satisfaction of these needs is linked directly to markers of well-being (Wilson, Mack, & Grattan, 2008), including SPA. For instance, in exercise settings, individuals who report greater fulfillment of the psychological needs for autonomy, competence, and relatedness also report lower SPA (Brunet & Sabiston, 2009; Thøgersen-Ntoumani & Ntoumanis, 2007). Furthermore, in a sample of undergraduate students, fulfillment of the three psychological needs was shown to mediate the SPA–exercise relationship, and perceived competence and relatedness served as unique mediators (Mack, Wilson, Sylvester, Gregson, Cheung, & Rimmer, in press). Thus, for people who are worried about physique evaluation, feelings of incompetence and social disconnectedness could deter exercise participation.

Finally, causality orientation theory delineates an individual's general orientation toward autonomous or controlled functioning (Deci & Ryan, 2002a). An autonomy orientation reflects the tendency to regulate behavior based on integrated values and in contexts that promote choice. A controlled orientation refers to the tendency to self-regulate according to external contingencies and pressures. Social contexts (e.g., exercise settings) that are perceived as controlling thwart the satisfaction of basic psychological needs and consequently lower self-determined motivation (Deci & Ryan, 2002a). Brunet and Sabiston (2009) have proposed that SPA serves as a controlling force over regulated behavior and that individuals higher in SPA should report lower psychological need satisfaction and more controlling motives regulating their exercise behavior. Support for this pattern of relationships was observed in a sample of young adults (Brunet & Sabiston, 2009).

Summary

Remarkably few investigations of self-presentation and exercise motivation have been guided by a theoretical framework. A few studies have employed the two-component model to examine dispositional factors associated with participation in exercise as an impression construction strategy. These studies have produced mixed support for their hypotheses. In other studies, self-presentational variables have been integrated with social-cognitive theories and constructs to test hypotheses regarding the effects of self-presentational variables on the mechanisms underlying exercise motivation. In general, these investigations have found theoretically consistent relationships between self-presentational variables and constructs captured by social-cognitive theory, the theory of planned behavior, and self-determination theory. It is particularly noteworthy that in these studies, SPA has shown statistically significant, theoretically meaningful relationships with social-cognitive determinants of exercise motivation. This pattern is in stark contrast to the inconsistent and weak (at best) relationships reported in studies of the direct relationship between SPA and measures of exercise participation and persistence. Thus, when self-presentational variables are examined within broader theoretical frameworks, they can play a predictable, meaningful role in explaining motivation.

Role of Self-Presentation in Exercise Motivation

Do self-presentational variables influence exercise participation? This is the primary question currently driving the self-presentation and exercise motivation literature. Based on the extant research, it would be reasonable to conclude that the influence of self-presentation on exercise motivation is weak, at best. But we think that this conclusion may be premature for at least two reasons:

1. Self-presentation variables are likely to have a greater effect on theory-based determinants of exercise participation and persistence than on exercise participation and persistence per se.

Most research on self-presentation and exercise has tested for a direct association between dispositional measures of self-presentation (e.g., SPA, impression motivation and construction, self-presentational motives) and measures of exercise participation. Although virtually all these studies were cross-sectional, many were premised on the notion that self-presentation can influence exercise behavior. In general, results indicate inconsistent, weak correlations between individual differences in self-presentation and exercise. But when these same self-presentational variables were conceptualized within broader social-cognitive theories of motivation, they were shown to correlate with factors that underlie exercise motivation in meaningful ways. From these observations, we conclude that dispositional measures of self-presentation are more strongly related to determinants of exercise motivation than to motivation per se.

This conclusion jives with contemporary approaches to conceptualizing and studying the role of individual difference variables in relation to exercise and other health-related behaviors. For example, personality and social-cognitive theorists share the perspective that personality does not have a direct effect on behavior (e.g., Bandura, 1999; Bermudez, 2006; Van Heck, 1997). From a personality theory perspective, however, it is possible that psychosocial factors and processes mediate the associations between individual difference factors and health-related behaviors (Van Heck, 1997). Indeed, within the exercise domain, Rhodes (2006) has suggested that personality and other personal characteristics may lead to physical activity through social-cognitive antecedents of motivation. This perspective is akin to Ajzen's (2009b) notion that dispositional variables (e.g., personality traits, individual orientations toward autonomous or controlling functioning, personal values) are "background factors" that influence motivated behavior vis-à-vis more proximal determinants of behavior, such as attitudinal, normative, and control beliefs. Although background factors provide valuable information about the origins of beliefs, their effects on behavior are not direct but rather are mediated by beliefs. Drawing from these perspectives, we think that self-presentational variables could enhance an understanding of the determinants of theoretically meaningful social cognitions that underlie motivation to exercise (see figure 10.4). These social cognitions are clearly delineated in the theories often favored by exercise psychologists (e.g., social-cognitive theory, theory of planned behavior, self-determination theory), but few investigators have examined them from a self-presentational perspective. Such investigations must be undertaken before concluding that the effects of self-presentation on exercise motivation are trivial.

Note that social-cognitive theorists would likely dispute the notion that dispositional self-presentational variables can function as antecedents of motivation. Bandura (1999) and others (e.g., Cervone, Shadel, Smith, & Fiori, 2006) refute the role of dispositions as sources of individual differences in health behavior (e.g., Bandura, 1999; Bermudez, 2006). According to Bandura (1999), the study of dispositional variables and behavior should focus on "how personal factors operate in causal structures in producing and

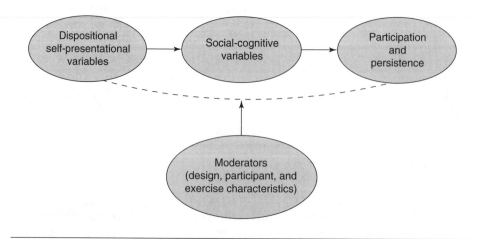

FIGURE 10.4 Model for studying the role of dispositional self-presentational variables in explaining exercise participation and persistence.

regulating behavior under the highly contingent conditions of everyday life" (p. 192). Bandura also states that in social-cognitive theory, "dispositions are personal factors such as self-beliefs, aspirations, and outcome expectations that regulate behavior" (pp. 192–193). Despite these claims, Ryan Rhodes' research has consistently shown an effect of one dispositional variable, the personality trait of extraversion, on exercise, independent of the effects of exercise-related social cognitions (for a review, see Rhodes, 2006). Rhodes has suggested that by virtue of its stability, extraversion (and the more specific facet trait of "activity") may be better than typically unrealistic, overoptimistic social cognitions for predicting exercise in the distal future. But as actual exercise opportunities become imminent, social cognitions may become more realistic and thus better predictors of proximal exercise behavior.

We strongly suspect that self-presentational variables exert their strongest influence on motivation *through* social-cognitive antecedents. Nevertheless, based on Rhodes' research and theorizing, there may be merit in examining whether dispositional measures of self-presentation can predict future exercise participation beyond the variance explained by social cognitions. To date, we are aware of only one published study that has examined a dispositional self-presentation variable as a predictor of future exercise participation (Treasure et al., 1998). Thus, before concluding that self-presentation has little to no effect on exercise motivation, investigators need to conduct prospective studies of the long-term direct and indirect effects of self-presentation on exercise participation.

2. The effects of self-presentation on motivation may be more evident when examined from a situational rather than a dispositional perspective.

The predominant approach to studying exercise and self-presentation has been to treat self-presentation as a dispositional phenomenon. A dispositional approach is problematic for a number of reasons. First, most of the trait measures of self-presentation used in exercise studies (the Social Physique Anxiety Scale [Hart et al., 1989] in particular) are not specific to exercise contexts. These measures provide indication of people's usual levels of SPA, fear of negative evaluation, and so on. But it would be naive to assume that how people think about self-presentation in most aspects of life (e.g., at school, at work, socializing with friends) is the same as how they think about self-presentation when they are exercising. Nonexercisers, in particular, would likely have different thoughts about impression motivation and construction in daily situations that they typically encounter compared to unfamiliar fitness settings. If study participants are not cued to think about exercise settings when they complete trait measures of self-presentation, then these measures are unlikely to predict their exercise motivation. We would also expect exercise-specific measures of self-presentation to be better predictors of exercise motivation than generic measures of self-presentation. Consistent with this hypothesis, studies of self-presentational motives for exercise have typically yielded much stronger correlations with exercise persistence than have studies of the non-exercise-specific trait of SPA.

A second problem with the dispositional approach is that many of the factors that prompt impression motivation and construction are transitory and situation specific (Leary, 1995; Leary & Kowalski, 1995). Manipulations of the exercise environment have been shown to lead to transitory changes in self-presentational thoughts and feelings, such as social anxiety (Martin & Fox, 2001), SPA (Amirthvasar & Bray, 2008; Kruisselbrink et al., 2004; Martin Ginis, Prapavessis, & Haase, 2008), and self-presentational efficacy (Fleming & Martin Ginis, 2004; Gammage, Martin Ginis, & Hall, 2004). Exercise environments that heighten self-presentational concerns can detract from motivation to exercise in those environments (Eklund & Crawford, 1994; Gammage, Martin Ginis, & Hall, 2004; Raedeke et al., 2007). By focusing on dispositional self-presentational predictors of exercise, researchers are overlooking the more proximal and presumably more potent situational self-presentational influences on exercise motivation. To gain better understanding of the role of self-presentation in exercise, researchers need to shift their attention away from dispositions and focus more closely on the situational elements of exercise environments that influence self-presentation.

Studying situational influences on self-presentation could have implications for understanding the longer-term effects of self-presentation on motivation (see figure 10.5). For instance, consider a situation whereby the presence of an evaluative audience prompts an exerciser to lift more weight (Rhea et al., 2003) or to run faster than usual (Worringham & Messick, 1983). An increase in maximum weight lifted or a decrease in usual time to run 5 kilometers would likely lead to an enhanced sense of self-efficacy and competence. Strengthening these perceptions is, of course, theoretically linked with greater

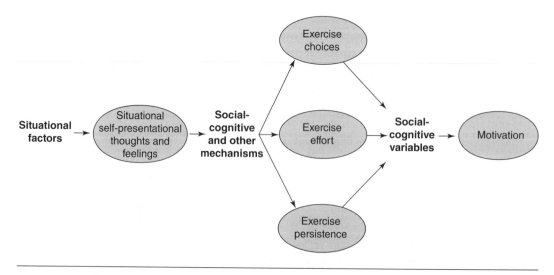

FIGURE 10.5 Model for examining the situational effects of self-presentation on exercise motivation and its longer-term motivational consequences.

or more adaptive forms of exercise motivation (cf. social-cognitive theory and self-determination theory). Thus, the situational effects of self-presentation could have positive trickle-down effects.

Some situational influences on self-presentation can also have negative long-term repercussions. Consider a novice exerciser who is trying out a group exercise class for the first time. Situational elements of the class (e.g., the instructor's appearance, Martin Ginis et al., 2008; the clothing worn by the participants, Crawford & Eklund, 1994) could elicit social anxiety and SPA. To avoid these negative feelings in the future, the exerciser may choose to exercise alone. Exercise adherence, however, is better when people exercise with others (Burke, Carron, Eys, Ntoumanis, & Estabrooks, 2006) who can provide social support, self-efficacy enhancement (i.e., through verbal persuasion and vicarious experiences), and distraction from the boredom and discomfort that may otherwise deter people from working out. Thus, some situational manifestations of self-presentation (i.e., maladaptive exercise choices) can create a cascade of negative effects on social cognitions and longer-term exercise motivation.

A third problem with the dispositional approach is that it has led to a reliance on general measures of exercise motivation and its theoretical determinants rather than measures that are specific to the exercise context. Most self-presentation studies have focused on assessing "usual" exercise behavior by way of summary measures of exercise (e.g., days per week or METS per week of activity) that merge all types of exercise performed across all types of environments (e.g., running outdoors, doing aerobics at home, lifting weights at a gym). But self-presentational concerns experienced in a particular environment should predict motivation to exercise in that environment better than they predict motivation to exercise in general. To maximize the likelihood of detecting relationships, investigators should be measuring contextually specific motivational determinants (Ajzen, 2002), such as intentions to exercise (e.g., Raedeke et al. 2007), need satisfaction, and self-efficacy for exercise in the setting of interest. Likewise, measures of exercise motivation should assess persistence, effort, and choice with regard to exercise performed in that setting. Until these recommendations are heeded, it is virtually impossible to discern whether the weak associations observed between self-presentation and exercise motivation are a consequence of measurement constraints or a weak correlation between these variables.

Practical Applications

In this section, we use research and theory to suggest ways in which self-presentational factors can be modified to improve exercise motivation. We suggest strategies that can be targeted to the exerciser, the exercise leader, and the exercise environment.

The Exerciser

One of the strongest findings in our literature review was that people who are motivated to exercise for self-presentational reasons do less exercise than those who are motivated for other reasons. Thus, strategies should be directed toward altering self-presentational motives for exercise. From a self-determination theory perspective, self-presentational motives are introjected, controlling forms of regulation (Thøgersen-Ntoumani & Ntoumanis, 2006, 2007), whereby behavior is regulated by internal pressures directed toward attaining reward (e.g., praise for changes in one's physical appearance), avoiding punishment (e.g., experiencing anxiety about wearing a bathing suit in public), or maintaining conditional self-worth (Deci & Ryan, 2002a). Introjected regulation may be valuable for prompting people to initiate an exercise program and for promoting short-term adherence (Thøgersen-Ntoumani & Ntoumanis, 2006). Indeed, the desire to alter one's physical appearance is a primary motive for starting an exercise program (Rodgers & Gauvin, 1994). But a transition from controlling to more autonomous exercise motives (e.g., valuing the behavior) is likely key to adherence (Ingledew, Markland, & Medley, 1998; Pelletier, Fortier, Vallerand, & Briere, 2001).

Various approaches can be employed to facilitate this transition. One approach is to use self-regulation strategies that increase perceptions of ownership and control over one's exercise regimen. Examples of such strategies include developing personally meaningful goals, exercise action plans (e.g., plans indicating where, when, and what types of exercise will be performed), and coping plans for overcoming exercise barriers (e.g., a plan for exercising despite bad weather). Both goal setting and planning have been shown to bolster perceptions of control over exercise (Arbour-Nicitopoulous, Martin Ginis, & Latimer, 2009; Elston & Martin Ginis, 2004; Latimer, Martin Ginis, & Arbour, 2006). Furthermore, simply taking responsibility for one's workouts, rather than leaving the planning in the hands of a personal trainer or fitness leader, can enhance feelings of autonomy and enhance intrinsic motivation. For example, people given the opportunity to select the intensity of a workout report stronger perceptions of autonomy and greater intrinsic motivation for exercise than those who have exercise intensity imposed on them (Vazou-Ekkekakis & P. Ekkekakis, 2009).

Another approach is to become more aware of the intrinsic pleasures and benefits of exercise while downplaying the importance placed on exercise as an appearance-altering strategy. Attention could be shifted to the intrinsic benefits by self-monitoring and paying greater attention to changes in the feeling states and energy levels that follow a workout. On a regular basis, exercisers also could take stock of the psychological and social benefits derived from their workouts. A shift away from appearance consciousness could be accomplished by participating in physical activities that draw attention inward and focus on how the body feels during movement rather than how it looks. Yoga and Feldenkrais movement classes (i.e., a form of somatic education that uses gentle movement and directed attention to teach body awareness; Feldenkrais, 1985) are examples of activities that may help in this regard. Preliminary studies suggest that women who do yoga (Prichard & Tiggemann, 2008) and girls who have participated in Feldenkrais activities (O'Brien, Martin Ginis, & Kirk, 2008) are less focused on their physical appearance and have lower SPA than those who participate in traditional forms of aerobic activity.

The Fitness Leader

The fitness leader is often cited as the single most important determinant of an exerciser's motivation to continue in an exercise program (Franklin, 1988). Characteristics of the fitness leader or instructor can influence self-presentational variables. For example, when exercisers perceive the instructor to be far more attractive than they are, such discrepancies can increase state SPA (Martin Ginis et al., 2008). Likewise, both routinely active and inactive women report lower self-presentational efficacy after exposure to a "perfect-looking" instructor than after exposure to a "normal-looking" instructor (Fleming & Martin Ginis, 2004). Social comparison processes are the likely mechanism behind these effects. That is, exposure to ultrafit leaders wearing physique-salient attire can elicit social comparisons between the exerciser and the leader (Greenleaf, McGreer, & Parham, 2006). For many women, these comparisons lead to feelings of inferiority and can subsequently trigger self-denigration and negative thoughts and feelings about themselves (Posavac, Posavac, & Weigel, 2001), including increased SPA and lower self-presentational efficacy. The negative self-perceptions that arise from such comparisons could have a negative effect on exercise adherence, particularly among exercise initiates (Martin Ginis et al., 2008).

Interestingly, preliminary data suggest that the exercise leader's sex does not influence self-presentational concerns. Lamarche and Gammage (2009) found no significant differences in self-presentational efficacy or state SPA among women who had just completed an aerobics exercise class with a male leader versus a female leader. As the authors noted, the leaders' actions during the class could override any effect of their sex on participants' self-presentational concerns. For instance, a male or female leader who is critical may make participants feel self-conscious, thus increasing their social anxiety (Martin & Fox, 2001). In addition, regardless of their sex, fitness leaders who emphasize the appearance-related benefits of exercise (e.g., decreased weight, increased muscle tone) may inadvertently increase participants' discomfort (cf. Raedeke et al., 2007) by drawing attention to their appearance and increasing concern about their self-presentational shortcomings.

With these possibilities in mind, fitness leaders and programmers can do several things to minimize self-presentational concerns (i.e., SPA, social anxiety) and maximize self-presentational efficacy. First, programmers should be sensitive to the propensity for people to make social comparisons by employing fitness instructors with a variety of body sizes and shapes. Such body diversity conveys the message that a fit and healthy body can take various forms. Consequently, when people make social comparisons with instructors, the discrepancy between their bodies and the instructors' bodies may not be as great.

Second, fitness leaders should avoid making comments or remarks that draw attention to physical appearance. Instructions such as "Let's work hard to get your legs toned so that they'll look good" should be replaced with cues such as "Let's work hard to get fit and healthy" (Raedeke et al., 2007). Furthermore, when teaching a group of beginner exercisers, leaders may want to avoid making any type of comment (e.g., praise for doing an exercise well or feedback to improve performance of a skill) that draws group attention to an individual exerciser. When people are learning a new exercise or are initiates to a new exercise class, evaluations by others can be a potent source of self-presentational concern and social anxiety (Martin & Fox, 2001). With time and experience, such concerns likely dissipate.

In fact, under certain conditions, the presence of other exercisers could help to alleviate social anxiety. In two scenario studies, Carron and colleagues (Carron, Estabrooks, Horton, Prapavessis, & Hausenblas, 1999; Carron & Prapavessis, 1997) found that being in the presence of friends reduced social anxiety during physique evaluative threat situations. When asked why they might feel less anxious in a group, study participants indicated that they are less likely to be the prime focus of an observer's attention when in a group than when alone. Participants also indicated that the presence of a group of friends provides security and comfort in situations of evaluative threat. Given this latter finding, our third recommendation is that fitness instructors should promote feelings of security and comfort among group members.

Strategies to enhance these feelings would likely parallel strategies used to increase feelings of group cohesion in exercise classes. For instance, Carron and Spink's (1993) team-building intervention for exercise classes includes techniques such as establishing group norms, providing opportunities for interaction among group members, and assigning roles and responsibilities to group members. The application of these techniques by an exercise class leader has been shown to improve group cohesion and reduce program dropouts. Presumably, a more cohesive group would also provide greater comfort to exercisers with self-presentational concerns.

The leader might also provide comfort and security vis-à-vis his or her leadership style. Martin and Fox (2001) found that exercisers reported less social anxiety when exposed to a leader who used a positive, supportive leadership style rather than a bland, disengaged leadership style. In addition, the quality of the relationship between leaders and exercisers could be maximized by the leader's demonstration of personal involvement—that is, dedicating psychological resources, such as time, energy, and affection (Deci & Ryan, 1991), to the exercise group. Edmunds and colleagues (Edmunds, Ntoumanis, & Duda, 2008) showed that an interpersonally involving exercise leadership style led to greater relatedness need satisfaction and exercise adherence compared to a typical leadership style. With greater feelings of relatedness could come greater feelings of comfort and security in situations that prompt self-presentational concern.

The Exercise Environment

Several characteristics of the exercise environment have been shown to influence self-presentational variables. The presence of men has been shown to increase women's state SPA in both imagined (Kruisselbrink et al., 2004; Amirthavasar & Bray, 2008) and real (Martin Ginis et al., 2011) exercise settings. The combined presence of other exercisers, a mirrored exercise environment, a male confederate, and the requirement to wear skimpy workout attire has been shown to reduce self-presentational efficacy and increase social anxiety (Gammage, Martin Ginis, & Hall, 2004).

Self-presentational variables are also related to exercise-setting preferences. As previously discussed, women with high SPA generally prefer to exercise in settings that minimize the likelihood of physique evaluation, such as private settings (Spink, 1992), at the back of a fitness studio (Brewer et al., 2004), and in classes where conservative exercise attire is the norm (Crawford & Eklund, 1994). Together, these findings provide some direction for creating exercise environments that minimize the self-presentational concerns that could ultimately weaken exercise motivation.

Our first recommendation is to provide all-women areas within fitness centers. The broader social anxiety and self-presentation literature shows that encounters with the other sex are anxiety arousing because of the social awards at stake in such encounters (e.g., the possibility of obtaining feedback that one is sexually desirable or acquiring a romantic partner; Leary & Kowalski, 1995). For women who are deterred from exercise by concerns about being evaluated by men, women-only gyms are a logical solution.

Interestingly, the existing (albeit limited) data suggest that the presence of the other sex does not have the same negative effects on male exercisers (Kruisselbrink et al., 2004). Although men may not be self-presentationally intimidated by the presence of women in the gym, they may be reluctant to enter into gyms where exercisers appear fitter and stronger than they are. As such, there may be some advantage to providing introductory strength and conditioning classes to male exercisers to increase their self-presentational efficacy and motivation for exercising in a new gym environment.

Our second recommendation has to do with the presence of mirrors. Stationary cycling exercise performed in front of a mirror has been shown to have negative psychological effects on women who are not usual exercisers (Martin Ginis et al., 2003, 2008). But in studies of active women (Katula & McAuley, 2001) and experiments involving more complex exercise activities, such as aerobics classes (Lamarche, Gammage, & Strong, 2009; Raedeke et al., 2007) and strength training (Chmelo, Hall, Miller, & Sanders, 2009), no such negative effects have been observed. Thus, for some women, some of the time, the presence of mirrors may exacerbate self-presentational concerns. We do not endorse, whatsoever, the removal of mirrors from exercise environments given the important visual performance feedback that they provide, but it may be feasible to provide some no-mirror areas in a fitness center. After beginner exercisers become confident in their self-presentational abilities, they can move into the mirrored areas.

Finally, we think that communities should continue to push for the construction of more trails, bike paths, tracks, and other outdoor exercise facilities. For the person who has self-presentational concerns about exercising with others, these types of facilities provide opportunity to exercise alone. Conversely, for the person who is motivated to exercise harder when other people are watching, the opportunity to work out in public could be a great self-presentational incentive.

Directions for Future Research

Given the primary direction of the research to date, coupled with the issues raised earlier, it is probably not surprising that the study of self-presentation has offered little to enhance our understanding of exercise motivation. But before throwing out the baby with the bath water and concluding that self-presentation has little relevance, we think that several important research questions remain to be addressed.

The models in figures 10.4 and 10.5 delineate the relationships proposed in the previous section. The models are designed to help investigators generate and test theory-driven research questions regarding the role of self-presentation in exercise motivation. The models do not supplant existing motivational theoretical frameworks (i.e., self-efficacy theory, self-determination theory, theory of planned behavior). Rather, they are to be used to identify the mediating and outcome variables that should be considered and measured when designing and conducting studies of self-presentation and exercise motivation. Tests of the hypotheses captured by the models should lead to a better understanding of the role of self-presentation.

Figure 10.4 is a model for examining the role that dispositional self-presentational variables play in explaining exercise persistence and participation. Moving from left to right, the model indicates that self-presentational variables—such as SPA, fear of negative evaluation, and physical self-presentation confidence—influence theory-based, social-cognitive antecedents of exercise motivation, such as self-efficacy, attitudes toward exercise, and psychological need satisfaction. In turn, these factors influence exercise participation and persistence. The dotted line allows for the possibility that under certain conditions (e.g., when predicting exercise well into the future; Rhodes, 2006), self-presentational variables may directly predict future exercise participation beyond variance explained by the social-cognitive variables. As shown in the model, the strength of the direct relationship may be moderated by characteristics of the study participants, the exercise being performed, or study design.

In presenting the direct relationship, we wish to underscore that in no way are we endorsing further cross-sectional study of the simple, direct relationship between dispositional measures of self-presentation and exercise. To advance this area of study, future investigations of the direct relationship must take into account mediators and moderators.

An example of a research question that can be tested within the model is whether SPA predicts adherence in an exercise training study. Using a longitudinal design, SPA would be measured at baseline followed by the researcher's choice of a manipulation that reflects theoretical determinants of motivation to exercise across the study period (e.g., 4 weeks, 6 months). Adherence to the exercise protocol would be measured. At the end of the study, regression, path, or structural equation modeling analyses would be conducted to examine the direct and indirect contributions of SPA to explaining variance in adherence. Participant characteristics (e.g., age, sex) would be examined as moderators of the direct relationship. At baseline, investigators could also measure the SPA that participants experience specifically within the context of the exercise training study environment. This approach would create measurement concordance between the predictor, mediator, and outcome variables and maximize the likelihood of detecting the hypothesized relationships.

Some preliminary support for the model can be seen in studies conducted by Brunet and Sabiston (2009) and Mack and colleagues (in press). Both investigations employed cross-sectional designs to test self-determination theory (Deci & Ryan, 2002a) variables as mediators of the SPA–physical activity relationship. Brunet and Sabiston showed that psychological need satisfaction and self-determined motivation mediate the relationship between SPA and physical activity. The direct relationship between SPA and physical activity was not significant. Similarly, Mack et al. found that perceived competence and relatedness mediated the SPA–physical activity relationship, but the direct relationship between SPA and physical activity was not statistically significant. Although the conclusions that can be drawn from these studies are somewhat limited by cross-sectional study designs, the results attest to the value of examining self-presentation and exercise through the sequence of relationships portrayed in figure 10.4.

Figure 10.5 is a model for examining the situational effects of self-presentation on acute and longer-term motivation. Moving from left to right, the model indicates that situations that elicit self-presentational concerns and feelings (e.g., self-presentational efficacy, state SPA) can affect exercise-related choices, effort, and persistence within that situation. The situational effects may be mediated by mechanisms other than, or in addition to, social cognitions. For example, in a situation that increases social anxiety, the anxiety may serve as a source of affective efficacy information, triggering a decrease in self-efficacy and negatively affecting exercise choice, effort, and persistence. Alternatively, the anxiety could lead to an increase in physiological arousal that facilitates exercise effort and persistence. Whether positive or negative, acute motivational effects could subsequently influence the social cognitions (e.g., self-efficacy, need satisfaction, attitudes toward exercise) that underlie motivation for longer-term exercise participation.

An example of a research question that can be addressed within this framework is, What are the immediate and longer-term effects of exposure to an exercise setting that elicits acute feelings of SPA and reductions in self-presentational efficacy? Of course, to answer this type of question, an experimental research design that allocates participants to experimental and control conditions is needed. Experimental manipulations that increase SPA or reduce self-presentational efficacy include asking study participants to wear revealing exercise attire, to exercise in a mixed-sex exercise class, or to exercise with a very fit, attractive instructor (Gammage, Martin Ginis, & Hall, 2004; Kruisselbrink et al., 2004, Martin Ginis et al., 2008). These manipulations are probably most effective for increasing SPA and decreasing self-presentational efficacy when administered to nonhabitual exercisers. Following the manipulation, changes in social cognitions and arousal would be measured, and an opportunity would be given for participants to demonstrate their immediate levels of motivation during an acute bout of exercise. Motivation could be operationalized and measured as exercise effort or persistence or choice of an exercise task. Following the exercise bout, the social-cognitive mechanism variables would be remeasured and used to predict future exercise motivation. Between-condition differences in motivation and the underlying mechanisms would be tested, along with the veracity of the proposed meditational framework.

A few studies have used designs that capture elements on the left-hand side of the model in figure 10.5 (e.g., Gammage, Martin Ginis, & Hall, 2004; Martin Ginis et al., 2008; Raedeke et al., 2007, 2009). For instance, Raedeke et al. (2007) manipulated the focus of an exercise class by having the instructor emphasize either appearance- or health-related elements throughout the class. Differences in postexercise affect, self-efficacy, enjoyment, and future intentions to exercise were measured and compared across the two exercise class conditions. Participants in the health-focused exercise class reported more positive affect and greater enjoyment. Enjoyment mediated the effects of class type on intentions for future exercise (Raedeke, Focht, & Scales, 2009). These results provide support for the chain of acute elements captured within our model. Unfortunately, neither Raedeke's studies nor any of the other self-presentation manipulation studies have examined the long-term consequences of their manipulations on exercise motivation on the right-hand side of the model. This next step is important for exercise and self-presentation researchers.

For this next step, we strongly urge investigators to look beyond effort and persistence as indices of motivation. In particular, we think that exercise choices are an understudied but potentially valuable jumping-off point for investigating the long-term implications of self-presentation. A self-presentational perspective could help investigators understand why people make exercise choices that undermine persistence, such as choosing to exercise alone or to stand at the back of an exercise class. As previously noted, people who exercise alone are less likely to adhere than those who exercise with a supportive group (Burke, Carron, & Eys, 2006). In a similar vein, women who choose to stand at the back of an exercise class may receive less instruction, feedback, and encouragement from the exercise leader than women who are positioned at the front of the class, which could lead to lower self-efficacy, a poorer sense of mastery and social connection, and ultimately poorer persistence (cf. Brewer et al., 2004). In both examples—exercising alone and at the back of a class— such maladaptive exercise choices may have been prompted by situations that elicited self-presentational concerns within exercise environments. In short, understanding the role of self-presentation in routine exercise choices may ultimately help to explain longer-term exercise motivation.

Summary

Self-presentational perspectives on exercise motivation have garnered considerable interest over the past 20 years. Yet, unfortunately, the general methodological approaches and research questions in this area have yielded little substantive information regarding the role of self-presentation in exercise motivation. In this chapter, we have highlighted what is currently known and have suggested ways in which investigators can move forward with theory-based self-presentation research. As evidenced in the final section of our chapter, we think that self-presentation influences exercise motivation in many ways and, consequently, offers many potential points of intervention. The challenge now is to provide the theoretical and empirical basis for such motivational interventions.

CHAPTER 11

Interventions for Physical Activity and Sedentary Behavior

Stuart J.H. Biddle, PhD
Loughborough University

Nanette Mutrie, PhD
University of Strathclyde

Trish Gorely, PhD
Loughborough University

Avril Blamey, PhD
Avril Blamey & Associates

The current public health problem of inactive lifestyles is no better illustrated than in two slides commonly shown at academic meetings on the topic. One shows a man using the escalator to avoid climbing about 15 steps to . . . the gym! The second depicts homo sapiens evolving from an ape to a lean, active hunter–gatherer and on to a sedentary person, sitting hunched up at a keyboard and screen. You can buy a T-shirt of the latter image accompanied by the caption "Something somewhere went terribly wrong!"

If such lifestyle changes are a true reflection of our propensity either to take the less active option or to spend large amounts of time in sedentary behaviors, why is this the case? One could argue, true to longstanding traditions in psychology, that the reasons lie in a combination of personal and environmental factors. As such, we should be able to reverse such problematic trends and improve physical and mental health, and quality of life, by modifying low levels of physical activity and high levels of sedentary behavior. Logically, strategies would include interventions to boost motivation and modifications to the environment to facilitate active behaviors.

The field of physical activity for health is now a rapidly expanding and important area. Often in the past, physical activity was not considered an important health behavior or was viewed simply as sport for youth or high-performance competitors. But physical activity is now a high priority in public health because it can have a significant effect on a wide range of health conditions and because population surveillance of physical activity levels suggests that large numbers of people are insufficiently active to gain such health benefits. For those reasons the population attributable risk of physical inactivity is extremely high (because the health benefits can be large and many people are affected), and therefore successful physical activity behavior change could have a significant effect on public health. Psychology has a clear role to play in the design and implementation of interventions that promote physical activity behavior change.

In this chapter, we address the issue of physical activity behavior change in various community settings. Specifically, after outlining some general frameworks, we consider issues of psychological and wider behavioral theory. These issues will be illustrated through various intervention projects, including the way in which the theory was applied, the results obtained from the intervention, and a discussion on the usefulness of theory. Moreover, we will address the dual behaviors of physical activity and sedentary behavior. The latter is a burgeoning field of contemporary research and focuses on behaviors that are primarily based on sitting, such as screen use and car travel (Owen, Healy, Matthews, & Dunstan, 2010).

Role of Motivation: Understanding the Ecological and Behavioral Epidemiology Frameworks

The adoption of an ecological framework is helpful because it highlights the multiple influences on physical activity and sedentary behavior (Stokols, 1992). Essentially, the ecological framework suggests that behavior can be the product of multiple influences, such as individual psychology, social circumstances, the surrounding physical environment, and wider sociopolitical influences (e.g., policy). This perspective is important to highlight in a chapter that has a focus on motivational psychology because such an approach can only be viewed properly in the wider context of an ecological framework. That is, motivational characteristics will be important, but they are not the only influences on behavior. For example, interventions might target individual motivation when people do not adopt the target behavior of physical activity yet operate in a favorable environment. On the other hand, motivated people might struggle to be as active as they wish if environmental constraints are severe. At the level of public (population) health, typically we need to address both areas because neither will be at an optimal level. That is to say, we need to create supportive environments in which people can operate and at the same time provide individuals with the psychological tools to change and regulate their own behavior.

The behavioral epidemiology framework provides a more focused approach in which to understand the role of psychology and motivation in health behavior change (Sallis & Owen, 1999). Behavioral epidemiology is concerned with the distribution and etiology of behaviors (e.g., smoking, lack of physical activity, sedentary behavior, diet) that may be associated with disease outcomes and how these relate to the occurrence of disease in the population. In relation to physical activity, this framework has five main phases, as illustrated in figure 11.1.

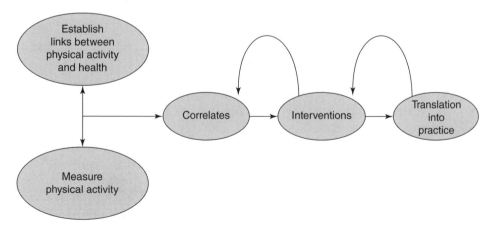

FIGURE 11.1   The behavioral epidemiological framework for physical activity.

1. *To establish the link between physical activity and health*. This connection is now well documented for many diverse health conditions and well-being in older adults (DiPietro, 2007), adults (Hardman & Stensel, 2009), and young people (Stensel, Gorely, & Biddle, 2008).

2. *To develop methods for accurate assessment of physical activity*. Despite new technologies, this task remains a significant challenge for researchers. Often, large-scale surveillance of population trends rely on self-report, a method that has significant problems with validity and reliability. "Objective" methods, such as accelerometers, heart rate monitors, or pedometers, are useful but do not necessarily give all the information required, such as type of activity or the setting in which the activity takes place. Nevertheless, it is recommended that objective assessment be undertaken, but the approach may need to be supplemented by other tools.

3. *To identify factors associated with different levels of physical activity*. It is important to identify factors that might be associated with the adoption and maintenance of behavior. This area is referred to as the study of correlates (association) or determinants (assuming some measure of causality) of physical activity (Biddle & Mutrie, 2008; Buckworth & Dishman, 2002).

4. *To evaluate interventions designed to promote physical activity*. After a variable is identified as a correlate of physical activity (e.g., self-efficacy), then interventions can manipulate this variable to test whether it is, in fact, a determinant (Baranowski, Anderson, & Carmack, 1998).

5. *To translate findings from research into practice*. If interventions work, it is appropriate to translate such findings into ecologically valid settings (i.e., enhance external validity).

We will now review the evidence concerning the correlates of physical activity (phase 3) before considering issues of intervention design and evaluation (phase 4).

Nonpsychological Correlates of Physical Activity

A great deal of research effort has been invested in the study of correlates of physical activity. Numerous reviews have focused on young people (Biddle, Whitehead, O'Donovan, & Nevill, 2005; Hinkley, Crawford, Salmon, Okely, & Hesketh, 2008; Sallis, Prochaska, & Taylor, 2000; van der Horst, A. Chin, Paw, Twisk, & Van Mechelen, 2007) and adults (Trost, Owen, Bauman, Sallis, & Brown, 2002). Correlates are typically grouped into demographic, biological, psychological, sociocultural, and environmental factors. A brief overview of nonpsychological correlates will be provided, followed by a more detailed look at psychological factors.

For demographic correlates, age and gender have been consistently associated with physical activity in youth; males and children often report more activity than females and adolescents. For adults, clear inverse associations were reported by Trost et al. (2002) in a review of studies on age. Males were shown to be more active than females. Lower levels of education and markers of socioeconomic status are generally associated with less physical activity, although this relationship can be complex (Stalsberg & Pedersen, 2010). Concerning biological correlates, weight status (e.g., BMI) has not been shown to be strongly related to physical activity in young people. For adults, however, an inverse association is evident between overweight or obesity and physical activity (Trost et al., 2002).

Previous physical activity and healthy diet are behavioral factors shown to be associated with physical activity in youth. In Trost et al.'s (2002) review of correlates of physical activity in adults, physical activity history in childhood and youth was not associated with activity as an adult. An association was found, however, for activity history during the period of adulthood. Other behavioral factors associated with physical activity for adults include smoking (negative) and healthy diet (positive). Sedentary behavior (e.g., TV viewing or playing computer games) at certain times, in particular during the after-school and weekend periods, is associated with less physical activity in youth (Atkin, Gorely, Biddle, Marshall, & Cameron, 2008). For adolescents, sport participation is related to overall physical activity levels (Biddle, Whitehead, O'Donovan, & Nevill, 2005; Vilhjalmsson & Kristjansdottir, 2003). Peer and parental support are important social correlates of physical activity for adolescents (Gustafson & Rhodes, 2006; Sallis, Prochaska, & Taylor, 2000). Moreover, social support is associated with physical activity in adults (Trost et al., 2002).

The study of environmental factors associated with physical activity is a more recent trend (Davison & Lawson, 2006). Reviews show that access to facilities (for children) and opportunities to exercise (for adolescents) are associated with higher levels of physical activity. In addition, time outdoors is associated with more activity in children, and this connection is likely to be related to spending less time on sedentary entertainment (Ferreira et al., 2006; Sallis, Prochaska, & Taylor, 2000). For adults, environmental factors that are related to physical activity include access to facilities and a positive environment, such as enjoyable scenery and neighborhood safety.

Psychological Correlates of Physical Activity

For children, little consistency was found in the results reported by Sallis et al. (2000) and van der Horst et al. (2007). Part of this may be explained by a simple lack of studies reported on some correlates. Across the two reviews, physical activity is positively associated with intentions and preference for physical activity, and self-efficacy (confidence) tends to be associated with greater levels of physical activity in children.

For adolescents, reviews show that higher levels of perceived competence and self-efficacy are associated with greater physical activity. Biddle et al. (2005) reported that the strength of the association between physical activity and self-efficacy for adolescent girls was small to moderate but only small for perceived competence. Although these two terms may appear to be synonymous, there is a distinction worth highlighting. Self-efficacy is situation-specific confidence to undertake a given behavior, in this case physical activity. Perceptions of competence typically refer to thoughts concerning one's ability to perform tasks at a certain level or to improve current levels. Perceptions of competence sometimes reflect levels of perceived ability. An overlap between the two constructs will be present, but most studies tend to refer to self-efficacy if they are investigating the adoption or maintenance of physical activity. Moreover, some tasks may require self-efficacy ("Can I find the time to cycle to school?") but not perceived competence ("I can easily cycle the required distance and over hilly terrain but have no efficacy to do it because of other constraints or preferences").

Goal orientation or motivation and achievement orientation were identified by van der Horst et al. and Sallis et al. as being positively associated with physical activity in adolescents. This construct is likely to be some form of task orientation—a style or orientation of motivation whereby the individual defines competence and success in self-referenced terms. The individual is motivated to learn from mistakes, to exert effort, and to improve. This literature is quite large but has tended to be restricted to young people in sport or physical education settings (Biddle, Wang, Kavussanu, & Spray, 2003; Roberts, Treasure, & Conroy, 2007). Related perspectives on intrinsic motivation (e.g., self-determination theory) have shown the importance of this approach for understanding physical activity (Mullan & Markland, 1997) and sedentary behavior (Ryan, Rigby, & Przybylski, 2006).

Another important correlate of physical activity is intention. The psychological literature is clear that the motivation to take part in behaviors of free choice, such as physical activity in leisure time, is predicted by strong intentions (Ajzen, 2001). This conclusion was supported in the review by Sallis et al. (2000). Intention is a key mediating variable in the theory of planned behavior and has been studied extensively in physical activity. Intentions to act are the immediate antecedent of behavior, and research supports an association between intentions and physical activity (Hagger, Chatzisarantis, & Biddle, 2002). Planning how best to implement intentions may strengthen this relationship further (Gollwitzer & Sheeran, 2006) and help close the gap between intentions and behaviors. This notion has led to the study of implementation intentions and other issues of self-regulation, planning, and goals (Lippke, Ziegelmann, & Schwarzer, 2004).

Issues of body image and appearance seem to be important for adolescent girls in physical activity and may be salient motivational variables. Typical assessments in this field include perceived body attractiveness, importance of appearance, and physical self-worth. These variables had small to moderate positive association with physical activity in adolescent girls (Biddle et al., 2005). In addition, such issues are often prominent in data derived from qualitative studies (Whitehead & Biddle, 2008). Evidence is less clear for boys and largely unimportant for younger children.

Trost et al.'s (2002) review of adult correlates of physical activity located 38 additional studies to those summarized by Sallis and Owen (1999) (i.e., 1998-2000). There was a positive association with physical activity, across both reviews, for the variables of enjoyment, expected benefits, intention, perceived health, self-motivation, self-efficacy, stage of behavior change, and self-schemata for exercise and a negative association for barriers and mood disturbance. The strongest evidence is for self-efficacy, and it is likely to be more important for behaviors that require effort, such as structured fitness programs.

Theories Typically Used in Physical Activity Interventions

A number of theories have been used to advance understanding of why people might choose to be active or not, and many adopt a social-psychological perspective. Theory provides a unifying framework from which to understand behavior change. It underpins the planning and implementation of physical activity research, particularly for interventions (Bartholomew, Parcel, Kok, & Gottlieb, 2001). More will be said on this topic later.

Typically, key theories have been social-cognitive theory (Bandura, 1986), theory of planned behavior (Ajzen, 2001; Hagger, Chatzisarantis, & Biddle, 2002), and the transtheoretical model (Marshall & Biddle, 2001; Prochaska & Marcus, 1994). Other theories or frameworks adopted in health psychology have been less frequently used in exercise psychology, yet they hold promise. These are the health action process approach (HAPA; Schwarzer, 2008), commonsense model of illness perceptions (Hagger & Orbell, 2003; Leventhal, Leventhal, & Contrada, 1998), and behavioral choice and economics theory (Epstein & Roemmich, 2001). The latter group of theories will not be discussed because of space limitations, but we do advise that researchers planning interventions consider them. Slavish adherence to singular theories can be harmful because important constructs for some populations may be missed. For example, the commonsense model of illness perceptions may be appropriate to use with some populations concerned about their health, but it may be less relevant for healthy populations. But both groups of people may benefit from being assessed on other constructs alongside the main theory of choice. In short, it may be better to consider what needs to be assessed rather than which theory is currently in favor or has been most used in the past.

Social-Cognitive Theory

Social-cognitive theory (SCT) can be attributed to the work of Bandura (1977b), who suggested that we learn and modify our behaviors through an interaction between personal, behavioral, and environmental influences. SCT comprises a self-regulation component whereby we regulate our behavior based on our goals, behaviors, and feelings. In addition, we reflect on our actions, such as by thinking about the consequences of our behaviors (outcome expectancies: "Will exercise help me lose weight?") and our own capabilities to do the behaviors of choice (efficacy expectancies: "Can I exercise more?").

The element of SCT concerned with self-reflection is self-efficacy, which is situation-specific confidence to undertake a certain behavior. This element has been identified as an important correlate of physical activity. Self-efficacy refers to efficacy beliefs (the "can I?" question). This element will be most influential for behaviors that challenge us, such as being more physically active, rather than for easy or habitual behaviors. If people believe that they can adopt and maintain the behavior in question, they are more likely to do so.

Four main sources of self-efficacy information will be important for intervention design if self-efficacy is a variable to be targeted:

- Prior behavior, such as success and performance attainment
- Watching and learning from others through imitation and modeling
- Encouragement from verbal and social persuasion
- Creation of feelings of relaxation and upbeat mood (otherwise referred to as judgments of physiological states)

Many physical activity interventions claim to use SCT as the theory underpinning their intervention, but rarely is it clear what exactly has been targeted from the theory and often only self-efficacy is the focus. Equally, some interventions may use self-efficacy alongside other theoretical constructs (Singh et al., 2006).

Theory of Planned Behavior

The theory of planned behavior (TPB) is based on the central role of attitudes and beliefs and assumes that intention is the immediate antecedent of behavior. Intention, in turn, is predicted from attitude, normative beliefs (subjective norms), and perceptions of behavioral control. Ajzen and Fishbein (1980) suggested that the attitude component of the model is a function of the beliefs held about the specific behavior, as well as the evaluation, or value, of the likely outcomes. Such beliefs can be instrumental (i.e., "Exercise helps me lose weight") and affective ("Exercise is enjoyable"). The latter may be more effective for sustained behavior change.

The subjective norm component is composed of the beliefs of significant others and the extent to which a person wishes to comply with such beliefs. Perceived behavioral control (PBC) is defined by Ajzen (1988) as "the perceived ease or difficulty of performing the behavior" (p. 132) and is assumed "to reflect past experience as well as anticipated impediments and obstacles" (p. 132). It is underpinned by a set of control beliefs and the perceived power of these beliefs. Control beliefs refer to the perceived presence of factors that may help or impede the behavior, and perceived power refers to the perceived effect that helping or inhibiting factors may have on the behavior (Ajzen, 1991).

Two meta-analyses have been conducted in physical activity research using the TPB. Hausenblas et al. (1997) showed that intention had a large effect on exercise behavior and that attitude had a large effect on intention. Hagger and colleagues (2002) reported similar findings.

Clearly, the correlation between intentions and behavior is less than perfect. To help bridge this gap, implementation intentions have been proposed (Gollwitzer, 1999). These are goals and plans that involve specifying when, how, and where performance of the behavior will take place. Evidence appears supportive of the role of implementation intentions in helping translate intentions into behavior (Gollwitzer & Sheeran, 2006).

Transtheoretical Model

Research concerning the transtheoretical model (TTM) in physical activity dates back to Marcus' work in the 1990s (Marcus et al., 1992). It is often seen as a useful and practical perspective by health professionals, although evidence on intervention effectiveness is not always clear cut and not all aspects of the theory are supported in the physical activity literature (Hutchison, Breckon, & Johnston, 2009; Marshall & Biddle, 2001; Riemsma et al., 2002).

The model proposes that behavior change involves movement through stages of change, although such movement may not be linear and may involve progression and regression between stages. The term *transtheoretical model* is used to describe the wider framework that encompasses both the when (stages) and the how of behavior change, including the processes (strategies) of change and mediators of change, such as decisional balance (pros and cons of change) and self-efficacy. Studies on physical activity assess the stages of precontemplation, contemplation, preparation, action, and maintenance. These are described for both physical activity and sedentary behavior in table 11.1.

The stages of change are concerned with the temporal patterning of behavior change. By identifying processes of change we are able to gain a better understanding of why and how this temporal shift might take place. Processes of change, therefore, are important for interventions by helping move people between stages. Processes of change are defined by Marcus et al. (1992) as various strategies and techniques that people use to help them progress through the various stages of change over time. Typically, 10 processes of change have been identified; 5 of these are described as cognitive, or thinking, strategies and the other 5 as behavioral, or doing, strategies. Cognitive processes (e.g., increasing knowledge of the risks of sedentary behavior) tend to peak during the action stage, whereas behavioral processes (e.g., enlisting support of friends and family) are thought to peak later, in the maintenance stage. Support for this proposed pattern for physical activity is less clear from the literature (Marshall & Biddle, 2001).

One strategy that can help people make successful behavior change is to weigh the advantages of change (pros) against the disadvantages, or costs, of change (cons). This decisional balance process is at the core of the TTM

TABLE 11.1

Defining the Stages of the Transtheoretical Model in Physical Activity and Sedentary Behavior

Stage	Physical activity		Sedentary behavior•	
	Meeting criterion level of physical activity?	Current physical activity behavior	Intention to meet criterion level of physical activity?	Application to sedentary behavior
Precontemplation	No	Little or no physical activity	No	Lack of intention to reduce sedentary behavior
Contemplation	No	Little or no physical activity	Yes	Considering ways to reduce sedentary behavior
Preparation	No	Small changes in physical activity	Yes	Small changes in sedentary behavior but below criterion level set
Action	Yes	Physically active for less than 6 months	Yes	Reduced sedentary time to desired level within the past 6 months
Maintenance	Yes	Physically active for more than 6 months	Yes	Reduced sedentary time to desired level for more than 6 months

in respect to behavior change. Research suggests that in the early stages of behavior change, the cons of change outweigh the pros. Those in preparation see more equality between the pros and cons, whereas those who are in maintenance will perceive more pros than cons. Changing perceptions of pros and cons (tipping the balance in favor of the advantages), therefore, may assist in behavior change. Marshall and Biddle (2001) also show that self-efficacy increases with each stage in the progression, as proposed by the model.

The TTM is not without its critics. Adams and White (2005) have questioned the long-term effectiveness of TTM-based interventions. But several commentators suggested that short-term effectiveness has been demonstrated and that further work is required before dismissing the model or replacing it with something else (Brug et al., 2005). A systematic review of TTM-based interventions in physical activity showed that most "fail to accurately represent all dimensions of the model" (p. 829), thus making it difficult to draw firm conclusions about its effectiveness (Hutchison, Breckon, & Johnston, 2009).

Types and Settings for Interventions

Interventions for increasing physical activity or decreasing sedentary behavior can take many forms and can be undertaken in various settings. Distinguishing the nature of the intervention by level may be helpful such that interventions target individuals, small groups, communities, or institutions or even operate at a national or international level, the latter usually being driven by policy initiatives (see table 11.2). This approach will have implications for the nature and design of interventions, such as whether randomization is possible or appropriate and what type of measurement is undertaken. One key issue here is that of sustainability. Interventions that rely heavily on a high level of resources, such as mass media campaign funding, may not be sustainable long term. Likewise, intensive interventions (e.g., one-to-one counseling) may prove effective but may not be sustainable unless they are rolled out to a wider audience in modified form. To this end there is usually a payoff between intensity of delivery and audience reach. Mass media campaigns have the potential to reach everyone but will have only small effects, at best, on individuals. On the other hand, intensive counseling may be highly effective for a few individuals but will have an extremely limited reach.

Behavior Change: Issues of Theory and Interventions

Exercise psychologists have conducted a plethora of cross-sectional observational studies, yet these are relatively weak designs in respect to building evidence for behavior change and causal links between psychology and behavior. More recently, a greater number of interventions have been undertaken and reported in the literature. In this section, we address the key issue of behavior change by discussing the important role that theory can play in designing and evaluating interventions.

TABLE 11.2

Levels and Types of Interventions

Level of intervention	Descriptor of typical design and examples
Individual	Targeting individuals through one-to-one counseling; GP advice
Small group	Exercise groups; rehabilitation or weight clinics
Community	Active travel schemes for companies; school-based initiatives for increasing PA or decreasing sedentary behavior (e.g., Planet Health); subsidized swimming for targeted groups (e.g., those in retirement)
National	Mass media campaigns (e.g., Change4Life, Verb); national policy and guidelines

The Importance of Theory

Systematic reviews have become an increasingly important aspect of designing intervention studies in physical activity. To design a good intervention, researchers must be aware of what is already known from the literature and where gaps in knowledge exist. One of the most important systematic reviews that have informed the design of interventions was that by Kahn et al. (2002). This review used changes in physical activity behavior and aerobic capacity as measures of effectiveness. The conclusions that are particularly relevant to interventions can be summarized as follows:

- There was insufficient evidence that family-based social support interventions effectively increased physical activity.
- There was strong evidence that strengthening local support networks through buddy systems, walking groups, and exercise contacts increased physical activity.
- There was strong evidence that personalized health behavior change programs, tailored to an individual's specific stage of behavior or interest, were effective in increasing physical activity. Activities such as goal setting, social support schemes, self-reward schemes, relapse prevention, and active living approaches to physical activity promotion were viewed as particularly effective. The interventions were delivered in groups, by mail, by telephone, or through other specific media. All such studies were based on a theoretical behavioral approach (e.g., transtheoretical model or theory of planned behavior), and all included goal setting and self-monitoring, self-reward and reinforcement, social support building, strategies for behavioral maintenance, and relapse prevention techniques. These cognitive and behavioral techniques are based on the knowledge of correlates and determinants of physical activity behavior that is a stage in the behavioral epidemiological framework described earlier. Kahn et al.'s review, therefore, provided strong evidence for the effectiveness of theoretically based interventions delivered at the level of the individual.

A recent systematic review of walking interventions made a similar conclusion (Ogilvie et al., 2007). Forty-eight studies that aimed to increase walking were reviewed. The analysis suggested that the most successful interventions were those following behavioral principles such as tailoring the approach to people's needs and targeting groups who were ready to change. Little evidence was found for effectiveness of interventions at the level of the community. An encouraging finding was that walking can be increased by targeting individuals, households, or groups with interventions that use principles of social psychology. But when considered from the perspective of public health, such strategies relate more to efficacy (showing that something can be done in a relatively controlled environment) than effectiveness (showing that the effects can be generalized to various settings). A gap in the literature appears to exist at the final stage of the behavioral epidemiology model where an attempt should be made to roll out successful controlled interventions in ecologically valid settings and across populations (i.e., have good external validity).

In the United Kingdom, the National Institute of Health and Clinical Excellence (NICE) reviewed all the available evidence on behavior change at population, community, and individual levels and issued guidance for practitioners based on that review (National Institute for Health and Clinical Excellence, 2007). The group of experts involved in developing the guidance said that they were influenced by theories and concepts from social science and behavioral science. They suggested that in trying to help any health-related behavior change, the psychological concepts shown in table 11.3 have evidence of effectiveness and could be applied.

Researchers who are planning intervention studies that aim to increase physical activity or decrease sedentary behavior, therefore, have access to several reviews that show the importance of basing the intervention approach on known principles from psychological theory. The choice of which theoretical approach to use should be informed by this literature. Designing an intervention study also requires careful planning and evaluation, as will be discussed next.

TABLE 11.3

Psychological Concepts Shown to Demonstrate Effectiveness in Behavior Change Interventions

Concept	Meaning and action
Outcome expectancies	Helping people develop accurate knowledge about the health consequences of their behaviors
Personal relevance	Emphasizing the personal salience of health behaviors
Positive attitude	Promoting positive feelings toward the outcomes of behavior change
Self-efficacy	Enhancing people's belief in their ability to change
Descriptive norms	Promoting the visibility of positive health behaviors in people's reference groups, that is, the groups they compare themselves to or aspire to
Subjective norms	Enhancing social approval for positive health behaviors in significant others and reference groups
Personal and moral norms	Promoting personal and moral commitments to behavior change
Intention formation and concrete plans	Helping people form plans and goals for changing behaviors over time and in specific contexts
Behavioral contracts	Asking people to share their plans and goals with others
Relapse prevention	Helping people develop skills to cope with difficult situations and conflicting goals

Theory-Based Versus Theory-Informed Interventions

The previous section demonstrated that psychological theory can play an important role in the development and implementation of effective physical activity behavior change interventions, and it identified a number of constructs, from a variety of theoretical perspectives, that could be employed in an attempt to change physical activity behavior. One of the first challenges facing interventionists interested in maximizing intervention effectiveness is to choose between this large number of competing constructs and theories. Choosing one theoretical perspective may make the design of an intervention easier but runs the risk of limiting effectiveness because key constructs from other theories are ignored. Bartholomew et al. (2001) outlined an intervention mapping process to guide these choices and assist in the planning, design, and evaluation of theoretically based interventions. Although intervention mapping is a detailed process that cannot be comprehensively presented here, the broad steps involved are the following:

1. Clearly specifying the objectives of the intervention
2. Selecting theory-based methods that are relevant to the target behaviors
3. Developing practical strategies based on the theory or theories chosen to achieve the objectives
4. Specifying adoption and implementation plans
5. Generating an evaluation plan

To be truly theory based rather than simply theory informed, an intervention must identify and report on explicit links between the theoretical constructs (e.g., social norms, attitudes) and the techniques employed to change them (Michie & Abraham, 2004). Unfortunately, many existing physical activity interventions do not provide this detail and therefore contain limited information about how behavior changes can be facilitated (Brug, Oenema, & Ferreira, 2005). In addition, few intervention studies have conducted mediation analysis (see later section) to assess whether any changes in behavior were influenced by changes in the constructs specified by the theory (Lubans, Foster, & Biddle, 2008; Michie & Abraham, 2004). If the field is to develop a range of theoretically sound and evidence-based behavior change techniques, these issues must be addressed (Michie & Abraham, 2004).

A Framework for Evaluating Interventions

In supporting the concept that approaches to increasing physical activity and decreasing sedentary time should be based on evidence-based psychological theory, we must also support the concept that these approaches must be properly evaluated. Such evaluation must take into account the theoretical basis of the interventions, work in relation to ecological models of physical activity behavior, and consider indicators that are relevant at the level of communities, populations, and settings rather than simply to the individual. Psychologists may need to learn a range of new evaluation skills to use these challenging strategies (Blamey & Mutrie, 2004).

One guide for designing and implementing interventions is the complex evaluation framework first suggested by the Medical Research Council (MRC) in the United Kingdom (Campbell et al., 2000). This framework suggested that for complex interventions (i.e., an intervention that has many parts such as one aimed at increasing physical activity in a community by a variety of means), several stages of design and development are required. Initial stages involve exploration of the literature, perhaps in the form of a systematic review, to ensure that the best theoretical intervention is chosen. Intermediate stages involve determining how elements of the intervention might influence behavior and testing the feasibility of the intervention in a realistic setting. This stage might involve pilot studies, qualitative work, and feasibility trials. A major stage of this framework includes conducting a definitive trial that will usually involve randomization and control conditions that can robustly determine the effect of the intervention. The final stage of this framework involves the implementation of the findings in more real-world settings to determine whether the intervention has the same effects in less-controlled conditions. This stage is similar to the final stage of the behavioral epidemiology model. The MRC framework was recently updated. The authors noted that the original framework had been influential but that more innovative approaches had since been developed; hence, a revision and update was required (Craig et al., 2008). In general, it could be said that the revised guidance suggests that the original framework was perhaps too rigid and offers a variety of alternatives that could apply in specific situations. The revised guidance again emphasizes that developing and evaluating interventions should proceed along a series of stages but adds that the progress might not be as linear as suggested in the original guidance, which strongly favored randomized controlled trials as the design best suited to evaluating outcomes in interventions. The revised guidelines, while still favoring experimental designs, offer a wider range of suggested designs that could be suitable. The revised guidance offers more emphasis on evaluation of the processes of how the observed changes may take place, but the authors note that outcomes are still the most critical element of intervention evaluation. Finally, the authors encourage researchers to report in more detail the interventions used so that replication may take place.

Intervention Planning and Evaluation

As highlighted in previously cited reviews (Kahn et al., 2002; Ogilvie et al., 2007), there is a need for enhanced evidence of what works in terms of promoting physical activity in the real world, that is, intervention effectiveness. There are several reasons for the current limitations in the evidence base and for the disappointing effect of some commonly utilized interventions (Blamey & Mutrie, 2004). These reasons include limitations in planning and implementation such as

- a lack of theory-driven interventions (those informed by psychological or behavioral theory that are appropriately tailored and targeted) and
- intervention plans that do not explicitly detail the following:
  - the anticipated steps between the selected intervention activities and the long-term outcomes (e.g., the short and interim outcomes), nor describe the actual mechanisms or psychological concepts, or mediators or correlates of behavior change that the planned activities are anticipated to trigger or change in their target population;
  - the likely reach of the interventions and the levels of exposure to the intervention that targeted participants will experience;
  - the evidence upon which the intervention activities are based; and
  - issues related to implementation failure, such as a lack of targeting and tailoring, or not delivering the intervention according to the evidence-informed plans agreed upon or in a consistent manner across multiple sites.

Additional explanations for the gaps in evidence are, in part, caused by evaluation issues such as a lack of an evaluative culture in many of our public sector agencies tasked with promoting physical activity, poor quality of many of the evaluations conducted, and a tendency to present evaluation findings without reflecting on where programs have been successful for some participants but not others and the underlying reasons for this (e.g., differential motivations and mediators for various target groups).

In an attempt to address these issues and improve the planning, implementation, and evaluation of social interventions, increasing emphasis has been placed on outcome-focused planning, improved process evaluation, and evaluation approaches that attempt to enhance attribution in complex real-life interventions (where controlled experiments are more difficult to conduct). The latter evaluation approaches are often referred to as theory based. These evaluation approaches, exemplified by theories of change and realistic evaluation (Blamey & Mackenzie, 2007; Fulbright-Anderson, Kubisch, & Connell, 1998; Pawson & Tilley, 1997), attempt to uncover the program theories (e.g., the prescriptive theory or program activities and their postulated links to the outcomes), as well as the more descriptive theories (e.g., the likely causal mechanisms that will motivate behavior change, such as reduction of known barriers to physical activity, like cost or time, or changes in psychological concepts or mediators) (Chen, 1990).

Outcome-focused planning encourages planning from right to left, meaning that plans detail the specific long-term outcomes and the interim and short-term outcomes that will be needed to achieve them. These outcomes then drive the selection of activities. The activities and interventions are, in turn, influenced by evidence (in terms of evaluative learning, review evidence, and tacit experience) of their likely effect on the agreed outcomes and for specific target groups. The reality is that planning processes in many public agencies are more influenced by left to right thinking—in other words, What can we achieve through the activities that we currently offer?

Evaluation approaches linked to theory, more so than traditional evaluation approaches, seek to understand the prescriptive and descriptive theory of an intervention (Chen, 1990; Weiss, 1998) by explicating the detailed program plans and their underlying assumptions about the psychological concepts and mediators that their planned activities are trying to change. As highlighted earlier, the uncovered theories are then used to drive the design of the subsequent evaluation and the methods that it will use. These approaches attempt, where feasible, to forge explicit links between process and outcome evaluation data and findings so that changes in longer-term outcomes might be more convincingly explained by data from the detailed process evaluation. As an example, changes in participants' levels of fitness and their disease risk factors, such as reduced hypertension or cholesterolemia, would more convincingly be seen to have resulted from their participation on an exercise referral program if detailed information was available about their attendance and adherence.

Theory-based evaluations would also ideally try to strengthen the underlying descriptive theory of the program by testing what key mediators had changed in those showing positive outcomes compared with those who did not. This might involve analyzing the changes in mediators (e.g., self-efficacy or attitudes) for these two groups and their explanation for these changes or exposure to particular aspects of the intervention (e.g., access to accurate knowledge or support from significant others, changed social norms because of family or peer support and approval) (see next section on mediation analysis). The limitations in planning processes detailed earlier and subsequently, however, often limit the extent to which evaluations are actually used to refine and enhance descriptive theory.

Both outcome-focused planning and theory-driven evaluations often use tools such as logic modeling (W.K. Kellogg Foundation, 2001) and the RE-AIM framework (Estabrooks & Gyurcsik, 2003; Glasgow, Vogt, & Boles, 1999) to enhance implementation plans. Where detailed plans and theories are not already available, theory-based evaluators often use such tools to develop an evaluation framework, identify key evaluation questions, and focus the subsequent design and methods. These approaches encourage right to left thinking so that the outcomes drive the selection of activities. They can help bring evaluative thinking into program design and thus test the linkages between activities and short-term, interim, and long-term outcomes through reference to available evidence and tacit professional or participant knowledge. The combination of such tools and approaches encourages greater consideration during planning of the prescriptive and descriptive theory, or the *how* (which intervention activities) and *why* (by changing the moderators or barriers) of behavior change.

If our existing evidence base for physical activity promotion is to be enhanced, those designing, planning, implementing, and evaluating interventions need to use the tools and approaches encouraged in outcome-focused planning and theory-driven evaluation and to consider more closely how different types of theory (prescriptive and descriptive) influence behavior change.

Mediation Analysis

Health behavior interventions are designed to target change in correlates of a behavior, which are hypothesized to lead to changes in actual behavior (MacKinnon & Fairchild, 2009). These correlates are often derived from theoretical models. For example, within social cognitive theory (SCT), it is hypothesized that self-efficacy influences physical activity participation (i.e., SCT suggests that a person with higher self-efficacy for physical activity will be more likely to participate in physical activity). Interventions based on SCT, therefore, would seek to employ strategies to increase self-efficacy for physical activity, which should then lead to increases in physical activity. Thus, correlates, in this case self-efficacy, act as a mediator of physical activity behavior change.

A mediator can be defined as "an intervening variable that is necessary to complete a cause–effect link between intervention program and physical activity" (Bauman, Sallis, Dzewaltowski, & Owen, 2002, p. 8). The mediation pathway is illustrated in figure 11.2. Within an intervention study and based on the definitions of Baron and Kenny (1986), a variable functions as a mediator when it meets the following conditions: (*a*) the intervention results in variations in the presumed mediator (e.g., the intervention results in changes in self-efficacy—path a in figure 11.2), (*b*) variations in the mediator significantly account for variations in the dependent variable (e.g., changes in self-efficacy are related to changes in physical activity behavior—path b), and (*c*) when paths a and b are controlled, a previously significant relation between the independent and dependent variables (e.g., between the intervention and

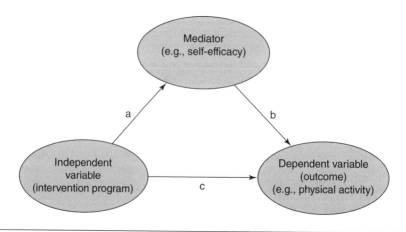

FIGURE 11.2 Overview of a mediation model.

physical activity behavior) is attenuated, and the strongest demonstration of mediation occurs when path c is zero.

Although many interventions are based on psychological theories, many studies do not systematically measure the mediating variables or assess the mediation pathways in the analysis (Baranowski, Anderson, & Carmack, 1998; Lubans, Foster, & Biddle, 2008). This limitation in the literature is significant for several reasons. Mediation analysis helps to identify critical components of interventions (MacKinnon, Krull, & Lockwood, 2000), providing evidence of what works for changing behavior (Lubans, Foster, & Biddle, 2008). This approach allows more effective interventions to be developed because factors identified as mediators can become the focus of future interventions and factors shown not to mediate the behavior change can be ignored (Bauman, Sallis, Dzewaltowski, & Owen, 2002; MacKinnon & Fairchild, 2009). In addition, mediation analysis can be used to refine and develop better theories of behavior change. For example, if an intervention results in change in behavior that is not explained by the hypothesized mediating variables within the underlying theoretical models, then the theory is incomplete and needs further development (Baranowski, Anderson, & Carmack, 1998).

There are several approaches to mediation analysis (see Baron & Kenny, 1986; MacKinnon, 2008), but it is beyond the scope of this chapter to outline them. But mediation analysis should become a fundamental component of intervention evaluation so that key mechanisms of behavior change are identified. This approach will enable the development of increasingly effective interventions and increase our understanding of how to facilitate health behavior change (Lubans, Foster, & Biddle, 2008).

Role of Qualitative Methods in Interventions

Sport and physical activity psychologists often use qualitative methodology in their work to gain a phenomenological insight into the experiences of performers and participants. We also believe that qualitative methods have several roles in considering interventions to promote physical activity or limit sedentary time. In the framework for designing and implementing complex interventions described earlier, qualitative methods may have many uses. Qualitative methodology can provide insight into the development of resources or approaches used in designing the intervention. For example, researchers need to know whether the materials that they have produced to support participants are clear and well received. Another role for qualitative work relates to finding evidence for the feasibility of putting the intervention in place from the view of the participants, as well as from the professionals and researchers involved. For example, when working in primary care settings the views of the whole primary care team about the time taken to arrange appointments and the person best suited to deliver the intervention must be taken into account. When conducting a randomized controlled trial there is added value in including elements of qualitative research to triangulate the outcome data and provide additional insight into the way in which participants responded to the intervention. Such methods may have a particularly important role in illuminating the processes that participants enjoyed and engaged with in comparison to aspects of the intervention that they did not engage with (McEachan, Lawton, Jackson, Conner, & Lunt, 2008).

In a randomized controlled trial of an exercise program for women with early stage breast cancer, we concluded that a supervised exercise program provided both psychological and functional benefits for women up to 6 months after beginning the exercise (Mutrie et al., 2007). The qualitative aspect of that study strongly underlined the motivation that the women had in attending these exercise opportunities. The women reported that they did not want to sit around talking about cancer and found exercise a positive alternative. They also reported that the safe environment created by a trained exercise leader was a critical component of their motivation (Emslie et al., 2007). Such insight may not be available from quantitative methods, and thus the qualitative approach adds value to the outcomes reported.

Examples of Physical Activity Behavior Change

In this section, we describe and analyze example interventions for increasing physical activity and decreasing sedentary behavior in an effort to illustrate some of the points discussed so far. We highlight key issues in method, results, and theory, building on prior text. First, for physical activity we highlight three types of interventions based on active commuting, community walking through use of pedometers, and a structured education approach for those with a high risk of type 2 diabetes, also including use of pedometers. We then outline issues from interventions for sedentary behaviors rather than physical activity.

The Walk In to Work Out Project

The transtheoretical model was used to inform the design of a trial to determine whether people could be encouraged to walk or cycle (actively commute) to work rather than use their cars (Mutrie et al., 2002). Such a change in behavior has become of interest not only for physical activity promotion but also as an element in campaigns to limit car use and congestion and potentially improve the environment. The first way that the theory was applied in this study concerned targeting people who were thinking about active commuting (contemplators) or preparing to commute actively (doing some irregular active commuting). A stages of change question was used as a screening tool for interested participants, and only contemplators and preparers were invited into the trial. The materials for the intervention group were delivered as a self-help instructional booklet, titled *Walk In to Work Out Pack*, designed for the contemplation and preparation stages. The pack contained written interactive materials that guided participants through elements of the transtheoretical model of behavior change, such as considering a decisional balance sheet (pros and cons) for increasing active commuting behavior, considering how to enhance self-efficacy for active commuting, and setting goals for increased walking or cycling to and from work. The pack also contained local information about distances and routes and safety information. The control group received the pack 6 months later.

The results showed that the intervention group was almost twice as likely to increase walking to work as the control group at 6 months. Contemplators (those who had been considering active commuting at the beginning of the trial) added more minutes per week to their walking than did those in the preparation stage, although the preparers also achieved an increase. The intervention was not successful at increasing cycling; few participants opted for that method of active travel.

One-quarter of the intervention group who received the pack at baseline were regularly actively commuting at the 12-month follow-up. The materials were updated and reproduced both in Scotland and England and are available to employers who wish to promote active commuting to their workforces, thus demonstrating good external validity and reaching phase 5 of the behavioral epidemiology framework. In this project, the transtheoretical model provided a practical approach to designing a self-instruction set of resources that appeared to influence behavior.

Pedometer-Based Studies

Besides being directed to active commuting studies, research has focused on walking more generally in local communities, and pedometers have become a popular addition to many studies that focus on walking. A recent review looked at the use of pedometers to increase physical activity and improve health (Bravata et al., 2007). The authors concluded that pedometer use is associated with significant increases in physical activity and decreases in body mass index and blood pressure. Overall, pedometer users were shown to increase physical activity by 26.7% over baseline.

What of the theory involved in pedometer use? Pedometers can provide daily feedback about the accumulated number of steps that a person has achieved. Some models provide additional feedback, such as the minutes spent in moderate-intensity activity or the weekly record of steps achieved. Thus, step counts provide the opportunity for both setting goals and receiving feedback. Indeed, having a step goal has been identified as a key predictor of an increase in activity, although evidence is lacking about the most appropriate goal to use. The pedometer, therefore, is a relatively cheap piece of technology that operates with known principles from the psychology of behavior change, such as goal setting and self-monitoring of progress. These principles are neatly illustrated by one participant in our walking studies:

> I think the pedometer was really useful at the beginning because you got tuned into it and checked it and I realised that my days at home and days at work were really quite different so I needed to make a special effort on my days off.

Evidence also suggests that a support structure that addresses social and cognitive factors is required for a pedometer-based intervention to be effective (Talbot, Gaines, Huynh, & Metter, 2003; Tudor-Locke et al., 2004). A physical activity consultation using a theoretically grounded framework constitutes one method of addressing these factors and has been demonstrated to promote physical activity (Kahn et al., 2002; Kirk, Mutrie, MacIntyre, & Fisher, 2003). Researchers have suggested that pedometers may provide an important point of discussion for in-depth physical activity consultations (Stovitz, VanWormer, Center, & Bremer, 2005), yet this is an area that has not been particularly well addressed by pedometer-based intervention studies.

In the work of the Scottish Physical Activity Research Collaboration (SPAR-Coll; www.sparcoll.org.uk), we have been conducting studies on walking using both pedometers and consultations. These studies have been planned with the use of the MRC's complex intervention framework already described. We conducted a systematic review of the literature relating to walking interventions (Ogilvie et al., 2007) and piloted approaches to using pedometers. We then designed a randomized controlled trial, Walking for Well-Being in the West (WWW), which aimed to promote and maintain increased walking behavior through the use of physical activity consultations and a pedometer-based walking program (Fitzsimons et al., 2008).

In the first part of our studies, 63 women and 16 men (49.2 years ± 8.8) were randomly assigned to either an intervention (physical activity consultation and 12-week pedometer-based walking program) or control (no action) group. The physical activity consultation followed principles of behavior change already described. The walking program involved a series of graduated step goals over 12 weeks. The goals were tailored to each individual's baseline level of daily steps and began with increasing step counts by 1,500 steps on 3 days of the week. By week 7 of the program the goals had been built up to achieving an additional 3,000 steps per day over baseline values on at least 5 days of the week. This goal equates to the public health recommendation of achieving 30 minutes of moderate-intensity activity on most days of the week.

We found significant increases in the intervention group for step counts, time spent in leisure walking, and positive affect. Significant decreases were found in this group for time spent in sitting, and no corresponding changes occurred in the control group. From this study we concluded that a pedometer-based walking program that incorporates a physical activity consultation is effective in promoting walking and improving positive affect over 12 weeks in community-based individuals (Baker et al., 2008).

In the second phase of our studies we followed up the participants 12 months after their initial engagement with the project. Those who were originally assigned to the control condition were given what we described as a minimal intervention, which involved the use of the pedometer and a walking program tailored to each person's baseline step count but not a physical activity consultation. We found that both the maximal intervention (which included the physical activity consultation) and the minimal intervention successfully increased and maintained step counts in low-active Scottish men and women over a 12-month period (Fitzsimons, Baker, Wright, Lowry, & Mutrie, 2009). No significant difference was found between groups in the number of participants who achieved a weekly step increase of 15,000 or more steps at 12 months (group 1, 13/24 [54%]; group 2, 9/23 [39%]). The maximal intervention, however, appeared to influence self-reported sitting time, using the IPAQ questionnaire (Craig et al., 2003; Fitzsimons, Baker, Brennan, & Mutrie, 2010).

What were the theoretical implications of these findings? The successful ingredient appears to be the graduated goals for increasing step counts in a walking program that uses pedometers to enable self-monitoring of progress toward those goals. The cognitive and behavioral skills addressed in the physical activity consultation have little added benefit for increasing walking but may have more influence on sitting time. Interventions relating to decreasing sedentary time are in their infancy, and these findings offer evidence of the psychological principles that may be needed to achieve behavior change in this domain (see later section on sedentary behavior interventions).

PREPARE: A Physical Activity Intervention for Individuals With Impaired Glucose Tolerance

The PREPARE program was a structured education intervention designed to increase physical activity and improve glucose tolerance in individuals with impaired glucose tolerance (IGT) (Yates, Davies, Gorely, Bull, & Khunti, 2008, 2009). People with IGT have an increased risk of developing type 2 diabetes and cardiovascular disease and are therefore an important population to target in health behavior interventions. The PREPARE program consists of a 3-hour single-session group educational program, usually having 5 to 10 participants, designed to increase physical activity by targeting perceptions and knowledge of IGT, physical activity self-efficacy, barriers, and self-regulatory skills.

The program takes a person-centered approach based on Chaiken's dual-process theory (Chaiken, 1987). This theory provides an outline for how information should be presented to participants and makes a distinction between heuristic and systematic processing. In heuristic processing the health professional is positioned as an expert who imparts knowledge to the passive patient. In contrast, systematic processing involves the individual taking an active role in the learning experience by looking for evidence, examples, reasoning, and logic within the information that is provided. The use of a systematic processing approach encourages people to scrutinize information, ask questions, and work things out for themselves. Systematic processing requires greater cognitive effort from participants but results in their making stronger links between theoretical concepts and their personal situation.

Three other social psychological theories underpin the content of the program: (1) Bandura's social-cognitive theory (Bandura, 1986), which identifies barriers, self-efficacy, and self-regulation as important influences on behavior; (2) Gollwitzer's implementation intentions (Gollwitzer, 1999), which focuses on self-regulation strategies, such as the formation of action plans outlining when, where, and how a behavioral goal will be achieved; and (3) Leventhal's commonsense model (Leventhal, Meyer, & Nerenz, 1980). This model postulates that individuals conceptualize and respond to a health threat in terms of their beliefs about the cause, consequence, identity, control, or treatment and timeline associated with the threat.

It has been demonstrated that illness perceptions and beliefs are linked to health behavior change in individuals with type 2 diabetes (Skinner, Davies, Heller, & Khunti, 2005), and although IGT is not a recognized disease, it was hypothesized that because people identified with IGT are likely to form perceptions and beliefs about IGT, targeting these perceptions and beliefs in the intervention would influence how participants cope with IGT in the future. The PREPARE program consists of four modules, which are briefly outlined in table 11.4.

TABLE 11.4

Outline and Theoretical Underpinning of the PREPARE Program

Module name	Content	Theoretical underpinning
Patient story	Participants are encouraged to share their knowledge and perceptions of IGT and highlight any issues that they would like addressed.	Commonsense model
Professional story	Using nontechnical language, open questions, and appropriate audiovisual aids, the educator provides an overview of healthy glucose metabolism, the etiology of prediabetes, and the risk factors and complications associated with prediabetes. Participants calculate their own risk scores.	Commonsense model Dual-process theory
Diet	The group educator provides an overview of the link between diet and metabolic dysfunction.	Social-cognitive theory Dual process theory
Physical activity	Using nontechnical language, open questions, and appropriate audiovisual aids, the educator helps participants • identify how physical activity improves glucose control, • understand current physical activity recommendations, • explore ways to incorporate physical activity into everyday life, • identify barriers to physical activity, and • form action plans and set personal goals. The educator encourages participants to use their physical activity diaries.	Social-cognitive theory Implementation intentions Dual-process theory

Adapted from *Patient Education and Counseling*, Vol. 73(2), T. Yates, M. Davies, T. Gorely, F. Bull, and K. Khunti, "Rationale, design and baseline data from the pre-diabetes risk education and physical activity recommendation and encouragement (PREPARE) programme study: A randomized controlled trial," pg. 264-271, Copyright 2008, with permission from Elsevier.

The PREPARE study was set up as a three-armed randomized controlled trial. Participants were randomized to receive either usual care (control group), the PREPARE program with pedometer use, or the PREPARE program without pedometer use. The two intervention groups received the identical program, except that in the pedometer version participants were given a pedometer and encouraged to set personalized steps-per-day goals, whereas in the alternative group participants were encouraged to set physical activity goals based on the generic recommendation of 30 minutes of moderate to vigorous physical activity on most days of the week.

Results showed that objectively measured ambulatory activity, self-reported walking, and overall moderate- to vigorous-intensity physical activity increased significantly in the pedometer group compared to those in the control group at 3, 6, and 12 months. In the group without pedometer use, ambulatory activity and self-reported walking and moderate- to vigorous-intensity physical activity increased significantly compared to those in the control group at 12 months, but no differences were found compared to the control group at 3 or 6 months.

The results of the PREPARE intervention study suggest that a structured education program can be effective in increasing physical activity in those with IGT. The study was limited, however, by the lack of a mediation analysis (see earlier section), so it is not possible to identify whether the theoretical constructs targeted by the intervention (e.g., self-efficacy, self-regulation) were related to the behavior change observed. As a result, critical components of the intervention were not identified. The inclusion of Leventhal's commonsense model is relatively rare; few other diabetes prevention programs include this approach. Qualitative work suggests that individuals identified with IGT experience uncertainty about their diagnosis, its consequences, and its treatment (Troughton et al., 2008). The commonsense model provides a theoretical basis for targeting these uncertainties within an intervention and may provide a framework to support and shape perceptions to enhance the likelihood of health-maintaining behaviors (Troughton et al., 2008). The use of implementation intentions is intuitively appealing, but the likelihood that participants will continue to sit down to set daily or weekly goals needs to be examined.

Three types of interventions to increase physical activity have been provided as exemplars and as anchors from which readers can apply some of the concepts described throughout this chapter. We now provide additional examples, but this time focused on changing sedentary behaviors.

Sedentary Behavior Change

Sedentary behavior includes a cluster of various behaviors primarily involving sitting. Although humans have always rested, the amount of sedentary time is likely to have increased significantly with motorized transport and attractive home-based entertainment systems, including TVs and computers (Katzmarzyk & Mason, 2009). Given that sedentary time is made up of multiple behaviors, it is often weakly associated with time spent in moderate to vigorous physical activity. This finding might also suggest that sedentary behaviors may have different correlates and require intervention strategies different from those targeting increasing physical activity. This point is important to note in the context of this chapter.

Surprisingly, no sedentary behavior interventions have been used with adults, although studies targeting physical activity have sometimes assessed sedentary time. But interventions have been designed to reduce sedentary time, usually screen time, in young people. In this section, we outline some example interventions, highlight some key issues, and conclude with a discussion on motivation and theory for sedentary behavior change.

Interventions to Reduce Sedentary Behavior in Young People

At least three types of sedentary behavior interventions for young people appear in the literature: recruiting from clinics (e.g., obesity research clinics, children's hospitals), population- or community-based interventions (e.g., child's home environment, community-based after school programs, school settings), and laboratory-based studies, all with varying intervention designs. Results show a small effect for intervention effectiveness but no moderators were significant (Biddle, O'Connell, & Braithwaite, 2011).

Laboratory-based studies show that positive reinforcement for reducing sedentary behavior and sedentary behavior being made contingent on being physically active can be successful in reducing sedentary behavior. These interventions tend to be with obese children (O'Connell, Biddle, & Braithwaite, 2009). Each type of intervention will be illustrated through examples.

Intervention With Clinic-Based Recruitment: Screen Time Reduction in Young Children

Epstein et al. (2008) recruited 4- to 7-year-old children and their families from a university children's hospital. The children were at or above the 75th percentile for BMI and were randomly assigned to either intervention or control groups. The former had TV allowance devices fitted in their homes to all TV sets and computers. This allowance device was accessed by a code, and monitors time spent on each machine. The intervention children were assessed for baseline screen time and then set targets of a 10% reduction per month up to a maximum of a 50% reduction. After the budget time had been reached, the screen could not be activated for the rest of that week. Financial incentives were offered. Results showed that although the control group reduced screen time by 5 hours per week, the intervention group reduced time by 18 hours. BMI reduction was greater in the intervention group.

The theory underpinning this intervention is not explicit in the paper, but the methods reflect behavioral choice theory (Epstein & Roemmich, 2001). In particular, the targeted sedentary behavior is made less accessible, and an alternative is reinforced with financial incentives. A relevant theoretical perspective that impinges on this study is self-determination theory (Ryan, Patrick, Deci, & Williams, 2008) because the authors claim that the allowance device enables the child to make decisions and have choice about screen time. They also argue that some may view such a device as controlling, which would be counterproductive to the development of intrinsic motivation for behavior change.

Community-Based Intervention: Planet Health

The Planet Health intervention was a randomized controlled field trial with five intervention and five control schools in the United States. It targeted children aged 11 to 12 years. A 2-year curriculum was taught, including reducing TV time and other health behaviors. The primary outcome measure was obesity, and prevalence was reduced in the intervention schools, but this was mainly in girls rather than in boys. TV time was reduced for both boys and girls in intervention schools by about 30 minutes per day. TV viewing time was related to the reduction of obesity in girls.

Planet Health was based on behavioral choice theory (Epstein & Roemmich, 2001) and social cognitive theory (SCT) (Bandura, 1986). Specifically, the authors targeted a reduction in TV viewing by offering alternatives and enabling more control and choice over active behaviors. Using SCT, the authors claimed that they provided cognitive and behavioral skills and time to practice skills to enhance perceived competence.

Laboratory-Based Intervention: Screen Time Contingent on Riding a Stationary Bicycle

Saelens and Epstein (1998) recruited 14 obese boys and girls aged 8 to 12 years. At baseline they were allowed a free choice of activities in a laboratory, including an exercise bike, computer games, books, and movies. On days 2 and 3, the intervention group's participation in watching movies and playing computer games was contingent on using the exercise bike because the bike powered the screens. The control group had no such restriction. Compared to baseline, the intervention group increased their physical activity, decreased the targeted sedentary behavior (i.e., screen time), but increased their time in other, nontargeted sedentary behaviors (e.g., reading, drawing). No changes occurred in the control group.

The theory underpinning the intervention design is not explicit in the paper. But it is clear from the discussion and from previous papers from Epstein's group that behavioral choice theory (Epstein & Roemmich, 2001) is supported when physical activity is made more accessible. This finding is consistent with reinforcement models and the Premack principle whereby a high-frequency activity (e.g., screen time) can be used as reinforcement for a low-frequency activity (e.g., physical activity). Note, however, that although the targeted sedentary behaviors were reduced, other sedentary behaviors increased. This result can be interpreted as good news in so far as the children did not completely abandon physical activity for alternative sedentary behaviors but instead were willing to be active to gain access to highly valued sedentary pursuits.

Sedentary Behavior: Issues for Psychologists

The field of motivation has been prominent in exercise psychology. Typical theories, as mentioned earlier in this chapter, include social-cognitive theory, theory of planned behavior, and the transtheoretical model. Other possible theories are numerous (see Bartholomew, Parcel, Kok, & Gottlieb, 2001). It is unclear at this stage whether these theories are equally applicable to sedentary behavior, although SCT has been used, as discussed earlier in some of the example interventions. Behavioral choice theory is prominent, and exercise psychologists may wish to consider others, including well-known motivational theories such as self-determination theory.

Sedentary behavior, though, is likely to operate in a different way from physical activity, as shown in table 11.5. The scenarios in table 11.5 are generalizations that will vary across individuals and behaviors, but they illustrate that it may be necessary to consider the behavior in more detail when planning the use of theoretical frameworks within interventions. For example, in reference to dietary behaviors, Kremers et al. (2007) said, "Theories of planned action may have limited use in the study of adolescent energy balance-related behaviors, since these behaviors are typically a natural part of adolescents' everyday lives that do not require much intentional effort" (p. 346). This point may also apply to sedentary behaviors, thus requiring intervention researchers to reconsider theoretical approaches and the role of conscious processing and habit.

TABLE 11.5

Possible Differentiating Qualities Between Physical Activity and Sedentary Behavior

Quality	Physical activity[1]	Sedentary behavior
Frequency across the day	Low; likely no more than once	High; regular, prolonged bouts of sedentary behavior likely
Duration	Short, at least for structured exercise (e.g., 30 minutes)	Long, such as 2 to 3 hours of TV viewing or prolonged sitting at work
Effort	Moderate to high	Low
Conscious processing	Moderate to high; requires planning	Low and habitual

[1]Physical activity can refer to many types of behavior. For the purpose of differentiating physical activity and sedentary behavior, we refer to physical activity as something done in planned bouts rather than throughout a day, such as NEAT (Levine, 2007).

Practical Applications

Interventions, almost by definition, are practical. They seek to apply principles of psychology and other disciplines to enhance behavior change. To do this effectively, the following key steps are suggested:

1. Identify modifiable correlates of physical activity that are important and relevant to the population of interest.
2. Seek information from the participants on how these correlates might be changed in ways that are possible, acceptable, and engaging.
3. Design the intervention based on good theory.
4. Consider how to prompt participants for behavioral maintenance.
5. Use good measures of the behavior.
6. Use outcome-focused planning that details the specific long-term outcomes and the interim and short-term outcomes that will be needed to achieve them.
7. Evaluate how the intervention is being delivered, as well as how it is being received and enacted by the participants (process evaluation).
8. Consider how best to enhance external validity for the current or a future intervention.

Directions for Future Research

1. *Sport and exercise psychology lacks a good evidence base on behavior change interventions.* There is a need to conduct cross-sectional and qualitative evidence of motivation in early stages of intervention development and, rather than stop at that point as is done in much of the literature, to integrate such findings into pilot interventions and full trials. This approach is consistent with the MRC guidelines alluded to earlier.
2. *Motivation research in behavior change studies needs to address how constructs such as intention can be translated better into behavior.* Theories tend to be biased toward understanding cognitions more than links to behavior itself. Clearly, better linkage is needed between elements of a theory and the way in which those elements are used for behavior change. Moreover, different psychological constructs may be more or less important for different behaviors (e.g. walking, playing sport, total physical activity) or in different settings.
3. *Motivation on its own may not be enough.* We also need to understand the wider social and environmental context of behaviors.
4. *Behavioral prompting may be a simple way to enhance engagement in behavior change.* To this end, researchers need to look to new technologies.

5. *Multimethod studies that combine qualitative and quantitative methods are needed.* Narrow-minded adherence to one or the other is neither appropriate nor helpful.

6. *Both physical activity and sedentary behavior appear to have significant links to health.* Both need to be addressed for behavior change, sometimes in combination. But we know little about the psychology of sedentary (sitting) behavior.

Summary

A key objective in writing this chapter has been to broaden the focus of motivation in the context of physical activity behavior change where health-related outcomes are the focus. Typically, motivation is seen as a personal or individual construct, and we have attempted to locate motivation in the wider context of an ecological model. Interventions to increase physical activity and reduce sedentary behavior will need to address personal motivation, and many of the key theories in this field are centered on individual cognitions. Moreover, we have argued that these can be successful in changing behavior. But the bigger picture must also be viewed to account for factors associated with social influence (e.g., family), communities, and related environmental factors, as well as societal norms and policies.

Psychologists interested in physical activity and health are likely to be well versed in psychological theory. These and other behavioral theories are required parts of behavior change intervention planning, and we have argued that this is a crucial step for researchers to take. A wider range of theories, however, may need to be considered. Space does not allow for expansion on these theories or for consideration of important topics such as counseling and interview skills (Breckon, Johnston, & Hutchinson, 2008).

We have covered the issues raised in this chapter to highlight important psychological and behavioral constructs and processes for the design, implementation, and evaluation of physical activity and sedentary behavior change interventions.

EPILOGUE

Of the three volumes in this series, this volume is the most balanced between theory, research, and application. This was our intent and the challenge we presented to the contributors. We wanted each chapter to present theoretically sound arguments supported by strong research findings. As befits a field that is applied in character, however, we wanted readers to be able to take away practical applications and ideas that would increase understanding of how to enhance motivation. Some of these applications we expected to be directly suggested in the text while other inferences and insights we thought would be stimulated by the text. We believe that each of the contributors successfully accomplished this goal. Each chapter clearly demonstrates that when theory, research, and practice interact, real progress can be made in addressing critical and pressing questions.

The field of motivation psychology in sport and exercise has come a long way since a symposium, organized by Glyn Roberts in November 1989 at the University of Illinois at Urbana-Champaign, served as the impetus for the first publication of the *Motivation in Sport and Exercise* book (Roberts, 1992). As evidenced by the chapters in this volume, we have progressed a great deal in our understanding of the thoughts and perceptions that have encompassed the motivation process since 1992. This progression is not only in terms of the quantity of research but, more important, in the quality of the research. Although there is much work still to be completed in regard to the development of our theoretical understanding, particularly in regard to parsimony, elegance, and conceptual coherence, we believe that the valuable insights garnered should now be applied to the myriad of contexts and conditions highlighted in this volume. When we state that motivation research in sport and exercise psychology has come of age, this is what we mean. It is time to accelerate the integration of our research knowledge into all aspects of applied practice touched on in this volume, ranging from coaching, teaching, and parenting to assisting in the health-related quality of life of cancer patients and broader public health policy decisions. In this way, the collective research of the contributors to this volume and others will become pivotal in facilitating optimal achievement striving, performance, well-being, and health.

REFERENCES

Abrahamsen, F.E., Roberts, G.C., & Pensgaard, A.M. (2008). Achievement goals and gender effects on multidimensional anxiety in national elite sport. *Psychology of Sport and Exercise, 9*, 449–464.

Abrams, M., & Hale, B.D. (2005). Anger: How to moderate hot buttons. In S. Murphy (Ed.), *The sport psychology handbook: A complete guide to today's best mental training techniques.* (pp. 93–112). Champaign, IL: Human Kinetics.

Adams, J., & White, M. (2005). Why don't stage-based activity promotion interventions work? *Health Education Research, 20*, 237–243.

Adie, J.W., Duda, J.L., & Ntoumanis, N. (2008). Autonomy support, basic need satisfaction and the optimal functioning of adult male and female sport participants: A test of basic needs theory. *Motivation & Emotion, 32*, 189–199. doi:10.1007/s11031-008-9095-z

Adler, A. (1956). Striving for superiority. In H.L. Ansbacher & R. Ansbacher (Eds.), *The individual psychology of Alfred Adler: A systematic presentation in selections from his writings* (pp. 101–125). New York: Harper Row.

Ajzen, I. (1985). From intentions to actions: A theory of planned behavior. In J. Kuhl & J. Beckmann (Eds.), *Action-control: From cognition to behavior* (pp. 11–39). Heidelberg, Germany: Springer.

Ajzen, I. (1988). *Attitudes, personality and behaviour.* Milton Keynes: Open University Press.

Ajzen, I. (1991). The theory of planned behavior. *Organizational Behavior and Human Decision Processes, 50*, 179–211.

Ajzen, I. (2001). Nature and operation of attitudes. *Annual Review of Psychology, 52*, 27–58.

Ajzen, I. (2002). *Constructing a TPB questionnaire: Conceptual and methodological considerations.* Retrieved from http://people.umass.edu/aizen/pdf/tpb.measurement.pdf

Ajzen, I. (2009a). *Behavioral interventions based on the theory of planned behavior.* Retrieved from www.people.umass.edu/aizen/tpb.html

Ajzen, I. (2009b). From intentions to behavior: Implementation intention, commitment and conscientiousness. *Journal of Applied Psychology, 39*, 1356–1372.

Ajzen, I., & Fishbein, M. (1980). *Understanding attitudes and predicting social behaviour.* Englewood Cliffs, NJ: Prentice-Hall.

Allen, J.B., & Shaw, S. (2009). Women coaches' perceptions of their sport organizations' social environment: Supporting coaches' psychological needs? *Sport Psychologist, 23*, 346–366. Retrieved from http://hk.humankinetics.com/TSP/journal-About.cfm

Allen, M.S., Jones, M.V., & Sheffield, D. (2010). The influence of positive reflection on attributions, emotions, and self-efficacy. *Sport Psychologist, 24*, 211–226.

Altman, D.G., Schulz, K.F., Moher, D., Egger, M., Davidoff, F., Elbourne, D., . . . Lang, T. CONSORT GROUP (Consolidated Standards of Reporting Trials). (2001). The revised CONSORT statement for reporting randomized trials: Explanation and elaboration. *Annals of Internal Medicine, 134*, 663–694.

Alvarez, M., S., Balaguer, I., Castillo, I., & Duda, J.L. (2009). Coach autonomy support and quality of sport engagement in young soccer players. *The Spanish Journal of Psychology, 12*, 138–148.

Amabile, T.M., DeJong, W., & Lepper, M. (1976). Effects of externally imposed deadlines on subsequent intrinsic motivation. *Journal of Personality and Social Psychology, 34*, 92–98.

American Cancer Society. (2010). *Cancer facts & figures 2010.* Atlanta, GA: American Cancer Society.

American College of Sports Medicine (ACSM). (2009). *ACSM's guidelines for exercise testing and prescription* (8th ed.). Baltimore, MD: Lippincott Williams & Wilkins.

Ames, C. (1984a). Achievement attributions and self-instructions under competitive and individualistic goal structures. *Journal of Educational Psychology, 76*, 478–487.

Ames, C. (1984b). Competitive, cooperative, and individualistic goal structures: A cognitive-motivational analysis. In C. Ames & R. Ames (Eds.), *Research on motivation in education: Vol. 1. Student motivation* (pp. 117–208). New York: Academic Press.

Ames, C. (1984c). Conceptions of motivation within competitive and noncompetitive goal structures. In R. Schwarzer (Ed.), *Self-related cognitions in anxiety and motivation*. Hillsdale, NJ: Erlbaum.

Ames, C. (1992a). Achievement goals and the classroom motivational climate. In D.H. Schunk & J.L. Meece (Eds.), *Student perceptions in the classroom*. (pp. 327–348): Hillsdale, NJ: Erlbaum.

Ames, C. (1992b). Achievement goals, motivational climate, and motivational processes. In G.C. Roberts (Ed.), *Motivation in sport and exercise* (pp. 161–176). Champaign, IL: Human Kinetics.

Ames, C. (1992c). Classrooms: Goals, structures, and student motivation. *Journal of Educational Psychology, 84*, 261–271. doi:10.1037/0022-0663.84.3.261

Amiot, C.E., Gaudreau, P., & Blanchard, C.M. (2004). Self-determination, coping, and goal attainment in sport. *Journal of Sport and Exercise Psychology, 26*, 396–411. Retrieved from http://hk.humankinetics .com/JSEP/journalAbout.cfm

Amiot, C.E., Vallerand, R.J., & Blanchard, C.M. (2006). Passion and psychological adjustment: A test of the person-environment fit hypothesis. *Personality and Social Psychology Bulletin, 32*, 220–229.

Amirthavasar, G., & Bray, S.R. (2008). Women exercisers' affective reactions to gender variations in class leaders and co-exercisers. *Journal of Sport and Exercise Psychology, 30*, S146–S147.

Amorose, A.J., & Anderson-Butcher, D. (2007). Autonomy-supportive coaching and self-determined motivation in high school and college athletes: A test of self-determination theory. *Psychology of Sport and Exercise, 8*, 654–670. doi:10.1016/j.psychsport.2006.11.003

Amorose, A.J., Anderson-Butcher, D., & Cooper, J. (2009). Predicting changes in athletes' well being from changes in need satisfaction over the course of a competitive season. *Research Quarterly for Exercise and Sport, 80*, 386–392. Retrieved from www.aahperd.org/rc/publications/rqes/

Anderson, D.M., & Dixon, A.W. (2009). Winning isn't everything: Goal orientation and gender differences in university leisure-skills classes. *Recreational Sports, 33*, 54–64.

Andrykowski, M.A., Beacham, A.O., Schmidt, J.E., & Harper, F.W.K. (2006). Application of the Theory of Planned Behavior to understanding intentions to engage in physical and psychosocial health behaviors after cancer diagnosis. *Psycho-Oncology, 15*, 759-771.

Anshel, M.H., & Eom, H. (2002). Exploring the dimensions of perfectionism in sport. *International Journal of Sport Psychology, 34*, 255–271.

Anshel, M.H., & Mansouri, H. (2005). Influences of perfectionism on motor performance, affect, goal setting and causal attributions in response to critical information feedback. *Journal of Sport Behaviour, 28*, 99–124.

Appleton, P.R., Hall, H.K., & Hill, A. (2006). *The relationship between perfectionism and athlete burnout in elite junior sport*. Paper presented at the International Association of Applied Psychology Congress, Athens, Greece.

Appleton, P.R., Hall, H.K., & Hill, A.P. (2009). The influence of perfectionism on junior-elite athlete burnout. *Psychology of Sport and Exercise, 10*, 457–465.

Appleton, P.R., Hall, H.K., & Hill, A.P. (2010). Family patterns of perfectionism: An examination of elite junior athletes and their parents. *Psychology of Sport and Exercise, 11*, 363–371.

Arbour-Nicitopoulous, K.P., Martin Ginis, K.A., & Latimer, A.E. (2009). Planning leisure-time physical activity, and coping self-efficacy in persons with spinal cord injury: A randomized controlled trial. *Archives of Physical Medicine and Rehabilitation, 90*, 2003–2011.

Armstrong, L., & Jenkins, S. (2001). *It's not about the bike. My journey back to life*. New York: Berkley Book.

Aron, A., Aron, E.N., & Smollan, D. (1992). Inclusion of other in the self scale and the structure of interpersonal closeness. *Journal of Personality and Social Psychology, 63*, 596–612.

Assor, A., Kaplan, H., & Roth, G. (2002). Choice is good, but relevance is excellent: Autonomy-enhancing and suppressing teacher behaviors predicting students' engagement in schoolwork. *British Journal of Educational Psychology, 72*, 261–278. doi:10.1348/000709902158883

Assor, A., Vansteenkiste, M., & Kaplan, A. (2009). Identified and introjection approach and avoidance motivations in school and in sport: The limited benefits of self-worth strivings. *Journal of Educational Psychology, 101*, 482–497. doi:10.1037/a0014236

Atkin, A.J., Gorely, T., Biddle, S.J.H., Marshall, S.J., & Cameron, N. (2008). Critical hours: Physical activity and sedentary behavior of adolescents after school. *Pediatric Exercise Science, 20*, 446–456.

Atkinson, J.W., & Feather, N.T. (1966). *A theory of achievement motivation*. New York: Wiley.

Averill, J.R. (1982). *Anger and aggression: An essay on emotion.* New York: Springer Verlag.

Baard, P.P., Deci, E.L., & Ryan, R.M. (2004). Intrinsic need satisfaction: A motivational basis of performance and well-being in two work settings. *Journal of Applied Social Psychology, 34,* 2045–2068.

Bain, L.L., Wilson, T., & Chaikind, E. (1989). Participant perceptions of exercise programs for overweight women. *Research Quarterly for Exercise and Sport, 60,* 134–143.

Baker, G., Gray, S., Wright, A., Fitzsimons, C., Nimmo, M., Lowry, R., et al. (2008). The effect of a pedometer-based community walking intervention "Walking for Wellbeing in the West" on physical activity levels and health outcomes: A 12-week randomized controlled trial. *International Journal of Behavioral Nutrition and Physical Activity, 5,* 44–49.

Balaguer, I., Duda, J.L., & Crespo, M. (1999). Motivational climate and goal orientations as predictors of perceptions of improvement, satisfaction, and coach ratings among tennis players. *Scandinavian Journal of Medicine and Science in Sports, 9,* 381–388.

Bandura, A. (1977a). *Social learning theory.* Englewood Cliffs, NJ: Prentice Hall.

Bandura, A. (1977b). Self-efficacy: Toward a unifying theory of behavioral change. *Psychological Review, 84,* 191–215.

Bandura, A. (1986). *Social foundations of thought and action: A social cognitive theory.* Englewood Cliffs, NJ: Prentice Hall.

Bandura, A. (1990). Perceived self-efficacy in the exercise of personal agency. *Journal of Applied Sport Psychology, 2,* 128–163.

Bandura, A. (1997). *Self-efficacy: The exercise of control.* New York: Freeman.

Bandura, A. (1999). A social cognitive theory of personality. In L. Pervin & O. John (Eds.), *Handbook of personality* (2nd ed., pp. 154–196). New York: Guilford. (Reprinted in D. Cervone & Y. Shoda [Eds.], *The coherence of personality.* New York: Guilford Press.)

Bandura, A. (2000). *Health promotion from the perspective of social cognitive theory.* Amsterdam: Harwood Academic.

Bandura, A. (2002). Social cognitive theory in cultural context. *Journal of Applied Psychology: An International Review, 51,* 269–290.

Bandura, A. (2006). Guide for creating self-efficacy scales. In F. Pajares & T. Urdan (Eds.), *Self-efficacy beliefs of adolescents* (pp. 307–337). Greenwich, CT: Information Age.

Bandura, A. (2009). A critical analysis of the quest for negative self-efficacy effects. Paper submitted for publication.

Bandura, A., & Cervone, D. (1983). Self-evaluation and self-efficacy mechanisms governing the motivational effects of goal systems. *Journal of Personal and Social Psychology, 45,* 1017–1028.

Bandura, A., & Locke, E.A. (2003). Negative self-efficacy and goal effects revisited. *Journal of Applied Psychology, 88,* 87–99.

Bandura, A., & Wood, R.E. (1989). Effect of perceived controllability and performance standards on self-regulation of complex decision-making. *Journal of Personal and Social Psychology, 56,* 805–814.

Baranowski, T., Anderson, C., & Carmack, C. (1998). Mediating variable framework in physical activity interventions: How are we doing? How might we do better? *American Journal of Preventive Medicine, 15,* 266–297.

Barber, B.K. (1996). Parental psychological control: Revisiting a neglected construct. *Child Development, 67,* 3296–3319. doi: 10.2307/1131780

Bargh, J.A. (1997). The automaticity of everyday life. *Advances in Social Cognition, 10,* 1–61. doi:10.2307/1131780

Barker, J.B., & Jones, M.V. (2008). The effects of hypnosis on self-efficacy, affect, and soccer performance. *Journal of Clinical Sport Psychology, 2,* 127–147.

Barker, J.B., Jones, M.V., Greenlees, I. (2010). Assessing the immediate and maintained effects of hypnosis on self-efficacy and soccer wall-volley performance. *Journal of Sport and Exercise Psychology, 32,* 243–252.

Barkoukis, V., Koidou, E., & Tsorbatzoudis, H. (2010). Effects of a motivational climate intervention on state anxiety, self-efficacy, and skill development in physical education. *European Journal of Sport Science, 10,* 167–177.

Barkoukis, V., Ntoumanis, N., & Nikitaras, N. (2007). Comparing dichotomous and trichotomous approaches to achievement goal theory: An example using motivational regulations as outcome variables. *British Journal of Educational Psychology, 77,* 683–702.

Barkoukis, V., Ntoumanis, N., & Thøgersen-Ntoumani, C. (2010). Developmental changes in achievement motivation and affect in physical education: Growth trajectories and demographic differences. *Psychology of Sport and Exercise, 11,* 83–90.

Barkoukis, V., Thøgersen-Ntoumani, C., Ntoumanis, N., & Nikitaras, N. (2007). Achievement goals in physical education: Examining the predictive ability of five different dimensions of motivational climate. *European Physical Education Review, 13,* 267–285.

Barnett, M.L. (1977). Effects of two methods of goal setting on learning a gross motor task. *Research Quarterly, 48,* 19–23.

Baron, R., & Kenny, D. (1986). The moderator-mediator variable distinction in social psychology research: Conceptual strategies and statistical concerns. *Journal of Personality and Social Psychology, 51,* 1173–1182.

Bartholomew, K., Ntoumanis, N., Ryan, R., & Thøgersen-Ntoumani, C. (2011). Psychological need thwarting in the sport context: Development and initial validation of a psychometric scale. *Journal of Sport and Exercise Psychology, 33,* 75–102.

Bartholomew, K.J., Ntoumanis, N., & Thøgersen-Ntoumani, C. (2009). A review of controlling motivational strategies from a self-determination theory perspective: Implications for sports coaches. *International Review of Sport and Exercise Psychology, 2,* 215–233. doi:10.1080/17509840903235330

Bartholomew, K.J., Ntoumanis, N., & Thogersen-Ntoumani, C. (2010). The controlling interpersonal style in a coaching context: Development and initial validation of a psychometric scale. *Journal of Sport and Exercise Psychology, 32,* 193–216. Retrieved from http://hk.humankinetics.com/JSEP/journalAbout.cfm

Bartholomew, L.K., Parcel, G.S., Kok, G., & Gottlieb, N.H. (2001). *Intervention mapping: Designing theory- and evidence-based health promotion programs.* Mountain View, CA: Mayfield.

Bassett, D.R., & Strath, S.J. (2002). Use of pedometers to assess physical activity. In G.J. Welk (Ed.), *Physical activity assessments for health-related research* (pp. 163–177). Champaign, IL: Human Kinetics.

Baum, J.R., & Locke, E.A. (2004). The relationship of entrepreneurial traits, skill, and motivation to subsequent venture growth. *Journal of Applied Psychology, 89,* 587–598.

Bauman, A., Sallis, J., Dzewaltowski, D., & Owen, N. (2002). Toward a better understanding of the influences on physical activity: The role of determinants, correlates, causal variables, mediators, moderators, and confounders. *American Journal of Preventive Medicine, 23*(2S), 5–14.

Baumeister, R.F., Bushman, B.J., & Campbell, W.K. (2000). Self-esteem, narcissism, and aggression: Does violence result from low self-esteem or from threatened egotism? *Current Directions in Psychological Science, 9,* 26–29.

Beiling, P.J., Israeli, A., Smith, J., & Antony, M.M. (2003). Making the grade: The behavioural consequences of perfectionism in the classroom. *Personality and Individual Differences, 35,* 163–178.

Beilock, S.L., & Carr, T.H. (2001). On the fragility of skilled performance: What governs choking under pressure? *Journal of Experimental Psychology: General, 130,* 701–725.

Beilock, S.L., & DeCaro, M.S. (2007). From poor performance to success under stress: Working memory, strategy selection, and mathematical problem solving under pressure. *Journal of Experimental Psychology: Learning, Memory, and Cognition, 33,* 983–998.

Berger, B.G., Pargman, D., & Weinberg, R.S. (2007). *Foundations of exercise psychology* (2nd ed.). Morgantown, WV: Fitness Information Technology.

Bermudez, J. (2006). Personality science, self-regulation, and health behavior. *Applied Psychology: An International Review, 55,* 386–396.

Besser, A., Flett, G.L., & Hewitt, P.L. (2004). Perfectionism, cognition, and affect in resonse to performance failure vs. success. *Journal of Rational Emotive and Cognitive Behavior Therapy, 22,* 301–328.

Beverly, E.A., & Wray, L.A. (2008). The role of collective efficacy in exercise adherence: A qualitative study of spousal support and Type 2 diabetes management. *Health Education Research.* Advance online publication. doi:10.1093/her/cyn032

Biddle, S.J.H. (2000). Exercise, emotions, and mental health. In Y. Hanin, *Emotions in sport,* (pp. 267–291). Champaign, IL: Human Kinetics.

Biddle, S.J.H. (2001). Enhancing motivation in physical education. In G.C. Roberts (Ed.), *Advances in motivation in sport and exercise* (pp. 101–127). Champaign, IL: Human Kinetics.

Biddle, S.J.H., Akande, A., Vlachopoulos, S., & Fox, K. (1996). Towards an understanding of children's motivation for physical activity: Achievement goal orientations, beliefs about sport success, and sport emotion in Zimbabwean children. *Psychology and Health, 12,* 49–55.

Biddle, S.J.H., Gorely, T., & Stensel, D.J. (2004). Health-enhancing physical activity and sedentary behaviour in children and adolescents. *Journal of Sport Sciences, 22,* 679–701.

Biddle, S.J.H., O'Connell, S., & Braithwaite, R.E. (2011). Sedentary behaviour interventions in young people: A meta-analysis. *British Journal of Sports Medicine, 45,* 937–942.

Biddle, S.J.H., & Mutrie, N. (2001). *Psychology of physical activity: Determinants, well-being, and interventions.* New York: Routledge.

Biddle, S.J.H., & Mutrie, N. (2008). *Psychology of physical activity: Determinants, well-being and interventions* (2nd ed.). London: Routledge.

Biddle, S.J.H., Wang, C.K.J., Kavussanu, M., & Spray, C.M. (2003). Correlates of achievement goal orientations in physical activity: A systematic review of research. *European Journal of Sport Science, 3*, 1–20. www.humankinetics.com/ejss.

Biddle, S.J.H., Whitehead, S.H., O'Donovan, T.M., & Nevill, M.E. (2005). Correlates of participation in physical activity for adolescent girls: A systematic review of recent literature. *Journal of Physical Activity and Health, 2*, 423–434.

Bigelow, B.J., Lewko, J.H., & Salhani, L. (1989). Sport-involved children's friendship expectations. *Journal of Sport and Exercise Psychology, 11*, 152–160.

Blais, M.R., Vallerand, R.J., Pelletier, L.G., & Brière, N.M. (1989). L'échelle de satisfaction de vie: Validation canadienne-française du "Satisfaction With Life Scale" [French-Canadian validation of the Satisfaction With Life Scale]. *Canadian Journal of Behavioural Sciences, 21*, 210–223.

Blamey, A., & Mackenzie, M. (2007). Theories of change and realistic evaluation: Peas in a pod or apples and oranges? *Evaluation, 13*, 439–455.

Blamey, A., & Mutrie, N. (2004). Changing the individual to promote health-enhancing physical activity: The difficulties of producing evidence and translating it into practice. *Journal of Sports Sciences, 22*, 741–754.

Blanchard, C.M., Amiot, C.E., Perreault, S., Vallerand, R.J., & Provencher, P. (2009). Cohesiveness, coach's interpersonal style and psychological needs: Their effects on self-determination and athletes' subjective well-being. *Psychology of Sport and Exercise, 10*, 545–551. doi:10.1016/j.psychsport.2009.02.005

Blanchard, C.M., Courneya, K.S., Rodgers, W.M., & Murnaghan, D.M. (2002). Determinants of exercise intention and behavior in survivors of breast and prostate cancer: An application of the theory of planned behavior. *Cancer Nursing, 25*, 88–95.

Blanchard, C.M., Courneya, K.S., & Stein, K. (2008). Cancer survivors' adherence to lifestyle behavior recommendations and associations with health-related quality of life: Results from the American Cancer Society's SCS-II. *Journal of Clinical Oncology, 26*, 2198–2204.

Blankstein, K.R., Lumley, C.H., & Crawford, A. (2007). Perfectionism, hopelessness, and suicide ideation: Revisions to diathesis-stress and specific vulnerability models. *Journal of Rational-Emotive and Cognitive-Behavior Therapy, 4*, 255–277.

Blatt, S.J., & Zuroff, D.C. (1992). Interpersonal relatedness and self-definition: Two prototypes for depression. *Clinical Psychology Review, 12*, 527–562.

Blatt, S.J., Zuroff, D.C., Hawley, L.L., & Auerbach, J.S. (2010). The impact of the two-configurations model of personality development and psychopathology on psychotherapy research: Rejoinder to Beutler and Wolf. *Psychotherapy Research, 20*, 65–70.

Blumenfeld, P.C. (1992). Classroom learning and motivation. Clarifying and expanding goal theory. *Journal of Educational Psychology, 84*, 272–281.

Boggiano, A.K., Barrett, M., Weiher, A.W., McClelland, G.H., & Lusk, C.M. (1987). Use of the maximal-operant principle to motivate children's intrinsic interest. *Journal of Personality and Social Psychology, 53*, 866–879. doi:10.1037/0022-3514.53.5.866

Boiché, J., Sarrazin, P.G., Grouzet, F.M.E., Pelletier, L.G., & Chanal, J.P. (2008). Students' motivational profiles and achievement outcomes in physical education: A self-determination perspective. *Journal of Educational Psychology, 100*, 688–701. doi:10.1037/0022-0663.100.3.688

Boixadós, M., Cruz, J., Torregrosa, M., & Valiente, L. (2004). Relationships among motivational climate, satisfaction, perceived ability, and fair play attitudes in young soccer players. *Journal of Applied Sport Psychology, 16*, 301–317.

Bonneville-Roussy, A., Lavigne, G., & Vallerand, R.J. (2010). When passion leads to excellence: The case of musicians. *Psychology of Music, 38*, 1–16.

Botterill, C., & Brown, M. (2002). Emotion and perspective in sport. *International Journal of Sport Psychology, 33*, 38–60.

Boutcher, S.H., Fleischer-Curtian, L.A., & Gines, S.D. (1988). The effects of self-presentation on perceived exertion. *Journal of Sport & Exercise Psychology, 10*, 270–280.

Boyce, B.A, Gano-Overway, L.A., & Love Campbell, A. (2009). Perceived motivational climate's influence on goal orientations, perceived competence, and practice strategies across the athletic season. *Journal of Applied Sport Psychology, 21*, 381–394.

Boyd, M.P. (1990). *The effects of participation orientation and success-failure on post-competitive affect in young adults.* (Unpublished dissertation.) University of Southern California, Los Angeles.

Bravata, D.M., Smith-Spangler, C., Sundaram, V., Gienger, A.L., Lin, N., Lewis, R., . . . Sirad, J.R. (2007). Using pedometers to increase physical activity and improve health: A systematic review. *JAMA: Journal of the American Medical Association, 298,* 2296–2304.

Bray, S.R. (2004). Collective efficacy, group goals, and group performance of a muscular endurance task. *Small Group Research, 35,* 230–238.

Bray, S.R., Gyurcsik, N.C., Martin Ginis, K.A., & Culos-Reed, S.N. (2004). The proxy efficacy exercise questionnaire: Development of an instrument to assess female exercisers' proxy efficacy beliefs in structured group exercise classes. *Journal of Sport and Exercise Psychology, 26,* 442–456.

Breckon, J.D., Johnston, L.H., & Hutchinson, A. (2008). Physical activity counseling content and competency: A systematic review. *Journal of Physical Activity and Health, 5,* 398–417.

Brett, J.E., & VandeWalle, D. (1999). Goal orientation and goal content as predictors of performance in a training program. *Journal of Applied Psychology, 84,* 863–874.

Brewer, B.W., Diehl, N.S., Cornelius, A.E., Joshua, M.D., & Van Raalte, J.L. (2004). Exercising caution: Social physique anxiety and protective self-presentational behaviour. *Journal of Science and Medicine in Sport, 7,* 47–55.

Brophy, J. (1987). Synthesis of research on strategies for motivating students to learn. *Educational Leadership, 5,* 40–48.

Brophy, J. (2005). Goal theorists should move on from performance goals. *Educational Psychologist, 40,* 167–176.

Brown, J., & Weiner, B. (1984). Affective consequences of ability and effort ascriptions: Empirical controversies, resolutions, and quandaries. *Journal of Educational Psychology, 76,* 146–158.

Brown, K.W., & Ryan, R.M. (2003). The benefits of being present: Mindfulness and its role in psychological well-being. *Journal of Personality and Social Psychology, 84,* 822–848.

Brown, L.J., & Malouff, J.M. (2005). The effectiveness of a self-efficacy intervention for helping adolescents cope with sport-competition loss. *Journal of Sport Behavior, 28,* 136–151.

Brug, J., Conner, M., Harre, N., Kremers, S., McKeller, S., & Whitelaw, S. (2005). The transtheoretical model and stages of change: A critique. Observations by five commentators on the paper by Adams, J. and White, M. (2004). Why don't stage-based activity promotion interventions work? *Health Education Research, 20,* 244–258.

Brug, J., Oenema, A., & Ferreira, I. (2005). Theory, evidence and intervention mapping to improve behavior nutrition and physical activity interventions. *International Journal of Behavioral Nutrition and Physical Activity, 2*(2).

Brunel, P.C. (1999). Relationship between achievement goal orientations and perceived motivational climate on intrinsic motivation. *Scandinavian Journal of Medicine and Science in Sports, 9,* 365–374.

Brunel, P.C. (2000). Achievement motivation: Toward interactive effects of dispositional and situational variables on motivation and social cognition. *Habilitation a diriger les researches,* University of Limoges, France.

Brunet, J., & Sabiston, C.M. (2009). Examining the relationship between social physique anxiety and physical activity: A self-determination perspective. *Psychology of Sport and Exercise, 10,* 329–335.

Buckworth, J., & Dishman, R.K. (2002). *Exercise psychology.* Champaign, IL: Human Kinetics.

Bueno, J., Weinberg, R.S., Fernandez-Castro, J., & Capdevila, L. (2008). Emotional and motivational mechanisms mediating the influence of goal setting on endurance athletes' performance. *Psychology of Sport and Exercise, 9,* 786–799.

Burke, R.J., & Fiskenbaum, L. (2009). Work motivations, work outcomes and health: Passion versus addiction. *Journal of Business Ethics, 84,* 257–263.

Burke, S.M., Carron, A.V., & Eys, M.A. (2006). Physical activity context: Preferences of university students. *Psychology of Sport and Exercise, 7,* 1–13.

Burke, S.M., Carron, A.V., Eys, M.A., Ntoumanis, N., & Estabrooks, P.A. (2006). Group versus individual approach? A meta-analysis of the effectiveness of interventions to promote physical activity. *Sport and Exercise Psychology Review, 2,* 13–39.

Burke, S.T., & Jin, D. (1996). Predicting performance from a triathlon event. *Journal of Sport Behavior, 19,* 272–287.

Burns, D.D. (1980). The perfectionists script for self-defeat. *Psychology Today, 14*(November), 34–51.

Burton, D. (1984, February). Goal setting: A secret to success. *Swimming World,* 25–29.

Burton, D. (1992). The Jekyll/Hyde nature of goals: Reconceptualizing goal setting in sport. In T. Horn (Ed.), *Advances in sport psychology* (pp. 267–297). Champaign, IL: Human Kinetics.

Burton, D., & Naylor, S. (2002). The Jekyll/Hyde nature of goals: Revisiting and updating goal setting in sport. In T. Horn (Ed.), *Advances in sport psychology* (pp. 459–499). Champaign, IL: Human Kinetics.

Burton, D., Naylor, S., & Holliday, B. (2001). Goal setting in sport: Investigating the goal effectiveness paradox. In R. Singer, H.A. Hausenblas, & C.M. Janelle (Eds.), *Handbook of research on sport psychology* (2nd ed., pp. 497–528). New York: Wiley.

Burton, D., Pickering, M., Weinberg, R.S., Yukelson, D., & Weigand, D. (2010). The competitive goal effectiveness paradox revisited: Examining the goal practices of prospective Olympic athletes. *Journal of Applied Sport Psychology, 22,* 72–86.

Burton, D., & Weiss, C.L. (2008). The fundamental goal concept: The path to process and performance success. In T. Horn (Ed.), *Advances in sport psychology* (3rd ed., pp. 339–375). Champaign, IL: Human Kinetics.

Butler, R. (1987). Task-involving and ego-involving properties of evaluation: Effects of different feedback conditions on motivational perceptions, interest, and performance. *Journal of Educational Psychology, 79,* 474–482.

Butler, R. (1988). Enhancing and undermining intrinsic motivation: The effects of task-involving and ego-involving evaluation on interest and performance. *British Journal of Educational Psychology, 58,* 1–14.

Butler, R., & Ruzani, N. (1993). Age and socialization effects on the development of social comparison motives and normative ability assessment in kibbutz and urban children. *Child Development, 64,* 532–543.

Campbell, J.D., & Di Paula, A. (2002). Perfectionistic self-beliefs: Their relation to personality and goal pursuit. In G.L. Flett & P.L. Hewitt (Eds.), *Perfectionism: Theory, research, and treatment* (pp. 181–198). Washington, DC: American Psychological Association.

Campbell, K.W., & Sedikides, C. (1999). Self-threat magnifies the self-serving bias: A meta-analytic integration. *Review of General Psychology, 3,* 23–43.

Campbell, M., Fitzpatrick, R., Haines, A., Kinmonth, A.L., Sandercock, P., Spiegelhalter, D., . . . Tyrer, P. (2000). Framework for design and evaluation of complex interventions to improve health. *British Medical Journal, 321*(7262), 694–696.

Carbonneau, N., Vallerand, R.J., Fernet, C., & Guay, F. (2008). The role of passion for teaching in intra and interpersonal outcomes. *Journal of Educational Psychology, 100,* 977–987.

Cardinal, B.J. (1997). Construct validity of stage of change for exercise behavior. *American Journal of Health Promotion, 12,* 68–74.

Cardon, M.S. (2008). Is passion contagious? The transference of entrepreneurial passion to employees. *Human Resource Management Review, 18,* 77–86.

Carmac, M.A., & Martens, R. (1979). Measuring commitment to running: A survey of runners' attitudes and mental states. *Journal of Sport Psychology, 1,* 25–42.

Carr, S. (2006). An examination of multiple goals in children's physical education: Motivational effects of goal profiles and the role of perceived climate in multiple goal development. *Journal of Sports Sciences, 24,* 281–297.

Carron, A.V., Estabrooks, P.A., Horton, H. , Prapavessis, H., & Hausenblas, H.A. (1999). Reductions in the social anxiety of women associated with group membership: Distraction, anonymity, security, or diffusion of evaluation? *Group Dynamics, 3,* 1–9.

Carron, A.V., Hausenblas, H.A., & Eys, M.A. (2005). *Group dynamics in sport* (3rd ed.). Morgantown, WV: Fitness Information Technology.

Carron, A.V., & Prapavessis, H. (1997). Self-presentation and group influence. *Small Group Research, 28,* 500–516.

Carron, A.V., & Spink, K.S. (1993). Team building in an exercise setting. *Sport Psychologist, 7,* 8–18.

Carver, C.S., & Scheier, M.F. (1998). *On the self-regulation of behavior.* New York: Cambridge University Press.

Caspersen, C.J., Powell, K.E., & Christenson, G.M. (1985). Physical activity, exercise, and physical fitness: Definitions and distinctions for health-related research. *Public Health Reports, 100,* 126–131.

Castelda, B.A., Mattson, R.E., MacKillop, J., Anderson, E.J., & Donovick, P.J. (2007). Psychometric validation of the Gambling Passion Scale (GPS) in an English-speaking university sample. *International Gambling Studies, 7,* 173–182.

Centers for Disease Control and Prevention. (2008). Preventing chronic diseases: Investing wisely in health: Preventing obesity and chronic diseases through good nutrition and physical activity. Retrieved from www.cdc.gov/nccdphp/publications/ factsheets/ prevention/pdf/obesity.pdf

Cervelló, E., Santos-Rosa, F.J., García Calvo, T., Jiménez, R., & Iglesias, D. (2007). Young tennis players' competitive task involvement and performance: The role of goal orientations, contextual motivational climate, and coach-initiated motivational climate. *Journal of Applied Sport Psychology, 19,* 304–321.

Cervone, D., Shadel, W.G., Smith, R.E., & Fiori, M. (2006). Self-regulation: Reminders and suggestions from personality science. *Applied Psychology: An International Review, 55,* 333–385.

Chaiken, S. (1987). The heuristic model of persuasion. In M. Zanna, J. Olson, & C. Herman (Eds.), *Social influence: The Ontario symposium* (5th ed., pp. 3–39). Hillsdale, NJ: Erlbaum.

Chalabaev, A., Sarrazin, P., Stone, J., & Cury, F. (2008). Do achievement goals mediate stereotype threat?: An investigation on females' soccer performance. *Journal of Sport and Exercise Psychology, 30*, 143–158.

Chantal, Y., Robin, P., Vernat, J.P., & Bernache-Assollant, I. (2005). Motivation, sportspersonship, and athletic aggression: A mediational analysis. *Psychology of Sport and Exercise, 6*, 233–249. doi:10.1016/j.psychsport.2003.10.010

Chase, M.A. (2001). Children's self-efficacy, motivational intentions, and attributions in physical education and sport. *Research Quarterly for Exercise and Sport, 72*, 47–54.

Chase, M.A. (2006). Competition plans and performance routines. In R. Bartlett, C. Gratton, & C. Rolf (Eds.), *Encyclopedia of international sports studies* (pp. 290–292). London: Taylor and Francis.

Chase, M.A., & Drummer, G.M. (1992). The role of sports as a social status determinant for children. *Research Quarterly for Exercise and Sport, 63*, 418–424.

Chatzisarantis, N.L.D., & Hagger, M.S. (2009). Effects of an intervention based on self-determination theory on self-reported leisure-time physical activity participation. *Psychology and Health, 24*, 29–48. doi:10.1080/08870440701809533

Chatzisarantis, N.L.D., Hagger, M.S., Biddle, S.J.H., Smith, B., & Wang, J.C.K. (2003). A meta-analysis of perceived locus of causality in exercise, sport, and physical education contexts. *Journal of Sport and Exercise Psychology, 25*, 284–306. Retrieved from http://hk.humankinetics.com/JSEP/journal-About.cfm

Chatzisarantis, N.L.D., Hagger, M.S., & Smith, B. (2007). Influences of perceived autonomy support on physical activity within the theory of planned behavior. *European Journal of Social Psychology, 37*, 934–954.

Chelladurai, P., & Saleh, S.D. (1980). Dimensions of leader behavior in sports development of a leadership scale. *Journal of Sport Psychology, 2*, 34–45. Retrieved from http://hk.humankinetics.com/JSEP/journalAbout.cfm

Chen, H.T. (1990). *Theory-driven evaluation.* London: Sage.

Chi, L. (1994). *The prediction of achievement related cognitions and behaviors in the physical activity domain: A test of the theories of goal perspectives and self-efficacy.* (Unpublished doctoral dissertation). Purdue University: West Lafayette, IN.

Chi, L., & Lu, S-E. (1995). *The relationship between perceived motivational climates and group cohesiveness in basketball.* Paper presented at the annual meetings of the North American Society for the Psychology of Sport and Physical Activity, Clearwater, FL.

Chmelo, E.A., Hall, E.E., Miller, P.C., & Sanders, K.N. (2009). Mirrors and resistance exercise, do they influence affective responses? *Journal of Health Psychology, 14*, 1067–1074.

Chow, G., & Feltz, D.L. (2008). Exploring new directions in collective efficacy and sport. In M. Beauchamp & M. Eys (Eds.), *Group dynamics advances in sport and exercise psychology: Contemporary themes.* London: Routledge.

Christodoulidis, T., Papaioannou, A., & Digelidis, N. (2001). Motivational climate and attitudes towards exercise in Greek senior high school: A year-long intervention. *European Journal of Sport Science, 1*, 228–241.

Chu, H., Bushman, B.A., & Woodward, R.J. (2008). Social physique anxiety, obligation to exercise, and exercise choices among college students. *Journal of American College Health, 57*, 7–13.

Ciani, K.D., & Sheldon, K.M. (2010). Evaluating the mastery-avoidance goal construct: A study of elite college baseball players. *Psychology of Sport and Exercise, 11*, 127–132.

Coakley, J. (2001). *Sport in society: Issues and controversies* (7th ed.). New York: McGraw-Hill.

Coatsworth, J.D., & Conroy, D.E. (2009). The effects of autonomy-supportive coaching, need satisfaction, and self-perceptions on initiative and identity in youth swimmers. *Developmental Psychology, 45*, 320–328. doi:10.1037/a0014027

Coen, S.P., & Ogles, B.M. (1993). Psychological characteristics of the obligatory runner: A critical examination of the anorexia analogue hypothesis. *Journal of Sport & Exercise Psychology, 15*, 338–354.

Cohen, J. (1982). A power primer. *Psychology Bulletin, 112*, 115–159.

Cohn, P.J. (1990). An exploratory study on sources of stress and athlete burn out in youth golf. *Sport Psychologist, 4*, 95–106.

Coleman, P.K., & Byrd, C.P. (2003). Interpersonal correlates of peer victimization among young adolescents. *Journal of Youth and Adolescents, 32*, 301–314.

Connell, J.P., & Wellborn, J. (1991). Competence, autonomy, and relatedness: A motivational analysis of self-system processes. In M. Gunar & A. Sroufe (Eds.), *Minnesota Symposium on Child Development* (pp. 43–77). Hillsdale, NJ: Erlbaum.

Conroy, D.E. (2004). The unique psychological meanings of multi-dimensional fears of failing. *Journal of Sport and Exercise Psychology, 26,* 484–491.

Conroy, D.E., & Coatsworth, J.D. (2007a). Assessing autonomy-supportive coaching strategies in youth sport. *Psychology of Sport and Exercise, 8,* 671–684. doi:10.1016/j.psychsport.2006.12.001

Conroy, D.E., & Coatsworth, J.D. (2007b). Coaching behaviors associated with changes in fear of failure: Changes in self-talk and need satisfaction as potential mechanisms. *Journal of Personality, 75,* 383–419. doi:10.1111/j.1467-6494.2006.00443.x

Conroy, D.E., & Elliot, A.J. (2004). Fear of failure and achievement goals in sport: Addressing the issue of the chicken and the egg. *Anxiety, Stress, and Coping, 17,* 271–285.

Conroy, D.E., Elliot, A.J., & Hofer, S.M. (2003). A 2x2 achievement goals questionnaire for sport: Evidence for factorial invariance, temporal stability, and external validity. *Journal of Sport and Exercise Psychology, 25,* 456–476.

Conroy, D.E., Kaye, M.P., & Coatsworth, J.D. (2006). Coaching climates and the destructive effects of mastery-avoidance achievement goals on situational motivation. *Journal of Sport and Exercise Psychology, 28,* 69–92.

Conroy, D.E., Kaye, M.P., & Fifer, A.M. (2007). Cognitive links between fear of failure and perfectionism. *Journal of Rational-Emotive and Cognitive-Behavior Therapy, 4,* 237–253.

Conroy, D.E., Motl, R.W., & Hall, E.G. (2000). Progress toward construct validation of the Self-Presentation in Exercise Questionnaire (SPEQ). *Journal of Sport and Exercise Psychology, 22,* 21–38.

Conroy, D.E., Willow, J.P., & Metzler, J.N. (2002). Multidimensional measurement of fear of failure: The performance failure appraisal inventory. *Journal of Applied Sport Psychology, 14,* 76–90.

Coudevylle, G., Martin Ginis, K., Famose, J-P., & Gernigon, C. (2009). An experimental investigation of the determinants and consequences of self-handicapping strategies across motivational climates. *European Journal of Sport Science, 9,* 219–227.

Coulter, A. (1998). Evidence based patient information is important, so there needs to be a national strategy to ensure it. *British Medical Journal, 317,* 225–226.

Coups, E.J., & Ostroff, J.S. (2005). A population-based estimate of the prevalence of behavioral risk factors among adult cancer survivors and noncancer controls. *Preventive Medicine, 40,* 702–711.

Coups, E.J., Park, B.J., Feinstein, M.B., Steingart, R.M., Egleston, B.L., Wilson, D.J., & Ostroff, J.S. (2009).

Correlates of physical activity among lung cancer survivors. *Psycho-Oncology, 18,* 395–404.

Courneya, K.S., Blanchard, C.M., & Laing, D.M. (2001). Exercise adherence in breast cancer survivors training for a dragon boat race competition: A preliminary investigation. *Psycho-Oncology, 10,* 444–452.

Courneya, K.S., Booth, C.M., Gill, S., O'Brien, P., Vardy, J., Friedenreich, C.M., . . . Meyer, M.D. (2008). The Colon Health and Life-Long Exercise Change trial: A randomized trial of the National Cancer Institute of Canada Clinical Trials Group. *Current Oncology, 15,* 271–278.

Courneya, K.S., & Friedenreich, C.M. (1997a). Determinants of exercise during colorectal cancer treatment: An application of the theory of planned behavior. *Oncology Nursing Forum, 24,* 1715–1723.

Courneya, K.S., & Friedenreich, C.M. (1997b). Relationship between exercise during treatment and current quality of life among survivors of breast cancer. *Journal of Psychosocial Oncology, 15,* 35–57.

Courneya, K.S., & Friedenreich, C.M. (1997c). Relationship between exercise pattern across the cancer experience and current quality of life in colorectal cancer survivors. *Journal of Alternative and Complementary Medicine, 3,* 215–226.

Courneya, K.S., & Friedenreich, C.M. (1999). Utility of the theory of planned behavior for understanding exercise during breast cancer treatment. *Psycho-Oncology, 8,* 112–122.

Courneya, K.S., Friedenreich, C.M., Arthur, K., & Bobick, T.M. (1999). Understanding exercise motivation in colorectal cancer patients: A prospective study using the theory of planned behavior. *Rehabilitation Psychology, 44,* 68–84.

Courneya, K.S., Friedenreich, C.M., Quinney, H.A., Fields, A.L., Jones, L.W., & Fairey, A.S. (2004). Predictors of adherence and contamination in a randomized trial of exercise in colorectal cancer survivors. *Psycho-Oncology, 13*(12), 857–866.

Courneya, K.S., Friedenreich, C.M., Quinney, H.A., Fields, A.L., Jones, L.W., Vallance, J.K., & Fairey, A.S. (2005). A longitudinal study of exercise barriers in colorectal cancer survivors participating in a randomized controlled trial. *Annals of Behavioral Medicine, 29,* 147–153.

Courneya, K.S., Friedenreich, C.M., Reid, R.D., Gelmon, K., Mackey, J.R., Ladha, A.B., . . . Segal, R.J. (2009). Predictors of follow-up exercise behavior 6 months after a randomized trial of exercise training during breast cancer chemotherapy. *Breast Cancer Research and Treatment, 114,* 179–187.

Courneya, K.S., Friedenreich, C.M., Sela, R.A., Quinney, H.A., & Rhodes, R.E. (2002). Correlates of adherence and contamination in a randomized controlled trial of exercise in cancer survivors: An application of the theory of planned behavior and the five factor model of personality. *Annals of Behavioral Medicine, 24,* 257–268.

Courneya, K.S., Jones, L.W., Mackey, J.R., & Fairey, A.S. (2006). Exercise beliefs of breast cancer survivors before and after participation in a randomized controlled trial. *International Journal of Behavioral Medicine, 13,* 259–264.

Courneya, K.S., Karvinen, K.H., Campbell, K.L., Pearcey, R.G., Dundas, G. Capstick, V., & Tonkin, K.S. (2005). Associations among exercise, body weight, and quality of life in a population-based sample of endometrial cancer survivors. *Gynecologic Oncology, 97,* 422–430.

Courneya, K.S., Katzmarzyk, P.T., & Bacon, E. (2008). Physical activity and obesity in Canadian cancer survivors: Population-based estimates from the 2005 Canadian Community Health Survey. *Cancer, 112,* 2475–2482.

Courneya, K.S., Keats, M.R., & Turner, A.R. (2000). Social cognitive determinants of hospital-based exercise in cancer patients following high dose chemotherapy and bone marrow transplantation. *International Journal of Behavioral Medicine, 7,* 189–203.

Courneya, K.S., Segal, R.J., Gelmon, K., Reid, R.D., Mackey, J.R., Friedenreich, C.M., . . . McKenzie, D.C. (2008). Predictors of supervised exercise adherence during breast cancer chemotherapy. *Medicine and Science in Sports and Exercise, 40,* 1180–1187.

Courneya, K.S., Segal, R.J., Mackey, J.R., Gelmon, K., Reid, R.D., Friedenreich, C.M., . . . McKenzie, D.C. (2007). Effects of aerobic and resistance exercise in breast cancer patients receiving adjuvant chemotherapy: A multicenter randomized controlled trial. *Journal of Clinical Oncology, 25,* 4396–4404.

Courneya, K.S., Vallance, J.K., Jones, L.W., & Reiman, T. (2005). Correlates of exercise intentions in non-Hodgkin's lymphoma survivors: An application of the theory of planned behavior. *Journal of Sport & Exercise Psychology, 27,* 335–349.

Covington, M.V. (1992). *Making the grade: A self-worth perspective on motivation and school reform.* Cambridge University Press.

Covington, M.V., & Mueller, K.J. (2001). Intrinsic versus extrinsic motivation: An approach/avoidance reformulation. *Educational Psychology Review, 13,* 157–176.

Covington, M.V., & Omelich, C.L. (1984). It's best to be able and virtuous too: Student and teacher evaluation response to successful effort. *Journal of Educational Psychology, 71,* 688–700.

Cox, A., Duncheon, N., & McDavid, L. (2009). Peers and teachers as sources of relatedness perceptions, motivation and affective responses in physical education. *Research Quarterly for Exercise and Sport, 80,* 765–773.

Cox, A., & Williams, L. (2008). The roles of perceived teacher support, motivational climate, and psychological need satisfaction in students' physical education motivation. *Journal of Sport and Exercise Psychology, 30,* 222–239.

Cox, B.J., Enns, M.W., & Clara, I.P. (2002). The multidimensional structure of perfectionism in clinically distressed and college student samples. *Psychological Assessment, 14,* 365–373.

Craig, C.L., Marshall, A.L., Sjostrom, M., Bauman, A.E., Booth, M.L., Ainsworth, B.E., . . . Oja, P. (2003). International physical activity questionnaire: 12-country reliability and validity. *Medicine and Science in Sports and Exercise, 35,* 1381–1395.

Craig, P., Dieppe, P., Macintyre, S., Mitchie, S., Nazareth, I., & Petticrew, M. (2008). Developing and evaluating complex interventions: The new Medical Research Council guidance. *British Medical Journal, 337,* 979–983.

Crawford, J.R., & Henry, J.D. (2004). The positive and negative affect schedule (PANAS). Construct validity, measurement properties and normative data in a large non-clinical sample. *British Journal of Clinical Psychology, 43,* 245–265.

Crawford, S. & Eklund, R.C. (1994). Social physique anxiety, reasons for exercise, and attitudes toward exercise settings. *Journal of Sport & Exercise Psychology, 16,* 70–82.

Cresswell, S.L., & Eklund, R.C. (2005a). Changes in athlete burnout and motivation over a 12-week league tournament. *Medicine and Science in Sports and Exercise, 37,* 1957–1966.

Cresswell, S.L., & Eklund, R.C. (2005b). Motivation and burnout among top amateur rugby players. *Medicine and Science in Sports and Exercise, 37,* 469–477. doi:10.1249/01.MSS.0000155398.71387.C2.

Crick, F., & Watson, J.D. (1953). A structure for deoxyribose nucleic acid. *Nature 171,* 737–738.

Crocker, J. (2002). Contingencies of self-worth: Implications for self-regulation and psychological vulnerability. *Self and Identity, 1,* 143–149.

Crocker, J., & Park, L.E. (2004). The costly pursuit of self-esteem. *Psychological Bulletin, 130,* 392–414.

Crocker, P.R.E., Sabiston, C.M., Kowalski, K.C., McDonough, M.H., & Kowalski, N.P. (2006). Longitudinal assessment of the relationship between physical self-concept and health related behaviour and emotion in adolescent girls. *Journal of Applied Sport Psychology, 18,* 185–200.

Crook, K., Beaver, B.R., & Bell, M. (1998). Anxiety and depression in children: A preliminary examination of the utility of the PANAS-C. *Journal of Psychopathology and Behavioral Assessments, 20,* 333–350.

Csikszentmihalyi, M. (1978). Intrinsic rewards and emergent motivation. In M.R. Lepper & D. Greene (Eds.), *The hidden costs of reward* (pp. 205–216). Hillsdale, NJ: Erlbaum.

Csikszentmihalyi, M., & Nakamura, J. (1989). The dynamics of intrinsic motivation: A study of adolescents. In C. Ames & R. Ames (Eds.), *Motivation in education. Vol. 3. Goals and cognitions.* (pp. 45–71). New York: Academic Press.

Csikszentmihalyi, M., Rathunde, K., & Whalen, S. (1993). *Talented teenagers: The roots of success and failure.* New York: Cambridge.

Culos-Reed, S.N., Brawley, L.R., Martin, K.A., & Leary, M.R. (2002). Self-presentation concerns and health behaviors among cosmetic surgery patients. *Journal of Applied Social Psychology, 32,* 560–569.

Cumming, J., Hall, C., Harwood, C., & Gammage, K. (2002). Motivational orientations and imagery use: A goal profiling analysis. *Journal of Sports Sciences, 20,* 127–136.

Cumming, S.P., Smoll, F.L., Smith R.E., & Grossbard, J.R. (2007). Is winning everything? The relative contributions of climate and won-lost percentage in youth sports. *Journal of Applied Sport Psychology, 19,* 322–336.

Cunningham, G.B., & Xiang, P. (2008). Testing the mediating role of perceived motivational climate in the relationship between achievement goals and satisfaction: Are these relationships invariant across sex? *Journal of Teaching in Physical Education, 27,* 192–204.

Cury, F., Biddle, S., Famose, J.P., Goudas, M., Sarrazin, P., & Durand, M. (1996). Personal and situational factors influencing intrinsic interest of adolescent girls in physical education: A structural equation modeling analysis. *Educational Psychology, 16,* 305–314.

Cury, F., Biddle, S., Sarrazin, P., & Famose, J.P. (1997). Achievement goals and perceived ability predict investment in learning a sport task. *British Journal of Educational Psychology, 67,* 293–309.

Cury, F., Da Fonséca, D., Rufo, M., & Sarrazin, P. (2002a). Perceptions of competence, implicit theory of ability, perception of motivational climate, and achievement goals: A test of the trichotomous conceptualization of endorsement of achievement motivation in the physical education setting. *Perceptual and Motor Skills, 95,* 233–244.

Cury, F., Da Fonséca, D., Rufo, M., Peres, C., & Sarrazin, P. (2003). The trichotomous model and investment in learning to prepare for a sport test: A mediational analysis. *British Journal of Educational Psychology, 73,* 529–543.

Cury, F., Elliot, A., Sarrazin, P., Da Fonseca, D., & Rufo, M. (2002). The trichotomous achievement goal model and intrinsic motivation: A sequential mediational analysis. *Journal of Experimental Social Psychology, 38,* 473–481.

Cury, F., & Sarrazin, P. (1998). Achievement motivation and learning behaviors in a sport task. *Journal of Sport and Exercise Behavior, 20,* S11.

Cury, F., Sarrazin, P., & Famose, J.P. (1997). Achievement goals, perceived ability and active search for information. In *European Yearbook of Sport Psychology* (Vol. 1, pp. 167–183). Sank Augustin.

Dale, D., Welk, G.J., & Matthews, C.E. (2002). Methods for assessing physical activity and challenges for research. In G.J. Welk (Ed.), *Physical activity assessments for health-related research* (pp. 19–34). Champaign, IL: Human Kinetics.

Damon, W. (1988). *The moral child: Nurturing children's natural moral growth.* New York: The Free Press.

Davis, C., Brewer, H., & Weinstein, M. (1993). A study of appearance anxiety in young men. *Social Behavior & Personality: An International Journal, 21,* 63–74.

Davison, K., & Lawson, C. (2006). Do attributes in the physical environment influence children's physical activity? A review of the literature. *International Journal of Behavioral Nutrition and Physical Activity, 3*(1), www.ijbnpa.org/content/3/1/19

de Bruin, A.P., Bakker, F.C., & Oudejans, R.R.D. (2009). Achievement Goal Theory and disordered eating: Relationships between female gymnasts' goal orientations, perceived motivational climate and disordered eating correlates. *Psychology of Sport and Exercise, 10,* 72–79.

deCharms, R. (1968). *Personal causation: The internal affective determinants of behavior.* New York: Academic Press.

deCharms, R. (1976). *Enhancing motivation.* New York: Irvington.

deCharms, R. (1984). Motivation enhancement in educational settings. In R. Ames & C. Ames (Eds.), *Research on motivation in education: Vol. 1. Student motivation* (pp. 275–310).

Deci, E.L. (1975). *Intrinsic motivation.* New York: Plenum.

Deci, E.L. (1992). The relation of interest to the motivation of behavior: A self-determination theory perspective. In A. Renninger, S. Hidi, & A. Krapp (Eds.), *The role of interest in learning and development* (pp. 43–70). Hillsdale, NJ: Erlbaum.

Deci, E.L., Driver, R.E., Hotchkiss, L., Robbins, R.J., & Wilson, I.M. (1993). The relation of mothers' controlling vocalizations to children's intrinsic motivation. *Journal of Experimental Child Psychology, 155,* 151–162.

Deci, E.L., Egharri, H., Patrick, B.C., & Leone, D.R. (1994). Facilitating internalization: The self-determination theory perspective. *Journal of Personality, 62,* 119–142. doi:10.1111/j.1467-6494.1994.tb00797.x

Deci, E.L., Koestner, R., & Ryan, R.M. (1999). A meta-analytic review of experiments examining the effects of extrinsic rewards on intrinsic motivation. *Psychological Bulletin, 125,* 627–668.

Deci, E.L., La Guardia, J.G., Moller, M.C., Scheiner, M.J., & Ryan, R.M. (2006). On the benefits of giving as well as receiving autonomy support: Mutuality in close friendships. *Personality and Social Psychology Bulletin, 32,* 313–327. doi:10.1177/0146167205282148

Deci, E.L., & Moller, A.C. (2005). The concept of competence: A starting place for understanding intrinsic motivation and self-determined extrinsic motivation. In A.J. Elliot & C.J. Dweck (Eds.), *Handbook of competence and motivation* (pp. 579–597). New York: Guilford Press.

Deci, E.L., & Ryan, R.M. (1980). The empirical exploration of intrinsic motivational processes. In L. Berkowitz (Ed.), *Advances in experimental social psychology* (pp. 39–80). New York: Academic Press.

Deci, E.L., & Ryan, R.M. (1985a). *Intrinsic motivation and self-determination in human behavior.* New York: Plenum.

Deci, E.L., & Ryan, R.M. (1985b). The general causality orientations scale: Self-determination in personality. *Journal of Research in Personality, 19,* 109–134.

Deci, E.L., & Ryan, R.M. (1987). The support of autonomy and the control of behavior. *Journal of Personality and Social Psychology, 53,* 1024–1037.

Deci, E.L., & Ryan, R.M. (1991). A motivational approach to self: Integration in personality. In R.A. Dienstbier (Ed.), *Nebraska symposium on motivation: Perspectives on motivation, Vol. 38* (pp. 237–288). Lincoln: University of Nebraska.

Deci, E.L., & Ryan, R.M. (1995). Human autonomy: The basis for true self-esteem. In M.H. Kernis (Ed.), *Efficacy, agency and self-esteem.* New York: Plenum.

Deci, E.L., & Ryan, R.M. (2000). The "what" and "why" of goal pursuits: Human needs and the self-determination of behavior. *Psychological Inquiry, 11,* 227–268. doi:10.1207/S15327965PLI1104_01

Deci, E.L., & Ryan, R.M. (2002a). *Handbook of self-determination research.* Rochester, NY: University of Rochester Press.

Deci, E.L., & Ryan, R.M. (2002b). The paradox of achievement: The harder you push, the worse it gets. In J. Aronson (Ed.), *Improving academic achievement: Contributions of social psychology* (pp. 59–85). New York: Academic Press.

Deci, E.L., & Ryan, R.M. (2008). Facilitating optimal motivation and psychological well-being across life's domains. *Canadian Psychology, 49,* 14–23.

Deci, E.L., Ryan, R.M., Gagné, M., Leone, D.R., Usunov, J., & Kornazheva, B.P. (2001). Need satisfaction, motivation, and well-being in the work organizations of a former Eastern Bloc country: A cross cultural study of self-determination. *Personality and Social Psychology Bulletin, 27,* 930–942.

Deci, E.L., Ryan, R.M., & Williams, G.C. (1996). Need satisfaction and the self-regulation of learning. *Learning and Individual Differences, 8,* 165–183.

Deci, E.L., Schwartz, A.J., Sheinman, L., & Ryan, R.M. (1981). An instrument to assess adults' orientations toward control versus autonomy with children: Reflections on intrinsic motivation and perceived competence. *Journal of Educational Psychology, 73,* 642–650. doi:10.1037/0022-0663.73.5.642

Deci, E.L., & Vansteenkiste, M. (2004). Self-determination theory and basic need satisfaction: Understanding human development in positive psychology. *Ricerche di Psicologia, 27,* 17–34.

Deffenbacher, J.L. (1999). Cognitive-behavioural conceptualisation and treatment of anger. *Journal of Clinical Psychology, 55,* 295–309.

Demark-Wahnefried, W., Clipp, E.C., Lipkus, I.M., Lobach, D., Snyder, D.C., Sloane, R., et al. (2007). Main outcomes of the FRESH START trial: A sequentially tailored, diet and exercise mailed print intervention among breast and prostate cancer survivors. *Journal of Clinical Oncology, 25,* 2709–2718.

Demark-Wahnefried, W., Clipp, E.C., McBride, C., Lobach, D.F., Lipkus, I., Peterson, B., et al. (2003). Design of FRESH START: A randomized trial of exercise and diet among cancer survivors. *Medicine and Science in Sports and Exercise, 35,* 415–424.

Demark-Wahnefried, W., Clipp, E.C., Morey, M.C., Pieper, C.F., Sloane, R., Snyder, D.C., et al. (2006).

Lifestyle intervention development study to improve physical function in older adults with cancer: Outcomes from Project LEAD. *Journal of Clinical Oncology, 24,* 3465–3473.

Demark-Wahnefried, W., Morey, M.C., Clipp, E.C., Pieper, C.F., Snyder, D.C., Sloane, R., et al. (2003). Leading the Way in Exercise and Diet (Project LEAD): Intervening to improve function among older breast and prostate cancer survivors. *Controlled Clinical Trials, 24,* 206–223.

Dennett, D.C. (1978). *Brainstorms: Philosophical essays on mind and psychology.* Montgomery, VT: Bradford.

Denson, T.F., Pederson, W.C., & Miller, N. (2006). The displaced aggression questionnaire. *Journal of Personality and Social Psychology, 90,* 1032–1051.

DeRue, D.S., Hollenbeck, J.R., Ilgen, D.R., & Feltz, D.L. (2010). Efficacy dispersion in teams: Moving beyond agreement and aggregation. *Personnel Psychology, 63,* 1–40.

Descartes, R. (1649/1972). Les passions de l'âme. In E.S. Haldane & G. Ross (Trans.), *The philosophical works of Descartes.* Cambridge, MA: Cambridge University Press.

DiBartolo, P.M., Frost, R.O., Dixon, A., & Almodovar, S. (2001). Can cognitive restructuring reduce the disruption associated with perfectionistic concerns? *Behaviour Therapy, 32,* 167–184.

Diehl, N.S., Brewer, B.W., Van Raalte, J.L., Shaw, D., Fiero, P.L., & Sorensen, M. (2001). Exercise partner preferences, social physique anxiety, and social discomfort in exercise settings among women university wellness center patrons. *Women in Sport and Physical Activity Journal, 10,* 89–101.

Diener, E., Emmons, R.A., Larsen, R.J., & Griffin, S. (1985). The Satisfaction With Life Scale. *Journal of Personality Assessment, 49,* 71–76.

Diener, E., Suh, M., Lucas, E., & Smith, H. (1999). Subjective well-being: Three decades of progress. *Psychological Bulletin, 125,* 276–302.

Digelidis, N., Papaioannou, A., Laparidis, K., & Christo-doulidis, T. (2003). A one year intervention in the 7th grade physical education classes aiming to change motivational climate and attitudes towards exercise. *Psychology of Sport and Exercise, 4,* 195–210.

DiPietro, L. (2007). Physical activity, fitness, and aging. In C. Bouchard, S.N. Blair, & W.L. Haskell (Eds.), *Physical activity and health* (pp. 271–285). Champaign, IL: Human Kinetics.

Dishman, R.K. (1982). Compliance/adherence in health-related exercise. *Health Psychology, 1,* 237–267.

Dithurbide, L., & Feltz, D.L. (in press). Self and collective efficacy. In G. Tenenbaum, R. Eklund, & A. Kamata (Eds.), *Handbook of measurement in sport and exercise psychology.* Champaign, IL: Human Kinetics.

Doebler, T.C., Schnick, C., Beck., B.L., & Astor-Stetson, E. (2000). Ego protection: The effects of perfectionism and gender on acquired and claimed self-handicapping and self-esteem. *College Student Journal, 34,* 524–537.

Dollard, J., & Miller, N.E. (1941). *Social learning and imitation.* London: Oxford University Press.

Donahue, E.G., Miquelon, P., Valois, P., Goulet, C., Buist, A., & Vallerand, R.J. (2006). A motivational model of performance-enhancing substance use in elite athletes. *Journal of Sport and Exercise Psychology, 28,* 511–520. Retrieved from http://hk.humankinetics.com/JSEP/journalAbout .cfm

Donahue, E.G., Rip, B., & Vallerand, R.J. (2009). When winning is everything: On passion, identity, and aggression in sport. *Psychology of Sport and Exercise, 10,* 526–534.

Dowrick, P.W. (1991). *Practical guide to using video in the behavioral sciences.* New York: Wiley.

Dowson, M., & McInerney, D.M. (2001). Psychological parameters of students' social and work avoidance goals: A qualitative analysis. *Journal of Educational Psychology, 93,* 35–42.

Doyle, C., Kushi, L.H., Byers, T., Courneya, K.S., Demark-Wahnefried, W., Grant, B., . . . Andrews, K.S. (2006). Nutrition and physical activity during and after cancer treatment: An American Cancer Society guide for informed choices. *CA: A Cancer Journal for Clinicians, 56,* 323–353.

Duckworth, A.L., Peterson, C., Matthews, M.D., & Kelly, D.R. (2007). Grit: Perseverance and passion for long-term goals. *Journal of Personality and Social Psychology, 92,* 1087–1101.

Duda, J.L. (1981). Achievement motivation in sport: Minority considerations for the coach. *Journal of Sport Behavior, 4,* 24–31.

Duda, J.L. (1988). The relationship between goal perspectives, persistence and behavioral intensity among male and female recreational sport participants. *Leisure Sciences, 10,* 95–106.

Duda, J.L. (1989). Relationship between task and ego orientation and the perceived purpose of sport among high school athletes. *Journal of Sport and Exercise Psychology, 11,* 318–335.

Duda, J.L. (1992). Motivation in sport settings: A goal perspective approach. In G.C. Roberts (Ed.),

Motivation in sport and exercise (pp. 57–91). Champaign, IL: Human Kinetics.

Duda, J.L. (1993). Goals: A social cognitive approach to achievement motivation in sport. In R. Singer, M. Murphy, & L. Tennant (Eds.), *Handbook of research on sport psychology* (pp. 421–436). New York: Macmillan.

Duda, J.L. (2001). Achievement goal research in sport: Pushing the boundaries and clarifying some misunderstandings. In G.C. Roberts (Ed.), *Advances in motivation in sport and exercise* (pp. 129–182). Champaign, IL: Human Kinetics.

Duda, J.L. (2005). Motivation in sport: The relevance of competence and achievement goals. In A.J. Elliot & C.S. Dweck (Eds.), *Handbook of competence and motivation* (pp. 318–335). New York: Guilford Press.

Duda, J.L. (2010). The PAPA project: A theory based intervention centered on promotion of an empowering motivational climate for young football players. In V. Mrowinski, M. Kyrios, & N. Voudouris (Eds.), *Abstracts of the 27th International Congress of Applied Psychology.* Melbourne, Australia.

Duda, J.L., Chi, L., Newton, M.L., Walling, M.D., & Catley, D. (1995). Task and ego orientation and intrinsic motivation in sport. *International Journal of Sport Psychology, 26,* 40–63.

Duda, J.L., Fox, K.R., Biddle, S.J., & Armstrong, N. (1992). Children's achievement goals and beliefs about success in sport. *British Journal of Educational Psychology, 62,* 313–323.

Duda, J.L., & Hall, H. (2001). Achievement goal theory in sport: Recent extensions and future directions. In R.N. Singer, H.A. Hausenblas, & C.M. Janelle (Eds.), *Handbook of sport psychology* (2nd ed.) (pp. 417–443). New York: Wiley

Duda, J.L., & Nicholls, J.G. (1992). Dimensions of achievement motivation in schoolwork and sport. *Journal of Educational Psychology, 84,* 290–299.

Duda, J.L., Olson, L.K., & Templin, T.J. (1991). The relationship of task and ego orientations to sportsmanship attitudes and the perceived legitimacy of injurious acts. *Research Quarterly for Exercise and Sport, 62,* 79–87.

Duda, J.L., & Whitehead, J. (1998). Measurement of goal perspectives in physical domain. In J. Duda (Ed.), *Advances in sport and exercise psychology measurement* (pp. 21–48). Morgantown, WV: Fitness Information Technology.

Duff, J., Evans, M.J., & Kennedy, P. (2004). Goal planning: a retrospective audit of rehabilitation process and outcome. *Clinical Rehabilitation, 18,* 275–286.

Dumas, J.E., Lynch, A.M., Laughlin, J.E., Smith, E.P., & Prinz, R.J. (2001). Promoting intervention fidelity: Conceptual issues, methods, and preliminary results from the EARLY ALLIANCE prevention trial. *American Journal of Preventive Medicine, 20*(1, Supplement), 38–47. Retrieved from www.ajpm-online.net/issues/

Duncan, S.C. (1993). The role of cognitive appraisal and friendship provisions in adolescents' affect and motivation toward activity in physical education. *Research Quarterly for Exercise and Sport, 64,* 314–323.

Duncan, T.E., & Stoolmiller, M. (1993). Modeling social and psychological determinants of exercise behaviors via structural equation systems. *Research Quarterly for Exercise and Sport, 64* (1), 1–16

Dunkley, D.M., & Blankstein, K.R. (2000). Self-critical perfectionism, coping, hassles and current distress: A structural equation modeling approach. *Cognitive Therapy and Research, 6,* 713–730.

Dunkley, D.M., Blankstein, K.R., Halsall, J., Williams, M., & Winkworth, G. (2000). The relation between perfectionism and distress: Hassles, coping, and perceived social support as mediators and moderators. *Journal of Counseling Psychology, 47,* 427–453.

Dunkley, D.M., Sanislow, C.A., Grilo, C.M., & McGlashan, T.H. (2006). Perfectionism and depressive symptoms 3 years later: Negative social interactions, avoidant coping, and perceived social support as mediators. *Comprehensive Psychiatry, 47,* 106–115.

Dunkley, D.M., Zuroff, D.C., & Blankstein, K.R. (2003). Self-critical perfectionism and daily affect: Dispositional and situational influences on stress and coping. *Journal of Personality and Social Psychology, 84,* 234–252.

Dunkley, D.M., Zuroff, D.C., & Blankstein, K.R. (2006). Specific perfectionism components versus self-criticism in predicting maladjustment. *Personality and Individual Differences, 40,* 665–676.

Dunn, J.C. (2000). Goal orientations, perceptions of the motivational climate, and perceived competence of children with movement difficulties. *Adapted Physical activity Quarterly, 17,* 1–19.

Dunn, J.G.H., Causgrove Dunn, J., & Syrotuik, D.G. (2002). Relationship between multidimensional perfectionism and goal orientations in sport. *Journal of Sport and Exercise Psychology, 24,* 376–395.

Dunn, J.G.H., Craft, J.M., Causgrove Dunn, J., & Gotwals, J.K. (in press). Comparing a domain-specific and global measure of perfectionism in competitive female figure skaters. *Journal of Sport Behaviour.*

Dunn, J.G.H., Gotwals, J.K., & Causgrove Dunn, J. (2005). An examination of the domain specificity of perfectionism among intercollegiate student-athletes. *Personality and Individual Differences, 38,* 1439–1448.

Dunn, J.G.H., Gotwals, J.K., Causgrove Dunn, J., & Syrotuik, D.G. (2006). Examining the relationship between perfectionism and trait anger in competitive sport. *International Journal of Sport and Exercise Psychology, 4,* 7–24.

Dupont, J.P., Carlier, G., Gérald, P., & Delens, C. (2009). Teacher-student negotiation and its relation to physical education students' motivational processes: An approach based on self-determination theory. *European Physical Education Review, 15,* 21–46. doi:10.1177/1356336X09105210

Durand, M., Cury, F., Sarrazin, P., & Famose, J-.P. (1996). Le Questionnaire du Succès en Sport: Validation Française du "Perception of Success Questionnaire." *International Journal of Sport Psychology, 27,* 251–268.

Dweck, C.S. (1975). The role of expectations and attributions in the alleviation of learned helplessness. *Journal of Personality and Social Psychology, 31,* 674–685.

Dweck, C.S. (1986). Motivational processes affecting learning. *American Psychologist, 41,* 1040–1048.

Dweck, C.S. (1998). The development of early self-conceptions: Their relevance for motivational processes. In J. Heckhausen & C.S. Dweck (Eds.), *Motivation and self-regulation across the lifespan* (pp. 258–283). New York: Cambridge University Press.

Dweck, C.S. (1999). *Self-theories: Their role in motivation, personality, and development.* Philadelphia: Psychology Press.

Dweck, C.S. (2006). *Mindset: The new psychology of success.* New York: Random House.

Dweck, C.S., & Leggett, E. (1988). A social-cognitive approach to motivation & personality. *Psychological review, 95,* 256–273.

Dworkin, J.B., Larson, R., & Hansen, D. (2003). Adolescents' accounts of growth experiences in youth activities. *Journal of Youth and Adolescence, 32,* 17–26.

Dykman, B.M. (1998). Integrating cognitive and motivational factors in depression: Initial tests of a goal orientation approach. *Journal of Personality and Social Psychology, 74,* 139–158.

Dzewaltowski, D.A., Karteroliotis, K., Welk, G., Johnston, J.A., Nyaronga, D., & Estabrooks, P.A. (2007). Measurement of self-efficacy and proxy efficacy for middle school youth physical activity. *Journal of Sport and Exercise Psychology, 29,* 310–332.

Eccles, J.S., & Harold, R.D. (1991). Gender differences in sport involvement: Applying the Eccles expectancy-value model. *Journal of Applied Sport Psychology, 3,* 7–35.

Edmonds, W.A., Tenenbaum, G., Kamata, A., & Johnson, M.B. (2009). The role of collective efficacy in adventure racing teams. *Small Group Research, 50,* 163–180.

Edmunds, J., Ntoumanis, N., & Duda, J.L. (2006a). A test of self-determination theory in the exercise domain. *Journal of Applied Social Psychology, 36,* 2240–2265.

Edmunds, J., Ntoumanis, N., & Duda, J.L. (2006b). Examining exercise dependence symptomatology from a self-determination perspective. *Journal of Health Psychology, 11,* 887–903.

Edmunds, J., Ntoumanis, N., & Duda, J.L. (2008). Testing a self-determination theory-based teaching style intervention in the exercise domain. *European Journal of Social Psychology, 38,* 375–388.

Egan, S.J., & Hine, P. (2008). Cognitive behaviour treatment of perfectionism: A single case experimental design series. *Behaviour Change, 25,* 245–258.

Eklund, R.C., & Crawford, S. (1994). Active women, social physique anxiety, and exercise. *Journal of Sport and Exercise Psychology, 16,* 431–448.

Elliot, A.J. (1994). *Approach and avoidance achievement goals: An intrinsic motivation analysis.* (Unpublished doctoral dissertation.) University of Wisconsin, Madison.

Elliot, A.J. (1997). Integrating "classic" and "contemporary" approaches to achievement motivation: A hierarchical model of approach and avoidance achievement motivation. In P. Pintrinch & M. Maehr (Eds.), *Advances in motivation and achievement* (vol. 10, pp. 143–179). Greenwich, CT: JAI Press.

Elliot, A.J. (1999). Approach and avoidance motivation and achievement goals. *Educational Psychologist, 34,* 149–169.

Elliot, A.J. (2005). A conceptual history of the achievement goal construct. In A. Elliot & C. Dweck (Eds.), *Handbook of competence and motivation* (pp. 52–72). New York: Guilford Press.

Elliot, A.J., & Church, M.A. (1997). A hierarchical model of approach and avoidance achievement motivation. *Journal of Personality and Social Psychology, 72,* 218–232.

Elliot, A.J., & Conroy, D.E. (2005). Beyond the dichotomous model of achievement goals in sport and exercise psychology. *Sport and Exercise Psychology Review*, 1, 17–25.

Elliot, A.J., Cury, F., Fryer, J.W., & Huguet, P. (2006). Achievement goals, self-handicapping, and performance attainment: A mediational analysis. *Journal of Sport & Exercise Psychology*, 28, 344–361.

Elliot, A.J., & Fryer, J.W. (2008). The goal construct. In J. Shah & W. Gardner (Eds.) *Handbook of motivation science* (pp. 235–250). New York: Guilford Press.

Elliot, A.J., & Harackiewicz, J.M. (1996). Approach and avoidance achievement goals and intrinsic motivation: A mediational analysis. *Journal of Personality and Social Psychology*, 70, 461–475.

Elliot, A.J., & McGregor, H.A. (1999). Test anxiety and the hierarchical model of approach and avoidance achievement motivation. *Journal of Personality and Social Psychology*, 76, 628–644.

Elliot, A.J., & McGregor, H.A. (2001). A 2x2 achievement goal framework. *Journal of Personality and Social Psychology*, 80, 501–519. doi:10.1037/0022-3514.80.3.501

Elliot, A.J., & Murayama, K. (2008). On the measurement of achievement goals: Critique, illustration, and application. *Journal of Educational Psychology*, 100(3), 613–628.

Elliot, A.J., & Thrash, T.M. (2001). Achievement goals and the hierarchical model of achievement motivation. *Educational Psychology Review*, 12, 139–156.

Elliott, E.S., & Dweck, C.S. (1988). Goals: An approach to motivation and achievement. *Journal of Personality and Social Psychology*, 54, 5–12.

Ellis, A. (1962). *Reason and emotion in psychotherapy.* New York: Lyle Stuart.

Ellis, A. (2003). The relationship of rational-emotive behavior therapy (REBT) to social psychology. *Journal of Rational-Emotive and Cognitive-Behavior Therapy*, 21, 5–20.

Elston, T.L., & Martin Ginis, K.A. (2004). The effects of self-set versus assigned goals on exercisers' self-efficacy for an unfamiliar task. *Journal of Sport and Exercise Psychology*, 26, 500–504.

Emslie, C., Whyte, F., Campbell, A., Mutrie, N., Lee, L., Ritchie, D., . . . Kearney, N. (2007). "I wouldn't have been interested in just sitting round a table talking about cancer"; exploring the experiences of women with breast cancer in a group exercise trial. *Health Education Research*, 22, 827–838.

Enns, M.W., Cox, B.J., Sareen, J., & Freeman, P. (2001). Adaptive and maladaptive perfectionism in medical students: A longitudinal investigation. *Medical Education*, 35, 1034–1042.

Epstein, J. (1988). Effective schools or effective students? Dealing with diversity. In R. Haskins & B. MacRae (Eds.), *Policies for America's public schools* (pp. 89–126). Norwood, NJ: Ablex.

Epstein, J. (1989). Family structures and student motivation: A developmental perspective. In C. Ames & R. Ames (Eds.), *Research on motivation in education* (Vol. 3, pp. 259–295). New York: Academic Press.

Epstein, L.H., & Roemmich, J.N. (2001). Reducing sedentary behaviour: Role in modifying physical activity. *Exercise and Sport Sciences Reviews*, 29, 103–108.

Epstein, L.H., Roemmich, J.N., Robinson, J.L., Paluch, R.A., Winiewicz, D.D., Fuerch, J.H., . . . Robinson, T.N. (2008). A randomised trial of the effects of reducing television viewing and computer use on body mass index in young children. *Archives of Pediatric and Adolescent Medicine*, 162, 239–245.

Erez, M., & Zidon, I. (1984). Effect of goal acceptance on the relationship of goal difficulty to performance. *Journal of Applied Psychology*, 69, 69–78.

Ericsson, K.A. (1996). The acquisition of expert performance: An introduction to some issues. In K.A. Ericsson (Ed.), *The road to excellence: The acquisition of expert performance in the arts and sciences, sports and games.* (pp. 1–50). Hillsdale, NJ: Lawrence Erlbaum.

Ericsson, K.A. (2006). The influence of experience and deliberate practice on the development of superior expert performance. In K.A. Ericsson, N. Charness, P. Feltovich, & R.R. Hoffman (Eds.), *Cambridge handbook or expertise and expert performance* (pp. 685–706). Cambridge, UK: Cambridge University Press.

Ericsson, K.A., & Charness, N. (1994). Expert performance: Its structure and acquisition. *American Psychologist*, 49, 71–76.

Eronen, S., Nurmi, J.E., & Salmela-Aro, K. (1998). Optimistic, defensive-pessimistic, impulsive, self-handicapping strategies in university environments. *Learning and Instruction*, 8, 159–177.

Escarti, A., & Gutierrez, M. (2001). Influence of the motivational climate in physical education on the intention to practice physical activity or sport. *European Journal of Sport Science*, 1, 1–12.

Escarti, A., & Guzman, J.F. (1999). Effects of feedback on self-efficacy, performance, and choice on an athletic task. *Journal of Applied Sport Psychology*, 11, 83–96.

Estabrooks, P., & Gyurcsik, N.C. (2003). Evaluating the impact of behavioral interventions that target physical activity: Issues of generalizability and public health. *Psychology of Sport and Exercise, 4*, 41–55.

Evans, J., & Roberts, G.C. (1987). Physical competence and the development of children's peer relations. *Quest, 39*, 23–35.

Evans, L., & Hardy, L. (2002). Injury rehabilitation: A goal-setting intervention study. *Research Quarterly for Exercise and Sport, 73*, 310–319.

Ewart, C.K., Taylor, C.B., Reese, L.B., & DeBusk, R.F. (1983). Effects of early postmyocardial infarction exercise testing on self-perception and subsequent physical activity. *American Journal of Cardiology, 51*, 1076–1080.

Ewing, M. (1981). *Achievement orientations and sport behaviors of males and females.* (Unpublished doctoral dissertation). University of Illinois at Champaign-Urbana.

Ey, S., Henning, K.R., & Shaw, D.L. (2000). Attitudes and factors related to seeking mental health treatment among medical and dental students. *Journal of College Student Psychotherapy, 14*, 23–39.

Feldenkrais, M. (1985). *The potent self: A guide to spontaneity.* San Francisco: Harper.

Feltz, D.L. (1982). A path analysis of the casual elements in Bandura's theory of self-efficacy and an anxiety-based model of avoidance behavior. *Journal of Personality and Social Psychology, 42*, 764–781.

Feltz, D.L. (1988). Gender differences in the causal elements of self-efficacy on a high-avoidance motor task. *Journal of Sport and Exercise Psychology, 10*, 151–166.

Feltz, D.L. (1994). Self-confidence and performance. In D. Druckman & R.A. Bjork (Eds.), *Learning, remembering, believing: Enhancing human performance* (pp. 173–206). Washington DC: National Academy Press.

Feltz, D.L., & Chase, M.A. (1998). The measurement of self-efficacy and confidence in sport. In J. Duda (Ed.), *Advances in sport and exercise psychology measurement* (pp. 63–78). Morgantown, WV: Fitness Information Technology.

Feltz, D.L., Chase, M.A., Moritz, S.A., & Sullivan, P.J. (1999). A conceptual model of coaching efficacy: Preliminary investigation and instrument development. *Journal of Educational Psychology, 91*, 765–776.

Feltz, D.L., Chow, G.M., & Hepler, T.J. (2008). Path analysis of self-efficacy and diving performance revisited. *Journal of Sport and Exercise Psychology, 30*, 401–411.

Feltz, D.L., Hepler, T.J., Roman, N., & Paiement, C. (2009). Coaching efficacy and volunteer youth sport coaches. *Sport Psychologist, 23*, 24–41.

Feltz, D.L., Landers, D.M., & Raeder, U. (1979). Enhancing self-efficacy in high avoidance motor tasks: A comparison of modeling techniques. *Journal of Sport Psychology, 1*, 112–122.

Feltz, D.L., & Lirgg, C.D. (1998). Perceived team and player efficacy in hockey. *Journal of Applied Psychology, 83*, 557–564.

Feltz, D.L., & Lirgg, C.D. (2001). Self-efficacy beliefs of athletes, teams, and coaches. In R.N. Singer, H.A. Hausenblas, & C.M. Janelle (Eds.), *Handbook of sport psychology* (pp. 340–361). New York: Wiley.

Feltz, D.L., & Mugno, D.A. (1983). A replication of the path analysis of the causal elements in Bandura's theory of self-efficacy and the influence of autonomic participation. *Journal of Sport Psychology, 5*, 263–277.

Feltz, D.L., & Payment, C. (2005). Self-efficacy beliefs related to movement and mobility. *Quest, 57*, 24–36.

Feltz, D.L., & Riessinger, C.A. (1990). Effects on in vivo emotive imagery and performance feedback on self-efficacy and muscular endurance. *Journal of Sport and Exercise Psychology, 12*, 132–143.

Feltz, D.L., Short, S.E., & Sullivan, P.J. (2008). *Self-efficacy in sport.* Champaign, IL: Human Kinetics.

Ferrari, J.R. (1995). Perfectionism cognitions with non-clinical and clinical samples. *Journal of Social Behaviour and Personality, 10*, 142–156.

Ferreira, I., van der Horst, K., Wendel-Vos, W., Kremers, S., van Lenthe, F.J., & Brug, J. (2006). Environmental correlates of physical activity in youth: A review and update. *Obesity Reviews, 8*, 129–154.

Fishbein, M., von Haeften, I., & Appleyard, J. (2001). The role of theory in developing effective interventions: Implications from Project SAFER. *Psychology, Health & Medicine, 6*, 223–238.

Fitzsimons, C., Baker, G., Brennan, G., & Mutrie, N. (2010). *Walking for Wellbeing in the West (WWW): Impact of maximal and minimal interventions on total sitting time over 24 months.* Paper presented at the International Congress on Physical Activity and Public Health, Toronto, Canada.

Fitzsimons, C., Baker, G., Wright, A., Lowry, R., & Mutrie, N. (2009). *Walking for Wellbeing in the West: Maximum versus minimum intervention.* Paper presented at the International Society for Behavioural Nutrition and Physical Activity Annual Meeting, Lisbon, Portugal.

Fitzsimons, C., Baker, G., Wright, A., Nimmo, M., Ward Thompson, C., Lowry, R., . . . Mutrie, N. (2008). The "Walking for Wellbeing in the West" randomised controlled trial of a pedometer-based walking programme in combination with physical activity consultation with 12 month follow-up: Rationale and study design. *BMC Public Health*, 8, 259.

Fleming, J.C., & Martin Ginis, K.A. (2004). The effects of commercial exercise video models on women's self-presentational efficacy and exercise task self-efficacy. *Journal of Applied Sport Psychology, 16*, 92–102.

Fletcher, G.J.O., Simpson, J.A., & Thomas, G. (2000). The measurement of perceived relationship quality components: A confirmatory factor analytic approach. *Personality and Social Psychology Bulletin, 26*, 340–354.

Flett, G.L., Besser, A., Davis, R.A., & Hewitt, P.L. (2003). Dimensions of perfectionism, unconditional self-acceptance, and depression. *Journal of Rational-Emotive and Cognitive-Behavior Therapy, 21*, 119–138.

Flett, G.L., Blankstein, K.R., Hewitt, P.L., & Koledin. (1992). Components of perfectionism and procrastination in college students. *Social Behaviour and Personality, 20*, 85–94.

Flett, G.L., Greene, A., & Hewitt, P.L. (2004). Dimensions of perfectionism and anxiety sensitivity. *Journal of Rational-Emotive and Cognitive-Behavior Therapy, 22*, 37–55.

Flett, G.L., & Hewitt, P.L. (2002). *Perfectionism: Theory, research and treatment*. Washington, DC: American Psychological Association.

Flett, G.L., & Hewitt, P.L. (2005). The perils of perfectionism in sports and exercise. *Current Directions in Psychological Science, 14*, 14–18.

Flett, G.L., & Hewitt, P.L. (2006). Positive versus negative perfectionism in psychopathology: A comment on Slade and Owen's dual process model. *Behavior Modification, 30*, 472–495.

Flett, G.L., & Hewitt, P.L. (2008). Treatment interventions for perfectionism-A cognitive perspective: Introduction to the special issue. *Journal of Rational Emotive and Cognitive Therapy, 26, 127–133.

Flett, G.L., Hewitt, P.L., Blankstein, K.R., & Dynin, C.B. (1994). Dimensions of perfectionism and type A behaviour. *Personality and Individual Differences, 16*, 477–485.

Flett, G.L., Hewitt, P.L., Blankstein, K.R., & Gray, L. (1998). Psychological distress and the frequency of perfectionist thinking. *Journal of Personality and Social Psychology, 75*, 1363–1381.

Flett, G.L., Hewitt, P.L., Blankstein, K.R., & O'Brien, S. (1991). Perfectionism and learned resourcefulness in depression and self-esteem. *Personality and Individual Differences, 12*, 61–68.

Flett, G.L., Hewitt, P.L., & DeRosa, T. (1996). Dimensions of perfectionism, psychosocial adjustment, and social skills. *Personality and Individual Differences, 20*, 143–150.

Flett, G.L., Hewitt, P.L., Endler, N.S., & Tassone, C. (1995). Perfectionism and components of state and trait anxiety. *Current Psychology, 13*, 326–350.

Flett, G.L., Hewitt, P.L., Whelan, T., & Martin, T.R. (2007). The perfectionism cognitions inventory: Psychometric properties and associations with distress and deficits in cognitive self-management. *Journal of Rational Emotive and Cognitive Therapy. 4*, 255–277.

Flett, G.L., Hewitt, P.L., Oliver, J.M., & McDonald, S. (2002). Perfectionism in children and their parents: A developmental analysis. In G.L. Flett & P.L. Hewitt, (Eds.), *Perfectionism: Theory, research and treatment.* (pp. 89-132). Washington, DC.: American Psychological Association.

Flett, G.L., Mardorsky, D., Hewitt, P.L., & Heisel, M. (2002). Perfectionism cognitions, rumination and psychological distress. *Journal of Rational-Emotive and Cognitive-Behaviour Therapy, 20*, 33–47.

Flett, G.L., Russo, F.A., & Hewitt, P.L. (1994). Dimensions of perfectionism and constructive thinking as a coping response. *Journal of Rational-Emotive and Cognitive-Behavior Therapy, 12*, 163–179.

Ford, M. (1992). *Motivating humans: Goals, emotions, and personal agency beliefs*. Boston: Sage.

Forest, J., Mageau, G.A., Sarrazin, C., & Morin, E.M. (2010). "Work is my passion": The different affective, behavioral, and cognitive consequences of harmonious and obsessive passion toward work. *Canadian Journal of Administrative Sciences*, DOI: 10.1002/cjas.170.

Forscher, B.K. (1963). Chaos in the brickyard. *Science, 142*, 3590.

Fortier, M.S., Williams, G.C., Sweet, S.N., & Patrick, H. (2009). Self-determination theory: Process models for health behavior change. In R.J. DiClemente, R.A. Crosby, & M.C. Kegler (Eds.), *Emerging theories in health promotion practice and research* (2nd ed.) (pp. 157–183). San Francisco, CA: Jossey-Bass.

Fox, K. (1988). The self-esteem complex and youth fitness. *Quest, 40*, 230–246.

Fox, K., Goudas M., Biddle, S., Duda, J., & Armstrong, N. (1994). Children's task and ego goal profiles in sport. *British Journal of Educational Psychology, 64,* 253–261.

Franklin, B.A. (1988). Program factors that influence exercise adherence: Practical adherence skills for the clinical staff. In R.K. Dishman (Ed.), *Exercise adherence: Its impact on public health* (pp. 237–239). Champaign, IL: Human Kinetics.

Frederick, C.M., & Ryan, R.M. (1993). Differences in motivation for sport and exercise and their relations with participation and mental health. *Journal of Sport Behavior, 16,* 124–146.

Frederick, C.M., & Ryan, R.M. (1995). Self-determination in sport: A review using cognitive evaluation theory. *International Journal of Sport Psychology, 26,* 5–23. Retrieved from www.cababstractsplus .org/abstracts/Abstract.aspx?AcNo=19951808917

Fredrickson, B.L. (2001). The role of positive emotions in positive psychology: The Broaden-and-Build Theory of positive emotions. *American Psychologist, 56,* 218–226.

Frese, M. (2006). Presidential address, International Association of Applied Psychology, presentation at 26th International Congress of Applied Psychology, Athens, Greece.

Friedenreich, C.M., & Cust, A.E. (2008). Physical activity and breast cancer risk: Impact of timing, type and dose of activity and population subgroup effects. *British Journal of Sports Medicine, 42,* 636–647.

Friedenreich, C.M., Gregory, J., Kopciuk, K.A., Mackey, J.R., & Courneya, K.S. (2009). Prospective cohort study of lifetime physical activity and breast cancer survival. *International Journal of Cancer, 124,* 1954–1962.

Friedman, R., Deci, E.L., Elliot, A.J., Moller, A.C., & Aarts, H. (2010). Motivational synchronicity: Priming motivational orientations with observations of others' behaviors. *Motivation and Emotion, 34,* 34–38.

Frijda, N.H., Mesquita, B., Sonnemans, J., & Van Goozen, S. (1991). The duration of affective phenomena or emotions, sentiments and passions. In K.T. Strongman (Ed.), *International review of studies on emotion* (Vol. 1, pp. 187–225). New York: Wiley.

Fromm, E. (1976). *To have or to be?* New York: Harper & Row.

Frost, R.O., Heimberg, R.G., Holt, C.S., Mattia, J.I., & Neubauer, A.L. (1993). A comparison of two measures of perfection. *Personality and Individual Differences, 14,* 119–126.

Frost, R.O., & Henderson, K.J. (1991). Perfectionism and reactions to athletic competition. *Journal of Sport and Exercise Psychology, 13,* 323–335.

Frost, R.O., Lahart, C.M., & Rosenblate, R. (1991). The development of perfectionism: A study of daughters and their parents. *Cognitive Therapy and Research, 15,* 469–489.

Frost, R.O., & Marten, P.A. (1990). Perfectionism and evaluative threat. *Cognitive Therapy and Research, 14,* 559–572.

Frost, R.O., Marten, P.A., Lahart, C., & Rosenblate, R. (1990). The dimensions of perfectionism. *Cognitive Therapy and Research, 14,* 449–468.

Fry, M.D. (2001). The development of motivation in children. In G.C. Roberts (Ed.), *Advances in motivation in sport and exercise* (pp. 51–78). Champaign, IL: Human Kinetics.

Fry, M.D., & Newton, M. (2003). Application of achievement goal theory in an urban youth tennis setting. *Journal of Applied Sport Psychology, 15,* 50–67.

Fulbright-Anderson, K., Kubisch, A., & Connell, J. (Eds.). (1998). *New approaches to evaluating community initiatives—Vol. 2: Theory, measurement, and analysis.* Washington, DC: Aspen Institute.

Fulmer, S.M., & Frijters, J.C. (2009). A review of self-report and alternative approaches in the measurement of student motivation. *Educational Psychology Review, 21,* 219–246. doi:10.1007/ s10648-009-9107-x

Gagné, F. (2007). Ten commandments for academic talent development. *Gifted Child Quarterly, 51,* 93–118.

Gagné, M., Ryan, R.M., & Bargmann, K. (2003). Autonomy support and need satisfaction in the motivation and well-being of gymnasts. *Journal of Applied Sport Psychology, 15,* 372–390. doi:10.1080/714044203

Galvan, Z.J., & Ward, P. (1998). Effects of public posting on inappropriate on-court behaviors by collegiate tennis players. *Sport Psychologist, 12,* 419–426.

Galway, K., Black, A., Cantwell, M., Cardwell, C.R., Mills, M., & Donnelly, M. (2008). Psychosocial interventions to improve quality of life and emotional wellbeing for recently diagnosed cancer patients. *Cochrane Database of Systematic Reviews, 2,* Art. No. CD007064.

Gammage, K.L., Martin Ginis, K.A., & Hall, C.R. (2004). Self-presentational efficacy: Its influence on social anxiety in an exercise context. *Journal of Sport & Exercise Psychology, 26,* 179–190.

Gammage, K.L., Hall, C.R., Prapavessis, H., Maddison, R., Haase, A., & Martin, K.A. (2004). Re-examination of the factor structure and composition of the Self-Presentation in Exercise Questionnaire (SPEQ). *Journal of Applied Sport Psychology, 16,* 82–91.

Gammage, K.L., Hall, C.R., & Martin Ginis, K.A. (2004). Self-presentation in exercise contexts: Differences between high and low frequency exercisers. *Journal of Applied Social Psychology, 34,* 1638–1651.

Gano-Overway, L.A., & Ewing, M.E. (2004). The longitudinal effects of the perceived motivational climate on physical education students' goal orientations. *Research Quarterly for Exercise and Sport, 75,* 315–325.

Garn, A., & Sun, H. (2009). Approach-avoidance motivational profiles in early adolescents to the PACER fitness test. *Journal of Teaching in Physical Education, 28,* 400–421.

Garnefski, N., Kraaij, V., De Graaf, M., & Karels, L. (2010). Psychological intervention targets for people with visual impairments: The importance of cognitive coping and goal adjustment. *Disability & Rehabilitation, 32,* 142–147.

Gaudreau, P., Amiot, C.E., & Vallerand, R.J. (2009). Trajectories of affective states in adolescent hockey players: Turning point and motivational antecedents. *Developmental Psychology, 45,* 307–319. doi:10.1037/a0014134

Gaudreau, P., & Antl, S. (2008). Athletes' broad dimensions of perfectionism: Examining change in life-satisfaction and the mediating role of motivation and coping. *Journal of Sport and Exercise Psychology, 30,* 356–382. Retrieved from http://hk.humankinetics.com/JSEP/journalAbout.cfm

George, T.R. (1994). Self-confidence and baseball performance: A causal examination of self-efficacy theory. *Journal of Sport and Exercise Psychology, 16,* 381–399.

George, T.R., Feltz, D.L., & Chase, M.A. (1992). The effects of model similarity on self-efficacy and muscular endurance: A second look. *Journal of Sport and Exercise Psychology, 14,* 237–248.

Georgiadis, M.M., Biddle, S.J.H., & Stavrou, N.A. (2006). Motivation for weight-loss diets: A clustering, longitudinal field study using self-esteem and self-determination theory perspectives. *Health Education Journal, 65,* 53–72.

Gernigon, C., d'Arripe-Longueville, F., Delignières, D., & Ninot, G. (2004). A dynamical systems perspective on goal involvement states in sport. *Journal of Sport and Exercise Psychology, 26,* 572–596.

Gill, D.L., & Deeter, T.E. (1988). Development of the sport orientation questionnaire. *Research Quarterly for Exercise and Sport, 59,* 191–202.

Gill, D.L., Gross, J.B., & Huddleston, S. (1983). Participation motivation in youth sports. *International Journal of Sport Psychology, 14,* 1–14.

Gillet, N., Berjot, S., & Gobancé, L. (2010). A motivational model of performance in the sport domain. *European Journal of Sport Science, 9,* 151–158. doi:10.1080/17461390902736793

Gillet, N., Vallerand, R.J., & Rosnet, E. (2009). Motivational clusters and performance in a real-life setting. *Motivation and Emotion, 33,* 49–62. doi:10.1007/s11031-008-9115-z

Gillison, F. (2007). *Maintaining adolescents' involvement in exercise and quality of life: A self-determination theory approach.* Unpublished doctoral dissertation. University of Bath, UK.

Gillison, F., Standage, M., & Skevington, S.M. (2006). Relationships among adolescents' weight perceptions, exercise goals, exercise motivation, quality of life and leisure-time exercise behaviour: A self-determination theory approach. *Health Education Research, 21,* 836–847.

Gillison, F., Standage, M., & Skevington, S.M. (2011). Motivation and body-related factors as discriminators of change in adolescents' exercise behavior profiles. *Journal of Adolescent Health, 48,* 44–51.

Gilson, T.A., Chow, G.M., & Feltz, D.L. (in press). Self-efficacy and athletic squat performance: Positive or negative influences at the within and between levels of analysis? *Journal of Applied Social Psychology.*

Gladwell, M. (2008). *Outliers: The story of success.* New York: Little, Brown.

Glasgow, R.E., Vogt, T., & Boles, S. (1999). Evaluating the public health impact of health promotion interventions: The RE-AIM framework. *American Journal of Public Health, 89,* 1322–1327.

Glasser, W. (1976). *Positive addiction.* New York: Harper & Row.

Glover, D.S., Brown, G.P., Fairburn, C.G., & Shafran, R. (2007). A preliminary evaluation of cognitive-behaviour therapy for clinical perfectionism: A case series. *British Journal of Clinical Psychology, 46,* 85–94.

Godin, G., & Shephard, R.J. (1985). A simple method to assess exercise behavior in the community. *Canadian Journal of Applied Sport Sciences, 10,* 141–146.

Gollwitzer, P.M. (1999). Implementation intentions: Strong effects of simple plans. *American Psychologist, 54,* 493–503.

Gollwitzer, P.M., & Sheeran, P. (2006). Implementation intentions and goal achievement: A meta-analysis of effects and processes. *Advances in Experimental Social Psychology, 38,* 69–119.

Goodger, K., Gorely, T., Lavallee, D., & Harwood, C. (2007). Burnout in sport: A systematic review. *Sport Psychologist, 21,* 127–151.

Gore, J.S., & Cross, S.E. (2006). Pursuing goals for us: Relationally autonomous reasons in long-term goal pursuit. *Journal of Personality and Social Psychology, 90,* 848–861. doi:10.1037/0022-3514.90.5.848

Gorley, T., & Gordon, S. (1995). An examination of the transtheoretical model and exercise behavior in older adults. *Journal of Sport and Exercise Psychology, 17,* 312–324.

Gotwals, J.K., & Dunn, J.G.H. (2009). A multi-method multi analytic approach to establishing internal construct validity evidence: The Sport Multidimensional Perfectionism Scale 2. *Measurement in Physical Education and Exercise Science, 13,* 71–92.

Gotwals, J.K., Dunn, J.G.H., & Wayment, H.A. (2002). An examination of perfectionism and self-esteem in intercollegiate athletes. *Journal of Sport Behavior, 26,* 17–38.

Goudas, M., Biddle, S., & Fox, K. (1994). Perceived locus of causality, goal orientations, and perceived competence in school physical education classes. *British Journal of Educational Psychology, 64,* 453–463.

Goudas, M., Biddle, S., Fox, K., & Underwood, M. (1995). It ain't what you do, it's the way you do it! Teaching style affects children's motivation in track and field lessons. *Sport Psychologist, 9,* 254–264.

Gould, D. (1996). Personal motivation gone awry: Burnout in competitive athletes. *Quest, 48,* 275–289.

Gould, D. (2006). Goal setting for peak performance. In J.M. Williams (Ed.), *Applied sport psychology: Personal growth to peak performance* (pp. 240–259). New York: McGraw-Hill.

Gould, D. (2010). Goal setting for peak performance. In J.M. Williams (Ed.), *Applied sport psychology. Personal growth to peak performances* (6th ed., pp. 201–220). New York: McGraw-Hill.

Gould, D., Dieffenbach, K., & Moffett, A. (2002). Psychological characteristics and their development in Olympic champions. *Journal of Applied Sport Psychology, 14,* 172–204.

Gould, D., Feltz, D., & Weiss, M.R. (1985). Motives for participating in competitive youth swimming. *International Journal of Sport Psychology, 16,* 126–140.

Gould, D., Guinan, D., Greenleaf, C., Medberty, R., & Peterson, K. (1999). Factors affecting Olympic performance: Perceptions of athletes and coaches from more and less successful teams. *Sport Psychologist, 13,* 371–394.

Gould, D., & Maynard, I. (2009). Psychological preparation for the Olympic Games. *Journal of Sports Sciences, 27,* 1393–1408.

Gould, D., Tammen, V., Murphy, S., & May, J. (1989). An examination of U.S. Olympic sport psychology consultants and the services they provide. *Sport Psychologist, 3,* 300–312.

Gould, D., Tuffey, S., Udry, E., & Loehr, J. (1996). Burnout in competitive junior tennis players: II. Qualitative analysis. *Sport Psychologist, 10,* 341–366.

Gould, D., Tuffey, S., Udrey, E., & Loehr, J. (1997). Burnout in competitive junior tennis players: III. Individual differences in the burnout experience. *Sport Psychologist, 11,* 257–276.

Gould, D., Udry, E., Bridges, D., & Beck, L. (1997). Coping with season-ending injuries. *Sport psychologist, 11,* 379–399.

Gould, D., Udry, E., Tuffey, S., & Loehr, J. (1996). Burnout in competitive junior tennis players: I. A quantitative psychological assessment. *Sport Psychologist, 10,* 332–340.

Gray, C.E., & Wilson, P.M. (2008). The relationship between organizational commitment, perceived relatedness, and intentions to continue in Canadian track and field officials. *Journal of Sport Behavior, 31,* 44–63. Retrieved from www.accessmylibrary.com/archive/2171–journal-of-sport-behavior.html

Greaven, S.H., Santor, D.A., Thompson, R., & Zuroff, D.C. (2000). Adolescent self-handicapping, depressive affect, and maternal parenting styles. *Journal of Youth and Adolescence, 29,* 631–646.

Greenberg, J., Pyszczynski, T., & Solomon, S. (1986). The causes and consequences of a need for self-esteem: A terror management theory. In R.F. Baumeister (Ed.), *Public self and private self* (pp. 189–212). New York: Springer-Verlag.

Greenleaf, C., McGreer, R., & Parham, H. (2006). Physique attitudes and self-presentational concerns: Exploratory interviews with female group aerobic exercisers and instructors. *Sex Roles, 54,* 189–199.

Greenlees, I.A., Graydon, J.K., & Maynard, I.A. (1999). The impact of collective efficacy beliefs on effort and persistence in a group task. *Journal of Sport Sciences, 17,* 151–158.

Greenlees, I.A., Graydon, J.K., & Maynard, I.A. (2000). The impact of individual efficacy on group goal selection and group goal commitment. *Journal of Sports Sciences, 18,* 451–459.

Greenspon, T.S. (2000). "Healthy perfectionism" is an oxymoron! Reflections on the psychology of perfectionism and the sociology of science. *Journal of Secondary Gifted Education*, 11, 197–208.

Greenspon, T.S. (2008). Making sense of error: A view of the origins and treatment of perfectionism. *American Journal of Psychotherapy*, 62, 263–282.

Grindrod, D., Paton, C.D., Knex, W.L., & O'Brien, B.J. (2006). Six minute walk distance is greater when performed in a group than alone. *British Journal of Sports Medicine, 40*, 876–877.

Grolnick, W.S., & Ryan, R.M. (1987). Autonomy in children's learning: An experimental and individual difference investigation. *Journal of Personality and Social Psychology, 52*, 890–898.

Grolnick, W.S., & Ryan, R.M. (1989). Parent styles associated with children's self-regulation and competence in school. *Journal of Educational Psychology, 81*, 143–154. doi:10.1037/0022-0663.81.2.143

Grolnick, W.S., & Seal, K. (2008). *Pressured parents, stressed-out kids: Dealing with competition while raising a successful child.* Amherst, NY: Prometheus Press.

Grossbard, J.R., Cumming, S.P., Standage, M., Smith, R.E., Smoll, F.L. (2007). Social desirability and relations between goal orientations and competitive trait anxiety in young athletes. *Psychology of Sport and Exercise*, 8, 491–505.

Grouzet, F.M.E., Kasser, T., Ahuvia, A., Dols, J.M.F., Kim, Y., Lau, S., . . . Sheldon, K.M. (2005). The structure of goal contents across 15 cultures. *Journal of Personality and Social Psychology, 89*, 800–816.

Guay, F., Mageau, G.A., & Vallerand, R.J. (2003). On the hierarchical structure of self-determined motivation: A test of top-down, bottom-up, reciprocal, and horizontal effects. *Personality and Social Psychology Bulletin, 29*, 992–1004.

Guivernau, M., & Duda, J.L. (1995b). Psychometric properties of a Spanish version of the Task and Ego Orientation in Sport Questionnaire (TEOSQ) and Beliefs about the Causes of Success Inventory. *Revista de Psicologia del Deporte, 5*, 31–51.

Gustafson, S.L., & Rhodes, R.E. (2006). Parental correlates of physical activity in children and adolescents. *Sports Medicine, 36*, 79–97.

Gustafsson, H., Hassmen, P., Kentta, G., & Johansson, M. (2008). A qualitative analysis of burnout in elite Swedish athletes. *Psychology of Sport and Exercise*, 9, 800–816.

Habke, A.M., & Flynn, C.A. (2002). Interpersonal aspects of trait perfectionism. In G.L. Flett & P.L. Hewitt. (Eds.), *Perfectionism: Theory, research and treatment.* (pp. 151–180). Washington, DC: American Psychological Association.

Hagan, A.L., & Hausenblas, H.A. (2003). The relationship between exercise dependence and perfectionism. *American Journal of Health Studies, 18*, 133–137.

Hagger, M.S., & Chatzisarantis, N.L.D. (2007). *Intrinsic motivation and self-determination in exercise and sport.* Champaign, IL: Human Kinetics.

Hagger, M.S., & Chatzisarantis, N.L.D. (2008). Self-determination theory and the psychology of exercise. *International Review of Sport and Exercise Psychology, 1*, 79–103.

Hagger, M.S., & Chatzisarantis, N.L.D. (in press). *Self-determination theory in sport and exercise.* Champaign, IL: Human Kinetics.

Hagger, M.S., Chatzisarantis, N.L.D., & Biddle, S.J.H. (2002). A meta-analytic review of the Theories of Reasoned Action and Planned Behaviour in physical activity: Predictive validity and the contribution of additional variables. *Journal of Sport & Exercise Psychology, 24*, 3–32.

Hagger, M.S., Chatzisarantis, N.L.D., & Harris, J. (2006). The process by which relative autonomous motivation affects intentional behavior: Comparing effects across dieting and exercise behaviors. *Motivation and Emotion, 30*, 307–321.

Hagger, M.S., Chatzisarantis, N.L.D., Hein, V., Pihu, M., Soós, I., & Karsai, I. (2007). The perceived autonomy support scale for exercise settings (PASSES): Development, validity, and cross-cultural invariance in young people. *Psychology of Sport and Exercise, 8*, 632–653. doi:10.1016/j.psychsport.2006.09.001

Hagger, M., Chatzisarantis, N.L.D., Hein, V., Soós, I., Karsai, I., Lintunen, T., & Leemans, S. (2009). Teacher, peer and parent autonomy support in physical education and leisure-time physical activity: A trans-contextual model of motivation in four nations. *Psychology and Health, 24*, 689–711. doi:10.1080/08870440801956192

Hagger, M.S., & Orbell, S. (2003). A meta-analytic review of the common-sense model of illness representations. *Psychology and Health, 18*, 141–184.

Hair, J.E., Anderson, R.E., Tatham, R.L., & Black W.C. (1998). *Multivariate data analysis* (5th ed.). Upper Saddle River, NJ: Prentice-Hall.

Hall, H.K. (1990). *A social-cognitive approach to goal setting: The mediating effects of achievement goals and perceived ability.* (Unpublished doctoral dissertation.) University of Illinois at Urbana-Champaign.

Hall, H.K. (2006). Perfectionism: A hallmark quality of world class performers, or a psychological impediment to athletic development? In D. Hackfort & G. Tenenbaum (Eds.), *Perspectives in sport and exercise psychology; essential processes for attaining peak performance* (Vol. 1, pp. 178–211). Oxford, UK: Meyer & Meyer.

Hall, H.K., & Byrne, A.T.J. (1988). Goal setting in sport: Clarifying recent anomalies. *Journal of Sport and Exercise Psychology, 10,* 184–198.

Hall, H.K., Hill, A.P., & Appleton, P.R. (2008). *Multidimensional perfectionism and primary exercise dependence: The mediating role of contingent self-worth and ruminative cognition.* Paper presented at the British Psychological Society Division of Sport and Exercise Psychology Conference.

Hall, H.K., Hill, A.P., & Appleton, P.R. (2009). *Multidimensional perfectionism and patterns of achievement striving.* Paper presented at the European College of Sport Science, Oslo, Norway.

Hall, H.K., Hill, A.P., Appleton, P.R., & Ariano, C. (2009). *Multidimensional perfectionism, trait anger and displaced aggression presentation.* Paper presented at the International Society of Sport Psychology World Congress, Marrakech, Morocco.

Hall, H.K., Hill, A.P., Appleton, P.R., & Kozub, S.A. (2009). The mediating influence of unconditional self-acceptance and labile self-esteem on the relationship between multidimensional perfectionism and exercise dependence. *Psychology of Sport and Exercise, 10,* 35–44.

Hall, H.K., & Kerr, A.W. (1997). Motivational antecedents of precompetitive anxiety in youth sport. *Sport Psychologist, 11,* 24–42.

Hall, H.K., & Kerr, A.W. (2001). Goal-setting in sport and physical activity: Tracing empirical developments and establishing conceptual direction. In G.C. Roberts (Ed.), *Advances in motivation in sport and exercise* (pp. 183–234). Champaign, IL: Human Kinetics.

Hall, H.K., Kerr, A.W., & Cawthra, I.W. (1997). Burnout: Motivation gone awry or a disaster waiting to happen? In R. Lidor & M. Bar-Eli (Eds.), *Innovations in sport psychology: Linking theory and practice. Proceedings of the 9th ISSP World Congress in Sport Psychology* (Vol. 1, pp. 306–308). Netanya, Israel: Ministry of Education, Culture and Sport.

Hall, H.K., Kerr, A.W., Kozub, S.A., & Finnie, S.B. (2007). Motivational antecedents of obligatory exercise: The influence of achievement goals and multidimensional perfectionism. *Psychology of Sport and Exercise, 8,* 297–316.

Hall, H.K., Kerr, A.W., & Matthews, J. (1998). Precompetitive anxiety in sport: The contribution of achievement goals and perfectionism. *Journal of Sport and Exercise Psychology, 20,* 194–217.

Halvari, H., & Kjormo, O. (1999). A structural model of achievement motives, performance approach and avoidance goals, and performance among Norwegian Olympic athletes. *Perceptual and Motor Skills, 89,* 997–1022.

Hamachek, D.E. (1978). Psychodynamics of normal and neurotic perfectionism. *Psychology, 15,* 27–33.

Hanrahan, S.J. (2007). Athletes with disability. In G. Tenenbaum & R.E. Eklund (Eds.), *Handbook of sport psychology* (3rd ed., pp. 845–858). Hoboken, NJ: Wiley.

Hanton, S., & Jones, G. (1999). The effects of a multimodal intervention program on performers: II. Training the butterflies to fly in formation. *Sport Psychologist, 13,* 22–41.

Harackiewicz, J.M. Barron, K.E. Elliot, A.J. Carter S.M., & Lehto A.T. (1997). Predictors and consequences of achievement goals in the college classroom: Maintaining interest and making the grade. *Journal of Personality and Social Psychology, 73,* 1284-1295.

Harackiewicz, J.M., Barron, K.E., Pintrich, P.R., Elliot, A.J., & Thrash, T.M. (2002). Revision of achievement goal theory: Necessary and illuminating. *Journal of Educational Psychology, 94,* 638–645.

Harackiewicz, J.M., Sansone, C., Blair, L.W., Epstein, J.A., & Manderlink, G.M. (1987). Attributional processes in behavior change and maintenance: Smoking cessation and continued abstinence. *Journal of Consulting and Clinical Psychology, 55,* 372–378.

Hardman, A.E., & Stensel, D.J. (2009). *Physical activity and health: The evidence explained* (2nd ed.). London: Routledge.

Hardy, C.J., Hall, E.G., & Prestholdt, P.H. (1986). The mediational role of social-influence in the perception of exertion. *Journal of Sport Psychology, 8,* 88–104.

Hardy, C.J., & Rejeski, W.J. (1989). Not what, but how one feels: The measurement of affect during exercise. *Journal of Sport and Exercise Psychology, 11,* 304–317.

Hardy, L. (1998). Responses to the reactants on three myths in applied consultancy work. *Journal of Applied Sport Psychology, 10,* 212–219.

Hardy, L., Jones, J.G., & Gould, D. (1996). *Understanding psychological preparation for sport: Theory and practice of elite performers.* Chichester, UK: Wiley.

Hardy, L., Maiden, D., & Sherry, K. (1986). Goal-setting and performance anxiety. *Journal of Sports Sciences, 4,* 223–234.

Hardy, L., & Nelson, D. (1988). Self control training in sport and work. *Ergonomics, 31,* 1573–1585.

Hart, E.A., Leary, M.R., & Rejeski, W.J. (1989). The measurement of social physique anxiety. *Journal of Sport & Exercise Psychology, 11,* 94–104.

Harter, S. (1974). Pleasure derived by children from cognitive challenge and mastery. *Child Development, 45,* 661–669.

Harter, S. (1981). A new self-report scale of intrinsic vs. extrinsic orientation in the classroom: Motivational and informational components. *Developmental Psychology, 17,* 300–312.

Hartup, W.W. (1996). The company they keep: Friendships and their developmental significance. *Child Development, 67,* 1–13.

Harwood, C.G. (2002). Achievement goals in sport: Working towards an alternative conceptual model. *BASES Conference,* Manchester, United Kingdom.

Harwood, C.G., Cumming, J., & Fletcher, D. (2004). Motivational profiles and psychological skills use within elite youth sport. *Journal of Applied Sport Psychology, 16,* 318–332.

Harwood, C.G., & Hardy, L. (2001). Persistence and effort in moving achievement goal research forward: A response to Treasure and colleagues. *Journal of Sport and Exercise Psychology, 23,* 330–345.

Harwood, C.G., Hardy, L., & Swain, A.B.J. (2000). Achievement goals in sport: A critique of conceptual and measurement issues. *Journal of Sport and Exercise Psychology, 22,* 235–255.

Harwood, C.G., Spray, C.M., & Keegan, R. (2008). Achievement goal theories in sport. In T.S. Horn (Ed.), *Advances in sport psychology* (3rd ed., pp. 157–185). Champaign, IL: Human Kinetics.

Harwood, C.G., & Swain, A.B.J. (1998). Antecedents of pre-competition achievement goals in elite junior players. *Journal of Sports Sciences, 16,* 357–371.

Harwood, C.G., Wilson, K., & Hardy, L. (2002). *Achievement goals in sport: Working toward an alternative model.* Paper presented at the British Association for Sport and Exercise Sciences Conference, Manchester, UK.

Haskell, W.L., Lee, I.M., Pate, R.R., Powell, K.E., Blair, S.N., Franklin, B.A., . . ., Bauman, A. (2007). Physical activity and public health: Updated recommendation for adults from the American College of Sports Medicine and the American Heart Association. *Medicine and Science in Sports and Exercise, 39,* 1423–1434.

Haslam, S.A., Wegge, J., & Postmes, T. (2009). Are we on a learning curve or a treadmill? The benefits of participative group goal setting become apparent as tasks become increasingly challenging over time. *European Journal of Social Psychology, 39,* 430–446.

Hassandra, M., Goudas, M., & Chroni, S. (2003). Examining factors associated with intrinsic motivation in physical education: A qualitative approach. *Psychology of Sport and Exercise, 4,* 211–223. doi:10.1016/S1469-0292(02)00006-7

Hatfield, E., & Walster, G.W. (1978). *A new look at love.* Reading, MA: Addison-Wesley.

Hatzigeorgiadis, A., Zourbanos, N., Goltsios, C., & Theodorakis, Y. (2008). Investigating the functions of self-talk: The effects of motivational self-talk on self-efficacy and performance in young tennis players. *Sport Psychologist, 22,* 458–471.

Hausenblas, H., Carron, A. V., & Mack, D. E. (1997). Application of the theories of reasoned action and planned behavior to exercise behavior: A meta-analysis. *Journal of Sport and Exercise Psychology, 19,* 36–51.

Hausenblas, H.A., Brewer, B.W., & Van Raalte, J.L. (2004). Self-presentation and exercise. *Journal of Applied Sport Psychology, 16,* 3–18.

Hausenblas, H.A., & Martin, K.A. (2000). Bodies on display: Predictors of social physique anxiety in female aerobic instructors. *Women in Sport and Physical Activity Journal, 9,* 1–14.

Hausenblas, H.A., & Symons Downs, D. (2002). Exercise dependence: A systematic review. *Psychology of Sport and Exercise, 3,* 89–123.

Hein, V., & Hagger, M.S. (2007). Global self-esteem, goal achievement orientations, and self-determined behavioral regulations in a physical education setting. *Journal of Sports Sciences, 25,* 149–159. doi:10.1080/02640410600598315

Hein, V., & Koka, A. (2007). Perceived feedback and motivation in physical education and physical activity. In M.S. Hagger & N.L.D. Chatzisarantis (Eds.), *Intrinsic motivation and self-determination in exercise and sport* (pp. 127–140). Champaign, IL: Human Kinetics.

Henschen, K. (2000). Maladaptive fatigue syndrome and emotions in sport. In Y.L. Hanin (Ed.), *Emotions in sport* (pp. 231–242). Champaign, IL: Human Kinetics.

Hepler, T.J. (2008). *Decision-making in sport: An examination of the take the first heuristic and self-efficacy theory.* Unpublished doctoral dissertation, Michigan State University, East Lansing.

Heuzé, J.P., Sarrazin P., Masiero, M., Raimbault R., & Thomas, J.P. (2006). The relationships of perceived motivational climate to cohesion and collective efficacy in elite female teams. *Journal of Applied Sport Psychology 18*, 201–218.

Hewitt, P.L., Caelian, C.F., Flett, G.L., Sherry, S.B., Collins, L., & Flynn, C.A. (2002). Perfectionism in children: Associations with depression, anxiety and anger. *Personality and Individual Differences, 32*, 1049–1061.

Hewitt, P.L., & Flett, G.L. (1991). Perfectionism in the self and social contexts: Conceptualization, assessment, and association with psychopathology. *Journal of Personality and Social Psychology, 60*, 456–470.

Hewitt, P.L., & Flett, G.L. (2004). *The multidimensional perfectionism scale: Technical manual.* Toronto, Canada: Multihealth Systems.

Hewitt, P.L., Flett, G.L., Besser, A., Sherry, S.B., & McGee, B. (2003). Perfectionism is multidimensional: A reply to Shafran, Cooper and Fairburn (2002). *Behaviour Research and Therapy, 41*, 1221–1236.

Hewitt, P.L., Flett, G.L., & Endler, N.S. (1995). Perfectionism, coping, and depression symptomatology in a clinical sample. *Clinical Psychology and Psychotherapy, 2*, 47–58.

Hewitt, P.L., & Genest, M. (1990). Ideal-self: Schematic processing of perfectionistic content in dysphoric university students. *Journal of Personality and Social Psychology, 59*, 802–808.

Hewitt, P.L., Mittelstadt, W.M., & Wollert, R. (1989). Validation of a measure of perfectionism. *Journal of Personality Assessment, 53*, 133–144.s

Higgins, J., Thompson, S.G., Deeks, J.J., & Altman, D.G. (2003). Measuring inconsistency in meta-analysis. *British Medical Journal, 327*, 1663–1682.

Hill, A.P., Hall, H.K., & Appleton, P.R. (2010). Perfectionism and athlete burnout in junior elite athletes: The mediating influence of coping tendencies. *Anxiety Stress and Coping, 23*, 415–430.

Hill, A.P., Hall, H.K., Appleton, P.R., & Kozub, S.A. (2008). Perfectionism and burnout in junior elite soccer players: The mediating influence of unconditional self-acceptance. *Psychology of Sport and Exercise, 9*, 630–644.

Hill, A.P., Hall, H.K., Appleton, P.R., & Murray, J.J. (2010). Perfectionism and burnout in canoe polo and kayak slalom athletes: The mediating influence of validation and growth-seeking. *Sport Psychologist, 24*, 16–34.

Hill, A.P., Hall, H.K., Duda, J.D., & Appleton, P.R. (in press). The cognitive, affective and behavioural response of self-oriented perfectionists following three successive failures on a cycle ergometer task. *International Journal of Sport and Exercise Psychology.*

Hill, R.W., Zrull, M.C., & Turlington, S. (1997). Perfectionism and interpersonal problems. *Journal of Personality Assessment, 69*, 81–103.

Hinkley, T., Crawford, D., Salmon, J., Okely, A.D., & Hesketh, K. (2008). Preschool children and physical activity: A review of correlates. *American Journal of Preventive Medicine, 34*(5), 435–441.

Hirschfeld, R.R., Thomas, C.H., & McNatt, D.B. (2008). Implications of self-deception for self-reported intrinsic and extrinsic motivational dispositions and actual learning performance: A higher order structural model. *Educational and Psychological Measurement, 68*, 154–173. doi:10.1177/0013164406299129

Hobden, K., & Pliner, P. (1995). Self-handicapping and dimensions of perfectionism: Self-presentation vs self-protection. *Journal of Research in Personality, 29*, 461–474.

Hodge, K., Allen, J.B., & Smellie, L. (2008). Motivation in masters sport: Achievement and social goals. *Psychology of Sport and Exercise, 9*, 157–176. doi:10.1016/j.psychsport.2007.03.002

Hodge, K., Lonsdale, C., & Jackson, S.A. (2009). Athlete engagement in elite sport: An exploratory investigation of antecedents and consequences. *Sport Psychologist, 23*, 186–202. Retrieved from http://hk.humankinetics.com/TSP/journalAbout.cfm

Hodge, K., Lonsdale, C., & Ng, J.Y.Y. (2008). Burnout in elite rugby: Relationships with basic psychological needs fulfillment. *Journal of Sports Sciences, 26*, 835–844. doi:10.1080/02640410701784525

Hodge, K., & Petlichkoff, L. (2000). Goal profile in sport motivation: A cluster analysis. *Journal of Sport and Exercise Psychology, 22*, 256–272.

Hodgins, H.S., & Knee, R. (2002). The integrating self and conscious experience. In E.L. Deci & R.M. Ryan (Eds.), *Handbook on self-determination research: Theoretical and applied issues* (pp. 87–100). Rochester, NY: University of Rochester Press.

Hodgins, H.S., Yacko, H.A., & Gottlieb, E. (2006). Autonomy and nondefensiveness. *Motivation and Emotion, 30*, 283–293.

Holick, C.N., Newcomb, P.A., Trentham-Dietz, A., Titus-Ernstoff, L., Bersch, A.J., Stampfer, M.J., . . . Willett, W.C. (2008). Physical activity and survival after diagnosis of invasive breast cancer. *Cancer Epidemiology, Biomarkers, and Prevention, 17*, 379–386.

Hollander, M.H. (1965). Perfectionism. *Comprehensive Psychiatry, 6*, 94–103.

Hollembeak, J., & Amorose, A.J. (2005). Perceived coaching behaviors and college athletes' intrinsic motivation: A test of self-determination theory. *Journal of Applied Sport Psychology, 17,* 20–36. doi:10.1080/10413200590907540

Holmes, M.D., Chen, W.Y., Feskanich, D., Kroenke, C.H., & Colditz, G.A. (2005). Physical activity and survival after breast cancer diagnosis. *Journal of the American Medical Association, 293,* 2479–2486.

Holt, N.L., Hoar, S., & Fraser, S.N. (2005). How does coping change with development? A review of childhood and adolescence sport coping research. *European Journal of Sport Science, 5,* 25–39.

Hom, H.L., Duda, J.L., & Miller, A. (1993). Correlates of goal orientations among young athletes. *Pediatric Exercise Science, 5,* 168–176.

Horn, T. (2008). Coaching effectiveness in the sport domain. In T. Horn (Ed.), *Advances in sport psychology,* Vol. 3, (pp. 239–267). Champaign, IL: Human Kinetics.

Horney, K. (1950). *Neurosis and human growth.* New York: Norton.

Hu, L., Motl, R.W., McAuley, E., & Konopack, J.F. (2007). Effects of self-efficacy on physical activity enjoyment in college-aged women. *International Journal of Behavioral Medicine, 14,* 92–96.

Hulleman, C.S., Durik, A.M., Schweigert, S.A., & Harackiewicz, J.M. (2008). Task values, achievement goals, and interest: An integrative analysis. *Journal of Educational Psychology, 100*(2), 398–416.

Hunter, J.E., & Schmidt, F.L. (1990). *Methods of meta-analysis: Correcting error and bias in research findings.* Newbury Park, CA: Sage.

Hutchison, A.J., Breckon, J.D., & Johnston, L.H. (2009). Physical activity behavior change interventions based on the Transtheoretical Model: A systematic review. *Health Education & Behavior, 36,* 829–845.

Hutchinson, J.C., Sherman, T., Martinovic, N., & Tenenbaum, G. (2008). The effect of manipulated self-efficacy on perceived and sustained effort. *Journal of Applied Sport Psychology, 20,* 457–472.

Ievleva, L., & Orlick, T. (1991). Mental links to enhanced healing: An exploratory study. *Sport Psychologist, 5,* 25–40.

Ingledew, D.K., & Markland, D. (2008). The role of motives in exercise participation. *Psychology & Health, 23,* 807–828.

Ingledew, D.K., Markland, D.A., & Medley, A.R. (1998). Exercise motives and stages of change. *Journal of Health Psychology, 3,* 477–489.

Irwin, M.L. (2009). Physical activity interventions for cancer survivors. *British Journal of Sports Medicine, 43,* 32–38.

Irwin, M.L., Crumley, D., McTiernan, A., Bernstein, L., Baumgartner, R., Gilliland, F.D, . . . Ballard-Barbash, R. (2003). Physical activity levels before and after a diagnosis of breast carcinoma: The Health, Eating, Activity, and Lifestyle (HEAL) study. *Cancer, 97,* 1746–1757.

Irwin, M.L., McTiernan, A., Bernstein, L., Billiland, F.D., Baumgartner, R., Baumgartner, K., & Ballard-Barbash, R. (2004). Physical activity levels among breast cancer survivors. *Medicine and Science in Sports and Exercise, 36,* 1484–1491.

Irwin, M.L., Smith, A.W., McTiernan, A., Ballard-Barbash, R., Cronin, K., Gilliland, F.D., . . . Bernstein, L. (2008). Influence of pre- and postdiagnosis physical activity on mortality in breast cancer survivors: The health, eating, activity, and lifestyle study. *Journal of Clinical Oncology, 26,* 3958–3964.

Isberg, L. (2000) Anger, aggressive behaviour and athletic performance. In Y.L. Hanin (Ed) *Emotions in Sport.* Champaign, IL: Human Kinetics.

Jaccard, J., Turrisi, R., & Wan, C.K. (1990). *Interaction effects in multiple regression.* Newbury Park, CA: Sage.

Jackson, S., & Roberts, G.C. (1992). Positive performance states of athletes: Toward a conceptual understanding of peak performance. *Sport Psychologist, 6,* 156–171.

Jackson, S.A., & Marsh, H.W. (1996). Development and validation of a scale to measure optimal experience: The Flow Scale. *Journal of Sport & Exercise Psychology, 18,* 17–35.

Jagacinski, C.M., & Nicholls, J.G. (1984). Conceptions of ability and related affects in task involvement and ego involvement. *Journal of Education Psychology, 76,* 909–919.

Jagacinski, C.M., & Nicholls, J.G. (1987). Competence and affect in task involvement and ego involvement: The impact of social comparison information. *Journal of Educational Psychology, 79,* 107–114.

Jang, H. (2008). Supporting students' motivation, engagement, and learning during an uninteresting activity. *Journal of Educational Psychology, 100,* 798–811. doi:10.1037/a0012841

Jerome, G.J., Marquez, D.X., McAuley, E., Canaklisova, S., Snook, E., & Vickers, M. (2002). Self-efficacy effects on feeling states in women. *International Journal of Behavioral Medicine, 9,* 139–154.

Johnson, J.G., & Raab, M. (2003). Take the first: Option-generation and resulting choices. *Organizational Behavior and Human Decision Processes, 91,* 215–229.

Jones, G., Hanton, S., & Connaughton, D. (2007). A framework for mental toughness in the world's best performers. *Sport Psychologist, 21*, 243–264.

Jones, G., & Hardy, L. (1990). Stress in sport: Experiences of some elite performers. In J.G. Jones & L. Hardy (Eds.), *Stress and performance in sport* (pp. 247–277). Chichester, UK: Wiley.

Jones, L.W., & Courneya, K.S. (2002). Exercise counseling and programming preferences of cancer survivors. *Cancer Practice, 10*, 208–215.

Jones, L.W., Courneya, K.S., Fairey, A.S., & Mackey, J.R. (2004). Effects of an oncologist's recommendation to exercise on self-reported exercise behavior in newly diagnosed breast cancer survivors: A single-blind, randomized controlled trial. *Annals of Behavioral Medicine, 28*, 105–113.

Jones, L.W., Courneya, K.S., Vallance, J.K., Ladha, A.B., Mant, M.J., Belch, A.R., . . . Reiman, T. (2004). Association between exercise and quality of life in multiple myeloma cancer survivors. *Supportive Care in Cancer, 12*, 780–788.

Jones, L.W., Courneya, K.S., Vallance, J.K., Ladha, A.B., Mant, M.J., Belch, A.R., & Reiman, T. (2006). Understanding the determinants of exercise intentions in multiple myeloma cancer survivors: An application of the theory of planned behavior. *Cancer Nursing, 29*, 167–175.

Jones, L.W., Guill, B., Keir, S.T., Carter, B.S.K., Friedman, H.S., Bigner, D.D., & Reardon, D.A. (2006). Patterns of exercise across the cancer trajectory in brain tumor patients. *Cancer, 106*, 2224–2232.

Jones, L.W., Guill, B., Keir, S.T., Carter, K., Friedman, H.S., Bigner, D.D., & Reardon, D.A. (2007a). Exercise interest and preferences among patients diagnosed with primary brain cancer. *Supportive Care in Cancer, 15*, 47–55.

Jones, L.W., Guill, B., Keir, S.T., Carter, K., Friedman, H.S., Bigner, D.D., & Reardon, D.A. (2007b). Using the theory of planned behavior to understand the determinants of exercise intention in patients diagnosed with primary brain cancer. *Psycho-Oncology, 16*, 232–240.

Jones, L.W., Peddle, C.J., Eves, N.D., Haykowsky, M.J., Courneya, K.S., Mackey, J.R., . . . Reiman, T. (2007). Effects of presurgical exercise training on cardiorespiratory fitness among patients undergoing thoracic surgery for malignant lung lesions. *Cancer, 110*, 590–598.

Jones, R.G. (1968). A factorial measure of Ellis's irrational belief system, with personality and maladjustment correlates. *Dissertation Abstracts International, 29*, 4379B–4380B.

Kahn, E.B., Ramsey, L.T., Brownson, R.C., Heath, G.W., Howze, E.H., Powell, K.E., et al. (2002). The effectiveness of interventions to increase physical activity: A systematic review. *American Journal of Preventive Medicine, 22*(4S), 73–107.

Kane, T.D., Marks, M.A., Zaccaro, S.J., & Blair, V. (1996). Self-efficacy, personal goals, and wrestlers' self-regulation. *Journal of Sport and Exercise Psychology, 18*, 36–48.

Kaplan, A., & Maehr, M.L. (1999). Achievement goals and student well-being. *Contemporary Educational Psychology, 24*, 330–358.

Kaplan A., & Maehr, M.L. (2002). Adolescent achievement goals: Situating motivation in sociocultural contexts. In T. Urdan & F. Pajares (Eds.), *Academic motivation of adolescents* (pp. 125–167). Greenwich, CT: Information Age.

Kaplan, A., & Maehr, M.L. (2007). The contributions and prospects of goal orientation theory. *Educational Psychology Review, 19*, 141–184.

Kaplan, R.M., Ries, A.L., Prewitt, L.M., & Eakin, E. (1994). Self-efficacy expectations predict survival for patients with chronic obstructive pulmonary disease. *Health Psychology, 13*, 366–368.

Karvinen, K.H., Courneya, K.S., Campbell, K.L., Pearcey, R.G., Dundas, G., Capstick, V., & Tonkin, K.S. (2007). Correlates of exercise motivation and behavior in a population-based sample of endometrial cancer survivors: An application of the Theory of Planned Behavior. *International Journal of Behavioral Nutrition and Physical Activity, 4*, 21.

Karvinen, K.H., Courneya, K.S., North, S., & Venner, P. (2007). Associations between exercise and quality of life in bladder cancer survivors: A population-based study. *Cancer Epidemiology, Biomarkers, and Prevention, 16*, 984–990.

Karvinen, K.H., Courneya, K.S., Plotnikoff, R.C., Spence, J.C., Venner, P.M., & North, S. (2009). A prospective study of the determinants of exercise in bladder cancer survivors using the Theory of Planned Behavior. *Supportive Care in Cancer, 17*, 171–179.

Karvinen, K.H., Courneya, K.S., Venner, P., & North, S. (2007). Exercise programming and counseling preferences in bladder cancer survivors: A population-based study. *Journal of Cancer Survivorship, 1*, 27–34.

Kasser, T. (2002). *The high price of materialism.* Cambridge, MA: MIT Press.

Kasser, T., & Ryan, R.M. (1993). A dark side of the American dream: Correlates of financial success as a central life aspiration. *Journal of Personality and Social Psychology, 65*, 410–422.

Kasser, T., & Ryan, R.M. (1996). Further examining the American dream: Differential correlates of intrinsic and extrinsic goals. *Personality and Social Psychology Bulletin, 22,* 280–287. doi:10.1177/0146167296223006

Kasser, V.M., & Ryan, R.M. (1999). The relation of psychological needs for autonomy and relatedness to health, vitality, well-being and mortality in a nursing home. *Journal of Applied Social Psychology, 29,* 935–954.

Katula, J.A. & McAuley, E. (2001). The mirror does not lie: Acute exercise and self-efficacy. *International Journal of Behavioral Medicine, 8,* 319–326.

Katula, J.A., McAuley, E., Mihalko, S.L., & Bane, S.M. (1998). Mirror, mirror on the wall . . . exercise environment influences on self-efficacy. *Journal of Social Behavior and Personality, 13,* 319–332.

Katz, I., & Assor, A. (2007). When choice motivates and when it does not. *Educational Psychology Review, 19,* 429–442. doi:10.1007/s10648-006-9027-y

Katzmarzyk, P.T., & Mason, C. (2009). The physical activity transition. *Journal of Physical Activity & Health, 6,* 269–280.

Kavussanu, M. (2006). Motivational predictors of prosocial and antisocial behaviour in football. *Journal of Sports Sciences, 24,* 575–588.

Kavussanu, M., & Boardley, I.D. (2009). The Prosocial and Antisocial Behavior in Sport Scale. *Journal of Sport & Exercise Psychology, 31,* 97–117.

Kavussanu, M., & Ntoumanis, N. (2003). Participation in sport and moral functioning: Does ego orientation mediate their relationship? *Journal of Sport & Exercise Psychology, 25,* 1–18.

Kavussanu, M., & Roberts, G.C. (1995, June). *Motivation and physical activity: The role of motivational climate, intrinsic interest, and self-efficacy.* Paper presented at the North American Society of Sport and Physical Activity. Asilomar, CA.

Kavussanu, M., & Roberts, G.C. (1996). Motivation in physical activity contexts: The relationship of perceived motivational climate to intrinsic motivation and self-efficacy. *Journal of Sport & Exercise Psychology, 18*(3), 264–280.

Kavussanu, M., & Roberts, G.C. (2001). Moral functioning in sport: An achievement goal perspective. *Journal of Sport & Exercise Psychology, 23,* 37–54.

Kavussanu, M., Roberts, G.C., & Ntoumanis, N. (2002). Contextual influences on moral functioning of college basketball players. *Sport Psychologist, 16,* 347–367.

Kavussanu, M., Seal, A.R., & Phillips, D.R. (2006). Observed prosocial and antisocial behaviors in male soccer teams: Age differences across adolescence and the role of motivational variables. *Journal of Applied Sport Psychology, 18,* 326–344.

Kavussanu, M., & Spray, C.M. (2006). Contextual influences on moral functioning of male football players. *Sport Psychologist, 20,* 1–23.

Kaye, M.P., Conroy, D.E., & Fifer, A.M. (2008). Individual differences in incompetence avoidance. *Journal of Sport & Exercise Psychology, 30,* 110–132.

Kearns, H., Forbes, A., & Gardiner, M. (2007). A cognitive behavioural coaching intervention for the treatment of perfectionism and self-handicapping in a nonclinical population. *Behaviour Change, 24,* 157–172.

Keats, M.R., & Culos-Reed, N. (2009). A theory-driven approach to encourage physical activity in pediatric cancer survivors: A pilot study. *Journal of Sport and Exercise Psychology, 31,* 267–283.

Keats, M.R., Culos-Reed, S.N., Courneya, K.S., & McBride, M. (2007). Understanding physical activity in adolescent cancer survivors: An application of the theory of planned behavior. *Psycho-Oncology, 16,* 448–457.

Keegan, R.J., Harwood, C.G., Spray, C.M., & Lavallee, D.E. (2009). A qualitative investigation of the motivational climate in early-career sport participants: The motivational influences of coaches, parents and peers. *Psychology of Sport and Exercise, 10,* 361–372.

Kennedy, P., Evans, M.J., Berry, C., Mullin, J. (2003). Comparative analysis of goal achievement during rehabilitation for older and younger spinal cord injury. *Spinal Cord, 41,* 44–52.

Kennedy, P., & Hamilton, L.R. (1999). The needs assessment checklist: A clinical approach to measuring outcome. *Spinal Cord, 37,* 136–139.

Kernis, M.H. (2003). Toward a conceptualization of optimal self-esteem. *Psychological Inquiry, 14,* 1–26.

Kingston, K.M., Harwood, C.G., & Spray, C.M. (2006). Contemporary approaches to motivation in sport. In S. Hanton & S.D. Mellalieu (Eds.), *Literature reviews in sport psychology* (pp. 159–197). New York: Nova Science.

Kingston, K.M., Horrocks, C.S., & Hanton, S. (2006). Do multidimensional intrinsic and extrinsic motivation profiles discriminate between athlete scholarship status and gender? *European Journal of Sport Science, 6,* 53–63. doi:10.1080/17461390500440889

Kingston, K.M., & Wilson, K.M. (2009). The application of goal setting in sport. In S. Mellalieu & S. Hanton (Eds.), *Advances in sport psychology: A review* (pp. 75–123). New York: Routledge.

Kirk, A.F., Mutrie, N., MacIntyre, P., & Fisher, B.M. (2003). Increasing physical activity in people with type 2 diabetes. *Diabetes Care, 26*(4), 1186–1192.

Klassen, R.M. (2004). Optimism and realism: A review of self-efficacy from a cross-cultural perspective. *International Journal of Psychology, 39*, 205–230.

Kleiber, D.A., & Roberts, G.C. (1987). High school play: Putting it to work in organized sport. In J. Block & N. King (Eds.), *School play* (pp. 193–218). New York: Garland.

Koestner, R., & Losier, G.F. (2002). Distinguishing three ways of being highly motivated: A closer look at introjection, identification, and intrinsic motivation. In E.L. Deci & R.M. Ryan (Eds.), *Handbook of self-determination research* (pp. 101–121). Rochester, NY: University of Rochester Press.

Koestner, R., Ryan, R.M., Bernieri, F., & Holt, K. (1984). Setting limits on children's behavior: The differential effects of controlling versus informational styles on children's intrinsic motivation and creativity. *Journal of Personality, 52*, 233–248.

Koivula, N., Hassmen, P., & Fallby. (2002). Self-esteem and perfectionism in elite athletes: Effects on competitive anxiety and confidence. *Personality and Individual Differences, 32*, 865–875.

Kouli, O., & Papaioannou, A. (2009). Ethnic/cultural identity salience, achievement goals and motivational climate in multicultural physical education classes. *Psychology of Sport and Exercise, 10*, 45–51.

Kowal, J., & Fortier, M.S. (2000). Testing relationships from the hierarchical model of intrinsic and extrinsic motivation using flow as a motivational consequence. *Research Quarterly for Exercise and Sport, 71*, 171–181. Retrieved from www.aahperd .org/rc/publications/rqes/

Kowalski, K.C., Mack, D.E., Crocker, P.R.E., Niefer, C.B., & Fleming, T.-L. (2006). Coping with social physique anxiety in adolescence. *Journal of Adolescent Health, 39* (275), e9–e16.

Kowalski, N.P., Crocker, P.R., & Kowalski, K.C. (2001). Physical self and physical activity relationships in college women: Does social physique anxiety moderate effects? *Research Quarterly for Exercise & Sport, 72*, 55–62.

Kremers, S.P.J., van der Horst, K., & Brug, J. (2007). Adolescent screen-viewing behaviour is associated with consumption of sugar-sweetened beverages: The role of habit strength and parental norms. *Appetite, 48*, 345–350.

Kristiansen, E., & Roberts, G. (2011). Media exposure and adaptive coping in elite football. *International Journal of Sport Psychology, 42*, 339–367.

Kristiansen, E., & Roberts, G.C. (2010). Young elite athletes and social support: Coping with competitive and organizational stress in "Olympic" competition. *Scandinavian Journal of Medicine and Science in Sport, 20*, 686–695.

Kristiansen, E., Roberts, G.C., & Abrahamsen, F.E. (2008). Achievement involvement and stress coping in elite sport. *Scandinavian Journal of Medicine and Science in Sports, 18*, 526–538.

Kristiansen, E., Sørensen, M., Lannem, A.M. , & Abrahamsen, F.E. (July, 2011). Winter Paralympians coping with the Vancouver Winter Paralympics. Paper presented at FEPSAC Annual Conference.

Krug, S.E. (1989). Leadership and learning: A measurement-based approach for analyzing school effectiveness and developing effective school leaders. In M.L. Maehr & C. Ames (Eds.), *Advances in motivation and achievement* (Vol. 3, pp. 73–105). New York: Academic Press.

Kruisselbrink, L.D., Dodge, A.M., Swanburg, S.L., & MacLeod, A.L. (2004). Influence of same-sex and mixed-sex exercise settings on the social physique anxiety and exercise intentions of males and females. *Journal of Sport and Exercise Psychology, 26*, 616–622.

Kuczka, K.K., & Treasure, D.C. (2005). Self-handicapping in competitive sport: Influence of the motivational climate, self-efficacy, and perceived importance. *Psychology of Sport and Exercise, 6*, 539–550.

Kutlesa, N., & Arthur, N. (2008). Overcoming negative aspects of perfectionism through group treatment. *Journal of Rational-Emotive and Cognitive-Behavior Therapy, 26*, 134–150.

Kyllo, L.B., & Landers, D.M. (1995). Goal setting in sport and exercise: A research synthesis to resolve the controversy. *Journal of Sport and Exercise Psychology, 17*, 117–137.

La Guardia, J.G., & Patrick, H. (2008). Self-determination theory as a fundamental theory of close relationships. *Canadian Psychology, 49*, 201–209.

Lafrenière, M.-A., Jowett, S., Vallerand, R.J., Donahue, E.G., & Lorimer, R. (2008). Passion in sport: On the quality of the coach-player relationship. *Journal of Sport and Exercise Psychology, 30*, 541–560.

Lafrenière, M.-A.K., Vallerand, R.J., Donahue, E.G., & Lavigne, G.L. (2009). On the costs and benefits of gaming: The role of passion. *CyberPsychology & Behavior, 12*, 285–290.

Lamarche, L., & Gammage, K.L. (2009). The effects of leader gender on self-presentational concerns in exercise. *Psychology & Health*, 1–13.

Lamarche, L., Gammage K.L., & Strong, H.A. (2009). The effect of mirrored exercise environments on self-presentational efficacy and social anxiety in women in a step aerobics class. *Psychology of Sport and Exercise, 10,* 65–71.

Lannem, A.M., & Sorensen, M. (in review). The role of exercise in the total physical workload for persons with incomplete spinal cord injury (SCI). Manuscript submitted for publication.

Lannem, A.M., Sorensen, M., Lidal, I.B., & Hjeltnes, N. (in press). Perceptions of exercise mastery in persons with complete and incomplete spinal cord injury. *Spinal Cord.*

Lantz, C.D., & Hardy, C.J. (1997). Social physique anxiety and perceived exercise behavior. *Journal of Sport Behavior, 20,* 83–93.

Larson, R.W., & Verma, S. (1999). How children and adolescents spend time across the world: Work, play, and developmental opportunities. *Psychological Bulletin, 125,* 701–736.

Latham, G.P., & Locke, E.A. (2007). New developments in and directions for goal-setting research. *European Psychologist, 12,* 290–300.

Latimer, A.E., & Martin Ginis, K.A. (2005). The importance of subjective norms for people who care what others think of them. *Psychology and Health, 20,* 53–62.

Latimer, A.E., Martin Ginis, K.A., & Arbour, K.P. (2006). The efficacy of an implementation intention intervention for promoting physical activity among individuals with spinal cord injury: A randomized controlled trial. *Rehabilitation Psychology, 51,* 273–280.

Lazarus, R.S. (1991). *Emotion and adaptation.* Oxford, UK: Oxford University Press.

Lazarus, R.S., & Folkman, S. (1984). *Stress, appraisal and coping.* New York: Springer.

Leary, M.R. (1983). A brief version of the Fear of Negative Evaluation Scale. *Personality and Social Psychology Bulletin, 9,* 371–376.

Leary, M.R. (1992). Self-presentational processes in exercise and sport. *Journal of Sport and Exercise Psychology, 14,* 339–351.

Leary, M.R. (1995). *Self-presentation: Impression management and interpersonal behavior.* Boulder, CO: Westview.

Leary, M.R., & Kowalski, R.M. (1990). Impression management: A literature review and two-component model. *Psychological Bulletin, 107,* 34–47.

Leary, M.R., & Kowalski, R.M. (1995). *Social anxiety.* New York: Guilford Press.

Leary, M.R., Tchividjian, L.R., & Kraxberger, B.E. (1994). Self-presentation can be hazardous to your health: Impression management and health risk. *Health Psychology, 13,* 461–470.

Lee, M.J., Whitehead, J., Ntoumanis, N., & Hatzigeorgiadis, A. (2008). Relationships among values, achievement orientations, and attitudes in youth sport. *Journal of Sport and Exercise Psychology, 30,* 5, 588–610.

Lemyre, P.-N., Hall, H.K., & Roberts, G.C. (2008). A social cognitive approach to burnout in elite athletes. *Scandinavian Journal of Medicine and Science in Sports, 18,* 221–224.

Lemyre, P.-N., Ommundsen, Y., & Roberts, C.C. (2000). Moral functioning in sport: The role of dispositional goals and perceived ability. *International Journal of Psychology, 35*(3–4), 23.

Lemyre, P.-N., Roberts G.C., & Ommundsen, Y. (2002). Achievement goal orientations, perceived ability and sportspersonship in youth soccer. *Journal of Applied Sport Psychology, 14,* 120–136.

Lemyre, P.-N., Roberts, G.C., Ommundsen, Y., & Miller, B.W. (2001). Parental and coach support or pressure on psychosocial outcomes of pediatric athletes in soccer. *Clinical Journal of Sport Medicine, 16,* 522–526.

Lemyre, P.-N., Roberts, G.C., & Stray-Gundersen, J. (2007). Motivation, overtraining, and burnout: Can self-determined motivation predict overtraining and burnout in elite athletes? *European Journal of Sport Science, 7,* 115–126. doi:10.1080/17461390701302607

Lemyre, P.-N., Stray-Gundersen, J., Treasure, D.C., Matt, K., & Roberts, G.C. (2004). Physiological and psychological monitoring of overtraining and burnout in elite swimmers. *Medicine and Science in Sports and Exercise, 36,* supplement, 144–145.

Lemyre, P.-N., Treasure, D.C., & Roberts, G.C. (2006). Influence of variability in motivation and affect on elite athlete burnout susceptibility. *Journal of Sport and Exercise Psychology, 28,* 32–48.

Lepper, M.R., Greene, D., & Nisbett, R.E. (1973). Undermining children's intrinsic interest with extrinsic rewards: A test of the "overjustification" hypothesis. *Journal of Personality and Social Psychology, 28,* 129–137.

Lerner, B.S., & Locke, E.A. (1995). The effects of goal setting, self-efficacy, competition, and personal traits on the performance of an endurance task. *Journal of Sport and Exercise Psychology, 17,* 138–152.

Leventhal, H., Leventhal, E., & Contrada, R.J. (1998). Self-regulation, health and behaviour: A perceptual cognitive approach. *Psychology and Health, 13,* 717–734.

Leventhal, H., Meyer, D., & Nerenz, D. (1980). The common-sense representation of illness danger. In S. Rachman (Ed.), *Contributions to medical psychology* (pp. 7–30). New York: Pergamon.

Levesque, C., & Pelletier, L.G. (2003). On the investigation of primed and chronic autonomous and heteronomous motivational orientations. *Personality and Social Psychology Bulletin, 29*, 1570. doi:10.1177/0146167203256877

Levine, J.A. (2007). Nonexercise activity thermogenesis: Liberating the life-force. *Journal of Internal Medicine, 262*, 273–287.

Li, F. (1999). The exercise motivation scale: Its multifaceted structure and construct validity. *Journal of Applied Sport Psychology, 11*, 97–115.

Li, F., & Harmer, P. (1996). Testing the simplex assumption underlying the Sport Motivation Scale: A structural equation modeling analysis. *Research Quarterly for Exercise and Sport, 67*, 396–405.

Lichacz, F.M., & Partington, J.T. (1996). Collective efficacy and true group performance. *International Journal of Sport Psychology, 27*, 146–158.

Lindwall, M. (2005). Examining the validity of a Swedish version of the Self-Presentation in Exercise Questionnaire. *Measurement in Physical Education and Exercise Science, 9*, 113–134.

Lippke, S., Ziegelmann, J.P., & Schwarzer, R. (2004). Behavioural intentions and action plans promote physical exercise: A longitudinal study with orthopaedic rehabilitation patients. *Journal of Sport and Exercise Psychology, 26*, 470–483.

Lloyd, J., & Fox, K. (1992). Achievement goals and motivation to exercise in adolescent girls: A preliminary intervention study. *British Journal of Physical Education Research Supplement, 11*, 12–16.

Lochbaum, M.R., & Roberts, G.C. (1993). Goal orientations and perceptions of the sport experience. *Journal of Sport and Exercise Psychology, 15*, 160–171.

Lochbaum, M.R., Stevenson, S., & Hilario, D. (2009). Achievement goals, thoughts about intense physical activity, and exerted effort: A mediational analysis. *Journal of Sport Behavior, 32*, 53–68.

Locke, E.A. (1968). Toward a theory of task motivation and incentives. *Organizational Behavior and Human Performance, 3*, 157–189.

Locke, E.A., & Latham, G.P. (1985). The application of goal setting to sports. *Journal of Sport Psychology, 7*(3), 205–222.

Locke, E.A., & Latham, G.P. (1990). *A theory of goal setting and task performance.* Englewood Cliffs, NJ: Prentice Hall.

Locke, E.A., & Latham, G.P. (2002). Building a practically useful theory of goal setting and task motivation: A 35-year odyssey. *American Psychologist, 57*, 705–717.

Locke, E.A., Shaw, K.N., Saari, L.M., & Latham, G.P. (1981). Goal setting and task performance: 1969–1980. *Psychological Bulletin, 90*, 125–152.

Loney, T., Standage, M., Thompson, D., Sebire, S.J., & Cumming, S.P. (2011). Self-report vs. objectively assessed physical activity: Which is right for public health? *Journal of Physical Activity and Health, 8*, 62–70.

Lonsdale, C., Hodge, K., & Rose, E. (2009). Athlete burnout in elite sport: A self-determination perspective. *Journal of Sports Sciences, 27*, 785–795. doi:10.1080/02640410902929366

Lonsdale, C., Hodge, K., & Rose, E.A. (2008). The behavioral regulation in sport questionnaire (BRSQ): Instrument development and initial validity evidence. *Journal of Sport and Exercise Psychology, 30*, 323–355.

Lonsdale, C., Sabiston, C.M., Raedeke, T.D., Ha, A.S.C., Sum, R.K.W. (2009). Self-determined motivation and students' physical activity during structured physical education lessons and free choice periods. *Preventive Medicine, 48*, 69–73.

Lubans, D.R., Foster, C., & Biddle, S.J.H. (2008). A review of mediators of behavior in interventions to promote physical activity among children and adolescents. *Preventive Medicine, 47*, 463–470.

Lundh, L.G. (2004). Perfectionism and acceptance. *Journal of Rational-Emotive and Cognitive-Behavior Therapy, 22*, 255–269.

Lundh, L.G., Saboonchi, F., & Wangby, M. (2008). The role of personal standards in clinically significant perfectionism. A person-oriented approach to the study of patterns of perfectionism. *Cognitive Therapy Research, 32*, 333–350.

Luszczynska, A. (2006). An implementation intentions intervention, the use of a planning strategy, and physical activity after myocardial infarction. *Social Science in Medicine, 62*, 900–908.

Lyubomirsky, S., King, L., Diener, E. (2005). The benefits of frequent positive affect: Does happiness lead to success? *Psychological Bulletin, 131*, 803–855.

Mack, D.E., Wilson, P.M., Sylvester, B.D., Gregson, J.P., Cheung, S., & Rimmer, S. (in press). The relationship between social physique anxiety and exercise behavior: Does the fulfillment of basic psychological needs matter? In T.M. Robinson (Ed.), *Social anxiety: Symptoms, causes, and techniques.* Hauppauge NY: Nova Science.

Mack, D.E., Wilson, P.M., Waddell, L., & Gasparotto, J. (2008). Social physique anxiety across physical activity contexts: A meta-analytic review. In J.N. Fuchs (Ed.), *Eating disorders in adult women* (pp. 1–17). Hauppauge NY: Nova Science.

MacKillop, J., Anderson, E.J., Castelda, B.A., Mattson, R.E., & Donovick, P.J. (2006). Divergent validity of measures of cognitive distortions, impulsivity, and time perspective in pathological gambling. *Journal of Gambling Studies, 22,* 339–354.

MacKinnon, D. (2008). *Introduction to statistical mediation analysis.* Mahwah, NJ: Erlbaum.

MacKinnon, D., & Fairchild, A. (2009). Current directions in mediation analysis. *Current Directions in Psychological Science, 18,* 16–20.

MacKinnon, D., Krull, J., & Lockwood, C. (2000). Equivalence of the mediation, confounding and suppression effect. *Prevention Science, 1,* 173–181.

Maddux, J.E. (1995). Looking for common ground: A comment on Kirsch and Bandura. In J.E. Maddux (Ed.), *Self-efficacy, adaptation and adjustment: Theory, research, and application* (pp. 377–386). New York: Plenum Press.

Maddux, J.E., Norton, L.W., & Leary, M.R. (1988). Cognitive components of social anxiety—an investigation of the integration of self-presentation theory and self-efficacy theory. *Journal of Social and Clinical Psychology, 6,* 180–190.

Maehr, M.L. (1983). On doing well in science. Why Johnny no longer excels; why Sarah never did. In S.G. Paris, G.M. Olsen, & H.W. Stevenson (Eds.), *Learning and motivation in the classroom* (pp. 179–210). Hillsdale, NJ: Erlbaum.

Maehr, M.L., & Braskamp, L.A. (1986). *The motivation factor: A theory of personal investment.* Lexington, MA: Lexington Books/Heath.

Maehr, M.L., & Nicholls, J.G. (1980). Culture and achievement motivation: A second look. In N. Warren (Ed.), *Studies in cross-cultural psychology* (Vol. 2, pp. 221–267). New York: Academic Press.

Maehr, M.L., & Zusho, A. (2009). Achievement goal theory: The past, present, and future. In K.R. Wentzel & A. Wigfield (Eds.), *Handbook of motivation in school* (pp. 77–104). New York: Taylor Francis.

Mageau, G., & Vallerand, R.J. (2003). The coach-athlete relationship: A motivational model. *Journal of Sports Sciences, 21,* 883–904. doi:10.1080/0264041031000140374

Mageau, G.A., & Vallerand, R.J. (2007). The moderating effect of passion on the relation between activity engagement and positive affect. *Motivation and Emotion, 31,* 312–321.

Mageau, G.A., Vallerand, R.J., Charest, J., Salvy, S., Lacaille, N., Bouffard, T., & Koestner, R. (2009). On the development of harmonious and obsessive passion: The role of autonomy support, activity valuation, and identity processes. *Journal of Personality, 77,* 601–645.

Mageau, G.A., Vallerand, R.J., Rousseau, F.L., Ratelle, C.F., & Provencher, P.J. (2005). Passion and gambling: Investigating the divergent affective and cognitive consequences of gambling. *Journal of Applied Social Psychology, 35,* 100–118.

Magyar, T.M., & Feltz, D.L. (2003). The influence of dispositional and situational tendencies on adolescent girls' sport confidence sources. *Psychology of Sport and Exercise, 4,* 175–190.

Magyar, T.M., Feltz, D.L., & Simpson, I.P. (2004). Individual and crew level determinants of collective efficacy in rowing. *Journal of Sport and Exercise Psychology, 26,* 136–153.

Maher, K.E. (2000). Radiation therapy: Toxicities and management. In C.H. Yarbro, M. Goodman, M. Frogge, & S.L. Groenwald (Eds.), *Cancer nursing: Principles & practice* (Vol. 5, pp. 323–351). Sudbury, MA: Jones & Bartlett.

Mallett, C.J., & Hanrahan, S.J. (2004). Elite athletes: Why does the fire burn so brightly? *Psychology of Sport and Exercise, 5,* 183–200.

Mandigo, J., Holt, N., Anderson, A., & Sheppard, J. (2008). Children's motivational experiences following autonomy-supportive games lessons. *European Physical Education Review, 14,* 407. doi:10.1177/1356336X08095673

Marcus, B.H., Banspach, S.W., Lefebvre, R.C., Rossi, J.S., Carleton, R.A., & Abrams, D.B. (1992). Using the stages of change model to increase the adoption of physical activity among community participants. *American Journal of Health Promotion, 6,* 424–429.

Marcus, B.H., & Owen, N. (1992). Motivational readiness, self-efficacy, and decision-making for exercise. *Journal of Applied Social Psychology, 24,* 489–508.

Markes, M., Brockow, T., & Resch, K.L. (2006). Exercise for women receiving adjuvant therapy for breast cancer. *Cochrane Database of Systematic Reviews* (4), CD005001.

Markland, D., & Hardy, L. (1997). On the factorial and construct validity of the intrinsic motivation inventory: Conceptual and operational concerns. *Research Quarterly for Exercise and Sport, 68,* 20–32.

Markland, D., Ryan, R.M., Tobin, V.J., & Rollnick, S. (2005). Motivational interviewing and self-determination theory. *Journal of Social and Clinical Psychology, 24,* 811–831.

Markland, D., & Tobin, V. (2004). A modification to the Behavioural Regulation in Exercise Questionnaire to include an assessment of amotivation. *Journal of Sport & Exercise Psychology, 26,* 191–196.

Markus, H., & Nurius, P. (1986). Possible selves. *American Psychologist, 41,* 954–969.

Maro, C., Roberts, G.C., & Sørensen, M. (2009). Using sport to promote HIV/AIDS education for at risk youths: An intervention using peer coaches in football. *Scandinavian Journal of Medicine and Science in Sports, 19,* 129–141.

Marsh, H. (1994). Sport motivation orientations: Beware of jingle-jangle fallacies. *Journal of Sport and Exercise Psychology, 16,* 365–380.

Marshall, H.H., & Weinstein, R.S. (1984). Classroom factors affecting students' self evaluations: An interactional model. *Review of Educational Research, 54,* 302–325.

Marshall, S.J., & Biddle, S.J.H. (2001). The Transtheoretical Model of behavior change: A meta-analysis of applications to physical activity and exercise. *Annals of Behavioral Medicine, 23,* 229–246.

Martens, R. (1969). Palmar sweating and the presence of an audience. *Journal of Experimental Social Psychology, 5,* 371–374.

Martens, R. (1987). *Coaches guide to sport psychology.* Champaign, IL: Human Kinetics.

Martin, E.H., Rudisill, M.E., & Hastie, P. (2009). The effectiveness of a mastery motivational climate motor skill intervention in a naturalistic physical education setting. *Physical Education and Sport Pedagogy, 14,* 227–240.

Martin, K.A., & Brawley, L.R. (2002). Self-handicapping in physical achievement settings: The contributions of self-esteem and self-efficacy. *Self and Identity, 1,* 337–351.

Martin, K.A., & Fox, L.D. (2001). Group and leadership effects on social anxiety experienced during an exercise class. *Journal of Applied Social Psychology, 31,* 1000–1016.

Martin, K.A., Leary, M.R., & O'Brien, J. (2001). Role of self-presentation in the health practices of a sample of Irish adolescents. *Journal of Adolescent Health, 28,* 259–262.

Martin Ginis, K.A., & Leary, M.R. (2004). Self-presentational processes in health damaging behavior. *Journal of Applied Sport Psychology, 16,* 59–74.

Martin Ginis, K.A., Lindwall, M., & Prapavessis, H. (2007). Who cares what other people think? Self-presentation in sport and exercise. In G. Tenebaum & R. Eklund (Eds.), *Handbook of sport psychology* (3rd ed., pp.136–157). New York: Wiley.

Martin Ginis, K.A., Murru, E., Conlin, C., & Strong, H.A. (2011). Construct validation of a state version of the Social Physique Anxiety Scale. *Body Image, 8,* 52–57.

Martin Ginis, K.A., O'Brien, J., & Watson, J.D. (2003). The importance of self-presentational motives for exercise: A preliminary cross-cultural comparison of Irish and American students. *Irish Journal of Psychology, 24,* 46–57.

Martin Ginis, K.A., Prapavessis, H., & Haase, A.M. (2008). The effects of physique-salient and physique non-salient exercise videos on women's body image, self-presentational concerns, and exercise motivation. *Body Image, 5,* 164–172.

Martin, L.J., Carron, A.V., & Burke, S.M. (2009). Team building interventions in sport: A meta-analysis. *Sport and Exercise Psychology Review, 5,* 3–16.

McArdle, S. (2010). Exploring domain-specific perfectionism. *Journal of Personality, 78,* 493–508.

McArdle, S., & Duda, J.D. (2008). Exploring the etiology of perfectionism and perceptions of self-worth in young athletes. *Social Development, 17,* 980–997.

McArthur, L.Z., & Baron, R.M. (1983). Toward an ecological theory of social perception. *Psychological Review, 90,* 215–283.

McAuley, E. (1985). Modeling and self-efficacy: A test of Bandura's model. *Journal of Sport Psychology, 7,* 283–295.

McAuley, E. (1991). Efficacy, attributional, and affective responses to exercise participation. *Journal of Sport and Exercise Psychology, 13,* 382–393.

McAuley, E. (1992). The role of efficacy cognitions in the prediction of exercise behavior in middle-aged adults. *Journal of Behavioral Medicine, 15,* 65–88.

McAuley, E. (1993). Self-efficacy and the maintenance of exercise participation in older adults. *Journal of Behavioral Medicine, 16,* 103–113.

McAuley, E., Blissmer, B., Katula, J., & Duncan, T.E. (2000). Exercise environment, self-efficacy, and affective responses to acute exercise in older adults. *Psychology and Health, 15,* 341–355.

McAuley, E., & Courneya, K.S. (1992). Self-efficacy relationships with affective and exertion responses to exercise. *Journal of Applied Social Psychology, 22,* 312–326.

McAuley, E., & Courneya, K.S. (1994). The Subjective Exercise Experiences Scales (SEES): Development and preliminary validation. *Journal of Sport and Exercise Psychology, 16,* 163–177.

McAuley, E., Courneya, K.S., Rudolph, D.L., & Cox, C.L. (1994). Enhancing exercise experience in middle-aged males and females. *Preventative Medicine, 23,* 498–506.

McAuley, E., Lox, D.L., & Duncan, T. (1993). Long-term maintenance of exercise, self-efficacy, and physiological change in older adults. *Journal of Gerontology, 48,* P218–P223.

McClelland, D.C. (1987). *Human motivation.* Cambridge, UK: Cambridge University Press.

McEachan, R., Lawton, R., Jackson, C., Conner, M., & Lunt, J. (2008). Evidence, theory and context: Using intervention mapping to develop a worksite physical activity intervention. *BMC Public Health, 8*(1), 326.

McFee, G. (2005). Why doesn't sport psychology consider Freud? In M. McNamee (Ed.), *Philosophy and the sciences of exercise, health and sport* (pp. 85–116). London: Routledge.

McNeely, M.L., Campbell, K.L., Rowe, B.H., Klassen, T.P., Mackey, J.R., & Courneya, K.S. (2006). Effects of exercise on breast cancer patients and survivors: A systematic review and meta-analysis. *Canadian Medical Association Journal, 175*(1), 34–41.

McNeill, M.C., & Wang, C.K. (2005). Psychological profiles of elite school sports players in Singapore. *Psychology of Sport and Exercise, 6,* 117–128. doi:10.1016/j.psychsport.2003.10.004

McRae, D. (2008). I'm striving for something I'll never achieve - I'm a mess. *The Guardian,* October 28, pp. 6–7.

Medic, N., Mack, D.E., Wilson, P.M., & Starkes, J.L. (2007). The effects of athletic scholarship of motivation in sport. *Journal of Sport Behavior, 30,* 292–306. Retrieved from www.accessmylibrary.com/archive/2171-journal-of-sport-behavior.html

Meyer, T.J., & Mark, M.M. (1995). Effects of psychosocial interventions with adult cancer patients: A meta-analysis of randomized experiments. *Health Psychology, 14,* 101–108.

Meyerhardt, J.A., Giovannucci, E.L., Holmes, M.D., Chan, A.T., Chan, J.A., Colditz, G.A., & Fuchs, C.S. (2006). Physical activity and survival after colorectal cancer diagnosis. *Journal of Clinical Oncology, 24,* 3527–3534.

Meyerhardt, J.A., Heseltine, D., Niedzwiecki, D., Hollis, D., Saltz, L.B., Mayer, R.J., . . . Fuchs, C.S. (2006). Impact of physical activity on cancer recurrence and survival in patients with stage III colon cancer: Findings from CALGB 89803. *Journal of Clinical Oncology, 24,* 3535–3541.

Michie, S., & Abraham, C. (2004). Interventions to change health behaviours: Evidence-based or evidence-inspired? *Psychology & Health, 19,* 29–49. doi:10.1080/0887044031000141199

Middleton, M.J., & Midgley, C. (1997). Avoiding the demonstration of lack of ability: An underexplored aspect of goal theory. *Journal of Educational Psychology, 89,* 710–718.

Miller, B.W., & Roberts, G.C. (2003). The effect of motivational climate on determinants of cheating among competitive Norwegian youth football players. In E. Müller, H. Schwameder, G. Zallinger, & V. Fastenbauer (Eds.), *Proceedings of the 8th Annual Congress of the European College of Sport Science* (pp. 311–312). Salzburg, Austria: University of Salzburg.

Miller, B.W., Roberts, G.C., & Ommundsen, Y. (2004). Effect of motivational climate on sportspersonship among young male and female football players. *Scandinavian Journal of Medicine and Science in Sports, 14,* 193–202.

Miller, B.W., Roberts, G.C., & Ommundsen, Y. (2005). The relationship of perceived motivational climate to moral functioning, moral atmosphere perceptions, and the legitimacy of intentionally injurious acts among competitive youth football players. *Psychology of Sport & Exercise, 6,* 461–477.

Milne, H.M., Wallman, K., Guilfoyle, A., Gordon, S., & Courneya, K.S. (2008). Self-determination theory and physical activity among breast cancer survivors. *Journal of Sport & Exercise Psychology, 30,* 23–38.

Milne, S., Orbell, S., & Sheeran, P. (2002). Combining motivational and volitional interventions to promote exercise participation: Protection motivation theory and implementation intentions. *Journal of Health Psychology, 7,* 163–184.

Milosis, D., & Papaioannou, A. (2007). Effects of interdisciplinary teaching on multiple goals, intrinsic motivation, self-concept and school achievement. In J. Liukkonen, Y. Vanden Auweele, B. Vereijken, D. Alfermann, & Y. Theodorakis (Eds.), *Psychology for physical educators.* (Vol. 2, pp. 175–198). Champaign, IL: Human Kinetics.

Milyavskaya, M., Gingras, I., Mageau, G.A., Koestner, R., & Gagnon, H. (2009). Balance across contexts: Importance of balanced need satisfaction across various life domains. *Personality and Social Psychology Bulletin, 35,* 1031–1045. doi:10.1177/0146167209337036

Mischel, W., & Shoda, Y. (1998). Reconciling processing dynamics and personality dimensions. *Annual Review of Psychology, 49,* 229–258.

Moller, A.C., Deci, E.L., & Ryan, R.M. (2006). Choice and ego-depletion: The moderating role of autonomy. *Personality and Social Psychology Bulletin, 32,* 1024–1036.

Moore, C.A., & Barrow, J.C. (1986). Perfectionistic thinking in university students: Implications for individual treatment. In *Counseling and psychotherapy with college students* (pp. 100–112). New York: Praeger.

Moran, A. (2009). Cognitive psychology in sport: Progress and prospects. *Psychology of Sport and Exercise, 10*, 420–426.

Morgan, K., & Kingston, K. (2008). Development of a self-observation mastery intervention programme for teacher education. *Physical Education and Sport Pedagogy, 13*, 109–129.

Morgan, K., Sproule, J., McNeill, M., Kingston, K., & Wang, C.K.J. (2006). A cross-cultural study of motivational climate in physical education lessons in the UK and Singapore. *International Journal of Sports Psychology, 37*, 299–316

Morgan, W.P. (1979). Negative addiction in runners. *The Physician and Sports Medicine, 7*, 57–77.

Moritz, S.E., Feltz, D.L., Fahrbach, K.R., & Mack, D.E. (2000). The relation of self-efficacy measures to sport performance: A meta-analytic review. *Research Quarterly for Exercise and Sport, 71*, 280–294.

Moritz, S.E., & Watson, C.B. (1998). Levels of analysis issues in group psychology: Using efficacy as an example of a multilevel model. *Group Dynamics: Theory, Research, and Practice, 2*, 285–298.

Morris, R.L., & Kavussanu, M. (2008). Antecedents of approach-avoidance goals in sport. *Journal of Sports Sciences, 26*, 465–476.

Morris, R.L., & Kavussanu, M. (2009). Approach-avoidance achievement goals in sport: Psychological correlates and a comparison with the dichotomous model. *International Journal of Sport and Exercise Psychology, 9*, 185–202.

Mossholder, K.W. (1980). Effects of externally mediated goal setting on intrinsic motivation: A laboratory experiment. *Journal of Applied Psychology, 65*, 202–210.

Motl, R.W., McAuley, E., Snook, E.M., & Gliottoni, R.C. (2009). Physical activity and quality of life in multiple sclerosis. *Psychology, Health, and Medicine, 14*, 111–124.

Mouratidis, A., Vansteenkiste, M., Lens, W., & Sideridis, G. (2008). The motivating role of positive feedback in sport and physical education: Evidence for a motivational model. *Journal of Sport and Exercise Psychology, 30*, 240–258. Retrieved from http://hk.humankinetics.com/JSEP/journalAbout.cfm

Mouratidis, A., Vansteenkiste, M., Lens, W., & Vanden Auweele, Y. (2009). Beyond positive and negative affect: Achievement goals and discrete emotions in the elementary physical education classroom. *Psychology of Sport and Exercise, 10*, 336–343.

Mullan, E., & Markland, D. (1997). Variations in self-determination across the stages of change for exercise in adults. *Motivation and Emotion, 21*, 349–362.

Mullan, E., Markland, D., & Ingledew, D.K. (1997). A graded conceptualisation of self determination in the regulation of exercise behaviour: Development of a measure using confirmatory factor analysis. *Personality and Individual Differences, 23*, 745–752.

Munroe-Chandler, K., Hall, C. & Fishburne, G. (2008). Playing with confidence: The relationship between imagery use and self-confidence and self-efficacy in youth soccer players. *Journal of Sport Sciences, 26*, 1539–1546.

Muraven, M. (2008). Autonomous self-control is less depleting. *Journal of Research in Personality, 42*, 763–770.

Muraven, M., & Baumeister, R.F. (2000). Self-regulation and depletion of limited resources: Does self-control resemble a muscle? *Psychological Bulletin, 126*, 247–259. doi:10.1037/0033-2909.126.2.247

Muraven, M., Gagne, M., & Rosman, H. (2008). Helpful self-control: Autonomy support, vitality, and depletion. *Journal of Experimental Social Psychology, 44*, 573–585. doi:10.1016/j.jrp.2007.08.002

Mutrie, N., Campbell, A.M., Whyte, F., McConnachie, A., Emslie, C., Lee, L., et al. (2007). Benefits of supervised group exercise programme for women being treated for early stage breast cancer: Pragmatic randomised controlled trial. *British Medical Journal, 334*(7592), 517–520B.

Mutrie, N., Carney, C., Blamey, A., Crawford, F., Aitchison, T., & Whitelaw, A. (2002). "Walk In to Work Out": A randomised controlled trial of a self help intervention to promote active commuting. *Journal of Epidemiology and Community Health, 56*, 407–412.

Myers, N.D., & Feltz, D.L. (2007). From self-efficacy to collective efficacy in sport. In G. Tenenbaum & R.C. Eklund (Eds.), *Handbook of sport psychology* (pp. 719–819). Hoboken, NJ: Wiley.

Myers, N.D., Feltz, D.L., Chase, M.A., Reckase, M.D., & Hancock, G.R. (2008). The Coaching Efficacy Scale II–High School Teams. *Educational and Psychological Measurement, 68*, 1059–1076.

Myers, N.D., Feltz, D.L., & Short, S.E. (2004). Collective efficacy and team performance: A longitudinal study of collegiate football teams. *Group Dynamics: Theory, Research, and Practice, 8*, 126–138.

Myers, N.D., Payment, C.A., & Feltz, D.L. (2004). Reciprocal relationships between collective efficacy and team performance in women's ice hockey. *Group Dynamics: Theory, Research, and Practice, 8*, 182–195.

Myers, N.D., Vargas-Tonsing, T.M., & Feltz, D.L. (2005). Coaching efficacy in intercollegiate coaches: Sources, coaching behavior, and team variables. *Psychology of Sport and Exercise, 6,* 129–143.

Myers, N.D., Wolfe, E.W., & Feltz, D.L. (2005). Coaching efficacy in intercollegiate coaches: Sources, coaching behavior, and team variables. *Psychology of Sport and Exercise, 6,* 129–143.

National Association for Sport and Physical Education (2006). *Quality coaches, quality sports: National Standards for Sport Coaches* (2nd ed.). Reston, VA: NASPE.

National Cancer Institute Office of Cancer Survivorship. (2009). Retrieved from www.cancercontrol.cancer.gov/ocs/office-survivorship.html

National Federation of State High School Associations (2007). *Fundamentals of Coaching.* Indianapolis, IN: NFHS.

National Institute for Health and Clinical Excellence. (2007). *The most appropriate means of generic and specific interventions to support attitude and behaviour change at population and community levels.* London: National Institute for Health and Clinical Excellence.

Newby, T.J. (1991). Classroom motivation: Strategies of first-year teachers. *Journal of Educational Psychology, 83,* 195–200. doi:10.1037/0022-0663.83.2.195

Newton, M., & Duda, J.L. (1993). The relationship of task and ego orientation to performance-cognitive content, affect, and attributions in bowling. *Journal of Sport Behavior, 16,* 209–220.

Newton, M., & Duda, J.L. (1999). The interaction of motivational climate, dispositional goal orientation and perceived ability in predicting indices of motivation. *International Journal of Sport Psychology, 30,* 63–82.

Neyrinck, B., Vansteenkiste, M., Lens, W., Duriez, B., & Hutsebaut, D. (2006). Cognitive, affective and behavioral correlates of internalization of regulations for religious activities. *Motivation and Emotion, 30,* 323–334.

Nicholls, A.R., Polman, R., & Levy, A.R. (2010). Coping self-efficacy, pre-competitive anxiety, and subjective performance among athletes. *European Journal of Sport Science, 10,* 97–102.

Nicholls, J.G. (1976). Effort is virtuous, but it's better to have ability: Evaluative responses to perceptions of effort and ability. *Journal of Research in Personality, 10,* 306–315.

Nicholls, J.G. (1978). The development of the concepts of effort and ability, perception of academic attainment, and the understanding that difficult tasks require more ability. *Child Development, 49,* 800–814.

Nicholls, J.G. (1979). Quality and equality of intellectual development: The role of motivation in education. *American Psychologist,* 1071–1084.

Nicholls, J.G. (1980). The development of the concept of difficulty. *Merrill-Palmer Quarterly, 26,* 271–281.

Nicholls, J.G. (1981, August). An intentional theory of achievement motivation. In W.U. Meyer & B. Weiner (Chairpersons), *Attributional approaches to human behavior.* Symposium presented at the Center for Interdisciplinary Studies, University of Bielefeld, Germany.

Nicholls, J.G. (1984). Achievement motivation: Conceptions of ability, subjective experience, task choice, and performance. *Psychological Review, 91,* 328–346.

Nicholls, J.G. (1989). *The competitive ethos and democratic education.* Cambridge, MA: Harvard University Press.

Nicholls, J.G. (1992). The general and the specific in the development and expression of achievement motivation. In G.C. Roberts (Ed.), *Motivation in sport and exercise* (pp. 31–57). Champaign, IL: Human Kinetics.

Nicholls, J.G., & Miller, A.T. (1983). The differentiation of the concepts of difficulty and ability. *Child Development, 54,* 951–959.

Nicholls, J.G., & Miller, A.T. (1984a). Development and its discontents: The differentiation of the concept of ability. In J.G. Nicholls (Ed.), *Advances in motivation and achievement, Vol.3, The development of achievement motivation* (pp. 185–218). Greenwich, CT: JAI Press.

Nicholls, J.G., & Miller, A.T. (1984b). Reasoning about the ability of self and others: A developmental study. *Child Development, 55,* 1990–1999.

Nicholls, J.G., Patashnick, M., & Nolen, S.B. (1985). Adolescents' theories of education. *Journal of Educational Psychology, 77,* 683–692.

Nideffer, R.M. (1989). Anxiety, attention and performance in sports: Theoretical and practical considerations. In D. Hackfort & C.D. Spielberger (Eds.), *Anxiety in sport: An international perspective* (pp. 117–136). New York: Hemisphere.

Nielsen, A.D., Hewitt, P.L., Han, H., Habke, A.M., Cockell, S.J., Stager, G., et al. (1997). *Perfectionistic self-presentation and attitudes toward professional help-seeking.* Paper presented at the Canadian Psychological Association, Toronto, Ontario.

Niemiec, C.P., Lynch, M.F., Vansteenkiste, M., Bernstein, J., Deci, E.L., & Ryan, R.M. (2006). The antecedents and consequences of autonomous self-regulation for college: A self-determination theory perspective on socialization. *Journal of Adolescence, 29*, 761–775.

Nien, C.L., & Duda, J.L. (2008). Antecedents and consequences of approach and avoidance achievement goals: A test of gender invariance. *Psychology of Sport and Exercise, 9*, 352–372. doi:10.1016/j.psychsport.2007.05.002

Niven, A., Fawkner, S., Knowles, A.M., & Stephenson, C. (2009). Social physique anxiety and physical activity in early adolescent girls: The influence of maturation and physical activity motives. *Journal of Sport Sciences, 27*, 299–305.

Nix, G.A., Ryan, R.M., Manly, J.B., & Deci, E.L. (1999). Revitalization through self-regulation: The effects of autonomous and controlled motivation on happiness and vitality. *Journal of Experimental Social Psychology, 35*, 266–284.

Ntoumanis, N. (2001a). A self-determination approach to the understanding of motivation in physical education. *British Journal of Educational Psychology, 71*, 225–242. doi:10.1348/000709901158497

Ntoumanis, N. (2001b). Empirical links between achievement goal theory and self-determination theory in sport. *Journal of Sports Sciences, 19*, 397–409. doi:10.1080/026404101300149357

Ntoumanis, N. (2002). Motivational clusters in a sample of British physical education classes. *Psychology of Sport and Exercise, 3*, 177–194. doi:10.1016/S1469-0292(01)00020-6.

Ntoumanis, N. (2005). A prospective study of participation in optional school physical education using a self-determination theory framework. *Journal of Educational Psychology, 97*, 444–453. doi:10.1037/0022-0663.97.3.444

Ntoumanis, N., Barkoukis, V., & Thøgersen-Ntoumani, C. (2009). Developmental trajectories of motivation in physical education: Course, demographic differences, and antecedents. *Journal of Educational Psychology, 101*, 717–728. doi:10.1037/a0014696

Ntoumanis, N., &. Biddle, S.J.H. (1998). The relationship between competitive anxiety, achievement goals, and motivational climates. *Research Quarterly for Exercise and Sport, 69*, 176–187.

Ntoumanis, N., & Biddle, S.J.H. (1999a). Affect and achievement goals in physical activity: A meta analysis. *Scandinavian Journal of Medicine and Science in Sports, 9*, 333–343.

Ntoumanis, N., & Biddle, S.J.H. (1999b). A review of motivational climate in physical activity. *Journal of Sports Sciences, 17*, 643–665.

Ntoumanis, N., Edmunds, J., & Duda, J.L. (2009). Understanding the coping process from a self-determination theory perspective. *British Journal of Health Psychology, 14*, 249–260. doi:10.1348/135910708X349352

Ntoumanis, N., Pensgaard, A.M., Martin, C., & Pipe, K. (2004). An idiographic analysis of amotivation in compulsory school physical education. *Journal of Sport and Exercise Psychology, 26*, 197–214. Retrieved from http://hk.humankinetics.com/JSEP/journalAbout.cfm

Ntoumanis, N., & Standage, M. (2009). Morality in sport: A self-determination theory perspective. *Journal of Applied Sport Psychology, 21*, 365–380. doi:10.1080/10413200903036040

O'Brien, J., Martin Ginis, K.A., & Kirk, D. (2008). The effects of a body-focused physical and health education module on self-objectification and social physique anxiety in Irish girls. *Journal of Teaching in Physical Education, 27*, 116–126.

O'Brien, M., Mellalieu, S., & Hanton, S. (2009). Goal-setting effects in elite and nonelite boxers. *Journal of Applied Sport Psychology, 21*, 293–306.

O'Connell, S., Biddle, S.J.H., & Braithwaite, R. (2009). *Are interventions aimed at reducing sedentary behaviours in young people successful? A systematic review.* Paper presented at the International Society for Behavioral Nutrition & Physical Activity Annual Conference, Lisbon, Portugal.

O'Connor, B.P., & Vallerand, R.J. (1994). Motivation, self-determination, and person-environment fit as predictors of psychological adjustment among nursing home residents. *Psychology and Aging, 9*, 189–194.

O'Connor, R.C., & O'Connor, D.B. (2003). Predicting hopelessness and psychological distress: The role of perfectionism and coping. *Journal of Counseling Psychology, 50*, 362–372.

O'Hagan, S. (2002). Inside the minds of Roy Keane. *The Observer.*

Ogilvie, D., Foster, C.E., Rothnie, H., Cavill, N., Hamilton, V., Fitzsimons, C.F., et al. (2007). Interventions to promote walking: Systematic review. *British Medical Journal, 334.* www.bmj.com, doi:10.1136/bmj.39198.722720.BE

Okurame, D.E. (2006). Role of self-efficacy in goal commitment: A case study of the 20th Nigerian university games chess event. *South African Journal for Research in Sport, Physical Education, and Recreation, 28*, 113–120.

Oliver, E.J., Markland, D., Hardy, J., & Petherick, C.M. (2008). The effects of autonomy-supportive versus controlling environments on self-talk. *Motivation and Emotion, 32*, 200–212.

Oliver, J.M., Hart, B.A., Ross, M.J., & Katz, B.M. (2001). Healthy perfectionism and positive expectation about counselling. *North American Journal of Psychology, 3*, 339–342.

Olmos, L.E., Freixes, O., Gatti, M.A., Cozzo, D.A., Fernandez, S.A., Villa, C.J., Agrati, P.E., & Rubel, I.F. (2008). Comparison of gait performance on different environmental settings for patients with chronic spinal cord injury. *Spinal Cord, 46*, 331–334.

Ommundsen, Y. (2004). Self-handicapping related to task and performance-approach and avoidance goals in physical education. *Journal of Applied Sport Psychology, 16*, 183–197.

Ommundsen, Y. (2006). Pupils' self-regulation in physical education: The role of motivational climates and differential achievement goals. *European Physical Education Review, 12*(3), 289–315.

Ommundsen, Y., & Kvalø Eikanger, S. (2007). Autonomy-mastery, supportive or performance focused? Different teacher behaviors and pupils' outcomes in physical education. *Scandinavian Journal of Educational Research, 51*, 385–413.

Ommundsen, Y., & Pedersen, B.H. (1999). The role of achievement goal orientations and perceived ability upon somatic and cognitive indices of sport competition trait anxiety. *Scandinavian Journal of Medicine & Science in Sports, 9*, 333–343.

Ommundsen, Y., & Roberts, G.C. (1999). Concomitants of motivational climate in team sport. *Scandinavian Journal of Medicine and Science in Sport, 9*, 389–397.

Ommundsen, Y., & Roberts, G.C. (2003). Juks og fanteri eller god idrettsmoral i fotball? Tre motivasjonsstudier blant unge spillere. *Tiddskrift for Norsk Psykologforening, 40*, 665–675.

Ommundsen, Y., Roberts, G.C., & Kavussanu, M. (1998). Perceived motivational climate and cognitive and affective correlates among Norwegian athletes. *Journal of Sports Sciences, 16*, 153–164.

Ommundsen, Y., Roberts, G.C., Lemyre, P.N., & Miller, B.W. (2005). Peer relationships in adolescent competitive soccer: Associations to perceived motivational climate, achievement goals and perfectionism. *Journal of Sports Sciences, 23*, 977–989.

Ommundsen, Y., Roberts, G.C., Lemyre, P.N., & Treasure, D. (2003). Perceived motivational climate in male youth soccer: Relations to social-moral functioning, sportspersonship and team norm perceptions. *Psychology of Sport and Exercise, 4*, 397–413.

Orlick, T. (2000). *In pursuit of excellence* (3rd ed.). Champaign, IL: Human Kinetics.

Orlick, T., & Partington, J. (1988). Mental links to excellence. *Sport Psychologist, 2*, 105–130.

O'Sullivan, R. (2004). *Ronnie*. London: Orion Books.

Owen, N., Healy, G.N., Matthews, C.E., & Dunstan, D.W. (2010). Too much sitting: The population health science of sedentary behavior. *Exercise and Sports Science Reviews, 38*, 105–113.

Owens, R.G., & Slade, P.D. (2008). So perfect it's positively harmful? Reflections on the adaptiveness and maladaptiveness of positive and negative perfectionism. *Behaviour Modification, 32*, 928–937.

Papaioannou, A. (1994). Development of a questionnaire to measure achievement orientations in physical education. *Research Quarterly for Exercise and Sport, 65*, 11–20. Retrieved from www.aahperd.org/rc/publications/rqes/

Papaioannou, A. (2006). Muslim and Christian students' goal orientations in school, sport, and life. *International Journal of Sport and Exercise Psychology, 4*, 250–282.

Papaioannou, A., Bebetsos, E., Theodorakis, Y., Christodoulidis, T., & Kouli, O. (2006). Causal relationships of sport and exercise involvement with goal orientations, perceived competence and intrinsic motivation in physical education: A longitudinal study. *Journal of Sports Sciences, 24*, 367–382.

Papaioannou, A., & Christodoulidis, T. (2007). A measure of teachers' achievement goals. *Educational Psychology, 27*, 349–361.

Papaioannou, A., & Karakanta, E. (2010). *Achievement goals and values* (translation from Greek). (Unpublished manuscript). University of Thessaly, Greece.

Papaioannou, A., Kosmidou, E., Tsigilis, N., & Milosis, D. (2007). Measuring perceived motivational climate in physical education. In J. Liukkonen (Ed.), *Psychology for physical educators* (Vol. 2., pp. 35–55). Champaign, IL: Human Kinetics.

Papaioannou, A., & Kouli, O. (1999). The effect of task structure, perceived motivational climate and goal orientations on students' task involvement and anxiety. *Journal of Applied Sport Psychology, 11*, 51–71.

Papaioannou, A., & Macdonald, A.I. (1993). Goal perspectives and purposes of physical education as perceived by Greek adolescents. *Physical Education Review, 16*, 41–48.

Papaioannou, A., & Milosis, D. (2009). Interdisciplinary teaching, goal orientations, self-determination and responsibility in life. In T.-M. Hung, R. Lidor, & D. Hackfort (Eds.), *Psychology of excellence* (pp. 75–90). Morgantown, WV: Fitness Information Technology http://www.pe.uth.gr/sk_cms/scriptlib/getblob.php?redir=../sk_cms/images/notfound.htm&table=publications&field=doc&id=388

Papaioannou, A., Milosis, D., Kosmidou, E., & Tsigilis, N. (2007). Motivational climate and achievement goals at the situational level of generality. *Journal of Applied Sport Psychology, 19,* 38–66.

Papaioannou, A., & Orfanidou, S. (2010). *Effects of different levels of task difficulty on achievement goals, perceived motivational climate and intrinsic motivation.* Paper under development. University of Thessaly, Greece.

Papaioannou, Sagovits, Ampatzoglou, Kalogiannis, & Skordala. (in press).

Papaioannou, A., Simou, T., Kosmidou, E., Milosis, D., & Tsigilis, N. (2009). Goal orientations at the global level of generality and in physical education: Their association with self-regulation, affect, beliefs and behaviours. *Psychology of Sport and Exercise, 10,* 466–480.

Papaioannou, A., Tsigilis, N., Kosmidou, E., & Milosis, D. (2007). Measuring perceived motivational climate in physical education. *Journal of Teaching in Physical Education, 26,* 236–259.

Papaioannou, A.G., Ampatzoglou, G., Kalogiannis, P., & Sagovits, A. (2008). Social agents, achievement goals, satisfaction and academic achievement in youth sport. *Psychology of Sport and Exercise, 9,* 122–141.

Papaioannou, A.G., Doxakis, G., Van Stam, W., & Bakker F. (2009). *Conflict strategies, achievement goals and motivational climate in sport.* Paper presented at the 12th World Congress of Sport Psychology, Marrakesh, Morocco, June 2009.

Parish, L., & Treasure, D.C. (2003). Physical activity and situational motivation during free-choice activity in physical education: Influence of perception of the motivational climate and personal ability. *Research Quarterly for Exercise and Sport, 74,* 173–182.

Parker, W.D., & Adkins, K.K. (1995). Perfectionism and the gifted. *Roeper Review, 17,* 173–175.

Parker, J.G., & Asher, S.R. (1987). Peer relations and later personal adjustment: Are low-accepted children at risk? *Psychological Bulletin, 102,* 357–389.

Parker, W.D. (1997). An empirical typology of perfectionism in academically talented children. *American Educational Research Journal, 34,* 545–562.

Pasxali, M., Kouli, O., Sidiropoulos, D., & Papaioannou, A. (2004). *Similarities and differences between three measures of achievement goals.* 8th Congress of the Hellenic Sport Psychology, Trikala, Greece, November 26–28, 2004.

Patall, E.A., Cooper, H., & Robinson, J.C. (2008). The effects of choice on intrinsic motivation and related outcomes: A meta-analysis of research findings. *Psychological Bulletin, 134,* 270–300.

Patrick, H., Knee, C.R., Canevello, A., & Lonsbary, C. (2007). The role of need fulfillment in relationship functioning and well-being: A self-determination theory perspective. *Journal of Personality and Social Psychology, 92,* 434–457. doi:10.1037/0022-3514.92.3.434

Pawson, R., & Tilley, N. (1997). *Realistic evaluation.* London: Sage.

Peddle, C.J., Au, H.J., & Courneya, K.S. (2005). Exercise motivation in colorectal cancer survivors: An application of self-determination theory. *Diseases of the Colon and Rectum, 51,* 1242–1248.

Peddle, C.J., Au, H.J., & Courneya, K.S. (2008). Associations between exercise, quality of life, and fatigue in colorectal cancer survivors. *Diseases of the Colon and Rectum, 51,* 1242–1248.

Peddle, C.J., Jones, L.W., Eves, N.D., Reiman, T., Sellar, C.M., Winton, T., & Courneya, K.S. (2009). Correlates of adherence to supervised exercise in patients awaiting surgical removal of malignant lung lesions: Results of a pilot study. *Oncology Nursing Forum, 36,* 287–295.

Peddle, C.J., Plotnikoff, R.C., Wild, T.C., Au, H.J., & Courneya, K.S. (2008). Medical, demographic, and psychosocial correlates of exercise in colorectal cancer survivors: An application of self-determination theory. *Supportive Care in Cancer, 16,* 9–17.

Pelletier, L.G., Fortier, M.S., Vallerand, R.J., & Brière, N.M. (2001). Associations among perceived autonomy support, forms of self-regulation, and persistence: A prospective study. *Motivation and Emotion, 25,* 279–306. doi:10.1023/A:1014805132406

Pelletier, L.G., Séguin-Lévesque, C., & Legault, L. (2002). Pressure from above and pressure from below as determinants of teachers' motivation and teaching behaviors. *Journal of Educational Psychology, 94,* 186–196. doi:10.1037/0022-0663.94.1.186

Pensgaard, A.M., & Roberts, G.C. (2000). The relationship between motivational climate, perceived ability and sources of stress among elite athletes. *Journal of Sport Sciences, 18,* 191–200.

Pensgaard, A.M., & Roberts, G.C. (2002). Elite athletes' perception of the motivational climate: The coach matters. *Scandinavian Journal of Medicine and Science in Sports, 12,* 54–59.

Perreault, S., Gaudreau, P., Lapointe, M., & Lacroix, C. (2007). Does it take three to tango? Psychological need satisfaction and athlete burnout. *International Journal of Sport Psychology, 38,* 437–451. Retrieved from www.ijsp-online.com/content/abstracts/

Pensgaard, A. M., Roberts, G.C., & Ursin, H. (1999). Motivational factors and coping strategies of Norwegian Paralympic and Olympic winter sport athletes. *Adapted Physical Activity Journal. 16,* 238–250.

Perreault, S., & Vallerand, R.J. (2007). A test of self-determination theory with wheelchair basketball players with and without disability. *Adapted Physical Activity Quarterly, 24,* 305–316. Retrieved from http://hk.humankinetics.com/APAQ/journalAbout.cfm

Petherick, C.M., & Weigand, D.A. (2002). The relationship of dispositional goal orientations and perceived motivational climates on indices of motivation in male and female swimmers. *International Journal of Sport Psychology, 33,* 218–237.

Philippe, F.L., & Vallerand, R.J. (2007). Prevalence rates of gambling problems in Montreal, Canada: A look at old adults and the role of passion. *Journal of Gambling Studies, 23,* 275–283.

Philippe, F.L., Vallerand, R.J., Andrianarisoa, J., & Brunel, P. (2009). Passion in referees: Examining their affective and cognitive experiences in sport situations. *Journal of Sport and Exercise Psychology, 31,* 1–21.

Philippe, F.L., Vallerand, R.J., Houlfort, N., Lavigne, G., & Donahue, E.G. (2010). Passion for an activity and quality of interpersonal relationships: The mediating role of emotions. *Journal of Personality and Social Psychology, 98,* 917–932.

Philippe, F.L., Vallerand, R.J., & Lavigne, G. (2009). Passion makes a difference in people's lives: A look at well-being in passionate and non-passionate individuals. *Applied Psychology: Health and Well-Being, 1,* 3–22.

Philippe, F.L., Vallerand, R.J., Richer, I., Vallières, E.F., & Bergeron, J. (2009). Passion for driving and aggressive driving behavior: A look at their relationship. *Journal of Applied Social Psychology, 39,* 3020–3043.

Pinder, C.C. (1984). *Work motivation.* Glenview, IL: Scott, Foresman.

Pinto, B.M., & Floyd, A. (2008). Theories underlying health promotion interventions among cancer survivors. *Seminars in Oncology Nursing, 24,* 153–163.

Pinto, B.M., Maruyama, N.C., Clark, M.M., Cruess, D.G., Park, E., & Roberts, M. (2002). Motivation to modify lifestyle risk behaviors in women treated for breast cancer. *Mayo Clinic Proceedings, 77,* 122–129.

Pintrich, P.R. (2000). The role of goal orientation in self-regulated learning. In M. Boekaerts & P.R. Pintrich (Eds.), *Handbook of self-regulation* (pp. 13–39). San Diego, CA: Academic Press.

Plant, R.W., & Ryan, R.M. (1985). Intrinsic motivation and the effects of self-consciousness, self-awareness, and ego-involvement: An investigation of internally-controlling styles. *Journal of Personality, 53,* 435–449.

Playford, E.D., Dawson, L., Limbert, V., Smith, M., Ward, C.D., & Wells, R. (2000). Goal-setting in rehabilitation: Report of a workshop to explore professionals' perceptions of goal-setting. *Clinical Rehabilitation, 14,* 491–496.

Poag, K., & McAuley, E. (1992). Goal setting, self-efficacy, and exercise behavior. *Journal of Sport and Exercise Psychology, 14,* 352–360.

Podlog, L., & Eklund, R.C. (2009). High-level athletes' perceptions of success in returning to sport following injury. *Psychology of Sport and Exercise, 10,* 535–544. doi:10.1016/j.psychsport.2009.02.003

Podlog, L., Lochbaum, M., & Stevens, T. (2010). Need satisfaction, well-being, and perceived return-to-sport outcomes among injured athletes. *Journal of Applied Sport Psychology, 22,* 167–182. doi:10.1080/10413201003664665

Podsakoff, P.M., MacKenzie, S.B., Lee, J.Y., & Podsakoff, N.P. (2003). Common method biases in behavioral research: A critical review of the literature and recommended remedies. *Journal of Applied Psychology, 88,* 879–903.

Posavac, H.D., Posavac, S.S., & Weigel, R.G. (2001). Reducing the impact of media images on women at risk for body image disturbance: Three targeted interventions. *Journal of Social and Clinical Psychology, 20,* 324–340.

Powers, W.T. (1973). *Behavior: The control of perception.* Chicago: Aldine.

Powers, W.T. (1978). Quantitative analysis of purposive systems: Some spadework at the foundations of scientific psychology. *Psychological Review, 85,* 417–435.

Powers, W.T. (1991). Commentary on Bandura's "human agency." *American Psychologist, 46,* 151–153.

Prapavessis, H. (Ed.) (2004). Self-presentation in exercise and sport [Special issue]. *Journal of Applied Sport Psychology, 16,* 1–2.

Preacher, K.J., & Hayes, A.F. (2008). Asymptotic and resampling strategies for assessing and comparing indirect effects in multiple mediator models. *Behavior Research Methods, 40,* 879–891.

Prichard, I., & Tiggemann, M. (2008). Relations among exercise type, self-objectification, and body image in the fitness centre environment: The role of reasons for exercise. *Psychology of Sport and Exercise, 9,* 855–866.

Prochaska, J.O., & DiClemente, C.C. (1983). Stages and processes of self-change of smoking: Toward an integrative model of change. *Journal of Consulting and Clinical Psychology, 51,* 390–395.

Prochaska, J.O., & DiClemente, C.C. (1984). *The transtheoretical approach: Crossing traditional boundaries of therapy.* Homewood, IL: Dow-Jones Irwin.

Prochaska, J.O., & Marcus, B.H. (1994). The transtheoretical model: Application to exercise. In R.K. Dishman (Ed.), *Advances in exercise adherence* (pp. 161–180). Champaign, IL: Human Kinetics.

Prusak, K.A., Treasure, D.C., Darst, P.W., & Pangrazi, R.P. (2004). The effects of choice on the motivation of adolescent girls in physical education. *Journal of Teaching in Physical Education, 23,* 19–29. Retrieved from http://hk.humankinetics.com/JTPE/journalAbout.cfm

Pyszczynski, T., & Greenberg, J. (1987). Self-regulatory perseveration and the depressive self-focusing style: A self-awareness theory of reactive depression. *Psychological Bulletin, 102,* 122–138.

Radel, R., Sarrazin, P., Legrain, P., & Wild, C. (in press). Social contagion of motivation between teacher and student: Analyzing underlying processes. *Journal of Educational Psychology.*

Radel, R., Sarrazin, P., & Pelletier, L. (2009). Evidence of subliminally primed motivational orientations: The effects of unconscious motivational processes on the performance of a new motor task. *Journal of Sport & Exercise Psychology, 31,* 657–674. Retrieved from http://hk.humankinetics.com/JSEP/journalAbout.cfm

Radloff, L. (1977). The CES-D Scale: A self-report depression scale for research in the general population. *Applied Psychological Measurement, 1,* 385–401.

Raedeke, T.D. (1997). Is athlete burnout more than just stress? A sport commitment perspective. *Journal of Sport and Exercise Psychology, 19,* 396–417.

Raedeke, T.D., Focht, B.C., & Scales, D. (2007). Social environmental factors and psychological responses to acute exercise for socially physique anxious females. *Psychology of Sport and Exercise, 8,* 463–476.

Raedeke, T.D., Focht, B.C., & Scales, D. (2009). Mediators of affective responses to acute exercise among women with high social physique anxiety. *Psychology of Sport and Exercise, 10,* 573–578.

Raedeke, T.D., & Smith, A.L. (2001). Development and preliminary validation of an athlete burnout measure. *Journal of Sport and Exercise Psychology, 23,* 281–306. Retrieved from http://hk.humankinetics.com/JSEP/journalAbout.cfm

Ramsey, D.C., & Ramsey, P.L. (2002). Reframing the perfectionist's catch-22 dilemma: A systems thinking approach. *Journal for Education of the Gifted, 26,* 99–111.

Ratelle, C.F., Baldwin, M.W., & Vallerand, R.J. (2005). On the cued activation of situational motivation.

Journal of Experimental Social Psychology, 41, 482–487. doi:10.1016/j.jesp.2004.10.001

Ratelle, C.F., Vallerand, R.J., Chantal, Y., & Provencher, P. (2004). Cognitive adaptation and mental health: A motivational analysis. *European Journal of Social Psychology, 34,* 459–476.

Ratelle, C.F., Vallerand, R.J., Mageau, G.A., Rousseau, F.L., & Provencher, P. (2004). When passion leads to problematic outcomes: A look at gambling. *Journal of Gambling Studies, 20,* 105–119.

Rawsthorne, L.J., & Elliot, A.J. (1999). Achievement goals and intrinsic motivation: A meta-analytic review. *Personality and Social Psychology Review, 3,* 326–344.

Reeve, J. (1998). Autonomy support as an interpersonal motivating style: Is it teachable? *Contemporary Educational Psychology, 23,* 312–330. doi:10.1006/ceps.1997.0975

Reeve, J. (2002). Self-determination theory applied to educational settings. In E.L. Deci & R.M. Ryan (Eds.), *Handbook of self-determination research* (pp. 183–203). Rochester, NY: University of Rochester Press.

Reeve, J. (2009). Why teachers adopt a controlling motivating style toward students and how they can become more autonomy supportive. *Educational Psychologist, 44,* 159–175. doi:10.1080/00461520903028990

Reeve, J., & Deci, E.L. (1996). Elements of the competitive situation that affect intrinsic motivation. *Personality and Social Psychology Bulletin, 22,* 24–33.

Reeve, J., Deci, E.L., & Ryan, R.M. (2004). Self-determination theory: A dialectical framework for understanding the sociocultural influences on motivation and learning. In D. M. McInerney, & S. van Etten (2004), *Big theories revisited* (Vol. 4, pp. 31-59). Greenwich, CT: Information Age Press.

Reeve, J., & Halusic, M. (2009). How K–12 teachers can put self-determination theory principles into practice. *Theory and Research in Education, 7,* 145–154.

Reeve, J., & Jang, H. (2006). What teachers say and do to support students' autonomy during a learning activity. *Journal of Educational Psychology, 98,* 209–218. doi:10.1037/0022-0663.98.1.209

Reeve, J., Jang, H., Carrell, D., Jeon, S., & Barch, J. (2004). Enhancing students' engagement by increasing teachers' autonomy support. *Motivation and Emotion, 28,* 147–169. doi:10.1023/B:MOEM.0000032312.95499.6f

Reinboth, M., & Duda, J. (2006). Perceived motivational climate, need satisfaction and indices of well-being in team sports: A longitudinal study. *Psychology of Sport and Exercise, 7,* 269–286.

Reinboth, M., & Duda, J.L. (2004). The motivational climate, perceived ability, and athletes' psychological and physical well-being. *Sport Psychologist, 18,* 237–251.

Reinboth, M., Duda, J.L., & Ntoumanis, N. (2004). Dimensions of coaching behavior, need satisfaction, and the psychological and physical welfare of young athletes. *Motivation and Emotion, 28,* 297–313. doi:10.1023/B:MOEM.0000040156.81924.b8

Reis, H.T., Sheldon, K.M., Gable, S.L., Roscoe, J., & Ryan, R.M. (2000). Daily well-being: The role of autonomy, competence, and relatedness. *Personality and Social Psychology Bulletin, 26,* 419–435.

Rejeski, W.J., Brawley, L.R., McAuley, E., & Rapp, S. (2000). An examination of theory and behavior change in randomized clinical trials. *Controlled Clinical Trials, 21,* 164S–170S.

Rhea, M.R., Landers, D.M., Alvar, B.A., & Arent, S.M. (2003). The effects of competition and the presence of an audience on weight lifting performance. *Journal of Strength and Conditioning Research, 17,* 303–306.

Rhodes, R.E. (2006). The built-in environment: The role of personality with physical activity. *Exercise and Sport Science Reviews, 34,* 83–88.

Rhodes, R.E., & Courneya, K.S. (2003). Investigating multiple components of attitude, subjective norm, and perceived control: An examination of the theory of planned behaviour in the exercise domain. *British Journal of Social Psychology, 42,* 129–146.

Rice, K.G., Ashby, J.S., & Slaney, R.B. (1998). Self-esteem as a mediator between perfectionism and depression: A structural equations analysis. *Journal of Counseling Psychology, 45,* 304–314.

Rice, K.G., Bair, C.J., Castro, J.R., Cohen, B.N., & Hood, C.A. (2003). Meanings of perfectionism: A quantitative and qualitative analysis. *Journal of Cognitive Psychotherapy, 17,* 39–58.

Rice, K.G., & Lapsley, D.K. (2001). Perfectionism, coping and emotional adjustment. *Journal of College Student Development, 42,* 157–168.

Rice, K.G., & Slaney, R.B. (2007). An efficient method for classifying perfectionists. *Journal of Counseling Psychology, 54,* 72–85.

Rice, K.G., Vergara, D., & Aldea, M.A. (2006). Cognitive-affective mediators of perfectionism and college student adjustment. *Personality and Individual Differences, 40,* 463–473.

Richman, L.S., Kubzansky, L.D., Maselko, J., Ackerson, L.K., & Bauer, M. (2009). The relationship between mental vitality and cardiovascular health. *Psychology and Health, 24,* 919–932.

Riemsma, R., Pattenden, J., Bridle, C., Sowden, A., Mather, L., Watt, I., et al. (2002). A systematic review of the effectiveness of interventions based on a stages-of-change approach to promote individual behaviour change. *Health Technology Assessment, 6*(24).

Riley, C., Lee, M., Cooper, Z., Fairburn, C.G., & Shafran, R. (2007). A randomised controlled trial of cognitive-behaviour therapy for clinical perfectionism: A preliminary study. *Behaviour Change, 25,* 245–258.

Rip, B., Fortin, S., & Vallerand, R.J. (2006). The relationship between passion and injury in dance students. *Journal of Dance Medicine and Science, 10,* 14–20.

Roberts, G.C. (1984). Achievement motivation in children's sport. In J.G. Nicholls (Ed.), *Advances in motivation and achievement, Vol.3. The development of achievement motivation* (pp. 251–281). Greenwich: JAI Press.

Roberts, G.C. (1989). When motivation matters: The need to expand the conceptual model. In J. Skinner (Ed.), *Future directions in exercise/sport research* (pp. 71–84). Champaign, IL: Human Kinetics.

Roberts, G.C. (1992). Motivation in sport and exercise: Conceptual constraints and convergence. In G.C. Roberts (Ed.), *Motivation in sport and exercise* (pp. 3–29). Champaign, IL: Human Kinetics.

Roberts, G.C. (2001). Understanding the dynamics of motivation in physical activity: The influence of achievement goals on motivational processes. In G.C. Roberts (Ed.), *Advances in motivation in sport and exercise* (pp. 1–50). Champaign, IL: Human Kinetics.

Roberts, G.C. (2008, September). The forgotten values of parsimony, elegance, and conceptual coherence in sport psychology research. The Coleman Griffith Lecture of AASP. Invited Keynote address, Association for Applied Sport Psychology, St. Louis, MO.

Roberts, G.C., Abrahamsen, F.E., & Lemyre, P-N. (2009). Motivation in sport and physical activity: An achievement goal interpretation. In A. Kaplan & S. Karabenick (Eds.), *Culture, self and motivation* (pp. 98–122). Charlotte, NC: Information Age.

Roberts, G.C., & Balague, G. (1989, July). *The development of a social cognitive scale of motivation.* Paper presented at the Seventh World Congress of Sport Psychology, Singapore.

Roberts, G.C., Hall, H.K., Jackson, S.A., Kimiecik, J.C., & Tonymon, P. (1995). Implicit theories of achievement and the sport experience: Goal perspectives and achievement strategies. *Perceptual and Motor Skills, 33,* 219–224.

Roberts, G.C., & Kristiansen, E. (2010). Motivation and goal setting. In S. Hanrahan & M.B. Anderson (Eds.), *Handbook of applied sport psychology* (pp. 490–499). Oxford, England: Routledge.

Roberts, G.C., & Ommundsen, Y. (1996). Effect of goal orientations on achievement beliefs, cognitions, and strategies in team sport. *Scandinavian Journal of Medicine and Science in Sport, 6,* 46–56.

Roberts, G.C., & Ommundsen, Y. (2003, July). The role of motivational variables on peer relationships in youth soccer. In R. Stelter (Ed.), *Proceedings of the XIth European Congress of Sport Psychology* (p. 141), Copenhagen, Denmark.

Roberts, G.C., Ommundsen, Y., Lemyre, N., & Miller, B. (2004). Cheating in sport. In C. Speilberger (Ed.), *Encyclopaedia of applied psychology* (pp. 313–322). San Diego, CA: Academic Press.

Roberts, G.C., & Treasure, D.C. (1995). Achievement goals, motivational climate, and achievement behaviors and strategies in sport. *International Journal of Sport Psychology.* 26(1), 64–80.

Roberts, G.C., & Treasure, D.C. (1992). Children in sport. *Sport Science Review, 2,* 46–64.

Roberts, G.C., & Treasure, D.C. (1994). Parental and individual determinants of children's physical activity involvement. *Enfance.* 2(3), 161–169.

Roberts, G.C., Treasure, D.C., & Balague, G. (1998). Achievement goals in sport: The development and validation of the Perception of Success Questionnaire. *Journal of Sports Sciences, 16,* 337–347.

Roberts, G.C., Treasure, D.C., & Conroy, D.E. (2007). Understanding the dynamics of motivation in sport and physical activity: An achievement goal interpretation. In G. Tenenbaum & R.E. Eklund (Eds.), *Handbook of sport psychology* (3rd ed., pp. 3–30). Hoboken, NJ: Wiley.

Roberts, G.C., Treasure, D.C., & Kavussanu, M. (1996). Orthogonality of achievement goals and its relationship to beliefs about success and satisfaction in sport. *Sport Psychologist, 10,* 398–408.

Roberts, G.C., Treasure, D.C., & Kavussanu, M. (1997). Motivation in physical activity contexts: An achievement goal perspective. In P. Pintrich & M. Maehr (Eds.), *Advances in motivation and achievement* Vol. 10 (pp. 413–447). Stamford, CT: JAI Press.

Rodgers, W.M., & Brawley, L.R. (1993). Using both self-efficacy theory and the theory of planned behavior to discriminate adherers and dropouts from structured programs. *Journal of Applied Sport Psychology, 5,* 195–206.

Rodgers, W.M., Hall, C.R., Blanchard, C.M., McAuley, E., & Munroe, K.J. (2002). Task and scheduling self-efficacy as predictors of exercise behavior. *Psychology and Health, 17,* 405–416.

Rodgers, W.R., & Gauvin, L. (1994). *Contributions and comparisons of personal strivings and outcome expectancies in the understanding of participation motives and exercise adherence.* (University of Alberta, Department of Physical Education and Sport Studies Rep. No. 922R010).

Rogers, C. (1959). A theory of therapy. Personality and interpersonal relationships as developed in the client-centered framework. In S. Koch (Ed.), *A study of a science: Formulations of the person and social context* (Vol. 3). New York: McGraw Hill.

Rogers, L.Q., Courneya, K.S., Robbins, K.T., Malone, J., Seiz, A., Koch, L., & Rao, K. (2008). Physical activity correlates and barriers in head and neck cancer patients. *Supportive Care in Cancer, 16,* 19–27.

Rogers, L.Q., Courneya, K.S., Verhulst, S., Markwell, S., Lanzotti, V., & Shah, P. (2006). Exercise barrier and task self-efficacy in breast cancer patients during treatment. *Supportive Care in Cancer, 14,* 84–90.

Rogers, L.Q., Hopkins-Price, P., Vicari, S., Markwell, S., Pamenter, R., Courneya, K.S., . . . Verhulst, S. (2009). Physical activity and health outcomes three months after completing a physical activity behavior change intervention: Persistent and delayed effects. *Cancer Epidemiology, Biomarkers and Prevention, 18,* 1410–1418.

Rogers, L.Q., Malone, J., Rao, K., Courneya, K.S., Fogleman, A., Tippey, A., . . . Robbins, K.T. (2009). Exercise preferences among patients with head and neck cancer: Prevalence and associations with quality of life, symptom severity, depression, and rural residence. *Head and Neck, 31,* 994–1005.

Rogers, L.Q., Markwell, S.J., Verhulst, S., McAuley, E., & Courneya, K.S. (2009). Rural breast cancer survivors: Exercise preferences and their determinants. *Psycho-Oncology, 18,* 412–421.

Rogers, L.Q., McAuley, E., Courneya, K.S., Humphries, M.C., & Gutin, B. (2007). Racial differences in physical activity associations among primary care patients. *Ethnicity and Disease, 17,* 629–635.

Rogers, L.Q., McAuley, E., Courneya, K.S., & Verhulst, S.J. (2008). Correlates of physical activity self-efficacy among breast cancer survivors. *American Journal of Health Behavior, 32,* 594–603.

Rogers, L.Q., Shah, P., Dunnington, G., Greive, A., Shanmugham, A., Dawson, B., et al. (2005). Social cognitive theory and physical activity during breast cancer treatment. *Oncology Nursing Forum, 32,* 807–815.

Rony, J.A. (1990). *Les passions (The passions)*. Paris: Presses Universitaires de France.

Rose, E.A., Markland, D., & Parfitt, G. (2001). The development and initial validation of the Exercise Causality Orientations Scale. *Journal of Sports Sciences, 19,* 455–462.

Rose, E.A., Parfitt, G., & Williams, S. (2005). Exercise causality orientations, behavioural regulation for exercise and stage of change for exercise: Exploring their relationships. *Psychology of Sport and Exercise, 6,* 399–414.

Rosenberg, M. (1979). *Conceiving the self.* New York: Basic Books.

Rosenholtz, S.J., & Simpson, S.H.(1984). The formation of ability conceptions: Developmental trend or social construction? *Sociology of Education Review, 54,* 31–43.

Roth, G., Assor, A., Niemiec, C.P., Ryan, R.M., & Deci, E.L. (2009). The emotional and academic consequences of parental conditional regard: Comparing conditional positive regard, conditional negative regard, and autonomy support as parenting practices. *Developmental Psychology, 45,* 1119–1142.

Rousseau, F.L., & Vallerand, R.J. (2008). An examination of the relationship between passion and subjective well-being in older adults. *International Journal of Aging and Human Development, 66,* 195–211.

Rousseau, F.L., Vallerand, R.J., Ratelle, C.F., Mageau, G.A., & Provencher, P. (2002). Passion and gambling: On the validation of the Gambling Passion Scale (GPS). *Journal of Gambling Studies, 18,* 45–66.

Rudolph, D.L., & McAuley, E. (1996). Self-efficacy and perceptions of effort: A reciprocal relationship. *Journal of Sport and Exercise Psychology, 18,* 216–223.

Rudolph, S.G., Flett, G.L., & Hewitt, P.L. (2007). Perfectionism and deficits in cognitive emotions regulations. *Journal of Rational-Emotive and Cognitive-Behavior Therapy, 4,* 343–357.

Russell, K.L., & Bray, S.R. (2009). Self-determined motivation predicts independent, home-based exercise following cardiac rehabilitation. *Rehabilitation Psychology, 54,* 150–156.

Russell, K.L., & Bray, S.R. (2010). Promoting self-determined motivation for exercise in cardiac rehabilitation: The role of autonomy support. *Rehabilitation Psychology, 55,* 74–80.

Russell, W.D. (2002). Comparison of self-esteem, body satisfaction and social physique anxiety across males of different exercise frequency and racial background. *Journal of Sport Behavior, 25,* 74–91.

Russell, W.D., & Cox, R.H. (2003). Social physique anxiety, body dissatisfaction, and self-esteems in college females of differing exercise frequency, perceived weight discrepancy and race. *Journal of Sport Behavior, 26,* 298–318.

Ryan, R.M. (1982). Control and information in the intrapersonal sphere: An extension of cognitive evaluation theory. *Journal of Personality and Social Psychology, 43,* 450–461.

Ryan, R.M. (1995). Psychological needs and the facilitation of integrative processes. *Journal of Personality, 63,* 397–427.

Ryan, R.M., Bernstein, J.H., & Brown, K.W. (2010). Weekends, work, and well-being: Psychological need satisfactions and day of the week effects on mood, vitality, and physical symptoms. *Journal of Social and Clinical Psychology, 29,* 95–122.

Ryan, R.M., & Connell, J.P. (1989). Perceived locus of causality and internalization: Examining reasons for acting in two domains. *Journal of Personality and Social Psychology, 57,* 749–761.

Ryan, R.M., & Deci, E.L. (2000a). Intrinsic and extrinsic motivations: Classic definitions and new directions. *Contemporary Educational Psychology, 25,* 54–67. doi:10.1006/ceps.1999.1020

Ryan, R.M., & Deci, E.L. (2000b). Self-determination theory and the facilitation of intrinsic motivation, social development, and well-being. *American Psychologist, 55,* 68–78. doi:10.1037//0003-066X.55.1.68

Ryan, R.M., & Deci, E.L. (2000c). The darker and brighter sides of human existence: Basic psychological needs as a unifying concept. *Psychological Inquiry, 11,* 319–338.

Ryan, R.M., & Deci, E.L. (2001). On happiness and human potentials: A review of research on hedonic and eudaimonic well-being. *Annual Review of Psychology, 52,* 141–166.

Ryan, R.M., & Deci, E.L. (2002). An overview of self-determination theory: An organismic perspective. In E.L. Deci & R.M. Ryan (Eds.), *Handbook of self-determination research* (pp. 3–33). Rochester, NY: University of Rochester.

Ryan, R.M., & Deci, E.L. (2003). On assimilating identities to the self: A Self-Determination Theory perspective on internalization and integrity within cultures. In M.R. Leary & J.P. Tangney (Eds.), *Handbook of self and identity* (pp. 253–272). New York: Guilford.

Ryan, R.M., & Deci, E.L. (2004). Avoiding death or engaging life as accounts of meaning and culture: Comment on Pyszczynski et al. (2004). *Psychological Bulletin, 130,* 473–477.

Ryan, R.M., & Deci, E.L. (2006). Self-regulation and the problem of human autonomy: Does psychology need choice, self-determination, and will? *Journal of Personality, 74,* 1557–1586.

Ryan, R.M., & Deci, E.L. (2007). Active human nature: Self-determination theory and the promotion and maintenance of sport, exercise and health. In Hagger M.S. & Chatzisarantis N.L.D. (Eds.), *Intrinsic motivation and self-determination in exercise and sport* (pp. 1–20). Champaign, IL: Human Kinetics.

Ryan, R.M., & Deci, E.L. (2008). Self-determination theory and the role of basic psychological needs in personality and the organization of behavior. In O.P. John, R.W. Robbins, & L.A. Pervin (Eds.), *Handbook of personality: Theory and research* (pp. 654–678). New York: Guilford Press.

Ryan, R.M., Deci, E.L., & Grolnick, W.S. (1995). Autonomy, relatedness and the self: Their relation to development and psychopathology. In D. Cicchetti & D.J. Cohen (Eds.), *Developmental psychopathology: Theory and methods* (pp. 618–655). New York: Wiley.

Ryan, R.M., & Frederick, C.M. (1997). On energy, personality and health: Subjective vitality as a dynamic reflection of well-being. *Journal of Personality, 65,* 529–565.

Ryan, R.M., Frederick, C.M., Lepes, D., Rubio, N., & Sheldon, K.M. (1997). Intrinsic motivation and exercise adherence. *International Journal of Sport Psychology, 28,* 335–354.

Ryan, R.M., Koestner, R., & Deci, E.L. (1991). Ego-involved persistence: When free-choice behavior is not intrinsically motivated. *Motivation and Emotion, 15,* 185–205. doi:10.1007/BF00995170

Ryan, R.M., Mims, V., & Koestner, R. (1983). Relation of reward contingency and interpersonal context to intrinsic motivation: A review and test using cognitive evaluation theory. *Journal of Personality and Social Psychology, 45,* 736–750.

Ryan, R.M., Patrick, H., Deci, E.L., & Williams, G.C. (2008). Facilitating health behaviour change and its maintenance: Interventions based on self-determination theory. *European Health Psychologist, 10,* 2–5.

Ryan, R.M., Rigby, C.S., & Przybylski, A. (2006). The motivational pull of video games: A self-determination theory approach. *Motivation and Emotion, 30,* 347–363.

Ryan, R.M., Sheldon, K.M., Kasser, T., & Deci, E.L. (1996). All goals are not created equal: An organismic perspective on the nature of goals and their regulation. In P.M. Gollwitzer & J.A. Bargh (Eds.), *The psychology of action: Linking cognition and motivation to behavior* (pp. 7–26). New York: Guilford Press.

Ryan, R.M., Weinstein, N., Bernstein, J., Brown, K.W., Mistretta, L. & Gagne, M. (2010). Vitalizing effects of being outdoors and in nature. *Journal of Environmental Psychology, 30,* 159–168.

Ryan, R.M., Williams, G.C., Patrick, H., & Deci, E.L. (2009). Self-determination theory and physical activity: The dynamics of motivation in development and wellness. *Hellenic Journal of Psychology, 6,* 107–124.

Ryckman, R.M., Robbins, M.A., Thornton, B., & Cantrell, P. (1982). Development and validation of a physical self-efficacy scale. *Journal of Personality and Social Psychology, 42,* 891–900.

Ryska, Todd A. (2003). Sportsmanship in youth athletes: The role of competitiveness, motivational orientation, and perceived purposes of sport. *Journal of Psychology, 137,* 273–293.

Saboonchi, F., & Lundh, L.G. (2003). Perfectionism, anger, somatic health and positive affect. *Personality and Individual Differences, 35,* 1585–1599.

Sachs, M.L. (1981). Running addiction. In M.H. Sachs & M.L. Sachs (Eds.), *Psychology of running* (pp. 116–126). Champaign, IL: Human Kinetics.

Saelens, B.E., & Epstein, L.H. (1998). Behavioral engineering of activity choice in obese children. *International Journal of Obesity, 22,* 275–277.

Sagar, S.S., & Stoeber, J. (2009). Perfectionism, fear of failure, and affective responses to success and failure: The central role of fear of experiencing shame and embarrassment. *Journal of Sport and Exercise Psychology, 31,* 602–627.

Sage, L., & Kavussanu, M. (2007). The effects of goal involvement on moral behaviour in an experimentally manipulated competitive setting. *Journal of Sport and Exercise Psychology, 2,* 190–207.

Sallis, J.F., Haskell, W.L., Fortmann, S.T., Vranizan, K.M., Taylor, C.B., & Solomon, D.S. (1986). Predictors of adaption and maintenance of physical activity in a community sample. *Preventative Medicine, 15,* 331–341.

Sallis, J.F., Hovell, M.F., Hofstetter, C.R., & Barrington, E. (1992). Explanation of various physical activity during two years using social learning variables. *Social Science and Medicine, 34,* 25–32.

Sallis, J.F., Hovell, M.F., Hofstetter, C.R., Faucher, P., Elder, J.P., Blanchard, J., . . . Christenson, G.M. (1989). A multivariate study of determinants of vigorous exercise in a community sample. *Preventative Medicine, 18,* 20–34.

Sallis, J.F., & Owen, N. (1999). *Physical activity and behavioral medicine.* Thousand Oaks, CA: Sage.

Sallis, J.F., Owen, N., & Fisher, E.B. (2008). Ecological models of health behaviour. In K. Glanz, B.K. Rimer, & K. Viswanath (Eds.), *Health behavior and health education: Theory, research, and practice* (4th ed., pp. 465–486). San Francisco: Jossey-Bass.

Sallis, J.F., Prochaska, J.J., & Taylor, W.C. (2000). A review of correlates of physical activity of children and adolescents. *Medicine and Science in Sports and Exercise, 32,* 963–975.

Sampson, R.J., Raudenbush, S.W., & Earls, F. (1997, August 15). Neighborhoods and violent crime: A multilevel study of collective efficacy. *Science Magazine, 277,* 918–924.

Sanderson, T. (2007). The challenges of measuring physical activity in postpartum women. *Midwifery Digest, 17,* 393–398.

Sarrazin, P., Roberts, G.C., Cury, F., Biddle, S., & Famose, J-P. (2002). Exerted effort and performance in climbing among boys: The influence of achievement goals, perceived ability, and task difficulty. *Research Quarterly for Exercise and Sport, 73,* 425–436.

Sarrazin, P., Tessier, D., Pelletier, L., Trouilloud, D., & Chanal, J. (2006). The effects of teachers' expectations about students' motivation on teachers' autonomy-supportive and controlling behaviors. *International Journal of Sport and Exercise Psychology, 4,* 283–301. Retrieved from www.ijsp-online.com/content/abstracts/

Sarrazin, P., Vallerand, R., Guillet, E., Pelletier, L., & Cury, F. (2002). Motivation and dropout in female handballers: A 21-month prospective study. *European Journal of Social Psychology, 32,* 395–418. doi:10.1002/ejsp.98

Schaufeli, W.B., & Salanova, M. (2007). Work engagement: An emerging psychological concept and its implications for organizations. In S.W. Gilliland, D.D. Steiner, & D.P. Skarlicki (Eds.), *Research in social issues in management (Vol. 5): Managing social and ethical issues in organizations* (pp. 135–177). Greenwich, CT: Information Age.

Schlenker, B.R. (1980). *Impression management: The self-concept, social identity, and interpersonal relations.* Monterey, CA: Brooks/Cole.

Schmidt, A.M., & DeShon, R.P. (2010). The moderating effects of performance ambiguity on the relationship between self-efficacy and performance. *Journal of Applied Psychology, 95,* 572–581.

Schmidt, G.W., & Stein, G.L. (1991). Sport commitment: A model integrating enjoyment, dropout, and burnout. *Journal of Sport and Exercise Psychology, 13,* 254–265.

Schmitz, K.H., Ahmed, R.L., Troxel, A., Cheville, A., Smith, R., Lewis-Grant, L., & Greene, Q.P. (2009). Weight lifting in women with breast-cancer-related lymphedema. *New England Journal of Medicine, 361,* 664–673.

Schmitz, K.H., Holtzman, J., Courneya, K.S., Masse, L.C., Duval, S., & Kane, R. (2005). Controlled physical activity trials in cancer survivors: A systematic review and meta-analysis. *Cancer Epidemiology, Biomarkers and Prevention, 14,* 1588–1595.

Schüler, J., Sheldon, K.M., & Fröhlich, S.M. (2010). Implicit need for achievement moderates the relationship between competence need satisfaction and subsequent motivation. *Journal of Research in Personality, 44,* 1–12. doi:10.1016/j.jrp.2009.09.002

Schwartz, S.H. (2008). Robustness and fruitfulness of a theory of universals in individual human values. In A. Tamayo & J. Porto (Eds.), *Valores e trabalho [Values and work].* Brasilia, Brazil: Editora Universidade de Brasilia.

Schwarzer, R. (2008). Modeling health behavior change: How to predict and modify the adoption and maintenance of health behaviors. *Applied Psychology: An International Review, 57,* 1–29.

Scorniaenchi, J.A., & Feltz, D.L. (2009). Coping self-efficacy in sport. In A.R. Nicholls (Ed.), *Coping in sport: Theory, methods, and related constructs* (pp. 279–292). New York: Nova.

Sebire, S.J., Standage, M., & Vansteenkiste, M. (2008). Development and validation of the Goal Content for Exercise Questionnaire. *Journal of Sport and Exercise Psychology, 30,* 353–377.

Sebire, S.J., Standage, M., & Vansteenkiste, M. (2009). Examining intrinsic versus extrinsic exercise goals: Cognitive, affective, and behavioral outcomes. *Journal of Sport and Exercise Psychology, 31,* 189–210.

Sebire, S.J., Standage, M., & Vansteenkiste, M. (in press). Predicting objectively assessed exercise behavior from the content and regulation of exercise goals: Evidence for a mediational model. *Journal of Sport and Exercise Psychology.*

Sedikides, C., & Gregg, A.P. (2003). Portraits of the self. In M.A. Hogg & J. Cooper (Eds.), *Sage handbook of social psychology* (pp. 110–138). London: Sage.

Sedikides, C., & Gregg, A.P. (2008). Self-enhancement: Food for thought. *Perspectives on Psychological Science, 3,* 102–116.

Sedikides, C., & Strube, M.J. (1997). Self-evaluation: To thine own self be good, to thine own self be sure, to thine own self be true, and to thine own self be better. In M.P. Zanna (Ed.), *Advances in Experimental Social Psychology, 29,* 209–269. New York: Academic Press.

Sedikides, C., Wildschut, T., Arndt, J., & Routledge, C. (2008). Nostalgia: Past, present, and future. *Current Directions in Psychological Science, 17,* 304–307.

Segal, R.J., Reid, R.D., Courneya, K.S., Malone, S.C., Parliament, M.B., Scott, C.G., et al. (2003). Resistance exercise in men receiving androgen deprivation therapy for prostate cancer. *Journal of Clinical Oncology, 21,* 1653–1659.

Séguin-Lévesque, C., Laliberté, M.-L., Pelletier, L.G., Blanchard, C.M., & Vallerand, R.J. (2003). Harmonious and obsessive passion for the Internet: Their associations with the couple's relationships. *Journal of Applied Social Psychology, 33,* 197–221.

Seifriz, J., Duda, J.L., & Chi, L. (1992). The relationship of perceived motivational climate to intrinsic motivation and beliefs about success in basketball. *Journal of Sport and Exercise Psychology, 14,* 375–391.

Sejits, G.H., Latham, G.P., Tasa, K., & Latham, B.W. (2004). Goal setting and goal orientation: An integration of two different yet related literatures. *Academy of Management Journal, 47,* 227–239.

Shafran, R., Cooper, Z., & Fairburn, G. (2002). Clinical perfectionism: A cognitive-behavioural analysis. *Behaviour Research and Therapy, 40,* 773–791.

Shafran, R., Egan, S., & Wade, T. (2010). *Overcoming perfectionism: A self-help guide using cognitive behavioural techniques.* Robinson Publishing.

Shafran, R., & Mansell, W. (2001). Perfectionism and psychopathology: A review of research and treatment. *Clinical Psychology Review, 21,* 879–906.

Shapira, Z. (1976). Expectancy determinants of intrinsically motivated behavior. *Journal of Personality and Social Psychology, 34,* 1235–1244.

Shapiro, C.L., & Recht, A. (2001). Side effects of adjuvant treatment of breast cancer. *New England Journal of Medicine, 344,* 1997–2008.

Shea, G.P., & Guzzo, R.A. (1987). Groups as human resources. In K. Rowland & G. Ferris (Eds.), *Research in personnel and human resources management* (Vol. 5, pp. 323–356). Greenwich, CT: JAI Press.

Sheeran, P., Webb, T.L., & Gollwitzer, P.M. (2005). The interplay between goal intentions and implementation intentions. *Personality and Social Psychology Bulletin, 31,* 87–98.

Sheldon, K.M. (2002). The Self-Concordance Model of healthy goal-striving: When personal goals correctly represent the person. In E.L. Deci & R.M. Ryan (Eds.), *Handbook of self-determination research* (pp. 65–86). Rochester, NY: University of Rochester Press.

Sheldon, K.M., & Bettencourt, B.A. (2002). Psychological need-satisfaction and subjective well-being within social groups. *British Journal of Social Psychology, 41,* 25–38.

Sheldon, K.M., & Elliot, A.J. (1998). Not all personal goals are personal: Comparing autonomous and controlled reasons for goals as predictors of effort and attainment. *Journal of Personality and Social Psychology Bulletin, 24,* 546–557. doi:10.1177/0146167298245010

Sheldon, K.M., & Elliot, A.J. (1999). Goal striving, need satisfaction, and longitudinal well-being: The self-concordance model. *Journal of Personality and Social Psychology, 76,* 482–497. doi:10.1037/0022-3514.76.3.482

Sheldon, K.M., & Filak, V. (2008). Manipulating autonomy, competence and relatedness support in a game-learning context: New evidence that all three needs matter. *British Journal of Social Psychology, 47,* 267–283.

Sheldon, K.M., & Gunz, A. (2009). Psychological needs as basic motives, not just experiential requirements. *Journal of Personality, 77,* 1467–1492. doi:10.1111/j.1467-6494.2009.00589.x

Sheldon, K.M., & Niemiec, C.P. (2006). It's not just the amount that counts: Balanced need satisfaction also affects well-being. *Journal of Personality and Social Psychology, 91,* 331–341. doi:10.1037/0022-3514.91.2.331

Shen, B., Chen, A., & Guan, J. (2007). Using achievement goals and interest to predict learning in physical education. *Journal of Experimental Education, 75*(2), 89–108.

Shen, B., McCaughtry, N., Martin, J.J., & Fahlman, M. (2009a). Effects of teacher autonomy support and students' autonomous motivation on learning in physical education. *Research Quarterly for Exercise and Sport, 80,* 44–53. Retrieved from www.aahperd.org/rc/publications/rqes/

Shen, B., McCaughtry, N., Martin, J.J., & Fahlman, M. (2009). Motivational profiles and their associations with achievement outcomes. *Journal of Teaching in Physical Education, 28,* 441–460.

Shields, D.L., & Bredemeier, B.J. (1995). Leadership, cohesion and team norms regarding cheating and aggression. *Sociology of Sport Journal, 12,* 324–336.

Short, S.E., & Vadocz, E.A. (2002). Testing the modifiability of the State Sport Confidence Inventory. *Perceptual and Motor Skills, 94,* 1025–1028.

Sideridis, G.D., & Mouratidis, A. (2008). Forced choice versus open-ended assessments of goal orientations: A descriptive study. *International Review of Social Psychology, 21,* 217–246.

Sierens, E., Vansteenkiste, M., Goossens, L., Soenens, B., & Dochy, F. (2009). The synergistic relationship of perceived autonomy support and structure in the prediction of self-regulated learning. *British Journal of Educational Psychology, 79,* 57–68. doi:10.1348/000709908X304398

Silk, J.S., Morris, A.S., Kanaya, T., & Steinberg, L. (2003). Psychological control and autonomy granting: Opposite ends of a continuum or distinct constructs? *Journal of Research on Adolescence, 13,* 113–128. doi:10.1111/1532-7795.1301004

Silva, M.N., Vieira, P.N., Coutinho, S.R., Minderico, C.S., Matos, M.G., Sardinha, L.S., & Teixeira, P.J. (2010). Using self-determination theory to promote physical activity and weight control: A randomized controlled trial in women. *Journal of Behavioral Medicine, 33,* 110–122.

Sinden, A.R., Martin Ginis, K.A., & Angove, J. (2003). Older women's reactions to revealing and nonrevealing exercise attire. *Journal of Aging and Physical Activity, 11,* 445–458.

Singh, A.S., Chin, A., Paw, M.J., Kremers, S.P.J., Visscher, T.L.S., Brug, J., & Van Mechelen, W. (2006). Design of the Dutch Obesity Intervention in Teenagers (NRG-DOiT): Systematic development, implementation and evaluation of a school-based intervention aimed at the prevention of excessive weight gain in adolescents. *BMC Public Health, 6*(304), www.biomedcentral.com/1471-2458/1476/1304

Skaalvik, E.M. (1997). Self-enhancing and self-defeating ego orientation: Relations with task and avoidance orientation, achievement, self-perceptions, and anxiety. *Journal of Educational Psychology, 89,* 71–81.

Skinner, E.A., & Belmont, M.J. (1993). Motivation in the classroom: Reciprocal effects of teacher behavior and student engagement across the school year. *Journal of Educational Psychology, 85,* 571. doi:10.1037/0022-0663.85.4.571

Skinner, E.A., & Edge, K. (2002). Self-determination, coping, and development. In E.L. Deci & R.M. Ryan (Eds.), *Handbook of self-determination research* (pp. 297–337). Rochester, NY: University of Rochester Press.

Skinner, T., Davies, M., Heller, S., & Khunti, K. (2005). To determine the effects of a structured educational programme on illness beliefs, quality of life and physical activity in individuals with newly diagnosed type 2 diabetes: Results from the DESMOND (Diabetes education and self-management for ongoing and newly diagnosed) pilot study. *Diabetes Medicine, 22*(Suppl. 2), 15.

Skjesol, K., & Halvari, H. (2005). Motivational climate, achievement goals, perceived sport competence, and involvement in physical activity: Structural and mediator models. *Perceptual and Motor Skills, 100,* 497–523.

Slade, P.D., & Owens, R.G. (1998). A dual process model of perfectionism based on reinforcement theory. *Behavior Modification, 22,* 372–390.

Slaney, R.B., & Ashby, J.S. (1996). Perfectionists: Study of a criterion group. *Journal of Counseling and Development, 74,* 393–398.

Slaney, R.B., Ashby, J.S., & Trippi, J. (1995). Perfectionism: Its measurement and career relevance. *Journal of Career Assessment, 3,* 279–297.

Smith, A., Balaguer, I., & Duda, J.L. (2006). Goal orientation profile differences on perceived motivational climate, perceived peer relationships, and motivation-related responses of youth athletes. *Journal of Sports Science, 24,* 1315–1327.

Smith, A., Ntoumanis, N., & Duda, J. (2007). Goal striving, goal attainment, and well-being: Adapting and testing the self-concordance model in sport. *Journal of Sport and Exercise Psychology, 29,* 763. Retrieved from http://hk.humankinetics.com/JSEP/journalAbout.cfm

Smith, A., Ntoumanis, N., Duda, J.L., & Vansteenkiste, M. (2011). Goal striving, coping, and well-being in sport: A prospective investigation of the self-concordance model. *Journal of Sport and Exercise Psychology, 33,* 124–145.

Smith, A.L. (1999). Perceptions of peer relationships and physical activity participation in early adolescence. *Journal of Sport and Exercise Psychology, 21,* 329–350.

Smith, A.L. (2003). Peer relationships in physical activity contexts: A road less travelled in youth sport and exercise psychology research. *Psychology of Sport and Exercise, 4,* 25–39.

Smith, J.M.J., & Harwood, C.G. (2001, September). The transiency of goal involvement states in match-play: An elite player case study Paper presented at the BASES conference, Newport, RI.

Smith, R.E. (1986). Toward a cognitive-affective model of athletic burnout. *Journal of Sport Psychology, 8,* 36–50.

Smith, M., Duda, J.L., Allen, J., & Hall, H. (2002). Contemporary measures of approach and avoidance goal orientations: Similarities and differences. *British Journal of Educational Psychology, 72,* 155–190.

Smith, R.E., Cumming, S.P., & Smoll, F.L. (2008). Development and validation of the Motivational Climate Scale for Youth Sport. *Journal of Applied Sport Psychology, 20,* 116–136.

Smith, R.E., Smoll, F.L., & Cumming, S.P. (2007). Effects of a motivational climate intervention for coaches on young athletes' sport performance anxiety. *Journal of Sport & Exercise Psychology, 29*, 39–59.

Smith, R.E., Smoll, F.L., & Curtis, B. (1978). Coaching behaviors in Little League baseball. In F.L. Smoll & R.E. Smith (Eds.), *Psychological perspectives on youth sports* (pp. 173–201). Washington, DC: Hemisphere.

Smoll, F.L., & Smith, R.E. (2002). Coaching behavior research and intervention in youth sports. In F.L. Smoll, & R.E. Smith (Eds.), *Children and youth in sport: A biopsychological perspective* (2nd ed., pp. 211–234). Dubuque, IA: Kendall/Hunt.

Smoll, F., & Smith, R. (2010). Youth enrichment in sport: An applied sport psychology perspective. *AASP Newsletter, 24*, 34–36.

Smoll, F.L., Smith, R.E., Barnett, N.P., & Everett, J.J. (1993). Enhancement of children's self-esteem through social support training for youth sport coaches. *Journal of Applied Psychology, 78*, 602–610. doi:10.1037/0021-9010.78.4.602

Smoll, F.L., Smith, R.E., Cumming, S.P. (2007). Effects of a motivational climate intervention for coaches on changes in young athletes' achievement goal orientation. *Journal of Clinical Sport Psychology, 1*, 23–46.

Snyder, M. (1984). When belief creates reality. In L. Berkowitz (Ed.), *Advances in experimental social psychology* (Vol. 18, pp. 248–305). Orlando, FL: Academic Press.

Soenens, B., Vansteenkiste, M., & Sierens, E. (2009). How are parental psychological control and autonomy-support related? A cluster-analytic approach. *Journal of Marriage and Family, 71*, 187–202. doi:10.1111/j.1741-3737.2008.00589.x

Solmon, M.A. (1996). Impact of motivational climate on students' behaviors and perceptions in a physical education setting. *Journal of Educational Psychology, 88*, 731–738.

Sorotzkin, B. (1998). Understanding and treating perfectionism in religious adolescents. *Psychotherapy, 35*, 87–95.

Sparkes, A.C. (2004). Bodies, narratives, selves and autobiography. The example of Lance Armstrong. *Journal of Sport & Social Issues, 28*, 397–428.

Speck, R.M., Courneya, K.S., Masse, L.C., Duval, S., & Schmitz, K.H. (2010). An update of controlled physical activity trials in cancer survivors: A systematic review and meta-analysis. *Journal of Cancer Survivorship, 4*, 87–100.

Spielberger, C.D. (1999). *State-trait anger expression inventory-2: Professional manual.* Odessa, FL: Psychological Assessment Resources.

Spiers Neumeister, K.L., Williams, K.K., & Cross, T.L. (2009). Gifted high-school students' perspectives on the development of perfectionism. *Roeper Review, 31*, 198–206.

Spink, K.S. (1990). Group cohesion and collective efficacy of volleyball teams. *Journal of Sport and Exercise Psychology, 12*, 301–311.

Spink, K.S. (1992). Relation of anxiety about social physique to location of participation in physical activity. *Perceptual and Motor Skills, 73*, 1075–1078.

Spray, C.M., & Wang, C.K.J. (2001). Goal orientations, self-determination and pupils' discipline in physical education. *Journal of Sports Sciences, 19*, 903–913. doi:10.1080/026404101317108417

Spray, C.M., Wang, C.K.J., Biddle, S.J.H., & Chatzisarantis, N.L.D. (2006). Understanding motivation in sport: An experimental test of achievement goal and self determination theories. *European Journal of Sport Science, 6*, 43–51. doi:10.1080/17461390500422879

Stajkovic, A.D., & Bandura, A. (2009). *Statistical machinations in the quest for negative self-efficacy effects.* Unpublished manuscript, University of Wisconsin.

Stalsberg, R., & Pedersen, A.V. (2010). Effects of socioeconomic status on the physical activity in adolescents: A systematic review of the evidence. *Scandinavian Journal of Medicine and Science in Sports, 20*, 368–383.

Standage, M. (2009, April). *Promoting adaptive engagement in health behaviour: A self-determination theory perspective.* Paper presented to the British Psychological Society Annual Conference, Brighton, England.

Standage, M., Duda, J.L., & Ntoumanis, N. (2003a). A model of contextual motivation in physical education: Using constructs from self-determination and achievement goal theories to predict physical activity intentions. *Journal of Educational Psychology, 95*, 97–110. doi:10.1037//0022-0663.95.1.97

Standage, M., Duda, J.L., & Ntoumanis, N. (2003b). Predicting motivational regulations in physical education: The interplay between dispositional goal orientations, motivational climate and perceived competence. *Journal of Sports Sciences, 21*, 631–647.

Standage, M., Duda, J.L., & Ntoumanis, N. (2005). A test of self-determination theory in school physical education. *British Journal of Educational Psychology, 75,* 411–433. doi:10.1348/000709904X22359

Standage, M., Duda, J.L., & Ntoumanis, N. (2006). Students' motivational processes and their relationship to teacher ratings in school physical education: A self-determination theory approach. *Research Quarterly for Exercise and Sport, 77,* 100–110. Retrieved from www.aahperd.org/rc/publications/rqes/

Standage, M., & Gillison, F. (2007). Students' motivational responses toward school physical education and their relationship to general self-esteem and health-related quality of life. *Psychology of Sport and Exercise, 8,* 704–721. doi:10.1016/j.psychsport.2006.12.004

Standage, M., Gillison, F., & Verplanken, B. (2010). *The use of incentives in the formation of healthy lifestyle habits following the school to work transition.* Unpublished raw data, University of Bath.

Standage, M., Sebire, S.J., & Loney, T. (2008). Does exercise motivation predict engagement in objectively assessed bouts of moderate-intensity exercise behavior? A self-determination theory perspective. *Journal of Sport & Exercise Psychology, 30,* 337–352.

Standage, M., Treasure, D.C., Hooper, K., & Kuczka, K. (2007). Self-handicapping in school physical education: The influence of the motivational climate. *British Journal of Educational Psychology, 77,* 81–99.

Standage, M., & Vallerand, R.J. (2008). Self-determined motivation in sport and exercise groups. In M.R. Beauchamp & M.A. Eys (Eds.), *Group dynamics advances in sport and exercise psychology: Contemporary themes* (pp. 179–199). New York: Routledge.

Starkes, J.L. (2000). The road to expertise: Is practice the only determinant. *International Journal of Sport Psychology, 31,* 431–451.

Starkes, J.L., & Ericsson, K.A. (Eds.). (2003). *Expert performance in sports: Advances in research on sport expertise.* Champaign, IL: Human Kinetics.

Steele, C.M. (1988). The psychology of self-affirmation: Sustaining the integrity of the self. *Advances in Experimental Social Psychology, 21,* 261–302.

Stensel, D.J., Gorely, T., & Biddle, S.J.H. (2008). Youth health outcomes. In A.L. Smith & S.J.H. Biddle (Eds.), *Youth physical activity and sedentary behavior: Challenges and solutions* (pp. 31–57). Champaign, IL: Human Kinetics.

Stenseng, F. (2008). The two faces of leisure activity engagement: Harmonious and obsessive passion in relation to intrapersonal conflict and life domain outcomes. *Leisure Sciences, 30,* 465–481.

Stephan, Y., Deroche, T., Brewer, B.W., Caudroit, J., & Le Scanff, C. (2009). Predictors of perceived susceptibility to sport-related injury among competitive runners: The role of previous experience, neuroticism, and passion for running. *Applied Psychology: An International Review, 58,* 672–687.

Steptoe, A., & Butler, N. (1996). Sports participation and emotional wellbeing in adolescents. *Lancet, 347,* 1789–1792.

Sternberg, R.J. (1986). A triangular theory of love. *Psychological Review, 93,* 119–153.

Stevenson, S.J., & Lochbaum, M.R. (2008). Understanding exercise motivation: Examining the revised social-cognitive model of achievement motivation. *Journal of Sport Behavior, 31,* 389–412.

Stevinson, C., Capstick, V., Schepansky, A., Tonkin, K., Vallance, J.K., Ladha, A.B., Steed, H., Faught, W., & Courneya, K.S. (2009). Physical activity preferences of ovarian cancer survivors. *Psycho-Oncology, 18,* 422–428.

Stevinson, C., Steed, H., Faught, W., Tonkin, K., Vallance, J.K., Ladha, A.B., ... Courneya, K.S. (2009). Physical activity in ovarian cancer survivors: Associations with fatigue, sleep, and psychosocial functioning. *International Journal of Gynecololgic Cancer, 19,* 73–78.

Stevinson, C., Tonkin, K., Capstick, V., Schepansky, A., Ladha, A.B., Vallance, J.K., Faught, W., Steed, H. & Courneya, K.S. (2009). A population-based study of the determinants of physical activity in ovarian cancer survivors. *Journal of Physical Activity and Health, 6,* 339–346.

Stoeber, J., & Becker, C. (2008). Perfectionism, achievement motives, and and attribution of success and failure in female soccer players. *International Journal of Psychology, 43,* 980–987.

Stoeber, J., Kempe, T., & Keogh, E.J. (2008). Facets of self-oriented and socially prescribed perfectionism and feelings of pride, shame, and guilt following success and failure. *Personality and Individual Differences, 44,* 1506–1516.

Stoeber, J., & Otto, K. (2006). Positive conceptions of perfectionism: Approaches, evidence and challenges. *Personality and Social Psychology Review, 10,* 295–319.

Stoeber, J., Otto, K., Pesheck, E., Becker, C., & Stoll, O. (2007). Perfectionism and competitive anxiety in athletes: Differentiating striving for perfection and negative reactions to imperfection. *Personality and Individual Differences, 42,* 959–969.

Stoeber, J., Stoll, O., Pesheck, E., & Otto, K. (2008). Perfectionism and goal orientations in athletes: Relations with approach and avoidance orientations in mastery and performance goals. *Psychology of Sport and Exercise, 9,* 102–121.

Stoeber, J., Stoll, O., Salmi, O., & Tiikkaja, J. (2009). Perfectionism and achievement goals in young Finnish ice-hockey players aspiring to make the under-16 national team. *Journal of Sports Sciences, 27,* 85–94.

Stoeber, J., Uphill, M.A., & Hotham, S. (2009). Predicting race performance in triathlon: The role of perfectionism, achievement goals, and personal goal setting. *Journal of Sport and Exercise Psychology, 31,* 211–245.

Stokols, D. (1992). Establishing and maintaining healthy environments: Toward a social ecology of health promotion. *American Psychologist, 47,* 6–22.

Stoll, O., Lau, A., & Stoeber, J. (2008). Perfectionism and performance in a new basketball training task: Does striving for perfection enhance or undermine performance? *Psychology of Sport and Exercise.* doi:10.1016/j.psychsport.2007.10.001, available early online.

Storch, E.A., Milson, V.A., Debraganza, N., Lewin, A.B., Geffken, G.R., Silverstein, J.H. (2007). Peer victimization, psychosocial adjustment, and physical activity in overweight and at-risk-for overweight youth. *Journal of Pediatric Psychology, 32,* 80–89.

Stott, C., Hutchison, P., & Drury, J. (2001). "Hooligans" abroad? Inter-group dynamics, social identity and participation in collective "disorder" at the 1998 World Cup Finals. *British Journal of Social Psychology, 40,* 359–384.

Stovitz, S.D., VanWormer, J.J., Center, B.A., & Bremer, K.L. (2005). Pedometers as a means to increase ambulatory activity for patients seen at a family medicine clinic. *Journal of the American Board of Family Practice, 18,* 335–343.

Strauss, B. (2002). Social facilitation in motor tasks: a review of research and theory. *Psychology of Sport and Exercise, 3,* 237–256.

Strong, H.A., Martin Ginis, K.A., Mack, D.E., & Wilson, P.M. (2006). Examining self-presentational exercise motives and social physique anxiety in men and women. *Journal of Applied Biobehavioral Research, 11,* 209–225.

Strube, M.J., Miles, M.E., & Finch, W.H. (1981). The social facilitation of a simple task: Field tests of

alternative explanations. *Personality and Social Psychological Bulletin, 7,* 701–707.

Stumpf, H., & Parker, W.D. (2000). A hierarchical structural analysis of perfectionism and its relation to other personality characteristics. *Personality and Individual Differences, 28,* 837–852.

Stuntz, C.P., & Weiss, M.R. (2009). Achievement goal orientations and motivational outcomes in youth sport: The role of social orientations. *Psychology of Sport and Exercise, 10,* 255–262.

Sturman, E.D., Flett, G.L., Hewitt, P.L., & Rudolph, S.G. (2009). Dimensions of perfectionism and self-worth contingencies in depression. *Journal of Rational-Emotive and Cognitive-Behavior Therapy, 27,* 213–231.

Sugiyama, T., Leslie, E., Giles-Corti, B., & Owen, N. (2008). Associations of neighbourhood greenness with physical and mental health: Do walking, social coherence and local social interaction explain the relationships? *Journal of Epidemiology and Community Health, 62*(5). doi:10.1136/jech.2007.064287

Sullivan, P.J., & Kent, A. (2003). Coaching efficacy as a predictor of leadership style in intercollegiate athletics. *Journal of Applied Sport Psychology, 15,* 1–11.

Swain, A.B.J., & Harwood, C.G. (1996). Antecedents of state goals in age group swimmers: An interactionist perspective. *Journal of Sport Sciences, 14,* 111–124.

Symons Downs, D., Hausenblas, H.A., & Nigg, C.R. (2004). Factorial validity and psychometric examination of the exercise dependence scale-revised. *Measurement in Physical Education and Exercise Science, 8,* 183–201.

Talbot, L.A., Gaines, J.M., Huynh, T.N., & Metter, E.J. (2003). A home-based pedometer-driven walking program to increase physical activity in older adults with osteoarthritis of the knee: A preliminary study. *Journal of the American Geriatrics Society, 51,* 387–392.

Tammen, V., Treasure, D.C., & Power, K.T. (1992). The relationship between competitive and mastery achievement goals and dimensions of intrinsic motivation. *Journal of Sport Sciences, 10,* 630.

Tauer, J.M., & Harackiewicz, J.M. (1999). Winning isn't everything: Competition, achievement motivation, and intrinsic motivation. *Journal of Experimental Social Psychology, 35,* 209–238.

Taylor, I.M., & Ntoumanis, N. (2007). Teacher motivational strategies and student self-determination in physical education. *Journal of Educational*

Psychology, 99, 747–760. doi:10.1037/0022-0663.99.4.747

Taylor, I.M., Ntoumanis, N., & Smith, B. (2009). The social context as a determinant of teacher motivational strategies in physical education. *Psychology of Sport and Exercise, 10,* 235–243. doi:10.1016/j.psychsport.2008.09.002

Taylor, I.M., Ntoumanis, N., & Standage, M. (2008). A self-determination theory approach to understanding the antecedents of teachers' motivational strategies in physical education. *Journal of Sport and Exercise Psychology, 30,* 75–94. Retrieved from http://hk.humankinetics.com/JSEP/journalAbout.cfm

Taylor, I.M., Ntoumanis, N., Standage, M., & Spray, C. (2010). Motivational predictors of physical education students' effort, exercise intentions, and leisure-time physical activity: A multilevel linear growth analysis. *Journal of Sport and Exercise Psychology, 32,* 99–120. Retrieved from http://hk.humankinetics.com/JSEP/journalAbout.cfm

Tenenbaum, G. (2004). Decision making in sport. *Encyclopedia of applied psychology, 1,* 575–584.

Tenenbaum, G., Lidor, R., Lavyan, N., Morrow, K., Tonnel, S., & Gershgoren, A. (2005). Dispositional and task-specific social-cognitive determinants of physical effort perseverance. *Journal of Psychology, 139,* 139–157.

Tessier, D., Sarrazin, P., & Ntoumanis, N. (2008). The effects of an experimental programme to support students' autonomy on the overt behaviours of physical education teachers. *European Journal of Psychology of Education, 23,* 239–253. Retrieved from www.springer.com/psychology/journal/10212

Tetlock, P.E., & Manstead, A.S.R. (1985). Impression management versus intrapsychic explanations in social-psychology—a useful dichotomy. *Psychological Review, 92,* 59–77.

Theeboom, M., De Knop, P., & Weiss, M.R. (1995). Motivational climate, psychological responses, and motor skill development in children's sport: A field-based intervention study. *Journal of Sport and Exercise Psychology, 17,* 294–311.

Theodorakis, Y., Malliou, P., Papaioannou, A., Beneca, A., & Filactakidou, A. (1996). The effect of personal goals, self-efficacy, and self-satisfaction on injury rehabilitation. *Journal of Sport Rehabilitation, 5,* 214–223.

Thøgersen-Ntoumani, C., & Ntoumanis, N. (2006). The role of self-determined motivation in the understanding of exercise-related behaviours, cognitions and physical self-evaluations. *Journal of Sports Sciences, 24,* 393–404.

Thøgersen-Ntoumani, C., & Ntoumanis, N. (2007). The self-determination theory approach to the study of body image concerns, self-presentation and self-perceptions in a sample of aerobic instructors. *Journal of Health Psychology, 12,* 301–315.

Thøgersen-Ntoumani, C., Ntoumanis, N., & Nikitaras, N. (2010). Unhealthy weight control behaviours in adolescent girls: A process model based on self-determination theory. *Psychology and Health, 25,* 535–550.

Thomassen, T.O., & Halvari, H. (2007). A hierarchical model of approach achievement motivation and effort regulation during a 90-min soccer match. *Perceptual and Motor Skills, 105,* 609–635.

Thompson, T. (1993). Characteristics of self-worth protection in achievement behaviour. *British Journal of Educational Psychology, 63,* 469–488.

Thorkildsen, T. (1988). Theories of education among academically precocious adolescents. *Contemporary Educational Psychology, 13,* 323–330.

Tomson, L.M., Pangrazi, R.P., Friedman, G., & Hutchison, N. (2003). Childhood depressive symptoms, physical activity and health related fitness. *Journal of Sport & Exercise Psychology, 25,* 419–439.

Toshima, M.T., Kaplan, R.M., & Ries, A.L. (1990). Experimental evaluation of rehabilitation in chronic obstructive pulmonary disease: Short-term effects on exercise endurance and health status. *Health Psychology, 9,* 237–252.

Tosun, L.P., & Lajunen, T. (2009). Why do young adults develop a passion for Internet activities? The associations among personality, revealing "true self" on the Internet, and passion for the Internet. *CyberPsychology and Behavior, 12,* 401–406.

Treasure, D.C. (1993). *A social-cognitive approach to understanding children's achievement behavior, cognitions, and affect in competitive sport.* (Unpublished doctoral dissertation). University of Illinois at Champaign-Urbana.

Treasure, D.C. (1997). Perceptions of the motivational climate and elementary school children's cognitive and affective response. *Journal of Sport & Exercise Psychology, 19,* 278–290.

Treasure, D.C. (2001). Enhancing young people's motivation in youth sport: An achievement goal approach. In G.C. Roberts (Ed.), *Advances in motivation in sport and exercise* (pp. 79–100). Champaign, IL: Human Kinetics.

Treasure, D.C., Duda, J.L., Hall, H., Roberts, G.C., Ames, C., & Maehr, M. (2001). Clarifying misconceptions and misrepresentations in achievement goal research: A response to Harwood, Hardy and Swain (2000). *Journal of Sport and Exercise Psychology, 23,* 317–329.

Treasure, D.C., Lemyre, N., Kuczka, K.K., & Standage, M. (2007). Motivation in elite level sport: A self-determination perspective. In M.S. Hagger & N.L.D. Chatzisarantis (Eds.), *Intrinsic motivation and self-determination in exercise and sport,* pp. 153–165.

Treasure, D.C., Lox, C.L., & Lawton, B.R. (1998). Determinants of physical activity in a sedentary, obese female population. *Journal of Sport & Exercise Psychology, 20,* 218–224.

Treasure, D.C., & Roberts, G.C. (1994a). Cognitive and affective concomitants of task and ego goal orientations during the middle school years. *Journal of Sport and Exercise Psychology, 16,* 15–28.

Treasure, D.C., & Roberts, G.C. (1994b). Perception of Success Questionnaire: Preliminary validation in an adolescent population. *Perceptual & Motor Skills, 79,* Spec. Issue, 607–610.

Treasure, D.C., & Roberts, G.C. (1995). Applications of achievement goal theory to physical education: Implications for enhancing motivation. *Quest, 47,* 475–489.

Treasure, D.C., & Roberts, G.C. (1998). Relationship between female adolescents' achievement goal orientations, perceptions of the motivational climate, belief about success and sources of satisfaction in basketball. *International Journal of Sport Psychology, 29,* 211–230.

Treasure, D.C., & Roberts, G.C. (2001a). Students' perceptions of the motivational climate, achievement beliefs and satisfaction in physical education. *Research Quarterly for Exercise and Sport, 72,* 165–175.

Treasure, D.C. & Roberts, G.C. (2001b). The effect of the motivational climate on the achievement beliefs and satisfaction of students in physical education. *Research Quarterly for Exercise and Sport. 72,* 165-175.

Triplett, N. (1897). The dynamogenic factors in pacemaking and competition. *American Journal of Psychology, 9,* 507–533.

Troiano, R.P., Berrigan D., Dodd, K.W., Masse, L.C., Tilert T., & McDowell, M. (2008). Physical activity in the United States measured by accelerometer. *Medicine and Science in Sports and Exercise, 40,* 181–188.

Trost, S.G., Owen, N., Bauman, A.E., Sallis, J.F., & Brown, W. (2002). Correlates of adults' participation in physical activity: Review and update. *Medicine and Science in Sports and Exercise, 34,* 1996–2001.

Troughton, J., Jarvis, J., Skinner, C., Robertson, N., Khunti, K., & Davies, M. (2008). Waiting for diabetes: Perceptions of people with pre-diabetes: A qualitative study. *Patient Education and Counseling, 72,* 88–93.

Trouilloud, D., Sarrazin, P., Bressoux, P., & Bois, J. (2006). Relation between teachers' early expectations and students' later perceived competence in physical education classes: Autonomy-supportive climate as a moderator. *Journal of Educational Psychology, 98,* 75–86. doi:10.1037/0022-0663.98.1.75

Tudor-Locke, C., Bell, R.C., Myers, A.M., Harris, S.B., Ecclestone, N.A., Lauzon, N., et al. (2004). Controlled outcome evaluation of the First Step Program: A daily physical activity intervention for individuals with type II diabetes. *International Journal of Obesity & Related Metabolic Disorders: Journal of the International Association for the Study of Obesity, 28,* 113–119.

Ullrich-French, S., & Cox, A. (2009). Using cluster analysis to examine the combinations of motivation regulations of physical education students. *Journal of Sport and Exercise Psychology, 31,* 358–379. Retrieved from http://hk.humankinetics.com/JSEP/journalAbout.cfm

Urdan, T., & Maehr, M.L. (1995). Beyond a two-goal theory of motivation: A case for social goals. *Review of Educational Research, 65,* 213–244.

Urdan, T., & Mestas, M. (2006). The goals behind performance goals. *Journal of Educational Psychology, 98,* 354–365.

Valentini, N.C., & Rudisill, M.E. (2004). An inclusive mastery climate intervention and the motor skills development of children with and without disabilities. *Adapted Physical Activity Quarterly, 21,* 330–347.

Vallance, J.K., Courneya, K.S., Jones, L.W., & Reiman, A.R. (2005). Differences in quality of life between non-Hodgkins lymphoma survivors meeting and not meeting public health exercise guidelines. *Psycho-Oncology, 14,* 979–991.

Vallance, J.K., Courneya, K.S., Jones, L.W., & Reiman, T. (2006). Exercise preferences among a population-based sample of non-Hodgkin's lymphoma survivors. *European Journal of Cancer Care, 15,* 34–43.

Vallance, J.K., Courneya, K.S., Plotnikoff, R.C., Dinu, I., & Mackey, J.R. (2008). Maintenance of physical activity in breast cancer survivors after a randomized trial. *Medicine and Science in Sports and Exercise, 40,* 173–180.

Vallance, J.K., Courneya, K.S., Plotnikoff, R.C., & Mackey, J.R. (2008). Analyzing theoretical mechanisms of physical activity behavior change in breast cancer survivors: Results from the activity promotion (ACTION) trial. *Annals of Behavioral Medicine, 35,* 150–158.

Vallance, J.K., Courneya, K.S., Plotnikoff, R.C., Yasui, Y., & Mackey, J.R. (2007). Randomized controlled trial of the effects of print materials and step pedometers on physical activity and quality of life in breast cancer survivors. *Journal of Clinical Oncology, 25,* 2352–2359.

Vallance, J.K., Courneya, K.S., Taylor, L.M., Plotnikoff, R.C., & Mackey, J.R. (2008). Development and evaluation of a theory-based physical activity guidebook for breast cancer survivors. *Health Education and Behavior, 35,* 174–189.

Vallance, J.K., Dunn, J.G.H., & Causgrove Dunn, J.L. (2006). Perfectionism, anger, and situation criticality in competitive youth ice hockey. *Journal of Sport and Exercise Psychology, 28,* 383-406.

Vallance, J.K., Lesniak, S., Belanger, L., & Courneya, K.S. (2010). Development and assessment of a physical activity guidebook for the Colon Health and Life-Long Exercise Change (CHALLENGE) Trial (NCIC CO.21). *Journal of Physical Activity and Health, 7,* 794–801.

Vallerand, R.J. (1997). Toward a hierarchical model of intrinsic and extrinsic motivation. In M.P. Zanna (Ed.), *Advances in experimental social psychology* (pp. 271–360). San Diego, CA: Academic Press.

Vallerand, R.J. (2001). A hierarchical model of intrinsic and extrinsic motivation in sport and exercise. In G. Roberts (Ed.), *Advances in motivation in sport and exercise* (pp. 263–319). Champaign, IL: Human Kinetics.

Vallerand, R.J. (2005, August). *Passion in sport. Theory and research.* Paper presented at the ISSP 11th World Congress of Sport Psychology. Sydney.

Vallerand, R.J. (2007). Intrinsic and extrinsic motivation in sport and physical activity: A review and a look at the future. In G. Tenenbaum & E. Eklund (Eds.), *Handbook of sport psychology* (3rd ed., pp. 59–84). New York: Wiley.

Vallerand, R.J. (2008). On the psychology of passion: In search of what makes people's lives most worth living. *Canadian Psychology, 49,* 1–13.

Vallerand, R.J. (2010). Passion for life activities: The dualistic model of passion. In M.P. Zanna (Ed.), *Advances in experimental social psychology.* New York: Academic Press.

Vallerand, R.J., Blanchard, C.M., Mageau, G.A.,

Koestner, R., Ratelle, C.F., Léonard, M., Gagné, M., & Marsolais, J. (2003). Les passions de l'âme: On obsessive and harmonious passion. *Journal of Personality and Social Psychology, 85,* 756–767.

Vallerand, R.J., Deci, E.L., & Ryan, R.M. (1987). Intrinsic motivation in sport. In K. Pandolf (Ed.,), *Exercise and sport science reviews, vol. 15* (pp. 389–425). New York: Macmillan.

Vallerand, R.J., & Fortier, M.S. (1998). Measures of intrinsic and extrinsic motivation in sport and physical activity: A review and critique. In J.L. Duda (Ed.), *Advancements in sport and exercise psychology measurement* (pp. 81–101). Morgantown, WV: Fitness Information Technology.

Vallerand, R.J., Fortier, M.S., Guay, F. (1997). Self-determination and persistence in a real-life setting: Toward a motivational model of high school dropout. *Journal of Personality and Social Psychology, 72,* 1161–1176.

Vallerand, R.J., & Houlfort, N. (2003). Passion at work: Toward a new conceptualization. In S.W. Gilliland, D.D. Steiner, & D.P. Skarlicki (Eds.), *Emerging perspectives on values in organizations* (pp. 175–204). Greenwich, CT: Information Age.

Vallerand, R.J., & Losier G.F. (1999). An integrative analysis of intrinsic and extrinsic motivation in sport. *Journal of Applied Sport Psychology, 11,* 142–169. doi:10.1080/10413209908402956

Vallerand, R.J., Mageau, G.A., Elliot, A.J., Dumais, A., Demers, M-A., & Rousseau, F.L. (2008). Passion and performance attainment in sport. *Psychology of Sport & Exercise, 9,* 373–392.

Vallerand, R.J., Mageau G.A., Ratelle, C., Leonard, M., Blanchard, C., Koestner, R., Gagne, M., & Marsolais, J. (2003). Les Pssions de l'ame:On obsessive and harmonious passion. *Journal of Personality and Social Psychology, 85,* 756-767.

Vallerand, R.J., Ntoumanis, N., Philippe, F.L., Lavigne, G.L., Carbonneau, C., Bonneville, A., Lagacé-Labonté, C., & Maliha, G. (2008). On passion and sports fans: A look at football. *Journal of Sport Sciences, 26,* 1279–1293.

Vallerand, R.J., Pelletier, L.G., Blais, M.R., Briere, N.M., Senecal, C., & Valliéres, E.F. (1992). The academic motivation scale: A measure of intrinsic, extrinsic, and amotivation in education. *Educational and Psychological Measurement, 52,* 1003–1017.

Vallerand, R.J., Pelletier, L.G., & Koestner, R. (2008). Reflections on self-determination theory. *Canadian Psychology, 49,* 257–262. doi:10.1037/a0012804

Vallerand, R.J., & Ratelle, C.F. (2002). Intrinsic and extrinsic motivation: A hierarchical model. In E.L.

Deci and R.M. Ryan (Eds.), *Handbook of self-determination research* (pp. 37–63). Rochester, NY: University of Rochester Press.

Vallerand, R.J., & Reid, G. (1984). On the causal effects of perceived competence on intrinsic motivation: A test of cognitive evaluation theory. *Journal of Sport Psychology, 6,* 94–102.

Vallerand, R.J., Rousseau, F.L., Grouzet, F.M.E., Dumais, A., & Grenier, S. (2006). Passion in sport: A look at determinants and affective experiences. *Journal of Sport & Exercise Psychology, 28,* 454–478.

Vallerand, R.J., Salvy, S.J., Mageau, G.A., Elliot, A.J., Denis, P., Grouzet, F.M.E., & Blanchard, C.M. (2007). On the role of passion in performance. *Journal of Personality, 75,* 505–534.

Vancouver, J.B., & Kendall, L.N. (2006). When self-efficacy negatively relates to motivation and performance in a learning context. *Journal of Applied Psychology, 91,* 1146–1153.

Vancouver, J.B., More, K.M., & Yoder, R.J. (2008). Self-efficacy and resource allocation: Support for a nonmonotonic, discontinuous model. *Journal of Applied Psychology, 93,* 35–47.

Vancouver, J.B., Thompson, C.M., Tischner, E.C., & Putka, D.J. (2002). Two studies examining the negative effect of self-efficacy on performance. *Journal of Applied Psychology, 87,* 506–516.

Vancouver, J.B., Thompson, C.M., & Williams, A.A. (2001). The changing signs in the relationships among self-efficacy, personal goals, and performance. *Journal of Applied Psychology, 86,* 605–620.

Van der Horst, K., Chin, A., Paw, M.J., Twisk, J.W.R., & Van Mechelen, W. (2007). A brief review on correlates of physical activity and sedentariness in youth. *Medicine and Science in Sports and Exercise, 39*(8), 1241–1250.

Van Heck, G. (1997). Personality and physical health: Toward an ecological approach to health-related personality research. *European Journal of Personality, 11,* 416–443.

Vansteenkiste, M., Lens, W., & Deci, E.L. (2006). Intrinsic versus extrinsic goal contents in self-determination theory: Another look at the quality of academic motivation. *Educational Psychologist, 41,* 19–31.

Vansteenkiste, M., Niemiec, C.P., & Soenens, B. (2010). The development of the five mini-theories of self-determination theory: An historical overview, emerging trends, and future directions. In T. Urdan & S. Karabenick (Eds.). *Advances in motivation and achievement, vol. 16: The decade ahead.* UK: Emerald.

Vansteenkiste, M., Simons, J., Lens, W., Sheldon, K.M., & Deci, E.L. (2004). Motivating learning, performance, and persistence: The synergistic effects of intrinsic goal contents and autonomy supportive contexts. *Journal of Personality and Social Psychology, 87,* 246–260.

Vansteenkiste, M., Simons, J., Soenens, B., & Lens, W. (2004). How to become a persevering exerciser? Providing a clear, future intrinsic goal in an autonomy-supportive way. *Journal of Sport and Exercise Psychology, 26,* 232–249.

Vansteenkiste, M., Soenens, B., & Duriez, B. (2008). Presenting a positive alternative to materialistic strivings and the thin-ideal: Understanding the effects of extrinsic relative to intrinsic goal pursuits. In S.J. Lopez (Ed.), *Positive psychology: Exploring the best in people* (Vol. 4, pp. 57–86). Westport, CT: Greenwood.

Vansteenkiste, M., Soenens, B., & Lens, W. (2007). Intrinsic versus extrinsic goal promotion in exercise and sport: Understanding the differential impacts on performance and persistence. In M.S. Hagger & N.L.D. Chatzisarantis (Eds.), *Intrinsic motivation and self-determination in exercise and sport* (pp. 167–180). Champaign, IL: Human Kinetics.

Van Yperen, N.W., & Duda, J.L. (1999). Goal orientations, beliefs about success, and performance improvement among young elite Dutch soccer players. *Scandinavian Journal of Medicine and Science in Sports, 9,* 358–364.

Vargas-Tonsing, T., & Batholomew, J.B. (2006). An exploratory study of the effects of pre-game speeches on team-efficacy beliefs. *Journal of Applied Sport Psychology, 36,* 918–933.

Vargas-Tonsing, T.M. (2009). An exploratory examination of the effects of coaches' pre-game speeches on athletes' perceptions of self-efficacy and emotion. *Journal of Sport Behavior, 32,* 92–111.

Vazou-Ekkekakis, S., & Ekkekakis, P. (2009). Affective consequences of imposing the intensity of physical activity: Does the loss of perceived autonomy matter? *Hellenic Journal of Psychology, 6,* 125–144.

Vazou, S., Ntoumanis, N., & Duda, J.L. (2005). Peer motivational climate in youth sport: A qualitative inquiry. *Psychology of Sport and Exercise, 6,* 497-516.

Vealey, R.S. (1986). Conceptualization of sport-confidence and competitive orientation: Preliminary investigation and instrument development. *Journal of Sport Psychology, 8,* 221–246.

Vealey, R.S., & Campbell, J.L. (1988). Achievement goals of adolescent figure skaters: Impact on self-confidence, anxiety and performance. *Journal of Adolescent Research, 3,* 227–243.

Vealey, R.S., & Greenleaf, C.A. (2010). Seeing is believing: Understanding and using imagery in sport. In J.M. Williams, (Ed.), *Applied sport psychology. Personal growth to peak performance* (6th ed., pp. 267–304). New York: McGraw-Hill.

Vealey, R.S., Hayashi, S.W., Garner-Holman, M., & Giacobbi, P. (1998). Sources of sport-confidence: Conceptualization and instrument development. *Journal of Sport and Exercise Psychology, 20*, 54–80.

Vierling, K.K., Standage, M., & Treasure, D.C. (2007). Predicting attitudes and physical activity in an "at-risk" minority youth sample: A test of self-determination theory. *Psychology of Sport and Exercise, 8*, 795–817. doi:10.1016/j.psychsport.2006.12.006

Vilhjalmsson, R., & Kristjansdottir, G. (2003). Gender differences in physical activity in older children and adolescents: The central role of organized sport. *Social Science & Medicine, 56*, 363–374.

Vlachopoulos, S., & Biddle, S.J.H. (1996). Achievement goal orientations and intrinsic motivation in a track and field event in school physical education. *European Physical Education Review, 2*, 158–164.

Vlachopoulos, S., & Biddle, S.J.H. (1997). Modeling the relation of goal orientations to achievement-related affect in physical education: Does perceived ability matter? *Journal of Sport and Exercise Psychology, 19*, 169–187.

Vlachopoulos, S., Ntoumanis, N., & Smith, A.L. (in press). The Basic Psychological Needs in Exercise Scale: Translation and evidence for cross-cultural validity. *International Journal of Sport and Exercise Psychology*.

Vlachopoulos, S.P., & Gigoudi, M.A. (2008). Why don't you exercise? Development of the amotivation toward exercise scale among older inactive individuals. *Journal of Aging and Physical Activity, 16*, 316–341. Retrieved from http://hk.humankinetics.com/JAPA/journalAbout.cfm

Vlachopoulos, S.P., Karageorghis, C.I., & Terry, P.C. (2000). Motivation profiles in sport: A self-determination theory perspective. *Research Quarterly for Exercise and Sport, 71*, 387–397. Retrieved from www.aahperd.org/rc/publications/rqes/

Vlachopoulos, S., Ntoumanis, N., & Smith, A.L. (2010). The basic psychological needs in exercise scale: Translation and evidence for cross-cultural validity. *International Journal of Sport and Exercise Psychology, 8*, 394–412.

Vlachopoulos, S.P., & Michailidou, S. (2006). Development and initial validation of a measure of autonomy, competence, and relatedness in exercise: The Basic Psychological Needs in Exercise Scale. *Measurement in Physical Education and Exercise Science, 10*, 179–201.

von Gruenigen, V.E., Gibbons, H.E., Kavanagh, M.B., Janata, J.W., Lerner, E., & Courneya, K.S. (2009). A randomized trial of a lifestyle intervention in obese endometrial cancer survivors: Quality of life outcomes and mediators of behavior change. *Health and Quality of Life Outcomes, 7*, 17.

Vosloo, J., Ostrow, A., & Watson, J.C. (2009). The relationship between motivational climate, goal orientations, anxiety and self-confidence among swimmers. *Journal of Sport Behavior, 32*, 376–393.

Wade, D.T. (1998). Evidence relating to goal planning in rehabilitation. *Clinical Rehabilitation, 12*, 273–275.

Walling, M.D., & Duda, J.L. (1995). Goals and their associations with beliefs about success in and perceptions of the purpose of physical education. *Journal of Teaching in Physical Education, 14*, 140–156.

Walling, M.D., Duda, J.L., & Crawford, T. (2002). Goal orientations, outcome, and responses to youth sport competition among high/low perceived ability athletes. *International Journal of Sport Psychology, 14*, 140–156.

Walsh, J.J., da Fonseca, R.S., & Banta, A. (2005). Watching and participating in exercise videos: A test of the theory of planned behaviour, conscientiousness, and the role of implementation intentions. *Psychology & Health, 20*, 729–741.

Wang, C.C., & Chu, Y.S. (2007). Harmonious passion and obsessive passion in playing online games. *Social Behavior and Personality, 35*, 997–1006.

Wang, C.C., & Yang, H.W. (2007). Passion and dependency in online shopping activities. *CyberPsychology & Behavior, 10*, 296–298.

Wang, C.K., & Biddle, S.J.H. (2001). Young people's motivational profiles in physical activity: A cluster analysis. *Journal of Sport & Exercise Psychology, 23*, 1–22

Wang, C.K.J., Biddle, S.J.H., & Elliot, A.J. (2007). The 2x2 achievement goal framework in a physical education context. *Psychology of Sport and Exercise, 8*, 147–168.

Wang, C.K.J., Chia Liu, W., Lochbaum, M.R., & Stevenson, S.J. (2009). Sport ability beliefs, 2x2 achievement goals, and intrinsic motivation: The moderating role of perceived competence in sport and exercise. *Research Quarterly for Exercise and Sport, 80*, 303–312.

Wang, C.K.J., Lim, B.S.C., Aplin, N.G., Chia, Y.H.M., McNeill, M., & Tan, W.K.C. (2008). Students' attitudes and perceived purposes of physical education in Singapore: Perspectives from a 2x2 achievement goal framework. *European Physical Education Review, 14*, 51–70.

Watson, D., Clark, L.A., & Tellegen, A. (1988). Development and validation of brief measures of positive and negative affect: The PANAS scales. *Journal of Personality and Social Psychology, 54,* 1063–1070.

Watson, J.D. (1996). *The double helix.* New York: Touchstone.

Waugh, C.E., & Fredrickson, B.L. (2006). Nice to know you: Positive emotions, self-other overlap, and complex understanding in the formation of new relationships. *Journal of Positive Psychology, 1,* 93–106.

Ward, J., Wilkinson, C., Vincent-Graser, S., & Prusak, K.A. (2008). Effects of choice on student motivation and physical activity behavior in physical education. *Journal of Teaching in Physical Education, 27,* 385–398. Retrieved from http://hk.humankinetics.com/JTPE/journalAbout.cfm

Watkins, B., Garcia, A.W., & Turek, E. (1994). The relation between self-efficacy and sport performance: Evidence from a sample of youth baseball players. *Journal of Applied Sport Psychology, 6,* 21–31.

Weinberg, R. (1985). Relationship between self-efficacy and cognitive strategies in enhancing endurance performance. *International Journal of Sport Psychology, 17,* 280–292.

Weinberg, R., Butt, J., Knight, B., & Perritt, N. (2001). Collegiate coaches' perceptions of their goal-setting practices: A qualitative investigation. *Journal of Applied Sport Psychology, 13*(4), 374–398.

Weinberg, R.S., Bruya, L.D., & Jackson, S. (1985). The effects of goal proximity and goal specificity on endurance performance. *Journal of Sport Psychology, 7,* 296–305.

Weinberg, R.S., Gould, D., & Jackson, A. (1979). Expectations and performance: An empirical test of Bandura's self-efficacy theory. *Journal of Sport Psychology, 1,* 320–331.

Weinberg, R.S., Gould, D., Yukelson, D., & Jackson, A. (1981). The effects of pre-existing and manipulated self-efficacy on a competitive muscular endurance task. *Journal of Sport Psychology, 4,* 345–354.

Weinberg, R.S., Yukelson, D., & Jackson, A. (1980). Effect of public and private efficacy expectations on competitive performance. *Journal of Sport Psychology, 2,* 340–349.

Weinberg, R.S., & Weigand, D. (1993). Goal setting in sport and exercise: A reaction to Locke. *Journal of Sport and Exercise Psychology, 15,* 88–96.

Weiner, B. (1972). *Theories of motivation: From mechanism to cognition.* Chicago: Markham.

Weinstein, N., & Ryan, R.M. (2010). When helping helps: Autonomous motivation for prosocial behavior and its influence on well-being for the helper and recipient. *Journal of Personality and Social Psychology, 98,* 222–244.

Weinstein, R.S. (1989). Perceptions of classroom processes and student motivation: Children's views of self-fulfilling prophecies. In C. Ames & R. Ames (Eds.), *Research on motivation in education* (Vol. 3, pp. 187–221). San Diego, CA: Academic Press.

Weiss, C.H. (1998). *Evaluation: Methods for studying programs and policies.* Upper Saddle River, NJ: Prentice Hall.

Weiss, M., & Ferrer-Caja, E. (2002). Motivational orientations and sport behavior. In T. Horne (Ed.), *Advances in sport psychology* (pp. 101–184). Champaign, IL: Human Kinetics.

Weissman, A.N., & Beck, A.T. (1978). *Development and validation of the dysfunctional attitudes scale.* Paper presented at the Association for the Advancement of Behavior Therapy, Chicago.

Wells, C., Collins, D., & Hale, B. (1993). The self-efficacy-performance link in maximum strength performance. *Journal of Sports Sciences, 11,* 167–175.

White, R.W. (1959). Motivation reconsidered: The concept of competence. *Psychological Review, 66,* 297–333.

White, S.A., & Duda, J.L. (1993). Dimensions of goals and beliefs among adolescent athletes with physical disabilities. *Adapted Physical Activity Quarterly, 10,* 125–136.

White, S.A., Duda, J.L., & Keller, M.R. (1998). The relationship between goal orientation and perceived purposes of sport among youth sport participants. *Journal of Sport Behavior, 21,* 474–483.

White, S.A., & Zellner, S.R. (1996). The relationship between goal orientation, beliefs about the causes of sport success, and trait anxiety among high school, intercollegiate, and recreational sport participants. *Sport Psychologist, 10,* 58–72.

Whitehead, S., & Biddle, S.J.H. (2008). Adolescent girls' perceptions of physical activity: A focus group study. *European Physical Education Review, 14*(2), 243–262.

Wiese, D.M., & Weiss, M.R. (1987). Psychological rehabilitation and the physical injury: Implications for the sports medicine team. *Sports Psychologist, 1,* 318–330.

Wigfield, A., & Eccles, J.S. (1992). The development of achievement task values: A theoretical analysis. *Developmental Review, 12,* 265–310.

Wild, T.C., & Enzle, M.E. (2002). Social contagion of motivational orientations. In E.L. Deci & R.M. Ryan (Eds.), *Handbook of self-determination research* (pp. 141–157). Rochester, NY: University of Rochester Press.

Wilkinson, E. (2008). Can you pay people to be healthy? *Lancet, 371,* 1325–1326.

Wilkinson, J. (2004). *My world.* London: Headline.

Wilkinson, J. (2008). *Tackling life.* London: Headline.

Williams, G.C., Cox, E.M., Hedberg, V., & Deci, E.L. (2000). Extrinsic life goals and health risk behaviors in adolescents. *Journal of Applied Social Psychology, 30,* 1756–1771.

Williams, G.C., Minicucci, D.S., Kouides, R.W., Levesque, C.S., Chirkov, V.I., Ryan, R.M., & Deci, E.L. (2002). Self-determination, smoking, diet and health. *Health Education Research, 17,* 512–521.

Williams, J.M. (2010). Relaxation and energizing techniques for regulation of arousal. In J.M. Williams (Ed.), *Applied sport psychology. Personal growth to peak performances* (6th ed., pp. 247–266). New York: McGraw-Hill.

Williams, J.M., & Andersen, M.B. (2007). Psychosocial antecedents of sport injury and interventions for risk reduction. In G. Tenenbaum & R.E. Eklund (Eds.), *Handbook of sport psychology* (3rd ed., pp. 379–424). Hoboken, NJ: Wiley.

Williams, J.M., & Krane, V. (2001). Psychological characteristics of peak performance. In J.M. Williams (Ed.), *Applied sport psychology. Personal growth to peak performance* (4th ed., pp. 162–178). Mountain View, CA: Mayfield.

Williams, L. (1998). Contextual influences and goal perspectives among female youth sport participants. *Research Quarterly for Exercise and Sport, 69,* 47–57.

Wilson, D.K., Evans, A.E., Williams, J., Mixon, G., Sirard, J.R., & Pate, R. (2005). A preliminary test of a student-centered intervention on increasing physical activity in underserved adolescents. *Annals of Behavioral Medicine, 30,* 119–124. doi:10.1207/s15324796abm3002_4

Wilson, K., & Brookfield, D. (2009). Effect on goal-setting on motivation and adherence in a six week exercise program. *International Journal of Sport and Exercise Psychology, 6,* 89–100.

Wilson, K.M., Hardy, L., & Harwood, C.G. (2006). Investigating the relationship between achievement goal orientations and process goals in rugby union players. *Journal of Applied Sport Psychology, 18,* 297–311.

Wilson, P.M., Blanchard, C.M., Nehl, E., & Baker, F. (2006). Predicting physical activity and outcome expectations in cancer survivors: An application of Self-Determination Theory. *Psycho-Oncology, 15,* 567–578.

Wilson, P.M., Longley, K., Muon, S., Rodgers, W.M., & Murray, T.C. (2006). Examining the contributions of perceived psychological need satisfaction to well-being in exercise. *Journal of Applied Biobehavioral Research, 11,* 243–264.

Wilson, P.M., Mack, D.E., & Grattan, K.P. (2008). Understanding motivation for exercise: A self-determination theory perspective. *Canadian Psychology, 49,* 250–256.

Wilson, P.M., & Rodgers, W.M. (2002). The relationship between exercise motives and physical self-esteem in female exercise participants: An application of self-determination theory. *Journal of Applied Biobehavioral Research, 7,* 30–43.

Wilson, P.M., & Rodgers, W.M. (2004). The relationship between perceived autonomy support, exercise regulations and behavioral intentions in women. *Psychology of Sport and Exercise, 5,* 229–242.

Wilson, P.M., Rodgers, W.M., Blanchard, C.M., & Gessell, J. (2003). The relationship between psychological needs, self-determined motivation, exercise attitudes, and physical fitness. *Journal of Applied Social Psychology, 33,* 2373–2392.

Wilson, P.M., Rodgers, W.M., & Fraser, S.N. (2002). Cross-validation of the revised motivation for physical activity measure in active women. *Research Quarterly for Exercise and Sport, 73,* 471–477.

Wilson, P.M., Rodgers, W.M., Fraser, S.N., & Murray, T.C. (2004). Relationships between exercise regulations and motivational consequences in university students. *Research Quarterly for Exercise and Sport, 75,* 81–91.

Wilson, P.M., Rodgers, W.M., Loitz, C., & Scime, G. (2006). It's who I am ... really! The importance of integrated regulation in exercise contexts. *Journal of Applied Biobehavioral Research, 11,* 79–104.

Wilson, P.M., & Rogers, W.T. (2008). Examining relationships between psychological need satisfaction and behavioural regulations in exercise. *Journal of Applied Biobehavioral Research, 13,* 119–142.

Wilson, P.M., Rogers, W.T., Rodgers, W.M., & Wild, T.C. (2006). The psychological need satisfaction in exercise scale. *Journal of Sport & Exercise Psychology, 28,* 231–251.

Wininger, S.R. (2007). Self-determination theory and exercise behavior: An examination of the psychometric properties of the Exercise Motivation Scale. *Journal of Applied Sport Psychology, 19,* 471–486.

W.K. Kellogg Foundation. (2001). Logic Model development guide: Using Logic Models to bring together planning evaluation and action update December 2001. www.exinfm.com/training/pdfiles/logicModel.pdf

Wolfson, S., & Neave, N. (2007). Coping under pressure: Cognitive strategies for maintaining confidence among soccer referees. *Journal of Sport Behavior, 30,* 232–247.

Woodgate, J., Martin Ginis, K.A., & Sinden, A.R. (2003). Physical activity and social physique anxiety in older women: The moderating effects of self-presentation efficacy. *Journal of Applied Biobehavioral Research, 8,* 116–127.

World Health Organization (WHO). (1989). *Guide to planning health promotion for AIDS prevention and control.* (Rep. No. 5). Geneva, Switzerland: WHO AIDS series.

World Health Organization (WHO). (2003). *Health and development through physical activity and sport.* Geneva, Switzerland: Author.

Worringham, C.J., & Messick, D.M. (1983). Social facilitation of running: An unobtrusive study. *Journal of Social Psychology, 121,* 23–29.

Wright, P.M., Ding, S., & Li, W. (2005). Relations of perceived physical self-efficacy and motivational responses toward physical activity by urban high school students. *Perceptual and Motor Skills, 101,* 651–656.

Wrosch, C., Scheier, M.F., Miller, G.E., Schulz, R., & Carver, C.S. (2003). Adaptive self-regulation of unattainable goals: Goal disengagement, goal reengagement, and subjective well-being. *Personality and Social Psychology Bulletin, 29,* 1494–1508. doi:10.1177/0146167203256921

Xiang, P., McBride, R., Bruene, A., & Liu, Y. (2007). Achievement goal orientation patterns and fifth graders' motivation in physical education running programs. *Pediatric Exercise Science, 19,* 179–191.

Yates, T., Davies, M., Gorely, T., Bull, F., & Khunti, K. (2008). Rationale, design and baseline data from the PREPARE (Pre-diabetes Risk Education and Physical Activity Recommendation and Encouragement) programme study: A randomized controlled trial. *Patient Education and Counselling.* doi:10.1016/j.pec.2008.06.010

Yates, T., Davies, M., Gorely, T., Bull, F., & Khunti, K. (2009). Effectiveness of a pragmatic education program designed to promote walking activity in individuals with impaired glucose tolerance: A randomized controlled trial. *Diabetes Care, 32,* 1404–1410.

Yeo, G.B., & Neal, A. (2006). An examination of the dynamic relationship between self-efficacy and performance across levels of analysis and levels of specificity. *Journal of Applied Psychology 91,* 1088–1101.

Yeung, R.R., & Hemsley, D.R. (1997). Personality, exercise, and psychological well-being: Static relationships in the community. *Personality and Individual Differences, 22,* 47–53.

Yin, Z. (2001). Setting for exercise and concerns about body appearance of women who exercise. *Perceptual and Motor Skills, 93,* 851–855.

Yli-Piipari, S., Watt, A., Jaakkola, T., Liukkonen, J., & Nurmi, J.E. (2009). Relationships between physical education students' motivational profiles, enjoyment, state anxiety, and self-reported physical activity. *Journal of Sports Science and Medicine, 8,* 327–336. Retrieved from www.jssm.org/vol8/n3/3/v8n3-3pdf.pdf

Zaccaro, S.J., Blair, V., Peterson, C., & Zazanis, M. (1995). Collective efficacy. In J.E. Maddux (Ed.), *Self-efficacy, adaptation, and adjustment: Theory, research, and application* (pp. 305–328). New York: Plenum Press.

Zaff, J.F., Smith, D.C., Rogers, M.F., Leavitt, C.H., Halle, T.G., & Bornstein, M.H. (2003). Holistic well-being and the developing child. In M.H. Bornstein, L. Davidson, C.L.M. Keyes, & K.A. Moore (Eds.), *Well-being: Positive development across the life course* (pp. 23–32). Mahwah, NJ: Erlbaum.

Zanna, M.P. & Fazio, R.H. (1982). The attitude-behavior relation: Moving toward a third generation of research. In M.P. Zanna, E.T. Higgins, & C.P. Herman (Eds.), *Consistency in social behavior* (pp. 283–301). Hillsdale, NJ: Erlbaum.

Zajonc, R.B. (1965). Social facilitation. *Science, 149,* 269–274.

Zhang, T. (2009). Relations among school students' self-determined motivation, perceived enjoyment, effort, and physical activity behaviors. *Perceptual and Motor Skills, 109,* 783–790. doi:10.2466/PMS.109.3.783-790

Zuckerman, H. (1977). *Scientific elite: Nobel laureates in the United States.* New York: Free Press.

Zuckerman, M., Porac, J., Lathin, D., Smith, R., & Deci, E.L. (1978). On the importance of self-determination for intrinsically-motivated behavior. *Personality and Social Psychology Bulletin, 4,* 443–446.

INDEX

Note: The italicized *f* and *t* following page numbers refer to figures and tables, respectively.

ABOUT THE EDITORS

Photo courtesy of Norwegian School of Sport Sciences.

Glyn C. Roberts, PhD, has been a professor of psychology at the Norwegian School of Sport Sciences since 1998. He was a professor of sport psychology in the department of kinesiology at the University of Illinois. His research has focused on the motivational determinants of achievement, and he has been particularly concerned with the motivation of children in the competitive sport experience. Dr. Roberts has focused on how coaches coach and how the climate the coach creates affects the motivation, achievement, and persistence of children and adolescents. He has been involved in research grants for over $2 million. He has over 200 publications, including 15 books and more than 70 book chapters. He has several distinguished scholar awards, including the Honour Award of the International Society of Sport Psychology (ISSP, 1997) and the Coleman Griffith Scholar Award for 2008 of the Association for Applied Sport Psychology (AASP). Dr. Roberts is a distinguished scholar of the North American Society for the Psychology of Sport and Physical Activity (NASPSPA, 1998). Dr. Roberts was president of NASPSPA (1981-82), president of the European Federation of Sport Psychology (1999-2003), founding president of Division 12 (Sport Psychology) of the International Association of Applied Psychology (IAAP, 1994-1998), and president of AASP (2010-11). He has also served as the secretary general of ISSP and has been on the board of directors of IAAP (1984-1996; 2006-2014). He is a fellow of the American Academy of Kinesiology and Physical Education and a founding fellow of AASP, and he is one of only two sport psychologists who have been elected a fellow of IAAP.

©Nike

Darren C. Treasure, PhD, is a former tenured associate professor at Arizona State University with an appointment in the department of kinesiology and an adjunct position in the department of psychology. Darren has held faculty positions at the University of Illinois at Urbana-Champaign and Southern Illinois University at Edwardsville. He has published over 50 scientific articles and book chapters on motivation and the psychology of peak performance and made invited keynote presentations at conferences in France, Norway, Finland, and the United Kingdom. Treasure currently resides in Portland, Oregon, where he consults with Nike in the role of high-performance director for the Oregon Project, a program that provides elite-level Nike-sponsored U.S. distance runners with the coaching, sports medicine, and sport science necessary for competing at the international level and ultimately winning medals at World Championships and the Olympic Games. From 2005 to 2009 Treasure was the author and lead consultant on a high-performance initiative in the athletic department at the University of California at Berkeley that enhances coaching, sports medicine, and sport science support systems. Dr. Treasure is the author of the hugely successful National Federation of State High School Associations' core coaching education course, Fundamentals of Coaching launched in 2007.

ABOUT THE CONTRIBUTORS

George Ampatzoglou, PhD, has a diploma in physical education and sport science from the Aristotle University of Thessaloniki, a master's degree in human performance and health, and a PhD in exercise and quality of life from Democritus University of Thrace. Since 1987 he has been working as a physical educator in elementary schools, and since 2007 he has been a physical education advisor. He has participated in numerous international and Greek conferences and has published in international and Greek journals. He is married with two children, and he likes jogging and playing tennis. His photo appears courtesy of University of Thessaly.

Paul R. Appleton, PhD, is a teaching and research fellow in the School of Sport and Exercise Sciences at the University of Birmingham, UK. Paul earned a first-class honors degree in sport and exercise science from De Montfort University in 2002 and completed a PhD in sport and exercise psychology at the University of Bedfordshire in 2009. Paul's research interests concern socioenvironmental and motivational processes in sport and other physical activity settings, including a developing program of research on perfectionism. His photo appears courtesy of Paul R. Appleton.

Stuart J.H. Biddle, PhD, is professor of exercise and sport psychology at Loughborough University, UK. He is a graduate of Loughborough University, Pennsylvania State University, and University of Keele.

Stuart's research adopts a wider approach in behavioral medicine through the study of the correlates and change of physical activity and sedentary behaviors. He has received funding from the Medical Research Council, British Heart Foundation, NHS Health Scotland, and industrial partners. In 2009-10 he chaired the Government Department of Health's Expert Group on Sedentary Behaviour and Obesity.

Stuart's research has been presented in more than 25 countries and published in over 150 articles. He is a member of several editorial boards, including the *International Journal of Behavioral Nutrition and Physical Activity, Preventive*

Medicine, and *Psychology of Sport & Exercise*. He has authored and edited several books, including the second edition of *Psychology of Physical Activity: Determinants, Well-Being and Interventions* (with Nanette Mutrie, 2008) and *Youth Physical Activity and Sedentary Behaviour: Challenges and Solutions* (with Al Smith, 2008).

Stuart enjoys active travel, especially through golf, in which he is often seriously challenged by his two sons. His photo appears courtesy of Loughborough University.

Avril Blamey, BEd, MEd, MPH, PhD, is a freelance planning and evaluation consultant. She is a graduate of Dunfermline College of Physical Education and Glasgow University in Scotland and has worked in academia and the UK National Health Service (NHS). She was a lecturer in the department of physical education and sport science and a research fellow in the department of public health and community-based sciences at Glasgow University. She was previously a senior manager in health promotion in Greater Glasgow Health Board and a senior public health advisor in the policy, evaluation, and appraisal team in NHS Health Scotland.

Avril has delivered, supported, and commissioned numerous complex evaluations for Scottish, UK, and local agencies. She has designed and evaluated interventions to promote stair climbing, active commuting, and exercise prescription schemes. She has published in numerous journals on the effectiveness of physical activity interventions and on evaluation methodology. Her PhD was on the use of theory-based evaluation methods in relation to community-based CHD prevention programs. She has been a freelance consultant since 2009, in which she provides support to public and voluntary sector agencies to enhance the health impact and evaluation of their programs and policies. Her photo appears courtesy of Avril Blamey.

Kerry S. Courneya, PhD, is a professor and Canada research chair in the faculty of physical education and recreation at the University of Alberta in Edmonton, Canada. He received his BA (1987) and MA (1989) in physical education from the University of Western Ontario and his PhD (1992) in kinesiology from the University of Illinois. He spent five years as an assistant and associate professor at the University of Calgary before moving to the University of Alberta in 1997. Courneya's research program focuses on physical activity and cancer, including primary prevention, coping with treatments, recovery after treatments, long-term survivorship, and secondary prevention and survival. His research interests include both the outcomes and determinants of physical activity and behavior change interventions. He has coauthored the American Cancer Society's physical activity and nutrition guidelines and the American

College of Sports Medicine's exercise guidelines for cancer survivors. He was the guest editor for a special issue on physical activity in cancer survivors in *Psycho-Oncology* in 2009 and also serves on the editorial boards of the *Journal of Cancer Survivorship* and *Annals of Behavioral Medicine*. His photo appears courtesy of University of Alberta.

Deborah L. Feltz, PhD, is professor and chairperson in kinesiology at Michigan State University. She received her BS degree from the State University of New York at Buffalo in 1974. Her MS (1976) and PhD (1980) degrees are from Pennsylvania State University under the direction of Daniel M. Landers. She has devoted more than 30 years to researching the relationships among efficacy beliefs, motivation, and performance in sport and physical activity contexts for athletes, exercisers, coaches, and teams. Her most recent scholarship has focused on group motivation gains in health games. She has over 130 peer-reviewed publications on these topics and one book, *Self-Efficacy in Sport*. She has received numerous awards for her work in these areas, including the Early Career Distinguished Scholar Award from the North American Society for the Psychology of Sport and Physical Activity (NASPSPA) and the *Research Quarterly for Exercise and Sport* Lecture Award from the Research Consortium of AAHPERD. She was also inducted into the National Academy of Kinesiology and served as its 61st president. She served as president of NASPSPA in 2008. She is a fellow of the American Psychological Association. Feltz remains a competitor in a local women's soccer league and in masters track in the 400-, 800-, and 1,500-meter distances. Her photo appears courtesy of Deborah L. Feltz.

Todd A. Gilson, PhD, is an assistant professor of sport and exercise psychology at Northern Illinois University. Todd earned his PhD at Michigan State University in 2008 under the guidance of Drs. Deborah Feltz and Martha Ewing. While at MSU, Todd received the Spencer Research and Training Grant to fund his research focused on the mental side of training for enhanced sport performance and was the student representative for the Association for Applied Sport Psychology (AASP). Todd has been published in the *Journal of Strength and Conditioning Research* and has forthcoming articles in the *Journal of Applied Social Psychology* and the *International Journal of Sport Psychology* focused on self-efficacy and motivation in sport training contexts. In addition to AASP, Todd is a professional member of the North American Society for the Psychology of Sport and Physical Activity (NASPSPA) and the National Strength and Conditioning Association (NSCA). In his free time, Todd enjoys Olympic weightlifting and watching deciding moments in almost any sporting event. His photo appears courtesy of Todd A. Gilson.

Kathleen A. Martin Ginis, PhD, is a professor of health and exercise psychology at McMaster University's department of kinesiology. Her research program focuses on psychosocial influences and consequences of physical activity participation. She has a particular interest in physical activity promotion among people living with spinal cord injury. Martin Ginis received her PhD from the University of Waterloo in 1996 and completed postdoctoral training at Wake Forest University. She is the recipient of several awards, including the Early Distinguished Career Award from the North American Society for the Psychology of Sport and Physical Activity and a New Investigator Award from the Canadian Institutes of Health Research. She has published more than 100 articles in journals such as *Health Psychology*, *Journal of Sport & Exercise Psychology*, *Annals of Behavioral Medicine*, and *Rehabilitation Psychology*. Her work has been featured in publications such as *O: The Oprah Magazine*, *Men's Health*, *Men's Fitness*, and *Shape*. Her photo appears courtesy of McMaster University.

Trish Gorely, PhD, is a senior research associate in the Institute of Youth Sport at Loughborough University, UK. She is a graduate of Otago University in New Zealand and the University of Western Australia.

Trish's research concentrates on understanding physical activity and sedentary behavior. Increasingly her focus is on intervention strategies to promote active lifestyles in young people. She has received funding from the Medical Research Council, British Heart Foundation, and industrial partners. In 2009-10 she was a member of the UK Government Department of Health's Expert Group on Sedentary Behaviour and Obesity. Trish's research has been presented in international journals and at multiple international and national conferences. Away from her desk, Trish enjoys keeping active by jogging, hill walking, and mucking around on climbing walls. Her photo appears courtesy of Loughborough University.

Howard K. Hall, PhD, is a professor of sport and exercise psychology in the faculty of health and life sciences at York St. John University. Howard began his academic life as a social geographer before training as a physical education teacher in the UK. Howard earned an MSc in sport psychology from the University of North Texas and a PhD in kinesiology from the University of Illinois at Urbana-Champaign. Howard has worked at various universities in the United States and the UK, teaching sport and exercise psychology and undertaking research on the psychological mechanisms that underpin both adaptive and maladaptive patterns of motivation. His most recent work seeks to understand the influence of perfectionism on patterns of cognition, affect, and behavior in sport participants. Howard served as vice president of the International Society of Sport Psychology from 1997 to 2005, and he is currently president of the International Association of Applied Psychology, Division 12. His photo appears courtesy of Howard K. Hall.

Andrew P. Hill, PhD, is a senior lecturer in youth sport and children's physical activity at York St. John University. He graduated from De Montfort University with a first-class honors degree in sport and exercise science in 2003 and earned a PhD in sport and exercise psychology from the University of Bedfordshire in 2010. Andy's research interests are focused on the motivational consequences of perfectionism in achievement context, and his work has been published in several international peer-reviewed journals. Andy is a reviewer for journals in sport and health psychology and is accredited by the British Association of Sport and Exercise Sciences (BASES) as a sport and exercise psychologist. His photo appears courtesy of Andrew P. Hill.

Elsa Kristiansen, PhD, has a master's degree in Norwegian (Nordic) language and literature from the University of Oslo (1995) as well as a master's in sport psychology (2005) with Glyn C. Roberts as her adviser. She completed her doctorate in sport psychology at the Norwegian School of Sport Sciences. The general conceptual basis of her PhD project was an investigation of the impact of organizational issues and, especially, the effect of media coverage on the perception of stress for elite athletes. Her research focus includes gender issues in sport, Paralympic participants, wrestling, and swimming. Her photo appears courtesy of Norwegian School of Sport Sciences.

Charalampos Krommidas, MSc, is a part-time lecturer and PhD student (PAPA project) in the department of physical education and sport sciences at the University of Thessaly in Greece. He received his MSc in exercise and quality of life at the Democritus University of Thrace and University of Thessaly, Greece. His main areas of interest are motivation, moral behavior, physical education, physical activity, and health. He has published articles in journals and congress proceedings in Greece. In his free time he likes playing basketball and jogging. His photo appears courtesy of University of Thessaly.

Diane Mack, PhD, is an associate professor in the department of physical education and kinesiology at Brock University. Research interests include understanding the mechanisms underpinning the relationship between physical activity and well-being. Outside the office, time with family (both two- and four-legged versions) contributes to her wellness. Her photo appears courtesy of Brock University.

Nanette Mutrie, PhD, is professor of exercise and sport psychology at the University of Strathclyde, Glasgow, Scotland. She has researched ways of increasing active living both in clinical populations and in the community with a particular interest in the mental health benefits. Current funded projects include the Scottish Physical Activity Research Collaboration (SPARColl, funded by NHS Scotland), the promotion of walking with the use of pedometers for older adults (funded by the Chief Scientist's Office), and the evaluation of the impact of structural changes to the environment on walking and cycling (funded by the Engineering and Physical Sciences Research Council).

Nanette is an accredited sport and exercise psychologist and honorary fellow with the British Association of Sport and Exercise Science (BASES). She is also a chartered psychologist with the British Psychological Society. With her students and colleagues, she has published over 100 peer-reviewed articles on exercise behavior and intervention strategies. Nanette has editorial roles with the *International Review of Sport and Exercise Psychology*, *Journal of Physical Activity and Health*, and *Mental Health and Physical Activity*. She has also contributed to national policy on active living and the National Institute of Health and Clinical Excellence (NICE) program on physical activity and the environment. Her photo appears courtesy of University of Strathclyde.

Nikos Ntoumanis, PhD, is a reader in exercise and sport psychology at the University of Birmingham, UK. He obtained his PhD at the University of Exeter in the UK. His research interests lie in the area of motivation in physical activity settings (sport, exercise, physical education). He has developed an interest in the regulation of weight-loss goals. Dr. Ntoumanis is a British Psychological Association chartered psychologist and serves as associate editor for the journal *Psychology of Sport and Exercise*. He also serves on the editorial board of five other journals, including the *Journal of Sport and Exercise Psychology*. His research has received awards from the European College of Sport Science, the North American Society for the Psychology of Sport and Physical Activity, the British Psychological Society, and the European Federation of Sport Psychology (FEPSAC). Dr. Ntoumanis is a member of the Hellenic Quality Assurance Agency for Higher Education. He has published 1 book, 5 book chapters, and about 80 articles in peer-reviewed journals. His research is funded by research councils and charities in the United Kingdom and overseas as well as by the European Union. His photo appears courtesy of University of Birmingham, UK.

Athanasios G. Papaioannou is professor of sport psychology and coordinator for the University of Thessaly of the Erasmus Mundus program European master's in sport and exercise psychology. He is a member of the managing council of the International Society of Sport Psychology (ISSP) and co-editor in chief of the *International Journal of Sport and Exercise Psychology* (IJESP). Papaioannou has been the scientific coordinator of projects promoting physical activity and healthy lifestyles of children and adolescents. He coauthored 3 books in the area of psychology and physical education, 2 books for public education in Greece, and more than 100 articles in journals and congress proceedings in the areas of motivational climate and goal orientations, self-regulation, and health-related behaviors. He has been an invited speaker on motivation in sport and exercise in several international and national congresses. He is married and has a young daughter, and he enjoys jogging. His photo appears courtesy of University of Thessaly.

Richard M. Ryan, PhD, is professor of psychology, psychiatry, and education at the University of Rochester and the director of clinical training. Having published over 250 articles and books, he is a widely cited researcher and theorist in the areas of human motivation and well-being. He is the codeveloper (with Edward L. Deci) of self-determination theory, an internationally influential framework for the study of motivation that has been applied in dozens of studies in sport and health-related settings as well as other areas such as development, education, work, relationships, medicine, psychotherapy, and cross-cultural psychology. Ryan has lectured in more than 60 universities worldwide and received numerous honors from professional organizations, including an honorary member of the German Psychological Society (DGP), a James McKeen Cattell fellow, and a visiting scientist at the Max Planck Institute for Human Development. He is also a practicing clinical psychologist and editor in chief of the journal *Motivation and Emotion*. His photo appears courtesy of University of Rochester.

Martyn Standage, PhD, is a senior lecturer in the department of health at the University of Bath, UK. He received his doctoral degree from the University of Birmingham in 2003. Organized mainly by self-determination theory, his research seeks to map the motivational determinants of adaptive and maintained engagement in health, exercise, sport, and education settings. Dr. Standage has authored more than 50 articles and book chapters, and his research has been supported by numerous grants, including awards from the Medical Research Council, the Economic and Social Research Council, and the British Academy. He currently serves as associate editor for *Motivation and Emotion* and *Frontiers in Movement Science and Sport Psychology*. He is the digest editor for the *Journal of Sport and Exercise Psychology*, serves on the editorial board for *Stress and Health*, and is a member of the peer-review college of the Economic and Social Research Council. His photo appears courtesy of Martyn Standage.

Jeff K. Vallance, PhD, is an assistant professor in the faculty of health disciplines at Athabasca University and an adjunct assistant professor in the department of oncology at the University of Calgary. He received his BHK (human kinetics) (2000) from the University of British Columbia and his MA (2002) and PhD (2007) from the faculty of physical education and recreation at the University of Alberta. He currently holds a Population Health Investigator Award from Alberta Innovates Health Solutions as well as a New Investigator Award from the Canadian Institutes of Health Research. Jeff's research program explores physical activity and related health outcomes, prevalence, and social-cognitive determinants in the context of cancer. His research focuses on developing and evaluating theoretically based strategies to facilitate physical activity behavior in survivors receiving treatments for cancer as well as in those who are post-treatment. His photo appears courtesy of University of Alberta.

Robert J. Vallerand, PhD, pursued postdoctoral studies in experimental social psychology at the University of Waterloo after receiving his PhD from the Université de Montréal. He has taught at Guelph University and has been an invited professor at McGill University. He is currently full professor of social psychology and director of the Laboratoire de Recherche sur le Comportement Social in the department of psychology. He has written or edited 5 books and well over 200 scientific articles and book chapters. Professor Vallerand has served as president of both the Quebec Society for Research in Psychology and the Canadian Psychological Association. He is currently president-elect of the

International Positive Psychology Association (IPPA). Professor Vallerand serves as consulting editor for several of the top international journals in the field. He has supervised to completion a number of students, including 17 who are now university professors across Canada and Europe. Professor Vallerand has received numerous awards and honors from over a dozen learned societies: including fellow of the International Association of Applied Psychology, the American Psychological Association, the Association for Psychological Science, the Society for Personality and Social Psychology, and the Canadian Psychological Association. He has also received the Adrien Pinard Career Award from the Quebec Society for Research in Psychology (the highest research award for a psychologist in Quebec) and the Sport Science Award from the International Olympic Committee. Vallerand is recognized as a leading international expert on motivational processes in which he has developed theories dealing with intrinsic and extrinsic motivation as well as passion for activities. His photo appears courtesy of Robert J. Vallerand.

Nikos Zourbanos, PhD, is a part-time lecturer and postdoctoral researcher (PAPA project) in the department of physical education and sport sciences at the University of Thessaly in Greece. He received his PhD at the University of Thessaly supported by the State Scholarships Foundation and his MSc in applied sport and exercise psychology at the University of Wales, Bangor, supported by the Onassis Foundation. His main areas of interest are self-talk, personality, psychological skills, and motivation. He has published articles in international and national journals and serves as a referee in scientific sport psychology journals. He is currently a member of the managing council of the European Network of Young Specialists in Sport Psychology (ENYSSP) and the managing council of the Hellenic Society of Sport Psychology (HSSP) and a member of three scientific bodies. In his free time he likes playing tennis and watching cinema. His photo appears courtesy of Nikos Zourbanos.